SURVEY OF

Chester County,

Pennsylvania,

Architecture

17th, 18th and 19th Centuries

Margaret Berwind Schiffer

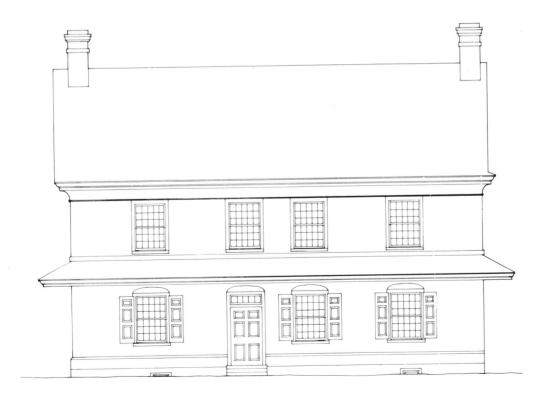

SCHIFFER PUBLISHING LTD.

Copyright © 1976, Schiffer Publishing Limited, Box E, Exton, Pa. 19341
All rights reserved
Library of Congress Catalog Card Number 76-4683
Printed in the United States of America
ISBN 0-916838-02-1

TO
Peter
&
Nancy

Survey of Chester County, Pennsylvania, Architecture

The purpose of this compilation is to present the facts and figures relating to architecture in Chester County, Pennsylvania from its 17th century beginnings thru the 19th century.

It is hoped that material garnered from all available manuscript and printed sources will be of interest not only to students of architectural history but to those primarily interested in social and economic history.

Once similar surveys are made of areas to the north and south of this first county of Pennsylvania, serious studies and interpretations of architectural history can be made.

Source material used included the following:

National Archives, Washington, D.C.

a. Ms. Bureau of Internal Revenue, Direct Tax 1798. Microfilm in Chester County Historical Society. Data found in the tax includes information on sod, log, plank, frame, brick and stone buildings standing that year—size, height, number of windows, number of panes of glass as well as the material used in the houses, barns and other out buildings.

b. Ms. Census, 1790-1850. Microfilm in Chester County Historical Society. Data includes number of people living in the county.

Court House, West Chester, Pa.

a. Ms. Deed and Mortgage Books prior to 1850 for mentions of trades.

b. Ms. Will Books prior to 1850 for mentions of trades and prior to 1815 for directions for building houses or for making additions to an existing house for the use of the widow.

c. Ms. Inventories prior to 1850 for data on trades, rooms and outbuildings.

Court House, Philadelphia, Pa.

a. Ms. Deeds, Wills and Inventories of people living in Chester County. These probate and land records are Chester County records filed there rather than in West Chester.

Chester County Historical Society, West Chester, Pa.

a. Ms. Tax assessments prior to 1850 for trades.

b. Ms. 1796 Tax assessments for East Fallowfield and West Nantmeal Townships for data of materials used for the construction of buildings.

c. 1799 Tax assessment for Charlestown, London Britain, Pikeland, West Marlboro and West Nottingham Townships for data of materials used for the construction of buildings.

d. Printed newspapers prior to 1850 for data on buildings in the county.

e. Printed 1883 Breau's Atlas for data on the materials used in the construction of houses and barns.

f. Ms. Report of Historic American Buildings Survey. Work done in Chester County under the auspices of the Chester County Historical Society.

g. Manuscripts, diaries and other related material.

Historical Society of Pennsylvania, Philadelphia, Pa.

a. Photostated Wills and Inventories of people living in Chester County for data on trades, instructions for building and mentions of rooms. Originals are in City Hall, Philadelphia, Pa.

Printed Reports of travellers passing through or near Chester County.

Printed. Local histories of towns, churches, etc. in Chester County for data on buildings.

The results of the research have been organized in this manner.

1. Brief history of the county.
2. Travellers' descriptions of the county.
3. Illustrations.
4. Extended notes on some buildings.
6. Architectural Drawings of Historic Buildings in Southeastern Pennsylvania by the office of John D. Milner, AIA

Settlement of Chester County

Chester County is one of the three original counties formed in 1682 in Pennsylvania by William Penn under Charter signed by King Charles II. Before this time Dutch, Swedes, Finns, and English lived along the Delaware River, the Schuylkill River, and tributary creeks in what was to become the southeastern portion of Pennsylvania. Originally Chester County included not only present-day Delaware County, but also an indefinite territory westwards, until the year 1729 when Lancaster County was formed. Its northern boundary was determined in 1752 when Berks County was established, and some twelve years later the southern boundary was determined by the Mason-Dixon Line. In 1789 the townships to the east and southeast were formed into a new county—Delaware. Today Chester County contains seven hundred and seventy-seven square miles.

The greatest number of settlers after 1682 came from the British Isles. Many English and Welsh Quakers and Baptists settled here in the 1680's, also Presbyterians and members of the Church of England. The English Quakers settled in the southeastern townships of Westtown, Thornbury and Birmingham as well as in the Great Valley. In the first quarter of the eighteenth century there was a migration of Irish Quakers and of Scotch Irish Presbyterians who settled chiefly in the southern and western townships. Finally, at the end of the first quarter of the eighteenth century the northern tier of townships received many settlers, the so-called Pennsylvania Dutch. A few French and other nationalities also settled within the county.

Land titles in the portion of Chester County which became Delaware County often go back to Dutch and Swedish colonists of the seventeenth century. A few buildings in this area date to pre-William Penn times. Today's Chester County has some late seventeenth century structures incorporated in existing buildings, but thus far research has not identified any one that can be definitely attributed in its entirety to the seventeenth century.

For over two hundred years the population of the county was primarily rural, conservative, and middle class with a strong Quaker element. Even though there was a constant flow of settlers westward, most family names found in the eighteenth century tax assessment lists were still found in the same township in 1850. Although the county was primarily agricultural it did not have a purely rural culture. The Quakers went to Philadelphia for Yearly Meetings and also to market and there they had the opportunity of seeing city styles which they could adapt to their own taste and ability.

The climate and available building materials are reflected in the architecture of a region. In 1682 it was observed that "the soil was fertile; the air mostly clear and healthy; the streams of water very good and plentiful; wood, for fire and building in abundance." William Penn mentions in 1683 that "The natural produce of the county, of vegetables, is trees, fruits, plants, flowers. The trees of most note, are the black walnut, cedar, cypress, chestnut, poplar, gum-wood, hickory, sassafrass, ash, beech, and oak of divers sorts, as red, white, and black; Spanish chestnut, and swamp, the most durable of all. Of which there is plenty, for the use of man."[1] In addition to those trees mentioned by William Penn, Chester County has pine, cherry, buttonwood and maple trees.

Building stone was available to the colonists. In the northern section of the county, in the Welsh mountains, there is a belt of red shale and sandstone and to the south of the mountain is an area of gneiss rock. In the Great Valley limestone and marble are found. South of the valley gneiss and mica slate cover the remaining southern section of the county. In the formation of gneiss and mica slate frequent beds of serpentine, hornblende trap-dykes, and deposits of pure feldspar occur. T. J. Wertenbaker noticed that if a line were drawn from Princeton, New Jersey to Wilmington, Delaware that in the region east of the line including Philadelphia, both banks of the Delaware and southern New Jersey, the houses were generally brick, whereas to the west the houses were almost invariabley of stone.[2] Chester County has some large eighteenth century brick houses in the southern townships but for the most part the better houses were built of stone.

The northern townships of Coventry, Nantmeal, and Vincent were the first to have an industrial development. By 1720 Coventry Forge was established and throughout the eighteenth century and until the Civil War, iron was a major industry in northern Chester County. The nineteenth century saw the same industry promote the growth of Coatesville, Phoenixville and Parkesburg.

From the 1680's until after the Centennial celebration of 1876 the rest of Chester County, due to its fertile soil and temperate climate, had chiefly an agricultural-dairying economy. The most important crop was wheat. Grain and flour were sold by the inhabitants of the county in Philadelphia and Wilmington. Many early mills, principally for flour and lumber, were built along the Brandywine, Elk, Octorara, Pickering, Valley, French and Pigeon creeks. Each section had a host of craftsmen but their product was chiefly for local consumption.

The first United States Federal Census was taken in 1790 just one year after Delaware County was formed from the southeastern part of Chester County. This census shows a total of four thousand four hundred and fifty-four families comprising 27,939 individuals. The rapid growth of the population of the county is reflected in the following figures from the Federal Census: 1800, 32,093; 1810, 39,597; 1820, 44,451; 1830, 50,910; 1840, 57,515 and in 1850, 66,438. By 1900 the population had increased to 96,628. Since the end of World War II, many areas of the county have become building developments, homes for employees in the industrial centers of Philadelphia, Chester and Wilmington. The 1960 Census listed 207,746 people in Chester County.

1.   Proud, Robert, *THE HISTORY OF PENNSYLVANIA IN NORTH AMERICA,* (Phila., Pa. 1797), p. 225.
2.   Ibid., p. 249.
3.   Wertenbaker, Thomas Jefferson, *THE MIDDLE COLONIES,* (New York, N.Y., 1963), p. 236.

Chester County as Seen by Travellers

Eighteenth and early nineteenth century accounts of travellers thru or near Chester County often provide interesting observations on the terrain and its buildings. Chronological extracts of printed reports follow.

A draft of a letter of Robert Parke to his sister Mary Valentine reads in part:

CHESTER TOWNSHIP the of the 10th Mo. 1725.
DEAR SISTER MARY VALENTINE,

...Land is of all Prices Even from ten pounds to one hundred pounds a hundred, according to the goodness or else the Situation thereof, & Grows dearer every year by Reason of Vast Quantities of People that come here yearly from Several Parts of the world, therefore thee & thy family or any that I wish well wod desire to make that Speed you can to come here and Sooner the better we have traveled over a Pretty deal of this country to seek for Land and (tho) we met with many fine Tracts of Land here and there in the country, yet my father being curious & somewhat hard to Please Did not buy any Land until the Second day of 10th mo: Last and then he bought a Tract of Land consisting of five hundred Acres for which he gave 350 pounds, it is Excellent good land but none cleared, Except about 20 Acres, with a small log house & Orchard Planted, We are going to clear some of it Directly, for our next Sumers fallow, we might have bought Land much cheaper but not so much to our satisfaction. We stayed in Chester 3 months & then Rented a Place 1 mile from Chester, with a good brick house & 200 Acres of Land for (?) pounds a year where we continue till next May.[1]

Docter Alexander Hamilton, in 1774, passes through Chester on his way to Darby:

We passed thro' Chester at seven o'clock at night, where we left Morison, Smith, and Howard; and the parson and I jogged on intending to reach Derby, a town about nine or ten miles from Chester.

Chester is a pretty neat and large village. Built chiefly of brick, pleasantly situated upon a small river of the same name that discharges itself into Delaware, about half a mile below where the village stands. Over this river is a wooden bridge, built with large rafters and planks in form of an arch. The State-house is a pretty enough building; this put me in mind of Chelsea near London, which it resembles for neatness, but it is not so large.

The parson and I arrived at Darby, our resting place, at half an hour after eight at night. This village stands in a bottom and partly upon the ascent of a hill, which makes it have a dull, meloncholy appearance. We put up at a publick house kept by one Thomas, where the landlady looked after everything herself, the land lord being drunk as a lord. The liquor had a very strange effect upon him, having deprived him of the use of his tongue. He sat motionless in a corner, smoaking his pipe and would have made a pretty good figure upon arras.

We were entertained with an elegant dispute between a young Quaker and the boatswain of a privateer, concerning the lawfulness of using arms against an enemy. The Quaker thee'd and thou'd it thro' the nose to perfection, and the privateer's boatswain swore just like the boatswain of a privateer, but they were so far from settling the point that the Quaker had almost acted contrary to his principles, clenching his fist at his antagonist to strike him for bidding God damn him. At nine Mr. Usher and I went to bed.[2]

Johann David Schoepf travelling in the confederation between 1783 and 1784 mentions:

On the low hills to the west of the river

[Schuylkill], made up likewise of limestone rock, loose quartz fragments are found in great quantity, frequently set off with fine crystals. These occur especially on Mr. Rambo's land, which is throughout based on the limestone. This observation, that crystals are very generally, if not always found on limestone soil, I have confirmed, in many other parts of America.

The Schuylkill is here commonly not so deep but one may ride through. . .

Between Swedes-Ford and Valley Forge there are to be seen many pits for burning lime; but on the surface along that road only common quartz and sandstone. The height, at the foot of which lies Valley-Forge, was over strewn with a quantity of hard, slatey, sandstones, in which here and there appeared little blackish points of what seemed to be shorl. The opposite hill consisted almost entirely of a brown rotten iron-ore mixed with mica. . .The works and buildings at the forge were burned down during the war. The ore which was smelted and worked here comes from a valley near-by.

The hills, over which the road lay from here, still seemed to be made up for the most part of a brown iron-mould, or of an earth similar to this. In one of the valleys there was limestone. But this whole region, far around, cannot boast of any particularly fertile soil; but little grain is raised, and there is a lack of meadows, the narrow low grounds along the Schuylkill excepted, which is the sole good land of the region. But the country is so much the more productive in iron-ore, which has been the occasion of setting up a good many forges and furnaces. The forests are everywhere thin and of young growth; for what with the lack of a systematic forest-economy here, the many iron-works could not but ravage the woods, and to their own hurt. The better land is used for farming, and the worse, where timber is left standing, produces a slow and poor growth. Moreover the game which at one time was very plentiful in the region has a great part been frightened off. . .The people who live in and among these hills seem not to be the most properous and their dwellings are not the best. But are not forgotten in the tax-levies; an

ordinary house e.g., with 100 acres of land, paid this year 20 Pd. Pensylv. Current. The owner, a German. . .

Coventry, another forge 15 miles from Valley-Forge, belongs to a Mr. Pott. On the road thither iron-mould is still to be seen, at times soft, at time hard, and divers other species of rock, scaly sound-stones, quartz, and breccia cemented with sand and iron; and a gneissic rock especially. The forge at Coventry stands in a narrow valley, running east and west. There are three hearths and three hammers. The hammers lie parallel with the shaft, the trunnions of which catch the helve at a little distance behind the hammer, and thus raise it with less power.

The bellows are of wood, and consist of two cylindrical casks, fitting closely the one into the other, and moving up and down between four wooden posts. The wind goes first through a leathern conduit, into an iron pipe, and so to the hearth. These simple bellows have the advantage that they may be set up without trouble or expense, need few repairs, and should last well. The best bar-iron is at this time sold here at 38 shillings Pensyl. Current the hundredweight, or about 5 pence the pound. Here, as everywhere, the assertion is made that American iron is in no way inferior to the best European. . .

Five miles father, over barren, stony, woody, and [illegible] hills, we come to Warwick Mine-holes, which in the district, are very famous iron-mines. The ore [illegible] here, (as very generally in America), heaped up [illegible] and shallow beneath the surface-mould. The surface of these hills is an iron-bearing sand; next, [illegible] lies a brown ochre-earth with little iron-stones intermixed beneath which is a bed, of no great depth, of sparse, red-brown ore, commonly soft; father down, [illegible] whiteish clayey stratum, still somewhat mixed with [illegible] bearing earth. The greatest depth they have is no more than 20 feet, a sufficient store being found above. Any knowledge of mining is superflous here, where there is neither shaft nor gallery to be [illegible], all work being at the surface or in great, wide [illegible] or pits.

From here we missed the prescribed road, and came through untravelled woodes and hills. . . Jones's Mine-holes, iron mines very little different from those just mentioned. Brown, sandy, [illegible] soft iron-stone lies shallow beneath the surface, but is very productive; 3000 pounds of ore are said to yield 2000 pounds of iron. Beneath and above the iron-stone there is a bed of gray, soft clayey earth which is called by the workmen soapstone. The work is carried on as mentioned above. That is to say, they dig here or there deep and wide, open pits, and when these grow inconvenient on account of depth, water, or other circumstances, they begin new ones. . .

The road to Lancaster lies through the fore-mentioned limestone valley, a fertile varies, and well [illegible] region. Along the road indeed one sees for the most part sorry cabins, for the better houses of the well-to-do landowners are all set a little off from the [illegible]. This, and the custom of always leaving some [illegible] next the road, brings it about that travellers [illegible] they are going through nothing but wilderness, when all around there are plantations and dwellings [illegible] away in the bush. On this road everybody I met addressed in German and they all answered me in the same language. . .

The limestone of the valley is the same coarse, black stone, as everywhere, and frequently comes to the surface. . .

The plantations and dwelling-houses in this region [illegible] scattered.[3]

Samuel Vaughan in 1787 mentions:

From Philadelphia to the Susquhannah the farmers are for the most part German and many publick houses on the road, the English Soldiers often, at times stood in need of a Linguist, but on crossing the River there are many Irish who are neigher so industrious, sober, or well informed in farming as the Germans who are the most valuable settlers.[4]

Mary Coburn Dewees, in 1787, mentions in her journal

. . .find the roads much better from Lancaster upwards than from Philad'a to Lancaster. . .[5]

Cazenove's Journal, in the year 1794, mentions:

November 14th, left McClahan's Tavern, through part of Lancaster [County], still fine land and beautiful meadows, 2 miles; then entered Chester County where for 10 miles the land is less level, more broken by very high hills, generally "barren land," but afterwards you go down in the valley and arrive at

Downing's Town [Downingtown], Chester County, 16-½ miles; stopped at Downing's, at the sign of Washington, very good inn. N.B. 33 miles from Philadelphia.

In this county, farms are generally about 300 acres, half of which remains as woods—generally lime-stone land; a farm with house and good barn, orchard, etc., sells for £12 [per acre] in the valley, and the price of land on the mountain, bordering the valley, called "hill-land," sells for £3 and is kept by the farmers for woodland for their farm use. Generally everything is grain-land or sown in clover, when they give it a rest. They fertilize their soil with lime, taken from their land, and with plaster of Paris; this latter gives a good yield of hay.

An acre in the good valley land generally yields 15 to 20 bushels of wheat, but these last 2 or 3 years they have been annoyed in this district by the Hessian fly and this year (1794) by mildew — so they cultivate corn more extensively, and sow their fields in clover, because when there is not enough wheat sown, the Hessian fly attacks barley; 30 to 35 bushels corn [per acre], 20 to 25 bushels barley, 1-½ to 2 or 2-½ tons of clover in 2 cuttings.

Send their flour and produce to Philadelphia — many mills, a few forges near the mountain, where there is plenty of wood, but no mines.

Very few Germans in this county, except in the 2 townships Spikland [Pikeland], Vincent, and Coventry. English Presbyterians and Quakers prevail in this county, also many Anabaptists in the 3 above townships.

The price for transportation from here to Philadelphia is 15 to 18 pence a 100 pounds, and 2s /6 for a barrel of flour.

You find very easy in this district workmen to help with harvest for 3f a day, with meals and a pint of whiskey.

Every house and barn is built of limestone, no brick-factories. The quality of land in Chester County is quite varied; the county is crossed in the north and south by 2 rows of mountains, not very high, but too high to be estimated of great value for cultivation. The land of the south mountains (chestnut) £ 3 an acre. The land of the north mountains, generally oak, for L.3 an acre.

The land south of the mountains is fair, and is worth £ 7 to £ 8 an acre, for 2 or 300 acre farms. The wood on the south mountains chiefly chestnut.

The valley where the land is level and "limestone." Farms with improvements, that is to say in activity [?] and ½ in cultivation, are worth £ 12 an acre.

The land in the north, beyond the mountains is sklit-stone, stony, but good for grain, is worth from £ 5 to £ 6 an acre, for 2 to 400 acre farms. N.B. The trees on the north mountains are generally oak

November 15th, left Downings T. [Downingtown], passing through a country partly level, partly broken with hills near [illegible] [arrived] at. . .Fornistak's Tavern, 10 miles, rather bad lodging, on the highway. . .

At Millers Tavern, [between Haverford and Bryn Mawr] 12 miles — good inn, on the road. Here farms are generally 150 acres. The price in general average, £ 10 an acre; "clay soil, poor ground, most worn out"; the short distance from Philadelphia is its great value.[6]

Thomas Fairfax, in 1799, traveling from Virginia to Salem, Massachusetts passes through Chester County:

Thence 10 miles to DOWNINGTOWN, and then 7 miles to a stone bridge over the west branch of BRANDYWINE. Here there was a Tavern at which the Stage going to LANCASTER, and myself, arrived together. I took this opportunity to relieve my horse in some measure by putting my trunk in the stage, to be left at LANCASTER. I then spoke for dinner and after waiting an hour, sat down to one of the most wretched meals that ever was served on a table. I was never more surprised, for from the appearance of the house, I expected at least to get something tolerable. I observed the kind of deception to be Common in this Country. You will see before you a large and handsome stone house, with a well painted sign and when you are taken with the bait, and go in, you find nothing but dirt, and the worst Accommodations. From hence I drove 12 miles to the SIGN OF PRESIDENT ADAMS and there lodged. At this house I had ample amends for my ill fare at the other, as every thing here was in the best order. Several Travelers had stopped for the night, and we spent an agreeable evening. The 25th early in the morning I left this and drove 5 miles to Breakfast at the SIGN OF THE SPREAD EAGLE, a German house. This is one of the handsome looking stone houses; however there was no description, for it was as fair within as without, and well provided. From hence it is 9 miles to LANCASTER.[7]

Robert Sutcliff, in 1806, mentions:
8th Month, 23d

This farm was in a good state of cultivation, with an excellent house, a very large barn, and stabling for many horses, with other conveniences on an extensive scale. The spring house, or dairy, in particular struck my attention, having a trench of spring water, about 2 feet wide and 4 or 5 inches deep, running all around the room, paved at the bottom, and inclosed at the sides with slabs of white marble.

I have before observed, that in the spring water which surrounds the floor of the dairies in this country, are placed the vessels contain the milk &c. and all is thus preserved sweet and cool, in the hottest part of the summer. Another conveniency I noticed in this farm-yard, was an appendage to the hog-sty, being a vault, near which was a stream of water, all within the inclosure wherein the hogs were confined. The advantages and comfort thus resulting to these animals, in hot weather must be obvious. On this farm, was an excellent orchard of several acres, the trees of which were at this time in their prime, and now in full bearing, and having been planted by the late Governor Mifflin, whose residence was here, they were well selected. Such abundance of fine fruit I never before beheld, in the same compass of ground; two or three of the best trees were literally broken down with the weight of the fruit. The rent G. A. proposed for his farm, with all these appendages, was about 20 s per acre: and, the quantity being short of 100 acres. The rent would amount to little more than the legal interest for the money which had been expended in buildings. As it was not more than an hour's ride from Philadelphia, and the land of good quality, I thought the price very reasonable.[8]

John Pearson, in 1821, mentions:

. . .Crossed the Welsh mountain, and came into a valley abounding with well cultivated farms, the inhabitants mostly Dutch; stopped at a store where an election was going on, the people were all as still as mice, and democratic was the order of the day. . .Slept at the second sign of General Green; and landlord had land to sell: at least the sherriff would take the trouble off his hands, and sell it for him. Land had been worth 70 to 80 dollars, but now would fetch but 20 per acre. (55th day) — Passed Downingtown. White wine dearer than in England. I travelled the old Chester road, which is both pleasanter and cheaper than the new road; the waggoners gave me this hint.[9]

. . .this brought me to Little Brandy Wine. . . Here were plenty of farms to sell cheap, with stone houses, stone barns, and stone spring houses, but an Englishmen whom I met, advised me not to make any purchase for the first year; he knew of plenty then in Brandy Wine Township, but he believed it was wrong time to make purchase. . .In the cool of the evening we moved on to a tavern five miles off; we were charged high for every thing. Married and single are accomodated in one bed-room, and as for certain utensils which are generally found under Englishmen's beds, and a certain description of small buildings, they are by no means common after you leave Philadelphia. . .[10]

Mrs. Anne Royall, in 1827, described West Chester

As the distance was short, and I had heard so much of the beauty of the country, and the superior manners, wealth and intelligence of the inhabitants of West Chester, a small town south of Philadelphia, I took a jaunt to that place. The road from Philadelphia to West Chester passes through one of the handsomest countries I have seen in my travels. As to wealth, fertility and cultivation, it excels. The farms are large and neat; the houses are built of stone principally, not very large, but remarkably for having small windows, their barns and stables are large, comfortable, close and costly. There is nothing like the barns, clover fields and cattle of Pennsylvania to be seen in any State. The whole country is chequered with fields of the rankest red clover. These were on each side of the road and in them stood droves of overgrown, sleek horses and cattle, gorged with clover, which was up to their knees. They were standing still, panting with their own weight. This is the case to West Chester, the twenty-eight miles.

I knew not which to admire most, the appearance of the country, or the neat plump Quaker and his wife, sitting side by side in their tight, comfortable, covered dearborn, going to the Philadelphia market. We met numbers of them in the course of the ride. They seemed to be the happiest people on earth, health on their cheeks, contentment on their countenance. Their white pails of butter sitting at their feet-richly and plainly dressed-their horse trembling with fat, secure from the sun and rain, they were enviable.

West Chester is a most delectable spot, near the Brandywine. It stands in the midst of a fertile country upon an even plain and is inhabited by the first people of the State. I found more taste, talent and refinement in West Chester, in proportion to the number of inhabitants than in any town, without exception, I have visited.***The citzens have built three meeting houses (one belongs to the Friends), and any parson of any sect has the privilege of preaching as often as he pleases, but not one cent of money does he receive. The citizens have entered into resolutions never to pay one cent of money to any priest.

See West Chester — let any man visit that town he will find it possessed of more virtue, hospitality, charity and inteligence than any town he has ever been in.

But West Chester speaks for itself. I never enjoyed myself more in any town. It is a perfect treat. They have a large collection (for the time) of choice books, minerals and a variety of productions of the terraqueous globe, all scentifically arrayed. This is the work of Dr. Darlington one of the most, if not altogether the most scientific man in the State of Pennsylvania. I was particularly struck with his cool, keen, steady penetrating eye.

They also have an athenaeum tastefully selected, and appear to be taking the lead in improving society. They seem to be aware of true happiness in the first place, and in the second place, they are in the right road to obtain it. There appears to be a harmony and mutual ambition for science and improvement, which can be met with in no other place. I had but a piece of day to spend there, which I deeply lamented, but I trust to spend some pleasant hours yet with those enviable people. I never was in a place where I saw less foppers. I believe it as clear of dandies as parsons. . .[11]

An English emigrant farmer writes in 1838:

June 1, 1838 Up at 5 started halfpast by railroad for Harrisburg passed through a good country, breakfasted at Paoli with about 100 passengers, it took about 5 munits, an excellent breakfast, passed throught a most beautiful cuntry th. I should like

to live there, it is a Quaker settlement. . .[12]

In 1836 a writer mentions:

The country between Philadelphia and Lancaster, is excelled by none in the United States in cultivation, fertility and beauty. It is all occupied by a thrifty and industrious population, whose comfortable farm houses, and substantial and capacious stone barns are scattered in very direction. In this part of Pennsylvania, until the construction of the rail road, all the houses, mills, barns, bridges and roads were made of stone. Solidity was the peculiar characteristic of the state. The fashion has changed, and there is now an iron road and wooden bridges.[13]

1. Myers, Albert Cook, *IMMIGRATION OF THE IRISH QUAKERS INTO PENNSYLVANIA 1682-1750 WITH THEIR EARLY HISTORY IN IRELAND,* (Swarthmore, Penna.), p. 70.
2. Hamilton, Alexander, *HAMILTON'S ITINERARIUM BEING A NARRATIVE OF A JOURNEY. . .1744,* (Saint Louis, Missouri, MCMVII), p. 18.
3. Schoeph, Johann David, *TRAVELS IN THE CONFEDERATION 1783-1784,* (Philadelphia, Penna., 1911), p.3.
4. Williams, Edward G., editor, *SAMUEL VAUGHAN'S JOURNAL OR MINUTES MADE BY S. W., FROM STAGE TO STAGE, ON A TOUR TO FORT PITT,* (The Western Pennsylvania Historical Magazine #194), p. 63.
5. *JOURNAL OF A TRIP FROM PHILADELPHIA TO LEXINGTON IN KENTUCKY KEPT BY MARY COBURN DEWEES IN 1787,* (Crawfordsville, Ind., 1936), p. 3.
6. Kelsey Rayner Wickersham, editor, *CAZENOVE JOURNAL 1784 A RECORD OF THE JOURNEY OF THEOPHILE CAZENOVE THROUGH NEW JERSEY AND PENNSYLVANIA,* (Haverford, Penna. 1922), p. 78.
7. Fairfax, Thomas, *JOURNAL FROM VIRGINIA TO SALEM MASSACHUSETTS,* (London, England, 1936), p. 26.
8. Sutcliff, Robert, *TRAVELS IN SOME PARTS OF NORTH AMERICA IN THE YEARS 1804, 1805 & 1806,* (Philadelphia, Penna. 1812), p. 291.
9. Pearson, John, *NOTES MADE DURING A JOURNEY IN 1821 IN THE UNITED STATES OF AMERICA.* (London, England, 1822), p. 59.
10. Ibid., p. 9.
11. *DAILY LOCAL NEWS,* (West Chester, Penna.), June 1905.
12. Wood, T. Kenneth, editor, *JOURNAL OF AN ENGLISH EMIGRANT FARMER,* (Lycoming Historical Society, Williamsport, Penna. 1928), June 1, 1838.
13. *A PLEASANT PEREGRINATION THROUGH THE PRETTIEST PARTS OF PENNSYLVANIA,* (Philadelphia, Penna. 1836), p. 39.

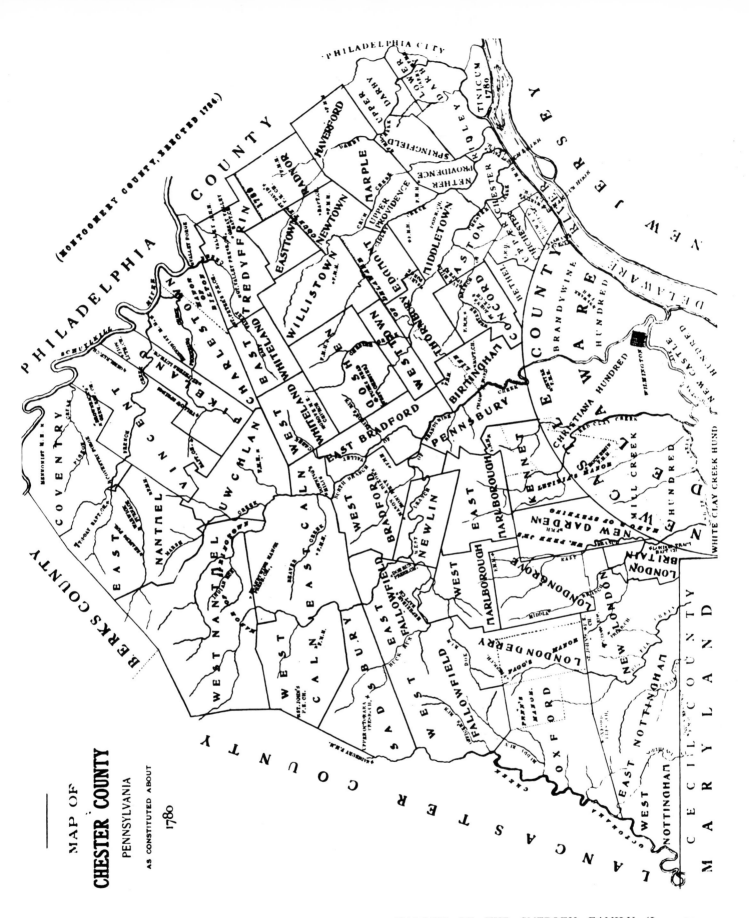

MAP OF CHESTER COUNTY PENNSYLVANIA AS CONSTITUTED ABOUT 1780. From Gilbert Cope, *GEN-EALOGY OF THE SMEDLEY FAMILY* (Lancaster, Penna., 1901), p. 47

SWEDISH LOG CABIN (LOWER) Built 1640-43

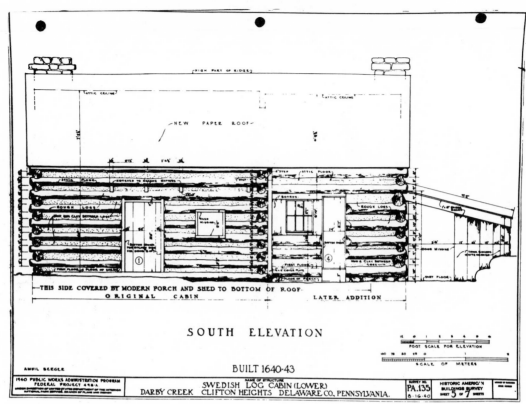

SOUTH ELEVATION

BUILT 1640-43

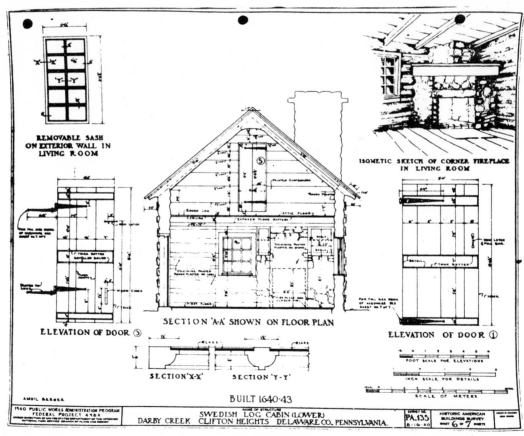

REMOVABLE SASH
ON EXTERIOR WALL IN
LIVING ROOM

ISOMETIC SKETCH OF CORNER FIREPLACE
IN LIVING ROOM

SECTION 'A-A' SHOWN ON FLOOR PLAN

ELEVATION OF DOOR ③

SECTION 'X-X'   SECTION 'Y-Y'

ELEVATION OF DOOR ①

BUILT 1640-43

SWEDISH LOG CABIN (Lower) Built 1640-43

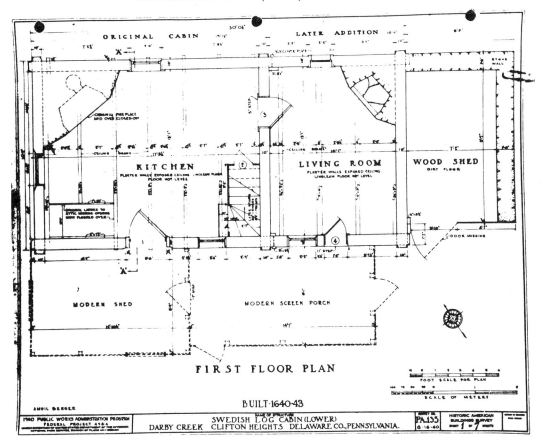

FIRST FLOOR PLAN

BUILT·1640-43

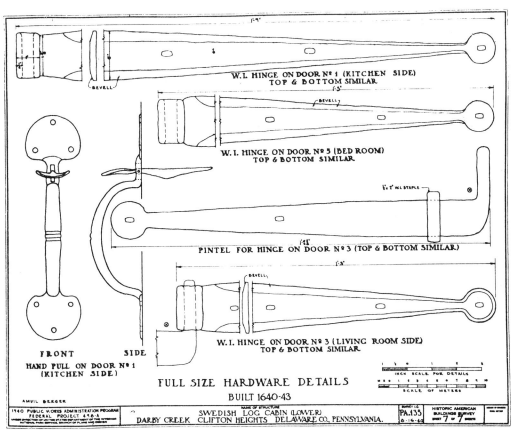

FULL SIZE HARDWARE DETAILS
BUILT 1640-43

PUSEY HOUSE, Upland First section built 1682, 21' x 18'; addition prior to 1696,   21' x 18'.

The Caleb Pusey house in Chester is considered to be the oldest surviving English built house in Pennsylvania. Caleb Pusey was born in 1651 and grew up in the hamlet of Chipping Lambourn in Berkshire, England. By 1675, Pusey had become a Quaker and had moved to London where he was a lastmaker, by trade. In 1681, when William Penn was selling off land in Pennsylvania, Pusey became a first purchaser. He paid £5 for two hundred and fifty acres. A group of Quaker investors, in England, had decided to put money into a grist mill, where wood could also be sawed for the colonists. Caleb Pusey was asked to become manager and agent of the mill. Richard Townsend, an experienced builder and miller, was to come to America to erect the mill and to build Caleb Pusey a house. The only record found of such a building having been brought to Chester County is from Richard Townsend's Account of his removal to Pennsylvania: "After some time I set up a mill, on Chester creek; which I brought ready framed from London; which served for grinding of corn, and sawing of boards; and was of great use to us."

In 1682, Caleb Pusey arrived in Pennsylvania and selected a site on the bank of Chester Creek, in Chester Township, for the mill. The rectangular stone house, twenty-four by eighteen and a half feet, had walls eighteen inches deep. The stone work is rough, many of the stones and boulders having been taken from the creek. The brick chimney is in the west gable end. The windows were double and single wood casements and the entrance had a batten door. The roof was low pitched and covered with wood shingles. The house resembles closely the medieval cottages that were familiar to Caleb Pusey, in Berkshire, England. Inside, the orginal house had one room on the ground floor with garret space above. Stairs are of the greatest

importance. The first colonists having built a one room house, with loft or garret above, used a ladder, either from the inside or the outside, to reach the space under the roof. As no evidence has been found in this house of an interior stair or opening in the second story floor for a ladder, the conclusion has been reached that the garret was entered by using an exterior ladder or stair. Along the west wall of the one room, there was a twelve foot cooking fireplace, with a brick hearth, a seat and a beehive bake oven which extended to the west. A low wooden shed was built against the exterior of the house, to the west, to protect the oven and the large exterior cooking kettle, used for brewing, candle making, dyeing, etc. The interior stone walls show evidence of having been whitewashed. There is a cellar fifteen by seven feet, ten inches and seven feet deep under the right section of the room reached by interior winding stone steps. There is also an outside cellar, just front of the west corner of the west room. Two of the walls are of red and black brick, laid in Flemish bond. The back wall of the cellar is below the front wall of the west room, indicating that the cellar preceeded the addition to the west.

Sometime, prior to 1696, when the Chester monthly meetings were held in the house, the stone addition twenty-one feet, ten inches was made to the west. At this time, the brewing kettle and well were enclosed in the house. The vault-like opening, on the front of the house, may well have been made at this time. Through the opening, fuel was fed to heat the large cooking kettle and oven at the back of the fireplace. Some seventeenth century home breweries, in England, have this arrangement for lighting the fire. In the eighteenth century, the pitched roof was changed to a gambrel, to afford more head room in the garret, and a dormer window was added.

MASSEY HOUSE, Marple Township
ca. 1692, 19' x 21'; ca. 1730, 20' x 19'; ca. 1860, 18' x 19'.

North side.

MASSEY HOUSE

Thomas Massey came to Pennsylvania at the age of twenty as an indentured servant to Francis Stanford, of Marple Township. In 1692, having served his time, he married Phebe Taylor and acquired three hundred acres in the township. The two and a half story brick house, laid in Flemish bond, nineteen by twenty-one feet is thought to have been an addition to an already existing log house. Thomas died in 1707/8, leaving his "plantation" to his eldest son, Mordecai, with the provision that Phebe should have "the lower room in the brick house" for as long as she did not remarry. About 1730, Mordecai tore down the log house and built the first stone addition, twenty by nineteen feet. The third addition, of stone, eighteen by nineteen feet, was made about 1860.

GILPIN HOUSE

About 1695, a one and a half story house, seventeen by twenty feet, of framed construction with brick masonry or "nogging" set in mortar between the uprights, the whole covered with clapboards was built. In 1745, a dated two and a half story stone addition was added to the west and in 1782, a dated story and a half stone wing, twenty-one by nineteen feet was added to the north. The house faces south which is usual in the county. The original house and

15

GILPIN HOUSE, Birmingham Township

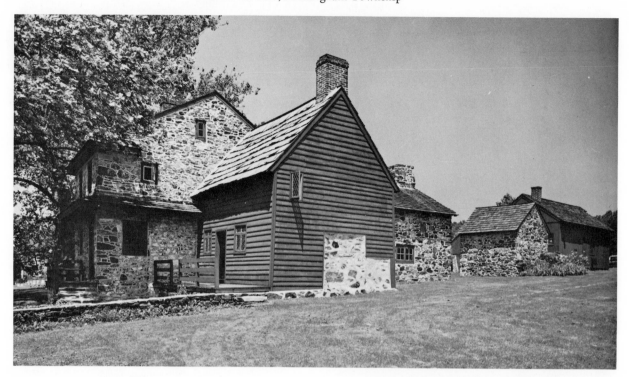

South front and east side

the addition to the north each had one room on a floor. The 1745 addition had two rooms on each floor and one in the garret.

On the 11th day of September 1777, there was taken and destroyed by the British Army under the command of General Howe from Gideon Gilpin 10 cows, 1 yoke of oxen, 7 yearlings, 6 calves, 48 sheep, 3 colts, wheat, corn, hay, buckwheat, potatoes, household line, clock, looking glass, a book, 4000 rails, £70 of fruit ana ther miscellaneous items. The following year, Gideon Gilpin petitioned the Justices of the Court of General Quarter Sessions for permission to establish a tavern. In 1825, when LaFayette returned to America, he visited Gideon Gilpin in this house.

This gunstock post detail, found where the staircase had been in the 1695 house, is apparently a unique detail in the county. The frames of the leaded glass casement window is original.

As found in the Gilpin house, many of the early stairs in the county were built in the gable-end, often sheathed in and making a half turn at the side of the fireplace. Sometimes a window was built into the gable wall to light the stairs. Occasionally, with each addition, as in the Gilpin House, stairs were built. The fireplace has no hearth. This is also noticed in a few other houses in this area built during this early period. The bake oven is outside the walls, covered with a shingled roof to protect it from the elements.

GILPIN HOUSE

1695 first floor

1745 addition, first floor

MARLBORO PLANK HOUSE, West Marlboro Township

South front and west side

This plank house, fifteen by twenty feet, was built in the early eighteenth century. The foundations are of stone. The interior must have been typical for the period: having board partitions, beamed ceilings and no baseboards. As late as 1798, many of the log houses in the county were fourteen or sixteen feet by twenty feet.

North and east sides

MARLBORO PLANK HOUSE

First floor, interior wall

Post and plank construction of East wall

BRINTON 1704 HOUSE, Birmingham Township

South front and west side

William Brinton and his wife, Ann, came from Staffordshire, England in 1684 and settled in Birmingham Township. They built a plank house, twenty-one by twenty-five feet in which they lived until 1704 when their son, William, built this two and a half story stone house, twenty-two by forty feet, known as "William Brinton's Great Houe". The frame addition is modern, built for the caretaker. The stone for the house came from a local quarry and is laid in courses of various thicknesses. The front and sides are symmetrical in the Renaissance style, while the back of the house follows the medieval traditions of placing openings for convenience, not balance. The steeply sloping dormer windows are typical of the early type surviving in the county.

North and west sides

BRINTON 1704 HOUSE

Fireplace

Candle Niche

The kitchen is in the west end of the cellar. Two stairways lead to the kitchen; one from the hall and one from outdoors to the east of the entrance. The latter would have been a great convenience when taking barrells and hogsheads to the cellar. The kitchen fireplace has a mantle tree above the opening but no mantlepiece. This is frequently found in the early houses. The bake oven opening is is the north wall of the kitchen fireplace and the oven itself extends under the steps leading to the first floor. There is no flue, the opening itself being left open while the oven was being heated. There were rarely doors to the early ovens. The fire embers would be made in the oven, the oven heated, the embers removed and the articles to be baked inserted. Indoors bake ovens are unusual in Chester County. The floor of the kitchen is flag stone. In the west end of the cellar, to the north, was a cold cellar probably with no glass in the windows and to the south, a warm cellar with glass in the windows. The floors of the cellars are a mixture of sand and lime stone that was dampened and tramped. In the north wall of the kitchen, there is a candle niche, a common feature of the eighteenth century houses.

BRINTON 1704 HOUSE

The first floor has two rooms, a hall and a lower room (parlor chamber); the second floor had two rooms when built, but the hall chamber was divided by 1750 when William Brinton's inventory was taken. The attic was unfinished. The attic rafters and collar beams are numbered. It was not until the early 1800's that anything was listed in an inventory as being in the attic. The ceilings in the first and second floors were plastered, but in the basement kitchen and the warm cellar, the beams were left exposed. The interiors of the outside walls of the house were plastered while the interior partitions were of vertical walnut boards. There were no baseboards. All of the fireplaces, except for the kitchen, had raised hearths. The closets in the hall, parlor chamber and parlor chamber upstairs have grills over the doors. The three closets in the west gable-end of the house all have small windows.

Attic

Raised hearth in chamber on first floor

BEEHIVE, Thornbury Township

Copy of photograph taken in the 1880's

The Beehive was built in 1705 by Richard Woodward, who settled on this tract of land in 1687. The site of an earlier house has not been discovered. The original two and a half story house is of stone, twenty-two by thirty feet. There were two rooms on the first and second stories divided by board partitions. The attic was one large room and a cellar is excavated under the west half of the house.

Originally, there was a stairway in both the east and west walls. The ceilings of the first and second story originally were plastered. The house never had baseboards. The summer beam extended below the plaster level. Sometime during the eighteenth century, a wing was added to the north which included a large cooking fireplace, and during the twentieth century, a number of partitions in the house were changed. The tile roof was put on in 1910.

South front and east side

BARNES BRINTON HOUSE, Pennsbury Township

Copy of photograph ca. 1905

William Barnes built this two and a half story brick house, twenty by forty feet, in what is now Pennsbury Township, sometime between 1704 and 1715. Brick, more widely used for houses than stone in colonies generally was employed rarely in Chester County and then mostly in the southern townships. The bricks are laid in Flemish bond in which the headers and stretchers alternate in each course. This gives an all-over diaper pattern to a building. The gable-end has a diaper design in the bricks and there are segmental brick arches over the small first floor windows on the side of the house. The roof is of steep pitch and is covered with wooden shingles. The pent eave originally went across the front of the house, the sides and three fifths of the back. The two chimney stacks are built in the walls of the gable-ends. On the north, there was once a lean-to or perhaps the original dwelling house of plank or log.

The first floor is divided into two rooms with a board partition. The second floor has a small hall at the head of the stairs and three chambers. There is also a garret. The house is unusual in that it has two winding stairs, one in each gable-end. Each stairway has a newel post and closed strings for a few steps before the winding stairs become enclosed. The fireplace ends are panelled with some of the best surviving early woodwork in the county. The kitchen fireplace has a built-in seat and window in it. The walls and ceilings are plastered and whitewashed and the space above the closet doors have grills.

First floor, east room

BARNES-BRINTON HOUSE

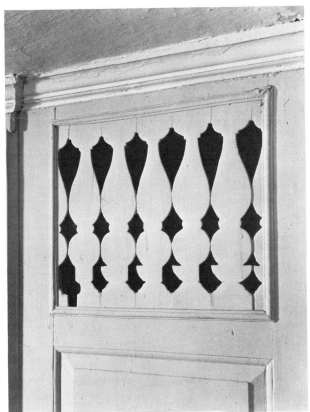

First floor, west room

Second floor, east room

Second floor, west room

CHADDS HOUSE, Birmingham Township

South front and east side

Francis Chadds came from Wiltshire, England to Chester County in 1689, and in 1702 he purchased the land in Birmingham Township on which he built a rubble masonry bank house. Rubble masonry is formed of stones, of varying sizes, but mostly rather small, which are sometimes roughly squared but frequently left quite irregular, and arranged without any order and set in mortar to form the walls. This was an economical way of building because almost every piece of stone, whether taken from a quarry or the field, was usable. Rubble masonry is in frequently found in the county and quoining is often employed on the houses built in this fashion. The house, twenty by thirty feet, is two and a half stories, plus a basement kitchen. The roof has a steep pitch and is covered with wooden shingles. Pent eaves were originally on the south, west and north sides. A bake oven extended from the fireplace in the basement kitchen. The porch, across the front of the house, appears to be very early as is the front door.

CHADDS HOUSE

Copy of photograph, ca. 1905

The entrance doorway is very typical for the period. The eighteenth century rectangular doorways usually had no more trim than the architrave itself. The door made of two thicknesses has eight panels on the exterior side while the inner side is made of boards running diagonally. Above the door, there is a rectangular glazed transom that lights the hall. The bars in the transoms are made of wood during the eighteenth century.

South front, first floor, exterior side of front door

CHADDS HOUSE

The first floor had two rooms divided by wide pine vertical board partitions which were later plastered over. The second story has a passage hall and two chambers and the garret has one large unfinished room. The exterior walls are plastered and the fireplace ends are panelled, some with built-in cupboards and shelves. On both the first and second stories, there are corner fireplaces. The house never had baseboards. The basement has a kitchen in the west half with an outside door and a cellar in the east. The floor of the kitchen was probably stone and the floor of the cellar earth. An interior stairway goes from the cellar to the first floor.

First floor

South front, first floor, interior side of front door

CHADDS HOUSE

First floor

Second floor

TEMPLE HOUSE
Bake oven on West Side

TEMPLE HOUSE, West Bradford Township

South front

Thomas Arnold, who owned a tract of land in West Bradford Township, probably built the two and a half story stone section of the Temple House in 1714. The 1798 Department of Revenue Direct Tax lists only the stone section twenty-one by seventeen feet. The roof has a steep pitch and is covered with wooden shingles. Across the front is a pent eave. The story and a half kitchen addition, eighteen by seventeen feet, must have been added shortly after 1798. The roof of the addition has been raised about three inches to give more head room to the kitchen chamber. The entrance door is made of two thicknesses of boards, the inner side having the boards running horizontally and studded with large headed hand forged nails running through both layers of the wood and clenched on the inside. The door is carried on strap hinges.

First floor, entrance door

TEMPLE HOUSE

The original Temple House has a small entrance hall from which straight closed string stairs ascend. There is a turned newel post, on the first step, and a simply moulded handrail. The wall under the stairs is panelled which is frequently found in the county at this period. In addition to the hall, there are two rooms on the first floor with corner fireplaces. On the second floor, over the larger down-stairs room, there are two rooms and a passage hall. There are board partitions between the rooms on the first and second stories. An interesting detail is the drawer under the window found in a few of the houses in Chester County. This house contains, in the original section, as much early woodwork as almost any other house in the county.

First floor

First floor

TEMPLE HOUSE

First floor

Basement, chimney arch

First floor

PARKE HOUSE, Caln Township

South front and east side

The Parke House, built before 1725, is one of the oldest surviving log houses not built by the Swedes in the county. It is fourteen by eighteen feet. As is usual with the early log houses, it is one and a half stories with foundations of stone. The roof is of medium pitch covered with wood shingles. The stone chimney is in the gable end built outside the house. On the first floor, there is evidence that there had been board partitions making two rooms on the first story with a loft above.

ST. DAVID'S PROTESTANT EPISCOPAL CHURCH, Newtown Township
Built 1715, 27' x 40'

ST DAVID'S CHURCH, BUILT 1717.

by C.L. Smith, Feby 4th 1862.   Bowen & Co lith Philada

From George Smith, *HISTORY OF DELAWARE COUNTY, PENNSYLVANIA, 1862.*

The Welsh Tract, in Chester County, was settled predominently by the Welsh members of the Church of England and the Welsh Quakers. The earliest date recorded of holding an organized Episcopal worship at Radnor was 1700 when Rev. Dr. Evans preached at the house of Mr. William Davis. Shortly after this time, tradition relates that the first church was built of logs in the neighborhood of present day Berwyn, in Easttown Township. In the Welsh Barony, Welsh was the common tongue. On December 7, 1714 the people at the southeastern end of the parish agreed to build a stone church and St. David's Church, in Newtown Township, was built in 1715. Fifteen families secured the land, quarried and hauled limestone from the Great Valley preparatory to burning lime, secured stone for the superstructure, obtained sand, felled, hewed and squared timbers and split and shaved shingles for the roof. The ceremonies of building a church were attended by both the English and Swedish clergymen. Israel Acrelius, one of the Swedish clergymen, mentions that: "On the 9th of May, 1715, Pastor Sandel (the Swedish missionary of Wicaoe, Philadelphia) was invited to attend the laying of the foundation of Radnor Church sixteen miles from Philadelphia. First a service with preaching was held in a private house; then they went in procession to the place where the church was to be built. Then a prayer was made, after which each of the clergymen laid a stone according to the direction of the master-mason."

The original church was twenty-seven by forty feet and eighteen feet to the square. It was a one story building with a roof of steep pitch. St. David's Church was laid out east and west, according to the custom of that day, with the main door on the south side. There were brick arches over both the panelled door and the windows. Over the years many improvements and changes were made to the building and grounds: in 1749, a school house was erected directly in front of the church within the graveyard walls; in 1765, Isaac Hughs was paid six pounds, seven shillings and six pence for laying the church floor and in 1767 there is a receipt for mason work for the vestry house. Until this time, there had not been pews in the church, people had supplied their own stools, benches and chairs. At this period, there are a number of records of individuals purchasing ground in the church on which to build their pew. In 1771, a large subscription secured the erection of a gallery at the west end which at the time built passed over the front door and joined the east wall. The gallery was

34

reached by an outside stone stairway. In 1776, Jonathan Hughes made a horse block; in 1784, a new gate was made for the graveyard; in 1809, the first addition was made to the graveyard. During the 1790's, the building was considerably repaired. At this time, the pews rented at two pounds each and the benches at ten shillings each per annum. In 1830, a number of changes were made to the building: that part of the gallery which passed over the front door was removed; the seventeen high backed pews were replaced with twenty-three low backed pews placed so that they faced the pulpit which was enlarged and removed from its old position, just east of the vestry room, to the eastern end of the church and surrounded by the chancel; the old sounding board was removed; lamp posts were placed in the alternate pews; new aisles of mortar were laid and a new vestry house, about seventeen feet square was built on the site of the older one. In 1840, the plaster ceiling of the church was blue washed; in 1844, a parsonage was built; in 1849, the graveyard was again enlarged; in 1858, a large and substantial receiving vault was built in the knoll in front of the church; in 1860, preparations were made for re-roofing the church; in the 1860's, the pulpit was entirely removed and the chancel was arranged very much as it is today, the lamp posts on the pews were removed and the church was illuminated by coal oil lamps, fastened in the wall; in the 1870's, stone walls were built and the church building itself, having become much dilapidated by the falling off of the plaster on the interior walls and the decay of the pointing on the exterior, in addition to the complete wreck of the vestry room, a large subscription was raised for the necessary repairs. A new vestry room, about eighteen by twenty-nine feet, was built and furnished as a Sunday School Room. The interior was painted, wainscoting was placed on the east wall and an arch over the chancel window was being installed. In time, the chancel window was replaced by wainscoting. In 1889, a new rectory was erected and during the twentieth century, a chimney was built on the west gable end and a building to house church offices and the Sunday School was built.

At the time that St. David's Church was built, it was one of the few stone churches in the province and it was constantly referred to as "The handsome stone church."

Horse Sheds

SPRINGFIELD MEETING, Springfield Township

BUILT 1738.

From George Smith, *HISTORY OF DELAWARE COUNTY*, 1862.

This meeting house was built in 1738.

UPPER OCTORARA PRESBYTERIAN CHURCH SESSIONS HOUSE, Sadsbury Township

Southwest to north side

The Upper Octorara Presbyterian Church Sessions House, in Sadsbury Township, was built between 1740 and 1745. It is one story, stone, fifteen by twenty feet. There is one door and two windows with shutters. Inside, there is one room with a corner fireplace and plastered walls. In Chester County, this building is a rare survival of a type once common to Presbyterian churches. In 1870, J. Smith Furthey wrote in, *HISTORICAL DISCOURSE...UPPER OCTORARA PRESBYTERIAN CHURCH* "In early times, it was very common to have these session houses —

study houses they used to be styled - in connection with every meeting house. I well remember hearing the term "study house" applied to this building in my young days. They were designed for the use of the ministers and elders of the church. Candidates for admission to church priviledges were there examined. The ministers were accustomed to use them in preparing for the services, when they arrived before the hour at which they began, and they would also resort to them to prepare for the after-noon service."

MORRISEIANNA, London Grove Township

First floor, original section

The original section of Morriseianna, in London Grove Township, was a small two story, stone house, sixteen by fifteen feet, built by Michael Harlan early in the eighteenth century. The house had one room on the first floor with a cooking fireplace eleven feet between the jams and five feet deep. There is a seat in the fireplace with a candle niche and there had been an oak lintel. The fireplace chimney is supported by an arch in the cellar. As is frequently found in early houses, the winding stairs to the second floor and to the cellar are placed to one side of the fireplace opening. The stairway to the second floor and the second story flooring are of oak. Diamond headed nails were used. The door to the basement is initialed "M H". When the inventory of Michael Harlan's estate was taken in 1729, only two beds were listed indicating he had not added to the original house. The original kitchen-hall is now one room of a center hall house to which later eighteenth century additions, a Greek Revival front porch and numerous other rooms have been added to form the present mansion. An unusual feature is a built-in clothes press on the second floor.

Clothes press

CHROME HOTEL, East Nottingham Township

South and west sides

The original center section of Chrome Hotel, in East Nottingham Township, was built of stone between 1715 and 1720. It was thirty by thirty feet. There were pent eaves on the south front, north and west sides. On the first floor, there was a large room on the south and two rooms on the north. On the second floor, there was one large south room, with a hinged partition, enabling two rooms to be made into one, and two rooms on the north side. The hinged partition is rare in Chester County. Before 1745, two wings were added. The west wing was one and a half stories, twenty-two by twenty-five feet and contained the kitchen and two very small rooms on the first floor and two rooms with board partitions on the second floor. There is an open string stair with ornamented step ends, a circular newel post, two turned balusters on each step, and a wainscotted dado on the wall opposite to the hand rail. The east wing was two and a half stories, eighteen by thirty feet. On the first floor, there were two rooms and on the second floor, there was a passage-hall and three small rooms. Most of the walls are plastered. The openings for doors and windows and the hardware seem to be original.

Chrome Hotel has the rarest, most elaborate front door found in the county. It is a panelled door, the top half in a diamond pattern made up of four diamonds and the bottom half with two rectangles and two squares. The door has a moulded wood enframement. The panelled shutter retains the original hardware. Many of the early eighteenth century houses show no evidence of having had shutters. When shutters were used on the early houses, they were used only on the ground floor, with louvered blinds on the second floor.

Corner fireplace, original section

CHROME HOTEL

Door

One of the few original "Dutch door" found thus far in the county

CHROME HOTEL

Swinging partition, original section

Shutter

PLUMSTOCK, Willistown Township early 18th century

HERR HOUSE

South and west sides

One of the most perfect surviving examples of German stone architecture is the house built by Christian Herr in 1719 in what was at that time a part of Chester County. The Herr House is built of sandstone from a natural outcroping in the southwest corner of the house. The house is rectangular, thirty-eight by thirty feet, with a sharply rising two story roof and a brick center chimney. Quoins have been used in the four corners of the house. There are no dormer windows, the second story and the garret being lighted from windows in the gable-end. Inscribed on the door lintel is "17 C H H R 19". This is the only house found thus far in the county to have stone framed casement openings. The surviving original stone framing around the windows retain the holes made for the hinges. There is a window in the west gable-end and two ventillators on the north wall.

The first floor is divided into three rooms. The door enters the kitchen in which there was the large cooking fireplace near the center of the house. No evidence of an oven has been found. The stairs to the second story and

HERR HOUSE

garret were in the southeast corner. The stairs from the second story to the garret are extremely steep and are formed from quartered logs. In the larger of the two remaining rooms on the first floor, there was probably a stove protruding from the kitchen fireplace. The exterior walls were plastered and the rooms were divided by board partitions. The ceilings were plastered between the joists. The second story was probably divided into two rooms, in one of which there was a fireplace. The vaulted cellar, running east to west on the north side of the house, is reached by exterior stone steps in the east gable-end. The floor is dirt.

Cellar

COVENTRY FORGE INN, South Coventry Township

The original section of Coventry Forge Inn, in South Coventry Township, was a two and a half story log house, eighteen by thirty-six feet, built about 1717. It consisted of two rooms on a floor. The log house had pent eaves on the south front. Sometime, before the Department of Revenue 1798 Direct Tax a stone addition, eighteen by twenty feet, was made to the north. Around 1800, a room was added to the northwest, thus making the house square. The pitch of the roof, of the original log house, was greatly changed at the time of the stone addition. The walls and ceilings are of plaster. The openings of doors and windows seem original. Although the house is plain on the outside, it has rather fine woodwork within, such as fireplace ends, built-in corner cupboards, chair rails and baseboards.

First floor

44

Copy of 1899 photograph

George Strode came from Southampton, England and purchased land in East Bradford Township in 1715, where he built a stone grist mill in 1721. In the stone quoining on the south wall, near the east end, the date "1721" has been cut into the stones. On the south side, the mill is two and a half stories, plus an almost clear basement above ground. It is about thirty by fifty-eight feet and has an entrance on both the north and east sides. The medium pitched roof today is covered with tin. Most of the openings are original and the windows show no evidence of ever having had shutters. A pent eave was on the east side of the mill. Inside, the original rafters are exposed. The size of the building, today, is the same as that mentioned in the Bureau of Internal Revenue Direct Tax for 1798. The frame addition to the west, the office and entry to the north were added during the twentieth century.

TOWN HALL, Chester
Built 1724 as a Court House

From George Smith, *HISTORY OF DELAWARE COUNTY*, 1862

THE OLD EAGLE SCHOOL, 1788

ABIAH TAYLOR HOUSE, East Bradford Township

HOUSE BUILT BY ABIAH TAYLOR IN 1724.

From Futhey and Cope, *HISTORY OF CHESTER COUNTY, 1881*

Abiah Taylor came from Berkshire, England in 1702 and built his first house in East Bradford Township. On the same tract of land, he later built a dated 1724 brick house. The date stone A 1724 D (with T above) is over the front door of the west front. The bricks for the house, laid in Flemish bond, were burnt on the property, a short distance south of the house. This two and a half story house is twenty by thirty feet. The Department of Revenue's 1798 Direct Tax shows that a stone kitchen, eighteen by twenty-one feet, was on the south of the house. This was apparently the original house, the outline clearly showing on the south gable today. The roof is of steep pitch and is covered with wooden shingles. Pent eaves were originally on the west front and south side. There were also "leaden window sash and glass" and segmental brick arches over the windows. There is no evidence of there having been shutters. The first floor consists of two rooms. The original cooking fireplace is in the north wall. The stairs to the second floor are to the left of the fireplace and a closet is on the right. Both the stairs and the closet have a small window. The second floor has one large room and two smaller rooms on the south side. The attic retains the old floors. The partitions are of plaster. The cellar is only dug out to the south of the chimney foundation. The opening to the cellar was originally outside the house.

ABIAH TAYLOR HOUSE

Window detail

SPRING MILL DATE STONE, East Whiteland Township

MARSHALLTON BLACKSMITH SHOP, West Bradford Township

North and west sides

Since the mid-eighteenth century, it appears that a shop has been on the property, in West Bradford Township, on which the Marshallton Blacksmith Shop stands today. The Department of Internal Revenue 1798 Direct Tax lists a stone building, eighteen by eighteen feet and a stone saddler's shop eighteen by eighteen feet. The present stone building, thirty by forty feet, one story to the west and two stories to the east may incorporate part of the earlier building. The blacksmith shop, to the west, has always been one large room with a shed to the south. The two story wheelwright shop, to the east, also consists of one room on each floor, with a shed to the south. On the roof of this shed, carriages could be taken thru large double doors to dry the paint. A ramp used to lead from the second floor drying porch to the ground. Except for this change, the building is almost unchanged thru the years.

MARSHALLTON BLACKSMITH SHOP

BIRTHPLACE OF BENJAMIN WEST, Swarthmore

South side

West and north sides

ASHBRIDGE HOUSE

The original early eighteenth century Ashbridge House, in East Caln Township, consisted of two rooms and a kitchen wing to the north. About 1755, a hall and two rooms were added making a center hall house with two rooms on either side of the hall and a kitchen wing. The main section of the house is thirty-three by fifty-one feet and the wing is eighteen by thirteen feet. About 1810, the original eighteenth century house was deepened and the pitch of the roof changed to match the 1755 addition. The old pent eaves remain on the west end of the south front and the west end of the north side.

The sloping shed dormer window over the original section of the house is a rare survival in Chester County. They had been used in England but were more frequently found in Wales and northern Europe. The shutters on the first story are panelled with cut out hearts.

ASHBRIDGE HOUSE

Stairs

About 1810, the interior woodwork of the west end was modernized, a second kitchen was made in the northwest room and a third arch was built in the west wall of the cellar to hold the present kitchen fireplace chimney. The original kitchen, to the north, became a summer kitchen and bake house. The window openings, interior trim, hardware and a stairway seem to be untouched since 1775 as is the stairway and trim in the 1810 addition. The floors are original and the walls are plastered. Cupboards are built into the plaster walls.

Stair detail

ASHBRIDGE HOUSE

First floor

Second floor

COLLINS MANSION, West Goshen Township

South front

Joseph Collins built the first section of a dated stone house in 1727 in West Goshen Township. Over the hood of the front door is a date stone inscribed I $\begin{smallmatrix} C \\ 1727 \end{smallmatrix}$ M for Joseph and Mary Collins. Above the door, it is not uncommon to find a cantilevered hood. On the Collins Mansion, the projecting hood is used with a pent roof. The beams of the main room of the house project thru the walls and support the pent eave and hood. The original house is two and a half stories, twenty-three by twenty-one feet, facing south. The front facade is built of dressed serpentine stone, from a local quarry to the north of the house, and the sides are built of field stone. The roof has a steep pitch and is today covered with composite shingles. Originally, the four windows on the south had leaded sash casement windows, with small fixed sash above. By 1760, Nathaniel Moore had added a field stone kitchen, twenty by twenty-three feet, to the original house.

Date stone

COLLINS MANSION

Kitchen fireplace

First floor

COLLINS MANSION

First floor

PUSEY HOUSE, London Grove Township

North side of the original house

The original stone section of the Pusey House, in London Grove Township, was built in 1728 by William Pusey. It was two and a half stories, twenty-seven by thirty-eight feet and faced south. There were two rooms downstairs and three rooms upstairs. In 1740, Joshua Pusey, the son of William, built a brick addition eighteen by thirty-nine feet. The addition had two rooms on each floor. The will of Joshua Pusey, proved in 1760 mentions: "...I give her [my loveing wife] all the Brick end of this my dwelling house with the Cellar under it during her widdowhood..."

In 1815, a brick addition was made to the west sixteen by thirty-five feet. This addition had two rooms on the first floor and three rooms on the second floor. The roof has a steep pitch and is covered with modern roofing material. The chimney of the original house is built of stone and those in both additions are built of brick. There are three staircases in the house, one for each section. On the first floor, the walls and ceilings are plastered except for the north room in the east wing which has an open beamed ceiling. On the second floor, the rooms are divided by board partitions. There is also a smoke chamber on the

PUSEY HOUSE

second floor of the original house.

In 1851, Jacob Pusey, a great grandson of William Pusey, said that he remembered as a youth seeing "W E P" [William and Elizabeth Pusey] on the gable of a portico over the front door and also that the date 1728 showed on a stone. On either side of the portico, at the front door, he remembered seeing benches attached to the house.

The inventory of Joshua Pusey, taken in 1760, lists this room as "his Desk room in the old House".

PUSEY HOUSE

Corner fireplace, first floor of 1740 addition

Smoke chamber on second floor of original house

WILLIAM MILLER HOUSE, Avondale

Cove cornice

The original section of the William Miller House, in Avondale, was a two and a half story, brick house built by William Miller in 1730. The bricks are laid in Flemish bond on a stone foundation. Across the front of the house, between the second story windows, are his initials and date "W M 1730" in black brick. The house was forty-three feet across the south front and forty-three feet deep which includes the kitchen wing which was probably built at the same time. In 1771, his son, William Miller, added a third story and between the third story windows are his initials and date "W M 1771" in black brick. There are also wavy lines in the gable ends formed of the black brick. The roof is of steep pitch and is covered with slate. There is a plaster cove cornice around the entire 1771 section. Pent eaves extended across the front of the house between the windows of the first and second stories and the original plaster cove of the two and a half story house remains between the windows of the second and third floor. The door and window openings on the front of the house are symetrical, while those on the sides are small and placed for convenience to give light to a closet or an attic. Over the entrance door, there were lights and a projecting hood. Benches were on either side of the doorway. Two brick additions were added, to the east, in the early nineteenth century but were destroyed by fire in the 1920's.

MILLER HOUSE

The first floor consists of a hall, a parlour on the right and a large kitchen and bake oven to the north. The second and third stories each have two large chambers with a small room between them. The kitchen wing has two rooms on the second floor and there are attics over the entire house. The house has much fine woodwork remaining and most of the board partitions. The stairway is particularly fine with its panelled newel posts and turned balusters extending to the fourth floor attic. There are chair rails and baseboards on three floors. The bollection moulding in the parlour, panelled ends, closets with grillwork over the doors are all exceptional for such a rural area. Except for the oven room, the early nineteenth century wings to the house have not been retained.

MILLER HOUSE

Second floor

Baking Room Oven

DOWNING HOUSE, East Caln Township

South front and east side

Thomas Downing, who came from Devonshire, England, purchased land in Caln Township, in 1739 without a house. The original south section of the stone house is two and a half stories high, twenty-two by thirty-two feet. A wing was added, before 1772, forty-two by thirty-two feet. The house has a gambrel roof, an unusual type in Chester County. The house has been considerably altered through the years. A dormer window and facilities for brewing are early features which remain.

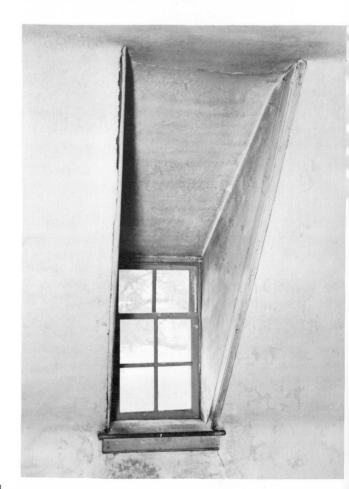

Dormer window

DOWNING HOUSE

First floor

Cellar-stone Arched Supports

SCONNELTOWN HOUSE, East Bradford Township

The Sconneltown House, in East Bradford Township, was probably built during the mid-eighteenth century. The Department of Revenue 1798 Direct Tax lists the property as belonging to John Dilworth and the house is described as being stone, one story, eighteen by twenty-six feet. There were five windows: two with five lights, two with four lights and one with three lights. The house faces west. The pitch of the roof is steep and is covered with wood shingles. The original shed dormer is rare for this area as is the shutter on the first floor window. There are two chimneys: one in the north gable and one corner chimney in the southwest corner. The house had two rooms on the first floor with board partitions. The cooking fireplace was off the north chimney with a bake oven. The small stairway was on one side of the fireplace and a small closet with a window was on the other. The ceilings, on the first floor, had open beaded beams four inches by nine inches. The windows had moulded sills and there were baseboards. The front door is original and retains the old hardware. Today, this house is a rare example of a type that was once very common - a story and half stone, log or frame house which the Department of Revenue 1798 Direct Tax proves to have been very prevalent in the county.

MT. PLEASANT, East Nantmeal Township

South front

The original field stone section of Mt. Pleasant, in East Nantmeal Township, which faces south, was probably erected in the 1730's when the property was part of the Reading Furnace tract. It was forty-one by twenty-one feet. In 1783, Colonel Thomas Bull purchased the property from Thomas Rutter and others and built the handsome present main section of the house with the west gable end, now the front of the building, facing the road. The addition is field stone, forty-four by twenty-two feet. The roof is of medium pitch and covered with wooden shingles. The chimney is brick. The door and window openings appear to be original. There were shutters on the first story windows. Over the first and third story windows of the addition, there are flat lentels and keystones of a rose coloured stone. The door sills, sink and the flashing for the pent eaves, of the original house were made of iron. There is also an outside bake oven in the original section of the house.

In the kitchen wing of Mt. Pleasant, there is an original dutch door, one of the few in the county, and open beamed ceilings. To the right of the fireplace opening, there is a door leading into the closet room that contains the iron sink which drains outside. The addition has a center hallway with a grained mahogany dado. The closed string stairs, in the back of the hall, have square newels and turned balusters. The stair landing leads off to one room and also turns and ascends to the second floor. The addition made to the original house contained some of the best panelling found in the county. In addition to wainscoting, there were windows with panelled reveals and seats, panelled fireplace ends, dentilled cornices and built in cupboards. Mt. Pleasant had fine interior trim on both the first and second stories, a feature not commonly found in this area.

MT. PLEASANT, East Nantmeal Township

PRIMITIVE HALL, West Marlboro Township

South front and east side

PRIMITIVE HALL, West Marlboro Township

Primitive Hall, in West Marlboro Township, was built by Joseph Pennock in 1738 as an addition to the first one and a half story stone house dating from ca. 1710. The original stone house became the kitchen of the new mansion. The bricks are laid in Flemish bond and there are arches over the doors and windows. There is a plaster cove cornice and pent eaves on three sides. The roof is of medium pitch and covered with wood shingles. The house does not have dormer windows, the large attic being lighted only by windows in the gable-ends. The door and window openings are not symetrical. The front entrance has a batten door over which there are lights. The windows have twelve over twelve lights on both the first and second stories. There are panelled shutters on the first story but there is no evidence of there having been shutters on the second story windows.

Primitive Hall is a center hall house and retains much of its fine original woodwork. The stairway is placed at the side of a large transverse stair hall which divides the four rooms and gives access to each one. The steps are wider and have a more gradual ascent than the stairs built before this period. The flight is straight to a landing across the end, then doubles back to reach the upper hall. There is a square newel post, boldly turned balusters which carry the handrail and originally there had been a panelled dado on the wall opposite to the handrail.

First floor

Stair landing

PRIMITIVE HALL

A number of houses have been found in the county, built at this period, that have a number of corner fireplaces. Primitive Hall is among the earliest. The over mantels of the house are either panelled without a mantel shelf or else have a mantel shelf and a simple fielded panel. The walls of the first floor are plastered and there are both chair rails and baseboards. There is a rare built-in corner cupboard with raised panels. The second floor has a hall from which each room is entered. Only one room, on the second floor has baseboards. There are board partitions.

Corner fireplace

Built-in corner cupboard

PRIMITIVE HALL

Corner Fireplace

A batten door retains the original wooden hardware. As are those in Primitive Hall, interior doors were usually panelled or of the batten type framed in a simple architrave. Batten doors are made from single thicknesses of vertical boards held in place by two or more horizontal boards.

Attic door

Built-in cupboard on stairway from first floor to cellar

JACKSON 1742 HOUSE, London Grove Township

"GREEN BANK."
RESIDENCE OF THOMAS M. HARVEY,
From Futhey and Cope, *HISTORY OF CHESTER COUNTY,* 1881

Joseph Jackson built a dated brick house in London Grove Township in 1742. The house is two and a half stories high. The main block is thirty-eight by nineteen feet plus an original wing, to the north, eighteen by twenty-two feet. This north wing was extended eleven feet sometime during the late eighteenth century. The west gable of the main block has a wavy pattern in black brick. Across the west side, in two foot figures, between the second story windows, is the date "1742". The house faces south, the foundations are of stone and the pitch of the roof is steep. The roof is covered by slate on the southern sections, the remainder of the roof is tin. Across the front of the house is the original plaster cornice. When the house was built, the cornice was also on the east and west sides.

The *DAILY LOCAL NEWS* (West Chester, Penna.) on March 23, 1879 mentions: "About a mile from the village of West Grove, on the Baltimore Central Railroad, is situated the fine old farm of Thomas M. Harvey. For a long distance over the neighboring hills Friend Thomas can see his broad acres stretching, and on the fertile meadows are as fine a herd of cattle as can be found in the county when its large size is considered. The old place was but recently purchased by him, but already the hand of improvement can be seen on every side. There have lately been erected a large addition to the barn, an immense corn crib, one of the most improved patters of milk house, a pig pen under cover and capable of holding 200 head of stock; and this year, he is building a tenement house on the hill between the old house and West Grove. The old farm house itself is a curiosity. On the northwest end, built of brick in the wall is the date 1742 in figures two feet long. The bricks for building the walls were brought from England. The interior division walls are quite substantial, being eighteen inches thick, of solid brick. The east walls of the rooms are in some cases covered with fine hard wood panelling, and cupboards and mantel shelves show very clearly that the carpenter of long ago was not afraid to rub a plane over the seasoned oak and ash. There is not so much as one cut nail in the whole house that was put there when it was built; all of these useful articles had formerly to be pounded out by hand, one at a time. The hinges on the doors, instead of being the neat affairs of to-day, are ponderous wrought iron bars, strong enough to resist the rust and wear of an eternity. The dining room contains four windows, no two of which are of the same size. In the march of improvement, the old house has been left undistrubed and friend Harvey likes the grand old place well enough to keep it as it stands."

JACKSON 1742 HOUSE

First floor

First floor

The first floor of the southern section of the house has two rooms. The fireplaces are in the outside end walls. The partitions between the rooms are of plaster. The doorway, chair rail and baseboard are all original. The original north wing contains one room and the stairway. The floor boards are oak.

JACKSON 1742 HOUSE

Second floor

The second story has three rooms in the south section with panelling or board partitions. Panelling of rooms, except for fireplace ends, is rare in Chester County. The woodwork on this floor is extremely fine for the county. The floor boards are pine. Much of the original hardware has survived. The cellar is under the south section of the house only. There is a vault which extends west from the cellar of the house and is reached by a short flight of stairs.

Second floor

WAYNESBOROUGH, Easttown Township

From Futhey and Cope, *HISTORY OF CHESTER COUNTY*, 1881

In 1742, Isaac Wayne built the first section of Waynesborough, a field stone house, in Easttown Township. It is two and a half stories, thirty-five by forty-five feet. In 1765, a wing was added to the northeast and in 1812, the house was again added to. There is a center hall with two rooms on either side and two wings. The walls are plastered and the openings for doors and windows seem original. A house was mentioned as being on this tract of land in 1723. By family tradition, it was built of logs.

SAINT PETER'S PROTESTANT EPISCOPAL CHURCH, East Whiteland Township   Built 1744, 63' x 28'

South front

For nearly fifty years, the two churches, St. David's in Radnor and St. Peter's in the Great Valley, formed one and the same parish. In 1744, instead of enlarging St. David's Church, St. Peter's Church, in East Whiteland Township, was built by private subscription by the Welsh people in the upper end of the parish. On a fly leaf of the old Vestry Book, dated 1744, is written, "Be it Remembered that this Year St. Peter's Church Was Built Under ye Care of Richd Richison, Math ^ah Davis, Jno Cuthbert and Morris Griffith." The original building was one story, stone, sixty-three by twenty-eight feet, with a steep roof covered with wooden shingles. There were semi-circular windows with oak shutters and iron hardware on either side of the doorway on the south front. At this time, there is no record that there were pews, a gallery, altar, pulpit, or paving. The congregation sat on whatever the individual members chose to supply for themselves. In 1749, the vestry took measures to provide uniform and orderly seating equipment. Thirty-two pews were ordered; twenty-six of which were eight feet long and twenty-eight inches wide and six pews were seven feet long and twenty-eight inches wide. In 1750, the vestry ordered that a gallery be built across the west end and along the south side of the church. Three years later, Edward Pearce was paid £ 6 toward building the gallery. In 1755, Edward Pearce received £ 2.0.0 for building sixteen pannels of post and rail fence along the front of the graveyard and in 1762, two stables were built by the same Edward Pearce for £ 2.15.0 and two stoves were ordered for £ 4.12.6 to accommodate the congregation. In 1765, Robt Rolston built five pews in the gallery and in 1770, John Gronow received 20 for building the wall in front of the graveyard. In 1787, "At a Vestary...it was ordered that Rich^d

Richison and Jno Potter should agree with some Joiner to Build a Pulpit, Reading Desk, and Communion Table and to floore and Banaster ye same and accordingly they agreed with Jn ^o   Wayne for £ 12.0.0 - To Do & Complete y^o same Workman Like". The altar stood beneath the large rounded east window. The high pulpit, with the reading desk for the clerk beneath it, stood against the north wall nearly opposite the main entrance which was the south door. The original sacristy was a small stone projection on the north side of the church with a doorway into the church just west of the pulpit. In 1823, Parson Brinckle organized a Sunday School. In 1830, the interior of the building was plastered, new low backed pews were installed, the pulpit was placed at the end of the church and a new vestry room was erected. In 1850, Parson Winchester wrote: "Edward Pearce may indeed be said to be the architect of the building, as he seemed to be the lever which reared the pile." In 1856, there were many changes made: the old vestry was torn down; a fifteen foot addition was made to the east; the exterior walls were pebble-dashed and whitewashed; the south gallery was removed; the roof was covered with tin; the then square windows were hung with green slat blinds and the walls and vaulted ceiling were painted a dull grey instead of white. About 1900, the next major changes and repairs were made which included replacing the pulpit, adding a parish house to the north of the 1856 Sunday School building, changing the windows back to having semi-circular heads and covering the old stone floor with wood. In 1939, the parishioners wished to restore St. Peter's Church, as much as possible, to its original appearance. R. Brognard Okie was the architect and the church today is the result of his research.

BIRMINGHAM FRIENDS MEETING, Birmingham Township

South and West side

Mounting block

Birmingham Friends Meeting was first authorized to be held in 1690 in William Brinton's one a half story plank house, twenty-one by twenty-five feet. The first meeting house was authorized to be built in 1718. Until that time, meetings had been held in members' homes. The original section of the present Birmingham Meeting House was erected in 1763. The diary of Benjamin Hawley mentions: "6th mo. 13th...P.S. Went to the raising of ye meeting house." This original, one story, fieldstone section was thirty-eight by forty-one feet. Inside, the usual Quaker plan was used of sliding partitions to divide the men's business meeting from that of the women at monthly meetings. There was a stove but no fireplace. The walls were plastered. It was here that the British took their wounded during the Battle of the Brandywine, September, 1777. In 1818, a stone addition was made making the building seventeen and a half feet longer. At this time, the sliding partitions were removed and new ones placed in the center of the enlarged building. The original roof was of wood shingles. The present slate roof was put on in 1864. The openings for doors and windows are original although the door to the grave yard, to the north, has been walled up. The doors and shutters are panelled and over each door there is a projecting hood.

CENTER CHIMNEY HOUSE, London Grove Township

The Center Chimney House was built about 1763 in London Grove Township. That year, Robert Baldwin petitioned the Justices of the Peace of the Court of Quarter Sessions for a license for a tavern: "...That your Petitioner hath settled on a Plantation on the grate Road leading from Lancaster to Newport on the Run Cauld the Pound Run on Which Said Place a good new Dwelling house shed & Stabling is now erected & your Petitioner Humbly Consaveing the Same may be a Suitable Place for a tavrin..." The house is built of stone, two and a half stories high, thirty by thirty-three feet and faces south. Later it was covered with plaster. The doors and windows are original. The roof has a fairly steep pitch and is covered with wooden shingles. In the basement, there is one large room in the east end and two rooms in the west end. There is also a fireplace and bake oven. The stone stairs, from the basement to the first floor, are on the west side of the center chimney. Both the first and second floors have four rooms each with plastered walls. The stairs between the first and second stories are enclosed. The attic is one large unfinished room. This is the only center chimney house that has been found in the county as it exists today. The Center Chimney House is particularly interesting as it was not built by a German.

The *AMERICAN REPUBLICAN* (West Chester, Penna.) on January 20, 1880 describes the Half Way House. "It is a 3-story stone building with roof projections, or point eaves covering the windows at sides and ends. At one corner of the wall near the main outer door, is a projecting stone, with a deep notch or slit out in it over which travelers threw the reins of bridles when alighting. The outer doors are very wide, with heavy oak double panneling with immense wrought iron hinges and locks, large enough for a jail. The chimney, which occupies a central position on the building, is a wonderful structure; being 18 feet wide and 5 feet deep. The fireplace had evidently been supplied with logs drawn in by a horse, for which there was abundance of room. In connection with this chimney, is a pair of very substantial stone steps, leading to the second story, and back of this the wine or liquor cellar. The roof is sustained by heavy, hewn rafters and purlings, with king-braces, strong enough for a barn roof. In the garret are old-time relics..."

MARSHALLTON FRIENDS MEETING, West Bradford Township

Picture courtesy of Mrs. Robert K. Long

The first meeting, for Bradford Township, was established in 1726 and the second in 1729. In 1765, when the present fieldstone meeting house, forty-five by thirty-eight feet, was built, the building previously used was moved to the farm of Abraham Marshall where it was used as a barn or stable for many years. The cornice and the door and window openings are original. The shutters and doors are panelled and over the door there is a projecting hood.

The 1765 Marshallton Friends Meeting House consisted of one room with the usual sliding partitions to separate the men's and women's business meetings. A most unusual addition to this general plan is the additional set of sliding partitions at right angles to the above with space for two rows of pews between it and the south wall. The center chimney is still in use with a stove and the walls are plastered.

MARSHALLTON FRIENDS MEETING, West Bradford Township

Sliding partitions closed

Sliding partitions with glass windows

"House of Nathan Sharpless Drawn by William P. Evans in 1856 or 1857"

WARRENPOINT, Warwick Township

South front

Warrenpoint is a stone house, two and a half stories high, built in the mid-eighteenth century, in Warwick Township. It is thirty-three by forty-four feet, plus a wing seventeen by twenty feet. There are three large stone chimneys. The roof, of medium pitch, is covered with wooden shingles. The house has shutters on the first floor but shows no evidence of having had shutters on the second story. The entrance door, instead of having lights in the transom, has lights in the door itself. The door, made of boards running horizontally, is hung on strap hinges. As is usual in masonry houses, the walls are thick and the door reveals are quite deep and, in this case, have been panelled. The cellar is under part of the house only and the porch, on the south front, was added during the twentieth century. Few other alterations have been made.

North and east sides

WARRENPOINT

The main section of Warrenpoint has a center hall with two rooms on either side. The kitchen wing is to the east. The walls and ceilings are plastered.

First floor

WARRENPOINT

The reveals of the windows are covered by wood panels. There are also window seats and panelled interior shutters which fold back into the jambs. The use of interior shutters is unusual in the county. A special characteristic of the better houses are the cupboard doors with arched heads, keystones and sometimes shaped shelves frequently used to flank parlour fireplaces. Warrenpoint contains some of the finest woodwork in the county.

First floor

WARRENPOINT

Second floor

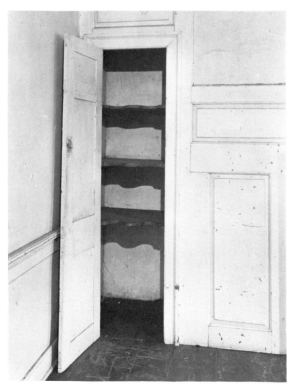

First floor

Basement

MOORE HALL, Schuylkill Township

South front and West side

Moore Hall, in Schuylkill Township, was built during the mid-eighteenth century for William Moore, Justice of the Peace, Judge, assemblyman, militia colonel and Chester County's most prominent loyalist in the Revolutionary War. The stone house is two and a half stories, twenty-nine by forty-five feet with a story and a half stone wing twenty-one by twenty-five feet. The house was much altered thru the years.

The interior of Moore Hall, today, fits the newspaper description which appeared in the AMERICAN REPUBLICAN (West Chester, Pa.,) on August 3, 1819: "Large and substantial stone house, four rooms and an entry on the lower floor, and five on the upper, with a large hall and kitchen adjoining."

First floor

TAYLOR PARKE HOUSE, West Bradford Township

North and west sides

The Taylor Parke House, in West Bradford Township, was built in 1768. The house is built of fieldstone, two and a half stories, thirty-seven by thirty-four feet, plus a one story kitchen wing twenty-six by twenty-one feet. The date stone, on the south front is inscribed "A $\frac{T}{1768}$, A" for Abiah and Ann Taylor. The front facade is built of dressed stone; the sides and back of field stone laid in random fashion. The door and window openings appear to be original except in the kitchen wing. As is frequently found in the county, solid shutters were used on the first story and louvred blinds on the second story. The shutters, on the first story, are made of two thicknesses of wood so that they are panelled when open and when closed, the boards run vertically. There is a batten front door, over which there are four lights with wood mullions. The stairway is directly opposite the front door. There is a square newel post with chamfered corners, a simple hand rail and panelling on the wall under the stairs. An interesting feature is the arched passage under the stairs connecting two rooms.

There are two corner fireplaces on the first floor, the over mantel of one is panelled and has a mantel shelf while over the second, there is a cupboard with glass doors. The house has both chair rails and baseboards.

TAYLOR PARKE HOUSE, West Bradford Township

First floor

First floor

First floor

MARTIN'S CORNER HOUSE, West Caln Township

The Martin's Corner House, in West Caln Township, erected about 1769, is built of hewn logs, saddle notched at the corners and chinked between the logs. The foundations and chimney are stone. The roof is of medium pitch covered with modern roofing materials. The house is two and a half stories, twenty-six by thirty-four feet, with four rooms on the first and second floors. On the first floor, some of the walls are plastered while others have the logs and chinking exposed. The beams in the ceiling are exposed. Both the first and second stories have fine board partitions. The stairway, in the northwest corner room, has been straightened, now making a quarter turn instead of the original half turn. The original cooking fireplace remains; the lintel is twenty-two inches high and eighteen inches wide.

MARTIN'S CORNER HOUSE

First floor, kitchen

This house has a number of features that have not been found in other houses: the door hinges and crane in the large cooking fireplace are made of wood instead of the usual metal and the floors are pegged. The niches found in the walls of this log house are also found in masonry houses. Except for the modern hood over the door, the stairs and parts of the house having been covered with plaster board, this house remains very much as built.

Wood crane in kitchen fireplace

MARTIN'S CORNER HOUSE

Door with wood hinges on second floor

First floor, detail of pegging

LOG HOUSE, East Bradford Township
Built ca. 1770, 18' x 20'.

South front and west side

Charles Wollerton, of East Bradford Township, in his will in 1781, left to his son, James, "house I know live in." The Department of Internal Revenue 1798 Direct Tax lists the house as being built of log eighteen by twenty feet, and in 1815, a newspaper advertisement mentions the house as being "a two story squared log house, two rooms on a floor, with a cellar under the whole, and a new piazza in front". This log house was probably built during the 1770's. The house has been chinked with stones set diagonally in mortar, each course set diagonally opposite to the preceeding one. Later additions have been made to the north and east of the original house and the stone chinking has been covered with clapboards for the most part. Very little interior trim remains.

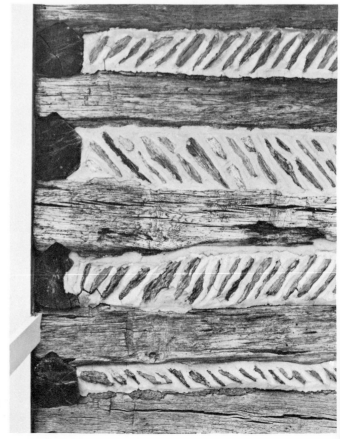

Southwest corner detail of saddle notched logs and chinking of stone

THOMAS MILL, Willistown Township

South front and east side

The Thomas Mill, in Willistown Township, was built in 1774 by Isaac Thomas, who in addition to being a grist miller, was a joiner, surveyor, farmer and clock maker. The mill was built of fieldstone, twenty-three by thirty-five feet. An early extension of sixteen feet was made to the north. The mill, which faces south, has been little changed since the time it was built. There are two and a half stories plus a basement. The stairway is built of quartered red logs and the timbers were fashioned with a broad axe. The openings for doors and windows appear to be original. There is a fireplace in the southwest corner on the lower floor. The works, today, are in the Smithsonian Institute in Washington, D.C.

93

THOMAS MILL

South front, first floor

First floor, quarter log stairs

HOOPES CURRYING SHOP, Caln Township

West front and south side

West front and north side

The Hoopes Currying Shop, in Caln Township, is listed as a stone currying shop in the Department of Internal Revenue Direct Tax for 1798. Except for the replacement of the roof, this building was unchanged until a few years ago, when it was torn down. The shop, built of rough fieldstone, is one and a half stories with basement, seventeen by eighteen feet, facing west, with a tin roof of medium pitch. The chimney is built outside the masonry gable wall. Shutters were originally on the front window on the first floor. The basement is one room with a fireplace, dirt floor and has exposed beams in the ceiling. There is no inside staircase to the first floor, but it is entered from a stairway leading to the porch which is supported by the first floor joists which extend thru the walls. On the first floor, there is one room with a chimney which has a stove flue on the south wall. The floors are old, the walls are rough plastered and the ceilings have open beams. There were never any baseboards. The stairs leading to the loft are in the northeast corner. Buildings, such as the Hoopes Currying Shop, in which a man lived and worked were prevalent in the county during the eighteenth century.

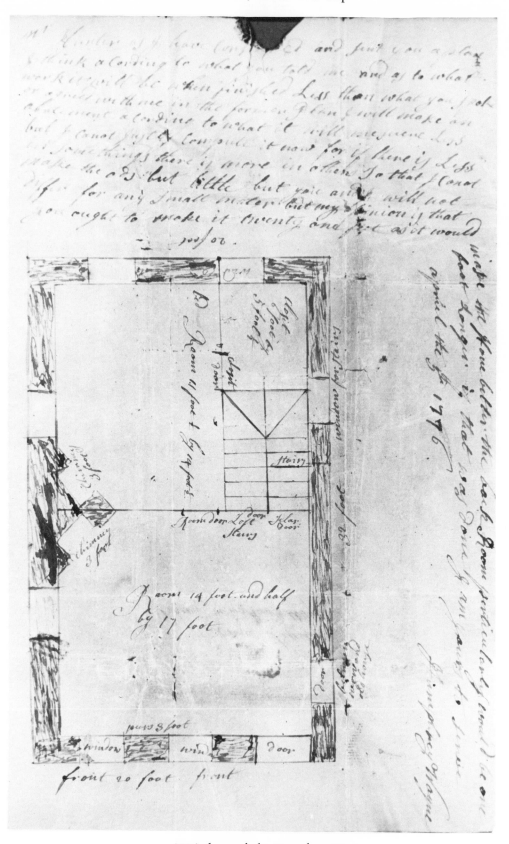

1776 plan made by Humphrey Wayne

HUMPHREY MARSHALL HOUSE, West Bradford Township

South front and west side

Humphrey Marshall was the son of Abraham Marshall, who came from Derbyshire, England to Chester County in 1707 and settled in West Bradford Township. Like his father, Abraham, Humphrey Marshall was a mason and built a dated stone house in 1773. The date stone is on the south side surrounded by bricks, set in a circle, over the door between the second story windows. Humphrey Marshall was a cousin of John Bartram and he filled many public offices. He is best remembered as being the author of *ARBUSTUM AMERICANUM: or, THE AMERICAN GROVE,* which was printed in 1785 by Joseph Cruikshank, in Philadelphia. In 1788, a French edition of the book was issued. Marshall corresponded widely with the leading natural scientists in America and Europe. With these men, he exchanged data; he also gathered together specimens for collectors.

The house is two and a half stories high, built of Wissahickon gneiss and diabase and vein quartz stone. On the front and sides of the house, the stones are laid in courses while on the back, the stones are irregularly laid. The house is twenty-eight by fifty-one feet and faces south. The roof, of steep pitch, is presently covered with asbestos shingles. There are shutters on the first floor windows.

The two most unusual features of the house are the flue from the first floor main room and the clock niche in the same room. The flue leads from the fireplace in the west wall at an angle back and across the room to a chimney in the gable end. From this second floor room, the flue runs along the wall in a series of steps to the west outer wall where the chimney is placed. This long flue, within the house, helped to heat the plant room on the first floor and the long room on the second floor. The long room also has a small wall safe built into the north wall. The woodwork of the house, especially that in the two rooms with corner fireplaces in the east end of the first floor, seems to be much earlier than the house itself. This is a characteristic of the county where there is considerable "cultural lag".

HUMPHREY MARSHALL HOUSE

First floor

HUMPHREY MARSHALL HOUSE

Kitchen fireplace

The inventory of the house, taken at the time of Humphrey Marshall's death in 1801, carefully lists all household items and the division into rooms is either carefully noted or else implied. The rooms today seem to have remained the same but with different uses. The room in the center of the house, with the stairway, has two rooms east of it with corner fireplaces over which there is panelling. To the west of this main room was the plant room, the back room downstairs and the kitchen. The kitchen fireplace has two bake ovens and the original crane. The rooms on the second floor remain the same, except for a back stairway which was removed. The small observatory that projected to the south from the long room on the second floor was removed late in the nineteenth century.

ALLEN HOUSE, Pocopson Township

South front and west side

The Allen House, in Pocopson Township, is a brick, bank house built in either 1780 or 1781. In the latter year, the place was taxed with improvements for the first time. Sometime between 1844 when the AMERICAN REPUB- LICAN (West Chester, Penna.) on November 26, mentions "...a good brick tenant house 18 by 12 feet, two stories high, with a good well at the door" and 1869 when the VILLAGE RECORD (West Chester, Penna.) on October 12 mentions: "Also two good Tenant Houses, one of which is brick and stone with stable attached". A stone addition, eight by fourteen feet was made to the original brick house. The two exterior doors, window openings and hardware are original. The sash is a replacement and there is no evidence of the house having had shutters. The chimneys are both of brick and are original. The porch is early for this section of Pennsylvania. The Allen House is a good example of what was once a very usual type of house in the county, a story and a half stone, brick or frame house which was later replaced, usually in the early nineteenth century by a larger mansion.

First floor

ALLEN HOUSE, Pocopson Township

First floor

The kitchen is in the basement. The enclosed winding stair is in the northwest corner of the brick section of the house. The first floor has two rooms with board partitions, exposed beams and no baseboards in the original eighteenth century section and one room in the later stone addition. The loft is one large room.

BRICK SHOP, Elk Township

South front and west side

A brick shop, twelve by fourteen feet, was built about 1790 in Elk Township. The bricks are laid in English bond. On the south front, there is a brick cornice, a door and a window. The chimney is in the west gable-end. The building is one story and a loft, a room on each floor with a ladder to reach the loft. The shop is practically unchanged since the time it was built. At different times, it was used by a spinning wheel maker, a turner and a shoemaker.

EDGE HOUSE, Caln Township
Built ca. 1784, 25' x 41' with wing 24' x 23'.

Kitchen drain

VODGES HOUSE, Willistown Township

First floor

First floor

The Vodges House, in Willistown Township, is a fine stone house with a date stone in the east gable "J$\underset{1795}{\overset{V}{}}$E" for Jacob and Elizabeth Vodges. The original section of the present house is two and a half stories, thirty by thirty-three feet, and faces south. The east wing, fifteen by twenty-one feet, was added after 1800, making it a center hall house. Although there have been changes made to the house throughout the years, much fine woodwork remains.

At the end of the eighteenth century, handsomer staircases with decorated open strings and balusters, which supported mahogany handrails, were coming into fashion in Chester County. Mantel pieces began to be decorated with gesso ornaments of leaves and classical motifs applied to the woodwork. Some of the gesso work was made by Robert Welford & Son of Philadelphia. Pilasters were also sometimes decorated as found in the Vodges House.

103

BRIDGE ON THE BRANDYWINE, Downingtown

The Bridge on the Brandywine, on the Horse Shoe
Road, at Downingtown was built about 1800. Benjamin
Henry Latrobe was the architect.

MILLTOWN HICKMAN PLANK HOUSE, East Goshen Township   Built ca. 1800, 15' x 25'.

East front and north side

West wall showing post and plank construction

MILLTOWN HICKMAN PLANK HOUSE

First floor, kitchen fireplace

CALHOON HOUSE
Built mid 18th Century, 15' x 18'

Log construction on first floor

PLEASANT GARDEN IRON WORKS, New London and East Nottingham Townships   Erected ca. 1803

VIEW OF THE PLEASANT GARDEN IRON-WORKS.

Situate on Big Elk Creek, Chester County, Penn.

South front

Although the Mary Rogers House, in West Goshen Township, bears the initials of Mary Rogers and the date 1807, William Rogers, her husband, started to build this stone house before he died. The original section, to the east, is two and a half stories, thirty-seven by thirty-one feet and faces south. The addition, to the west, made about 1815, is seventeen feet long. The front of the house is built of dressed serpentine stone and the sides and back of field stone. The roof has a medium pitch and is covered with wood shingles. The cornice is unusually elaborate for the county. The front has three arched dormer windows with bold dentillation and fluted pilasters. There is a semi-circular lunette or fanlight over the panelled front door and pilasters on either side of the doorway. The exterior workmanship of this house is among the finest in the county.

MARY ROGERS HOUSE

There is a center hall with two rooms on either side of the hallway. The hall is divided by an eliptical arch. The open string stairs are placed at the side. They have a mahogany hand rail and reeded square balusters. The landing is lighted by a window having an arched head, keystone and panelled reveals.

Detail of dormer window, cornice and date stone

Palladium window on stair landing

MARY ROGERS HOUSE

Hall

Hall

MARY ROGERS HOUSE

First floor

There are plastered walls, baseboards and chair rails. The fireplaces have applied plaster decoration and marble surrounds. The *CHESTER AND DELAWARE FEDER-ALIST,* (West Chester, Pa.,) on November 27, 1811 mentions:"WILL BE SOLD...the buildings consist of a new two story dwelling, and kitchen, all built of stone - the new house elegantly finished..."

HOPEWELL ACADEMY, Hopewell

Front

Hopewell Academy, in Hopewell, was built as a two and a half story school about 1814. It is now a three story brick building fifty-three by twenty feet with a wing extending to the north thirty-four by nineteen feet. The bricks are laid in Flemish bond. The roof is flat and covered with slate and tin. The doorway is one of the most elaborate in the county. The panelled door is flanked by two narrow windows or sidelights and all three elements are topped by a graceful elliptical arched fanlight. The doorway has gouged wood carving and a keystone.

Front

HOPEWELL ACADEMY

First floor

There are six rooms on the first floor, eight on the second and twelve lodging rooms on the third floor. The walls are plastered and there are baseboards, chair rails and cornices. The fireplaces are carved using delicate fluting and pateras. Cupboards have been built into the side walls of the fireplaces.

First floor

HOUSE OF CHARLES D. PHILLIPS, West Chester

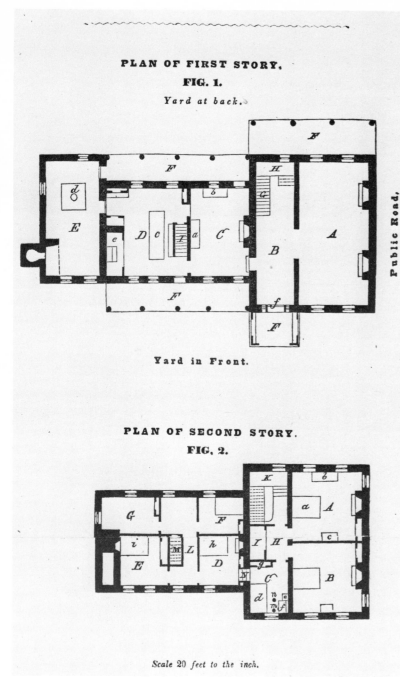

PLAN OF FIRST STORY.

FIG. 1.

Yard at back.

Public Road.

Yard in Front.

PLAN OF SECOND STORY.

FIG. 2.

Scale 20 feet to the inch.

FIGURE 1—FIRST STORY.

A—Unfinished Parlor, used as a Chamber.
B—Main Entrance Hall.
C—Dining or Sitting Room.
  a—Sofa.
  b—Settee.
D—Kitchen.
  c—Kitchen Table.
  e—Fire-place with Cooking Stove.
E—Wash-house or Back Kitchen.
  d—Pump.
F F F F—Front and Back Piazzas.
  f—Front Door.
G—Main Stairs.
H—Landing of Main Stairs.
I—Back Stairs.

FIGURE 2—SECOND STORY.

A—Phillips' Chamber.
  a—Bed in Phillips' Chamber.
  b—Settee   do.   do.
  c—Secretary do.   do.
B—Spare Chamber.
C—Lennard's Chamber, 11 ft. 10 in. long by 9 ft. wide.
  d—Bed in Lennard's Chamber, 6 ft. 7 in. long by 4 ft. 8 in. wide.
  e—Chair in   do.   do.   1 ft. 6 in. long by 1 ft 6 in. wide.
  f—Desk in corner of Lennard's Chamber, 2 ft. 10 in. long by 2 ft. 3 in. wide and 2 ft. 11 in. high.
  g—Closet, projecting 1 ft. 1 in. into the room.
  m—The place where Phillips stood when the pistol discharged.
  n—The place where Bartholomew stood when the pistol discharged.
D—Lewis' Chamber.
  h—Bed in Lewis' Chamber.
E—Women's Chamber.
  i—Bed in the Women's Chamber.
F and G—Chambers.
H—Passage between Chambers, 5 ft. 2 in. wide by 8 ft. long
I—Large Closet.
K—Landing of Main Stairs.
L—Passage.
M—Back Stairs.
N—Steps from Lennard's to Lewis' Chamber.

Used as an illustration reporting a murder trial.

BELL SCHOOL, East Caln Township

Built 1818   Copy of photograph

FRIENDS SCHOOL, East Caln Township

Copy of a drawing

DIAMOND ROCK SCHOOL,   Tredyffrin Township

South front

The Diamond Rock School, in Tredyffrin Township, is an octagonal, stone, one story school house built in 1818. It faces south and is ten feet on a side. The land on which the school was built was leased by George Beaver, Jr. to a group of trustees as tenants in common for nine hundred and ninety-nine years or as long as the school was used as such. The building was erected by a group of local inhabitants, chiefly of Welsh and German descent. The openings for the door and windows are original, although the frame for the door and the door itself are replacements. The shutters are also replacements. Inside the building there is one room. The *MESSENGER* (Phoenixville, Penna.) on March 6, 1909 mentions:

"The furniture consisted of long desks with benches for seats. The pupils sat facing the wall and the windows. The door was flanked on either side by open cupboards for the kettles and dinner baskets; but no provision was made for clothing beyond a few pegs.

In the middle of the room stood a large tenplate stove with a capacious door that would admit a good sized log. The sawing and splitting of the wood for this stove formed a drill in athletics that is not in fashion in our modern schools. The building was opened in the spring of 1818. During the winter term at times, as many as sixty scholars attended. They were mostly men and women, as the younger children were only allowed to go during the spring and fall."

BUCKWALTER HOUSE, East Nantmeal Township

Built in 1821, 31' x 35'

First floor

Date stone and cornice detail

PARKE HOUSE, Parkesburg

Built ca. 1825   West side

Ironwork

South front of porch

PARKE HOUSE, Parkesburg

First floor

Stairway

MT. ROCKY METHODIST CHURCH, Elk Township

Copy of 1899 or 1900 photograph

In 1829, Thomas and Elizabeth Wilson sold ninety-six perches of land in Elk Township to Richard Mahan, et. al., trustees, to build a Methodist meeting house. *THE DAILY LOCAL NEWS*, (West Chester, Penna.,) on July 29, 1885 mentions: "This is one of the oldest church buildings in the lower part of Chester County having been erected in 1831". This log church was a story high with a loft. The squared logs were notched into the upright corner posts, a most unusual type of log construction in Chester County. Mortar was set between the logs. The foundations were stone. The building faced south and had a steep pitched roof that was covered with wooden shingles. The door was on the south side with two windows and there were two windows on the north side. There were shutters at the sash windows. The chimney was in the center of the one room fitted for a stove. The interior walls were plastered. *THE JEFFER-SONIAN*, (West Chester, Penna.,) on October 16, 1869 mentions: "The house has been crowded to its utmost capacity, and many are unable to obtain admittance. A larger church is greatly needed, and, we learn, the building of an addition to the present house is contemplated. The meetings will be continued during this week". To-day the church has fallen down.

Northwest corner

DAVID TOWNSEND HOUSE, West Chester

West side

The David Townsend House, in West Chester, was started about 1785 when a one and a half story brick house, twenty-four by sixteen feet, was built. In 1830, a two and a half story brick addition was made to the south, twenty-eight by thirty-six feet, designed by Thomas U. Walter. The addition had an entry and two rooms on the first floor and three rooms on the second floor. The 1785 house became the kitchen wing with one room downstairs and two above, reached by an enclosed winding stairway. In the cellar, there is a large arch which supported the kitchen fireplace. In 1849, David Townsend added a wing to the south, thirty-one by sixteen feet. At this time, the chimney of the cooking fireplace was removed and a new chimney built for a small fireplace in the small original house and for the kitchen range in the new kitchen. Today, the walls are of brick, covered with plaster and marked off to imitate marble. In 1874, the original half story was raised a full story with a low garret over it. The front door is simply framed with a fanlight above.

Landing detail

DAVID TOWNSEND HOUSE

Hall

Inside, there is a hallway along one side of the house from which one enters the two principal rooms, the back wing, or passes out to the porch. An unusual feature is one iron baluster, on the landing, used to stiffen the handrail.

The walls are plastered, have baseboards but there are no chair rails or cornices. The two principal rooms on the first floor have fireplaces with Valley Forge marble facings and hearths and built-in cupboards. On the second floor, the fireplaces have received a simpler treatment. The two third floor rooms have flues for small stoves. This house is an excellent example of a late eighteenth century house that has been added to and modernized as fashions changed.

Stair detail

DAVID TOWNSEND HOUSE

First floor

Second floor

MARKET HOUSE OFFICE, West Chester

Built 1831, Architect, Thomas U. Walter

MANSION HOUSE, West Chester

Copy of photograph ca. 1902.

The Chester County Hotel, in West Chester, was built in 1832 by William Everhart. William Strickland was the architect. This was the last of the large hotels to be built in the town. It started as a temperance house, but changed to a licensed house almost immediately. Due to the hotel's location, across the street from the Court House, it became very popular and continued as a hotel until it was demolished. In 1846, it became known as the Mansion House. The original plans for the building are unknown and over the years, there have been many remodellings and changes. It was brick, three and a half and four stories high, sixty-eight by ninety-six feet.

PARKESBURG HOUSE, Parkesburg

Built ca. 1830   Wall painting depicting house on first floor

PARKESBURG HOUSE

Wall painting on first floor

PARKSBURG HOUSE

Wall painting on first floor

PARKSBURG HOUSE

PARKSBURG HOUSE

UP AND DOWN SAW MILL, West Pikeland Township

Built ca. 1830.

FIRST PRESBYTERIAN CHURCH, West Chester

North and West sides. The remodelled Sunday School building is at the left.

The Presbytery of New Castle, Delaware, had supplied West Chester with preachers, off and on, from the time the county seat was moved to West Chester in 1786. The meetings were held in the Court House. In 1832, the corner stone of the present First Presbyterian Church was laid. The architect was Thomas U. Walter. His fee is not known. The estimated cost of $5,000 for the church was exceeded. The original building was one story, stone, roughcast, forty-five by seventy-five feet and twenty-three feet high. There was a basement in the rear of the building. An important feature is the front facade with a recessed porch with two Ionic columns in antis, all placed in an enclosed area on either side. Within one of these enclosed areas, a stairway leads to a gallery, and the other serves as a cloakroom. The ceiling is supported by the king post truss principle. A pediment extended over the front facade. The original furnishings have been replaced and additions have been made to the original building.

SOUTHEAST NATIONAL BANK, West Chester

1836 water colour by Thomas U. Walter

The Bank of Chester County was chartered in 1814, the first in Chester County. Its first place of business was in the Record Office, (which was a separate building from the Court House) at the northwest corner of High and Gay Streets. In 1818, the Bank of Chester County purchased a lot and building on the opposite side of High Street, present day 13 North High Street. The bank remained there until the present banking building was ready for occupancy on May 30, 1837. In 1864, the bank became known as the National Bank of Chester County; in 1930 as the National Bank of Chester County and Trust Company and in 1970 as the Southeast National Bank. *THE UNITED STATES GAZETTE,* on February 9, 1832 showed the Bank of Chester County to be the third largest bank in Pennsylvania outside of Philadelphia. In 1970 it was named the Southeast National Bank.

Thomas U. Walter was the architect for the present building, his fee being $1000.00. The building is marble, on a stone foundation, two stories high, forty-five by ninety feet. The cost of the building was $35,000. The marble came from the quarry of Jacobs and Cornog, in West Whiteland Township; the marble work was supervised by Tennant and Highlands; the stonework by Chalkley Jefferis; James Powell was the master carpenter and the plaster work was supervised by Yearsley Miles. The Building Committee Minutes for May 13, 1835 mention: "Resolved, that the Basement be faced with good rubble Stone pointed, and that the water table be composed of Marble of an inferior quality."; "Resolved that all the Marble in the Building be backed with Bricks" and "Resolved, that the roof be covered with Copper." The same minutes for September 23, 1836 resolved that: "N. H. Sharples be authorized and requested to procure a furnace of Suitable description for the Same. . .And that William Williamson be authorized and requested to procure Six Marble Mantels, and Six Coal grates of Suitable Size and description for the said Banking House."

For design, Walter based the fine portico on Stuart and Revett's *ANTIQUITIES OF ATHENS* published in London, in 1762 Volumn 1, plate 1V. The bank was to be erected on a narrow lot, between two already stnading structures that would block any view of the building except the front facade. The bank has a small Doric portico and was one of the more academic Greek Revival buildings in Pennsylvania.

The ground plan of the bank is the only one known of a small bank of this period. Today, after several alterations and additions, the plan of the main banking room is basically the same as that shown on the plan. The Bank has been lengthened and a wing added to the south. The major changes were made in 1874, 1905 and 1928. In the latter year, the changes included the only change ever made to the west front of the building that of lowering the floor of the bank and of the central section of the portico, making these levels only three steps from the sidewalk rather than the original eight.

SOUTHEAST NATIONAL BANK

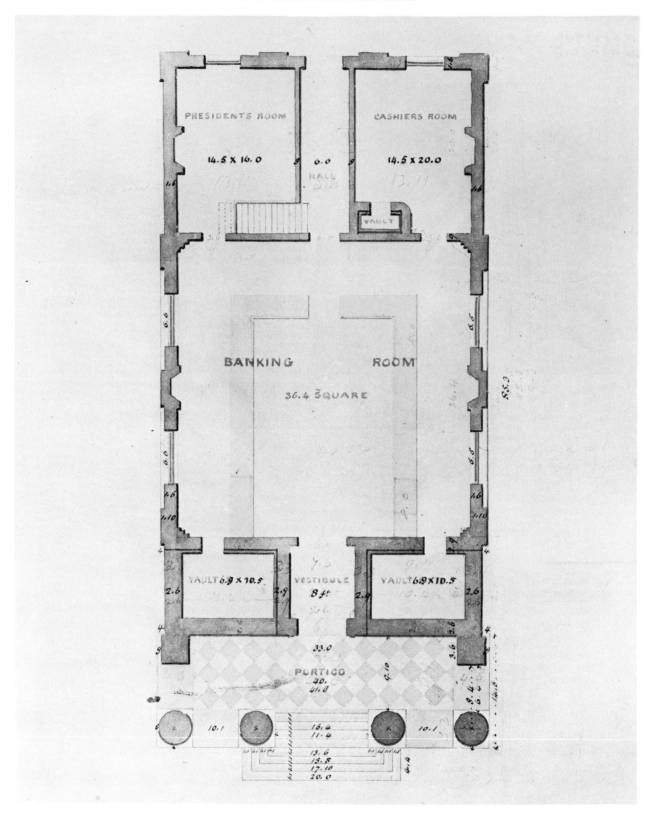

Plan of first story of Thomas U. Walter

SOUTHEAST NATIONAL BANK

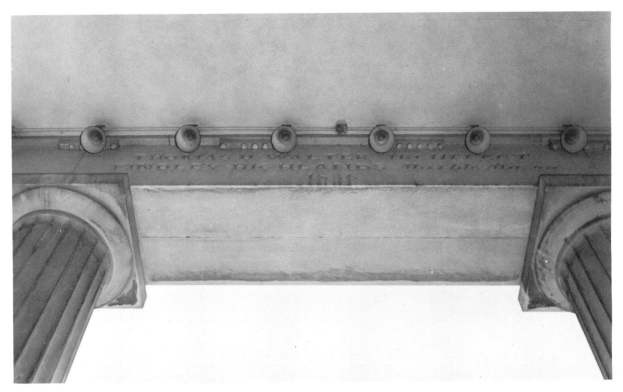

Inside portico. The inscription read: "Thomas U. Walter, Architect. Findley Highlands, Marble Mason, 1836."

North front and east side

OFFICE BUILDING, West Chester

A brick, three and a half story office building wasbuilt in West Chester in 1833 or 1834. The north front is twenty feet, the south side is twenty-seven feet and the depth is thirty-nine feet. It is built on stone foundations. The dormer window, brick cornice, chimney and door are original. The windows, except for the east wall and the cellar, which have been bricked closed, are also original. Each floor has a hall with a staircase on the west side of the building, and two offices with fireplaces and double doors between them off the hall. The walls are of plaster. The *VILLAGE RECORD*, (West Chester, Penna.) on May 2, 1868 mentions: "Squire Everhart is putting up a handsome balcony, from the foundry of Jacob Baily, corner of 15th and Wood Streets, Philadelphia, intended for the convenience of public speakers, at the Republican headquarters of Chester county, a few doors east of the Mansion House, in front of the building, lately the printing office of the *AMERICAN REPUBLICAN.*"

OFFICE BUILDING

Ironwork

LYCEUM, West Chester

Front Elevation

Designed in 1835. Never built.

Architect Thomas U. Walter

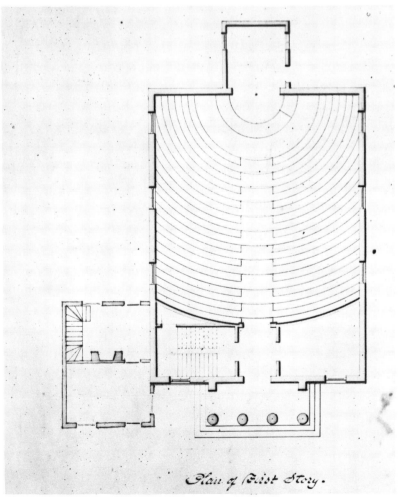

Plan of First Story.

ISABELLA FURNACE, West Nantmeal Township

Copy of 1892 photograph

Isabella Furnace, in West Nantmeal Township, was constructed in 1835. The hugh circular furnace was sixty feet high; the stone walls tapering from about four or five feet at the base to about two feet. A winding stairway of iron lead to the circular dias which was twenty-five feet in diameter. Other buildings necessary to the successful manufacture of iron were built nearby: a brick oven-like structure to effect steam heat so as to increase the output of iron; a brick water pump house; a stone building to house a large iron pump; a charcoal stock house; limestone bins and a railroad siding with a track leading into the charcoal stockhouse which adjoined the furnace. To withstand the strain upon the walls (the track being elevated so that the charcoal can be quickly dumped) an abutment of heavy masonry fifty feet high was erected against the southern end of the stock house. The last blast was made at Isabella Furnace in 1894 due to the great improvements in anthracite furnaces.

ISABELLA FURNACE

East front

Inside furnace

MT. JORDAN POTTERY, Oxford, Chester County, Pa.

.R. J. GRIER, Proprietor.   From Futhey and Cope, *HISTORY OF CHESTER COUNTY, PENNSYLVANIA, 1881.*

AMERICAN WOOD PAPER COMPANY, SPRING CITY

HUGH BURGESS, MANAGER,   From Futhey and Cope, *HISTORY OF CHESTER COUNTY, PENNSYLVANIA, 1881.*

SADSBURY WOOLEN MILLS, Sadsbury Twp., Chester Co., Pa.

From Futhey and Cope, *HISTORY OF CHESTER COUNTY, PENNSYLVANIA, 1881.*

E. T. COPES SONS' MANUFACTORY AND RESIDENCE, EAST BRADFORD TWP.

From Futhey and Coppe, *HISTORY OF CHESTER COUNTY, PENNSYLVANIA, 1881.*

SHARPLESS HOUSE, Birmingham Township

Built 1838

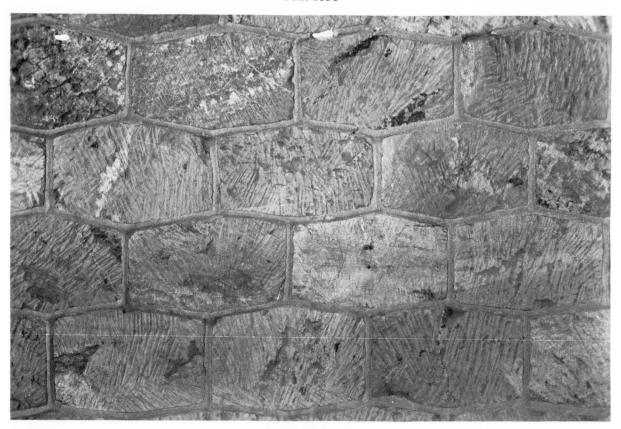

Detail of stone work

DOWNINGTOWN LIBRARY, Downingtown

North front

The Downingtown Library, in Downingtown, is a two and a half story stone building, thirty-two by twenty-eight feet, facing north, built during the 1830's as a girls' boarding school. Typical of its period there are four windows and a doorway on the first floor and five windows on the second story. The shutters on the first story are solid and those on the second story are louvered. The dormer windows are among the finest in the county. The cornice has punched and grooved woodwork. The doorway has two engaged columns, a fan light, a keystone and punched and grooved carving.

North front

DOWNINGTOWN LIBRARY

There is a center hall with two rooms on either side. The open string stairway ascends from the back of the hall. The newel posts curve outward and the plain instead of turned balasters support a mahogany handrail. There are two landings on the stairway. The rooms to the left of the hall have very fine punched and grooved woodwork surrounding the fireplace openings, on the chair rails and in one room under the windows which also have panelled reveals. The fireplaces have marble facings and hearths. The punched and grooved carving in this house is among the finest in the county.

First floor

First floor

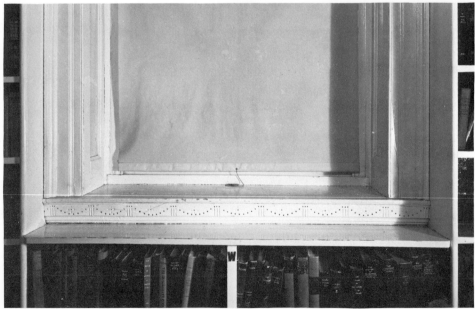

OCTAGONAL HOUSE, East Fallowfield Township

The porch and wing have been removed and the window-doors that opened out onto the porch have been made solid. There are four chimneys but no fireplaces. Inside, the house has baseboards, a dumb waiter from the cellar to the first floor, and many of the interior doors have adjustable transoms. The jambs of the windows are rounded and the walls are of plaster. Beneath the cellar, in the center of the house, there is a vault reached by steep stone steps.

A. BOIMAR'S BOARDING SCHOOL FOR BOYS, West Chester

Copy of 1840-1860 oil painting, artist unknown

The West Chester Young Ladies Seminary, in West Chester, was built by a joint stock company in 1838 at a cost of over $30,000. Thomas U. Walter was the architect. His fee is not known. The original red brick building was of three part construction: a four story center block and two three-story side wings one hundred and thirty by forty-five feet and two, two-story galleries to the north, each one hundred feet long. The foundations are of stone. The center block and two wings were topped with a simple cornice and five small windows. The roof was nearly flat and there was a cupola somewhat similar to that on the prison. The building faced south.

The exterior has been greatly changed thru the years: a large granite chapel and mansard roof were added, the cupola was removed and the brick has been plastered over.

The building has been used for many purposes: between 1838 and 1840 by the West Chester Young Ladies Seminary; between 1840 and 1860 by Jean Claude Antoine Brumin de Bomar as a boys' school; between 1860 and 1866 by the Pennsylvania Military Academy; between 1866 and 1871 by William F. Wyers as a school; between 1871 and 1873 by Robert M. McLellan and between 1873 to the present time by the Sisters, Servants of the Immaculate Heart of Mary. (It has been recently torn down)

The first floor interior seems to be very much as originally planned by Thomas U. Walter. The main stairway rises from the first floor in two flights to a landing and then continues from the landing in one flight to the second floor. The door and window openings appear to be original and the walls are plastered. This entrance floor is simple and yet impressive.

PRISON, West Chester

Copy of 1839 water colour by J. R. Smith

The Chester County Prison, in West Chester, was built in 1838. Thomas U. Walter was the architect. His fee was $1500.00 and the cost of the building was $39,021.82. The original plans have not been found. William Ingram and Chalkley Jefferis were the contractors. This prison is one of the few American prisons to be built in the Greek Revival style rather than the more usual Gothic. The County Commissioners desired a new prison whose plan was based on John Haviland's 1828 Eastern Penitentiary and Thomas U. Walter's 1835 Moyamensing Prison in Philadelphia. There was a great deal of local interest in prison reform at this time due in part to the strong Quaker element in the county.

The original masonry building had a three-story center block one hundred and six by forty-four feet and two, two-story side wings twenty-four feet deep. The projecting center bay, on the south facade, had two Doric columns in the recessed porch framed by large rusticated granite piers. The roof was of low pitch and there was an octagonal cupola. The projecting center bay was often found in Georgian architecture; the rusticated granite piers were used in place of the Greek Antae and the cupola, a popular architectural feature of American Georgian buildings is unknown in Greek architecture, although a feature used locally by Walter.

The warden's quarters were in the east wing, the offices were in the main block and the west wing and the kitchens were in the rear of the center block. In 1871, eighteen new cells were added at a cost of $12,588.54. The stone work was done by Coburn; the brick work by Taylor and Hampton, the carpenter work by Joseph Hunt and the bricks were purchased from H. R. Guss, in West Chester. The principle of confining each prisoner in a cell of his own, from which he was not removed for the duration of his sentence, came to be known as the Pennsylvania system.

In 1885, a porch was added to the warden's quarters, a new gate was placed in the prison yard and heating and electricity were introduced into the building. Hangings took place in the courtyard and prison until 1912. The prison has been demolished.

PRISON, West Chester

First floor

Octagonal cupols

METHODIST EPISCOPAL CHURCH, West Chester

M. E. CHURCH, WEST-CHESTER, PENNA.

Charlie C. Taylor. Delin.

Copy of drawing by Charles C. Taylor

Built 1841-1842
Architect, Thomas U. Walter

SHARPLESS HOUSE, West Chester

South front   Built 1838. Three story section 33' x 32'; kitchen wing 15' x 45'

PORTICO ROW, West Chester

Built ca. 1848

COURT HOUSE, West Chester

"Chester County Court House. T. U. Walter, Arch. MDCCCXLVI Printed by R. Kuhl, Philada.
Executed on stone by W. H. Rease, No. 17 So 5th St Philada."

COURTHOUSE

The present Court House, in West Chester, was built in 1846 at a cost of $55,345.98. Thomas U. Walter was the architect for a fee of $1911.70. The construction bid of $44,749.67 by William Ingram, Chalkley Jefferis, James Powell and David H. Taylor was accepted. The original plans are not known. The building was built of brick and stone, two stories, sixty-two by one hundred and nineteen feet with a twelve foot pentice. The foundations are of stone, the first floor being supported by heavy stone and brick arches and groins. The two foot brick walls were first covered with mastic, a cement-like stucco, and later, when that pealed, with Pictou stone. The original entrance, on the east facade, has a portico supported by six cast iron columns an inch thick and filled with brick masonry, Corinthian columns, capitals and an entablature. Only one iron worker, Edge T. Cope, is mentioned in the list of workmen and suppliers. He had a large iron foundry in East Bradford Township. It is possible that the columns were made at that foundry. The doorway on the south front has been made into a window. The other window openings appear to be original and they never had shutters. The roof, of low pitch, was originally covered with copper which was replaced in 1856 with tin. The tower has an octagonal base. The four chimneys are original.

The interior shows very little change. The first floor has a corridor which runs from east to west with county offices on either side. Each office had both an iron and a wooden door. The court rooms are on the second floor. The stairway in the southeast corner leading to the court room and tower seem to be original. The original floors have been covered with cement, and the walls are plastered. The Court House is as nearly fireproof as construction of the time made possible. In 1895, an addition, fifty by one hundred and fifty-eight feet, built of Indiana limestone, was designed by T. Roney Williamson at a cost of $75,030.00. Plummer E. Jefferis was the contractor.

In the last decade, there has been a need for additional room. An Annex to the Court House was built between 1964 and 1966 for a proposed three million dollars. The architects were Young and Schultze, of Philadelphia. It is a five-story building constructed of limestone with aluminum windows and doors with a finish of anodized light bronze. The building contains two court rooms and offices and is connected with the other building by a passage made of metal and glass.

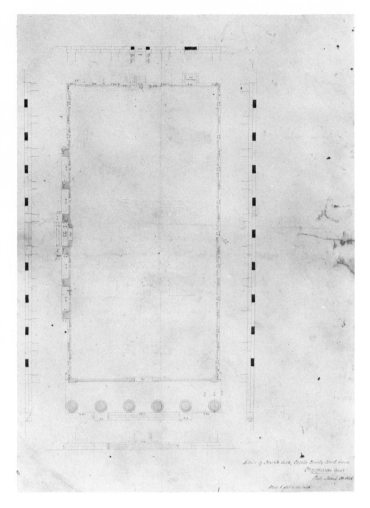

1846 details of marble work by architect

HORTICULTURAL HALL

Exterior in the 1870's

Horticultural Hall was built in 1848. It was the last building designed by Thomas U. Walter to be built in West Chester and the only one not built in the Greek Revival style. Instead it is a pseudo-Gothic building having gabled ends. The front facade with its recessed Norman arch was built of local cut serpentine stone. The remainder of the structure is built of brick covered with mastic. It was built for the Chester County Horticultural Society which was founded in 1845. The building, of brick and stone, was one story and basement, forty-five by seventy-five feet. The roof is of medium pitch and covered with tin. The heavily riveted front door is original.

The floor plans for Horticultural Hall have not been found. The exhibition hall occupied the ground floor and the basement was fully excavated. Besides the exhibitions of the society, the building became the town meeting hall and from 1850 on hundreds of men and women in every field lectured here such as Horace Greeley, Lueretia Mott, Sojourner Truth and Ralph Waldo Emerson. Nearly all of West Chester's church, school and larger social events were held here. In 1873, the building was sold at sheriff's sale to Uriah H. Painter, who built the Lafayette Theatre in Washington, D. C. At this period, many changes were made to the building as it was used as a theatre for many road

HORTICULTURAL HALL

Interior in the 1870's

shows. In 1870, a gallery was hung from the rafters across the west front and north and south sides of the main room and an extension was made to the rear of the structure for a stage and dressing rooms and the roof was raised; in 1872, a lobby addition was made; in 1880, the old benches were removed and replaced by chairs; in 1882, fire escapes were installed, two on each of the north and south sides and one from the balcony and one from the first floor; in 1883, the ticket office was changed; in 1885, an outside two story addition to the northwest of the main building, designed by E. F. Bertolette, was added to house a ticket office and stairs to the balcony and electric lights were installed; in 1894, the stage was enlarged; about 1930, the balcony was removed; in 1937, the old stage was removed and a modern fireproof library designed by Price and Walton, of Philadelphia, was added and in 1942, the new addition was finished and occupied by the Chester County Historical Society.

YELLOW SPRINGS, OR CHESTER SPRINGS, West Pikeland Township

Wagner & McGuigan's Lith. 116, Chestnut St. Philad.

1 Hotel,
2 Hall,
3 Cottage,
4 Baths and
   Fountain,

5 Our House,
6 Barracks,
7 Mountain,
   House, Spring.
8 Piazzas 800 ft.
   in length.

YELLOW SPRINGS, OR CHESTER SPRINGS,

CHESTER COUNTY, PENNSYLVANIA, 32 MILES FROM PHILA.

THIS Watering Place will be ready to receive visitors after the Fifteenth of May, Inst. The Proprietor having added a spacious dining room, and otherwise enlarged and improved his Establishment, has also engaged an experienced gentleman as Superintendent, and secured the services of the best cooks, Confectioners and Servants, by which efforts he hopes to render his Establishment both agreeable and stylish.

This place, so long celebrated for its Chalybeate Baths, unrivalled in the cure of Chronic Disease, was selected by General Washington as an Army Station, for its healthfulness and beauty, and teems with historical recollections. It is Dr. Lingen's intention, after the first of September to appropriate part of the Establishment (which will be open during the whole year) to patients under Homeopathic or Hydropathic treatment, the variety of waters being eminently adapted to the latter purpose. Besides being a Post Office station, there are facilities for arrival and departure twice a day by the Reading, Columbia and Norristown Rail Roads. Letters to the Proprietor (post paid) are to be addressed to

DR. GEORGE LINGEN,
Chester Springs, Chester Co., Pa.

Copy of Broadside 1845-1847, 8" x 10½" issued by "Wagner and McGuigan's Lith, 116 Chestnut Street, Phila."

The open air Chester Springs Bath House, in West Pikeland Township, was built in 1842. By tradition, Mrs. Holman employed Thomas U. Walter, as architect. It is one story, stone, plastered over in imitation of marble, twenty-six by thirty-four feet, facing west. The door is original and the roof is covered with shingles. Inside there is one room with the bath, plastered walls and a paved floor. Yellow Springs, also called Chester Springs, was a very early spa in the United States. There were open air baths here from the first half of the nineteenth century.

BATH HOUSE, Chester Springs, West Pikeland Township

West front

Interior

SUMMER HOUSE, Chester Springs, West Pikeland Township

The octagonal Chester Springs Summer House, in West Pikeland Township, was built before 1845 when it was shown on the prospectus of Dr. George Lingen. The building is frame, one story, and measures fifteen feet across. In the center of the summer house, there is a medicinal spring. One enters from the north. The floor is paved and the roof is covered with wood shingles.

RAILROAD STATION, West Chester

North and West sides

In mid-nineteenth century, a brick railroad station, seventy-two by forty-six feet, was built in West Chester. There was a flat projection on the north front of the building. The windows were arched and on the second floor arranged in pairs.

Inside, across the front, there was the waiting room with a ticket office on the right. The freight office was in the back wing alongside the railroad tracks. This building contained some of the most elaborate brick work done in the county, especially in the cornice. It was demolished in 1968.

Brick cornice

158

MAYFIELD, West Chester

Residence of W. Ebbs

From "Map of the Borough of West Chester, Chester Co., Pa., Survey & Drawn by Martin & Kennedy" 1856

Mayfield, in West Chester, was built between 1848 and 1851 by William Ebbs, a Pittsburgh industralist. The architect is not known. It was built of brick, on stone foundations, two and a half stories, facing south. The main block is forty-eight by forty-five feet plus wings and porches. The pediment of the Greek Revival portico was supported by four Doric columns made of wood. The roof was of medium pitch covered with tin. The door and window openings appear to be original.

A wide center hall runs through Mayfield. To the east is a large drawing room with two original marble fireplaces and the original plaster cornice. In the west end of the original house, there were two rooms with a stairway between the rooms. The kitchen was in the basement. The original conservatory was rebuilt in 1915 at which time a service wing, to the north, was also added and in 1950 the east porch was enclosed.

BAPTIST CHURCH, West Chester

BAPTIST CHURCH

The corner stone for the Baptist Church, in West Chester, was laid on July 4, 1854 and the church was dedicated on August 29th and 30th, 1857. The architect is not known. The cost was $10,811.67. The original brick building was one story, with a full basement, forty-one by eighty-one feet. In the basement, there was a lecture room used by the Sunday School. The floor above was the church proper. The pulpit was on the west side and there was a baptismal font. In 1886, a small addition was made to the south side for a baptistry and the pulpit. Rev. Clarence Larkin, of Kennett Square, was the architect for this addition. At this time, chairs replaced the original pews. In 1899, the pulpit was changed back to the east end of the building. In the early twentieth century a Sunday School, forty by fifty feet, was added to the east of the old building. The portico on the west front was added in 1930. The architect, for the portico, was Ralph Minick aided by George E. Merrill. At this time, there were also changes made to the interior of the building.

CEDARCROFT, East Marlboro Township

South side

Cedarcroft, built by Bayard Taylor in 1859 in East Marlboro Township, may well be the most pretentious mid-nineteenth century building in the county. It is sixty-five by sixty-two feet. The foundations are stone and the corners are faced with marble. The bricks were burned on the property. There is a central projecting flat pavillion topped by a five-story tower. The tower has an arched entrance and an iron balcony. The roofs are of slate and modern composition shingles. Granite quoins and slabs have been used for ornamentation. Mouldings of brick, to mark the floor levels, are found on the tower. Special windows in which the sill is on the floor level making it possible to open the windows and pass out to porches and terraces have been employed.

A narrow hallway runs through Cedarcroft from which one enters the principal rooms. The kitchen wing is to the north. The main open string stairway ascends from the center of the hall and has two newel posts which curve out from the stairs and two hand rails. On the landing, the stairs divide having a stair on both the right and left sides to the second floor. The interior walls are brick, plastered. Plaster cove cornices are used in some rooms on the first floor. There are marble facings on some of the fireplaces, some parquet floors and a few of the windows have interior shutters. Bayard Taylor was a famous traveller and author.

CEDARCROFT

First floor showing window which can be raised

First floor

BARTRAM'S BRIDGE, Willistown Township

North and West sides

Bartram's Bridge was built in 1860, over Crum Creek, in Willistown Township, between Chester and Delaware Counties. The contract was given to Ferdinand Wood for $1133. Both of the counties paid half of the cost. It is a frame bridge, built on stone foundations, on one level, eighty-one feet long and seventeen feet wide. The roof has a low ptich and is covered with wood shingles. In 1940, the Commissioners of Chester and Delaware Counties built a new concrete bride over Crum Creek, moving the old covered bridge to the south of the new one. This is the only covered bridge that it is planned to save in the county.

Arch

LOCH AEIRE, West Whiteland Township

Built 1865. Architect Addison Hutton

A wide hall runs through Loch Aerie with a drawing room to the west and a library and dining room to the east. The service wing is at the east end of the main block. The main stairway, of walnut, is unusual as it ascends from the center of the hall having open strings, two newel posts which curve out from the stairs and two handrails. At the landing, the stairs divide having a stair on both the right and left sides to the second floor. Dividing the first floor hallway there is an elliptical arch supported by corbels. The walls are plastered, there are cornices and fireplaces in every room in addition to the original heating system. In the library, the fireplace is under the window with flues on either side of the window opening. The house was lighted by gas chandeliers.

LOCHAEIRE

South side and lake

First floor

BRINTON SERPENTINE HOUSE, 311 Church St., West Chester

West front — East side

NORTH HILL

"North Hill" Residence of Joshua Hartshorne, West Chester. Architect, Addison Hutton. Built 1869.
From Futhey and Cope, *HISTORY OF CHESTER COUNTY PENNSYLVANIA, 1881.*

LANGOMA, West Nantmeal Township

Built 1890, 165' x 107'   Architect Theophilus P. Chandler

167

HOLY TRINITY PROTESTANT EPISCOPAL CHURCH, West Chester

Northeast and south side

On November 23, 1835 a meeting was held of those interested in organizing an Episcopal Church. With the help of Reverend Levi Bull a congregation was formed. In 1838, the first church was built on the north side of Gay Street. It was thirty-nine by ninety-seven feet and cost $3695.00. Benjamin F. Haines was the contractor.

The corner stone for the present Holy Trinity Church was laid on July 3, 1868 and the first service was held there on January 25, 1870. John Bolton, the rector, was the architect for the building. The contract was let to Bentley Worth for $17,000. The original section of the church is built of green serpentine stone, from the Brinton quarries, with red brick used as a contrasting trim. It faces east, is one story high, and is fifty-five by one hundred and two feet. A tower, twenty feet square, was started in 1871 and finished in 1890 at a cost of $8200. The Sunday School, built from plans drawn by John Bolton, was finished in 1882 at a cost of $10,263.25. It is sixty-five by eighty-eight feet. The rectory was erected in 1886 at a cost of $5937. John Bolton was the architect and William H. Burns was the contractor for the tower and Sunday School. In 1901, the buttresses and walls were strengthened at a cost of $6,971.97 and in 1957 repairs were made to the roof and some of the windows after a fire.

East front and north side

FOUNTAIN, West Chester

Copy of 1869-1879 photograph

A stone drinking fountain was erected in West Chester in 1869. The architect was the Reverend John Bolton. Garrett & Jones, of West Chester, were the marble manufacturers and David Jones, of West Chester, was the marble cutter. The height of the fountain is eighty-two inches and the base is thirty-two by thirty-six inches. In 1960, the fountain was moved from its position in front of the Court House to the garden of the David Townsend House in West Chester.

NORMAL SCHOOL, West Chester

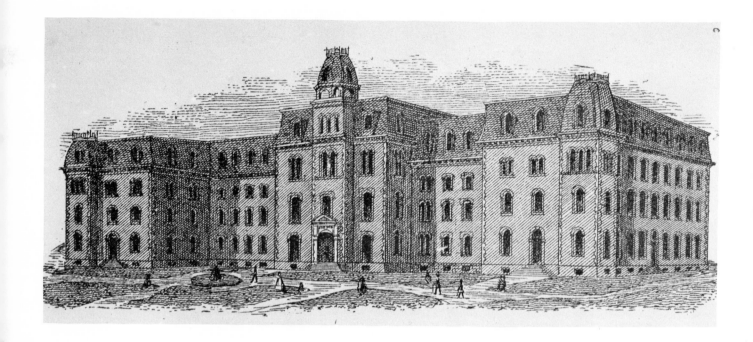

East front and north side

The Normal School, in West Chester, was built in 1870. Addison Hutton was the architect and Messrs. Yarnall & Cooper, of Philadelphia, were the builders. The main building was four stories, sixty by one hundred and fourteen feet with two wings forty-five by fifty-two feet, making the entire front one hundred and fifty feet. The mansard roof was boarded over closely; the curved parts for slate and the flat parts for tin. The building was faced with green serpentine stone from the quarry of Joseph H. Brinton, in Westtown Township. White marble, from the quarry of J. Preston Thomas, in West Whiteland Township, was used to face the building up to four feet above ground level, for the steps, for the arches over the doors and windows and for the door sills. Both the serpentine stone and the marble were dressed and fitted for the building in sheds upon the grounds. The large front doors were walnut.

The first floor had a wide entry at the end of which there was a dining room forty-two by sixty feet with frescoed walls. The staircase ascended from each end of the hall. The second floor had a long corridor on either side of which there were both class and teacher's rooms. There was also a chapel, fifty-two by sixty feet. It was an elegant high ceiled room, twenty-five feet in the clear, fitted up with desks and benches. At one end, there was a raised platform and on three sides, there was a gallery. The chapel seated one thousand people. The kitchen was in the basement. The ceilings of the first floor were twelve feet; the second floor main building, fourteen feet; the second floor wings, eleven feet; the third floor, eleven feet; the fourth floor, nine and a half feet and the cellar, eight feet in the clear. There were stationary wash stands and bathtubs on every floor and the building was heated with steam heat. In front of the Normal School, there was a low stone wall surmounted by an ornamental iron fence. The building has been demolished.

MONAGHAN HOUSE PLANS, West Chester

Front   Built in 1872   Architect, Addison Hutton

Side

MONAGHAN HOUSE PLANS, West Chester

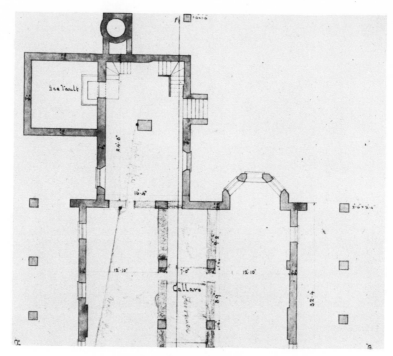

Plan of Basement Floor

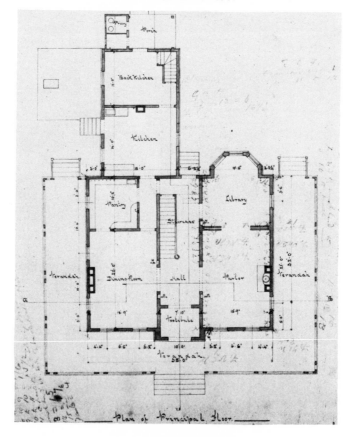

Plan of Principal Floor

MONAGHAN HOUSE PLANS, West Chester

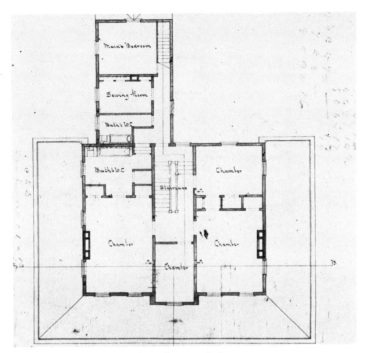

Plan of Second Floor

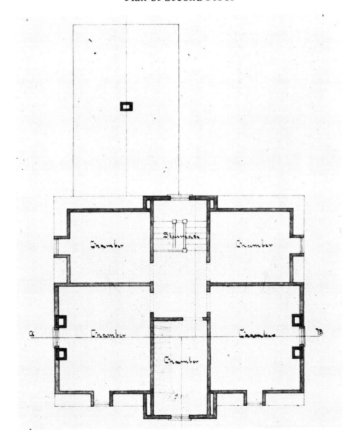

Plan of Third Floor

CEDAR HOLLOW RAILROAD STATION, Tredyffrin Township

Cedar Hollow Railroad Station, in Tredyffrin Township, is a frame, two-story building built in 1872 at a cost of approximately $4150. The north section, eighteen by forty-five feet, contains the office, waiting room and freight rooms on the first floor and bedrooms on the second floor. The south section, twenty-five by twenty-eight feet, contains the kitchen, living room and dining rooms on the first floor. The building is almost entirely as built. The chimney is brick. The openings for doors and windows are original and the walls are plastered. Cedar Hollow Railroad Station is probably the only combination freight and passenger station attached to a dwelling house left in the county.

North front and west side

STRAFFORD RAILROAD STATION, Tredyffrin Township

South and East

This building was built in Japan in 1876 for the Centennial in Philadelphia. In 1887, it was erected at Strafford as a railroad station.

PLAN of a improvet Tract of Land, containing Acres, situated in Vincent Township, Chester County, State of Pennsylvania.
"Sold to Godfrey Gebler"

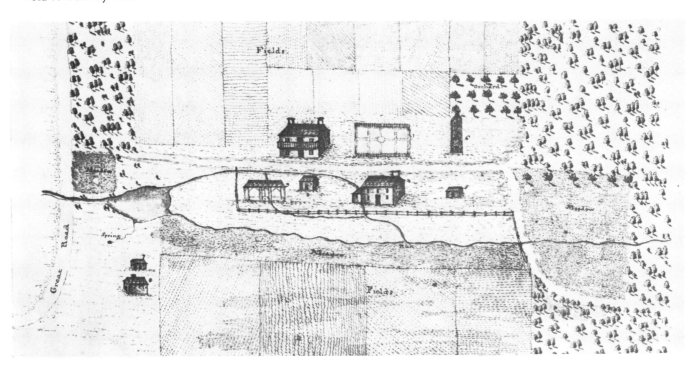

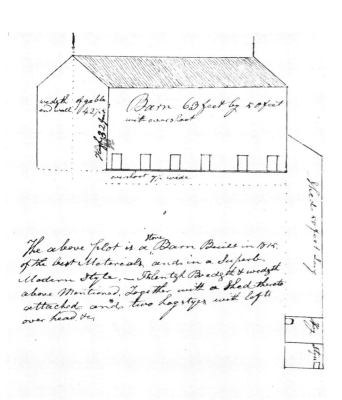

"Draft or Plot of John Beavers, Esq. Dwelling House and Barn, as well as other out buildings, Together with there Several Demantions &c. &c."

"House of Nathan Sharpless Drawn by William P. Evans in 1856 or 1857"

HAUSE SMOKE HOUSE, East Nantmeal Township

South front and west side

A log smoke house, on a stone foundation, was built in the eighteenth century in East Nantmeal Township. It is nine by eleven feet and faces south. The roof has a low pitch and there is one door on the south side.

CALHOON ROOT CELLAR

This rootcellar was built in the mid-nineteenth century.

ZOOK BARN, East Whiteland Township

West side

The Zook Barn, of Swiss type, was built by John Zook, in East Whiteland Township, prior to 1798. It is built of squared logs with stone clinking set in mortar, twenty-five by sixty feet. The foundations are of stone. As is often found in log house construction, the gable end from the plate ot the roof top is built of vertical boards. Inside, the first level is used for the stabling of the farm animals and the second level for the storage of hay and straw. The hay mows are formed of squared logs notched at the corners.

ZOOK BARN

Roof frame work

Log mow

HOPPER BARN, East Whiteland Township

South and west sides

The Hopper Barn, in East Whiteland Township, was built during the latter part of the eighteenth century. It is twenty-five by twenty-five feet and constructed of stone and wood.

BRINTON 1704 HOUSE PRIVY, Birmingham Township

GILPIN ROOT CELLAR, Birmingham Township

MILLER BARN, Avondale

HALLY BARN, Warwick Township

GILPIN CART HOUSE, Birmingham Township

The Gilpin Cart House, in Birmingham Township, was built in 1798. In the east gable-end there is a date stone "$^{I}1798^{G}$". The Bureau of Internal Revenue 1798 Direct Tax lists the cart house as being twenty-three by twenty-three feet, its present size. The ground floor is earth, the sides of the building are field stone and there is a wooden floor above. The south front is open. Probably most buildings of this type have had the front enclosed in modern times.

WILSON SPRING HOUSE, Tredyffrin Township

North side

The Wilson Spring House, in Tredyffrin Township, is a masonry building built in the eighteenth century. The Bureau of Internal Revenue Direct Tax for 1798 lists it as being half the present size of fifteen by twenty-three feet plus a chimney three by eight feet in the northeast corner. The building has three levels: the spring level which is divided into two rooms; the first floor level which is also divided into two rooms with oak floors and plastered walls and one room in the loft. The door is on the first floor level. Each floor has three windows without shutters. The roof is of medium pitch covered with wood shingles.

South front and west side

1804 BARN, West Bradford Township

East side

John and Mary Romans built a dated field stone and frame, barn, in East Bradford Township, in 1804. It is built on three levels forty-six by forty-four feet. The date stone "L$_{1804}^{R}$M" is in the east gable end. The roof is of wooden shingles. This barn has the usual southeastern Pennsylvania type of barn construction: stables and yard on the lower level, threshing floor on the second level and mows on the third level. There have been no additions made to this barn.

1806 BARN, Charlestown Township

South and east sides

The Williams Barn, in Charlestown Township, was built in 1806 by Joseph and Mary Williams. Joseph Williams was a mason. The date stone "J $\begin{smallmatrix}M\\AD\end{smallmatrix}$ W" is in the east gable end. It is a stone and frame bank barn, fifty-eight by sixty feet, having the usual plan for a Pennsylvania bank barn. There is a forebay, to the south, supported by four columns. The stable doors have bars that pull out of the masonry walls similar to those found on the Lowndes Taylor Barn. The openings seem original and the roof, of medium pitch, is covered with wood shingles.

LOWNDES TAYLOR BARN, West Goshen Township

South and west side

Lowndes Taylor built a serpentine stone barn, in West Goshen Township, in 1820. It is forty-five by thirty-four feet. The south front and east and west sides are of dressed serpentine stone; the north side is built of field stone. The medium pitched roof is covered with slate. The lower level contains stalls having an entrance from the south: the upper level is entered by a bridgeway from the north. Mows are on both sides of this upper level. The mason, Albin Hall, scratched his name and date, 1820, in two places on the south wall of the barn.

South side, Stable door

187

BRICK BARN, Franklin Township

Dated 1853, 59' x 49'

TOOL HOUSE

From *PENNSYLVANIA FARM JOURNAL*, 1854

"Wheatland Villa", Residence of George Young, Newlin Township

From Futhey and Cope, *HISTORY OF CHESTER COUNTY, PENNSYLVANIA, 1881*

"Willow Dale Farm", Residence of William Evans, Willistown Township

From Futhey and Cope, *HISTORY OF CHESTER COUNTY, PENNSYLVANIA, 1881*

189

Edgefield Institute, Residence of A. Fetters, Upper Uwchlan Township

From Futhey and Cope, *HISTORY OF CHESTER COUNTY, PENNSYLVANIA, 1881*

Residence of George Little, East Bradford Township

From Futhey and Cope, *HISTORY OF CHESTER COUNTY, PENNSYLVANIA, 1881*

1743 Tomb Stone of Catherine Reese

St. Peter's Protestant Episcopal Church,
East Whiteland Township

1748 Tombstone of Jane Hathorn
In graveyard at Lewisville, Elk Township

1796 Tombstone of Anthony Wayne

In St. David's Protestant Episcopal Church,
Newtown and Easttown Townships

1811 Tombstone of John Wilson

In graveyard at Lewisville, Elk Township

APPLE KILN

The 1798 Direct Tax lists four apple kilns: three of stone, the mean size being 130 square feet, and one of unspecific material, 10 x 9 feet.

ARCHITECT

Architect is defined by Bailey (ed. 1735) as "a Master-builder, a Surveyor of the Building", by Sheridan (ed. 1789) as "a professor of the art of building; a builder" and by Webster (ed. 1828) as "A person skilled in the art of building; one who understands architecture, or makes it his occupation to form plans and designs of buildings, and superintend the artificers employed."

RICHARD ARMITT

Richard Armitt's account book between the years 1785 and 1790, mentions carpentry work and that he worked on bridges. His inventory taken in Chester County, in 1790, lists "Architecture 2 Vols"[1] and "Unfinished Joiner Work."[2]

1.   Ms. #3630 Chester County Historical Society, (West Chester, Pa.)
2.   Chester County Inventory #4132.

L. C. BAKER, JR.

A newspaper mentions in 1892 that "L. C. Baker, Jr., architect of Philadelphia. . .improving dwelling of Major L. G. McCauley"[1] in West Chester.

1.   *DAILY LOCAL NEWS* (West Chester, Pa.) Feb. 17, 1892.

BAKER AND DALLETT

L. C. Baker, Jr. and James E. Dallet, of Philadelphia, were the architects for The First National Bank, in West Chester, which opened in March 1913.[1]

1.   *DAILY LOCAL NEWS* (West Chester, Penna.) March 21, 1913.

MR. BEAM

A newspaper mentions in 1858 "NEW BARN. . .This building is 80 feet by 45, and is over 20 feet to the square, with double spans. Upwards of ninety persons were engaged upon it, and it occupied the entire day. Through the skillful managment of the architect, Mr. Beam, everything went well, and it was raised to the square and the top plates put on without a single accident. Mr. B. ranks high among the first class framers and builders."[1]

1.   *VILLAGE RECORD* (West Chester, Penna.) June 15, 1858.

JOHN BOLTON

The Reverend John Bolton designed the Holy Trinity Church, in West Chester, in 1868 and a drinking fountain, also in West Chester, in 1869.

THEOPHILUS P. CHANDLER

Theophilus P. Chandler was the architect of "Langoma" started by Joseph D. Potts in 1890 in West Nantmeal Township.

CULVER AND ROGERS

A newspaper mentions in 1888 that "Culver & Rogers, architects, are now engaged building Queen Anne cottages at Devon"[1] in Easttown Township.

1.   *DAILY LOCAL NEWS* (West Chester, Pa.) April 25, 1888.

JAMES E. DALLET

A newspaper mentions in 1883 that Thomas W. Marshall, of West Chester, was "enlarging his stable and carriage house. . .E. James Dallett is the architect."[1] The following year he is mentioned again: "The Work of Architects. — The people of West Chester are indebted to the skill of two architects for some of the recent improvements in the town. . .and James E. Dallet. . .J.E. Dallet was the artist who planned the improvements made to the present residence of Mr. Waddell, on High Street."[2]

1.   *DAILY LOCAL NEWS* (West Chester, Pa.) Oct. 27, 1883.
2.   Ibid., July 2, 1884.

N. B. DOBB

A newspaper mentions in 1875 that the Mason Street School, in Phoenixville, had "designs furnished by Mr. N. B.

Dobb of New York."[1]

1. *PHOENIXVILLE MESSENGER* (Phoenixville, Penna.) Aug. 7, 1875.

COL. N. M. ELLIS

A newspaper mentions, in 1874, that "Col. N. M. Ellis made drafts 60.10 by 49.8"[1] for the new school at Phoenixville.

1. *DAILY LOCAL NEWS* (West Chester, Pa.) Aug. 14, 1874.

EDWARD ENTWISLE

A newspaper mentions, in 1873, that the "plans & specifications & drawings for store and house by Edward Entwisle"[1] for Francis Ecock, of Phoenixville.

1. *PHOENIXVILLE MESSENGER* (Phoenixville, Pa.) Sept. 27, 1873.

RICHARD A. GILPIN

A newspaper mentions in 1858 that "For all these improvements the congregation [for the church of Holy Trinity, West Chester] is indebted to Richard A. Gilpin, Esq. residing on his farm near West Chester, who is a thoroughly educated architect and certainly one of the most accomplished draughtsmen that we know of."[1] His obituary mentioned that his death had occured suddenly at his home in Delaware County on May 15, 1887 and that he had studied civil engineering and architecture.[2]

1. *AMERICAN REPUBLICAN* (West Chester, Pa.) Sept. 28, 1858.
2. *DAILY LOCAL NEWS* (West Chester, Pa.) May 18, 1887.

ADDISON HUTTON

Addison Hutton designed the Harthshorne House, now the Barclay Home, and the main building of the State Normal School in West Chester, the main building of Westtown School, in Westtown Township and Loch Aerie in West Whiteland Township as well as numerous private homes in Chester County.

BENJAMIN HENRY LATROBE

Benjamin Henry Latrobe designed the Bridge over the Brandywine, on the Horse Shoe Road, at Downingtown about 1800.

WILLIAM McFARLAN

The inventory of William McFarlan, taken in 1782 in

East Caln Township, mentions "Carpenters Book".[1]

1. Chester County Inventory #3244.

DAVID McKIM, JR.

The inventory of David McKim, Jr., taken in Sadsbury Township, in 1816 lists a "Book of Architecture."[1]

1. Chester County Inventory #6326.

SIDNEY & NEFF

THE DEDICATION OF THE OAKLANDS CEMETERY, in 1854, mentions: Having secured the proper location, the managers employed Sidney [James C. Sidney] & Neff, of Philadelphia, to lay the grounds out and prepare them for interments. Mr. Sidney having much experience and excellent taste as an Engineer in this department, performed his task with great credit to himself and satisfaction to the managers. The drives and walks being all laid out and graded — five hundred lots staked out — a small lake created — the grounds enclosed with a substantial pale fence — a receiving vault built and a cottage for the superintendent with a beautiful gateway erected, it was thought proper to dedicate the premises by suitable ceremonies on the afternoon of Saturday, December 10th, 1853.[1]

1. *DEDICATION OF THE OAKLANDS CEMETERY* (West Chester, Pa., 1854), pp. 3,4.

SAMUEL SLOAN

Samuel Sloan was born on March 7, 1815 at Beaver Dam in Chester County. During his earlier years he was a carpenter. Later he became a well known architect and author. He planned some of the finest buildings in the country specializing in hospitals and colleges. Some of the residences in West Chester were planned by him. On July 19, 1884 he died in Raleigh, North Carolina.

WILLIAM B. SLOAN

A newspaper mentions in 1869 that the "New School House [in Honey Brook Borough] built of brick and was designed by Wm. B. Sloan, 33 by 60 feet, two stories containing four large school rooms, and was contracted for $5100."[1]

1. *VILLAGE RECORD* (West Chester, Penna.) Dec. 7, 1869.

WILLIAM STRICKLAND

A newspaper mentions in 1870 that "The new Hotel, erected by William Everhart upon a plan furnished by Mr. Strickland."[1] In 1817 he had designed the first Paoli Monument.

1. *AMERICAN REPUBLICAN* (West Chester, Penna.) Dec. 6, 1870.

DAVID H. TAYLOR

A newspaper mentions in 1855:

THE NEW POOR HOUSE.

The Poor House for Chester County is nearly completed under the superintendence of Mr. David Taylor. The walls are all up and roofed in, the floor laid and the plastering of the main building in progress—the wings being completed. The plastering is done by Mr. Wm. B. Gause of Newlin. It is not designed to occupy the building until April next, by which time it will be thoroughly dry and ventilated. The edifice is one of magnificent proportions—140 front and 53 feet deep; with two wings running back, 57 by 30 feet—the whole three stories high and cellared under the whole.—It is built of brick in the most substantial and durable manner. A stream of water flowing near by may be conducted over the whole building.—There are about 60 rooms in the building and twelve cells for the insane. A portion of the first floor is appropriated to the Steward and family—the remainder being for the use of the paupers. In the rear of the entire building is an extensive enclosure with a brick wall eight feet high, so that escape at night from the yard would be difficult, should any of the paupers escape the vigilence of the keeper in the house. The entire cost to the county will be about thirty thousand dollars.[1]

Another newspaper mentions:

The design is by David Taylor of this county, a builder of considerable experience and possessing a thorough knowledge of his business. . .

The main building is provided with a hall which runs the entire length. In this a double stairway rises from the middle of the building, and together with the hall is lighted from the roof. An arrangement which conflicts with our idea of a complete separation of the sexes. There are, however, separate stairways in the wings.

The architect has of course followed the general directions given him by the Directors. The appearance of the proposed structure will be precisely what is desirable, that of a plain, substantial and commodious building, imposing from its size and the fine position it will occupy, but without unnecessary ornament. It is proposed to be placed just to the west of the present house, extending across the lane and its front a little forward of the old building.[2]

1. *VILLAGE RECORD* (West Chester, Penna.) Sept. 18, 1855.
2. *AMERICAN REPUBLICAN* (West Chester, Penna.) Jan. 31, 1854.

ELLIS P. TOWNSEND

In 1857 Ellis P. Townsend advertised himself as "ARCHITECT AND ENGINEER, Office of Central Real Estate Agency, CHATHAM, Chester County, Pa. — LAND SURVEYING and CIVIL ENGINEERING carefully attended to, Real Estate Sales made on reasonable terms. All kinds of LEGAL WRITINGS accurately drawn."[1]

1. *VILLAGE RECORD* (West Chester, Penna.) May 23, 1857.

GEORGE WALTERS

George Walters is mentioned as being an architect, forty years old and that he had been born in Pennsylvania in the 1850 Census return for East Vincent Township.

THOMAS U. WALTER

Between 1832 and 1848 Thomas U. Walter designed the Methodist and Presbyterian Churches, Cabinet Hall, the Bank of Chester County, the West Chester Young Ladies Seminary, the Court House, Prison, Horticultural Hall, the Market House office, Judge Bell's house at 101 South Church Street, the Misses Price's School on West Union Street, and perhaps Mayfield and the David Townsend House.

LEWIS WERNWAG

Lewis Wernwag is listed as being an architect in an 1817 deed for Charlestown Township.[1] "In 1816 they [Cadwalader and Benjamin Morris] engaged Lewis Wernwag, German engineer in charge of the Phoenix Iron works, to plan and build their house, which they called The Knoll. . .The original Morris residence was said to follow much the same plan as that of the impressive house built by Wernwag, for his own family overlooking French Creek. . . The Knoll is of stone, with a covering of stucco, spacious rooms, fireplaces and handsome woodwork throughout. The porch which angles around two sides was added by the

Survey of Chester County, Pennsylvania, Architecture

Reeves family, who also built a glassed in sunporch."[2]

1.   Chester County Deed Book Z-2, p. 566.
2.   *DAILY REPUBLICAN* (West Chester, Penna.) Feb. 17, 1964.

DAVID WILLIAMS

The inventory of David Williams taken in Goshen Township in 1726 mentions "A Book of Architecture."[1]

1.   Chester County Inventories #208.

T. RONEY WILLIAMSON

Architect of the new Court House Addition and the Assembly Building now in course of Erection.

Of more than usual interest, at this time is a biographical sketch of Mr. T. Roney Williamson, the architect of the Court House Addition, and the Assembly Building in West Chester. A detailed description of both these buildings will be found in this issue of the DEMOCRAT.

A NATIVE OF WEST CHESTER.

T. Roney Williamson was born in West Chester, in October, 1852. He is the son of Edward H. Williamson, a well known lawyer of Philadelphia, and the grandson of William Williamson, a prominent lawyer of this borough and State Senator during Governor Shank's administration.

Mr. Williamson was educated at Philadelphia, and resided in that city until six years ago, at which time he removed to West Chester, where he has since lived.

He studied the profession of architecture with the late Henry A. Sims, at that time, and up to his death, the most prominent architect in Philadelphia. Since Mr. Sim's decease, Mr. Williamson has practiced for himself.

The large insurance building at 136 South Fourth Street, Philadelphia, was designed by Mr. Williamson, and his main office is located there. A branch office at Grand Rapids, Michigan, is under the management of his brother, Mr. William Williamson.

PROMINENT IN HIS PROFESSION.

Mr. Williamson has attained distinction during his professional career, and many buildings have been erected under his supervision within the limits of his native town as well as elsewhere. A list of them here includes the principal buildings in the borough, such as the new Public School, and the chapel and gymnasium of the State Normal School. He has prepared drawings for the Recitation Hall of the latter institution and also for the new home of Prof. Phillips, the principal.

In this connection must be enumerated the Assembly Building, the Addition of the Court House, the new Public

Library, the engine houses of the West Chester and Fame fire companies as well as the chapel of the Methodist Church, and the tower of the Church of the Holy Trinity, and nearly all the private residences erected in West Chester since 1880. Among the latter are the homes of Jerome B. Gray, S. P. Darlington, Wm. M. Hayes and Jos. Murtagh

Mr. Williamson's long run of prosperity is sufficient evidence that the fair borough of West Chester shows a proper appreciation for its public spirited citizens.[1]

In 1889 a newspaper mentions:
          Nearly Completed.
A committee from the School Director's Association of Chester County, of which Supt. Walton is Chairman, has prepared a 50 page book upon the subject of building, lighting, ventilating and repairing school houses. The committee were appointed last February but only now finishing their work. The book will be well illustrated and is now in the hands of the printer. It was written by Architect T. R. Williamson, West Chester.[2]

1.   *CHESTER COUNTY DEMOCRAT* (West Chester, Penna.) Sept. 17, 1891.
2.   *DAILY LOCAL NEWS* (West Chester, Penna.) Oct. 15, 1889.

JAMES H. WINDRIM

In 1876 the Iron Bank, in Phoenixville, was described as being "26 x 52½, 2 story, walls dressed stone, slate roof, designed by James H. Windrim."[1]

1.   *PHOENIXVILLE MESSENGER* (Phoenixville, Penna.) Nov. 4, 1876.

During the latter half of the 19th century the newspapers declared the need for architects in the county.
A GREAT WANT.—An Architect with sound, practical views, and possessing good taste in designing is wanted to locate himself somewhere in this section of our county. We have already the best of mechanics to execute, but we greatly need the services of an Architect to uproot this Quaker style of building which prevails hereabouts at present. It is uncouth in appearance, inconvenient in arrangement, and if persevered in will mar the beauty of our scenery. From the rapid improvement which is taking place in this part of the County, an Architect would derive profitable business, and if one of the right sort would locate himself hereabouts he sould be regarded as a public benefactor.[1]

          Suburban Residence.
MAJOR MOORE:—Seeing a move made to build on a beautiful hill adjoining the town, I have often wondered why our citizens were content to huddle

196

together within prescribed limits in the very heart of town on lots of 25 to 50 feet front, when so many beautiful sites lie adjacent to, and in our Borough limits unoccupied. Why do not our builders spread themselves, and dot our hills with villas that will attract the attention of capitalists who may wish a cozy mansion with a few acres surrounding it? I have heard it frequently remarked by Philadelphians "that if you would have us come amongst you, offer us some neat cottages. Build them not too costly, but comfortable, and you will find customers." Let us try it, builders and owners.

BUILDER[2]

ABOUT ARCHITECTURE.—The internal arrangements of modern dwelling houses, as compared with those of twenty years ago, possesses so many advantages and conveniences that it is difficult to understand how our fathers and mothers managed to get along without heaters, ranges, hot and cold water in every room, gas, wardrobes, etc., with which the new style structures abound. The architect who has the faculty of multiplying these so called conveniences to the greatest possible extent, and especially in the line of cupboards and closets, is in most demand. A lady architect is making a fortune simply by possessing the ability to plan a house with from five to twenty closets on each floor. This feature commends such houses to the female heads of houses.[3]

Hints to Carpenters.

The *AMERICAN BUILDER* believes that there is much labor in vain in the ornamentation of houses, especially in wooden houses. It tells carpenters, before making and fixing a quantity of ornament, to see that it is good, and goes on to say: There are many things that you do, and many others that an architect—if there be one in the case—will often instruct you to do, which are neither tasteful nor in good construction. Of course there are exceptions. You may be sure of this, however, that the more elaborate with ornament and carving a building is, the more you are going on the wrong track. Real beauty consists not in adding features but in the body of the work itself, and this fact should always be borne in mind.

The principle of carving wood for outside ornament is wrong. We would not say it is to be discarded altogether, but, still, we have that leaning. Cut wood, and that of the simplest kind, is the best. Complexity in forms and ornaments is mostly bad. It not only requires unnecessary labor to produce, but there is actually vexation in the mind of the spectator. When people see a thing that is crowded with intricate work, that it takes them trouble to make out, it is tolerably good evidence that such work is not exactly what is wanted.

Give great attention to sizes and proportion of doors and windows, and pay especial attention to the construction; and never if possible, conceal its principles, but let them form the basis of ornament.

Molding, cornices, and miters are not to be put in exposed positions.

It is surprising what an excellent effect can be produced by cutting even with little or no molding or carving.

We would not stick much molding or carving about a ship. How plain and yet how beautiful it is, simply because of its proportions and because—it looks like work.[4]

1. *KENNETT ADVERTISER*, (Kennett Square, Penna.) Sept. 25, 1855.
2. *AMERICAN REPUBLICAN*, (West Chester, Penna.) Aug. 8, 1871.
3. *DAILY LOCAL NEWS*, (West Chester, Penna.) May 1, 1873.
4. *PHOENIXVILLE MESSENGER*, (Phoenixville, Penna.) Sept. 2, 1871.

ASH HOUSE

The inventory of Enoch Jones, Tredyffrin Township, taken in 1820 mentions: "1 Lot. of Do [Sundries] in the ash house".[1]

1. Chester County Inventories #6801.

AWNING

The newspaper advertisements mention:

1868 "A substantial Wooden Awning has been put up adjoining the kitchen, which can be used for washing or cooking purposes in summer"[1] Robin W. Levis (West Chester)
1886 "will erect a new wooden awning over the pavement fronting his property"[2] J.B. Roecker (West Chester)

The newspaper advertisements mention before 1876 three other awnings, one of which was described as being of wood.

1. *VILLAGE RECORD* (West Chester, Penna.) March 3, 1868.
2. *DAILY LOCAL NEWS* (West Chester, Penna.) April 21, 1886.

BAKE HOUSE
BAKERY

Bake is defined by Sheridan (ed. 1789) as "To heat any thing in a close place; to dress in an oven; to harden at the fire; to harden with heat." A bake house or bakery is the building in which baking is done.

The 1798 Direct Tax lists five bake houses: four of stone, the mean size being 189 square feet and one of log 12 x 10 feet. The newspaper advertisements mention:

1843 "dwelling and store house is about 70 by 25 ft., part

of which is two stories high, now occupied as a bakery"[1] John L. Phillips (Phoenixville)

1850 "Wash house and Bake house underneath"[2] Nathan Dorlan (Honey Brook Twp.)

1853 "Bakery 20 x 36 with a room in front fitted up for the sale of Bread and confectionary"[3] William and Ea. A. Grant (Phoenixville)

The newspaper advertisements between 1855 and 1859 mention one two story brick bake house 20 x 17 feet.

1. *AMERICAN REPUBLICAN* (West Chester, Penna.) Sep. 19, 1843.
2. Ibid., Sep. 3, 1850.
3. *VILLAGE RECORD* (West Chester, Penna.) Aug. 30, 1853.

BALCONY

Balcony is defined by Bailey (ed. 1735) as "a Frame before the Window of an House", by Sheridan (ed. 1789) as "a frame of wood or stone, before the window of a room" and by Webster (ed. 1828) as "A frame of wood, iron or stone, in front of a house or other building, supported by column, pillars or consoles, and encompassed with a balustrade. Balconies are common before windows."

The newspaper advertisements mention:

1813 "There is a balcony and piazza along the front of the house"[1] James Given (East Caln Twp.)

1855 "House is plastered frame. . .commodious balcony on three sides"[2] John Hipple (Parkesburg)

1876 "House has a balcony with iron railing at the front"[3] J. S. Furthy (West Chester)

The newspaper advertisements mention before 1877 nine other balconies.

1. *AMERICAN REPUBLICAN* (West Chester, Penna.) Aug. 10, 1813.
2. Ibid., Nov. 20, 1855.
3. *VILLAGE RECORD* (West Chester, Penna.) April 1, 1876.

BANK

The newspaper advertisements mention between 1865 and 1874 one brick, three story, bank 58 x 22 feet and two of unstated material: one 52 x 25 feet and another 60 x 24 feet. In 1876 the Iron Bank, in Phoenixville, was described as being "26 x 52½, 2 story, walls dressed stone, slate roof, designed by James H. Windrim."[1]

1. *PHOENIXVILLE MESSENGER* (Phoenixville, Penna.) Nov. 4, 1876.

BANKED STRUCTURE

The Brinton diary mentions that "The cellar of the Willis house [standing in 1792 and afterwards] was in the side of a bank, & arched over."[1]

The newspaper advertisements mentioned:

1803 "house. . .three story stone building 50 feet front, 28 deep, the first story being banked in the rear"[2] David Llewellyn (Easttown Twp.)

1. John H. Brinton Diary Vol. #1, p. 87 under date April 20, 1858 Chester County Historical Society (West Chester, Penna.).
2. *PENNSYLVANIA GAZETTE* (Phila., Penna.) Feb. 2, 1803.

BAR ROOM
SALOON

Bar is defined by Sheridan (ed. 1789) as "an inclosed place in a tavern where a house-keeper sits" and by Webster (ed. 1828) as "The inclosed place of a tavern, inn or coffee house, where the landlord or his servant delivers out liquors, and waits upon customers."

The 1798 Direct Tax lists William Burns of Upper and Lower Chichester Townships as having a frame bar 14 x 14 feet. The newspaper advertisements between the years 1878 and 1899 mention one saloon as being one story frame 32 x 16 feet.

BARK MILL (HOUSE)

The 1798 Direct Tax lists seven bark mills: one wood 15 x 12 feet; one stone 25 x 20 feet; one log 20 x 20 feet; one frame 34 x 22 feet and three that did not mention the material of construction the mean size being 681 square feet. The newspaper advertisements between 1835 and 1840 list a frame bark house 40 x 23 feet and one that did not mention the material of construction 30 x 28 feet. Between 1855 and 1860 one stone and frame bark bill 58 x 30 feet and one frame mill 35 x 25 feet are mentioned.

BARN

Barn is defined by Bailey (ed. 1735) as "a Repository for any Sort of Grain", by Sheridan (ed. 1789) as "a place or house for laying up any sort of grain, hay, or straw" and by Webster (ed. 1828) as "A covered building for securing grain, hay, flax, and other productions of the earth. In the northern states of America, the farmers generally use barns for stabling their horses and cattle; so that among them, a barn is both a cornhouse or grange, and a stable."

Peter Kalm, a Swedish naturalist, travelling in the Delaware Valley between 1748 and 1751 mentioned:

> neither the English nor the Swedes had any stables; but the Germans and Dutch had preserved the custom of their country and generally kept their cattle in barns during the winter. Almost all the old Swedes say, that on

their first arrival in this country they made barns for their cattle, as is usual in Sweden; but as the English came and settled among them, and left their cattle in the fields all winter, as is customary in England, they left off their former custom, and adopted the English one. They owned, however, that the cattle suffered greatly in winter...[1]

The barns in the Delaware Valley were described by many men at different times. Lewis Evans, the map maker, in 1753, in *"A Brief Account of Pennsylvania"* mentions:

It is pretty to behold our back Settlements, where the barns are large as pallaces, while the Owners live in log hutts; a sign tho' of thriving farmers.[2]

In 1789 Thomas Anburey, a Britisher, whose *"Travels Through the Interior Parts of America"* mentions:

The farmers in Pennsylvania, and in the Jerseys, pay more attention to the construction of their barns than their dwelling-houses. The building is nearly as large as a common country church, the roof very lofty, and covered with shingles, declining on both sides, but not very steep, the walls are about thirty feet; in the middle is the threshing floor, and above is a loft for the corn unthreshed; on one side is a stable, and on the other a cow-house and the small cattle have their particular stables and styes.[3]

Benjamin Rush in *"An Account of the Manners of the German Inhabitants of Pennsylvania"* in 1789:

The barn and stables are generally under one roof, and contrived in such manner as to enable them to feed their horses and cattle, and to remove their dung, with as little trouble as possible.[4]

John Beale Bordley, a Maryland farmer who moved to Philadelphia in 1791 wrote in 1799 in *"Essays and Notes on Husbandry and Rural Affairs"*:

Farmers in Pennsylvania have a commendable spirit for building good barns, which are mostly of stone. On the ground floor are stalls in which their horses and oxen are fed with hay, cut-straw, and rye-meal; but not always their other beasts. Roots are seldom given to their live-stock, being too little thought of. The second floor with the roof, contains their sheaves of grain, which are thrashed on this floor. A part of their hay is also here stored. Loaded carts and wagons are driven in, on this second floor; with which the surface of the earth is there level; or else a bridge is built up to it, for supplying the want of height in the bank, the wall of one end of the house built close to the bank of a hill cut down. For giving room to turn waggons within the house, it is built thirty-six to forty feet wide; and the length is given that may be requisite to the design or size of the farm.[5]

6th Month, 8th, 1806. I attended the Valley meeting [Tredyffrin Twp.] at which I noticed some of the Dunkers...After dinner he showed me his fine barn, stables, &c. which are most complete I have seen either in England or America. The barn is of stone and stands on descending ground, having a south aspect. It is about 40 yards in length by 10 in breadth, and 9 yards high in front. Along the north side of the barn is a range of vaults which communicate with it, and are on the same level with the barn. The centre vault, which communicates with the cow-house, is fitted up as a dairy; and the other vaults are made use of to preserve roots, &c. for the cattle, such as beets, carrots, turnips, potatoes, pumpkins, &c. As the carriage-road into the barn runs over the vaults, as high as the topmost floor of the barn, the vaults are preserved cool in the summer, and free from frost in winter. The whole of the ground floor of the barn being set apart for stables and cow-houses as is commonly the case with barns in Pennsylvania, there is accommodation for a great number of horses and cows. Along the front of the barn, about 8 feet from the ground, a wooden stage projects about six feet from the wall, inclosed overhead six or seven feet high, and also at the ends and side, forming a gallery the length of the building; having several communications or door-ways out of the barn into it. In the floor of this gallery are several trap doors, through which they throw fodder for the cattle into the yard during the winter months. It is obvious that an appendage of this sort must be very useful in a farm-yard as it affords a comfortable shelter to the cattle from rain and snow.[6]

In 1825 and 1826 His Highness, Bernhard, Duke of Saxe-Weimar Eisenach mentioned in *"Travels Through North America During the Years 1825 and 1826:"*

[Through Chester County] The whole country is cultivated in a most excellent manner, and covered with handsome farms, many barns look like large churches.[7]

Charles B. Trego in *"A Geography of Pennsylvania"*, in 1843, mentions:

The traveller in the older settled parts of Pennsylvania is particularly struck with the neat and substantial appearance of the buildings, fences, &c., as well as the order and convenience of the whole domestic arrangement of a well regulated farm. The pride of a Pennsylvania farmer is his barn, many of which are from 60 to 120 feet in length and substantially built, either wholly of stone, or the lower story of stone and the superstructure of wood, handsomely painted or whitewashed. The interior arrangement of stables, thrashing floor, granaries, places for depositing hay, &c., is admirably convenient and useful. The horses, cattle and other domestic animals are comfortably sheltered during the winter, and like their master and family, enjoy the plenty provided by good husbandry and provident industry.[8]

In 1854 a country gentlemen writes:

In passing from Philadelphia to Lancaster, the first twenty-five miles presented nothing very notable, except what may be seen in all parts of the country settled by the Dutch. The farm houses are not large, or of tasty design, but the barns are large, substantial, and commodious structures, well calculated as storehouses for grain, and to afford comfortable shelter for the cattle. Many of them are built of stone, and they, as well as other farm buildings, are mostly white washed externally and look clean and healthy.[9]

In 1855 the "Guide for the Pennsylvania Railroad..." mentions:

[Main Line] thickly dotted with neat farmhouses and barns, with all sorts of comfortable out-houses for pigs, and poultry, sheep, cattle, and horses...

[Chester Valley] noted for its fertility and beautiful farms. As the cars descend the hill, on an easy grade, the passenger may take in at one view many miles of this magnificent panorama, interspersed with comfortable and neat farmhouses, spacious barns, and other necessary buildings.[10]

In the Court Records for Chester County in 1689 there is the following complaint:

"JOHN NEELD pl[t]f

in an action of the Case for Breach of Articles

JOHN MADOX Defd[t]

Declaration

John Neelde of the Town of Aston in the said County yeoman Complains against John Madox of Ridly Joyner in an action on the Case for that whereas the said Def[dt] was to Build for the said pl[t]f Severall Buildings as by Two Articles of agreem[t] under the hand and Seale of Boath partyes will make it appeare In the first agreem[t] the said Def[dt] was to Build for the pl[t]f Two peeses of Building one

to be fifteen foote Long and Twelve foot wide w[th]in and Ten foote and half high of the Wall and the other to be Eighteen foot Long and fifteen foot Wide w[th]in Ten foot and a half of the Wall and to make One Doore and a Doore plase in Each them Windowes att the End to hich in att and to Lay barens over One End for a threshing place and to Lay a flore of plankes but the s[d] pl[t]f was to Cleave the plankes and to Sett on Two Locks, And all the Worke was to be Compleated and Don by the 24th day of the 4th month And the pl[t]f was to pay Said Def[dt] Two Steares and fouer bushalls Indian Corne when the Worke was ffinished. . ."[11]

The newspapers mention:

1761 "a good Barn, about five feet of good Stone Wall, and a good Frame upon it; two Bays, and a Threshing Floor in the Middle; a good Cart-house, and a Stable at one End, with a Floor over both to put Hay in"[12] James Day (Springfield Twp.)

1763 "Barn, two Stables, two Cow-houses, Sheep-house, Cart house &c. with a large Hay loft over them all"[13] Capt. Cruickshank (Haverford Twp.)

1766 "double barn, 60 feet long, and 26 wide, together with stables, cowhouses"[14] William Kerr, (Londonderry Twp.)

1825 "barn is new. . .well built and boarded with pine"[15] Caleb Brinton (West Fallowfield Twp.)

1858 "NEW BARN. . .This building is 80 feet by 45, and is over 20 feet to the square, with double spans. Upwards of ninety persons were engaged upon it, and it occupied the entire day. Through the skillful management of the architect, Mr. Beam, everything went well, and it was raised to the square and the top plates put on without a single accident. Mr. B. ranks high among the first class framers and builders.[16]

1858 "double floored Barn 36 x 51 with dormitory"[17] Thomas Lamborn (New Garden Twp.)

1859 "Barn 47 x 120, built upon the most approved plan, wall to the first story 2½ feet thick, from there up 2 feet, the whole of the threshing story is laid tight with white pine"[18] Mary R. Cox (West Whiteland Twp.)

1870 "Barn, 56 x 65 feet. . .2 driving floors, entries mortared and planked"[19] (Benj. Phillips, New Garden Twp.)

1872 "stone Barn 48 by 45 feet, gothic windows, dormer back. It is built in English style"[20] (Henry Webster, Highland Twp.)

1872 "John Garrett of East Goshen built new barn for Joseph Miller 55 by 70 feet, first story stone 9 feet high the above of frame is 15 feet with two threshing floors in middle each 15 feet with bays at the end 20 feet, 85 feet of shedding and hay loft 17 to 20 feet wide. It is well lighted up with dormer and other windows"[21] (Pennsbury Twp.)

1873 "Barn 45 by 60 feet, straw House 60 feet, another Barn as wing to first 66 by 18 feet and 14 feet to square"[22] Elizabeth Evans (South Coventry Twp.)

1873 "Wm. H. Wilson used in new Barn 40,000 of hewed timber, 12,282 oak scantling, 9,012 feet of oak boards, 9,043 feet lath, 20,000 feet stock boards, 7,643 feet stripping, 10,000 shingles, 1,000 feet worked boards, 3,000 worked hemlock, 1760 feet hemlock joice"[23] (Valley Twp.)

1873 "new Barn 50 by 50 feet, stone and frame, 40 feet high to comb of roof"[24] Charles S. Carter, (East Bradford Twp.)

1876 "barn 62 x 55½ containing 18,000 ft sawed timber"[25] (Upper Oxford Twp.)

The 1798 Direct Tax lists forty-one barns, without mentioning the material of construction, the mean size being 774 square feet. The same tax for East Caln and West Whiteland Townships lists Joseph Downing with "1 dwelling house and Barn Connect[d]". The 1796 tax assessment for East Fallowfield Township lists one barn, without mentioning the material of construction of 900 square feet. The 1799 tax assessment for West Marlboro and West Nottingham Townships lists two barns, without mentioning the material of construction, the mean size being 767 square feet. In Honey Brook Township the 1799 tax assessment lists Abraham Curtz with "A Dwelling house and barn of Logs Covered with Straw and Shingles under one Roof".

1. Benson, Adolph B., editor, *PETER KALM'S TRAVELS IN NORTH AMERICA* (New York, N.Y., 1937), Vol. 1, p. 236.
2. Shoemaker, Alfred L., *PENNSYLVANIA BARN* (Lancaster, Pa., 1955), p. 12.
3. Ibid., p. 13.
4. Ibid., p. 14.
5. Ibid., p. 19.
6. Sutcliff, Robert, *TRAVELS IN SOME PARTS OF NORTH AMERICA IN THE YEARS 1804, 1805 & 1806* (Phila., Pa., 1812) p. 241.
7. Shoemaker, Alfred L., *PENNSYLVANIA BARN* (Lancaster, Pa., 1955), p. 16.
8. Ibid., p. 17.
9. Ibid., p. 9.
10. *GUIDE FOR THE PENNSYLVANIA RAILROAD WITH AN EXTENSIVE MAP: INCLUDING THE ENTIRE ROUTE, WITH ALL ITS WINDINGS, OBJECTS OF INTEREST AND INFORMATION USEFUL TO THE TRAVELLER 1855.*
11. Colonial Society of Pennsylvania *RECORD OF THE COURTS OF CHESTER COUNTY PENNSYLVANIA 1681-1697*, (Philadelphia, Penna., 1910) p. 190.
12. *PENNSYLVANIA GAZETTE* (Phila., Penna.) Jan. 29, 1761.
13. Ibid., Oct. 27, 1763.
14. Ibid., Nov. 6, 1766.
15. *AMERICAN REPUBLICAN* (West Chester, Penna.) Aug. 31, 1825.
16. *VILLAGE RECORD* (West Chester, Penna.) June 15, 1858.
17. Ibid., Dec. 11, 1858.
18. Ibid., Oct. 11, 1859.
19. Ibid., Oct. 4, 1870.
20. Ibid., Nov. 19, 1872.
21. Ibid., Oct. 1, 1872.
22. *AMERICAN REPUBLICAN* (West Chester, Penna.) Nov. 14, 1873.
23. *DAILY LOCAL NEWS* (West Chester, Penna.) May 30, 1873.
24. *AMERICAN REPUBLICAN* (West Chester, Penna.) Nov. 25, 1873.
25. *AMERICAN REPUBLICAN* (West Chester, Penna.) June 20, 1876.

The following information pertaining to the materials used in the construction of barns was obtained, when possible, from the Bureau of Internal Revenue Direct Tax. Since a few townships have not been found in that tax, a tax assessment in date as near to 1798 as possible has been used: 1796 for East Fallowfield Township and 1799 for Charlestown, London Britain, Pikeland, West Marlboro and West Nottingham Townships.

BARNS	Brick No.	Brick Mean	Frame No.	Frame Mean	Log No.	Log Mean	Mud Walls No.	Mud Walls Mean	Stone No.	Stone Mean	Stone & Frame No.	Stone & Frame Mean
Brandywine			2	735	77	888			7	1377	1	1120
Charlestown			6	1274	51	840			37	1425		
Coventry					36	851	1	1800	26	1667	4	1367
East Bradford	1	1380	15	1039	15	802			12	1915	2	1550
East Caln			4	961	18	852			23	1979	1	2160
East Fallowfield			2	736	35	675			1	1500	2	689
East Nantmeal			1	875	60	822			28	1709		
East Whiteland			2	870	20	907			19	1473		
London Britain					11	694			2	1162		
Pikeland					47	670			18	1415	1	741
Sadsbury			4	990	39	767			14	1586	2	1920
Tredyffrin			3	565	34	619			33	1694		
Uwchlan			3	1032	42	757			27	1626	1	748
Vincent			4	612	52	842			26	1594	1	1800
West Bradford			25	1132	37	765			5	1668	1	1620
West Caln			3	680	62	719			3	1333		
West Marlboro			28	593	19	874			7	1407		
West Nottingham			2	500	13	685			1	900		
West Whiteland	1	2450	4	765	6	676			13	693	1	800

	Log & Frame		Brick & St.		Wood & Stone		Log & Stone		Stone, Log & Frame		No Material Given	
	No.	Mean	No.	Mean	No.	Mean	No.	Mean	No.	Mean	No.	Mean
Brandywine							6	741			1	440
Charlestown					1	416	7	1106				
Coventry							11	1186			7	776
East Bradford												
East Caln	1	600					6	1137			4	705
East Fallowfield							1	900			1	1200
East Nantmeal							4	917				
East Whiteland											1	720
London Britain												
Pikeland							12	1014				
Sadsbury							10	869				
Tredyffrin							2	1229				
Uwchlan							11	1024	1	1876		
Vincent							9	1004			15	932
West Bradford	1	756									1	1000
West Caln												
West Marlboro	1	1350	1	2000							1	860
West Nottingham											1	860
West Whiteland	1	640			1	1000	3	573			8	1200

BARNS	Frame		Log		Stone		Wood		Stone & Frame		Log & Frame		Wood & Stone		No Material Given	
	No.	Mean	No.	Mean	No.	Mean	No.	Mean	No.	Mean	No.	Mean	No.	Mean	No.	Mean
Aston																
Bethel																
Birmingham	19	939	10	712	5	1398			1	600	2	1000				
Chester	26	801	6	760	4	1076			1	1200	2	834				
Concord																
Darby																
Edgemont																
Haverford																
Middletown & part Lower Providence	34	848	19	548	11	1459			2	1165	4	925			1	700
Newtown & part Marple					9	1291	63	540					11	1221		
Radnor																
Ridley																
Springfield & part Lower Providence	20	740	8	755	5	1335			10	1543	3	1050				
Thornbury			3	583	2	1840			3	766	4	700				
Tinicum																
Upper & Lower Chichester	35	696	5	502	2	1434			1	600	1	1485			3	495
Upper Darby																
Upper Darby & part Marple																

BREAU'S 1883 ATLAS

The following information pertaining to barns was obtained from *BREAU'S OFFICIAL SERIES OF FARM MAPS, CHESTER COUNTY, PENNSYLVANIA: COMPILED, DRAWN AND PUBLISHED FROM PERSONAL EXAMINATIONS & SURVEYS BY W. H. KIRK & CO., PHILADELPHIA, 1883.*

BARNS	Brick	Stone	Frame	Total Number
Birmingham	1	21	26	48
Caln	1	41	42	84
Charlestown			50	50
East Bradford	1	68	51	120
East Brandywine		67	34	101
East Caln		23	20	43
East Coventry		85	37	122
East Fallowfield		23	104	127
East Goshen		60	38	98
East Marlboro	3	1	102	106
East Nantmeal		107	33	140
East Nottingham	1		122	123
East Pikeland		1	69	70
East Vincent		102	11	113
East Whiteland		88	116	204
Easttown	1	43	68	112
Elk		2	100	102
Franklin	2	6	84	92
Highland	10	4	103	117
Honey Brook	1	13	96	110
Kennett		18	91	107
London Britain	1	14	76	91
London Grove	1			1
Londonderry		3	98	101
Lower Oxford	1	3	83	87
New Garden	2	36	144	182
Newlin		15	46	61
New London		4	112	116
Penn	3	1	81	85
Pennsbury	1	16	72	89
Pocopson	3	12	51	66
Sadsbury		12	36	48
Schuylkill		69	66	135
South Coventry			39	39
Thornbury		5	20	25
Tredyffrin		78	152	230
Upper Oxford	1	2	93	96
Upper Uwchlan	1	98	34	133
Uwchlan	4	97	25	126
Valley	3	59	55	117
Wallace		50	25	75
Warwick	3	156	53	212

BARNS	Brick	Stone	Frame	Total Number
West Bradford	24	98	101	223
West Brandywine	2	96	30	128
West Caln	3	123	83	209
West Fallowfield	60	32	70	162
West Goshen	37	68	35	140
West Marlboro	25	93	51	169
West Nantmeal		109	39	148
West Nottingham	14	18	106	138
West Pikeland	2	69	30	101
West Sadsbury	3	65	40	108
West Vincent	6	158	26	190
West Whiteland	3	127	81	211
Westtown	26	77	29	132
Willistown	11	161	77	249

BANK

The newspapers mention:

1820 "a large bank barn"[1] John Myers, Jr., W. Robinson (Honey Brook Twp.)

1843 "Frame bank BARN, Stone Stable high 30 by 39 ft."[2] Jas. Marrow (East Caln Twp.)

Between 1825 and 1849 the newspapers mention four other bank barns: two mention dimensions; one 16 x 22 feet and the other 64 x 40 feet. Between 1850 and 1875 twenty-one bank barns are mentioned: six mention dimensions; 50 x 52, 60 x 30, 35 x 25, 80 x 40, 40 x 60 and 35 x 58 feet.

1. *VILLAGE RECORD* (West Chester, Penna.) March 22, 1820.
2. Ibid., June 6, 1843.

BRICK

The newspapers mention:

1773 "new brick barn, which is cellared under, and divided for the feeding of horses and cattle"[1] Joseph Allen (London Grove Twp.)

1818 "brick Swizer barn"[2] George & John Long (Brandywine Twp.)

The newspapers mention before 1800, one other brick barn: between 1825 and 1850 two brick barns are mentioned the dimensions being 60 x 36 and 38 x 48 feet; between 1850 and 1875 ten brick barns are mentioned, the dimensions given were 60 x 42, 50 x 60, 60 x 61, 45 x 35 and 20 x 24 feet.

The 1798 Direct Tax lists two brick barns the mean size being 1915 square feet.

1. *PENNSYLVANIA GAZETTE* (Phila., Penna.) Dec. 15, 1773.
2. *AMERICAN REPUBLICAN* (West Chester, Penna.) Dec. 8, 1818.

BRICK & STONE

The 1799 tax assessment for West Marlboro Township lists one brick and stone barn of 2000 square feet.

FRAME

The newspapers mention:

1750 "large framed Barn, about three years old"[1] William Hewel (Upper Chichester Twp.)

1762 "Frame Barn of a well grown Pine"[2] Edward Bennett (Thornbury Twp.)

1823 "Frame barn with 4 stables and 2 entries front to back under it"[3] Henry Hoopes (Pennsbury Twp.)

1847 "double floored frame Barn (the under part stone) 50 by 36 feet with garners between floors, and large dormer back, which makes a good shelter for a cart, ploughs, harrows, &c."[4] John C. Dorat (London Grove Twp.)

1852 "frame Barn, recently built 68 by 55 feet, sixteen feet high all around to the square, two floors and roofed with the best quality of pine shingles"[5] David Williams (East Fallowfield Twp.)

1854 "frame Barn, stone stable high, 40 x 115 eighteen feet to the square, shed at east end 27 ft."[6] William D. Haines (West Goshen Twp.)

1867 "Barn...The frame is all pine...The bridge wall of the Barn is 30 feet in length, 14 ft. high, with a large vault arched with brick"[7] Thomas J. Edge (New Garden Twp.)

The 1798 Direct Tax lists two hundred and four frame barns, the mean size being 840 square feet. The 1796 tax assessment for East Fallowfield Township lists two frame barns, the mean size being 736 square feet. The 1799 tax assessment for Charlestown, West Marlboro, and West

Nottingham Townships list thirty-six frame barns, the mean size being 789 square feet.

1. *PENNSYLVANIA GAZETTE* (Philadelphia, Penna.) March 6, 1750.
2. Ibid., Aug. 10, 1762.
3. *VILLAGE RECORD* (West Chester, Penna.) Jan. 22, 1823.
4. *AMERICAN REPUBLICAN* (West Chester, Penna.) Aug. 31, 1847.
5. Ibid., July 20, 1852.
6. *VILLAGE RECORD* (West Chester, Penna.) Oct. 31, 1854.
7. Ibid., Sept. 14, 1867.

LOG

The newspapers mention:

1762 "sawed Log Barn"[1] James Day (Middletown Twp.)

1763 "square Log Barn"[2] John Mendenhall (East Caln Twp.)

1770 "a barn, 70 feet in length, 23 in breadth, of good peeled chestnut logs, with 2 stables"[3] William Graham (Londonberry Twp.)

1801 "a barn 44 by 25 feet, cellared under with stone, hewed logs above, with an overshoot"[4] Isaac Zigler (West Caln Twp.)

1809 "Barn; the under story of which is of stone, and the upper part of squared logs"[5] Matthew Grier (Brandywine Twp.)

1811 "new square log barn, 52 feet by 25"[6] John Wheeler (Upper Oxford Twp.)

1812 "square log barn, 56 by 27 feet"[7] John C. Hamill (West Fallowfield Twp.)

1814 "chestnut log Barn"[8] Samuel Cochran (Upper Oxford Twp.)

1820 "barn of Hewed logs, stone stable high 60 by 30"[9] John Zook (East Whiteland Twp.)

1843 "swisser barn. .built with pleted logs and weatherboarded, stone stabling"[10] William S. Michiner (Upper Oxford Twp.)

The newspapers during this period mention two other square log barns.

The 1798 Direct Tax lists five hundred and ninety-six log barns, the mean size being 739 square feet. In East Caln Township there were three hewn log barns and in West Whiteland Township there were nine round log barns. The 1796 tax assessment for East Fallowfield Township lists thirty-five log barns, the mean size being 675 square feet. The 1799 tax assessment for Charlestown, London Britain, West Marlboro and West Nottingham Townships lists thirty-six log barns, the mean size being 773 square feet. The tax assessment for Honey Brook Township lists Abraham Curtz with "A dwelling house and barn of Logs Covered with Straw and Shingles under one Roof."

1. *PENNSYLVANIA GAZETTE* (Philadelphia, Penna.) April 1, 1762.
2. Ibid., May 2, 1763.
3. Ibid., May 31, 1770.
4. Ibid., Dec. 6, 1801.

5. *AMERICAN REPUBLICAN* (West Chester, Penna.) Nov. 28, 1809.
6. Ibid., Nov. 5, 1811.
7. Ibid., Feb. 22, 1812.
8. *CHESTER & DELAWARE FEDERALIST* (West Chester, Penna.) Dec. 14, 1814.
9. *AMERICAN REPUBLICAN* (West Chester, Penna.) Nov. 21, 1820.
10. Ibid., Dec. 19, 1843.

LOG & FRAME

The 1798 Direct Tax lists nineteen log and frame barns the mean size being 887 square feet. The 1799 tax assessment for West Marlboro Township lists one log and frame barn of 1350 square feet.

LOG & STONE

The 1798 Direct Tax lists seventy-four log and stone barns, the mean size being 972 square feet. The 1796 tax assessment for East Fallowfield Township lists one log and stone barn of 900 square feet. The 1799 tax assessment for Charlestown Township lists seven log and stone barns, the mean size being 1106 square feet.

MUD

The 1798 Direct Tax for Coventry Township lists George Fritz with "one Barn of Mode Walls 60 x 30" and Christopher Holderman with a "Barn Mode Walls." The 1796 tax assessment for New London Township lists Isaac Ryan with "mud house and barn".

STONE

The newspapers mention:

1769 "stone Barn, 144 feet by 14, which is divided into 12 stalls, each sufficient to contain a team of horses"[1] William Gibbons (West Nantmeal Twp.)

1814 "stone barn, 70 by 52 feet with stables under the whole, plastered inside and the heads and sills of the doors marble"[2] John Miller Est. (Tredyffrin Twp.)

1829 "a Stone Barn, 72 by 35 feet. . .the barn yard is enclosed by a neat stone wall. . .There is a shed at one end covering the horse power of a threshing machine, which is attached to the barn"[3] Nathan Walton (New Garden Twp.)

1834 "large bridged STONE BARN, 40 by 60 feet, finished, stalled, garnered &c."[4] John Van Amringe (Upper Oxford Twp.)

1836 "sand stone barn"[5] Frederick March (Coventry Twp.)

1836 "new stone barn 52 by 40 feet. . .plastered inside and out"[6] Isaac Z. Coffman (Charlestown Twp.)

1838 "stone barn double floored, 35 by 45 ft. with a dormer 20 by 23 ft."[7] Joseph Eavenson (East Bradford Twp.)

1841 "stone Barn, with ample root cellars"[8] Jabez Jenkins (West Whiteland Twp.)

1850 "stone Barn 57 by 30 feet, with an overshot 20 feet wide, wagon house adjoining to each end with shedding under, one 23 feet and the other 15 feet wide"[9] John Huey (East Nantmeal Twp.)

1859 "Barn 75 x 55, 22 feet from floor to square; ventilator 9 feet square by 15 feet high and is 62 feet high from the ground to the top of the ventilator. It is built of stone, with a slate roof"[10] John Dampman (West Nantmeal Twp.)

1861 "stone Barn, 60 x 40 frame dormer over bridgeway, frame straw house 15 x 100 supported by wall and stone pillars"[11] Jacob E. John (East Goshen Twp.)

1863 "stone Barn 30 x 60 (22 feet story)"[12] Levi H. Crouse (Wallace Twp.)

1872 "stone Barn 48 by 45 feet, gothic windows, dormer back. It is built in English style"[13] Henry Webster (Highland Twp.)

1894 "To Build a Fine Barn. Samuel Steele, carpenter and builder, of Mendenhall, has been awarded the contract to build a new barn at Ercildoun Stock Farm for N. P. Boyer to replace the one burnt a short time since.

The one destroyed was one of the largest and finest double-decker barns in the country, being built in the form of the letter T: was 125 feet long by 100 wide; the main building was of stone, nearly 50 feet to square, being covered with slate roof, and would hold 200 tons of hay besides the other crops of the farm. It was the only barn in the county with stables three stories high that you could enter from the ground to all of them.

The new barn will be 125 feet long by 70 feet wide"[14]

The 1798 Direct Tax lists two hundred and ninety-two stone barns, the mean size being 1502 square feet. The 1796 tax assessment for East Fallowfield Township lists one stone barn 1500 square feet. The 1799 tax assessment for Charlestown, London Britain, West Marlboro and West Nottingham Townships lists forty-seven stone barns, the mean size being 1223 square feet.

1. *PENNSYLVANIA GAZETTE* (Philadelphia, Penna.) Jan. 20, 1769.
2. *CHESTER & DELAWARE FEDERALIST* (West Chester, Penna.) Dec. 14, 1814.
3. *AMERICAN REPUBLICAN* (West Chester, Penna.) Oct. 6, 1829.
4. Ibid., Sept. 9, 1834.
5. *REGISTER & EXAMINER* (West Chester, Penna.) Oct. 11, 1836.
6. *AMERICAN REPUBLICAN* (West Chester, Penna.) Oct. 11, 1836.
7. *VILLAGE RECORD* (West Chester, Penna.) Oct. 2, 1838.
8. Ibid., Dec. 14, 1841.
9. Ibid., Sept. 17, 1850.
10. Ibid., Sept. 6, 1859.
11. Ibid., Oct. 5, 1861.
12. Ibid., Oct. 24, 1863.
13. Ibid., Nov. 19, 1872.
14. *DAILY LOCAL NEWS* (West Chester, Penna.) Aug. 24, 1894.

STONE & FRAME

The newspapers mention:

1770 "frame barn, with stables under the whole, well under-pinned with stone"[1] John Briggs (Thornbury Twp.)

1858 "double decker Barn 33 by 50 feet, stone and frame, with double dormer 10 by 15 feet and frame overshoot or straw house 20 by 20 feet roofed with slate"[2] William & John J. McCrery (Lower Oxford Twp.)

1859 "new double decker Barn 35 by 40 feet, stone and frame, weather boarded with Frame Dormer 15 feet square"[3] William Tuton (East Fallowfield Twp.)

1859 "stone Barn 45 x 90, with frame overshoot; frame straw house about 90 feet long supported by pillars"[4] Samuel Beaver (Tredyffrin Twp.)

1863 "new stone Barn 60 x 70 with a wing 33 x 16 of frame 21 feet to square"[5] Joseph Hoopes (Pennsbury Twp.)

1872 "John Garrett of East Goshen built new barn for Joseph Miller 55 by 70 feet, first story stone 9 feet high the above of frame is 15 feet with two threshing floors in middle each 15 feet with bays at the end 20 feet, 85 feet of shedding and hay loft 17 to 20 feet wide. It is well lighted up with dormer and other windows"[6] (Pennsbury Twp.)

1873 "new Barn 50 by 50 feet, stone and frame, 40 feet high to comb of roof"[7] Charles S. Carter (East Bradford Twp.)

The 1798 Direct Tax lists thirty-three stone and frame barns, the mean size being 1231 square feet. The 1796 tax assessment for East Fallowfield Township lists one stone and frame barn of 689 square feet.

1. *PENNSYLVANIA GAZETTE* (Philadelphia, Penna.) Feb. 22, 1770.
2. *VILLAGE RECORD* (West Chester, Penna.) Oct. 2, 1858.
3. Ibid., Dec. 17, 1859.
4. Ibid., Jan. 8, 1859.
5. Ibid., Nov. 7, 1863.
6. Ibid., Oct. 1, 1872.
7. *AMERICAN REPUBLICAN* (West Chester, Penna.) Nov. 25, 1873.

STONE & WOOD

The 1798 Direct Tax lists twelve stone and wood barns, the mean size being 1110 square feet. The 1799 tax assessment for Charlestown Township lists one stone and wood barn 416 square feet.

SWISS

The newspapers mention:

1810 "Swisher stone barn"[1] John Moore, Est. (Sadsbury Twp.)

1818 "brick Swizer barn"[2] George & John Long (Brandywine Twp.)

1831 "a switzer barn, part stone and part log"[3] Henry Shunkel Est.(Coventry Twp.)

1843 "swisser barnn...built with pleted logs and weatherboarded, stone stabling"[4] William S. Michiner (Upper Oxford Twp.)

The newspapers mention between 1825 and 1849 ten Swiss barns, the dimensions being 63 x 36, 46 x 30 and 50 x 40 feet. Between 1850 and 1875 six Swiss barns are mentioned: two give dimensions: 20 x 40 and 65 x 40 feet.

1. *CHESTER & DELAWARE FEDERALIST* (West Chester, Penna.) Jan. 31, 1810.
2. *AMERICAN REPUBLICAN* (West Chester, Penna.) Dec. 8, 1818.
3. Ibid., Dec. 27, 1831.
4. Ibid., Dec. 19, 1843.

WOOD

The 1798 Direct Tax lists sixty-three wood barns, the mean size being 540 square feet.

BARRACK

Peter Kalm mentions between 1748 and 1751 that in the Delaware Valley hay was stored in haystacks and barracks as well as in the barns:

> However, many people, especially in the environs of Philadelphia, had haystacks with roofs which could be moved up and down. Near the surface of the ground were some poles laid, on which the hay was put, that the air might pass freely through it.[1]
>
> However, in Philadelphia, and in a few other places, I saw that those people who made use of the latter kind of haystacks, viz. that with movable roofs, commonly had built them so that the hay was put a fathom or two above the ground, on a floor of boards, under which the cattle could stand in winter when the weather was very bad. Under this floor were partitions of boards on all the sides, which however stood far enough from each other to afford the air a free passage.[2]

The 1798 Direct Tax lists three barracks: one of frame 18 x 18 feet and two that did not mention the material of construction, the mean size being 162 square feet. The 1799 tax assessment for Charlestown Township

lists four barracks: one of frame 12 x 12 feet and three that did not mention the material of construction, the mean size being 160 square feet.

The newspaper advertisements between 1775 and 1799 mention one frame barrack 20 x 12 feet and between 1800 and 1876 one frame barrack or grain house 30 x 16 feet.

"Hay in the Barracks"[3] is included in the inventory of David Jones, of Tredyffrin Township in 1771.

1. Adolph B. Benson, editor, *PETER KALM'S TRAVELS IN NORTH AMERICA*, (New York, N.Y., 1937), Vol. 1, p. 264.
2. Ibid., pp.264, 265.
3. Chester County Inventories #80.

BATH HOUSE

Bath is defined by Bailey (ed. 1735) as "a Place to bathe or wash in" and by Webster (ed. 1828) as "A bath for bathing; a convenient vat or receptacle of water for persons to plunge or Wash their bodies in." A bath house is a building in which baths may be taken.

The 1798 Direct Tax lists John Ross, of Haverford Township, with a bath house, one story, 20 by 10 feet. The newspaper advertisements mention:

1831 "a brick bath house"[1] George B. Norris (West Chester)

1833 "mineral springs and Bath Houses"[2] A.O. Olwine, "Washington Hotel" (Pikeland Twp.)

1840 "A shower and plunging bath in a well shaded back yard"[3] William Fahnestock, "Warren Tavern" (East Whiteland Twp.)

1849 "stone house, 54 by 32 feet, stone kitchen, Milk house and Bath house attached"[4] Dr. Edmund C. Evans (Tredyffrin Twp.)

Before 1877 the newspaper advertisements mention three other bath houses and one bath house attached.

In 1856 is was observed:

> A PUBLIC BATH HOUSE.—WE have notices with some degree of pride how attentive and how ready the proprietors of our ice cream saloons and mineral water establishments are to tickle the palates of a warm, tired and dusty customer with a dose of their cold and sparkling refreshments, but we have often wondered why no person had been energetic enough to fit up a public bath house to accommodate that portion of humanity who are sweltering under the summer's heat, and to whom a bath would be more refreshing than a water-ice. There are a great many who feel an inclination to take a daily bath, for the double purpose of cleanliness and refreshment. With the inclination unfortunately, there are no means of gratifying it. While many citizens have

bath houses attached to their dwellings, and are enabled to indulge in ablutions at their pleasure there are still, hundreds who are not so fortunately situated in this respect, and who would if it were started in the Borough, liberally patronize a well kept bathing establishment. It is certainly singular that some enterprising individual has not ere this, opened a bath house here. That it would be a profitable investment, we can entertain no doubt. The question then is, shall those who now feel the absence of it, soon have an opportunity of patronizing such an establishment? We hope so.[5]

1. *AMERICAN REPUBLICAN* (West Chester, Penna.) April 19, 1831.
2. Ibid., Dec. 19, 1833.
3. Ibid., Nov. 24, 1840.
4. Ibid., Jan. 2, 1849.
5. *VILLAGE RECORD* (West Chester, Penna.) June 24, 1856.

BEAM HOUSE

The 1798 Direct Tax lists five beam houses: two of stone, the mean size being 354 square feet; one of frame 18 x 15 feet: one of log 14 x 14 feet and one of unspecified material, 24 x 20 feet.

BEE HOUSE

The 1796 tax assessment for East Whiteland Township lists one frame bee house.

BENCH

Bench is defined by Bailey (ed. 1735) as "A Seat to sit on" and by Webster (ed. 1828) as "A long seat, usually of board or plank, differing from a stool in its greater length."

Henry Graham Ashmead, in 1883, describes the Logan house, in Chester, built in 1700 as "Built of brick, two stories in height, with a tent-like roof forming an attic within, with steep sides. Over first story windows was a pent roof. . .and a porch at the front door, with seats at each side of the door, at right angles to the building. . .Wide doorway gave access to spacious hall."[1]

1. Henry Graham Ashmead, *HISTORICAL SKETCH OF CHESTER, ON DELAWARE* (The Republican Steam Printing House, 1883), p. 73.

BIRD HOUSES

The 1798 Direct Tax lists one poultry house, that did not mention the material of construction, 59 x 30 feet.

The 1798 Direct Tax lists Thomas Truman, of Sadsbury Township, as having "1 stone hog & hen house under the same roof." J. Lee Englebert, of West Chester advertises in 1870 "A Henery recently erected with Trellis 8 feet high. Roosts, Nests, &c., for 200 Fowls."[1]

The 1799 tax assessment for Charlestown Township lists one stone fowl house and for New London Township one pidgeon house.

In 1881 a newspaper mentions: "A Mansion for Birds. — A large bird-house has just been made for the lawn of the Everhart residence, in this borough. The building is four stories high and contains no less than fifty little rooms for the feathery tribe. It will be surmounted by a large spire, and will be placed on a pole sixteen feet high. It is a very neat and attractive piece of work, and the birds will doubtless appreciate it very much."[2]

The newspaper advertisements between 1877 and 1900 list two chicken houses but do not mention the material of construction, the mean size being 228 square feet. In 1880 William H. Phillips, of Kennett Square advertised a chicken house "30 feet long by 7 feet wide and has a glass front facing south."[3]

1. *VILLAGE RECORD* (West Chester, Penna.) Oct. 22, 1870.
2. *DAILY LOCAL NEWS* (West Chester, Penna.) March 16, 1881.
3. Ibid., March 6, 1880.

BLADE MILL

The 1798 Direct Tax lists two blade mills: one of stone, 28 x 26 feet and one of stone and frame, 31 x 18 feet.

BOARD

Board is defined by Bailey (ed. 1735) as "a Plank, a Table" and by Sheridan (ed. 1789) as "a piece of wood of more length and breadth than thickness; a table."

The newspapers mention:

1810 "log house boarded"[1] Richard Woodward (Newlin Twp.)

1825 "the barn is new. . .well built and boarded with pine"[2] Caleb Brinton (West Fallowfield Twp.)

1831 "first rate garden, enclosed with a pine board fence"[3] John Babb (Sadsbury Twp.)

1834 "frame store house lined inside with boards"[4] Thos. H. B. Jacobs (Charlestown Twp.)

1840 "frame store house, 33 by 17 feet, platered without and lined with boards within"[5] Charles Buffington (East Marlboro Twp.)

1840 "barn 45 by 48 ft boarded and roofed with pine"[6] John Swayne (West Marlboro Twp.)

1855 'Frame house (boarded on the outside)"[7] Joshua Lee (East Fallowfield Twp.)

1856 "part log & frame House, all boarded on the outside"[8] Joshua Lee (East Fallowfield Twp.)

1859 "board carriage House"[9] Abner Baldwin (East Caln Twp.)

1871 "frame cottage...The inside is lathed and plastered in the usual manner but the outside is first covered with boards, which are overlaid with a sheet of felting, and then covered with slate from Vermont after the fashion of the mansard roofs"[10] Thomas H. Hall (West Chester)

1. *CHESTER & DELAWARE FEDERALIST* (West Chester, Penna.) Sept. 12, 1810.
2. *VILLAGE RECORD* (West Chester, Penna.) Nov. 16, 1831.
3. *AMERICAN REPUBLICAN* (West Chester, Penna.) Aug. 31, 1825.
4. Ibid., Dec. 16, 1834.
5. Ibid., Dec. 1, 1840.
6. Ibid., Aug. 25, 1840.
7. *VILLAGE RECORD* (West Chester, Penna.) Sept. 11, 1855.
8. Ibid., Jan. 8, 1856.
9. Ibid., Nov. 12, 1859.
10. *AMERICAN REPUBLICAN* (West Chester, Penna.) Dec. 12, 1871.

BOOKS

The inventories of the county list a few men during the eighteenth century who owned books pertaining to building. In 1726 David Williams, of Goshen Township, had "A Book of Architecture";[1] in 1782, William McFarlan, of Chester County, had "Carpenter Book & many tools"[2] and in 1790 Richard Armitt, of Chester County, had "Architecture, 2 Vols."[3]

In 1797 *The Practical House Carpenter's Directory* which contains a list of sponsoring tradesmen and a detailed statement of architectural details and prices charged for them was printed in West Chester. The pamphlet is reprinted in full:

THE
PRACTICAL HOUSE CARPENTER'S
DIRECTORY:
Containing,
A GENERAL LIST OF PRICES
FOR LABOUR;
Arranged In Alphabetical Order,
And
Interspersed
with useful and important notes,

WEST-CHESTER:

Printed for the proprietors,
By Derrick & Sharples,
1797.

SUBSCRIBERS' NAMES

Benjamin Baldwin
Samuel Bell
Gershom Bates
Thomas Burnet
Jacob Chamberlin
Joseph Davis
Joseph Ezra
James Edwards
David Hains
Joseph Hawley
Imlah Hoopes
Seth Hoopes
Jacob Howell
Peter Hannum
Joseph Jefferies

Thomas Kenney
Thomas Lindsey
Mordecai Laurence
Isaac M'Farland
Joel Mendenhall
Isaac Mason
Jesse Passmore
Joseph Parker
Samuel Plankenton
Jesse Reece
Daniel Register
Davis Richards
Job Sharpless
Joseph Taylor
Silas Walton

ADVERTISEMENT

The utility of a publication like the present, will, we trust, be sufficiently evident in itself, to render any further illustration necessary on our part. To speculative as well as to practical readers, such circumlocution would be equally tedious and disinteresting.

We shall therefore only inform our readers of the principal motives, for laying the following pages before them. Such as have had occasion to be engaged in buildings, have doubtless experienced considerable disadvantages in consequence of their being deprived of a work of this nature to refer to. Nor was this the only evil, that presented itself to view. If the Carpenter chanced to be called on to execute orders in a stile different from that he usually was accustomed to perform, frequently, for want of proper rules and instructions to govern himself by, rather chose to accept any price, (however desicient it might be, to what he in justice was entitled) than have any difference with his employer on that account.

These circumstances we presume, will amply convince our readers, of the obvious necessity of a publication like the present. We do not however offer it as a complete work, for much remains yet to be added, which time alone must bring to maturity. Yet not withstanding this work may not be on a scale altogether as large as we would wish, we still indulge a hope, that it may not only be highly acceptable to the generality of our readers, but also prove a valuable acquisition to The practical House Carpenter.

West-Chester)
) THE PROPRIETORS.
Feb. 18th, 1797.)

THE
PRACTICAL HOUSE CARPENTER'S
DIRECTORY.

	L.	s.	d.
ARCHITRAVES, single faced 5 inches and under on ground per foot run	0	0	4
Ditto, exceeding 5 inches add per inch	0	0	0 1-2
Ditto, double faced 5 inches on the ground per foot run	0	0	5
If kneed add for each knee	0	0	11
Circular part of ditto per foot run	0	2	0
Ditto, 6 inches on the ground per foot	0	0	6
If kneed add for each knee	0	1	0
Circular part of ditto per foot	0	2	0
Ditto, of 7 inches on the ground per foot	0	0	7
If kneed add for each knee	0	1	1
Circular part of ditto, per foot	0	2	2
Ditto, of 8 inches on the ground per foot	0	0	8
If kneed add for each knee	0	1	2
Ditto, circular part of do, per foot	0	2	8
Ditto, of 9 inches on the ground per foot	0	0	9
If kneed add for each knee	0	1	4
Circular part of ditto per foot	0	3	2
Ditto, 10 inches on the ground per foot	0	0	10
If kneed add for each knee	0	1	6
Circular part per foot	0	3	8
Do. 11 inches on the ground per foot	0	0	11
If kneed add for each knee	0	1	6
Circular part per foot	0	4	0
Ditto, 12 inches on the ground per foot	0	1	0
If kneed add for each knee	0	2	0
Circular part per foot	0	4	6

Note, All Architraves are to be measured at the extreme edge of the straight or circular part of the moulding, glued on and well proportioned at those prices, if there are any plinth blocks, proper imposts or keys to the aforementioned architraves, they must be valued according to the work.

Ovolos, 2 inches on the ground per foot	0	0	2
If kneed for each knee	0	0	4
Ditto, two and half inch on the ground per foot		2	1-2

B

Back and barge boards per foot run	0	0	2
A tabernacle frame on breast chimney	1	2	6
Ditto, faced, fluted, and cheese moulding properly broke with other mouldings in proportion	2	5	0
Designs on breast chimney	0	11	3
Ditto, on an angle chimney	0	7	6

Note, The cornice, mantle and architraves on ditto, to be measured separately.

C

Sash casing from 4 to 9 lights	0	1	10 1-2
Ditto, from 9 to 12 lights	0	2	0
Ditto, from 9 to 15 lights	0	2	6
Ditto, from 15 to 24 lights	0	3	6
Ditto, hanging any of the above sizes	0	1	10 1-2
Ditto, for superior casing		3	9
Jamb casing for doors and windows six inches wide, per foot run	0	0	2
Ditto, from 6 to 9 inches per foot	0	0	3
Ditto, from 9 to 12 inches per foot	0	0	4 1-2
Ditto, half casting per foot run	0	0	3
Ceiling penthouses, piazzas per square	0	15	0
Single faced and cornice round rooms per foot run	0	0	6
Plain inside cornice per foot superficial and add two projections for each brake around chimnies and other places	0	0	10
Modillion cornice per foot superficial and add as before in case of a brake	0	1	3
If either of the above have a dentle bed mould add per foot	0	0	3
Plain box cornice, per foot superficial	0	0	7
Plain block cornice add 1-4			
Modillion cornice per foot superficial	0	1	0
If either of the 2 last have a dentle bed mould, per foot	0	0	2
Raking cornice, if plain add 1-4 to the price before mentioned. And if modillion or block cornice be raking add one third more than the level.			
Taking dimensions of out-side cornice measure on the longest sillit for the length			
Note, the covering of the cornice on the returns of the gable end of houses per foot run	0	0	8
But in case it runs across the end, charge for the facia cornice and covering board per foot run	0	1	0
Counters for flores and shops per square	0	15	0
Casings, door jambs in frame buildings, rabbted, measure per foot run	0	0	2
Stud casing for windows per foot run	0	0	3
If the sill be of plank or scantling rabbeted for the shutter, charge for each sill	0	1	0
Ditto, not rabbeted	0	0	9

D

Plain door frames with only a rabbet and bead, per foot run	0	0	3
Ditto, with moulding worked out of the solid, per foot	0	0	5
Ditto, with a Transum, per foot run	0	0	6

Window frames plain, with proper rabbets			
Without moulding or boxing for weights per foot	0	0	4 1-2
Ditto with proper rabbets and boxing for weights without mouldings per foot run	0	0	5
Ditto, with moulding on the face, without boxing for weights per foot run	0	0	5
Window frames with mouldings and boxed for weights, without shutter rabbets	0	0	5 1-2
Ditto, full trimmed	0	0	6
Case frames made of plank, boards or scantling, with a lath between the sashes and inside casing per foot	0	0	9
Ditto, with rabbets deep enough to receive sashes of 2 inches thick, per foot	0	0	10
For circular part of such frames, charge per foot	0	2	6
Moulding the sill of such frames	0	2	0
Inside door frames made of scantling, per foot run	0	0	3
Ditto, made of boards and framed together	0	0	4
Ditto, one part framed and planted on to for a rabbet	0	0	4
Cellar doors with stone sills and cheeks	0	11	3
Ditto, of sawed scantling	0	13	6
Ditto, of hewed	0	17	6
For lining cellar doors	0	2	6
Note. Cellar doors are supposed to be double hung, if not, deduct	0	2	0
For common trap-doors scribed down	0	7	6
Ledge doors, per yard	0	2	6
Ditto, if gauged to a thickness per yd.	0	3	3
Ditto, batten per yd.	0	4	6
Ditto if framed per yd.	0	6	0
Doors of 2 thicknessess, both sides planed and grooved per yd.	0	5	0
Two pannel doors framed with 1-2 inch, quarter round on one side per yd.	0	5	7 1-2
4 Pannels framed as above per yd.	0	6	0
Double ditto, and pannels raised on both sides per yd.	0	7	6
6 Pannels ditto framed as per yard	0	6	6
Double ditto and pannels raised on both sides	0	8	6
8 Pannels ditto, framed as above per yard	0	10	0
Double ditto, and pannels raised on both sides per yd.	0	12	6
Note. If any of the aforesaid doors should be framed with a moulding on the back of the stiles and raised on one side, charge per yard. for said moulding	0	1	0
Two or four pannels ditto framed with a			

5-8 quarter round per yd.	0	6	0
Ditto, double framed and single raised per yd.	0	7	6
Ditto double framed and raised on both sides per yd.	0	2	6
If any of said doors should be framed with ovolo or ogee add per yd.	0	0	2
Outside 4 pannel doors framed with 5-8 quarter bound lined as common per yd.	0	8	0
6 Pannel doors lined as common per yd.	0	10	0
Ditto if double hung add	0	3	0
8 Pannel doors lined as common per yd.	0	12	0
Ditto, double hung add	0	4	0
6 Pannel doors double work and single hung per yd.	0	11	0
Ditto, double hung	0	4	0
8 Pannel doors double work and single hung per yd.	0	11	3
Ditto, double hung	0	4	0
If framed with an ogee or ovolo add per yd.	0	0	2
If the pannels have a moulding on add per yd. for each side done	0	0	2
If any of these doors are bead and slush charge the same price as ovolo or ogee and pannel raised with mouldings on both sides			
6 Pannel doors framed with a 3-4 round lined and single hung per yd.	0	11	3
Ditto, double hung, per yd.	0	4	0
8 Pannel doors framed with 3-4 round lined and single hung, per yard	0	12	0
Ditto, double hung, per yard	0	4	0
6 Pannel doors two inch thick and lined as common and single hung per yard	0	14	0
Ditto, double hung, per yd.	0	4	0
If any of the aforesaid doors should be arched, charge for the arched part four times that of the straight buffet doors: if they be framed in four parts with six pannels, with ovolo or ogee, per yd.	0	7	6
Sash doors per light	0	1	0
For the wainscot part of such doors ls 6d more per yard, than for the same kind in other doors.			
Flat dormants of 9 or 12 lights, and with board cheeks each	0	18	9
Flat dormers of 12 or 15 lights, 8 by 10, single cornice with board cheeks each	1	5	0
Ditto with shingle cheeks each	1	10	0
Ridged dormers of 12 or 15 lights with board cheeks each	2	0	0
Arched ditto of 12 or 15 lights with block and knee, and bracketed with the brackets turned up, and with scroll			

and shingle cheeks each	3	15	0
Ditto, with double cornice, rusticated pilasters carved, bracketed, and shingle cheeks each	7	10	0
Dresser made of plank, per foot superficial	0	0	4 1-2
For narrow shelves and uprights in do. per foot superficial	0	0	4
Lining behind ditto, per square	0	15	0

F

Floors laid with boards only jointed per square	0	5	0
Ditto, grooved	0	7	6
Ditto, planed and grooved	0	10	6
Ditto, sapt and grooved, strait-joints per square	0	12	6
Ditto, laid of oak planed and grooved strait-joints per square	0	15	0
Ditto, planed on both sides and beaded, straight laid per square	1	0	0
Ditto, poplar or pine boards planed on one side, straight laid per square	0	10	6
Ditto planed on both sides and beaded per square	0	14	3
Ditto, floors laid with 1 1-4 boards strait laid per square	0	1	6
Ditto, if not grooved, deduct	0	3	9

Note. The board is supposed to be from 6 to 9 inches in the aforesaid floors and nailed in sight.

Ditto, from 3 to 6 inches wide and nailed in the edge per square	1	0	0
Ditto, if the heading joints tongued and nailed as ditto	1	2	6
Ditto if dowelled per square	1	5	0
Plank floors for stores per square	0	7	6
Framing common floors, from 3 to 4s per square			
Ditto, if trimmed over cellar doors or windows per square	0	1	6
Ditto, if one girder and joist 8 inches deep per square, and the joist 1 foot 6 inches between	0	6	0
Ditto, if trimmed over cellar doors and windows per square	0	1	0
Ditto, if two girders, add 1-3			
Ditto, if 9 inches deep and 1 foot 6 between, per square	0	6	3
Ditto, 10 inches deep 1 foot 6 inches between, per square	0	6	6
Ditto, 11 inches deep, and do. per square	0	7	0
Ditto, 12 inches deep and do. per square	0	7	6

Note. If any of the floors be framed with the joice nearer or farther apart, add or diminish according to the distance.

Laying sleepers per square from 4 to 5s			
Ceiling joice per square	0	5	0
Framing houses, if close studded, per square	0	7	6
Ditto, truss partitions of the plainest kind per square	0	8	0
Ditto, of the best kind, per square	0	17	6
Wall plaits, raising pieces and lintels per foot run	0	0	1
Framing common roofs without collar beams per square	0	3	0
Framing ditto with collar beams per square	0	6	0

Note. The rafters are supposed to be 20 inches in the clear.

Framing roofs with 3 rafters and collar beams, with the upper rafters to make a flat on the top	0	7	6
Ditto, with collar beams, the upper one plank, and sawn so as to form a pitch both ways, per square	0	8	0
Ditto, with collar beams and purlins per square	0	15	0
Ditto, with collar beams, king posts, hammer posts, and purlins per square	1	2	6
For hip roof take the girt of the facia per square	0	7	6
Fences made of rough boards, per square	0	2	0
Ditto board jointed	0	3	0
Ditto, grooved or sprung	0	5	0
Ditto, planed on one side and grooved	0	7	0
Ditto, on both sides and grooved	0	9	0
Capping on ditto with moulding on one side per foot run	0	0	3
Capping on ditto with mouldings on both sides per foot run	0	0	4 1-2
Common paling round gardens with posts, rails, and pales split and pointed per pannel, 5s 6d, per pannel for shaving the pales 6d			
Ditto, if the rails be sawed, per ditto	0	4	0
Ditto, of 3 rails and sawed, per ditto	0	4	6
Ditto, posts hewed, per pannel	0	3	0
Ditto, all planed per pannel	0	7	6
Ditto, if top rail rabbeted, per pannel	0	0	6

Note. Charge the same for a gate, as for a pannel of the kind, supposing the pannel 10 foot long

Palisade fence of the roughest kind per foot run	0	2	3
Ditto, pales notched in the rails and architraves on one side	0	3	6
Ditto, architraves on both sides	0	4	3
Ditto, with the pales morticed thro' the rails and architraves on both sides	0	5	0
Charge for each ramp in the rail	0	5	0

Ditto, for each gate per foot run	0	7	6
Flats laid with plank, or double boarded per square, bridging included	1	2	6
Post and rails on ditto, with the rails nailed on per foot run	0	0	9
Pales morticed through the posts	0	1	0
Ditto, made of plank and capt with moulding under the capping	0	2	0

G

Grounds for architraves of the best kind per foot run	0	0	2
Gutters made of cedar plank and shingled in at the eaves, per foot run	0	0	9
Ditto, made of boards, per foot run	0	0	6
Ditto, worked in the cornice per foot run	0	0	4 1-2
Measure the cornice separately, and charge for each knee	0	0	9
Ditto made of cedar scantling, per do.	0	0	4 1-2
Ditto, made of cedar plank and shingled behind chimnies and other places per foot run	0	1	0
Gutters made to hang under eaves of scantling from 3 to 4 inches thick, and 5 or 6 inches broad per foot run	0	0	6
If these gutters have an architrave add	0	0	1

L

Step ladders not exceeding 2 feet wide per step	0	0	8
Common ladders per round	0	0	6
Lintels made to represent stone over doors or windows are worth each	0	5	6

M

Mantle for a small fire place, with only a facia cornice and shelf charge	0	3	9
Mantle with stiles and frize with small fire mould bed mould and cornice, plain	0	11	3
Ditto, with a contracted frize	0	15	0
Ditto, with stiles and frize architraves, Tablet bed mould broke over the tablet cornice, straight	1	2	6
Ditto, with grounds framed wide enough, to receive an architrave and pilaster, and with the same the pilasters running up to the plancier bed mould broke round them and the cornice likewise, and a tablet the thickness of the under part of the bed mould and the upper part not broke.	2	6	0
Ditto, of the same kind with fluted pilasters and fret bed mould	2	10	6
Ditto, in another manner or form charge in proportion to the trouble			

Kitchen mantles including facia cornice per foot run	0	1	0
Ditto, without cornice do.	0	9	0
Inch mouldings of all kinds per foot run	0	0	1 1-2
Ditto, inch and 1-4 moulding per do.	0	0	2
And charge per each knee in ditto	0	0	4

N

Necessary houses, if framed in the readiest manner and finished accordingly	1	0	0
Ditto, if weather boards be planed, grooved and covered with cedar and oak shingles, with seats and all included per piece	1	15	0
If double charge accordingly			
Ditto, if stone, charge as for other work, of like nature			

P

Partitions rough for plaistering per square	0	6	6
Ditto, partitions of pine or poplar planed on both sides and grooved	0	15	0
Ditto, if planed on one side and grooved per square	0	11	0
Common lets, partitions in cellars per yd	0	2	0
Ditto the best kind per yard	0	3	0
And for doors in each kind add 1-4. Pent eves cornice and facia per foot run	0	0	6
Plain pediments including the frize for doors not exceeding 3 foot 4 inches wide	1	15	0
Ditto, with a dentle bed mould	2	0	0
If either of them have trusses add 1-4 And for open pediments add 1-8. Plain porches, each at	0	15	0
Ditto, capt posts and completed with ankle board	1	10	0
Planing joists per foot run	0	0	1
Ditto, girders per foot run	0	0	2
Open pilaster or doors, charge per foot run	0	0	11 1-4
If suitable capt and base			
Ditto, fluted and capt, and base as above, per foot	0	1	6

R

Rabbet strips, per foot run	0	0	1 1-2

S

Sashes of 8 by 10 per light	0	0	7
Ditto, 9 by 11 do.	0	0	8
Ditto, 9 by 12 do. stuff 1 1-2 thick	0	0	10
Ditto, 10 by 12, or 12 by 14, 15 or 16, stuff 2 inches	0	1	0
The arched part per light	0	3	0
Common shelves for closets, per foot superficial	0	0	3

And for scolloping, add for each shelf	0	1	10
Stores, shelves and uprights with the edges round per square	0	16	8
If the shelves and uprights be planed to a thickness and the astickle planted on the edges and mitered, per square	1	5	6
For lining behind shelves, per square	0	12	6
Lathing and shingling, new roofs per square, if the cornice be 4 1-2 long	1	5	0
Ditto, if 6 inches	0	17	6
Ditto, if 8 inches	0	12	6
Ditto, if 9 inches	0	10	0
Ditto, if 10 inches	0	9	0
Ditto, if 12 inches	0	8	0

Note. The shingles are supposed to be dressed.

For shingling penthouses and the like places, add double.

Inside shutters made to fold in a box the outside ones framed with a small moulding, the others clampt, per foot superficial	0	1	2
The inner ditto, framed square	0	1	3
Ditto framed with mouldings	0	1	6
Ditto all clampt	0	0	9
Outside shutters inlaid or framed, for four pannels, per yard	0	10	0
Six pannels ditto, framed	0	12	6

Note. If they be formed with a 5-8 ovolo or ogee, add per yard

Bead and flush doors, per yard	0	13	0
Ditto, made of plank per yard	0	15	0
Lining for shutters per foot superficial	0	0	3
Common wash board with a bead per foot run	0	0	3
And add for each brake	0	0	1
Ditto, with belection, per foot run	0	0	4
Ditto, with a bead and moulding planted on	0	0	5
Ditto raking down stairs	0	1	0
Common winding stairs planed on one side per step	0	1	4
Ditto, planed on both sides per step	0	1	8
Common winding stairs per step	0	1	0
And for newel in such stairs per foot run	0	0	5 1-2
But if boards per foot superficial	0	0	3
Open newel stairs with strait hand rails and string-boards, including the bannisters per step	0	10	0
Ditto common bracketed with two bannisters on a step	0	12	6
Ditto, with 3 on a step	0	14	0
If the steps raisers, and mouldings glued together add to each step	0	1	6
For a circular rail charge	0	17	6
For a twist rail of one revolution	5	0	0

For 1 1-2 revolution	7	0	0
For two revolutions	9	0	0
For half hand rails, charge per foot run	0	1	0
For rampt in ditto	0	10	0
For ditto, in hand rails charge	0	17	6
Plain open pilasters under half hand rails full capt and base	0	5	0
Ditto, single capt and base	0	3	0
For a circular string-board	0	13	6
For half space or quarter charge	0	9	0
If nailed on the edges add to each	0	2	6
Common ledge shutters for 9 or 12 lights, single hung with hooks and straps each	0	3	9
Ditto, double hung with do.	0	4	6
Ditto, two thicknesses crossing each other of pine or poplar from 9 to 16 lights, double hung per pair	0	10	6
Common surbass per foot run	0	0	6
Ditto, if the facia ornamented, per foot run with a suitable moulding	0	1	0
Ditto, mouldings ornamented per foot run	0	1	6
Ditto, like half-hand sides of entrys, per foot run	0	0	8

T

Trunks made square to convey water down walls, per foot run	0	0	7
Circular part per foot run	0	1	0
Charge for each knee in ditto	0	0	8

W

Wainscoting framed, square raised pannels per yard	0	2	6
Ditto frame double and pannels raised on both sides per yard	0	8	3
Ditto, planed on both sides per yard	0	6	6
Ditto, pannels raised on both sides per yard	0	4	6
Ditto, framed with ovolo or ogee and raised ditto	0	5	0
Panels raised and beaded, per yard	0	0	2
Ditto, planed on both sides per yard	0	6	6
Ditto, with 5-8 ovolo or ogee and pannels raised and beaded per yard	0	6	0
Ditto, planed on both sides	0	6	6
Ditto, double framed pannels raised on both sides	0	9	0

Wainscoting framed with ovolo or ogee on one side, and flush and bead on the other, charge as if double framed, raised and pannel beaded.

Narrow wainscoting for door or window jambs, per yard	0	7	6
Ditto, if plank, per yard	0	8	0
Angular about stairs	0	8	6
And for each rampt pannel	0	3	9

Wall covering with boards or shingles and
    corniced and facia on one side, per
    foot run   0 1 6
Ditto, if 2 sides do.   0 2 0
Ditto, pitching but one way, per foot run   0 1 3
Ditto, without cornice, per foot do.   0 1 1
Ditto, without cornice and facia, per foot do   0 . 0 9
    Note. The boards are supposed to be
grooved.
Weather boarding without jointing, per
    square   0 3 0
Ditto, jointed and beaded, per do.   0 4 3
Ditto, jointed grooved and beaded   0 6 0
Ditto, planed grooved sprung or plowed,
    per square   0 9 0
Ditto, notched on the studs and laped
    per do.   0 7 6
Well-curbs made to sink per piece   0 7 6
Common wash boards, per foot   0 0 4
Well-curbs with windlass and caped   1 2 6
Ditto, if the stuff be hewed   1 10 0
Ditto, made to go round pumps of plank
    dowel together   0 18 9

STONE BARNS

Under framing in stone or frame barns, sides
    of entries or dividing off for stalls including
    the boarding, per square   0 7 0
Framing joist in girder or sill, per square   0 2 6
If two girders or sills and tenented on both
    ends, per square   0 3 0
Joist cut to a length and laid down loose,
    per square   0 1 6
Framing roofs in stone or frame barn pur-
    lined measure only the superficial con-
    tents of the roofs and include the fram-
    ings of the plaits and purlines and cross
    beams in at those prices, per square   0 7 6
Principal rafter and purlines, per square   0 8 0
Ditto, two purlines or more add in pro-
    portion
Framing with two interties, per square and
    single breast   0 5 6
Ditto, two interties and double breast,
    per square   0 6 0
Ditto, 1 do. and single do. do.   0 4 6
    Note. The sides of the floors in frame
barns charge, per square   0 3 0
and in stone barns charge, per square   0 1 6
If the front be framed and the interties
    tenented in the posts and likewise in
    the back door posts the same as frame
    barns   0 3 0
Large doors in stone or frame barns with
    four arms, per square   0 15 0

Ditto, with three arms do.   0 13 0
Ditto, if plowed and grooved add, per
    square   0 3 9
Front doors charge if double hung per door   0 5 0
Ditto, if planed and grooved add per door   0 1 10 1-2
Ditto, stable doors in the front and frame,
    per piece   0 7 6
Ditto, planed and beaded add, per door   0 1 10 1-2
Ditto, if the frames be planed and rabbeted
    for the door and beaded, charge for the
    rabbet, per foot run   0 0 1
Ditto, window frames with rounds 15
    inches high and two feet wide, per frame   0 2 6
Ditto if no sill   0 2 0
Ditto, if sill, planed and beaded, add   0 1 0
Ditto, no sill and do. add   0 0 9
Ditto, if a shutter and hung add 1-2
Ditto, if planed and grooved add 2-3 of
    the prices of the frames they belong to.
If 2 feet wide and 3 feet high with
    slanting board   0 5 0
Ditto, if planed and the frame beaded   0 7 6
Common racks top and bottom sawed,
    rounds split, per round   0 0 2
Ditto, if all split, per do.   0 0 3
Mangers with slanting boards and proper
    fastned to the studs or wall   0 0 7
Ditto, if kneed add for each knee   0 0 6
Half stalls for cattle, per piece   0 2 6
Ditto, for horses   0 6 6
Ditto, well finished, per do   0 3 9
Extra work for doors or gates, in the
    division of stables, charge according
    to form.
Barn floors laid down from the saw,
    per square   0 1 0
Ditto, jointed and laid down, per square   0 8 3
Ditto, jointed and pinned down, per square   0 15 0
Ditto, do. plowed and lathed, per square   1 0 0
    Note. The said floors are supposed to
be without lining, if lined charge according
to the work.
Clapboarding of any frame, per square   0 10 0
Silling old frame barns, per foot run   0 0 6
For splicing old posts, per splice not ex-
    ceeding two feet long   0 2 6
New tenents only, per tenent   0 1 0

SHINGLES.

Making oak shingles, per hundred 3 feet
    long   0 4 6
Ditto, laying per hundred   0 1 6
Ditto, 2 feet 8 inches long charge for

making	0	3	9
If the stuff be cut by some other person, charge for making, per hundred	0	3	0
Dressing cedar shingles, if three feet long, charge per hundred	0	1	10 1-2
If 2 feet long per hundred	0	0	9
Hewing timber of any size, take half the girt and multiply it by the length, and charge for every superficial foot that it contains	0	0	3
Hewed on but three sides charge, per foot run	0	0	2 1-2
Hewed on two sides, per foot do.	0	0	2
Hewed on one side, do.	0	0	1 1-2
Making flax breaks with 5 slotes single headed, per piece	0	11	3
Ditto, 7 slotes single headed	0	15	0
Ditto, do. double headed	0	18	9
Common farm gate stuff sawed, per gate	0	4	6
Ditto, with top rail and brace and head of scantling slotes morticed through	0	12	6
Ditto, planed add, per gate	0	2	6
Ditto, planed and beaded and the brace mitered at the heel and top, per gate	0	18	9

FINIS.

More architectural books are known to have been used during the nineteen century. In 1816 David McKim, Jun., of Sadsbury Township, had a "Book of Architecture"[5] Moses Baily owned *THE PRACTICAL BUILDER, OR WORKMAN'S GENERAL ASSISTANT* by William Pain, Architect and Joiner, published in Boston in 1792 and George Mason owned *THE YOUNG CARPENTER'S ASSISTANT: OR, A SYSTEM OF ARCHITECTURE, ADAPTED TO THE STYLE OF BUILDING IN THE UNITED STATES* by Owen Biddle, House Carpenter, and Teacher of Architectural Drawing in Philadelphia, published in 1810. In Philadelphia, architectural books were available at the Carpenter's Company and the Library Company of Philadelphia.

1. Chester County Inventories #208.
2. Ibid., #3244.
3. Ibid., #4132.
4. Original copy of pamphlet in Chester County Historical Society (West Chester, Penna.)
5. Chester County Inventories #6328.

BREWHOUSE

A few inventories list the contents of brewhouses:
1716 John Hoskins, Chester[1]
"In the Brewhouse
a Larg Copper

3 Long brewing tubbs
A Cooler
A hand mill
2 larg Trough
4 Bushells of Mault"
1742/3 Archibald McNeille, Kennett Township[2]
"11th In the Brew House
one Copper ffurnace
One Hashing Kowe and 18 old Barrels
A Quantity of Ground Malt
Earthen pots and Glass Bottles
One tea pot Silver spoons and other things necessary for a Tea Table
Five earthen Dishes one plate and one Bason"
1786 Henry Hayes, Darby Township[3]
"Over Brewhouse N:9
A Bed bedsteds & furniture
An other bed do do
A Chaff do do do
A Close Stool Chair & pan, looking Glass & Cloath baskett"
1787 John Kerlin, East Whiteland Township[4]
"To Sundrey barrells in the brew house
To the Copper in the brew house"
The 1799 tax assessment for Charlestown Township lists a frame brew house 20 x 16 feet. The newspaper advertisements between 1775 and 1800 mention one stone brew house 25 x 18 feet.

1. Chester County Inventories #27.
2. Ibid., #842.
3. Ibid., #3832.
4. Ibid., #3884.

BRIDGEWAY

A newspaper advertisement mentions:
1859 "STONE HOUSE, four stories, 40 by 36 feet, divided into convenient rooms, with double Piazza front. Has been used as a first class Boarding House, accommodating from 40 to 50 boarders; also a GOOD BRICK HOTEL, 35 by 20 feet, two stories high, with Bar room, waiting room Post and Ticket Offices on the first floor, and four lodging rooms and two bath rooms on the second floor, with cellars complete; both buildings being supplied with water by a force and lift pump between the two buildings, which are connected by a bridgeway from the second stories."[1]
Mifflin Lewis, est. (Tredyffrin Twp.)

1. *VILLAGE RECORD* (West Chester, Penna.) Oct. 1, 1859.

BUTTRESS

Henry Graham Ashmead, in 1883, describes the Logan house, in Chester, built in 1700 as "Built of brick, two stories in height, with a tent-like roof...Large buttresses were built against the gables for strength, and smaller ones to guard the brick walls on each side of main building."[1]

1. Henry Graham Ashmead *HISTORICAL SKETCH OF CHESTER, ON DELAWARE,* (The Republican Steam Printing House, 1883), p. 73.

CABIN

Cabin is defined by Bailey (ed. 1735) as "Cabbin, a Cottage or Hut" and by Sheridan (ed. 1789) as "a cottage, or small house."

Henry Graham Ashmead mentions in 1883 that on Sept. 12, 1682, Nossiter conveyed this estate to John Sharpless. The latter came from Ratherton, in Cheshire, England, accompanied by his wife, Jane Moor (they were then in middle life), and their children, landing at Chester on the 14th of Sixth month, 1682, two months prior to the arrival of William Penn. The family history, published in 1816, states that they settled on Ridley Creek, about two miles northwest from Chester, "where they fell a large tree, and took shelter among the boughs thereof about six weeks, in which time they built a cabin against a rock, which answered for their chimney-back, and now contains the date of the year when the cabin was built viz., 1682, in which they dwelt, about twenty years, and where they all died, except the mother and three sons, in which time Joseph learned the trade of house-carpenter, and when of age built the dwelling-house, which is now standing, and occupied by one of their descendants. Part of the original floors are still in use, being fastened down with wooden pins of about an inch in diameter instead of nails. It is a sizable two-story dwelling, the walls of stone."[1]

A diary describes the early cabins of the Brinton and Thatcher families. The "Brinton cabin of 1684 – The cabin was yellow poplar plank, sawed three or four inches thick, dovetailed, probably one story high with a loft, downstairs two rooms[2]...It was constructed out of plank sawed from poplar trees, felled on the premises[3]...The trees were sawed into plank with a whip saw[4]...Cabin of yellow poplar, near a spring[5]...Was of poplar plank, sawed with a whip saw—Some two inches thick[6]...Wm. Brinton built a cabin in which monthly meetings were held—lived in it 14 years."[7] The Thatcher cabin is mentioned as "built of 3 inch yellow poplar plank, sawed by a whip saw & remained sound to the last."[8]

The 1798 Direct Tax lists Daniel Bailey, of East Fallowfield township, as having an "Old Cabben"; Caleb Cobourn, of Chester, as having a "cabin"; Richard Humphton Esq., of West Bradford Township, with "1 Log Cabben small" and Robert Young, of West Bradford Township as having "1 Log Cabben Small".

"In the year 1800, there was a man (Barnitt) who lived in a small Cabin east of the Ford, near the bank who kept a Scow, and took across wagons. Later a coloured man, Brown, lived in the same Cabin & kept a skiff to carry across foot travellers."[9]

1. Ashmead, Henry Graham *HISTORY OF DELAWARE COUNTY, PENNSYLVANIA* (Philadelphia, Pa., 1884), p. 653.
2. Brinton, John Hill, Ms. Diary, (Chester County Historical Society, West Chester, Penna.), Vol. 2, p. 58, under date Feb. 11, 1876.
3. Ibid., Vol. 3, p. 6, under date, April 20, 1879.
4. Ibid., Vol. 1, p. 20, under date 1845.
5. Ibid., Vol. 1, p. 25, under date March 1858.
6. Ibid., Vol. 1, p. 124, under date Dec. 2, 1866.
7. Ibid., Vol. 3, p. 1, no date.
8. Ibid., Vol. 3, p. 23 under date May 13, 1879.
9. Ibid., Vol. 1, p. 93, under date March 30, 1860.

CART HOUSE

Cart is defined by Bailey (ed. 1735) as "a Cart to carry any thing in", by Sheridan (ed. 1789) as "a wheel-carriage, used commonly for luggage" and by Webster (ed. 1828) as "A carriage with two wheels, fitted to be drawn by one horse, or by a yoke of oxen, and used in husbandry or commercial cities for carrying heavy commodities...In America, horse-carts are used mostly in cities, and ox-carts in the country."

The 1798 Direct Tax lists eighteen cart houses: one of stone and frame 23 x 23 feet, ten of frame, the mean size being 288 square feet; three of stone, the mean size being 494 square feet and two of log the mean size being 410 square feet. The 1796 tax assessment for West Whiteland Township lists and describes six cart houses: George Gray and George Hoofman each had "1 Cart House on Posts, Straw Roof" George Hoofman also had a "Cart House on Posts"; John Jacobs had "1 Old Cart House on Pillars" and John Jones had "1 Brick Cart House Granary aloft." The 1799 tax assessment for West Marlboro Township lists two cart houses that did not mention the material of construction, the mean size being 166 square feet.

CAVE

Cave is defined by Bailey (ed. 1735) as "a Den or dark hollow Place under Ground", by Sheridan (ed. 1789) as "a cavern, a den" and by Webster (ed. 1828) as "A hollow place in the earth; a subterraneous cavern; a den. This may be natural or artificial..."

A diary mentions a few of the early caves that the settlers first lived in. "Gilpin cave. It was dug into a side of a bank. Probably the earth side of the cave was lined with boards...Gilpin lived in a cave in 1694 in Birmingham.[1] Several children born in cave. Built a small wooden house by the cave & then lived in it...in 1758 his son added to it a brick addition. Frame torn down in 1835 & a stone building put in its place[2]...Gilpin cave was not in the side of the hill. The ground was level & it was dug into like a cellar. (Most probably then covered over & sodded over for a roof J.H.B.)[3]...I have a pair of silver candlesticks which were used by the colonist Gilpin. He was here 1694."[4]

A deed to Isaac Haines, dated 1710, mentions "& he made a cave soon after that & had several children born in cave. Afterwards a frame house was built, then the present west end stone, now used as a kitchen."[5] Francis Hickman also "lived in a cave. Some of Francis Hickmaan's children born in that cave."[6]

1. John H. Brinton Diary #1, p. 128 under date Jan. 16, 1867, Chester County Historical Society, (West Chester).
2. John H. Brinton Diary #2, p. 7 under date Jan. 1855, Chester County Historical Society, (West Chester).
3. John H. Brinton Diary #3, p. 2 Feb. 25, 1878, Chester County Historical Society, (West Chester).
4. John H. Brinton Diary #1, p. 45 under date 1846, Chester County Historical Society (West Chester).
5. Ibid., p. 99 under date July 22, 1862, Chester County Historical Society (West Chester).
6. Ibid., p. 87 under date April 20, 1858, Chester County Historical Society (West Chester, Penna.).

CEILING

Ceiling is defined by Bailey (ed. 1735) as "the inner Roof of a House" and by Webster (ed. 1828) as "The covering which overlays the inner roof of a building, or the timbers which form the top of a room. This covering may be of boards, or of lath and plastering. Hence ceiling is used for the upper part of a room."

John F. Watson mentions:

> From his maternal grandfather Rambo, who had been one of the earliest settler, Mr. Jacob Bengston, had learned that the board ceilings in the first colonial houses had been covered with earth to prevent the heat from escaping through the top. No dirt is used now, only thin boards, and not any too many of these.[1]

The newspaper advertisements mention:

1764 "Brick Messuage. . .Kitchen, Work Shop. . .ceiled and finished, two Story high"[2] Dennis M'Loughlin (Chester)

1775 "three ceiled garrets"[3] David Jackson (Chester)

1788 "four good rooms on each of the two first floors and two ditto in the garret, all of them ceiled"[4] Jesse Sharpless (Darby)

1832 "third story which is ceiled and plastered"[5] Daniel Vondersmith (Downingtown)

1839 "Stone House. . .two parlors and an entry on the first floor, three rooms on the second, and two rooms in the garret ceiled and plastered"[6] George A. Fairlamb (Downingtown)

1839 "stone tavern house. . .the 1st and third floors are counterceiled"[7] Randall Evans, "Franklin Tavern", (Tredyffrin Twp.)

1843 "two story stone house. . .all ceiled"[8] Samuel Williamson, Est.(Uwchlan Twp.)

The newspaper advertisements mention before 1849 thirty-one ceiled garrets, two ceiled attics, four garrets ceiled and plastered, one third floor ceiled and plastered

and one ceiled and plastered garret.

1. John F. Watson, *ANNALS OF PHILADELPHIA AND PENNSYLVANIA IN THE OLDEN TIME* (Philadelphi, Penna., 1909), Vol. 2, p. 727.
2. *PENNSYLVANIA GAZETTE* (Philadelphia, Penna.) Sept. 13, 1764.
3. Ibid., Jan. 11, 1775.
4. Ibid., Jan. 23, 1788.
5. *VILLAGE RECORD* (West Chester, Penna.) Nov. 7, 1832.
6. *AMERICAN REPUBLICAN* (West Chester, Penna.) Jan. 29, 1839.
7. Ibid., Nov. 5, 1839.
8. Ibid., Oct. 10, 1843.

CHAIR HOUSE

Chair is defined by Bailey (ed. 1735) as ". . .also a Sedan or open Chaise," by Sheridan (ed. 1789) as "a two wheeled vehicle which contains two persons and is drawn by a single horse" and by Webster (ed. 1828) as ". . .A sedan; a vehicle on poles borne by men." A chair house is a building to house chairs.

The 1798 Direct Tax lists twenty-eight chair houses: nineteen of frame, the mean size being 228 square feet; six of stone, the mean size being 289 square feet; one of slab 15 x 10 feet; one of log 15 x 15 feet, and one of unspecified material of construction, 15 x 10 feet. The 1796 tax assessment for West Whiteland Township lists George Massey as having "1 frame Chair house Granary & Loft."

CHEESE HOUSE

The 1798 Direct Tax lists three cheese houses: one of frame, 120 square feet and two of stone, the mean size being 234 square feet.

The newspapers mention:

1776 "cheese house"[1] William Dilworth (Birmingham Twp.)

1790 "stone spring house with an excellent cheese room over the same"[2] Benjamin Powell (East Bradford Twp.)

1. *PENNSYLVANIA GAZETTE* (Philadelphia, Penna.) Feb. 7, 1776.
2. Ibid., Oct. 6, 1790.

CHIMNEY

Chimney is defined by Bailey (ed. 1735) as "a kind of Funnel, &c. for the Conveyance of Smoak", by Sheridan (ed. 1789) as "the passage through which the smoke ascends from the fire in the house: the fireplace" and by Webster (ed. 1828) as "In architecture, a body of brick or stone, erected in a building, containing a funnel or funnels, to convey smoke, and other volatile matter through the roof, from the hearth or fire-place, where fuel is burnt. . .2. A fireplace; the lower part of the body of brick or stone which confines and conveys smoke."

John F. Watson, in 1830 mentions:

> From an old man, Martin Garet [Martin Garret], seventy-five, I learned the following observations: he said he had never seen or heard of any Swedes who used dampers, but he had heard them say that they used them in Sweden. However, he himself had made a cover which he placed over the chimney on cold nights, thereby retaining much more heat then usual. But it was a lot of trouble to climb up on the roof of the house every night and morning.[1]

In 1884 Henry Graham Ashmead mentions that the mansion of the Governor at Tinicum had had "chimney said to have been made of small foreign made bricks of a pale yellow color."[2]

The wills mention:

1735 "Priviledge of my Lodging Room with my best bed beding and furniture thereunto belonging and my son Joseph shall build her a Corner Chimney of Brick in the said Room"[3] Joseph Baker (Edgemont Twp.)

1754 "a round Log House Sixteen feet Square with a Chimney made of wood and Lath'd & filled with Clay, with two Boarded Floors dores and Windows"[4] Joseph McClackey (Chester County)

1790 "Executors to build a House...sixteen feet by Twenty, one story and a half high with two floors, viz upper and lower floor with a corner chimney"[5] Samuel Futhey (West Fallowfield Twp.)

The newspapers mention:

1761 "square Log House, Brick Chimney"[6] Jane Jenkins, Nathaniel Pennock (New Garden Twp.)

1762 "Log House, a Stone Chimney, with two Hearths"[7] Lydia, Samuel & Thomas Jones (Tredyffrin Twp.)

1763 "Frame Dwelling house...Stone Gable-end, with a Chimney to each Story"[8] Daniel John (Charlestown Twp.)

1764 "Dwelling house with two Chimneys...shop...with a chimney"[9] Jacob Yarnall (Willistown Twp.)

1766 "Log House, with two Stone Chimneys"[10] Susannah James & David Davis (Coventry Twp.)

1768 "framed dwelling house, with a stone chimney"[11] Robert Elliot (Radnor Twp.)

1776 "log house with a stone chimney"[12] Richard Fawkes (Newtown Twp.)

1777 "two story log house, a room built of stone, with a double chimney of stone and lime built last summer"[13] Henry Saunderson (Londonderry Twp.)

1779 "frame house, with two rooms on a floor, and a chimney in each"[14] James Butland (Chester County)

1783 "two log dwelling houses, with two stone chimneys in each"[15] Mordecai Evans (Uwchlan Twp.)

1783 "stone store house with a chimney in the back room"[16] Joseph Shippen Jr., (Kennett Square)

1786 "stone dwelling house, having three rooms on the lower floor, and four on the upper, with chimney places in the house"[17] Daniel Yarnall (Willistown Twp.)

1833 "Stone Spring House, 12 feet by 16, containing fire place and chimney"[18] John Williamson (West Nantmeal Twp.)

1876 "fire place and chimney, having a breast of twelve and a depth of five feet"[19] (East Goshen Twp.)

The newspapers, before 1877 mention two other houses with stone chimneys, twelve log houses with stone chimneys, one log house with chimney, one house with chimney and one other shop with a chimney as well as those already quoted.

After 1877 a few chimneys were described in the newspapers:

1881 "Harry Darlington residing near Birmingham Meeting House, has torn down the stone chimneys of his dwelling house, and built them up with brick and placed upon them terra cotta tops"[20] (Birmingham Twp.)

1886 "old Williamson house...the chimneys being eight feet square and built heavy and solid"[21] (East Goshen Twp.)

1891 "...began tearing down the residence of Patrick Cook on South High Street..when the lath and plaster was stripped off of the outside that the structure was of logs...The chimneys, two in number, stood in the northwest and southwest corners respectively and were built across the corners, filling considerable space"[22] (West Chester)

1. John F. Watson, *ANNALS OF PHILADELPHIA AND PENNSYLVANIA IN THE OLDEN TIME* (Philadelphia, Penna., 1909), Vol. 2, p. 727.
2. Henry Graham Ashmead, *HISTORY OF DELAWARE COUNTY, PENNSYLVANIA* (Philadelphia, Penna., 1884), p. 277.
3. Chester County Will Book 1, p. 34.
4. Ibid., #3, p. 473.
5. Ibid., #8, p. 420.
6. *PENNSYLVANIA GAZETTE* (Philadelphia, Penna.) March 19, 1761.
7. Ibid., March 11, 1762.
8. Ibid., March 10, 1763.
9. Ibid., Jan. 19, 1764.
10. Ibid., March 6, 1766.
11. Ibid., Feb. 18, 1768.
12. Ibid., Oct. 9, 1776.
13. Ibid., April 16, 1777.
14. Ibid., May 26, 1779.
15. Ibid., Dec. 3, 1783.
16. Ibid., July 16, 1783.
17. Ibid., Feb. 1, 1786.
18. *AMERICAN REPUBLICAN* (West Chester, Penna.) Sept. 3, 1833.
19. *DAILY LOCAL NEWS* (West Chester, Penna) May 27, 1876.
20. Ibid., April 12, 1881.
21. Ibid., April 14, 1886.
22. Ibid., May 13, 1891.

CIDER HOUSE
CIDER PRESS

The 1798 Direct Tax lists seven cider houses: two of frame, the mean size being 228 square feet; two of unspecified material, the mean size being 250 square feet; two cider presses on stone pillars, the mean size being 271 square feet and one of log 20 x 10 feet.

CLAPBOARD

Clapboard is defined by Bailey as "a Board cut ready to make Casks, &c." and by Webster (ed. 1828) as "A thin narrow board for covering houses. In England, according to Bailey, a clapboard is also what in America is called a stave for casks." The Oxford English Dictionary (ed. 1733) defines clapboard as "1. orig. A smaller size of split oak, imported from north Germany, and used by coopers for making barrel-staves; in later times also for wainscoting. App. now obsolete. b. In U.S. A board, thinner at one edge, used to cover the sides or roofs of houses, each board being made to overlap that below it; a weather-board."

The earliest mention of clapboard found for Chester County thus far is in the Court Records of 1684 "The Testimony of Henry Hastings Who being Attested declareth that he had agreed with Richard Frend to Build a Cattle house of Clap boards 24 foot long and 16 foot Board for William Oly for which he was to receive L. 6.5."[1]

The Brinton diary has three mentions of clapboard. The house of the Bennett family, in Birmingham Township, was "Made of plank, clapboarded, & filled in."[2] A later entry mentions that materials had been taken from an earlier house to use on a later one: "Father got bricks from early 1713 house, also doors, windows, boards, & clapboards. They were painted a Venetian red."[3] and "Edward Brinton — built [house] about 1724, frame, at first, afterwards clapboarded by Edward B. Darlington (d. in 1823-4) & painted yellow."[4]

The newspaper advertisements mention:

1855 "frame beaming and sizing room clapboarded"[5] Francis Bonner (Phoenixville)

1855 "Frame engine & Boiler House clapboarded. Frame stable clapboarded. Frame Office clapboarded... Frame Blacksmith shop clapboarded"[6] Keystone Mining Co. (Schuylkill Twp.)

1857 "Frame wagon house clapboarded"[7] Francis Hoopes (London Grove Twp.)

1857 "stone House with end clapboarded"[8] Wm. W. Wilson (New Garden Twp.)

1857 "frame summer kitchen clapboarded...a frame woodshed and water closet, clapboarded"[9] William White (Tredyffrin Twp.)

1858 "frame House, clapboarded"[10] Charles T. Glasgow

(East Nottingham Twp.)

1858 "new 2 story shop 24 by 30 feet, lower story stone, upper story clapboarded"[11] David E. Taylor (New Garden Twp.)

1858 "stone House, plastered in and outside...frame and clapboarded and porch in front"[12] Thomas Peck (East Brandywine Twp.)

1859 "log House clapboarded"[13] James H. Boyd (East Nottingham Twp.)

1859 "back of four frame Houses clap boarded 16 x 24"[14] Pennsylvania Smelting Co. (Schuylkill Twp.)

1859 "new frame carriage house clap boarded"[15] Samuel Beaver (Tredyffrin Twp.)

In the newspaper advertisements before 1860 eighteen frame houses, one log house and two frame offices were mentioned as being clapboarded in addition to those already described. Between 1860 and 1869 thirty-four buildings were mentioned as being clapboarded: nine frame houses, two log houses, two frame summer kitchens and four frame kitchens.

1. Colonial Society of Pennsylvania, *RECORDS OF THE COURTS OF CHESTER COUNTY PENNSYLVANIA 1681-1697* (Philadelphia, Penna., 1910), p. 41.
2. Joseph H. Brinton diary Vol. #1, p. 88 under date June 3, 1858 Chester County Historical Society (West Chester, Penna.)
3. Ibid., Vol. #2, p. 2 under date May 2, 1868.
4. Ibid., p. 57 under date Feb. 17, 1876.
5. *VILLAGE RECORD* (West Chester, Penna.) Sept. 18, 1855.
6. *AMERICAN REPUBLICAN* (West Chester, Penna.) March 18, 1855.
7. *VILLAGE RECORD* (West Chester, Penna.) Nov. 21, 1857.
8. Ibid., Nov. 21, 1857.
9. *AMERICAN REPUBLICAN* (West Chester, Penna.) March 24, 1857.
10. *VILLAGE RECORD* (West Chester, Penna.) July 10, 1858.
11. Ibid., Nov. 27, 1858.
12. Ibid., July 10, 1858.
13. Ibid., Sept. 17, 1859.
14. Ibid., Oct. 18, 1859.
15. Ibid., Jan. 8, 1859.

CLOSET

Closet is defined by Bailey (ed. 1735) as "a small Apartment in a Room", by Sheridan (ed. 1789) as "a small room of privacy and retirement, a private repository of curiosities" and by Webster (ed. 1828) as "...3. A small close apartment or recess in the side of a room for repositing utensils and furniture."

Henry Graham Ashmead, in 1883, describes the Old Hoskins (Graham) house, in Chester, built in 1688 as having "In the rooms on the first and second floors on the north side of the house, the high old-fashioned wooden mantels over the large fireplaces are flanked by enormous closets, which are lighted by small windows in the outer walls."[1] The Barber house, in Chester, built between 1699 and 1708 he describes as "in the chambers above on each side of the fireplaces were large closets, similiar to those mentioned in Hoskins and Logan Houses."[2] The Logan house, in Chester, built in 1700 he mentions as having had "Large closets were on each side of the wide chimney places, lighted by windows in the outer walls,"[3] and the Old Porter (Lloyd) house, in Chester, built in 1721 "Was stone. . .with closet and milk house adjoining."[4]

Two wills mention:

1759 "and the fire Room & Closet above Stairs"[5] David Jones (Tredyffrin Twp.)

1790 "to have a Corner cupboard built and put up in either of the Rooms she my wife shall direct"[6] John Pugh (East Nottingham Twp.)

Newspaper advertisements mention closets, cupboards and clothes presses:

1762 "House. . .hath 13 Rooms in it, besides Closets"[7] Jane and James Jenkins (New Garden Twp.)

1763 "Frame Dwelling-house, two Stories high, two Rooms and Convenient Closets, on each floor"[8] Daniel John (Charlestown Twp.)

1856 "Adjoining the dining room are two large china closets with other closets within the room...5 Chambers and Dressing Rooms fully supplied with convenient closets"[9] Parsonage, Church of Holy Trinity (West Chester)

1864 "clothes presses and closets in every room"[10] Joseph Davis (West Chester)

1866 "lodging rooms...with closets and drawers"[11] Hickman James (West Chester)

1867 "chambers with closets in each"[12] Thomas S. Young (Coatesville)

1868 "closets in every available part of the house"[13] Isaac T. Lewis (Uwchlan Twp.)

1869 "House...supplied with cupboards, closets and clothes presses"[14] Mary A. G. Miles (West Chester)

1870 "closets & wardrobes"[15] E. V. Garrett (West Chester)

1872 "closets and shelves"[16] Webb A. Nichols (Kennett Square)

1872 "bed rooms with two large closets or clothes presses"[17] Reeves Mansion (Phoenixville)

1873 "coat closets"[18] J. B. Roecker (West Chester)

1876 "15 large closets"[19] J. R. Gilpin (Birmingham Twp.)

In the newspaper advertisements before 1877 there are thirteen other mentions of closets in houses, two of cupboards and closets and one bed rooms with closet in each.

1. Henry Graham Ashmead, *HISTORICAL SKETCH OF CHESTER, ON DELAWARE*, (The Republican Steam Printing House, 1883), p. 67.
2. Ibid., p. 121.
3. Ibid., p. 73.
4. Ibid., p. 111.
5. Chester County Will Book 4, p. 177.
6. Chester County Will Book 8, p. 469.
7. *PENNSYLVANIA GAZETTE* (Philadelphia, Penna.) March 11, 1762.
8. Ibid., March 11, 1763.
9. *AMERICAN REPUBLICAN*, (West Chester, Penna.) Feb. 5, 1856.
10. *VILLAGE RECORD*, (West Chester, Penna.) Feb. 9, 1864.

11. Ibid., Dec. 8, 1866.
12. Ibid., Feb. 2, 1867.
13. Ibid., Sept. 19, 1868.
14. Ibid., Nov. 30, 1869.
15. Ibid., Aug. 30, 1870.
16. Ibid., Nov. 23, 1872.
17. *PHOENIXVILLE MESSENGER* (Phoenixville, Penna.) April 27, 1872.
18. *AMERICAN REPUBLICAN* (West Chester, Penna.) Dec. 23, 1873.
19. *VILLAGE RECORD* (West Chester, Penna.) April 15, 1876.

CLOVER MILL

The newspaper advertisements between 1815 and 1819 list one stone clover mill 45 x 25 feet and between 1845 and 1854 one stone clover mill 40 x 30 feet and one frame clover mill 20 x 15 feet.

COACH SHOP

Coach is defined by Bailey (ed. 1735) as "a large sort of Chariot", by Sheridan (ed. 1789) as "the carriage of pleasure or state" and by Webster (ed. 1828) as "A close vehicle for commodious traveling, bourne on four wheels, and drawn by horses or other animals. It differs from a chariot in having seats in front, as well as behind."

The 1799 tax assessment for Honey Brook Township lists one stone coach shop. The newspaper advertisements mention:

1836 "frame COACH SHOP, 24 by 20 feet, 2 stories high, and platform in front"[1] Hazael Thomas (Downingtown)

1843 "two story Frame Coachmaker Shop with platform"[2] Thomas Wood (West Fallowfield Twp.)

1847 "Wheelwright and Coachmaker Shop, lathed and plastered, wood shop in the basement, paint, drying, trimming and harness rooms in 2nd story, a good stone Blacksmith shop adjoining"[3] Henry L. Pratt (Willistown Twp.)

The newspaper advertisements between 1835 and 1839 mention one coachmaker's shop that did mention the material of construction 50 x 18 feet.

1. *VILLAGE RECORD* (West Chester, Penna.) Oct. 5, 1836.
2. *AMERICAN REPUBLICAN* (West Chester, Penna.) Sept. 26, 1843.
3. Ibid., Sept. 28, 1847.

COAL HOUSE

The 1798 Direct Tax lists nine coal houses: four of stone, the mean size being 1855 square feet; one of frame 37 x 25 feet; one of log 18 x 12 feet and three of unspecified material, the mean size being 440 square feet. The 1796 tax assessment for East Fallowfield Township lists one frame and stone coal house 50 x 30 feet. The newspaper advertisements, between 1850 and 1854, list one stone coal house 40 x 40 feet and 40 feet high, and one of frame, 20 x 20 feet.

COLONADE

Colonade is defined by Bailey (ed. 1735) as "a Range of Pillars running quite round a building, and standing within the Walls of it" by Sheridan (ed. 1789) as "Colonnade...or series of columns, disposed in a circle; any series or range of pillars" and by Webster (ed. 1828) as "In architecture, a peristyle of a circular figure, or a series of columns, disposed in a circle, and insulated within side."

The newspaper advertisements mention:

1871 "Mansard roof, two colonades"[1] Phoenix Hotel (Phoenxville)

1.   *PHOENIXVILLE MESSENGER* (Phoenixville, Penna.) Jan. 14, 1871.

COLOR EXTERIOR

The Brinton diary, which describes a few of the early houses in the county, mentions that a man had taken "bricks, from early 1713 house. also doors, windows, boards, & clapboards. They were painted a Venetian red."[1] The house of Joseph Brinton, built ca. 1711, "was of frame resting on a stone foundation, a story & a half high, the woodwork outside painted a redish brown. A well was sunk on the south side."[2] The "1712 Brinton house. Fronted south — the cellar was walled & above that the super-structure was plank painted red & it was known as the red house."[3] "Edward Brinton — built about 1724 frame at first, afterwards clapboard by Edward B. Darlington (d. in 1823-4) & painted yellow & a stone end added on the east. This house was known as the Yellow House."[4]

The inventories, before 1850, and the walls, before 1814, do not mention any exterior color on buildings. The newspapers mention:

1770 "new log house, weatherboarded and painted, well finished with sash windows, about 35 feet front, and 18 deep, three stories high"[5] Yellow Springs (Pike-land Twp.)

1818 "stone dwelling house...with piazza 45 by 10, ceiled and painted"[6] Moses Hoopes, David Wilson (East Goshen Twp.)

1847 "spring house was repaired and painted last spring, the grounds around it were laid out and a new painted ornamental fence surrounds the whole"[7] Alfred Weeks (East Marlboro Twp.)

1866 "many dwellings have been rejuvenated this spring with a coat of paint"[8] (West Chester)

1866 "House...with a tin roof painted on both sides"[9] H. G. Malin (Tredyffrin Twp.)

1868 "east end rubble masonry and painted"[10] Masonic Hall (Downingtown)

1871 "new stable painted"[11] William Nichols (Coatesville)

1872 "front is built of serpentine stone...and the painting is pure white, making a very clean appearance"[12] Hammond & Kervey Drug store (West Chester)

1872 "Frame house, painted"[13] Samuel J. Reyburn (Oxford Twp.)

1873 "The whole woodwork has been painted a modest white, unrelieved by strips or stain. And now with its painted walls of gray stone"[14] Friends Meeting (Uwchlan Twp.)

1874 "frame, 35 by 50 feet. Without is coated with a dark brown color, inside white. The seatbacks, pulpit, altar railings &c are painted in imitation of walnut"[15] Methodist Episcopal Church (Kennett Twp.)

1874 "outside of entire structure to be painted in imitation of granite"[16] Presbyterian Church (West Chester)

1874 "Wm. S. Snare has just painted his store front in imitation of walnut"[17] (West Chester)

1874 "stone, pointed on the outside with white mortar: The window caps and sills of green serpentine stone, with window frames painted the same color. The walls are white"[18] Baptist Church (West Goshen Twp.)

1875 "will be plastered and marbleized on outside"[19] Baptist Church (Malvern)

1876 "three story painted brick house"[20] J. Smith Futhey (West Chester)

Before 1877 the newspaper advertisements mention fourteen other houses painted and three weatherboarded houses painted.

1880 "house...J. F. Walton...It has been kalsomined from top to bottom by Mr. Walton"[21] (West Whiteland Twp.)

1883 "The homestead in itself with its peaked gables, its beetle-browned porches and extensive court serves to recall all the architectural intricaries of the reign of Queen Anne, while from its square plaza upon the roof-top one commands an impressive view of far-reaching valleys, moorlands of irregular shape and wood freighted slopes"[22] John Patterson "Glen Cairn" (Wallace Twp.)

1883 "Addison May...addition built to his residence...of pressed brick with red mortar"[23] (West Chester)

1884 "[House] The bricks as well as the wood work of the exterior are receiving a coat of paint"[24] A. McLear (West Chester)

1886 "house...and within a day or two the roof has been painted and beautiful metallic ornaments placed on the combs of the roof"[25] N. Hayes (West Chester)

1888 "stable dug and serpentine stone hauled to the spot.

The building will be painted in plain white"[26] William Wayne (Easttown Twp.)

1893 "improvements on the residence of Jerome B. Gray ...The old dormer window in the front got to leaking...Now that section of the front is being covered with galvanized iron, and the woodwork of the whole exterior of the house is being painted white. Later a touch of lemon will be added"[27] (West Chester)

1. John H. Brinton diary Vol. #2, p. 2 under date May 2, 1868, Chester County Historical Society (West Chester, Penna.)
2. John H. Brinton, Account of William Brinton, p. 3. Chester County Historical Society (West Chester, Penna.)
3. John H. Brinton diary Vol. #3, p. 36, June 2, 1891, Chester County Historical Society (West Chester, Penna.)
4. John H. Brinton diary Vol. #2, p. 57 under date Feb. 11, 1876, Chester County Historical Society (West Chester, Penna.)
5. *PENNSYLVANIA GAZETTE* (Philadelphia, Penna.) March 1, 1770.
6. *VILLAGE RECORD* (West Chester, Penna.) Sept. 16, 1818.
7. *AMERICAN REPUBLICAN* (West Chester, Penna.) Oct. 19, 1847.
8. Ibid., June 12, 1866.
9. *VILLAGE RECORD* (West Chester, Penna.) Nov. 24, 1866.
10. Ibid., July 11, 1868.
11. Ibid., Sept. 23, 1871.
12. *AMERICAN REPUBLICAN* (West Chester, Penna.) Oct. 1, 1872.
13. *VILLAGE RECORD* (West Chester, Penna.) Nov. 9, 1872.
14. *PHOENIXVILLE MESSENGER* (Phoenixville, Penna.) March 9, 1873.
15. *DAILY LOCAL NEWS* (West Chester, Penna.) June 8, 1874.
16. Ibid., Sept. 16, 1874.
17. *VILLAGE RECORD* (West Chester, Penna.) Oct. 10, 1874.
18. *AMERICAN REPUBLICAN* (West Chester, Penna.) Dec. 1, 1874.
19. *DAILY LOCAL NEWS* (West Chester, Penna.) July 20, 1875.
20. *VILLAGE RECORD* (West Chester, Penna.) April 1, 1876.
21. *DAILY LOCAL NEWS* (West Chester, Penna.) May 3, 1880.
22. Ibid., Jan. 26, 1883.
23. Ibid., June 8, 1883.
24. Ibid., July 18, 1884.
25. Ibid., May 6, 1886.
26. Ibid., Oct. 5, 1888.
27. Ibid., May 17, 1893.

COLOR INTERIOR

Henry Graham Ashmead, in 1883, describes the Logan house, in Chester, built in 1700, as having had "a wainscoted hallway...All the rooms were wainscoted also, and the panels were painted or stained in imitation of mahogany."[1]

The wills and inventories mention interior colors:

1716 "The Blew roome"[2] John Hoskins (Chester)

1773 "Blue Parlour"[3] Joseph Hoskins (Chester)

1777 "Green Parlour"[4] John Knowles (Ridley Twp.)

1784 "Blue Chamber"[5] John Smith (Lower Chichester Twp.)

1826 "White room"[6] Jacob Bennett (Birmingham Twp.)

1827 "White Chamber"[7] William Clinglan (West Fallowfield Twp.)

The inventories, before 1850, mention in addition to those already quoted four blue rooms and one yellow room upstairs.

The newspapers mention:

1858 "The walls and ceiling are painted in plain fresco or distemper, and was colored by Mr. Lamor, an accomplished artist of Philadelphia, being the same individual who executed so beautifully the fresco painting in the new brown sand stone building of our townsman David Meconkey Est. The painting of the wood work in oil, and the lettering of the panels back of the pulpit, attest the good taste and harmonious blending of colors of one of our workmen John Miller"[8] Church of Holy Trinity (West Chester)

1866 "many dwellings have been rejuvenated this spring with a coat of paint"[9] (West Chester)

1867 "new white paint"[10] Methodist Church (West Bradford Twp.)

1870 "east end to be lathed and plastered, ceiling and walls to be frescoed and painted"[11] Baptist Church (West Chester)

1870 "court room painted, stairway and hall whitewashed overhead, walls fine brown coating of paint"[12] Court House (West Chester)

1872 "walls painted, woodwork grained"[13] Depot (Phoenixville)

1872 "Brick Cottage...three coats of best paint and paper"[14] Wm. B. Laslett (Parkesburg)

1872 "The whole woodwork has been painted a modest white, unrelieved by strips or stain. And now with its painted walls of gray stone"[15] Friends Meeting (Uwchlan Twp.)

1873 "Parlor 18 by 22 feet, finished in white with marbleized slate mantle"[16] J. B. Roecker, (West Chester)

1874 "frame, 35 by 50 feet. Without is coated with a dark brown color, inside white. The seat backs, pulpit, alter railings &c are painted in imitation of walnut"[17] Methodist Episcopal Church (Kennett Twp.)

1874 "Two story brick building, mansard roof, 40 by 33 feet, back building 58 by 32 feet. The whole inside is finished in imitation of walnut...Wm. Armstrong, painter"[18] Mary Hoopes (London Grove Twp.)

1874 "stone, pointed on the outside with white mortar. The window caps and sills of green serpentine stone, with window frames painted the same color. The walls are white"[19] Goshen Baptist Church (West Goshen Twp.)

1874 "The walls and ceiling, too will also put on a new dress at the hands of the fresco artist. The ceiling will be clad in sky blue for a body tint, with neat ornamentations of hues to contrast in pleasing and deceptive relief in the developing of the scroll and panel designs, which the improvement committee have selected. The walls will be similarly decorated, only the body color will be of a different shade — that of a light purple tint."[20] Presbyterian Church (West Chester)

1. Henry Graham Ashmead, *HISTORICAL SKETCH OF CHESTER, ON DELAWARE* (The Republican Steam Printing House, 1883), p. 73.
2. Chester County Inventory #27.
3. Chester County Inventory #2775.
4. Chester County Inventory #3138.
5. Chester County Inventory #3578.
6. Chester County Inventory #7909.
7. Chester County Inventory #8033.
8. *AMERICAN REPUBLICAN* (West Chester, Penna.) Sept. 28, 1858.
9. Ibid., June 12, 1866.
10. Ibid., May 28, 1867.
11. Ibid., April 12, 1870.
12. Ibid., Sept. 13, 1870.
13. *PHOENIXVILLE MESSENGER* (Phoenixville, Penna.) Oct. 26, 1872.
14. *VILLAGE RECORD* (West Chester, Penna.) Nov. 30, 1872.
15. *PHOENIXVILLE MESSENGER* (Phoenixville, Penna.) March 9, 1873.
16. *AMERICAN REPUBLICAN* (West Chester, Penna.) Dec. 23, 1873.
17. *DAILY LOCAL NEWS* (West Chester, Penna.) June 8, 1874.
18. *AMERICAN REPUBLICAN* (West Chester, Penna.) June 2, 1874.
19. Ibid., Dec. 1, 1874.
20. Ibid., Dec. 1, 1874.

CORN CRIB

The 1798 Direct Tax lists two frame corn cribs, the mean size being 327 square feet. The 1796 tax assessment for East Fallowfield Township lists George Welch as having "1 frame Wagon House and Corn Crib above 15 by 20 feet." The 1799 tax assessment for West Marlboro Township lists one frame corn crib 40 x 24 feet. The newspaper advertisements described a few corn cribs: James H. Ray, of New London Township, in 1856 "corn crib separate 5 by 30 feet high";[1] Enoch Passmore, of Kennett Township, in 1858, "corn crib 18 by 20 feet with work shop overhead, pig pen attached"[2] and John Traynor Jr., of Lower Oxford Township, in 1858, "frame corn crib about 35 feet long, five feet wide and nine feet high."[3] The newspaper advertisements between 1860 and 1876 mentioned the dimensions of two corn cribs one 27 x 5½ feet and the other 35 x 35 feet.

1. *VILLAGE RECORD* (West Chester, Penna.) Nov. 15, 1856.
2. Ibid., Feb. 6, 1858.
3. Ibid., March 6, 1858.

CORNICE

Cornice is defined by Bailey (ed. 1735) as "the third and highest Part of the Entablature, and commonly signifies the uppermost Ornament of any Wainscot, &c.", by Sheridan (ed. 1789) as "the highest projection of a wall or column" and by Webster (ed. 1828) as "A little projecture in joinery or masonry, as the cornice of a chimney."

The newspaper advertisements mention:

1865 "The wood work of the room is beautifully oaked, and the ceiling handsomely corniced"[1] First National Bank (West Chester)

1867 "New cornice will be put around the entire building"[2] Town Hall (Coatesville)

1870 "house 39 by 33 feet, ceilings corniced"[3] Jas. R. Cummings (New Garden Twp.)

1870 "Lower room corniced and ornamented with centers"[4] Benjamin Phillips (New Garden Twp.)

1870 "ceiling being 10 feet high and finished with cornice and center pieces"[5] J. W. Barnard (West Chester)

1872 "The ceilings of each room have massive cornices run with plaster paris while the wood work of the new buildings is trimmed with walnut and ash, having a beautiful grain and evidently selected with great care"[6] Reeves Mansion (Phoenixville)

1873 "new stable...a tin roof, with heavy cornice and ornamental brackets"[7] Mansion House Hotel (West Chester)

1. *VILLAGE RECORD* (West Chester, Penna.) March 21, 1865.
2. *AMERICAN REPUBLICAN* (West Chester, Penna.) June 23, 1867.
3. *VILLAGE RECORD* (West Chester, Penna.) Sept. 10, 1870.
4. Ibid., Oct. 4, 1870.
5. *AMERICAN REPUBLICAN* (West Chester, Penna.) Sept. 20, 1870.
6. *PHOENIXVILLE MESSENGER* (Phoenixville, Penna.) April 27, 1872.
7. *AMERICAN REPUBLICAN* (West Chester, Penna.) May 20, 1873.

COTTAGE

Cottage is defined by Sheridan (ed. 1789) as "a hut, a mean habitation" and by Webster (ed. 1828) as "a hut; a small mean habitation." The English Oxford Dictionary (ed. 1933) defines cottage as 1. A dwelling-house of small size and humble character, such as is occupied by farm-labourers, villagers, miners, etc. 2. A small temporary erection used for shelter; a cot, hut, shet, etc. Obs...4. The term cottage has for some time past been in vogue as a particular designation for small country residences and detached suburban houses, adopted to a moderate scale of living, yet with all due attention to comfort and refinement. While, in this sense of it, the name is divested of all associations with poverty, it is convenient, inasmuch as it frees from all pretentions and parage and restraint. In this sense, the appellation cottage orne (ornee) was in vogue, when picturesqueness was aimed at. b. In U.S. spec. A summer residence (often on a large and suptuous scale) at a water-place, or a health or pleasure resort."

The 1796 tax assessment for London Grove Township lists seven cottages: four of log, two of stone and one that did not mention the material of construction.

The newspapers mention:

1833 "good cottage with stabling, convenient for a tenant"[1] Jacob Lindley (London Grove Twp.)

1835 "Cottage for tenant"[2] Nicholas Mendenhall (New Garden Twp.)

1851 "The Dwelling house is newly built in handsome

cottage style, with portico front"[3] William Edge (Downingtown)

1854 "Cottage House 16 x 24, 2 stories"[4] Hamilton Graham (East Caln Twp.)

1854 "COTTAGE, 30 by 40 feet"[5] John Rutter (West Whiteland Twp.)

1855 "stone Cottage"[6] J. Marshall (West Chester)

1856 "Rectory or Parsonage House...being a beautiful English Cottage built of the green serpentine stone of this locality...The walls are all studded, lathed and plastered on the interior, thus rendering the house entirely dry...House has a wide hall, with a large library room on one side and a commodious parlor on the other. In the back building is a dining room with a fine large basement kitchen, cellars...vault for cooling hydrant water...range in kitchen with hot and cold water which is conducted to a bath room on second story...There is also a heating apparatus in the cellar with flues to convey the heat to different apartments in the first and second stories...Adjoining the dining room are two large china closets with other closets within the room...On second besides bathroom, 5 chambers and Dressing Rooms fully supplied with convenient closets...Third story three chambers ...Gas and water in first and second stories. House completed in 1849"[7] Church of Holy Trinity (West Chester)

1856 "Cottage – Two story stone building, 85 feet front with two ends or wings extending back..."[8] Chester Springs (West Pikeland Twp.)

1856 "frame cottage"[9] Edwin H. Coates (West Pikeland Twp.)

1858 "a number of BEAUTIFUL COTTAGES, similar to those in West Philadelphia have been erected this present season."[10] (West Chester)

1859 "new cottage" 33 feet square, with a porch front and observatory on top "a model house"[11] David Mamall (West Vincent Twp.)

1859 "two stories stone MANSION HOUSE, in the cottage style, with verandas on three sides"[12] Hewson Cox Est. (West Chester)

1861 "frame COTTAGE SCHOOL HOUSE"[13] Edith B. Chalfant (East Marlboro Twp.)

1864 "Brick Cottage House"[14] Alexander Marshall (West Chester)

1865 "Cottage School, frame 24 x 36"[15] (East Whiteland Twp.)

1871 "This Cottage is architecturally the most complete, perfect and beautiful in West Chester"[16] C. C. Sellers (West Chester)

1873 "building highly ornamental frame cottage"[17] R. E. Monaghan (West Chester)

1873 "Cottages – Virginia Avenue. It has long been our day dream to own a cottage – not one of those

low-eaved, straw-thatched houses, one story high, of which our shcoolbooks, drawing descriptions from the poets, tell us, but a good, substantial edifice of stone and mortar, with appropriate porches around it, bay windows, and vines climbing up the pillars and over the doors.

Adverse, fate, however, has not yet permitted us to realize our desires, yet, without any envious feeling, we are always glad to see any of our friends in the enjoyment of a well-built cottage.

Until recently the style of building in our pleasant little town was exceedingly rectangular and monotonous; most of the houses were built on the same pattern of the same kind of red brick, and with the same close, glaring white window-shutters below and green blinds above.

If our town, looking very pleasant even under such monotony, had been suddenly denuded of its shade trees, it would have exhibited a most melancholy spectacle.

We are glad, however, to see within the last ten years a better taste has prevailed and citizens have found out that beauty of architecture can well be blended with comfort and economy.

In our loitering around the borough, seeking our daily "locals," we occasionally came in sight of the cottages on Virginia Avenue, and as we have not been on the Avenue recently, we paid it a Sunday visit yesterday morning.

Four gentlemen of taste, breaking away from the conventional style of building that has hitherto prevailed, and owning beautiful lots on the highest land in the western part of the town, determined to erect their homes in a style that should give pleasure to the eye and comfort and convenience at the same time to themselves without much more expense than that involved in the erection of an ordinary dwelling.

They consulted an architect of taste and ability and received designs from him, which, whilst different in details, were yet on the same general principle of Cottage architecture.

Their buildings are all of the beautiful green serpentine stone of our neighborhood, which is growing into such high favor in our cities for churches and other public buildings but which is much better adapted for cottages in a country place, as it harmonizes so well with the outside rural surroundings.

Their dwellings are all set back from the Avenue, and have neat porches, handsome bay windows, slated roofs and tiled chimneys. They have extensive lawns before their dwellings well set with grass, which is rapidly becoming as smooth and soft to the tread as a Turkish carpet. These lawns have been planted with flowers, which have been well in bloom this Spring, and their shrubbery, though young and tender, is of great variety, and in that kindly soil will have a rapidity of growth that will require but a few years to prove greatly ornamental. All of them but one, have no fences to their lawns. They are open to the Avenue. They have trusted to the good taste, honor and sense of the people to save them from intrusion, and we trust that no boy or man will break a twig or pull a flower, for they have planted them for the gratification of the public eye as well as their own.

A row of evergreens that extends along the ridge back of some of their houses protect them against the cold blasts of winter, and is an excellent aid to the development of their gardens in the early spring."[18]

1886 "cottages...The first story of these will be what is known as the "broken range (stone) and the other parts will be frame"[19] (Easttown Twp.)

1888 "Plummer E. Jefferis has erected a fine residence for himself on South High Street, between Miner and Barnard streets. It is a three storied cottage with slate roof. It contains eleven rooms, and is finished in cyprus throughout, except the stairway, which is of oak, and the bath room, which is finished in cherry"[20] (West Chester)

1. *VILLAGE RECORD* (West Chester, Penna.) Nov. 27, 1833.
2. Ibid., Sept. 30, 1835.
3. *AMERICAN REPUBLICAN* (West Chester, Penna.) Feb. 18, 1851.
4. *VILLAGE RECORD* (West Chester, Penna.) Dec. 23, 1854.
5. Ibid., Sept. 14, 1854.
6. *AMERICAN REPUBLICAN* (West Chester, Penna.) April 24, 1855.
7. Ibid., Feb. 5, 1856.
8. Ibid., Jan. 1, 1856.
9. *VILLAGE RECORD* (West Chester, Penna.) Oct. 21, 1856.
10. *AMERICAN REPUBLICAN* (West Chester, Penna.) Dec. 16, 1858.
11. *VILLAGE RECORD* (West Chester, Penna.) May 17, 1859.
12. Ibid., July 9, 1859.
13. Ibid., Dec. 10, 1861.
14. Ibid., Oct. 11, 1864.
15. Ibid., Oct. 21, 1865.
16. Ibid., Oct. 31, 1871.
17. *AMERICAN REPUBLICAN* (West Chester, Penna.) Aug. 12, 1873.
18. *DAILY LOCAL NEWS* (West Chester, Penna.) June 23, 1873.
19. Ibid., Dec. 13, 1886.
20. Ibid., Nov. 17, 1888.

COTTON FACTORY

The newspapers, between 1815 and 1824 mention three cotton factories but do not mention the material of construction, the mean size being 1252 square feet. Betwen 1830 and 1849 twelve cotton factories were mentioned; four of stone, the mean size being 2433 square feet and eight that did not give the material of construction the

mean size being 2210 square feet. On January 6, 1830 Elisha Phipps, of West Marlboro Township, advertised "factory is built with stone, three stories high, well constructed and lighted with windows."[1] Between 1855 and 1876 the newspapers mention seven cotton factories: four of stone, the mean size being 2740 square feet; one stone and frame 25 x 20 feet; one brick 40 x 33 feet with an addition 33 x 15 feet and one that did not mention the material of construction 40 x 30 feet. One stone factory was described as being five stories 80 x 45 feet 75 feet high.

1. *VILLAGE RECORD* (West Chester, Penna.) Jan. 6, 1830.

COW HOUSE

The earliest description of a cow house found thus far is the following: "The Testimony of Henry Hastings Who being Attested declareth that he had agreed with Richard Frend to Build a Cattle house of Clap boards 24 foot long and 16 foot Broad for William Oly for which he was to receive Ł. 6 5."[1] The Testimony was given at a Court held in Chester in 1684.

The 1798 Direct Tax lists sixteen cow houses: six of stone, the mean size being 285 square feet; five of frame, the mean size being 404 square feet; one of stone and log 40 x 16 feet; one of stone 30 x 20 feet and three that did not mention the material of construction, the mean size being 636 square feet.

The 1798 Direct Tax lists one log calf house 20 x 11 feet.

1. Colonial Society of Pennsylvania, *RECORD OF THE COURTS OF CHESTER COUNTY PENNSYLVANIA 1681–1697* (Patterson & White Co., Philadelphia, Penna. 1910), p. 41.

CUPOLA

The newspaper advertisements mention:

1881 "The cupola on the barn is thirty feet high"[1] Abram Fetters (Upper Uwchlan Twp.)

1883 "erection of a new coachhouse...surmounted by a beautiful cupola"[2] "Bellevue" (East Goshen Twp.)

1884 "House...New cornice will be added, also a cupola"[3] Larissa D. Matlack (West Goshen Twp.)

1. *DAILY LOCAL NEWS* (West Chester, Penna.) Aug. 6, 1881.
2. Ibid., Nov. 7, 1883.
3. Ibid., Oct. 13, 1884.

DISTILLERY

The 1798 Direct Tax lists nine distilleries: six of log, the mean size being 321 square feet; two of stone, the mean size being 756 square feet and one of stone and log 24 x 18 feet. Joseph Cowen, of Sadsbury Township, had "1

Distillary Under his house." The newspaper advertisements between 1815 and 1835 mention four distilleries: three of stone, the mean size being 773 square feet and one that did not mention the material of construction two stories, 45 x 40 feet.

DOG HOUSE

The 1796 tax assessment for West Whiteland Township lists one stone dog house.

DOORS

Henry Graham Ashmead, in 1883, mentions that the Boar's Head Inn, in Chester, where Penn resided in 1682–1683 "The doors were peculiar in the manner in which they were hung, a peg or projection from the door above and below fitted into holes made in the frames, and on these they swung instead of hinges...In the kitchen on the side opening to the west was a large double door through which a cart load of wood could be drawn if desired."[1]

The newspapers described a few doors:

1831 "brick house...with 15 light windows, 10 by 12 glass together with side glass at the front or hall door and large handsome top"[2] James Grier (West Nottingham Twp.)

1833 "The house can be conveniently divided into two comfortable houses as there are two front and three back doors"[3] William Lent (Downingtown)

1844 "two story dwelling...has been occupied for many years as a fancy store; it has two front doors and a bulk window"[4] Joseph Jones (West Chester)

1873 "large walnut doors"[5] Normal School (West Chester)

1874 "Church...At the front entrance of the room it is intended to have a small vestibule with self closing doors"[6] Presbyterian Church (West Chester)

1874 "Church...As we entered the building, we found a very neat audience room separated from the vestibule by double doors covered with green baize"[7] Baptist Church (West Goshen Twp.)

1875 "varnished doors, sash &c."[8] John Griffin (Phoenixville)

1875 "Panel doors"[9] Yearsleys's (West Caln Twp.)

1876 "the dining room can be enlarged for extra occasions by pushing back the sliding doors"[10] J. R. Gilpin (Birmingham Twp.)

1. Henry Graham Ashmead, *HISTORICAL SKETCH OF CHESTER, ON DELAWARE* (The Republican Steam Printing House, 1883), p. 63.
2. *AMERICAN REPUBLICAN* (West Chester, Penna.) Dec. 20, 1831.
3. Ibid., Oct. 22, 1833.
4. Ibid., Feb. 6, 1844.
5. *VILLAGE RECORD* (West Chester, Penna.) April 15, 1873.
6. *DAILY LOCAL NEWS* (West Chester, Penna.) July 30, 1874.
7. Ibid., Sept. 16, 1874.
8. *PHOENIXVILLE MESSENGER* (Phoenixville, Penna.) Aug. 28, 1875.
9. Ibid., Oct. 16, 1875.
10. *VILLAGE RECORD* (West Chester, Penna.) April 15, 1876.

DRYING HOUSE

The 1798 Direct Tax lists one stone drying house 25 x 20 feet and one stone and frame drying house 49 x 20 feet. The 1796 tax assessment for Uwchlan Township lists Robert Allison Jr., as having "1 house for drying paper 2 story stone & 1 story frame." The newspaper advertisements between 1830 and 1834 list one two story frame drying house 40 x 20 feet and one four story brick drying house 1500 square feet.

DUMB WAITER

The newspaper advertisements mention:

1855 "dumb waiter"[1] M. Thomas & Sons (West Chester)

1861 "dumb waiter from kitchen to dining room"[2] James Beale, "Exton Hotel" (West Whiteland Twp.)

The newspaper advertisements mention before 1876 one other dumb waiter.

1. *AMERICAN REPUBLICAN* (West Chester, Penna.) April 24, 1855.
2. Ibid., June 24, 1861.

FARM HOUSE

The 1798 Direct Tax lists George Willing, of Haverford Township, as having a farm house 28 x 18 feet.

FIREPLACE

Fireplace is defined by Webster (ed. 1828) as "The part of a chimney appropriated to the fire; a hearth."

The newspaper advertsisements mention:

1721 "Stone House two Storey high, and a cellar under all with a Fire-Place therin"[1] James Thomas (Whiteland Twp.)

1762 "Brick-House, two Story high, with four Fire Places, two below and two above...square Log House, 24 Feet Square, two Story high, three Rooms on a Floor, three Fire-Places, two below, and one above"[2] Wm. Lindsey (Lower Providence Twp.)

1763 "Square Log Dwelling House, with a Fire-place"[3] Thomas Vaughan (Haverford Twp.)

1763 "saw'd Log Loom Shop and Kitchen, with a good

Stone Chimney and Stove"[4] Rober M'Mallin (Upper Darby Twp.)

1764 "Stone Spring house, with Fire-place"[5] Samuel Hall (Willistown Twp.)

1766 "two Story Stone House with three Rooms on a Floor, five Fire-places, and a large Stone Kitchen, with two Fire-places"[6] Thomas Canvell (Middletown Twp.)

1767 "Stone Dwelling House, consisting of four Fire Rooms"[7] Charles Cruikshank (Haverford Twp.)

1770 "bathing springs...are inclosed by a good new frame house, 35 feet front and 16 feet deep. Each bath has a drawing room, and one fire place in it"[8] Yellow Springs (Pikeland Twp.)

1771 "new square log house...stone chimney with two fire-places"[9] George Evans (part of the place is in Chester County)

1784 "log dwelling house, two rooms on a floor, fire places in each, and two above"[10] George Yarnall (Willistown Twp.)

1791 "stone dwelling house, two stories high, two rooms on the lower floor and three on the second, with convenient fire-places"[11] Sarah White, Est. (Willistown Twp.)

1810 "a stone milk-house, 18 by 16, with a room and a fire place above"[12] Matthew Stanley (Brandywine Twp.)

1816 "there are fire-places in all the rooms on the first and second stories excepting one room in the second story; the chimneys are well constructed, there is not a room in the house which as been known to be infested with smoke"[13] Joseph Jackson (West Chester)

1820 "stone milk house...accommodated with a fire place and chimney adjoining for washing &c."[14] J. Menough (New London Twp.)

1834 "Mill house is 28 feet by 28, with a fire place, and a carding room adjoining; the second story is occupied as a dwelling having 2 rooms and a kitchen and 2 fireplaces"[15] Robert Wilson (West Nantmeal Twp.)

1839 "with a kitchen and oven, fire place, boiler &c. attached"[16] Samuel Pennock (Kennett Square)

1846 "wash house...fire place"[17] Walter Calvert (Kennett Twp.)

1861 "kitchen with stone fire place"[18] John & Elizabeth Welsh (West Bradford Twp.)

1872 "House...Library with open Fire Place"[19] James H. Bradford (West Chester)

The newspaper advertisements, before 1877, mention seventy-seven houses as having two hundred and fifty-six fire places; eleven houses mention fireplaces in all the rooms; three spring houses, four milk houses and two wash houses have fire places.

1. *AMERICAN MERCURY* (Philadelphia, Penna.) Oct. 12, 1721.
2. *PENNSYLVANIA GAZETTE* (Philadelphia, Penna.) Sept. 23, 1762.
3. Ibid., Feb 10, 1763.
4. Ibid., Feb. 10, 1763.
5. Ibid., March 8, 1764.
6. Ibid., July 24, 1766.
7. Ibid., April 16, 1767.
8. Ibid., March 1, 1770.
9. Ibid., Dec. 19, 1771.
10. Ibid., March 17, 1784.
11. Ibid., Oct. 5, 1791.
12. *AMERICAN REPUBLICAN* (West Chester, Penna.) June 17, 1810.
13. *CHESTER & DELAWARE FEDERALIST* (West Chester, Penna.) Oct. 2, 1816.
14. *VILLAGE RECORD* (West Chester, Penna.) Oct. 11, 1820.
15. *WAYNESBURG PRESS* (Waynesburg, Penna.) Feb. 12, 1834.
16. *VILLAGE RECORD* (West Chester, Penna.) Dec. 10, 1839.
17. Ibid., Dec. 15, 1846.
18. Ibid., July 13, 1861.
19. Ibid., Aug. 17, 1872.

FIREPLACE BENCHES

Henry Graham Ashmead in 1883 mentions that the Boar's Head Inn, in Chester, built before 1682 "The chimney was an enormous affair, nearly sixteen feet in width and the wide-mouthed old fireplace was spacious enough to hold entire cord wood sticks on great iron dogs, while on either side in the fireplace were benches"[1] and that the Hoskins House, built in 1688 in Chester had a "kitchen which is built in an L. is large, the fireplace comprising almost the entire eastern end...could seat themselves on either end of the chimney on benches."[2]

The Brinton diary mentions that the John Harris House built in 1690 was a "Frame house. It had a very large fire place, with a seat in one end...in the chimney corner."[3] The fire place of Edward Brinton's house built about 1723 "would take in wood eight feet long, but half that length was used, a corner in arch of the fireplace accommodated a sitter."[4] The diary mentions that the Brinton 1704 house, Joseph Brinton house built 1713, Wm. Brinton's house built 1713, Ann Brinton Cox, Joseph Eavenson and the Mercer house were all stone houses that had "fire places for wood cord length, with seat in the corner."[5]

1. Henry Graham Ashmead, *HISTORICAL SKETCH OF CHESTER, ON DELAWARE* (The Republican Steam Printing House, 1883) p. 63.
2. Ibid., p. 67.
3. John H. Brinton Diary #1, p. 93 under date March 30 1860. Chester County Historical Society (West Chester, Penna.)
4. John H. Brinton Diary #2, p. 57 under date Feb. 17, 1876. Chester County Historical Society (West Chester, Penna.)
5. John H. Brinton Diary #3, p. 24 under date Feb. 6, 1885. Chester County Historical Society (West Chester, Penna.)

FIREPLACE CORNER

Jasper Dancraets, a Dutch traveler, in 1678 stayed over night in a log house in the Delaware Valley. "The house although not much larger than where we spent the last night, was somewhat better and tighter, being made according to the Swedish mode...but the chimney stands in the corner."[1] Henry Graham Ashmead in 1883 mentions that a Swedish characteristic of building was that "The chimneys with huge fire-places, were occasionally built of gray sandstone, in the corners of the rooms, but oftener the stacks were erected of turf on the outside of the houses and in the middle of the gables."[2] He also mentions that the Old Porter (Lloyd) House, built in 1721 in Chester "had open corner chimney-place."[3]

The will of Joseph Baker, of Edgemont Township, in 1731 gives to his wife: "Priviledge of my Lodging Room with my best bed beding and furniture therunto belonging and my son Joseph shall build her a Corner Chimney of Brick in the said Room."[4]

Peter Kalm, a Swedish naturalist, travelling through the Delaware Valley between 1748 and 1751 mentions that "The houses which the Swedes built when they first settled here were very bad...The chimneys were made in a corner, either with gray sandsone, or in places where no stone was to got, by mere clay which they laid very thick in one corner of the house. The ovens for baking were always in the rooms."[5]

The will of Samuel Futhey, of West Fallowfield Township, in 1790 instructs his executors to build a house for his wife "Sixteen feet by twenty, one story & a half high with two Floors, viz an upper & lower floor with a corner chimney."[6] A newspaper article describes the White Hall Hotel, in West Chester, built originally about 1794 as "In the old building the rooms were small, the ceilings low and all the fire places were built in the corners, with heavy hand worked mantles."[7]

In 1830 John F. Watson wrote "The fireplaces made at the time were built in a corner of the dwelling room...They are now called Swedish fireplaces here, and are said to be quite rare. The most common ones now are English, which are as large as our kitchen hearth, though the bottom of them is not higher than the floor of the room."[8]

1. Harold Donalson Eberlain and Cortlandt V. D. Hubbard, *HISTORIC HOUSES AND BUILDINGS OF DELAWARE* (Dover, Del., 1963), p. 5.
2. Henry Graham Ashmead, *HISTORIC SKETCH OF CHESTER, ON DELAWARE* (The Republican Steam Printing House, 1883), p. 4.
3. Ibid., p. 111.
4. Chester County Will Book 1, p. 34.
5. Henry C. Mercer, *THE ORIGIN OF LOG HOUSES IN THE UNITED STATES* (Bucks County Historical Society, Doylestown, Pa., 1924) p. 577.
6. Chester County Will Book 8, p. 420.
7. *AMERICAN REPUBLICAN* (West Chester, Penna.) Oct. 21, 1873.
8. John F. Watson, *ANNALS OF PHILADELPHIA AND PENNSYLVANIA IN THE OLDEN TIME* (Philadelphia, Penna., 1909), Vol. 2, p. 727.

FIREPROOF

The newspapers mention:

1816 "garret, which is fire proof"[1] William Downy (West Caln Twp.)

1823 "all ceiled and plastered, with a fire proof garret floor"[2] Dilman Ziegler (West Caln Twp.)

1825 "There is a fire cistern in the back yard, which is paved"[3] Elisha Ingram (West Chester)

1849 "garret lathed and fire proof plastered"[4] Caleb James (East Goshen Twp.)

1865 "(fire proof) being covered with slate"[5] W.E. Haines (Franklin Twp.)

1874 "caught fire, roof burned off, further progress of fire was prevented by mortar floor in garrett"[6] Jesse Hickman (Thornbury Twp.)

1. *AMERICAN REPUBLICAN* (West Chester, Penna.) Dec. 24, 1816.
2. Ibid., Nov. 12, 1823.
3. Ibid., Nov. 23, 1825.
4. *VILLAGE RECORD* (West Chester, Penna.) Sept. 25, 1849.
5. Ibid., Jan. 7, 1865.
6. *AMERICAN REPUBLICAN* (West Chester, Penna.) Jan. 20, 1874.

FLOOR

Henry Graham Ashmead in 1884 mentions that the Friends Meeting House, in Birmingham Township, built about 1763 was built of stone and the floor was oak.[1] In Bethel Township, one schoolhouse, built prior to 1780, had a floor laid in bricks.[2]

The newspapers mention:

1822 "in the cellar of which is a milk house handsomely flagged"[3] Hannah B. Stalker (East Caln Twp.)

1853 "cellars...vault...floor of which, together with one under the dwelling, is plastered"[4] Catharine Evans Est. (West Chester)

1871 "directors contemplate...tile floor"[5] Bank (Phoenixville)

1872 "The ground floor is beautifully laid with marble tile."[6] Hammond & Kervey Drugstore (West Chester)

1873 "just remodelled store...The floor is handsomely laid with tri-colored tile"[7] Jesse Thatcher (West Chester)

1873 "piazza with roof. The floor of which is a model of workmanship, it being composed of yellow pine, and it heavily oiled and laid in white lead...The first story was a hall 7 feet wide, with a vestibule about 7 feet square, handsomely inlaid with tile of rare finish and exquisite design"[8] Henry Buckwalter (West Chester)

1874 "Dr. Jones laying new floor, alternate strips of ash and cherry"[9] (West Chester)

1879 "Fine improvement — J. Curtis Smith Esq...A very pretty floor has been laid in the vestibule of Minton tile, by Mr. A. M. Garrett, proprietor, of the Marble Works, corner of Market and Matlack streets"[10] (West Chester)

1880 "The floor of the hallways, both up and down stairs, is composed of a combination of walnut and ash, as is also the two bathroom floorsrs"[11] Dr. Ingram (West Chester)

1. Henry Graham Ashmead, *HISTORY OF DELAWARE COUNTY, PENNSYLVANIA* (Philadelphia, Penna. 1884) p.317.
2. Ibid., p. 309.
3. *VILLAGE RECORD* (West Chester, Penna.) July 17, 1822.
4. Ibid., Feb. 13, 1853.
5. *PHOENIXVILLE MESSENGER* (Phoenixville, Penna.) Aug. 5, 1871.
6. *AMERICAN REPUBLICAN* (West Chester, Penna.) Oct. 8, 1872.
7. *DAILY LOCAL NEWS* (West Chester, Penna.) Dec. 9, 1873.
8. Ibid., Dec. 5, 1873.
9. Ibid., March 17, 1874.
10. Ibid., March 26, 1879.
11. Ibid., Oct. 1, 1880.

FORGE

Forge is defined by Bailey (ed. 1735) as "a Place where a Smith heats his Iron; a large Furnace where Iron Ore is melted" by Sheridan (ed. 1789) as "the place where iron is beaten into form; any place where any thing is made or shaped" and by Webster (ed. 1828) as "A furnace in which iron or other metal is heated and hammerered into form..."

Peter Kalm travelling in Pennsylvania in 1748 and 1749 mentions: "About two English miles behind Chester I passed by an iron forge, which was to the right hand by the road side. It belonged to two brothers, as I was told. The ore, however, is not dug here, but thirty or forty miles from hence, where it is first melted in the oven, and then carried to this place. The bellows were made of leather, and both they and the hammers, and even the hearth [were] but small in proportion to ours. All the machines were worked by water. The iron was wrought into bars."[1]

The 1798 Direct Tax lists four forges: one of stone 32 x 20 feet; one stone and frame 40 x 40 feet and two that did not mention the material of construction, the mean size being 1225 square feet. In 1857 the Pleasant Garden Iron Works, of New London Township, had a "stone Forge 50 by 40 feet, covered with slate."[2]

1. Henry Graham Ashmead, *HISTORY OF DELAWARE COUNTY, PENNSYLVANIA* (Philadelphia, Penna. 1884) p. 743.
2. *AMERICAN REPUBLICAN* (West Chester, Penna.) March 10, 1857.

FOUNDRY

The newspapers mention between 1830 and 1849 one stone foundry 65 x 30 feet and one stone and frame foundry 40 x 30 feet. Between 1860 and 1874 the newspapers mention one brick foundry 40 x 40 feet, one four story foundry 44 x 40 feet, two frame foundries, the mean size being 1680 square feet and two that did not mention the material of construction, the mean size being 707 square feet.

FULLING MILL

Fuller is defined by Bailey (ed. 1735) as "one who fulls, mills, or scours Cloth." Sheridan (ed. 1789) mentions "To Full, to cleanse cloth from its oil or grease."

The 1798 Direct Tax lists thirteen fulling mills: ten of stone, the mean size being 379 square feet and three of log, the mean size being 334 square feet. The 1799 tax assessment for West Nottingham Township lists two stone fulling mills the mean size being 702 square feet. The newspaper advertisements between 1830 and 1834 list one fulling mill 28 x 28 feet.

GABLE

Gable is defined by Bailey (ed. 1735) as "the upright and triangular End, from the Eaves to the Top", by Sheridan (ed. 1789) as "the sloping roof of a building" and by Webster (ed. 1828) as "The triangular end of a house or other building from the cornice or eaves to the top. In America, it is usually called the gable-end."

The newspapers mention:

1763 "Frame Dwelling house...Stone Gable-end, with a Chimney to each Story"[1] Daniel John (Charlestown Twp.)

1763 "square Log House, with a Stone Gable end"[2] John Best (Tredyffrin Twp.)

1773 "log dwelling house, with a stone gable end and chimney"[3] Amos David (Goshen Twp.)

1774 "square log house with a gable end stone chimney"[4] Thomas Roberts (Charlestown Twp.)

1871 "The structure is a frame cottage with four gables and four bay windows"[5] Thomas H. Hall (West Chester)

1. *PENNSYLVANIA GAZETTE* (Philadelphia, Penna.) March 10, 1763.
2. Ibid., June 2, 1763.
3. Ibid., Sept. 29, 1773.
4. Ibid., March 16, 1774.
5. *AMERICAN REPUBLICAN* (West Chester, Penna.) Dec. 12, 1871.

GALLERY

Gallery is defined by Bailey (Ed. 1735) as "a kind of Balcony that surrounds a Building, or a Passage leading to several Apartments in a great House" by Sheridan (ed. 1789) as "a kind of walk along the floor of a house, into which the doors of the apartments open; the upper seats in a church; the seats in a playhouse above the pits, in which the meaner people sit" and by Webster (ed. 1828) as "In architecture, a covered part of a building, commonly in the wings, used as an ambulatory or place for walking...In Churches, a floor elevated on columns and furnished with pews or seats; usually ranged on three sides of the edifice. A similar structure in a play-house."

The newspaper advertisements mention:

1839 "with two galleries, each one hundred feet long, and two stories high"[1] Young Ladies Seminary (West Chester)

1855 "sky light Gallery in Hemphill's Building"[2] (Highland Twp.)

1865 "in front of the Director's room, a gallery runs around the entire open space from which a fine view is to be seen of what transpires in and outside of the building"[3] First National Bank (West Chester)

1873 "organ gallery"[4] M. E. Church (Wallace Twp.)

1874 "2nd story 25 feet high with galleries overhead"[5] Young Men's Literary Union (Phoenixville)

1. *AMERICAN REPUBLICAN* (West Chester, Penna.) Sept. 24, 1839.
2. Ibid., April 24, 1855.
3. *VILLAGE RECORD* (West Chester, Penna.) March 21, 1865.
4. *DAILY LOCAL NEWS* (West Chester, Penna.) July 30, 1873.
5. Ibid., Feb. 4, 1874.

GARDEN HOUSE

The 1798 Direct Tax lists John Ross, of Haverford Township, as having a one story garden house 22 x 15 feet.

GAS

The newspapers mention:

1853 "new brick Dwelling House...Gas has been introduced into the house"[1] B.V. Thorn (West Chester)

1853 "three 3 story brick dwelling Houses...Gas introduced in all of them, together with gas fixtures, Chandoliers &c."[2] Wm. Apple (West Chester)

1856 "Gas introduced into the Parsonage of the Church of Holy Trinity"[3] (West Chester)

The newspapers, before 1877, mention thirty other houses and one other Church with gas.

1. *VILLAGE RECORD* (West Chester, Penna.) July 5, 1853.
2. Ibid., Dec. 20, 1853.
3. *AMERICAN REPUBLICAN* (West Chester, Penna.) Feb. 5, 1856.

GEAR HOUSE

Gear is defined by Bailey (ed. 1735) and Sheridan (ed. 1789) as "stuff." A gear house is a building which houses stuff.

The 1798 Direct Tax lists seven gear houses: three of frame, the mean size being 131 square feet; two of log, the mean size being 202 square feet; one of wood 13 x 12 feet and one that did not mention the material of construction 10 x 10 feet.

GLASS

Glass is defined by Bailey (ed. 1735) as "a transparent Substance artificially made of Flints, Sand, Ashes, &c." and by Sheridan (ed. 1789) as "an artificial substance made by fusing salt and flint or sand together, with a vehement fire."

Henry Graham Ashmead, in 1884, mentions that an ancient house in Darby, part of which dates from 1725 had a double door with bull's eyes glass on northern eastern and on inside door all going into dining room.[1]

A few inventories give interesting mentions of glass:

1688 "for 2 Casments & 2 other panes of Glass 11 14 00"[2] George Gleave (Springfield Twp.)

1763 "parcel of Glass with Window Lead"[3] Thomas Martin (Middletown Twp.)

1772 "¼ Box 8 by 10 Window Glass"[4] John Trimble (Concord Twp.)

1823 "a lot of Mahogany Sash and Glass"[5] Jacob Fertig (Charlestown Twp.)

1834 "Box Glass 8 by 10...Do 10 by 12"[6] Charles Rarke (East Caln Twp.)

The newspapers mention:

1831 "new and substantial brick house 30 by 29 feet, with 3 rooms and half entry on the first floor, and the same on the 2d in modern style, with 15 light windows 10 by 12 glass together with side glass at the front or hall door and large handsome top"[7] James Grier ' Jordon Pottery" (West Nottingham Twp.)

1858 "The only Iron Front Store...two large Show Windows, and Glass Door in centre."[8] L. W. H. Kervey (West Chester)

1864 "Brick Grape House...with glazed roof"[9] Alexander Marshall (West Chester)

1870 "House...long deep windows Gothic style, plate and stained Glass"[10] J. Lee Englebert (West Chester)

1871 "Store room 16 by 45 feet, with plate glass front"[11] Joseph Murdogh (Oxford)

1872 "bulk windows, each of single plate of French Glass"[12] G. C. M. Eicholtz (Downingtown)

1873 "show windows, with plate glass fronts 5½ by 8½ feet"[13] J. B. Roecker (West Chester)

1874 "erection of sliding glass partitions by which it [lecture room] can be divided into rooms"[14] Presbyterian Church (Oxford)

1876 "French plate Glass show window 23 x 31"[15] Andrew Ferrell (West Chester)

1. Henry Graham Ashmead, *HISTORY OF DELAWARE COUNTY, PENNSYLVANIA* (Philadelphia, Penna. 1884) p. 531.
2. Colonial Society of Pennsylvania *RECORD OF THE COURTS OF CHESTER COUNTY PENNSYLVANIA 1681–1697* (Philadelphia, Penna., 1910) p. 218.
3. Chester County Inventory #2084.
4. Chester County Inventory #2711.
5. Chester County Inventory #7380.
6. Chester County Inventory #9095.

7. *AMERICAN REPUBLICAN* (West Chester, Penna.) Dec. 20, 1831.
8. Ibid., Aug. 3, 1858.
9. *VILLAGE RECORD* (West Chester, Penna.) Oct. 11, 1864.
10. Ibid., Oct. 22, 1870.
11. Ibid., Jan. 24, 1871.
12. *AMERICAN REPUBLICAN* (West Chester, Penna.) May 21, 1872
13. Ibid., Dec. 23, 1873.
14. *VILLAGE RECORD* (West Chester, Penna.) Nov. 28, 1874.
15. *DAILY LOCAL NEWS* (West Chester, Penna.) Dec. 26, 1876.

GRANARY

Granary is defined by Bailey (ed. 1735) as "a Place where Corn is Kept, a Store house for Corn" by Sheridan (ed. 1789) as "a store-house for threshed corn" and by Webster (ed. 1828) as "A store house or repository of grain after it is thrashed; a corn house."

The 1798 Direct Tax lists thirty-three granaries: nine of frame, the mean size being 189 square feet; nine of log, the mean size being 261 square feet; seven of stone, the mean size being 259 square feet; two of wood, the mean size being 284 square feet; one of plank 18 x 15 feet; one of brick 18 x 15 feet and one of brick and stone 15 x 15 feet. Robert Valentine of East Caln and West Whiteland Townships had "low wagon shed & granary over it", and Joseph Baker of Middletown and part of Lower Providence Townships, had "log granary or shop 15 x 14 feet." The 1796 tax assessment for East Fallowfield Township lists one stone granary 16 x 12 feet and John Hollis as having '1 frame Wagon house with a Granary above". The 1796 tax assessment for West Whiteland Township lists George Masey as having "1 frame Chair house Granary a loft." The 1799 tax assessment for Pikeland Township lists one frame granary 21 x 15 feet and for West Marlboro Township it lists one frame granary 33 x 20 feet. The newspaper advertisements between 1830 and 1849 mention one frame granary 30 x 20 feet and three that do not mention the material of construction, the mean size being 900 square feet.

GRAVEL

Gravel is defined by Bailey (ed. 1735) as "the larger and stony sort of Sand" by Sheridan (ed. 1789) as "hard sand" and by Webster (ed. 1828) as "Small stones or fragments of stone, or very small pebbles, larger than the particles of sand, but often intermixed with them."

The newspaper advertisements mention:
1863 "barn...a large gravel roof"[1] G. Grover Lewis (West Marlboro Twp.)
1863 "buildings are beautifully laid out in gravelled walks"[2] George W. Richards (Phoenixville)
1869 "one mile of gravel walks"[3] T.S.C. Lowe (Schuylkill Twp.)

1. *VILLAGE RECORD* (West Chester, Penna.) Nov. 21, 1863.
2. Ibid., June 9, 1863.
3. Ibid., Oct. 9, 1869.

GREEN HOUSE
HOT HOUSE

The newspaper advertisements mention:
1855 "green house"[1] M. Thomas & Sons (West Chester)
1857 "hot house"[2] William White (Tredyffrin Twp.)
1860 "wagon gouse with hot beds along one side"[3] Miles Murphy (Pocopson Twp.)
1864 "a Brick Grape House, in back yard with glazed roof 52 feet by 12"[4] Alexander Marshall (West Chester)
1869 "Green House...20 by 60 feet, requiring 60,000 square feet of glass roof to cover the same"[5] Kift (West Chester)
1870 "TWO GREENHOUSES 50 by 19 feet with furnaces for heating"[6] Joseph Hill (East Nottingham Twp.)

Before 1876 the newspapers mentioned three other greenhouses and one other hot house. Between 1876 and 1900 the newspaper advertisements mentioned one green house 80 x 15 feet and one 202 x 22 feet 13 feet high.

1. *AMERICAN REPUBLICAN* (West Chester, Penna.) April 24, 1855.
2. Ibid., March 24, 1857.
3. *VILLAGE RECORD* (West Chester, Penna.) Aug. 28, 1860.
4. Ibid., Oct. 11, 1864.
5. *AMERICAN REPUBLICAN* (West Chester, Penna.) July 13, 1869.
6. *VILLAGE RECORD* (West Chester, Penna.) Oct. 11, 1870.

GRIST OR MERCHANT MILL

Grist is defined by Bailey (ed. 1735) as "Corn ground, or fit for grinding" and by Sheridan (ed. 1789) as "corn to be ground." Grist mill is defined by Webster (ed. 1828) as "A mill for grinding grain."

The 1798 Direct Tax lists seven grist mills: six of stone, the mean size being 1215 square feet and one that did not mention the material of construction 36 x 33 feet. The 1796 tax assessment for East Fallowfield Township lists four grist mills: two of stone, the mean size being 923 square feet, one stone and log 22 x 17 feet and one that did not mention the material of construction 60 x 30 feet. The 1796 tax assessment for East Fallowfield Township lists four grist mills: William Mode's as "1 Grist Mill 17 by 22 under part Stone upper part Logs. A single Geer'd Mill for one Day it goes two Days it Stands Still"; Crosby Phipps as "1 Double Geer'd Grist Mill 30 by 60 feet with two pair of Stones one pair burs and the other Country Stones", Benjamin Powel's as "Grist Mill 40 x 25 with 2 pair of Stones, one Burs and the Other Country Stones" and that of Thomas Worth's as "1 Stone Grist Mill 24 by 36 feet with two pair of Stones one Burs and the Other Country Stones."

The newspaper advertisements, between 1750 and 1774, list twelve grist mills, ten of stone the mean size being 1729 square feet, one stone and brick 40 x 32 feet and one that did not mention the material of construction 60 x 50 feet. Between 1775 and 1799 the newspapers mention seven grist mills: four stone, the mean size being 1472 square feet and three that did not mention the material of construction the mean size being 1448 square feet; between 1800 and 1824 two were mentioned, the mean size being 1556 square feet; between 1825 and 1849 twenty-one grist mills are mentioned; seven of stone, the means size being 2070 square feet and fourteen that did not mention the material of construction, the mean size being 1468 square feet. The newspapers mention between 1850 and 1874 fifty-four grist mills; twenty six of stone the mean size being 1975 square feet; five of stone and frame, the mean size being 1841 square feet; two of brick, the mean size being 2397 square feet and twenty-one that did not mention the material of construction, the mean size being 1821 square feet.

HAY HOUSE

The 1798 Direct Tax lists sixty-nine hay houses: thirty-one of log, the mean size being 312 square feet; seventeen of frame, the mean size being 640 square feet; five of stone and frame, the mean size being 730 square feet; four of wood, the mean size being 630 square feet; one of stone and log 50 x 30 feet and eleven that did not mention the material of construction, the mean size being 369 square feet. Thomas Pimm of East Caln and West Whiteland Townships had "1½ story old round log hay house 50 x 24." the 1799 tax assessment for Charlestown, Pikeland and West Marlboro Townships list nine hay houses: three of log, the mean size being 272 square feet; three of frame, the mean size being 657 square feet and three that did not mention the material of construction, the mean size being 551 square feet. The newspaper advertisements between 1835 and 1839 list one hay house 50 x 16 feet.

HEATING

The newspapers mention:

1856 "every apartment is warmed by heaters"[1] Sunny Side Seminary (East Fallowfield Twp.)

1856 "There is also a heating apparatus in the cellar with flues to convey the heat to the different apartments in the first and second stories"[2] Parsonage of Church of Holy Trinity (West Chester)

1857 "heated by furnace in the cellar, furnished with gas pipes"[3] William White (Tredyffrin Twp.)

1857 "heater in cellar, constructed to heat every part of the house...circulating bath boiler"[4] C. A. Walborn (West Whiteland Twp.)

1858 "The HOUSE is in good order, warmed by heated air"[5] Yardley Warner (East Whiteland Twp.)

1858 "A large Patent Range in the kitchen from which the dining room is heated"[6] John P. Rawlings (West Chester)

1860 "furnaces walled in [house]"[7] Moses Lewis, Sr., (Upper Uwchlan Twp.)

1860 "furnace in wash house"[8] Robert C. Hemphill (West Chester)

1860 "heater in cellar"[9] Francis E. Wilcox (Willistown Twp.)

1862 "heating apparatus"[10] Thomas Bateman (West Chester)

1867 "House...heated with hot air furnace"[11] David Meconkey (West Chester)

1870 "cold air ventilators...Furnace in cellar"[12] J. W. Barnard (West Chester

1872 "VENTILATION from the FLOORS [a house]"[13] Charles L. Warner (West Chester)

1873 "House...water heaters, flews and registers"[14] Sharpless & Hall (West Chester)

1. *VILLAGE RECORD* (West Chester, Penna.) Nov. 29, 1856.
2. *AMERICAN REPUBLICAN* (West Chester, Penna.) Feb. 5, 1856.
3. Ibid., March 24, 1857.
4. *VILLAGE RECORD* (West Chester, Penna.) Sept. 12, 1857.
5. Ibid., Feb. 9, 1858.
6. Ibid., Feb. 20, 1858.
7. Ibid., Oct. 6, 1860.
8. Ibid., Dec. 25, 1860.
9. *AMERICAN REPUBLICAN* (West Chester, Penna.) Sept. 4, 1860.
10. *VILLAGE RECORD* (West Chester, Penna.) May 24, 1862.
11. Ibid., Oct. 15, 1867.
12. *AMERICAN REPUBLICAN* (West Chester, Penna.) Sept. 20, 1870.
13. *VILLAGE RECORD* (West Chester, Penna.) Jan. 13, 1872.
14. *DAILY LOCAL NEWS* (West Chester, Penna.) March 28, 1873.

HOG HOUSE

The 1798 Direct Tax lists two stone hog houses the mean size being 112 square feet. The tax lists Thomas Truman, of Sadsbury Township, as having "1 stone hog & hen house under the same roof."

The newspaper advertisements mention:

1829 "a large hog house well paved"[1] Nathan Walton (New Garden Twp.)

1845 "Hog house 30 by 13 feet, 2 stories high, paved with stone"[2] Hayes Jackson (East Marlboro Twp.)

The newspapers mention before 1850 one stone hog house 65 x 25 feet and one hog house that did not mention the material of construction 20 x 18 feet. Between 1850 and 1877 four hog houses that did not mention the material of construction had a mean size of 544 square feet.

Another is mentioned as being 60 x 14 feet with a ceiling of 8 feet.

1. *AMERICAN REPUBLICAN* (West Chester, Penna.) Oct. 6, 1828.
2. *VILLAGE RECORD* (West Chester, Penna.) Sept. 30, 1845.

HOUSE

House is defined by Bailey (ed. 1735) as "a Home, a Place of Abode", by Sheridan (ed. 1789) as "a building erected for human abode; any building" and by Webster (ed. 1828) as "In a general sense, a building or shed intended or used as a habitation or shelter for animals of any kind; but appropriately, a building or ediface for the habitation of man; a dwelling place, mansion or abode for any of the human species. It may be of any size and composed of any materials whatever, wood, stone, brick, &c."

William Penn recommended in 1684 in his "Information and Directions to Such Persons as are inclined to America, more Especially Those related to the Province of Pennsylvania..." the following directions for building houses. He advised the colonists:

To build them an House of thirty foot long and eighteen foot broad with a partition near the middle, and another to devide one end of the House into two small Rooms. There must be eight Trees of about sixteen inches square, and cut off to Posts of about fifteen foot long, which the House must stand upon, and four pieces, two of thirty foot long and two of eighteen foot long, for Plates, which must lie upon the top of these Posts, the whole length and breadth of the House, for the Gists to rest upon. There must be ten Gists of twenty foot long to bear the Loft, and two false Plates of thirty foot long to lie upon the ends of the Gists for the Rafters to be fixed upon, twelve pare of Rafters of about twenty foot to bear the Roof of the House, with several other small pieces, as Windbeams, Braces, Studs, &c., which are made out of the Waste Timber. For covering the House, Ends and Sides, and for the Loft we use Clabboard, which is Rived feather-edged, of five foot and a half long, that, well Drawn, lyes close and smooth. The Lodging Room may be lined with the same, and filled up between, which is very warm. These houses usually endure ten years without repair.

For the Carpenters work for such an House,
I and my Servants assisting him, together with his Diet	07 00 00
For a Barn of the same Building and Dimensions	05 00 00
For Nailes, and other things to finish Both	03 10 00

The lower floor is the Ground, the upper Clabbord. This may seem a mean way of Building, but 'tis sufficient and safest for ordinary beginners. 'Tis true, some of our Folks have exceeded much, even in Villages; but how wise they were in it, is the Question. An ordinary House, and a

good Stock, is the Planters Wisdom; else, some of our Neighbouring Provinces, improv'd by persons, whom Necessity had made ingenious and provident, had not succeeded so well as they have done. Howbeit, if better are desired, people may have them suitable to their abilities.

This house may be finished by the middle of November, the Barn by the Spring, but there being little use for it, till the next fall, it may be built at Leasure, and the Winter imploy'd to clear Land for the Spring, by which time, they may easily clear'd fifteen Acres...[1]

The Hoskins (Graham) House, in Chester, built in 1688 was

> Two stories in height with attics...steps and porch...Hallway runs through the center of the building...a wide easily ascended staircase rises from the rear of the entry...Balustrade is fashioned of hard wood and is very massive... steps of ash...Windows in lower rooms deeply recessed and old-time seats constructed therein ...Heavy beams supporting upper floors stand prominently out from ceiling. In the rooms on the first and second floors on the north side of the house, the high old-fashioned wooden mantels over the large fireplace are flanked by enormous closets, which are lighted by small windows in the outer walls...Floors are hardwood, and the flooring boards are wide. Ceilings are lofts...Steep roof. Kitchen, which is built in an L, is large, the fireplace comprising almost the entire eastern end...could seat themselves on either end of the chimney on benches...Was portico or veranda in rear...An old oven was attached to the house.[2]

The Barber House, in Chester, built between 1699 and 1708 had

> Pent roof over second story window, originally had porch. Has two doors. Eastern one leading into the parlor, and the western door into the hallway a room of the same size as the one on the opposite side. Stairway ascended from hall. Back of this was the sitting room while in the rear of the parlor was a dining room. The fireplaces had hearths in the hall-room and the parlor was laid in blue tiles, presenting scenes from Scriptural history, and in the chambers above on each side of the fireplace were large closets, similar to those mentioned in Hoskins and Logan Houses.[3]

1. William Penn, *INFORMATION AND DIRECTIONS TO SUCH PERSONS AS ARE INCLINED TO AMERICA MORE ESPECIALLY THOSE RELATED TO THE PROVINCE OF PENNSYLVANIA* Historical Society of Pennsylvania, (Philadelphia, Penna.), Vol. 4, p. 331.
2. Henry Graham Ashmead, *HISTORICAL SKETCH OF CHESTER, ON DELAWARE* (Chester, Penna., 1883), p.67.
3. Ibid., p. 121.

The following information pertaining to the materials used in the construction of houses was obtained, when possible, from the Bureau of Internal Revenue Direct Tax. Since a few townships have not been found in that tax, a tax assessment in date as near to 1798 as possible has been used. 1796 for East Fallowfield Township and 1799 for Charlestown, London Britain, Pikeland, West Marlboro and West Nottingham Townships.

HOUSES	Brick		Brick & Stone		Brick, Stone & Frame	
	No.	Mean	No.	Mean	No.	Mean
Aston	6	813	1	1284	1	408
Bethel	3	885				
Birmingham	6	833				
Chester	42	1013	3	1048		
Concord	12	1110	2	942		
Darby	23	693	1	1462		
Edgemont	2	1180	1	1034		
Haverford	1	720	2	1240		
Middletown & part Lower Providence	9	764	2	845		
Newtown & part Marple	4	812	2	1290		
Radnor						
Ridley	8	1259	1	1471		
Springfield & part Lower Providence	7	891	2	1410	1	1152
Thornbury	1	440				
Tinicum	1	1188				
Upper & Lower Chichester	27	692	2	1130		
Upper Darby	13	968	4	1338		
Upper Providence & part Marple	1	1778				

HOUSES	Brick		Brick & Stone		Brick, Stone & Frame	
	No.	Mean	No.	Mean	No.	Mean
Brandywine						
Charlestown						
Coventry						
East Bradford	3	1100	1	1208		
East Caln	4	1095				
East Fallowfield						
East Nantmeal						
East Whiteland	2	830				
London Britain	1	616				
Pikeland						
Sadsbury						
Tredyffrin	1	1285	1	1071		
Vincent						
West Bradford	4	1191	2	1248		
West Caln						
West Marlboro	5	906			1	1410
West Nottingham						
West Whiteland	2	1671				

HOUSES	Frame		Frame, Brick & Stone		Frame & Stone		Frame, Stone & Log		Frame & Log	
	No.	Mean	No.	Mean	No.	Mean	No.	Mean	No.	Mean
Aston	5	785	1	408						
Bethel	3	495								
Birmingham	1	468								
Chester	27	426			1	510			1	589
Concord	5	740			1	786			2	392
Darby	31	470			2	396			3	318
Edgemont	1	975			1	1112				
Haverford	5	533								
Middletown & part Lower Providence	2	630			1	486	1	680	1	480
Newtown & part Marple										
Radnor	1	360								
Ridley	2	544								
Springfield & part Lower Providence	7	404	1	1152	2	757			1	220
Thornbury	5	947			2	1207			1	320
Tinicum	6	493								
Upper & Lower Chichester	29	388			3	493			3	1894
Upper Darby	6	618			1	360			1	888
Upper Providence & part Marple										

HOUSES	Frame		Brick & Stone		Frame & Stone	
	No.	Mean	No.	Mean	No.	Mean
Brandywine	1	960				
Charlestown	1					
Coventry						
East Bradford	2	454			2	720
East Caln	2	2675				
East Fallowfield						
East Nantmeal						
East Whiteland						
London Britain	2	328				
Pikeland	2	830			2	479
Sadsbury						
Tredyffrin	1	820				
Vincent						
West Bradford	3	517			1	990
West Caln	1	448				
West Marlboro	4	407	1	1410	1	662
West Nottingham						
West Whiteland	1					

HOUSES	Log		Log & Boarded		Log Weather Boarded		Log & Plank	
	No.	Mean	No.	Mean	No.	Mean	No.	Mean
Aston	23	366	2	573				
Bethel	11	444						
Birmingham	42	397					1	640
Chester	28	356						
Concord	22	499						
Darby	11	367						
Edgemont	8	420						
Haverford	35	443						
Middletown & part Lower Providence	48	284						
Newtown & part Marple								
Radnor	13	507					1	736
Ridley	18	548						
Springfield & part Lower Providence	28	368			1	1147		
Thornbury	33	315						
Tinicum	2	505						
Upper & Lower Chichester	40	267						
Upper Darby	22	355						
Upper Providence & part Marple	8	765						

HOUSES	Log	
	No.	Mean
Brandywine	89	471
Charlestown	86	443
Coventry	98	458
East Bradford	50	437
East Caln	50	466
East Fallowfield	60	464
East Nantmeal	38	276
East Whiteland	21	384
London Britain	23	349
Pikeland	61	418
Sadsbury	63	393
Tredyffrin	60	386
Vincent	129	479
West Bradford	73	393
West Caln	94	418
West Marlboro	444	380
West Nottingham	32	337
West Whiteland		

HOUSES	Mud	
	No.	Mean
Brandywine		
Charlestown		
Coventry	1	384

HOUSES	Slab	
	No.	Mean
Aston		
Bethel		
Birmingham		
Chester		
Concord		
Darby		
Edgemont		
Haverford		
Middletown & part Lower Providence	1	480
Newtown & part		
Marple		
Radnor		
Ridley		
Springfield & part Lower Providence	1	240
Thornbury		
Tinicum		
Upper & Lower Chichester		
Upper Darby		
Upper Providence & part Marple		

HOUSES	Stone		Stone Roughcast		Stone & Brick		Stone & Frame	
	No.	Mean	No.	Mean	No.	Mean	No.	Mean
Aston	20	587			1	1284	1	408
Bethel	9	777						
Birmingham	17	681						
Chester	26	706			3	1048		
Concord	31	733			2	942		
Darby	21	862			1	1462		
Edgemont	35	796			1	1034		
Haverford			1	1512	2	1240		
Middletown & part Lower Providence	52	686			2	845		
Newtown & part Marple	42	816			2	1290		
Radnor	54	793	1	408				
Ridley	24	800			1	1471		

HOUSES	Stone		Stone Roughcast		Stone & Brick		Stone & Frame	
	No.	Mean	No.	Mean	No.	Mean	No.	Mean
Springfield & part Lower Providence	35	947			2	1410	1	1152
Thornbury	22	805						
Tinicum	2	1002						
Upper & Lower Chichester	16	610			2	1130		
Upper Darby	31	773			4	1338		
Upper Providence & part Marple	29	785						

HOUSES	Brick, Stone Frame		Stone & Log		Stone, Log & Frame		Stone & Timber		Stone & Wood	
	No.	Mean	No.	Mean	No.	Mean	No.	Mean	No.	Mean
Aston			9	642						
Bethel										
Birmingham			1	486						
Chester	1	510								
Concord	1	786	5	711						
Darby	2	396								
Edgemont	1	1112								
Haverford										
Middletown & part Lower Providence	1	486	9	462	1	680				
Newtown & part Marple									6	1222
Radnor			4	636					6	568
Ridley			2	998						
Springfield & part Lower Providence	2	757	2	353						
Thornbury	2	1207	1	936						
Tinicum										
Upper & Lower Chichester	3	493	2	870						
Upper Darby	1	360	1	585						
Upper Providence & part Marple							3	698		

HOUSES	Stone		Stone & Brick		Stone, Brick & Frame		Stone & Frame		Stone & Log	
	No.	Mean	No.	Mean	No.	Mean	No.	Mean	No.	Mean
Brandywine	42	792								
Charlestown	74	763							3	1324
Coventry	29	991								
East Bradford	50	854	1	1208			2	720		
East Caln	51	1095								
East Fallowfield	21	656							3	603
East Nantmeal	4	239							1	176
East Whiteland	40	932								
London Britain	5	696								
Pikeland	41	708					2	479	17	604
Sadsbury	49	864							4	713
Tredyffrin	60	809	1	1071					11	677
Vincent	43	731								
West Bradford	34	835	2	1248			1	990	3	817
West Caln	39	704								
West Marlboro	38	747			1	1410	1	662	2	617
West Nottingham	8	539								
West Whiteland	30	1031								

BRICK

Henry Graham Ashmead in 1883 mentions that the Logan house, in Chester has a date stone inscribed "J & C Y 1700" for Jasper and Catharine Yeates set in a gable-end. The house was

> Built of brick, two stories in height, with a tentlike roof forming an attic within, with steep sides. Over first story windows was a pent roof...and a porch at the front door, with seats at each side of the door, at right angles to the building...Wide doorway gave access to spacious hall, many small diamond-shaped panes of glass set in lead, in the large window sashes...and casements at the head of the stair landing... wainscoted hallway...All the rooms were wainscoted also, and the panels were painted or stained in imitation of mahogany. Large closets were on each side of the wide chimney places, lighted by windows in the outer walls. Under the high wooden mantel pieces in the parlour and the room opposite, across the hall, the fireplaces were lined with illuminated tiles, delineating incidents of Scriptural history. Large buttresses were built against the gables for strength, and smaller ones to guard the brick walls on each side of main building.[1]

The Parker House, also in Chester, was built in 1700. It was a two-stories brick house, of respectable dimensions, built in 1700, had much of old-fashioned wooden wainscotting. In the chambers upstairs the pannels were curiously painted in a congeries of colours, not unlike yellow mahogany. The house had originally small glass panes, set in leaded frames, of which a few speciments still remained in the casements on the stairway, large closets were on each side of the chimneys, large enough for small beds, which were lighted by small windows in the outer walls; on the side of the house stood a one-story office, which had long contained the records of Chester County...[2]

The 1798 Direct Tax lists one hundred and eighty-two brick houses the mean size being 685 square feet. The 1799 tax assessment for London Britain and West Marlboro Townships lists six brick houses, the mean size being 253 square feet.

The newspapers give a few interesting descriptions of the use of brick:

1862 "Frame House 16 by 24 feet, weatherboarded and filled in with brick"[3] Oliver Stoops (East Nottingham Twp.)

1866 "House 36 by 30 feet of mortar brick"[4] Richard Jacobs (Atglen)

1869 "THE HOUSE (Brick sanded)"[5] Sidney D. Pennock (Kennett Square)

1872 "BRICK COTTAGE...Pressed brick front"[6] Wm. B. Haslett (Parkesburg)

1873 "Yesterday Mr. Henry Buckwalter, took possession of the new and handsome residence corner of High and Union streets. This building is composed of two residences, the northern portion being now for sale. Its erection was contracted for and put in progress by the Talley Brothers, in September 1872. It fronts on High street 50 feet, running back a distance of 34 feet, where an extension 36 feet wide, by 62 feet deep, completes the ground limits of the structure. It is three stories high the first one being 12 feet, the second 11 feet, and the third 10 feet. We shall briefly describe Mr. Buckwalter's residence, insomuch the other end or house is almost a perfect facsimile of the one occupied by him.

The first story has a hall 7 feet wide with a vestibule about 7 feet square, handsomely inlaid with tile of rare finish and exquisite design. The parlor is 16 by 32 feet, having a beautiful ceiling centre-piece and a neat molding around the entire room. A very pretty Italian marble mantle also adds its beauty to this department.

The dining room is 17 by 19 feet, with oak grained wood-work and slate mantel. Back of this last named room is the breakfast room with its oiled pine wood-work, pantry sink with hot and cold water heated by a range. In this apartment are located all the call bells, the wires of which extend to all parts of the house. The kitchen back of the breakfast room is an apartment combining more little accessories to comfort and utility than is ordinarily seen, and in a word, its appointments may be embodied in the word "perfection." The large Clilson range in this apartment is a very complete affair and dispenses comfort to three chambers above.

The second story is reached by back and front stair-ways, with massive railings and ash steps. Taking the front means so provided is reached a wide ample landing above, from which we could either enter the library or a well-planned bath room. The library is a handsome room of about 17 by 20 feet, with slate mantel and walnut grained wood-work. A nobby little covered piazza is one of the comforts to this room, and is a feature which gives to it a liberal amount of pleasantness, besides adds to the appearance of the building. The bath room should be seen to be fully appreciated, possessing as it does so many modern appliances and accessories to comfort, as to render a pen description a futile attempt to do it justice.

Besides these already described apartments on the second story are three chambers, large and elegant in all their architectural appointments. The two in the front portion of the building immediately over the parlor are arranged with beautiful wash-stands, so as to accommodate the inmates of both rooms, and is a novel feature of luxuriance and genuine comfort. These apartments also have toilet gaslights, the arrangement of which show that Mr. Buckwalter has an eye single for facilitating the irksome duties attached to the present fashion in which the ladies dress their hair.

The third story is divided off into five chambers, possessing all the modern appliances to ease and repose, and in no one part is there the least discrepancy in finish exhibited.

The cellar presents the same regard to order and comfort, as the more assuming apartments above. It is divided and subdivided into vault and pantry, with bins for coal, wood and ashes. One of Reynold's famous heaters is here located, to the use of warming the entire house, and in which duty Mr. B., informs us, it is abundantly equal to the task.

The walls of the building are all hollow and hence they are dry and pleasant, the vacuum carrying off all dampness, which otherwise would find its way into the inner apartments. The wood finish of the parlor is of a new design and is very pretty, reflecting credit upon Mr. Buckwalter who planned its symmetrical proportions. The windows all have elegant stone caps, lintels, and casings, while the inside finish is walnut, open and shut blinds made in such a manner as to attract the most unobserving eye with their beauty. Around the entire front portion of the building is a light, airy-fashioned piazza with roof, the floor of which is a model of workmanship, it being composed of yellow pine, and it heavily oiled and laid in white lead. The large massive walnut doors leading from High street entrance, are the work of Mr. Baldwin of sash factory renown, and are a credit to his skill as a finished workman...

The walls of the building are composed of 135,000 brick..." (West Chester)

1880 "Yesterday Dr. Ingram moved into his new dwelling house...The building is a two-story brick, with a marble base in front to the depth of about four feet, and a fine large flight of white marble steps. The vestibule is entirely of walnut, while the woodwork of the parlor and his two offices and the rooms upstairs are of a dark color, which makes it very neat and substantial looking. The floor of the hallways, both up and down stairs, is composed of a combination of walnut and ash, as is also the two bath room floors. This makes a clean and seasonable floor and well dispenses with carpets, oilcoth, and matting, which would otherwise be used as a covering. The stairs leading to the rooms in the upper stories are of solid walnut, and on each landing is a window composed of red, white, blue and yellow stained glass, which add much to the appearance of the surroundings, and more especially when the sun shines through them. The two offices contain everything convenient for the transaction of business. The parlor is a large and spacious one, the windows of which are finished with inside walnut blinds. The dining room is also a commodious one, finished in light hard wood. A dumb waiter is so constructed in this room upon which the necessaries of life are lowered and hoisted to and from the vault in the cellar with much ease. A door leads from the dining room to a porch built on the side of the house. The kitchen make up is similar to the dining room, only smaller in size. The sitting room extends over the size of the dining room and kitchen, in the second story, and this also is built of the same material of wood as the two rooms just mentioned, and also has a door leading to the side porch. The bedrooms are large and comfortable, the woodwork of which is after the color of walnut. Two water-closets have been built in the building, which are connected with the main chimney of the house, and are thereby ventilated." (West Chester)[8]

1883 "Addison May...addition built to his residence...of pressed brick with red mortar"[9](West Chester)

1883 "Samuel G. Moore, of East Marlboro, is making preparations to build an elegant residence on his farm on the Street Road, next spring. The walls will be of enameled brick and will be furnished by William H. Evans, of Waynesbury, Ohio."[10]

1884 "Commenced...four new houses...mortar which is being used in the brick work of the four houses now building on Dean street is black" (West Chester)[11]

1884 "[house] The bricks as well as the wood work of the exterior are receiving a coat of paint"[12] A. McLear (West Chester)

1894 "THREE STORY BRICK DWELLING...The house has a large porch along the whole front, contains 13 rooms with every modern convenience and improvement, and is in firstclass repair. The library is wainscotted, ceiled and pannelled in white oak; the dining room has a side board refrigerator built in; the kitchen is a large double one, well arranged. There are two bath rooms, one on the first floor finished in cherry, and one on the second floor, both with hot and cold water; water closet on both first and second floors. The house is lighted throughout with both gas and electricity, is fitted with electric burglar alarm, and heated by two good furnaces; good cellar with

vault...House is carpeted throughout."[13] (West Chester)

1. Henry Graham Ashmead, *HISTORICAL SKETCH OF CHESTER, ON DELAWARE* (Republican Steam Printing House, 1883) p. 73.
2. Henry Graham Ashmead, *HISTORY OF DELAWARE COUNTY, PENNSYLVANIA* (Philadelphia, Penna. 1884) p. 307.
3. *AMERICAN REPUBLICAN* (West Chester, Penna.) June 24, 1862.
4. *VILLAGE RECORD* (West Chester, Penna.) Nov. 10, 1866.
5. Ibid., Jan. 12, 1869.
6. Ibid., Nov. 30, 1872.
7. *DAILY LOCAL NEWS* (West Chester, Penna.) Dec. 5, 1873.
8. Ibid., Oct. 1, 1880.
9. Ibid., June 8, 1883.
10. Ibid., Jan. 1, 1883.
11. Ibid., June 28, 1884.
12. Ibid., July 18, 1884.
13. *CHESTER COUNTY DEMOCRAT* (West Chester, Penna.) Sept. 30, 1894.

BRICK & FRAME

The 1798 Direct Tax lists six brick and frame houses, the mean size being 557 square feet.

BRICK & PLANK

The 1798 Direct Tax lists one brick and plank house of 648 square feet.

FRAME

Frame construction was used in Chester County as soon as there were saw mills. In the Court Records for the county in 1689 there is the following complaint:

"JOHN NEELD pl[tf]

in an action of the Case for Breach of Articles

JOHN MADOX Def[dd]

Decleration...

And in the Second aggreem[t] the said Def[dt] was to build for the Said pl[tf] A Dwelling house Twenty four foot in Lengh and Eighteen foot in Width and Ten foot in hight Betwen Sell and Wale plate Two perticions below and a Closett and One pertion above and a Closett And to face the Roof wth Clapboards in the Inside and to make the Botom fflore wth Sufecient plank and the first Loft wth sufecient inch board and to Cover the house Sufeciently wth Shingles and to doe all the Timber Worke about the making on one Chimley, and to make ffouer Windowes two below and two above and a porch to the ffront of the house and little windowes to the afore Said Closett[d], and one peare of Staires and to face all thewhole house in the Inside and the Def[dt] doth promise to make the house Sufecient to live in att or before the 25th of the Tenth Month next ensuing the Date of the said agreem[t] and in Nine months after to ffinish the whole worke belonging to the house. And the said pl[tf] is to

242

pay unto the said Def^dt Sixteen pounds Ten Shillings as ffol. in Three Cattle that is Two Cowes and a bullock Twelve pounds in Bacon Twenty Shillings att Six pence the pound a paire of Boots and spurs att Twenty Shillings and som other Goods to the value of ffifty Shillings. Now the said Def^dt hath not Pformed his part in Eith of the Two Articles of agreem^t And Delayes soe to doe although the pl^tf on his part hath allways Supplyed the Def^dt wth pay ans is Redy to make him paym^t wth the Remainder Soe that the said Def^dt had finished the said Buildings But he Neglects soe to doe soe that the pl^tf is Damnifyed In the full sume of five pounds Lawfull money of this Province whereupon the pl^tf brings this sute and Craves Judgment of this Court against the said def^dt wth Cost of Sute"[1]

Henry Graham Ashmead mentions in 1883 that the Boar's Head Inn, in Chester, where Penn resided in 1682-1683 was "One story and a half high, with peaked roof...just below the eaves projected the crane from which the old sign of a boar's head was suspended. House constructed of heavy frame timber, filled in with brick, and outside as well as inside the laths which were interlaced in a kind of basket pattern, were covered with plaster made of oyster shell lime and mud, while in place of hair, swamp grass was employed to hold the composition together. The doors were peculiar in the manner in which they were hung, a peg or projection from the door above and below fitted into holes made in the frames, and on these they swung instead of hinges. The windows, with the exception of the one in the kitchen were small; the glasses 4 by 3 in size, were let in lead. The sashes were not hung with weights, a comparatively modern improvement, and when it was desired that the lower sashes should be raised, they were supported by pieces of wood which fitted into the groves in the frames, or a turn buckle placed half way up sustained the weight. The large window in the kitchen was made to slide one sash past the other. The roof was of split shingles and the kitchen floor was laid in flagging some of which were as large as 6 by 8 feet, and under these was a body of eighteen inches of sand on which they rested. In the kitchen on the side opening to the west was a large double door through which a cart load of wood could be drawn if desired. The chimney was an enormous affair, nearly sixteen feet in width and the wide-mouthed old fireplace was spacious enough to hold entire cord wood sticks on great iron dogs, while on either side in the fireplac were benches...The cellar, which was under the front part of the building...It was of dressed stone, the joints were true, every stone set square...The front room, which was used as a sleeping room, was spacious, as the sitting room back of it, but both these apartments, as well as the ones above were without means of warmth in winter."[2]

The newspapers mention frame houses but only two framed:

1768 "framed dwelling house, with stone chimney, two rooms on a floor"[3] Robert Elliot (Radnor Twp.)

1773 "framed dwelling house"[4] Abraham Marshall, Est. (Upper Darby Twp.)

The 1798 Direct Tax lists one hundred and forty-five frame houses, the mean size being 583 square feet, and thirteen frame and log houses the mean size being 637 square feet and six brick and frame houses, the mean size being 557 square feet. The 1799 tax assessment for London Britain, Pikeland and West Marlboro Townships lists eight frame houses the mean size being 521 square feet. In 1862 Oliver Stoops, of East Nottingham Township had a "Frame House, 16 by 24 feet, weatherboarded and filled in with brick".[5]

1. Colonial Society of Pennsylvania, *RECORD OF THE COURTS OF CHESTER COUNTY PENNSYLVANIA 1881-1697* (Philadelphia, Penna.) p. 190.
2. Henry Graham Ashmead, *HISTORICAL SKETCH OF CHESTER, ON DELAWARE.* (Republican Steam Printing House, 1883) p. 63.
3. *PENNSYLVANIA GAZETTE* (Philadelphia, Penna.) Feb. 18, 1768.
4. Ibid., May 12, 1773.
5. *AMERICAN REPUBLICAN* (West Chester, Penna.) June 24, 1862.

INDIANS

William Penn, in 1683, described the houses of the Delaware Indians.

> Their Houses are Mats, or Bark of Trees set on Poles, in the fashion of an English Barn, but out of the power of the Winds, for they are hardly higher than a Man; they lie on Reeds or Grass. In Travel they lodge in the Woods about a great Fire, with the Mantle of Duffels they wear by day, wrapt about them, and a few Boughs stuck round them.[1]
>
> If an European comes to see them, or calls for Lodging at their House or Wigwam they give him the best place and first cut.[2]

1. Myers, Albert Cook, *WILLIAM PENN HIS OWN ACCOUNT OF THE LENNI LENAPE OR DELAWARE INDIANS 1683* (Moylan, Penna., 1937) p. 31.
2. Ibid., p. 32.

IRON

In 1883 a newspaper mentions:

SOMETHING NEW UNDER THE SUN IN THE WAY OF A RESIDENCE.

George L. Huston, of Parkesburg, Chester county, will build a palatial private mansion for himself entirely of iron, the foundations of solid rock. The architect is an Englishman, whom Mr. Huston recently met while abroad. The iron-work is now being turned out at

Coatesville, as the superstructure is to be of iron entirely. The floor of the hall, vestibule and library will be laid with polished cast-iron tiles, in which different qualities of iron will be used to produce the same variety of color as in ordinary tile flooring. All the other floors of the house will be of stout iron plates firmly bolted to the iron joists. The outside wall and inside partitions all through the structure will be composed of two courses of iron plates, firmly bolted together so as to be air-tight. These hollow iron walls and partitions will be used instead of chimneys and for conveying heat to different parts of the house, and for ventilation. The hot smoke and gases from the furnaces passing through the sides of the rooms in this way, it is claimed, be almost sufficient to keep the house comfortable in the coldest weather, so that the heating can be done with about one-half the fuel required in ordinary houses. All the doors and window sashes will also be iron, but be constructed in such a light way and so nicely balanced upon hinges and weights as to open and shut as easily as those made of wood. All the inside walls and partitions will be handsomely painted and frescoed so as to present the appearance of any ordinary house finished in plaster. Outside, the style of architecture will be light and graceful, and it will be painted and ornamented so as to look as if it was built of wood. The roof will be of strong boiler plate, and the top, at the convergence of the four gables, will be a handsome observatory supported at the four corners by four Ironic pillars of iron. Inside the ornaments will be made of the same material. In the parlor will be a mantel of polished steel, handsomely ornamented. There will be a similar one in the dining room, upon which will be engraved hunting scenes. In the library will be a massive mantel so constructed that it will look as if it were made of pig iron fused together. Quite a curiosity in this room will be a cabinet for the exhibition of specimens of iron. This will be constructed entirely of strongly magnetized iron, so that all the specimens will adhere to the back of it, held in place solely by magnetic attraction. In order to guard against the bungling which would take place in such a solid iron structure on account of the contraction and expansion caused by the heat and cold, there will be breaks in the iron at intervals, which will be filled with rubber, so that when expansion takes place there will be room for it without producing any change in

the contour of the frame work. As much as possible of the furniture will also be of iron, so that if it takes fire in any part, nothing can burn but the carpets and the few articles of wood that may be within reach of the flames. The house will be an architectural and scientific curiosity. Mr. Huston admits that it may cost twice or three times as much as any ordinary house; but claims that with a little attention it will last for centuries without repairs, and will never cost a cent for insurance.[1]

1.   *DAILY LOCAL NEWS* (West Chester, Penna.) Jan. 4, 1883.

LOG

The will of Henry Shengle, of Coventry Township, in 1785 instructed "my Estate Shall build a little House thereon for her [wife] Use the Logs to be Cut twenty feet Long and Eighteen feet wide One Story high with a Stone Chimney & floors fitting for her to live in."[1]

John Hill Brinton's diary mentions that "When going to Wilmington in 1797 the only stone houses from the Turk at West Chester was 5/8 of a mile below West Chester — then the old 1704 house[2]...All the other houses were log along the road."[3]

The 1798 Direct Tax lists one thousand one hundred and fifty-three log houses, the mean size being 418 square feet; two log and boarded houses, the mean size being 573 square feet; one log house weatherboarded of 1147 square feet; five log and stone houses, the mean size being 948 square feet and two log and plank houses the mean size being 688 square feet. The 1796 tax assessment for East Fallowfield Township lists sixty log houses, the mean size being 464 square feet. The 1799 tax assessment for Charlestown, London Britain, Pikeland, West Marlboro and West Nottingham Townships lists two hundred and forty-six log houses the mean size being 385 square feet. In West Nottingham Township Joseph Coulson had "2 log houses Under one roof 1 Story high"; Jacob Juss had "2 old Log houses Under one roof" and Joseph Brown has "2 little Log houses Under one roof." In Honey Brook Township Abraham Curtz had "A Dwelling house and barn of Logs Covered with Straw and Shingles under one Roof."

The newspapers mention in 1814 "a chestnut log Dwelling House" belonging to Samuel Cochran, In West Fallowfield Township.[4] A few of the early log houses are described:

1884 "Two of the plaster and lath houses which are being raised to the ground on South High street was originally log huts"[5] West Chester

1887 "The old log house...being raised to ground...said to be one of first built in this section...This house being built of white ash logs."[6] Kennett Square

1887 "Among the old landmarks which lie near the village of Berwin...It consists of a story and a half log cabin, built upon the slope of a hill...[chimney] The wall at this end of the house is of stone, and measures over six feet in thickness. The original thatched roof has given place to one of shingles...The same rafters and joists remain...The joists penetrate and project beyond the outer walls several inches. They are hewed by hand and are remarkable true. The house is built upon a large rock, which may be seen in the cellar."[7]

1954 "The log dwelling probably had been at first a house of one room downstairs and two above. The stairway circling the chimney. The great fireplace on the east end of the house served for cooking and for the family gathering place. A one-story lean-to was an early addition on the east, perhaps to shelter an oven. The west end was also extended one step down and two stories high to provide a workshop and loft. The loft was reached by a stairway in this west addition. The outer logs were exposed in those days, but the house is now covered with clapboards, painted cream-color, with green trim and in good order."[8]

Log houses continued to be built in the twentieth century: "The handsome log cabin on the John Wyeth property in Thornbury Township is entirely completed...It is 40 x 60 feet and built of the finest North Carolina pine logs. The grounds are artistically laid out and planted with many trees."[9]

1. Chester County Will Book 7, p. 339.
2. John Hill Brinton, Ms. Diary, Chester County Historical Society (West Chester, Penna.) Vol. 2, p. 131.
3. Ibid., Vol 1, p. 132.
4. *CHESTER & DELAWARE FEDERALIST* (West Chester, Penna.) Dec. 14, 1814.
5. *DAILY LOCAL NEWS* (West Chester, Penna.) July 19, 1884.
6. Ibid., April 6, 1887.
7. Ibid., July 2, 1887.
8. Ibid., Jan. 7, 1954.
9. Ibid., Sept. 12, 1903.

LOG HEWN

The Morten Mortenson log house which is located at Prospect Park near Essington is described by C. A. Weslager as "The earliest section, a dwelling of closely-fitted hewn oak logs, dovetailed and flush at the corners...A second unit of hewn pine and chestnut logs also dovetailed and flush at the corners, was built alongside the first at a later date (1698 is usually given for this unit and 1654 for the earlier one, but I have been unable to substantiate either date), and the two cabins were connected by a passage. The older unit has the characteristic Swedish-Finnish corner fireplace and chimney."[1]

The earliest mentions of hewn log houses found in the newspapers are:

1761 "hewn Log House"[2] Francis Wayne (Willistown Twp.)
1773 "hewn log house, cellared underneath, and covered with ceder"[3] Jason Cloud (West Nantmeal Twp.)
1785 "stone dwelling house and kitchen, part stone and part hewed logs"[4] Samuel Vanleer (Easttown Twp.)
1787 "hewn log dwelling house, 20 by 30 feet, 4 rooms on the lower floor...loft and cellar"[5] Jesse Reynolds (West Nottingham Twp.)
1818 "two story hewed log dwelling house, 20 by 22 feet, with a porch in front"[6] Jesse Thomas (Londonderry Twp.)

Before 1820 the newspapers mention eight other hewn log houses and one other stone and hewn log house. The 1798 Direct Tax lists for East Caln Township ten hewn log houses, four hewn log houses with stone "chunking", one hewn log partly plank house, one round and hewn log house, one hewn log kitchen and one hewn log section of a house. The tax for West Whiteland Township lists six hewn log houses with stone "chunking", four hewn log houses, two hewn log kitchens and one hewn log section of a house.

1. C. A. Weslager, *THE LOG CABIN IN AMERICA FROM PIONEER DAYS TO THE PRESENT* (New Brunswick, New Jersey, 1969), p. 166, 167.
2. *PENNSYLVANIA GAZETTE* (Philadelphia, Penna.) March 5, 1761.
3. Ibid., April 28, 1773.
4. Ibid., Aug. 31, 1785.
5. Ibid., Feb. 28, 1787.
6. *VILLAGE RECORD* (West Chester, Penna.) Aug. 12, 1818

LOG ROUND

Two seventeenth century round log houses are described by C. A. Weslager. The earliest said to have been erected between 1643 and 1653 "the top ends of the logs are cut in pear shape to mesh with the V notch in the bottom of each log. This dwelling has two rooms but in reality it was constructed as two cabins butting against each other, and each has the distinctive corner fireplace. The presence of corner fireplaces in these early cabins appears indicative of their Scandinavian antecedents. Nearby at Clifton Heights is a second round-log cabin also of Scandinavian origin said to have been erected about 1650. Although this date has not been authenticated, the dwelling is unquestionably a seventeenth century survival. Like the first, it, too, consists of two rooms, although the logs are saddle-notched with their ends extending well beyond the corners of the walls."[1]

The will of Joseph McClackey, farmer, in Chester County, in 1754 mentions "a round Log House Sixteen feet Square with a Chimney made of wood and Lath'd & fil'd with Clay, with two Boarded Floors dores and Windows."[2]

The 1798 Direct Tax for East Caln Township lists thirty-two round log houses and one round and hewn log house. For West Whiteland Township the tax lists seventeen round log houses and one round log kitchen.

The newspapers mention:

1762 "round Log House, with a stone Chimney, and an Oven"[3] Richard Thatcher (Kennett Twp.)

1771 "round log house, two stories high"[4] Alexander Boyd (Easttown Twp.)

1. C. A. Weslager, *THE LOG CABIN IN AMERICA FROM PIONEER DAYS TO THE PRESENT* (New Brunswick, New Jersey, 1969), pp. 167, 168.
2. Chester County Will Book 3, p. 472.
3. *PENNSYLVANIA GAZETTE* (Philadelphia, Penna.) April 8, 1762.
4. Ibid., Oct. 24, 1771.

LOG SAWED

The 1798 Direct Tax for Middletown and part of Lower Providence Townships lists Levi Lewis with a stone house, 1 story 24 x 18 with a kitchen one hundred years old of sawed logs and in Radnor Township Jacob Siter had a two story house 45 x 19 "Saw'd logs weather boarded".

The will of Charles Humphrey, of Haverford Township, in 1785 mentions: "I order my Executors to build them the said Tom & Judy [servants] a good Sawed Log House with Stone Chimney."[1]

The newspapers mention:

1761 "sawed Log-house"[2] Rowland Perry (Haverford Twp.)

1795 "dwelling house...part stone and part sawed log"[3] George King, Est. (Willistown Twp.)

1833 "Frame house, part stone and part sawed log, plastered inside and out"[4] Benjamin Windle (East Marlboro Twp.)

During this period the newspapers mention one other sawed log dwelling house.

1. Chester County Will Book 8, p. 32.
2. *PENNSYLVANIA GAZETTE* (Phila., Penna.) April 30, 1761.
3. Ibid., Jan. 21, 1795.
4. *AMERICAN REPUBLICAN* (West Chester, Penna.) Oct. 29, 1833.

SQUARED LOG

In the newspapers squared log houses were the most frequently mentioned:

1742 "new square Logg House, Cellared under"[1] Robert Mickle (East Marlboro Twp.)

1761 "square Log House, Brick Chimney"[2] Jane Jenkins, Nathaniel Pennock (New Garden Twp.)

1763 "Dwelling House, Part Stone and Part Square Logs"[3] John Rogers (Sadsbury Twp.)

1763 "square Log-house, with a Stone Gable end"[4] John Best (Tredyffrin Twp.)

1766 "Stone House, and square Log House adjoining"[5] John Bocas (Sadsbury Twp.)

1770 "square log house, lately raised, 30 feet square"[6] William Graham (Londonderry Twp.)

1772 "dwelling house is part brick with stone, and part with squared logs"[7] Alexander Sumrall (Sadsbury Twp.)

1773 "squared log house, 30 feet by 20"[8] Thomas Elliot (Easttown Twp.)

1781 "two story stone dwelling house, with a squared log kitchen adjoining"[9] Thomas Mateer (Birmingham Twp.)

1783 "square log house, 20 by 32 feet, one and a half story high"[10] William Harris

1792 "square log house 32 by 30 feet...two stories high with four rooms below and four above stairs, five fire places"[11] Jonathan Valentine (West Bradford Twp.)

1799 "square log house, nearly new, 26 feet by 18"[12] Michael Lapp (East Whiteland Twp.)

1813 "square log dwelling house and store, with a stone kitchen adjoining"[13] James Miller (New Garden Twp.)

1814 "square-log house chunk'd with stone"[14] Jacob Binder (Pikeland Twp.)

1815 "square log house, chunked with stone"[15] William Williams (Brandywine Twp.)

The newspapers mention before 1812 forty-one other squared log houses, three square log houses with gable ends, two stone houses with square log houses adjoining, and two other stone houses with squared log kitchens adjoining.

1. *PENNSYLVANIA GAZETTE* (Phiadelphia, Penna.) March 10, 1742.
2. Ibid., March 19, 1761.
3. Ibid., April 7, 1763.
4. Ibid., June 2, 1763.
5. Ibid., May 8, 1766.
6. Ibid., May 31, 1770.
7. Ibid., Aug. 12, 1772.
8. Ibid., Jan. 20, 1773.
9. Ibid., Aug. 22, 1781.
10. Ibid., Nov. 19, 1783.
11. Ibid., Feb. 29, 1792.
12. Ibid., Feb. 20, 1799.
13. *CHESTER & DELAWARE FEDERALIST* (West Chester, Penna.) Nov. 3, 1813.
14. *AMERICAN REPUBLICAN* (West Chester, Penna.) June 7, 1814.
15. Ibid., Oct. 17, 1815.

LOG SWEDISH

C. A. Weslogen in *The Historical Society of Delaware Bulletin* complied the following descriptions of log buildings built by the Swedish in Chester County:

> FORT NEW GOTHENBURG ON TINICUM ISLAND: "a strong fort, made of hemlock logs laid one upon the other." (Andries Hudde, "Report" in The Instruction for John Printz... ed. by Amandus Johnson [Phila. 1930], p. 257).

PRINTZ HALL (PRINTOFF) ON TINICUM ISLAND: constructed in 1644 and in all likelihood built of hewn logs, two stories high, some interior woodwork brought from Sweden, two or more fireplaces made of bricks; the house had glass windows. The "Fama" in 1644 brought six thousand bricks for use in chimneys and fireplaces; twenty-four pieces of window glass were brought from Sweden in the same year (Johnson, Instruction for Printz, pp. 26-27; Johnson, Swedish Settlements, 1, 348). There was a log storehouse on the land site of the island where merchandise and provisions were stored. (Johnson, Swedish Settlements, 1, 364).

CHURCH ON TINICUM ISLAND was erected of wood, not in 1649 as stated by Tobias Biorck, Graduation Dissertation (translated by Nothstein [1943], p. 18), but was erected in 1646, made of logs with a clapboard roof. (Johnson, Instruction for Printz, pp. 33, 131). Two thousand clapboards for the roof were bought from the English. (Johnson, Swedish Settlements, 1, 366).

"On this point [Tinicum Island] three or four houses are standing, built by the Swedes, a little Lutheran Church made of logs, and the remains of the large block-house which served them in place of a fortress, with the ruins of some log huts." (Jaspar Dankets and Peter Sluyter, Journal of a Voyage to New York and Tour...1679-80 [Brooklyn, 1867], p. 178, published as Vol. 1 of the Memoirs of the Long Island Historical Society).

BATHHOUSE. A "bastu" made of logs on Tinicum Island was built for the use of Printz and his family. (Johnson, Swedish Settlements, 1, 358).

FORT VASA AT KINGSESSING. Here Printz built "a fine house" (Johnson, Instruction for Printz, p. 131), which was also called a "strong building." (Hudde, "Report," ibid., p. 257). It was later described as "five families dwelt together in houses two stories high built of white nut tree (hickory) which at that time was reguarted as the best material for building houses, but in later times was altogether disapproved of for such purposes." (Acrelius, History, p. 46). "It was not properly a fort, but substantial log houses, built of good strong, hard hickory, two stories high." (Campanius, Description, p. 81).

BLOCKHOUSE AT UPLAND (Chester, Pennsylvania). Built in 1643, it was described by Printz as "a strong wooden house." (Johnson, Instruction for Printz, p. 112). Since Printz uses identical words to describe Fort Korsholm which we know to have been of logs, it seems reasonable to suppose that the Upland blockhouse was also built of logs.

GRIST MILL ON COBB'S CREEK was built by the summer or autumn of 1646 (Ibid., p. 33). The settlement at the mill was called "Molndal." (Johnson, Swedish Settlements, 1, 328). "There was no fort near it, but only a strong dwelling house built of hickory [logs]" (Campanius, Description, p. 81).[1]

Jasper Dancraerts, a Dutch traveler, in 1678 stayed overnight in a log house in the Delaware Valley constructed in the Swedish fashion:

> The house although not much larger than where we spent the last night, was somewhat better and tighter, being made according to the Swedish mode, and as they usually build their houses here, which are blockhouses, or houses of hewn logs being nothing else than entire trees, split through the middle or somewhat squared out of the rough, these trees are laid in the form of a square upon each other as high as they wish to have the house, the ends of these timbers are let into each other, about a foot from the ends of them. So stands the whole building without nail or spike, the ceiling and the roof do not show much finer work, except among the most particular who also have all the ceilings planked and also a glass window. The doors are wide enough but very low, so that everyone must stoop to enter in, always these houses are tight and warm, but the chimney stands in the corner.[2]

Peter Kalm, a Swedish naturalist, traveling in the Delaware Valley between 1748 and 1751 mentioned:

> The houses which the Swedes built when they first settled here were very bad. The whole house consisted of one little room, the door of which was so low that one was obliged to stoop in order to get in. As they had brought no glass with them, they were obliged to be contented with little holes, before which a board was fastened. They found no moss, or at least none which could have been serviceable when stopping holes or cracks in the walls. They were forced to close them both without and within with clay. The chimneys were made in a corner, either with gray sandstone, or in places where no stone was to be got, by mere clay which they laid very thick in one corner of the house. The ovens for baking were always in the rooms.[3]

The Swedes' houses were formerly all of wood, with clay daubed between the logs, no doubt like those the Irish now build here. They have no glass in the windows, but small open holes with a shutter or sliding board in front, so were quite like our Finnish cabin window.[4]

1. C.A. Weslager, *LOG STRUCTURES IN NEW SWEDEN DURING THE SEVENTEENTH CENTURY* (Delaware History Magazine, 1952) Vol 5, pp. 84, 85.
2. Harold Donaldson Eberlain and Cortlandt V. D. Hubbard, *HISTORIC HOUSES AND BUILDINGS OF DELAWARE* (Dover, Del., 1963), p. 5.
3. Henry C. Mercer, *THE ORIGIN OF LOG HOUSES IN THE UNITED STATES* (Bucks County Historical Society, Doylestown, Penna., 1924), p. 577.
4. Harold R. Shurleff, *THE LOG CABIN MYTH* (Harvard University Press, Cambridge, Mass., 1939), p. 176.

LOG & BOARDED

The 1798 Direct Tax lists two log and boarded houses, the mean size being 573 square feet.

MUD

The 1798 Direct Tax for Coventry Township lists the house of Elizabeth Hofacker as "Sones Wols of Moth Cracked", Martin Rinehart with "Mud Walls of stone" kitchen 30 x 28, 1½ stories high. John High with house "Moth wols of stone 33 x 26" and Rudolph Harles with house "Moth wols of stone 32 x 23 1 story." The same tax for Vincent Township lists the heirs of Laurence Hipple as having "Stone wols of Mode with kitchen 30 x 19". The 1796 tax assessment for New London Township lists Isaac Ryan as having a mud house and barn and Samuel Ramsey, of Londonderry Township, with "old mud wall house." The 1799 tax assessment lists Thomas Simmons, of Londonderry Township, with "old Mud house", Isaac Tyan, of New London Township, with "Mud wol House old" and Ezekiel Hopkins, of Upper Oxford Township, with one mud house.

PLANK

The Brinton diary mentions the following use of plank. The Brinton cabin was "Poplar plank 4½ inches thick, by some 15 inches wide — sawed G. B. thinks with a whip saw — yellow poplar — which the Emigrants selected always — dovetailed at the ends — Wood used in later house for lintels over windows, & rail for stairs."[1] The Bennett house was "Made of plank, clapboarded, & filled in".[2] The Thatcher cabin "was built of 3 inch yellow poplar plank, sawed by a whip saw & remained sound to the last."[3] The "1712 Brinton house. Fronted south — the cellar was walled & above that the superstructure was plank painted red & it was known as the red house."[4] The original Pierce

house was a "Small building, of poplar plank, dovetailed, & three planks were pinned together perpendicularly which made it strong."[5] The Chadd's mill had a "sound plank floor & sleepers".[6]

The newspaper advertisements mention:

1780 "stables, the floor planked and divided into five stalls"[7] Printer

1815 "a complete shop built of plank, 14 feet by 18"[8] James Morton (New Garden Twp.)

The 1798 Direct Tax lists fourteen plank houses, the mean size being 181 square feet.

1. John H. Brinton Diary #1, p. 86 under date Nov. 4, 1857, Chester County Historical Society (West Chester, Penna.)
2. Ibid., under date June 3, 1858.
3. Ibid., #3, p. 23 under date May 13, 1884.
4. Ibid., p. 36 under date June 2, 1891.
5. Ibid., #1, p. 122 under date July 27, 1861.
6. Ibid., p. 88 under date July 6, 1864.
7. *PENNSYLVANIA GAZETTE* (Phila., Penna.) May 10, 1780.
8. *AMERICAN REPUBLICAN* (West Chester, Penna.) Aug. 15, 1815.

PALISADE CONSTRUCTION

Palisade construction, as in the earliest timber construction in England, thus far, has not been found in the county altho there has been a rumor of such construction used in lower Berks county. Gawen Lawrie, in 1684, mentions of the houses of the first British settlers in East Jersey:

> The poor sort set up a house of two or three rooms themselves, after this manner; the walls are of cloven timber about eight or ten inches broard, like planks set one end to the ground, and the other vailed to the rising, which they plaster within.[1]

Since this method of building was used in the Delaware Valley there is a possibility that it was also used in Chester County.

1. Samuel Smith, *THE HISTORY OF THE COLONY OF NOVA-CAESARIA, OR NEW-JERSEY* (Burlington, N.J., 1765), p. 180.

SLAB

The 1798 Direct Tax lists Mary Vernon, of Springfield and part of Lower Providence Townships with "Slab House very indifferent 24 x 22"; John Worall, of Springfield and part of Lower Providence Townships, with "Slab House very ordinary 20 x 12".

STONE

John H. Brinton's diary mentions that "The old stone

houses were built of stones something like bricks, thin & laid in layers"[1] and that the "Brinton 1704 house, Joseph Brinton 1712, Wm. Brinton 1713, Ann Brinton Cox, Joseph Eavenson, Mercer house. They were the first stone houses. Very steep roofs, a story high, with garret rooms, fire places for wood cord length, with seat in the corner, lead sash, very thick walls, small one pane windows in places. In 1712 house the kitchen was detached. Steep roof owing to an early idea of heavy snows."[2]

The 1798 Direct Tax lists nine hundred and thirty-six stone houses, the mean size being 781 square feet. The 1796 tax assessment for East Fallowfield Township lists twenty-one stone houses, the mean size being 656 square feet. The 1799 tax assessment for Charlestown, London Britain, Pikeland, West Nottingham and West Marlboro Townships lists one hundred and sixty-six houses the mean size being 690 square feet.

The newspapers mention a few interesting stone houses:

1821 "John Marshall's Old House. It was built in Revolutionary War Days in 1776...The walls of stone are as smooth and even as glass, and boards 3½ feet wide were used in its makeup...Another feature of this ancient building is the old fashioned water-eve, and there is the proverbial "hole in the wall."[3]

1866 "[house] one of oldest in West Chester, its walls being stone and of immense thickness"[4] High Street (West Chester)

1869 "building fine pointed stone building for store & dwelling"[5] Franklin Diermer, (Spring City)

1871 "House is built of Cut Stone, squared and pointed on all sides."[6] J. W. Barnard (West Goshen Twp.)

1880 "An Old House Torn Down — One of the oldest, if not the oldest stone dwelling house in East Vincent Township...It was built by Philip Thomas, in 1755, and in its erection clay was used instead of mortar made with lime and sand"[7]

1. John H. Brinton diary #2, Chester County Historical Society (West Chester, Penna.) p. 21 under date Sept. 14, 1869.
2. John H. Brinton diary #2, Chester County Historical Society (West Chester, Penna.) p. 23, under date Feb. 6, 1885.
3. Source cannot be found.
4. *AMERICAN REPUBLICAN* (West Chester, Penna.) Sept. 4, 1866.
5. Ibid., Nov. 2, 1869.
6. *VILLAGE RECORD* (West Chester, Penna.) Sept. 23, 1871.
7. *DAILY LOCAL NEWS* (West Chester, Penna.) July 8, 1880.

STONE, BRICK AND FRAME

The 1798 Direct Tax lists two stone, brick and frame houses, the mean size being 780 square feet. The 1799 tax assessment for West Marlboro Township lists one stone brick and frame house 1410 square feet.

STONE AND FRAME

The 1798 Direct Tax lists seventeen stone and frame houses, the mean size being 591 square feet. The 1799 tax assessment for Pikeland and West Marlboro Townships list three stone and frame houses, the mean size being 570 square feet.

STONE AND LOG

The 1798 Direct Tax lists fifty-five stone and log houses, the mean size being 631 square feet. The 1796 tax assessment for East Fallowfield Township lists three stone and log houses, the mean size being 603 square feet and the 1799 tax assessment for Charlestown, Pikeland and West Marlboro Townships lists twenty-two stone and log houses, the mean size being 848 square feet.

STONE, LOG AND FRAME

The 1798 Direct Tax lists one stone, log and frame house of 680 square feet.

STONE AND BRICK

The 1798 Direct Tax lists twenty-seven stone and brick houses, the mean size being 1203 square feet.

A newspaper mentions:

1888 "Joseph Murtagh has now nearly completed a fourteen roomed residence at the corner of Church and Biddle streets. It is constructed in the main of stone, but the upper stories of the rear building are of brick. The stone consists of unhewn boulders of large size, and are neatly pointed. It is roofed with shingles stained green by means of creosote. It will be fitted up with both gas and electric light, electric bells, hot and cold water and furnaces for heating the building throughout."[1] (West Chester)

1. *DAILY LOCAL NEWS* (West Chester, Penna.) Nov. 17, 1888.

STONE AND TIMBER

The 1798 Direct Tax lists three stone and timber houses, the mean size being 698 square feet.

STONE AND WOOD

The 1798 Direct Tax lists twelve stone and wood houses, the mean size being 859 square feet.

TIMBER

The 1798 Direct Tax lists seven timber houses; the mean size being 547 square feet.

WOOD

The 1798 Direct Tax lists sixty-three wood houses, the mean size being 466 square feet. The 1799 tax assessment for Charlestown Township lists one wood house 480 square feet.

ARCHITECTURAL DETAILS FOUND IN CHESTER COUNTY WILLS

The following chronological list of quotes will illustrate the sort of details found in the county wills prior to 1816.

1731 "[wife] Priviledge of my Lodging Room...my son Joseph shall build her a Corner Chimney of Brick in the said Room" Joseph Baker (Edgemont Twp.)[1]

1747 "use of the new building at the East end of my sd house with the buttery thereto adjoining" John Brinton (Kennett Twp.)[2]

1753 "[executors] build for my loving wife a round log house sixteen foot square with a chimney made of wood and lath'd & filled with clay, two boarded floors, doors and windows" Joseph McClosky (Chester County)[3]

1756 "[son] shall Build a Convenient House upon some convenient place near my dwelling House. The House to be built is to be made with Stone Walls fifteen feet in breadth and twenty feet in length in the Clear and twelve feet in height to the Square of Said House, the said House to be completely furnished" Llewellin David (Charlestown Twp.)[4]

1760 "my two sons shall build her a Convenient house upon my Plantation of sixteen feet by twenty and make it Commodious for her to dwell in" Joseph Smith (Oxford Twp.)[5]

1762 "[wife] my stone Kitchen adjoining my dwelling House" Henry Lawrence (Haverford Twp.)[6]

1762 "[wife] my Springhouse and one half of the wash and Bakehouse adjoining there" Henry Lawrence (Haverford Twp.)[7]

1764 "Allow her a Room in my now dwelling House with a Chimney in it to be partitioned off from the Kitchen door to Room door"[8] Thomas Yarnall (Edgemont Twp.)

1768 "[wife] stone Messuage commonly called Grandfather's Room" Cadwallader Evans (Edgemont Twp.)[9]

1779 "Son David to build a good Frame Kitchen at the Plantation adjoining to the House the width of the same" David Cowpland (Chester)[10]

1779 "[wife] but if she chuses to live by her self in the little house at the end of my Dwelling house" William Brown (East Nantmeal Twp.)[11]

1780 "my Executor herein named to Build a house Sixteen feet Square" John Smith Sen. (Oxford Twp.)[12]

1782 "Wife Should Incline or be Desirous to finish a Small Stone House which I have begun which I am Rather Desirous that She might according to my Plan" Justice Linderman (Coventry Twp.)[13]

1783 "[wife] Benefits of my stone Building with the Appurtenances at the East end of my old wooden Building" Isaac Allen (New Garden Twp.)[14]

1784 "my Estate Shall build a little House thereon for her use the Logs to be Cut twenty feet Long & Eighteen feet wide One Story high with a Stone Chimney & floors fitting for her to live in likewise Rails & Stakes for fencing...I do order a Small Stable be built for her twelve feet Square to be covered Straw and to be Raised So high as will be Sufficient to hold Hay enough at one time to winter a Cow" Henry Shengle (Coventry Twp.)[15]

1785 "I order my Executors to build them the said Tom & Judy [servants] a good Sawed Log House with a Stone Chimney" Charles Humphrys (Haverford Twp.)[16]

1788 "priviledge of our Lodging Room which may be enlarged to the front door by a partition if she shall think it needful and a small room up stairs over the same (which may be made by a partition) & part of the Cellar at the East Corner which may be also partition" William Lamplugh (Upper Chichester Twp.)[17]

1790 "to have a Corner cupboard built and put up in either of the Rooms she my wife shall direct, and in case she think fit to have a partition put in the Kitchen loft and Cellar" John Pugh (East Nottingham Twp.)[18]

1790 "Executors to build a House...Sixteen feet by Twenty, one story & a half high with two Floors, viz an upper & lower floor with a corner chimney" Samuel Futhey (West Fallowfield Twp.)[19]

1795 "one half the Cellar to be Partitioned off for her [wife] own use" John Phipps (Uwchlan Twp.)[20]

1795 "[nephew] to Build and finish her the first year a good Warm Room fourteen feet Square with A good fire place so that She may Cook & to put A good ten plate Stove & Pipe in the room and said Room to be build adjoin the dwelling house" John Smith (Coventry Twp.)[21]

1797 "[wife] all that my Stone dwelling house last built at the east end of my other Stone House with the Seller underneath the same" Isaac Mendenhall (Pennsbury Twp.)[22]

1798 "[wife] Sole use of my stone House and Kitchen

adjoining two Rooms in the Loghouse one up and one down stairs" Samuel Lewis (West Whiteland Twp.)[23]

1799 "[wife] stone end of the house and the bed room adjoining it in the log end" Richard Peirsol (Chester County)[24]

1803 "[wife] One room below stairs beside the Kitchen or the Room over the Kitchen should she chuse the latter the partition to be moved the length of two Joices to enlarge her room" John Showalter (Tredyffrin Twp.)[25]

1815 "[son] Shall Previously to his bringing a Wife into the family Build a convenient dwelling house of a proper Size and dimensions Chair house and Stable all Stone buildings the Stable Shall be large Enough to Contain two horses & two Cows Comfortably...He Also Shall dig a Well near sd house a Sufficient depth to furnish a good Supply of Water in the dryest Seasons Wall the Same and put a good pump therein and keep the whole in good repair" Thomas Downing (East Caln Twp.)[26]

1. Chester County Will Book 1, p. 448.
2. Ibid., Book 3, p. 21
3. Ibid., p. 472.
4. Ibid., Book 4, p. 36.
5. Ibid., p. 222.
6. Ibid., p. 447.
7. Ibid., p. 557.
8. Ibid., p. 474.
9. Ibid., Book 7, p. 93.
10. Ibid., Book 6, p. 287.
11. Ibid., Book 8, P. 254.
12. Ibid., Book 7, p. 64.
13. Ibid., p. 100.
14. Ibid., p. 225.
15. Ibid., p. 339.
16. Ibid., Book 8, p. 32.
17. Ibid., p. 187.
18. Ibid., p. 460.
19. Ibid., p. 420.
20. Ibid., Book 9, p. 394.
21. Ibid., Book 10, p. 185.
22. Ibid., p. 425.
23. Ibid., p. 59.
24. Ibid., p. 167.
25. Ibid., Book 11, p. 130.
26. Ibid., Book 12, p. 112.

DOWER RIGHTS

Frequently in the wills, before 1816, the dower rights of a widow to a house, a section of a house or simply a room in a house, with or without privileges are specifically mentioned: one room (124 times); end of house (55 times); two rooms (36 times); a house (30 times); end of house with privileges (21 times); two rooms and cellar (14 times); half of house (12 times); a room and privilege of kitchen and cellar (7 times); three rooms and privilege of kitchen and cellar (3 times); four rooms and privilege of kitchen and cellar (3 times); son to build a new room (3 times); the house until son comes of age and then two rooms (2 times); a room and privilege of kitchen (2 times); two rooms and use of vault (2 times); a room and cellar (2 times); house and cellar (2 times); a room and privilege of cellar, kitchen and spring house (2 times); three rooms and privilege of cellar (2 times); three rooms and use of cellar, kitchen and well (2 times); four rooms (2 times); two rooms and kitchen (2 times); two rooms and privilege of kitchen and cellar (2 times) and three rooms and cellar (2 times).

The following are mentioned in the wills a single time: stone house and cellar, leanto, room with fireplace, lodging room and fireplace, house until son comes of age and then a new house, liberty to dwell in the house, room and privilege of cellar and dairy house, leanto with chambers and cellars belonging; parlour, room over the parlour, room at the head of stairs and the cellar; upper and lower room and cellar; parlour, room over the parlour and privilege of cellar and kitchen; west end of the house and privilege of kitchen, bake oven and milk house; parlour, chamber, kitchen and cellar; two rooms and privilege in other house and cellar; room, chamber above and privilege of the stairs, kitchen and cellar; two parlours, vault and privilege of the wash house, draw well and bake oven; two rooms and half of cellar; two lower rooms, cellar and liberty of pump or well in kitchen; parlour and room above; new building at the end of house, buttery and privilege of cellar and spring house; one room and half the cellar; new part of house and half of the kitchen; a room and privilege of milk house, oven, draw well and pump; two rooms, garden and privilege of fireplace and apartment in cellar; a room and privilege of cellar and dairy house; to build a log house; to build a stone house; privilege of three rooms, cellar, kitchen, oven, pump, half of the garden and half of the well house; two rooms and privilege of kitchen; one third of house, barn and stables; two rooms, half the cellar and privilege of the garden; a room, closet and cellar; two rooms and privilege of kitchen, cellar, oven and draw well; a room, part of the cellar and privilege of the oven; room with bake oven etc, in house adjoining; rooms and the use of the kitchen oven; a room, corner in the cellar and privilege of the kitchen; end of house and privilege of kitchen, oven and cellar; a room, cellar and garden; two and a half rooms and the use of the kitchen; a room and privilege of cellar, kitchen and well; two rooms and part of the cellar and milk house; three rooms, cellar and build her a milk house; four rooms, cellars and privilege of the well house and kitchen; two rooms, arch in the cellar and privilege of the kitchen; two rooms and privilege of kitchen, cellar and oven; two rooms, half of the cellar, kitchen and part of the spring and well house; three rooms and privilege of cellar, garret and entry; four rooms and cellar; three rooms and privilege of the kitchen, oven, cellar, arch and garret; three rooms and the use of the cellar, spring house and kitchen and three rooms and the use of the cellar and porch.

During this period some wills bequeath rooms and privileges extended to other members of the family. For a daughter: a room (9 times); two rooms (3 times); upper house of new building (1 time) two rooms and privilege of cellar, kitchen and draw well (1 time); the kitchen, half the cellar, parlour, half the spring house and half of the wash and bake house (1 time); three rooms (1 time); three rooms, garret and privilege of cellar (1 time); two rooms and cellar (1 time) and build her a house (1 time). A daughter-in-law is granted two rooms and part of the cellar. In three cases sisters are bequeathed: front parlour and privilege of the common room; one room and privilege of out kitchen; two rooms and one room. One son orders that a house be built for his father and one man orders that a log house be built for the servants.

Eight out of the forty-five Chester County inventories before 1700 mention room names:

1685	William Wood	Garret, Kitchen, Parlour chamber, Parlour, Chamber
1688	George Gleave	Upper room, Parlour
1688	John Harding	Chamber, Cork loft, Kitchen, Shed
1689	Richard Flow	Upper chamber, Two back rooms, Kitchen, Cellar
1693	Joshua Fearn	Large parlour, Little parlour, Chamber
1697	Maurice Trent	Lower chamber, Hall chamber, Kitchen, Hall
1698	Robert Wade	Chamber next the river, Back chamber from the river, Chamber on the ground floor, Servant's room, Kitchen
1698	John Hodgssins	Fore street chamber, Middle chamber, Great fore room above stairs, Common room below, Dining room, Kitchen, Best room, Little room, Buttery, Parlour

Garret is defined by Bailey (ed. 1735) as "the uppermost Floor in an House", by Sheridan (ed. 1789) as "a room on the highest floor of the house" and by Webster (ed. 1828) as "That part of a house which is on the upper floor, immediately under the roof. Kitchen is defined by Bailey (ed. 1735) as "a Room where Meat is dressed, &c., also Kitchen Stuff, i.e. grease", by Sheridan (ed. 1789) as "the room in a house where provisions are cooked" and by Webster (ed. 1828) as "A cook-room in a house where the provisions are cooked." Parlour is defined by Bailey (ed.

1735) as "a low Room to receive Company in", by Sheridan (ed. 1789) as "a room in houses on the first floor, elegantly furnished for reception or entertainment" and by Webster (ed. 1828) as "Primarily, the apartment in a nunnery where the nuns are permitted to meet and converse with each other; hence with us, the room in a house where the family usually occupy when they have no company, as distinguished from a drawing room intended for the reception of company, or for a dining room, when a distinct apartment is allotted for that purpose. In most houses, the parlor is also the dining room."

Chamber is defined by Bailey (ed. 1735) as "an Apartment or Room in a House", by Sheridan (ed. 1789) as "an apartment in a house, generally used for those appropriated to lodging" and by Webster (ed. 1828) as "An apartment in an upper story, or in a story above the lower floor of a dwelling house; often used as a Lodging room. Any retired room; any private apartment which a person occupies..." Loft is defined by Bailey (ed. 1735) as "an upper Floor of a House" by Sheridan (ed. 1789) as "a floor; the highest floor" and by Webster (ed. 1828) as "Properly, an elevation; hence, in a building, the elevation of one story or floor above another; hence a floor above another; as the second loft, third loft; fourth loft. Spenser seems to have used the word for the highest floor or top, and this may have been the original signification." Shed is defined by Bailey (ed. 1735) as "a Penthouse or Shelter made of Boards", by Sheridan (ed. 1789) as "a slight temporary covering" and by Webster (ed. 1828) as "A slight building; a covering of timber and boards, &c. for shelter against rain and the inclemencies of weather; a poor house, or hovel; as a horse-shed." Cellar is defined by Bailey (ed. 1735) as "the lowest Part of a Building under Ground", by Sheridan (ed. 1789) as "a place under ground, where stores are reposited; where liquors are kept" and by Webster (ed. 1828) as "A room under a house or other building, used as a repository of liquors, provisions, and other stores for a family."

Hall is defined by Bailey (ed. 1735) as "a large Room at the Entrance of an House", by Sheridan (ed. 1789) as "the first large room at the entrance of a house" and by Webster (ed. 1828) as "In architecture, a large room at the entrance of a house or palace." Bailey (ed. 1735) did not define dining room. It was defined by Sheridan (ed. 1789) as "the principle apartment of the house", and by Webster (ed. 1828) as "A room for a family or for company to dine in; a room for entertainments." Buttery is defined by Bailey (ed. 1735) as "a Place where Victuals is set up", by Sheridan (ed. 1789) as "the room where provisions are laid up" and by Webster (ed. 1828) as "An apartment in a house, where butter, milk, provisions and utensils are kept."

Twenty-one out of the seventy-eight inventories between 1700 and 1710 mention rooms.

1701 John Rhoades   Hall, Parlour, Chamber, Out shed

1701 Peter Dicks   Parlour, Hall, Cellar, Chamber, Garret

1702 Henry Gibbons   Hall, Parlour, Kitchen, Kitchen chamber, Shed chamber, Kitchen chamber, Workhouse

1702 Nathaniell Parcks   Lodging room, Shed, Upper chamber, Lower chamber, Cellar

1702 John Radley   Chamber, Hall, Sheds

1703/4 Edmond Pritchard   Hall, Little house, House chamber

1703 Edmund Cartlidge   Hall, Parlour, Outshed, House chamber, Parlour chamber, Outshed to the house, Cellar

1704 James Mill   Closet, Room over the kitchen, Room next the street, Little room next the street, Another room next the street, Kitchen, Cellar

1704 Walter Faucatt   Old chamber, New garret, Parlour, Common room, Kitchen, Middle room, Cellar

1705 John Kirk   Hall, Parlour, Parlour chamber, Hall chamber, Garret, Cellar

1705 Thomas Smith   Kitchen, Passage, Old room, Passage chamber, Cellar room

1706 Richard Woodward   Common house, Kitchen, Parlour, Sheds, Chamber, Another chamber, Back kitchen, Work house, Cellar

1707 John Bethell   Hall, Closet, Chamber over the hall, Garret chamber, Chamber over the old house, Kitchen, Cellar under the hall, Cellar under the old house, Porch, corn Mill chamber, Toll garner

1707 Joseph Bushell   Kitchen, Chamber, Buttery

1708 Isaac Bartram   Dwelling house, Parlour, Parlour chamber, House chamber, Parlour over cellar, Kitchen

1708 Thomas Hope   Great chamber, Little chamber, Garret, Lower Room, Cellar

1708 Robert Scothome   House, Parlour, Kitchen, Kitchen chamber, Chamber over the house, Shed chamber, Shed over the well

1708 Ralph Fishbourn   Parlour, Outward room, Inward chamber, Garret, Shop, Porch, Kitchen, Cellar, New house, Closet, Outward room, Chamber, Cellar

1708 Peter Boss   Lower Room, Chamber, Garret

1709 Elizabeth Fishbourn   Shop, New house, Cellar, Parlour, Outer room, Garret, Chamber over the outer room, Chamber over the parlour, Kitchen

1709 John Bennett   Chamber, Garret, Kitchen

Closet is defined by Bailey (ed. 1735) as "a small Apartment in a Room", by Sheridan (ed. 1789) as "a small room of privacy and retirement, a private repository of curiosities" and by Webster (ed. 1828) as "A small close apartment or recess in the side of a room for repositing utensils and furniture."

Fifteen out of one hundred and five inventories between 1710 and 1720 mention room names:

1713 Francis Chads   Chamber where he died, Upper chamber, Kitchen

1714 Edward Beeson   Best room, Next room, Room in the leanto, Kitchen, Cellar, Loft

1714 Thomas Powell   Room over the parlour, Room over the porch, First room over the hall, Second room, Third room, Over the kitchen, Kitchen, Parlour

1714 John Smith   Parlour, Kitchen, Kitchen chamber, Parlour chamber, Garret, Cellar

1716 Jane Smith — Hall, First chamber, Second chamber, Third chamber, Fourth chamber, Kitchen, Parlour, Old house, Oven house

1716 John Hoskins — Large lower room on first floor, Third lodging room, Little room, Cellar, Kitchen, Buttery or closet, Large room on first floor, Blue room, Little room, Garret, Brewhouse

1716 John Blunston, Jr. — Kitchen, Cellar, Coopers shop & bake house, Bolting house

1717 George Woodyer — House and shed, Upper chamber, Cellar

1717 John Tyler — Fore room, Chamber, Garret, Kitchen

1717 Thomas Hood — Dwelling house, Chamber over the house, Shop, Chamber over the shop, Passage between the house and shop, Old house chamber

1718 John Test — Lodging room, Other chamber, Garret, Hall, Other room down stairs, Kitchen, Cellar

1718 Edward Lewis — Hall, Hall chamber, Kitchen, Kitchen chamber, Cellar

1718 William Poulson — Hall, Parlour, Kitchen

1718 Morton Mortonson — Old house and chamber over it, New house and chamber

1719 Walter Martin — Upstairs, Downstairs, Back shed, Cellar and end shed

Between 1720 and 1730 eleven of the two hundred and ninety-one inventories mention room names.

1720 John Fred — Lower room, First room above stairs, Second room above, Kitchen, Cellar

1721 Benjamin Head — Parlour, Outer parlour, Upper chamber, Another upper room, Kitchen, Kitchen cellar

1722 Andrew Job — Parlour, Closet, Middle room, Upstairs, Cellar, Kitchen, Shop

1723 John Cartlidge — House, Parlour, Study, Front chamber, Chamber closet, Parlour chamber, Garret, Cellar, Kitchen and chamber

1723 Joseph Coeburn — House, New room above stairs, Children's room, Buttery and closet, Kitchen, Cellar

1723 John Blunston — Chamber over hall, Chamber over kitchen, Porch chamber, Cellar chamber, Cellar, Passage

1726 Isreal Taylor — Lower kitchen, Back room, Cellar, Hall and 2 back rooms, Junior room, Front room, Closet, Garret

1726 Henry Nayles — Low-room of ye stone house, ye upper room of Same, Kitchen

1726 Thomas Codery — Bed chamber, Upper chamber, Kitchen

1727 Thomas Bradshaw — House, Parlour, Chamber, Back room, Hall, Chamber, Cellar, Kitchen

1729 John Marshall — Hall, First chamber, Second chamber, Parlour

A study is defined by Bailey (ed. 1735) as "...also a Closet to study in, a Library", by Sheridan (ed. 1789) as "apartments set off for literary employment" and by Webster (ed. 1828) as "A building or an apartment devoted to study or to literary employment."

Twenty out of three hundred and thirty inventories mention room names between 1730 and 1740.

1730 John Hannums — Dwelling House, Best chamber, Upper chamber inward, Upper chamber outward, Kitchen, Pantry, Cellar

1731 David Lloyd — Dining room, Lodging room, Parlour, Milkhouse, Closet, Chambers upstairs, Garret,

Cellar, Kitchen, Wash house, Chamber over wash house, Cider house

1731 William Lewis — Lodging room, Stove room, front room above stairs

1731 Josiah Ffearn — Hall, Room over cellar, Passage, Closet, Best chamber, Passage chamber, Chamber over hall, Shop, Shop chamber, Cellar, Chamber over vault

1731 Nathaniel Newlin — Garret, Back room above stairs, Front room above stairs, Common room below, Outward room in the kitchen, Inward room of ditto, Kitchen chamber, Cellar

1732 Samuel Hood — Upper room, Back shed, Kitchen

1732 John Wills, Jr. — Lodging room, Out room, Lower room

1732 Robert Johnson — Parlour, Next room, Room above parlour, At the stairs head, Kitchen, Cellar, Kitchen loft

1732 Joseph Roades — Upper room in new house, Lower room in new house, Little parlour, Shed room, Old house chamber

1732 James Miller — Lower room, Room above stairs, Other room

1734 Andrew Haydon — First room, Second room, Third room, Milk house, Kitchen

1736 Michael Blunston — Hall, Parlour, Chamber over parlour, Chamber over hall, Garret, Kitchen chamber, Little parlour and Kitchen, Cellar

1736 John Hunter — House, Rooms over house, Middle chamber, Chamber over parlour, Kitchen, Parlour

1736 Richard Parker — Parlour, Hall, Kitchen, Cham-

bers, Cellar, Shed, Kitchen chamber

1736 Henry Osbourne — Parlour, Upper room, Another room, Another room, Garret

1738 John Evans — Forefront chamber, Back chamber, Second front do, Lower front do, Closet annexed, Closet under stairs, Common room, Lodging room annexed, Closet, Above stairs in do, Cellar, Outward kitchen, Coopers shop

1738 Roger Evans — Lodging room, Kitchen, Loft, Cellar

1739 Jacob Bonsall — New room, Old parlour, Old house, Kitchen, New chamber, Old chambers, Chamber, Garret

1739 William Trehorn — Clock room, Room above clock room, Common lodging room, Kitchen, Room over kitchen, Room over common lodging room, Cellars

1739 John Salkeld — Parlour, Common room, Room over common room, Room over parlour, Kitchen

Pantry is defined by Bailey (ed. 1735) as "a Room or Closet where Bread and cold Meat are kept", by Sheridan (ed. 1789) as "a room in which provisions are reposited" and by Webster (ed. 1828) as "An apartment or closet in which provisions are kept."

USE OF SECOND HAND MATERIALS

John H. Brinton mentions in his diary that second hand materials were used in new houses. "Father got bricks from early 1713 house, also doors, windows, boards, & clapboards. They were painted a Venetian red. My father used the clapboards in building his kitchen. They were of white oak, riven & shaved, some five feet in length & six inches in width. He shingled the kitchen with the shingles (cedar). The doors & windows of the kitchen were there of the old house, & some window frames of our house were from the old house. Our chimneys were, in part at least, tipped off with the old bricks. The passage door between our house & kitchen was one of the doors of the old house.

I tore down my kitchen & built a new one of stone & raised my house a story, tore out windows, &c..."[1] The woods in an early cabin were "used in later house for lintels over windows, & hand rail for stairs."[2]

1. John H. Brinton Diary #2, Chester County Historical Society (West Chester, Penna.) p. 2.
2. Ibid., #1, p. 86.

HOUSE & BARN OR STABLE ATTACHED

At a Court of Quarter Sessions held at Chester for the said County on August 28 and 29, 1705 the testimony mentions that James Gibbons "...with force and arms &c. a certain stable being part of the dwelling and mansion house of John Hoskins at Chester in the County aforesaid about the hour of two in the night of the same day feloniously and burglariously did break and enter and one gelding of a sorril color of the price of eight pounds of the goods & chattels of the said John Hoskins then and there being found then & there feloniously and burglarly did steal take & lead away against the peace of our said lady the Queen her crown and dignity."[1] The 1798 Direct Tax for East Caln and West Whiteland Townships lists Joseph Downing with "1 dwelling house and Barn Connect[d]". The 1799 tax assessment for Honey Brook Township lists Abraham Curtz with "A Dwelling house and barn of Logs Covered with Straw and Shingles under one Roof."

1. Colonial Society of Pennsylvania, *RECORD OF THE COURTS OF CHESTER COUNTY PENNSYLVANIA 1681-1697,* (Patterson & White Co., Phila., Penna., 1910) Vol. 2, p.132

HOUSE CARPENTERS

1695	Francis Coebourn	Chester
	Thomas Coebourn	Chester, Middletown
1707	John Piggott	Birmingham
1747	Robert Brown	Kennett
1755	John Townsent	Westtown
1756	Caleb Evans	Radnor
	William Lewis	Darby
1759	Thomas Coebourn	Chester
	William Coebourn	Chester
	Kingsman Dutton	Chichester
1762	Joshua Evans	Tredyffrin
1763	Joshua Evans	Tredyffrin

1771	William Edwards	Ridley
	Lawrence Rice	West Whiteland
	Isaac Taylor	Upper Providence
1773	John Crozier	Springfield
	Samuel Cunningham	West Nantmeal
	Ledeklah W. Graham	Chester
1775	Ledekah W. Graham	Chester
1783	Ezekiel Bowen	East Marlboro
1785	George Harlan	West Marlboro
1788	Benjamin White	Sadsbury
1789	John Caldwell	Chester
1793	Joshua Hunt	Westtown
	John Davis	Charlestown
1794	Abraham Harlan	London Grove
1795	Edward Brooks	Brandywine
	Joshua Hunt	Westtown
1797	Joseph Calvert	Sadsbury
	Samuel Huzzard	Tredyffrin
	George McFarlin	East Marlboro
1798	John Harshbarger	West Fallowfield
1799	Joseph Moore	Sadsbury
1800	Jacob Howell	Chester
1801	William McKim	Sadsbury
	Benjamin White	Sadsbury
	David Crosby	Upper Oxford
1802	John Guthrie	Brandywine
1803	John Hoyt	Sadsbury
	Moses Baily	East Marlboro
	James Bodley	Charlestown
	David Hains	Westtown
1804	William Fox	Londonderry
1805	Daniel Russell	Sadsbury
	John Davis	Charlestown
	Adam Glendening	West Fallowfield
1806	Isaac Hoffman	Goshen

	Thomas Lindsey	Willistown
	Robert Britt	East Nantmeal
1807	Isaac Hoffman	Goshen
	Isaac Houlden	East Marlboro
	John Hoyt	Sadsbury
	Adam Glendening	West Fallowfield
1809	Obadiah Hannum	Kennett
	Benjamin Frederick	Coventry
1810	Frederick March	Coventry
	Elizah Walton	Londonderry
1811	Isaac Hawley	East Caln
	Josiah Philips Jr.	Uwchlan
1812	Isaac Hawley	East Caln
	William Reed	Westtown
	Isaac Buffington	East Fallowfield
	John Buffington	East Fallowfield
	Benedict Darlington	Westtown
1813	Samuel Newlin	New London
	George Bailey	Honey Brook
1815	John Kennedy	East Caln
1816	James McKee	East Whiteland
	John Cochran	West Fallowfield
1817	Lewis Goodwin	Westtown
1818	John Meredith	Tredyffrin
	George Miller	Waynesburg
1819	Septimus Harrar	London Britain
1821	William White	Honeybrook
1822	Robert Baldwin	Sadsbury
1823	Joseph Kurtz	East Whiteland
1824	Joseph Kurtz	East Whiteland
	Benjamin Bunn	Honeybrook
1827	Septimus Harrar	London Britain
	Jesse Pennypacker	Vincent
	Christian Groff	Honeybrook
1828	Samuel Newlin	London Grove
	James Williamson	London Grove
	George Bailey	Honeybrook

	John Cochran	West Fallowfield
	James Guest	West Nantmeal
1829	George Bailey	Honeybrook
	Jacob Chamberlin	West Chester
1831	John Dampman	West Nantmeal
1833	Thomas Walker	West Whiteland
	Joshua Fulton	Sadsbury
1835	John Meredith	Tredyffrin
1838	Isaac Gray	Kennett
1839	William W. Taylor	Phoenixville
1840	John Thompson	Kennett
1841	Adam Hipple	North Coventry
1842	John Benner	North Coventry
	George Brown	Pennsbury
	Emmor Bruce	West Whiteland
	Jacob Buckwalter	South Coventry
	Joshua Cloud	Pennsbury
	John Collins	West Whiteland
	Amer Frame	Pennsbury
	George Fred	South Coventry
	Jacob Geuinter	South Coventry
	William Lamborn	Pennsbury
	Elis Mendenhall	Pennsbury
	Amos Stephens	Pennsbury
	John Taggert	Pennsbury
	Joseph Vandever	Pennsbury
	John Walker	Pennsbury
	Sharpless Windle	Pennsbury
1843	Peter Overdeer	West Chester
1846	Isaiah Wells	West Chester

HOVEL

Hovel is defined by Sheridan (ed. 1789) as "a shed open on the sides, and covered overhead; a mean habitation, a cottage" and by Webster (ed. 1828) as "A shed, a cottage; a mean house."

The 1798 Direct Tax lists Mary Reece, of Newtown and part of Marple Townships, as having: 1 story wood house 22 x 16 feet, 2 story wood and stone Barn 63 x 33 feet, wood hovel 11 x 10 feet, stone cart house 28 x 23 feet, wood shed 16 x 16 feet and a one story wood and stone stable 21 x 17 feet.

ICE HOUSE

The 1798 Direct Tax lists five stone ice houses, the mean size being 206 square feet. In the newspaper advertisements John P. and Aaron P. Osmond, of London Britain Township, advertised in 1859 "stone ice house with frame cover, weatherboarded", and Samuel Pugh, of New Garden Township, advertised in 1861 "stone ice house 18 feet square and 7 feet deep."[2] In the newspaper advertisements between 1860 and 1876 one stone and frame ice house was 25 x 10 feet and three that did not mention the material of construction had a mean size of 1037 square feet.

In 1873 the following directions were given for building an ice house:

> Ice House...Dig a hole about 15 feet square and 15 deep. Place all around this, one foot from the outside, a frame of slabs from the saw mill or split timber, and fill in between the earth with tan bark or saw dust; cover with a roof of pales, straw and earth, and you have an ice house that will keep your supplies all summer.[3]

1. *VILLAGE RECORD,* (West Chester, Penna.) Dec. 3, 1859.
2. Ibid., March 5, 1861.
3. *AMERICAN REPUBLICAN,* (West Chester, Penna.) Dec. 2, 1873.

IMITATION

EXTERIOR

The newspapers mention:

1833 "stone house, plastered in imitation of marble"[1] James Sloan (Honey Brook Twp.)

1833 "three story Brick Building, fifty three by 32 plastered in front in imitation of granite"[2] Odd Fellows (West Chester)

1840 "Dwelling House, 38 by 28 feet, one half Brick, the other half log, plastered outside and in and finished in front in imitation of Brick"[3] Charles Buffington (East Marlboro Twp.)

1874 "outside of entire structure to be painted in imitation of granite"[4] Presbyterian Church (West Chester)

1874 "Wm. S. Snare has just painted his store front in imitation of walnut"[5] (West Chester)

1. *AMERICAN REPUBLICAN* (West Chester, Penna.) Nov. 26, 1833.
2. Ibid., Dec. 3, 1833.
3. Ibid., Dec. 1, 1840.
4. *DAILY LOCAL NEWS* (West Chester, Penna.) Sept. 16, 1874.
5. *VILLAGE RECORD* (West Chester, Penna.) Oct. 10, 1874.

INTERIOR

Henry Graham Ashmead in 1883 mentions that the Logan House, in Chester, built in 1700 had a "wainscoted hallway...All the rooms were wainscoted also, and the panels were painted or stained in imitation of mahogany."[1]

The newspapers mention:

1873 "The dining room is 17 by 19 feet, with oak grained wood-work...Library is a handsome room of about 17 by 20 feet, with slate mantel and walnut grained wood-work" Henry Buckwalter (West Chester)[2]

1874 "frame, 35 by 50 feet. Without is coated with a dark brown color, inside white. The seat backs, pulpit, altar railings &c are painted in imitation of walnut"[3] Hamerton M. E. Church (Kennett Twp.)

1874 "Two story brick building, mansard roof, 40 by 33 feet, back building 58 by 32 feet. The whole inside is finished in imitation of walnut...Wm. Armstrong, painter"[4] Mary Hoopes (London Grove Twp.)

1. Henry Graham Ashmead, *HISTORICAL SKETCH OF CHESTER, ON DELAWARE* (The Republican Steam Printing House, 1883), p. 73.
2. *DAILY LOCAL NEWS* (West Chester, Penna.) Dec. 5, 1873.
3. Ibid., June 8, 1874.
4. *AMERICAN REPUBLICAN* (West Chester, Penna.) June 2, 1874.

INCUBATOR

Incubate is defined by Bailey (ed. 1735) as "to lie or sit upon, as a Hen" and by Webster (ed. 1828) as "To sit, as on eggs for hatching." An incubator is a place where birds sit on eggs for hatching.

A newspaper mention in 1882 that "Dr. Morris, of Birmingham Township, is now erecting a large incubator on his premises which is about seventy-five feet long by twenty-five feet wide. The northern portion of the structure is built against a bank, which gives the building a southern exposure. The foundation is a solid rock. Glaziers are now at work putting the glass in the roof, which will take about 1200 panes."[1]

1. *DAILY LOCAL NEWS* (West Chester, Penna.) Jan. 18, 1882.

IRON

The newspaper advertisements mention iron:

1855 "Forge, partly covered with sheet iron."[1] Springton Forge (Wallace Twp.)

1858 "iron veranda around three sides of house...yard...enclosed by iron fence"[2] S. Snyder & A.S. Leidy (Westtown Twp.)

1860 "Brick House, with iron porch in front."[3] W.B. Mendenhall (Coatesville)

1863 "Valley Creek bridge to be of iron."[4]

1866 "School House...roof is of sheet iron."[5] (West Marlboro Twp.)

1868 "a heavy iron fence of elegant design fixed with marble coping."[6] Joseph Baugh (Downingtown)

1870 "two verandahs 10 feet wide with heavy iron columns, pilasters and railing mostly wrought."[7] J. Lee Englebert (West Chester)

1872 "evergreen hedge replaced by iron fence made by Evans, Griffith & Thomas, West Chester...3 Houses... with galvanized iron door and window finishes."[8] (West Chester)

1873 "Evans Barnard & Co. making Iron Shutters."[9] (West Chester)

1874 "938 feet by 90, principal material is rolled or wrought iron, roof being slate."[10] Phoenix Iron Co. (Phoenixville)

1874 "in front low stone wall surmounted by ornamental iron fence."[11] Normal School (West Chester)

1874 "two iron rod doors placed at doors."[12] Prison (West Chester)

1875 "warehouse, roofed with iron."[13] David Mercer (Newlin Twp.)

1876 "house has a balcony with iron railings at the front and double verandas ten feet wide at the side, with iron railings and posts."[14] J.S. Futhey (West Chester)

In 1874 the newspapers mentioned that Evans Barnard & Co., of West Chester, made iron fences for Shaner Chrisman, of West Vincent Township,[15] and for Jos. Perdue and Dr. Jones.[16] In 1875 Evans & Baird, of West Chester, made iron fences for Samuel Diemer and David Finkbinner.[17]

Before 1877 the newspapers mentioned thirteen other iron fences, two other iron verandas and seven other iron porches.

In 1883 "SOMETHING NEW UNDER THE SUN IN THE WAY OF A RESIDENCE.

> George L. Huston, of Parkesburg, Chester county, will build a palatial private mansion for himself entirely of iron, the foundations of solid rock. The architect is an Englishman, whom Mr. Huston recently met while abroad. The iron-work is now being turned out at Coatesville, as the superstructure is to be of iron entirely. The floor of the hall, vestibule and library will be laid with polished cast-iron tiles, in which different qualities of iron will be used to produce the same variety of color as in ordinary tile flooring. All the other floors of the house will be of stout iron plates firmly bolted to the iron joists. The outside wall and inside partitions all through the structure will be composed of two courses of iron plates, firmly bolted together so as to be air-tight. These hollow iron walls and partitions will be used instead of chimneys and for conveying heat to different parts of the house, and for

ventilation. The hot smoke and gases from the furnaces passing through the sides of the rooms in this way, it is claimed, be almost sufficient to keep the house comfortable in the coldest weather, so that the heating can be done with about one-half the fuel required in ordinary houses. All the doors and window sashes will also be iron, but be constructed in such a light way and so nicely balanced upon hinges and weights as to open and shut as easily as those made of wood. All the inside walls and partitions will be handsomely painted and frescoed so as to present the appearance of any ordinary house finished in plaster. Outside, the style of architecture will be light and graceful, and it will be painted and ornamented so as to look as if it was built of wood. The roof will be of strong boiler plate, and on the top, at the convergence of the four gables, will be a handsome observatory supported at the four corners by four Ionic pillars of iron. Inside the ornaments will be made of the same material. In the parlor will be a mantel of polished steel, handsomely ornamented. There will be a similar one in the dining room, upon which will be engraved hunting scenes. In the library will be a massive mantel so constructed that it will look as if it were made of pig iron fused together. Quite a curiosity in this room will be a cabinet for the exhibition of specimens of iron. This will be constructed entirely of strongly magnetized iron, so that all the specimens will adhere to the back of it, held in place solely by magnetic attraction. In order to guard against the bungling which would take place in such a solid iron structure on account of the contraction and expansion caused by the heat and cold, there will be breaks in the iron at intervals, which will be filled with rubber, so that when expansion takes place there will be room for it without producing and change in the contour of the frame work. As much as possible of the furniture will also be of iron, so that if it takes fire in any part, nothing can burn but the carpets and the few articles of wood that may be within reach of the flames. The house will be an architectural and scientific curiosity. Mr. Huston admits that it may cost twice or three times as much as any ordinary house; but claims that with a little attention it will last for centuries without repairs, and will never cost a cent for insurance.[18]

In 1889 the Iron Works, at Coatesville, was described as "This mamouth structure is built of iron, and is about

150 x 200 feet in dimensions with a fifty foot roof. The supports are laid on solid brick and stone piers and extend several feet below the surface of the ground..."[19] In 1893 a newspaper mentions "improvements on the residence of Jerome B. Gray [West Chester]...The old dormer window in the front got to leaking...Now that section of the front is being covered with galvanized iron, and the woodwork of the whole exterior of the house is being painted white. Later a touch of lemon will be added."[20]

1. *AMERICAN REPUBLICAN* (West Chester, Penna.) Sep. 25, 1855.
2. *VILLAGE RECORD* (West Chester, Penna.) June 12, 1858.
3. Ibid., Nov. 3, 1860.
4. Ibid., May 12, 1863.
5. Ibid., April 10, 1866.
6. Ibid., Nov. 24, 1868.
7. Ibid., Oct. 22, 1870.
8. *AMERICAN REPUBLICAN* (West Chester, Penna.) June 18, 1872.
9. *DAILY LOCAL NEWS* (West Chester, Penna.) Dec. 24, 1873.
10. *VILLAGE RECORD* (West Chester, Penna.) April 28, 1874.
11. *AMERICAN REPUBLICAN* (West Chester, Penna.) April 7, 1874.
12. *DAILY LOCAL NEWS* (West Chester, Penna.) Oct. 22, 1874.
13. *VILLAGE RECORD* (West Chester, Penna.) Jan 12, 1875.
14. Ibid., April 1, 1876.
15. *DAILY LOCAL NEWS* (West Chester, Penna.) April 22, 1874.
16. Ibid., April 22, 1874.
17. *VILLAGE RECORD* (West Chester, Penna.) June 26, 1875.
18. *DAILY LOCAL NEWS* (West Chester, Penna.) Jan. 4, 1883.
19. Ibid., Sep. 16, 1889.
20. Ibid., May 17, 1893.

IRON FOUNDRY

The newspaper advertisements mention between 1830 and 1849 one stone foundry 65 x 30 feet and one stone and frame foundry 40 x 30 feet and between 1850 and 1876 one brick foundry 40 x 40 feet; one, four story, foundry 44 x 40 feet; one foundry 35 x 21 feet; one two story, frame foundry 60 x 32 feet; one two story frame foundry 60 x 24 feet and one foundry 34 x 20 feet.

LANDSCAPING

The Brinton diary mentions that an early settler had used flowers outside his plank house: "And so are blue bottles which were brought from England and planted in the garden, as flowers."[1] Peter Kalm, the Swedish-Finnish naturalist, who travelled in Pennsylvania in 1748 noticed that "Almost all the enclosures round the corn fields and meadows hereabouts, were made of planks fastened in a horizontal direction...for the people here take posts from four to six feet in height, and make two or three holes in them so that there was a distance of two feet and above between them. Such a post does the same service as two, and sometimes three poles are scarce sufficient. The posts were fastened in the ground, at two or three fathoms distance from each other, and the holes in them kept the planks, which were nine inches, and sometimes a foot board, and lay above each other from one post to the next. Such an enclosure there looked at a distance like hurdles in which we enclose the sheep at night in Sweden. They were really no closer than hurdles, being only destined to keep out the greater animals, such as cows and horses,"[2] and "I frequently was surprised at the prudence of the inhabitants of this country. As soon as one has bought a piece of ground, which is neither built upon nor sown, his first care is to get young apple trees, and to make a garden. He next proceeds to built his house and lastly prepares the uncultivated ground to receive corn. For it is well known that the trees require many years before they arrive to perfection, and this makes it necessary to plant them first."[3] In the town of Chichester he mentions "many gardens, which are full of apple-trees sinking under the weight of innumerable apples."[4]

The newspapers mention:

1745 "Close Yard, a spacious Garden, well paled"[5] Edmund Bourk (Chester)

1764 "Garden, with a Stone Wall along the Northeast end"[6] John Yarnall (Willistown Twp.)

1766 "good Garden fenced in with Cedar Boards"[7] Thomas Smith (Chester)

1770 "garden paled in...and walks, with rows of shady trees"[8] Yellow Springs (Pikeland Twp.)

1773 "a stone wall round the garden"[9] Enoch Wells (Uwchlan Twp.)

1802 "kitchen and garden fenced with pales and boards"[10] Joseph Shippen (Westtown Twp.)

1803 "between the house and the turnpike is a large piece of semicircular land thrown open for the convenience of wagons, carriages, &c."[11] David Llewellyn "Spring House Tavern" (Easttown Twp.)

1815 "with good garden ground and about an acre of ground in front of the house, planted with trees descending from the house until it terminates at the great road in a regular handsome slope"[12] Dennis Whelen, S. Babb Yellow Springs (Pikeland Twp.)

1816 "[land]enclosed with good fence; a great part being stone walls, and post and rails"[13] George Young (Pikeland Twp.)

1816 "[enclosed] by good fences, clear of hedges"[14] Peter Hartman, John Fetters (Pikeland Twp.)

1820 "fences, composed of stone and part of chestnut rails"[15] Jacob Waitneight (Chester County)

1821 "divided into convenient fields, with thorn fences"[16] Wm. Neill Est. (Tredyffrin Twp.)

1822 "The whole enclosure in good fence, the front paled on a good wall"[17] John Kennedy (Downingtown)

1824 "a large Garden walled in under cedar roof...three miles of Virginia thorn hedge: near a mile of stone wall"[18] James Jones (Brandywine Twp.)

1825 "the gardens attached are enclosed by a substantial board fence, and there is a fine cistern in the back yard which is paved"19 Elisha Ingram (West Chester)

1831 "first rate garden, enclosed with a pine board fence"20 John Babb (Sadsbury Twp.)

1832 "yard is large and paved"21 Daniel Vondersmith (Downingtown)

1833 "a three feet alley paved with brick, extends from the street to the back yard, which is also paved with brick"22 Lewis W. Williams (West Chester)

1834 "yard having considerable shrubbery"23 William Sloanaker (Easttown Twp.)

1834 "enclosed by good post and rail fences and hedges"24 Caspar Wistar Est. (Pennsbury Twp.)

1836 "a large garden handsomely laid out and planted with a great variety of shrubs, flowers and European and native grape vines"25 Josiah Ankrim (Penn Twp.)

1837 "spacious and beautiful pleasure ground planted with various shrubbery"26 Margaret Holman "Mansion House" (West Chester)

1838 "yard neatly paled in, and planted with trees in front"27 David Meconkey (Upper Oxford Twp.)

1840 "The ground surrounding the house is beautifully laid off and enclosed, and planted with a variety of evergreen and other ornamental trees"28 Jesse Pusey (East Marlboro Twp.)

1841 "stone MANSION...It is situated on an eminence in a lawn of about 3 acres, which is planted with ornamental and fruit trees and shrubbery"29 Jabez Jenkins (West Whiteland Twp.)

1841 "divided into 9 fields, chiefly with thorn hedges"30 Benedict Darlington (Westtown Twp.)

1845 "large yard round the house with shade trees therein"31 Hayes Jackson (East Marlboro Twp.)

1847 "the grounds around it were laid out and a new painted ornamental fence surrounds the whole"32 Alfred Weeks (East Marlboro Twp.)

1848 "handsomely shaded with a Sugar Maple in front"33 Joseph E. Clark (East Marlboro Twp.)

Before 1830 the newspaper advertisements mention eighteen gardens pailed in; three yards and gardens pailed in; one fence of cedar boards; two paved yards; one thorn hedge; one board fence; one garden with stone walls; one garden enclosed with stone wall and pail fence and two houses with shrubbery besides those already quoted. Between 1830 and 1849 the newspaper advertisements mention twenty-eight gardens pailed in and fourteen yards pailed in as well as those already quoted.

In 1847 G. A. Macartney, Auctioneer, advertises:

Fruit and Shade Trees

WILL be sold, at public sale, on Wednesday and Thursday, the 31st of March and 1st of April, at the West Chester Rail-road Depot, in the Borough of West Chester, an extensive and select assortment of Fruit Trees and Vines, consisting of Apple, Pear, Peach, Plum, Cherry, Nectarine, Quince, Sibernian Crab, Grape Vines, English Walnuts, English Chestnuts, White and red Dutch Currants, large English Gooseberries, Antwerp Raspberries, Hovey Seedling and other varieties of Strawberries. Also 150 Shade Trees, of good size and thrift growth, and a lot of Tobolsk Rhubarb roots. Sale to commence at one o'clock, p.m.34

The following year Paschall Morris and Ezra Stokes advertise:

NEW NURSERY AT WEST CHESTER. THE subscribers have associated under the firm of MORRIS & STOKES, for carrying on the NURSERY business, at West Chester, in all its various branches, of Fruit and Ornamental Trees, Shrubbery, Grape Vines, &c. One of the partners having served an apprenticeship of several years to the business, at one of the principal Nurseries in the Union, and more recently had the entire management of one in an adjoining State, we hope to be able to offer to the public, trees which can be relied on for genuineness and healthy growth. Every care will be taken by his personal attention to the insertion of buds and grafts, that no tree shall be sold from this establishment of doubtful character. It is also intended to connect with it a specimen orchard, for testing the different kinds of fruit, and from which buds can be obtained.

A correspondence has been established with two of the principal nurseries in England, from which we expect to receive the present Spring, and hereafter, whatever is valuable and desirable from that quarter.

JOSHUA EMBREE, of Marshallton, (the high character of whose trees is well known through Chester county, and all of which have been warranted true to their name) having declined the business, the undersigned have purchased his entire stock, which with the addition of a considerable portion of E. Stokes' former establishment, grown under his immediate direction, and which will be removed to West Chester, enable us to offer to the public the present spring, a full supply of apple trees, comprising over a hundred select kinds, and a moderate supply of other fruits, and a good stock of ornamentals.

Out of about 130 different kind of apples, the following are selected. The remainder, many of them of local name and character, can be obtained at the Nursery.

SUMMER APPLES.

Bough	Red Juneating, or E.
Birmingham	Red Margaret
Old English Codin	Summer Rose
Knowles Early	Hoopes' Seedling
Maiden's Blush	Summer Queen
Prince's Harvest	Summer Vandiver
Summer Pearmain	Betsey
White Juneating	Caleb.

FALL APPLES.

American Red Streak	Porter
Cabbage Head	Republican Pippin
Delaware Red Streak	Rambo
Boston Fall Pippin	Wistar Pippin
White Fall Pippin	White Seek no-further
Gloria Mundi	Gravenstein
Hays	Hagloe
Holland Pippin	Morgan

WINTER APPLES.

Baldwin	Ladies' Sweeting
Newtown Pippin	Lady Apple
Blue Pearmain	Ohio Bellflower
Beauty of the West	Ohio Winter Green
Smith's cider apple	Rhode Island Greening
Minister	Roxbury Russet
Michael Henry Pippin	Roman Stem
Cooper's Reding	Sheep Nose
Domine	Tewksbury Winter Blush
Esopus Spitzenburg	White Bellflower
Fallawater	Yellow Bellflower
Galliflower	Wine Sap
Hubbardston's non such	Danver's Winter Sweet
Jersey Greening	Monmouth Pippin
Long Island Russet	Swaar

PEARS

Bartlett	Frederic de Wirtemberg
Belle de Brussels	Fulton
Belle de Flanders'	Golden Beurre de Bolboa
Benset Winter	English Jargonelle
Beurre Bosc	Louise Bonne de Jersey
Beurre Diel	Marie Louise
Beurre de Capiaumont	Queen of the Low
Beurre Brown	Countries
White Doyenne or butter	Seckel
Colmar	Surpasse Marie Louise
Duchesse de Angouleme	Tyson
Dix	Urbanisie

Early Catharine	Vanmon's Leon le clerc
Easter Bergamot	Washington
Easter Beurre	

PEACHES

Crawford's Early Mele coton	Morris White
Crawford's late do	Old Mixon Free
Early York	Red-cheek Melecoton
George the Fourth	Red Rare Ripe
La Grange	Smock
Late Hearth	Yellow Rare Ripe

PLUMS

Coe's Golden Drop	Jefferson
Yellow Gage	Imperial Gage
Hewling's Superb	Green Gage
Washington's Bolmar	Early Violet
Magnum Bonum	

CHERRIES

American Amber	English May Duke
Belle de Choisey	June Duke
Black Partarlan	Kentish White Heart
Black Eagle	Napoleon Bigarrean
Bleeding Heart	Virginia May
Downer's late Red	Ox Heart
Elton	Knight's early Black

APRICOTS

Perche	Hemshirke
Moorpark	Brussels or Breda

NECTARINES

Temple's	Pitmaster Orange
Dounton	Duc du Telliers
Red Roman	

ORNAMENTAL TREES & SHRUBS

Horse Chestnut	European Linden
Silver Leaved Maple	Umbrella Magnolia
Norway Maple	Purple Magnolia
Ash Leaved Maple	Glaucus Magnolia
English Cork do	European Mountain Ash
Sugar Maple	Flowering Ash
European Sycamore	Maple Leaved Poplar
Catalpa	European Larch
Honey Locust	Exmouth Elm
Tulip Tree	Scotch Elm

Abele or Silver Leaf Poplar	Red Elm
Golden Twigged Poplar	Red Fringe
American Aspen	White Fringe
Weeping Willow	Purple Beech
	Osage Orange

EVERGREENS

Cedar of Lebonon	White Pine
Norway Spruce Fir	Tree box
European Silver Fir	American Arbor Vitae
Scotch Mountain Fir	Hemlock
White Spruce	American Juniper
Black Spruce	American Holly
Pinaster or Cluster Pine	Mountain Laural
Balm of Gilead	

GOOSEBERRIES, GRAPEVINES, &C

Trees packed so as to carry any distance,
and delivered in Philadelphia if desired.
PASCHALL MORRIS,
EZRA STOKES.[35]

The newspaper advertisements mention:

1852 "handsome lawn in front, adorned with splendid shade and fruit trees"[36] Robert Smith (Uwchlan Twp.)

1853 "an evergreen grove, handsomely arranged with fine flowers"[37] John Cadwallader (East Marlboro Twp.)

1853 "Garden paled in, eight feet high and planted with Fruit Trees"[38] Mary Preston "Caln Depot" (Valley Twp.)

1855 "The house is surrounded by Forrest and Locust trees, making a very cool and delightful retreat in a warm summer day"[39] Robert H. Strawbridge (East Nottingham Twp.)

1855 "yard planted with ornamental and evergreen trees such as Norway fur, white pine"[40] Thomas C. Chandler (Pennsbury Twp.)

1856 "The play grounds are laid out in walks and well supplied with shade trees, flowers &c."[41] Sunnyside Seminary (East Fallowfield Twp.)

1856 "a garden beautifully laid out in walks, and set with ornamental trees and shrubbery"[42] Deny Sharwood (Schuylkill Twp.)

1856 "Cottage...a porch extending along two sides and the front; it is also connected with the "Hotel" and "Hall" by a covered promenade of about 120 feet in length. Bath Houses Nos 1 and 2, and the "Iron and Yellow" and "Sulphur Springs" are in a grove laid out in walks containing summer houses and swings, and is situated in front of the main or Hotel Building"[43] Chester Springs (West Pikeland Twp.)

1857 "On the lot is one of the handsomest gardens in town, with a vine arbor, the beds planted with box wood around, containing a variety of choice shrubs and flowers"[44] William Garrett (Phoenixville)

1858 "Tavern...adorned by a raised yard, sheltered by beautiful shade trees"[45] S.C. Harry (London Grove Twp.)

1858 "front yard...enclosed by iron fence"[46] S. Snuer & A. S. Leidy (Westtown Twp.)

1859 "The ground is beautifully laid out in lawns, flower, fruit and vegetable gardens, partly enclosed with iron railings"[47] Mifflin Lewis Est. (Tredyffrin Twp.)

1859 "beautiful Lawn, surrounded with over 30 of the finest variety of evergreens and ornamental trees, also a number of shade trees"[48] Enos Smedley (Easttown Twp.)

1860 "yard enclosed with pale and lattice fence"[49] Elisha W. Huyck (Franklin Twp.)

1860 "Brick House...grape vine and arbor along one end of house...side yard enclosed by iron and pale fence"[50] Mary Ann Reese (Phoenixville)

1860 "enclosed by ornamental and board fence"[51] Robert C. Hemphill (West Chester)

1861 "Brick House...is connected by frame passageway with messuage...yard enclosed by new pale fence, set with shade and ornamental trees, grape vines and arbors, and is laid out in pebbled walks"[52] James E. Giffin (Coatesville)

1861 "grape vine arbor along side of brick and frame kitchen"[53] John Moher (West Chester)

1862 "Grape vines and Bower over Kitchen door"[54] Emmor Townsend (West Chester)

1863 "buildings are beautifully laid out in gravelled walks"[55] George W. Richards (Phoenixville)

1866 "grape arbor along front of kitchen"[56] Clinton Frame (West Chester)

1867 "Latice arched verandahs covered with evergreens and grapes surround the entire premises"[57] William B. Torbert (West Whiteland Twp.)

1868 "yard elevated with brick walk around"[58] Isaac T. Lewis (Uwchlan Twp.)

1868 "The dwelling has a large front and side yard well laid out with flower borders, fruit and evergreen trees and walks paved with brick; the whole is surrounded with a heavy iron fence of elegant design fixed upon marble coping"[59] Joseph Baugh (Downingtown)

1869 "large yard well shaded nearly one mile of gravel walks and filled with choice flowers"[60] T. S. C. Lowe (Schuylkill Twp.)

1869 "Lawn Terraced and set with evergreens"[61] George Y. Passmore (West Brandywine Twp.)

1871 "lot enclosed with hedges, iron and wood fences of pretty designs, and is beautifully laid out with walks"[62] C. C. Sellers (West Chester)

1871 "House...approached by an Avenue, boarded on either side by a beautiful hedge"[63] (West Pikeland Twp.)

1871 "avenue leading to the buildings is ornamented by rows of shade trees"[64] P. W. B. Brinton Est. (West Whiteland Twp.)

1873 "House...The whole enclosed with a substantial picket fence"[65] D. B. Hinman (Penn Twp.)

1874 "Mr. Jones Tustin is making preparations for planting an osage orange hedge"[66] (Schuylkill Twp.)

1874 "shrubbery, running fountains, walks"[67] Rosedale Homestead (West Caln Twp.)

1874 "evergreen hedge replaced by iron fence made by Evans Griffith and Thomas West Chester in front low stone wall surmounted by an ornamental iron fence."[68] Normal School, (West Chester)

1875 "Samuel Diemer & David Finbinner new iron-fences furnished by Evans & Baird, West Chester"[69] (Spring City)

1875 "farm inclosed...by a stone wall laid in foundation, about 4 feet high" "Yearseley's"[70] (West Caln Twp.)

1875 "building a sort of pavillion which will ward off the afternoon sun from their rooms...west side will be formed of lattice work, the same to be ornamented with a vigorous climatis"[71] Darlington Marshall (West Chester)

1876 "Lawn, enclosed at the front with new iron post and galvanized cable wire fence 580 feet long, each post set in stone"[72] John R. Gilpin (Birmingham Twp.)

Between 1850 and 1877 the newspapers mention nine gardens enclosed with stone walls; ten yards enclosed with stone wall and pale fence; four yards enclosed by pale and board fence and stone wall; ten yards enclosed by pale and board fence; two yards enclosed with board fence; sixty-two gardens enclosed by pale fence; one lawn with ornamental trees and shrubbery; one lawn with fruit, shade and ornamental trees; one thorn hedge; one ornamental fence, eleven iron fences; one box wood and evergreens; one osage orange hedge and one lawn terraced as well as those already quoted.

In 1841 a course was offered in

LANDSCAPING GARDENING And Rural Economy. A COURSE of four Lectures upon Landscape Gardening and Rural Economy, embracing the laying out of Grounds, the formation of Roads, the management of Water, the construction of Farm Houses and Village Residences, Draining, Irrigation, the analysis and amelioration of Soils, and the application of the principles of the Picturesque and beautiful, to the improvement of Farms and Village Property, will be delivered by THOMAS DUNN ENGLISH, M.D., at the Horticultural Hall...[73]

Twenty one years later in 1862:

"Landscape Gardening ALEXANDER MARSHALL OFFERS his Professional services to the public as LANDSCAPE GARDENER. He will lay out Lawns of smaller gardens — group trees and shrubbery by marking the location for each, so as to form a combination that will present the best view from prominent stand points — will locate and LAY OUT FLOWER BEDS — select trees, shrubbery and flowers for his customers at either of the West Chester Nurseries and, if required, will superintend their planting — will also SELECT FRUIT TREES, GRAPE VINES, &c., and may be consulted on any branch of Horticulture. He may be called on Personally, at No. 64 South High Street (corner of Barnard) or addressed by mail through the Post Office, West Chester. His charge will be moderate."[74]

In 1873 Gerold Altorfer, of West Chester, advertised that he was a "LANDSCAPE GARDENER AND FLORIST."[75]

In 1850 A. Marshall & Co., West Chester, advertises: "Osage Orange for hedging, Shade and Ornamental trees, Evergreens, Flowering Shrubs, Dwarf box edging for walks and flower beds. A choice Variety of Roses and Green house plants, (Green House opposite the Horticultural Hall.)".[76] The same year Morris & Stokes' Nursery and Garden, West Chester, advertise: "..Osage Orange for hedging, Chinese Arbor Vitae for do. Box Edging &c. &c. Their ornamental department embraces most of the desirable native and exotic trees and plants, and is annually enriched by their own importations from abroad. They are also erecting a spacious Green House...Catalogues furnished gratis."[77]

The newspapers also mention the fences and hedges found in the county:

1857 "WHITEWASHING, — Judging from the exceedingly white appearance of the fences and out buildings throughout the county, it seems as if the whitewash fever had broken out, and was raging with unmitigated fury. In every direction, during the pleasant weather, the ladies with their sun bonnets on, may be seen endeavoring to assuage the attack by applying heavy coats of lime and water"[78]

1867 "Rustic Fence — We observe a new fancy iron fence, newly erected and enclosing two front yards on Miner Street, in this Borough. The design is to represent the knotty branches of the hickory tree. We learn it comes from the manufactory of MR. GEORGE LADLEY, of West Chester, and is at once strong and beautiful"[79] (West Chester)

1870 "OAK AND CHESTNUT POSTS from 5 to 10 feet long PINE AND HEMLOCK RAILS 12, 16, 20 and

24 feet long. PICKETS, FENCE BOARDS, &c. Constantly on hand"[80] Sharples & Hall (West Chester)

1872 "IRON FENCE. We are prepared at short notice to furnish WROUGHT IRON FENCE, of any style, to suit customers. Also, CAST BRACKETS, POSTS, and RAILINGS FOR PORCHES. Give us a call"[81] Evans, Griffith & Thomas, (West Chester)

1871 "The fence is composed of iron posts set in stone, with wire rails as follows: We use for posts, iron bars, about sixteen inches long (common iron) 1¼ inches wide and half inch thick, cut into lengths 4 ft 3½ inches, and drilled with five holes, quarter inch in diameter; the two upper holes being about nine inches apart"[82]

1874 "Local Option. One day we walked to West Chester, distance about five miles from our camp, and have to say respecting it, it is one of the prettiest towns of its size we have ever seen. Its streets are usually wide and level, and all run paralled with the points of the compasses, its sidewalks all lined with ornamental shade trees, its buildings magnificent...THE FARMS are generally larger than those in Berks...HEDGES, for fences, for enclosing and dividing their lands, and we understand that they are becoming more popular every year. Not only do the hedges greatly improve the appearance of the lands, but also avoid the continual bore of repairing and re-erecting..."[83]

1876 "The posts are iron, set in rock and a mound of earth has been raised reaching to the lower wire thus preventing hogs or sheep from getting under the fence."[84]

1880 "A Farm Fenced with Beautiful Hedges. J. S. Worman, of East Coventry township, has his farm fenced entirely with hedges, some of which are honey locust, but the greater portion is osage orange. These hedges are all kept neatly trimmed, and give his farm a most beautiful appearance. It is doubtless the best fenced farm in the county, and attracts the attention of all passers-by."[85]

1885 "Oakbourne is a superb estate, belonging to Mr. James C. Smith, a Philadelphia gentleman of wealth and refinement and a brother-in-law to the well-known banker Anthony J. Drexel. Oakbourne is one of the lovliest spots in Chester county and is situated on the line of the West Chester Railroad, a few rods from Hemphill station, and some twenty-five miles from Philadelphia. It contains about 147 acres, all under the highest state of cultivation and ornamentation. Mr. Smith has converted the estate from a forlorn looking place into a little earthly paradise and he has spent a vast sum of money in improvements, 150 workmen and skilled artisans being employed for a long time on the various improvements. The vast estate is surrounded by a substantial stone wall and iron railing, within which stands on an eminence a stately and costly family mansion, surrounded by a large lawn of surpassing beauty and fountains, statuary, miniature lakes, rivulets, rustic bridges, green-houses, stately oak trees, flower beds, shrubbery, hedges and everything that money could obtain or exquisite taste suggest to make the place beautiful and attractive.

The mansion is built of dark stone and contains eighteen rooms, superby furnished. A feature consists in a massive ornamental copper gable end and cornice of great value, and a large tower runs up to a considerable height, from the top of which a magnificent view is obtained. Everything about the estate is in keeping with the lawn and mansion, and there are quite a number of elegant buildings, Lodges, etc. Mr. Smith devotes much time to raising live stock, and he possesses many valuable horses, cows, etc. Five thousand loads of dirt were used in grading Oakbourne, and over $5,000 were expended in the simple work of making paths and carriage-ways alone."[86] (Westtown Twp.)

The wills before 1814 mention

1776 "with the Garden fronting South of the House, & the Garden Call'd the Bean Garden now fenced in at the Lower Corner of the Orchard"[87] John Gronow (Tredyffrin Twp.)

OAKLANDS CEMETERY.

A newspaper sales notice describes Oaklands Cemetery, in West Goshen Township, in 1853:

THE OAKLANDS CEMETERY.
FIVE HUNDRED BURIAL LOTS FOR SALE. — The improvements at the "Oaklands Cemetery" being in a sufficient state of forwardness to allow of interments, the Managers will expose at Public Sale, at the Cemetery, on Saturday the 15th of October, at 1 o'clock, P.M., Five Hundred Burial lots, if that number should be demanded. These lots contain from 100 to 600 square feet, each are located in ten different sections of the Cemetery, and in a great variety of situations, affording an opportunity for all tastes to be suited. The cemetery is beautifully located, within a mile and a half of the Court House, is traversed by two streams of water, is delightfully undulating in its surface, and affords an opportunity for the erection of vaults, tombs, mausoleums, and monuments of every character. It is shaded by a beautiful growth of native forest trees, and has been laid out with great care and excellent taste

by J. C. Sidney, one of the most experienced engineers in the country, in this department, and when the improvements in progress are completed will be one of the most beautiful rural cemeteries our State can boast. The rapidly increasing repugnance to burial in our borough graveyards, and the growing desire, in a large portion of our community, to deposit the remains of departed friends in more suitable places than our present burial grounds present, have induced the managers to spare no pains to render the Oaklands Cemetery a desirable place of sepulture; and they earnestly call the attention of the citizens of the borough and the surrounding neighborhood to its many advantages, among which is the important one, that the enclosure of the grounds and the supervision of the superintendent will prevent any violation of the graves of the dead...".88

MARSHALL SQUARE

In 1878 the newspapers give an excellent description of Marshall Square in West Chester:

Marshall Square.

The work of giving beauty and refinement to Marshall Square was commenced to-day in reality, and the prospects are that the hands and hearts so engaged will neither tire nor relax their energies until that place has been made to conform with the beauty of our Borough in general.

Mr. Josiah Hoopes has the supervision of the work of ornamentation, which is sufficient to guarantee that it will be performed in no second rate manner both as to design and completeness.

There will be twenty beds filled with all the rarest and most beautiful bedding plants, among them many tropical ones, and the manner of their arrangement is in accordance with Mr. Hoopes' well considered plans.

When this feature of ornamenting these splendid grounds has been completed, Mr. H. will proceed to erect a Swiss cottage, the plan of which will be after one located in Fairmount Park. This structure will be 35 feet in length by 12 feet in width, with a little "annex" to be used as a tool house. The cottage is to have plain board entries, and will be divided into two rooms, one for ladies, the other for gentlemen. It will be supplied with water closets, washstands, tables and seats, and other little accessories necessary to comfort. The exterior will show the nicely dressed work of the frames, while between these timbers halved cedars will form a rustic and pretty finish. The roof will project considerably on all sides, which with the rustic porches and rounded shingle adornments, will form a very pretty appearance. Over the entire structure trailing vines will be led to add their part of the ornamental work, but it will take time before they can be made to fill the idea projected for them.

This building will be located about midway between the center of the Square and the south-east corner.

In the centre of the Square it is proposed to erect at an early day a large summer-house, where music can be dispensed, and a sort of general retiring place to all who may wish to sit at their ease after taking a stroll of the town or the grounds.

Near the corner opposite the Hon. Washington Townsend's residence, also at a point near the fountain, two more rustic houses are to be located, in style to be entirely different from the two above referred to. They will partake of the "umbrella" style, and being supplied with seats, will serve as cosy places for loving couples to sit and have their conversation without being interfered with by the visiting throng.

In addition to the above, seats will be scattered throughout the entire Square, and it is the hope of those having the matter in hand that the people of the town will subscribe a sum of money sufficient for the procurement of four very large vases to be placed at different points in the grounds.

Mr. Hoopes has his whole heart enlisted in the work; he has been selected to superintend, and the major part of it he has very generously offered to donate the borough, if the Council will push the matter along with the vim the project demands.

With what is already accomplished and the prospects for what we have above imperfectly and hurriedly described, it is but fair to look forward to Marshall Square being early made a place of resort that will be a credit to West Chester and its people.89

A monument was erected in West Chester in 1887. A newspaper mentions:

The monument which is to-day unveiled is 50 feet high from the bottom of the first base stone to the top of the soldier's head. It is of Ryegate granite, from South Ryegate, Vermont, and was made by the Ryegate Granite Works, of which R. F. Carter is President, A. F. Mulliken Secretary and Treasurer, and P. McGinn General Traveling Agent, who is here and put this beautiful monument in position. Its construction is as follows:

Bases—1st-12 feet square by 1 foot thick
       2d-10 ft. 4 in. square by 1 ft. thick
       3d- 8 ft. 8 in. square by 1 ft. thick
       4th- 7 ft. 2 in. square by 1 ft. thick

Plinths—6 feet square, with moulding on top, and 2 feet thick. A second and smaller plinth upon which rests the die, 5 feet 4 inches square and 1 foot thick, cut with bases to receive the columns.

Die—This is a polished stone 3 feet 4 inches square and 4 feet high, with columns at the four columns also polished.

On the die are the following inscriptions:

South Face.

Organized at
Camp Everhart and
Camp Wayne,
West Chester,
Pennsylvania,
Oct. 29, 1861.
Companies
A, B, C, E, F, H and K
From Chester County.
Companies D, G, and I
From Delaware County.
Mustered out of Service
At Weldon,
North Carolina,
August 28, 1865.

West Face.

Erected by the Surviving Members
of
The Ninety-Seventh Regiment,
Pennsylvania Volunteers,
to the
Memory of Its Dead.
Dedicated Oct. 29, 1887.

North Face.

Fort Clinch,
James Island,
Secessionville,
Seige of Charleston,

Wagner and Gregg,
Drury's Bluff,
Cold Harbor,
Petersburg Heights,
Cemetery Hill,
Mine Explosion,
Deep Bottom,
Charles City Road,
Darby Town Road,
Fort Fisher,
Wilmington,
Surrender of Johnson.

East Side.

Field and Staff Officers at the Organization of the Regiment:

Colonel Henry R. Gus,
Lieut.-Colonel Augustus P. Duer,
Major Galusha Pennypacker,
Surgeon John R. Everhart, M.D.,
Asst. Sur. George W. Miller, M.D.,
Adjutant Henry W. Carruthers,
Quartermaster David Jones,
Chaplain, Rev. Wm. E. Whitehead.

Surmounting the dies is a frieze extending over the capitals and cut in such a manner as to relive the die from the capitals. The frieze is 6 feet 2 inches square and 2 feet thick. On his frieze is a plinth with shields embossed upon the four faces: South face, 24th Army Corps badge; west face, 18th Army Corps badge, north face, 10th Army Corps badge, east face the figures "97" being the number of the regiment. Above this plinth is another stone, which is 5 feet 4 inches square 10 inches thick, and embellished as follows: South side, an anchor; west side, crossed muskets; north side, crossed cannon; east side, crossed sabres. The next piece is a moulding 3 feet 6 inches square and 1 foot 2 inches thick, on which rests the shaft, which is in three pieces. The first section is 6 feet long and 2 feet 9 inches square at its base and finished with a moulding 1 foot thick. The next section is 7 feet long and 2 feet 7 inches thick at the base, also finished with a one-foot moulding. The third section is 7 feet long and 2 feet 5 inches thick at the base, finished at the top with a moulding. On this rests a composite capital 3 feet 6 inches square with a pedestal ornamented with carving, which is 2 feet 8 inches square and 1 foot thick. The soldier stands upon this pedestal. The statue is that of a soldier at parade rest, and is a handsome piece of workmanship 8 feet high and weighs two tons. The entire weight of the monument is 104 tons.

In The Box.

Between the third and fourth bases a tin box was placed by Officer Robert O. Jefferis, who collected the following articles for it:

A copy of the 97th Regiment, a muster out roll presented by Ellwood Baldwin, a nicely painted card upon which were the seal of the borough of West Chester and the names of the Chief and Second Burgess, the Council and standing committees, also the names of the members of the Board of Health, besides a slip of paper upon which were written the names of the police force, a badge of the Fame Fire Company, also a G. A. R. badge, printed by-laws of Chieftain's League Improved Order of Red Men, also those of WestChester Lodge, No. 42, I. O. O. F., the ticket upon which were printed the names of officers of Lodge No. 322, F. & A. M., a card of invitation to the ceremonies of the unveiling, a piece of Continental money bearing date 1756, a ten-cent piece contributed by Hon. Washington Townsend, and a five-cent piece contributed by W. A. Brooke, a fourth annual reunion ticket of the regiment, cards with the following names upon them: P. Maginn, W. L. Davis, R. O. Jefferis, Winslow Gheen and copies of the Daily News, Village Record, American Republican, Jeffersonian and Chester County Democrat.

Between the first and second sections of the shaft Sergeant St. Julien Ogier, of Co. I (Wayne Fencibles, had a copper case about ten inches long and four wide, containing the muster and pay roll of the above company. On the case, which was presented by Theo. P. Apple, was the following inscription:

Muster and Pay Roll
Of Co. I (Wayne Fencibles), Sixth Regt,
N. G. P.
West Chester, Pa.
Copper from roof of Nat. Bank Chester Co.[90]

The following men are listed in the public records of the county as gardeners: Edward Leet, East Marlboro Township in 1739; William Lemon, Westtown Township in 1810; Henry Souders, East Whiteland Township in 1811; Samuel Faulkner, Westtown Township in 1820; John Jackson, London Grove Township in 1821 and Thomas Murphy, East Nantmeal Township in 1842.

1. John H. Brinton Diary #1, p. 40 under date April, 1846. Chester County Historical Society (West Chester, Penna.)
2. Adolph B. Benson, *PETER KALM'S TRAVELS IN NORTH AMERICA,* (New York, 1937) Vol 1, pp 71, 72.
3. Ibid., p. 58.
4. Henry Graham Ashmead, *HISTORY OF DELAWARE COUNTY,* Pennsylvania, (Philadelphia, Pa., 1884), p. 460.
5. *PENNSYLVANIA GAZETTE,* (Philadelphia, Pa.) May 9, 1745.
6. Ibid., March 8, 1764.
7. Ibid., May 8, 1766.
8. Ibid., March 1, 1770.
9. Ibid., Oct. 27, 1773.
10. Ibid., Dec. 29, 1802.
11. Ibid., Feb. 2, 1803.
12. *CHESTER & DELAWARE FEDERALIST,* (West Chester, Penna.) Feb. 22, 1815.
13. *AMERICAN REPUBLICAN* (West Chester, Penna.) Nov. 19, 1816.
14. Ibid., Nov. 19, 1816.
15. Ibid., Oct. 31, 1820.
16. *VILLAGE RECORD,* (West Chester, Penna.) Jan. 10, 1821.
17. Ibid., Jan. 30, 1822.
18. Ibid., July 28, 1824.
19. *AMERICAN REPUBLICAN,* (West Chester, Penna.) Nov. 23, 1825.
20. *VILLAGE RECORD,* (West Chester, Penna.) Nov. 16, 1831.
21. Ibid., Nov. 7, 1832.
22. *AMERICAN REPUBLICAN,* (West Chester, Penna.) June 11, 1833.
23. Ibid., Oct. 14, 1834.
24. Ibid., Dec. 2, 1834.
25. *VILLAGE RECORD,* (West Chester, Penna.) July 27, 1836.
26. *AMERICAN REPUBLICAN,* (West Chester, Penna.) June 27, 1837.
27. Ibid., Oct. 23, 1838.
28. Ibid., July 14, 1840.
29. Ibid., Dec. 14, 1841.
30. Ibid., Sept. 21, 1841.
31. *VILLAGE RECORD,* (West Chester, Penna.) Sept. 30, 1845.
32. *AMERICAN REPUBLICAN,* (West Chester, Penna.) Oct. 19, 1847.
33. *VILLAGE RECORD,* (West Chester, Penna.) Aug. 22, 1848.
34. Ibid., March 23, 1847.
35. Ibid., April 11, 1848.
36. *AMERICAN REPUBLICAN,* (West Chester, Penna.) Nov. 2, 1852.
37. *VILLAGE RECORD,* (West Chester, Penna.) Nov. 29, 1853.
38. Ibid., Nov. 22, 1853.
39. *AMERICAN REPUBLICAN,* (West Chester, Penna.) Dec. 11, 1855.
40. *VILLAGE RECORD,* (West Chester, Penna.) Nov. 6, 1855.
41. *AMERICAN REPUBLICAN,* (West Chester, Penna.) Nov. 25, 1856.
42. Ibid., April 8, 1856.
43. Ibid., Jan. 1, 1856.
44. *VILLAGE RECORD,* (West Chester, Penna.) May 23, 1857.
45. Ibid., Nov. 23, 1858.
46. Ibid., June 12, 1858.
47. Ibid., Oct. 1, 1859.
48. Ibid., Dec. 3, 1859.
49. Ibid., Feb. 11, 1860.
50. Ibid., Sept. 29, 1860.
51. Ibid., Dec. 25, 1860.
52. Ibid., Feb. 23, 1861.
53. Ibid., April 6, 1861.
54. Ibid., June 7, 1862.
55. Ibid., June 9, 1863.
56. Ibid., July 3, 1866.
57. Ibid., Dec. 31, 1867.
58. Ibid., Sept. 19, 1868.
59. Ibid., Nov. 24, 1868.
60. Ibid., Oct. 9, 1869.
61. Ibid., Dec. 25, 1869.
62. Ibid., Oct. 3, 1871.
63. Ibid., Sept. 30, 1871.
64. *AMERICAN REPUBLICAN,* (West Chester, Penna.) Nov. 7, 1871.
65. *VILLAGE RECORD,* (West Chester, Penna.) Feb. 1, 1873.
66. *PHOENIXVILLE MESSENGER,* (Phoenixville, Penna.) Aug. 8, 1874.

67. *VILLAGE RECORD*, (West Chester, Penna.) June 6, 1874.
68. *AMERICAN REPUBLICAN*, (West Chester, Penna.) April 7, 1874.
69. *VILLAGE RECORD*, (West Chester, Penna.) June 26, 1875.
70. *PHOENIXVILLE MESSENGER*, (Phoenixville, Penna.) Oct. 16, 1875.
71. *DAILY LOCAL NEWS*, (West Chester, Penna.) July 23, 1875.
72. *VILLAGE RECORD*, (West Chester, Penna.) April 15, 1876.
73. *AMERICAN REPUBLICAN*, (West Chester, Penna.) Nov. 18, 1841.
74. *VILLAGE RECORD*, (West Chester, Penna.) Sept. 13, 1862.
75. Ibid., March 15, 1873.
76. *AMERICAN REPUBLICAN*, (West Chester, Penna.) Feb. 26, 1850.
77. Ibid., March 5, 1850.
78. *VILLAGE RECORD*, (West Chester, Penna.) May 19, 1857.
79. Ibid., July 6, 1867.
80. Ibid., April 9, 1870.
81. Ibid., Aug. 20, 1872.
82. *KENNETT ADVERTISER*, (Kennett Square, Penna.) June 10, 1871.
83. *DAILY LOCAL NEWS*, (West Chester, Pena.) Sept. 2, 1874.
84. *AMERICAN REPUBLICAN*, (West Chester, Penna.) June 13, 1876.
85. *DAILY LOCAL NEWS*, (West Chester, Penna.) May 21, 1880.
86. Ibid., Nov. 17, 1885.
87. Chester County Will Book 6, p. 162.
88. *VILLAGE RECORD*, (West Chester, Penna.) Oct. 11, 1853.
89. *DAILY LOCAL NEWS*, (West Chester, Penna.) May 22, 1878.
90. Ibid., Oct. 29, 1887.

LEANTO

Leanto is not defined by Baily (ed. 1735), Sheridan (ed. 1789) and Webster (ed. 1828). It is defined by the Oxford English Dictionary (ed. 1933) as "A building whose rafters pitch against or lean on to another building or against a wall (Qwilt): a penthouse."

The 1798 Direct Tax lists four leantos: one of stone 18 x 10 feet; one of frame 34 x 18 feet and two that did not mention the material of construction, the mean size being 810 square feet. The 1799 tax assessment for Charlestown Township lists one leanto 26 x 11 feet and for Pikeland Township one log leanto. In the newspaper advertisements William Moore, of West Caln Township, advertised in 1782 a "log dwelling house with a stone end and a leanto adjoining"[1]; Benjamin Bartholomew, of East Whiteland Township, advertised in 1785 a "stone dwelling house, two stories high, four rooms on the first floor and entry, six on the second, with a leanto kitchen"[2] and Abraham Musgrave, of Upper Darby Township, advertised in 1787 a "log house, with frame leantoos, a part finished on purpose for a store."[3]

1. *PENNSYLVANIA GAZETTE* (Phila., Penna.) April 3, 1782.
2. Ibid., Jan. 19, 1785.
3. Ibid., March 7, 1787.

LEATHER HOUSE

The 1799 tax assessment for Honey Brook Township lists one stone leather house.

LIME HOUSE

The 1798 Direct Tax lists one lime and lumber house of stone 20 x 17 feet in Springfield and Lower Providence Townships.

LUMBER HOUSE

The 1798 Direct Tax lists ten lumber houses: three of stone, the mean size being 620 square feet; two of frame, the mean size being 304 square feet; two of log, the mean size being 184 square feet; one of wood 18 x 15 feet and two that did not mention the material of construction, the mean size being 192 square feet.

LYCEUM

The newspapers mention:
1858 "one story. stone House called a Lyceum 20 x 24 feet" John R. McClung (New Garden Twp.)

1. *VILLAGE RECORD* (West Chester, Penna.) Dec. 18, 1858.

MALT HOUSE

The 1798 Direct Tax lists six malt houses: two of stone, the mean size being 1004 square feet; one of brick 50 x 20 feet; one of log and stone 60 x 20 feet; one of log 64 x 20 feet and one that did not mention the material of construction 60 x 21 feet. The 1799 tax assessment for West Marlboro Township lists one stone malt house 70 x 23 feet. The newspaper advertisements mention between 1750 and 1774 two stone malt houses the mean size being 1800 square feet and one of brick 95 x 22 feet. Between 1825 and 1850 one stone malt house 100 x 24 feet and two that did not metion the material of construction, the mean size being 2725 square feet are listed in the advertisements.

MARBLE

Marble is defined by Bailey (ed. 1735) as "a Sort of fine Stone, extremely hard and solid, dug out of the Quarries", by Sheridan (ed. 1789) as "stone used in statues and elegant buildings, capable of a bright polish" and by Webster (ed. 1828) as "The popular name of any species of calcarious stone or mineral, of a compact texture, and of a beautiful appearance, susceptible of a good polish. The varieties are numerous, and greatly diversified in color. Marble is limestone, or a stone which may be calcined to lime, a carbonate of lime; but limestone is a more general name, comprehending the calcarious stones of an inferior texture, as well as those which admit a fine polish. Marble is much used for statues, busts, pillars, chimney pieces, monuments, &c."

The newspaper advertisements mention:

1828 "Marble Mantles, Tombs &c. THE subscriber having taken the establishment on the Philadelphia and Lancaster turnpike, 23 miles from Philadelphia, and 5 from West Chester, formerly occupied by JOHN GARD, intends keeping a general assortment of marble Mantles, Tombs, Grave-Stones, Curriers' tables &c. Door and window sills, steps &c. furnished at the shortest notice, on the most reasonable terms. John Woodward. N.B. All orders directed to the subscriber, East Whiteland, Chester county, will be promptly attended to."[1]

1832 "Marble Cutting Establishment. JOHN CORNOG, respectfully informs the inhabitants of the Boro' of West Chester and its vicinity, that he has commenced the MARBLE CUTTING in all its branches, in Market-st. West Chester..."[2]

1842 'MARBLE MANUFACTORY. THE SUBSCRIBER takes this method of returning thanks to his customers and friends, for the very liberal patronage he has received. He has considerably enlarged his stock, and is now prepared to furnish on sight HEAD & FOOT STONES, TOMBS & TABLE tops, DOOR & WINDOW SILLS, PLATFORMS & STEPS, DATE STONES, PAINT STONES & MULLARS Engraved with ROMAN or ITALIC, GERMAN TEXT, or ENGLISH Letters, as cheap as can be had at Philadelphia or Lancaster city. THOMAS PARKE. Downingtown."[3]

1844 "MARBLE CUTTING...in West Chester...MONU-MENTS also furnished...He also has on hand a number of ready finished MANTLES of both foreign and Chester county marble of various patterns, and other under way...JAMES PARK."[4]

1846 NEW MARBLE YARD. In the Borough of West Chester...THOMAS MOORE"[5]

1853 "Marble Slab For Sale. A MARBLE SLAB, that has been used as a Currying table, it is 10 feet in length by 3 feet 9 or 10 inches wide...JACOB SHARP-LESS."[6]

1855 "DOWNINGTOWN MARBLE WORKS — The subscriber having lately received a large addition to his stock would say to his friends and the public in general if you wish to obtain at very low prices a neat and handsome head and foot stone, a chaste and reposing Couch, a lofty and towering Monument, or a modest and assuming set of Quaker Stones with their bold and expressive inscriptions, call at the Downingtown MARBLE WORKS. All work delivered if requested. THOMAS PARK."[7]

1855 "Downingtown Marble Works...MONUMENTS both Italian and American...THOMAS PARKE."[8]

1856 "NEW MARBLE YARD...Always on hand MANTLES, MONUMENTS, TOMBS and STATUARY. ABM. M. GARRETT."[9]

1857 "PARKESBURG MONUMENT AND GRAVESTONE WORKS...A book of designs can be seen at the establishment to select from. WILLIAM B. McCOY."[10]

1862 "New Marble Works...No. 83 Gay Street...Marble Mantles, Toys for counters, bureau tables or wash-stands, as well as Steps, Sills, and all kinds of Building Work...W. J. ILLINGWORTH."[11]

1865 "McClintock's Marble Works DOWNINGTOWN, PA... that he has commenced the Marble business...to furnish Monuments, Tombs, Head and Foot Stones, Mantle work in all its branches, Furniture Slabs..."[12]

1868 "NEW MARBLE YARD IN WAYNESBURG. Mr. William Green..."[13]

1871 "CROSS & KRAMER'S PHOENIX MARBLE WORKS..."[14]

1871 "Geo E. Jones OXFORD Marble Works..."[15]

1872 "Public Sale of Personal Property...JOHN S. ASHTON...AT THE MARBLE YARD...West Chester..."[16]

1873 "HANDSOME TOMBSTONE Mr. David Jones' marble yard, a handsomely wrought stone destines to commemorate the resting place of Daniel Nields, dec'd. This tribute is of Italian marble, resting on an American marble vase..."[17]

1. *VILLAGE RECORD* (West Chester, Penna.) Feb. 27, 1828.
2. Ibid., May 16, 1832.
3. *AMERICAN REPUBLICAN* (West Chester, Penna.) March 8, 1842.
4. Ibid., Feb. 20, 1844.
5. *VILLAGE RECORD* (West Chester, Penna.) Dec. 22, 1846.
6. Ibid., Sept. 20, 1853.
7. *AMERICAN REPUBLICAN* (West Chester, Penna.) April 10, 1855.
8. *VILLAGE RECORD* (West Chester, Penna.) March 27, 1855.
9. Ibid., March 1, 1856.
10. Ibid., Aug. 8, 1857.
11. *AMERICAN REPUBLICAN* (West Chester, Penna.) April 1, 1862.
12. *VILLAGE RECORD* (West Chester, Penna.) April 18, 1865.
13. *AMERICAN REPUBLICAN* (West Chester, Penna.) March 17, 1868.
14. *PHOENIXVILLE MESSENGER* (Phoenixville, Penna.) April 29, 1871.
15. *KENNETT ADVERTISER* (Kennett Sq., Penna.) Jan. 28, 1871.
16. *VILLAGE RECORD* (West Chester, Penna.) Aug. 20, 1872.
17. *DAILY LOCAL NEWS* (West Chester, Penna.) April 2, 1873.

EXTERIOR

The newspapers mention:

1814 "stone barn, 70 by 52 feet with stables under the whole, plastered inside and the heads and sills of the doors marble, a stone Spring House, sufficient to hold the milk of twenty cows paved with marble set in terraces"[1] John Miller Est. (Tredyffrin Twp.)

1828 "Door and window sills, steps &c furnished"[2] John Woodward (West Whiteland Twp.)

1833 "stone house, plastered in imitation of marble"[3] James Sloan (Honey Brook Twp.)

1852 "marble steps on platform in front"[4] Susan Lungren (West Chester)

1855 "2 story stone House, nearly new, 38 by 42 feet with marble window and door sills"[5] Townsend Hoopes (East Caln Twp.)

1859 "three story House and office with marble first story"[6] David Meconkey (West Chester)

1866 "Brick House...marble sills and lintels to the windows and doors"[7] #273 High Street (West Chester)

1867 "House, three story with white marble 25 ft."[8] David Meconkey (West Chester)

1869 "House...marble steps at the front door"[9] Thomas S. Valentine Est. (West Chester)

1870 "The base of the building, from the ground to the line of first floor, will be faced with white marble. The steps, window and door sills, are all to be of white marble"[10] Normal School (West Chester)

1870 "The marble arches over the windows and doors... They are dressed and fitted for the building in sheds upon the ground"[11] Normal School, (West Chester)

1871 "New Bank Proposed...marble or brown stone, 24 by 60 feet"[12] (Phoenixville)

1872 "window...Marble Heads and Sills"[13] Charles L. Warner (West Chester)

1873 "marble steps and caps from quarries of J. Preston Thomas, West Whiteland"[14] Normal School (West Chester)

1874 "new Brick House with marble corners and pressed brick front"[15] Charles L. Warner (West Chester)

1875 "House, pressed brick front, marble finish"[16] Joseph Speakman Est. (West Chester)

1876 "Bank...Built of Blue Lime Stone with Marble Corners"[17] Bank of Brandywine (West Chester)

1. *CHESTER AND DELAWARE FEDERALIST* (West Chester, Penna.) Dec. 14, 1814.
2. *VILLAGE RECORD* (West Chester, Penna.) Feb. 27, 1828.
3. *AMERICAN REPUBLICAN* (West Chester, Penna.) Nov. 26, 1833.
4. Ibid., Feb. 10, 1852.
5. *VILLAGE RECORD* (West Chester, Penna.) Oct. 23, 1855.
6. *AMERICAN REPUBLICAN* (West Chester, Penna.) Jan. 25, 1859.
7. *VILLAGE RECORD* (West Chester, Penna.) Nov. 3, 1866.
8. Ibid., Oct. 15, 1867.
9. Ibid., Nov. 27, 1869.
10. *AMERICAN REPUBLICAN* (West Chester, Penna.) July 12, 1870.
11. Ibid., Oct. 4, 1870.
12. *PHOENIXVILLE MESSENGER* (Phoenixville, Penna.) April 1, 1871.
13. *VILLAGE RECORD* (West Chester, Penna.) Jan. 13, 1872.
14. Ibid., April 15, 1873.
15. *DAILY LOCAL NEWS* (West Chester, Penna.) Jan. 16, 1874.
16. *VILLAGE RECORD* (West Chester, Penna.) Nov. 6, 1875.
17. Ibid., March 14, 1876.

INTERIOR

The newspapers mention:

1828 "intends keeping a general assortment of marble Mantles"[1] John Woodward (West Whiteland)

1832 "[spring] flows into the Wash House into a Marble Basin"[2] Charles Worrall (East Bradford Twp.)

1832 "brick dwelling...and 2 rooms 17 feet square and 10 ft 6 in in height with marble mantles in each"[3] George B. Norris (West Chester)

1841 "2 parlors on the first floor one of which is finished with mahogany folding doors, marble mantle, jambs and hearth, and the other with marble jambs, hearth &c."[4] John Aitken (Upper Oxford Twp.)

1842 "...with marble mantels on the 1st and second story"[5] Wm. Ingram (West Chester)

1844 "a marble table and large drying room"[6] George Massey, tannery, (West Whiteland Twp.)

1852 "two marble mantels on the first floor"[7] Susan Lungren (West Chester)

1857 "Italian Marble Mantels...hot and cold water conveyed to marble top wash stands in all the principal chambers and bath room"[8] C. A. Wolborn (West Whiteland Twp.)

1865 "A neat high counter, with marble top"[9] First National Bank, (West Chester)

1870 "House...permanent Marble Washstands"[10] Benjamin Phillips (New Garden Twp.)

1872 "marble soda fountain"[11] G.C.M. Eicholtz (Downingtown)

1872 "The ground floor is beautifully laid with marble tile"[12] Hammond & Kervey Drug store (West Chester)

1872 "have erected a very handsome white marble soda fountain of the cottage pattern with German jasper panels"[13] Hammond & Kervey Drug store (West Chester)

1873 "large show cases on the marble top counter"[14] Jesse Thatcher (West Chester)

1873 "lately put in a very fine white marble octagon fountain with Tennessee marble panels"[15] Hammond & Kervey Drug Store (West Chester)

1876 "white marble mantel in the parlor"[16] J.S. Futhey (West Chester)

The newspaper advertisements before 1876 mention ten other marble mantels and one other marble basin.

1. *VILLAGE RECORD* (West Chester, Penna.) Feb. 27, 1828.
2. *REGISTER AND EXAMINER* (West Chester, Penna.) Oct. 16, 1832.
3. *AMERICAN REPUBLICAN* (West Chester, Penna.) April 19, 1832.
4. Ibid., Sep. 21, 1841.
5. *VILLAGE RECORD* (West Chester, Penna.) Jan. 26, 1842.
6. Ibid., Aug. 6, 1844.
7. *AMERICAN REPUBLICAN* (West Chester, Penna.) Feb. 10, 1852.
8. *VILLAGE RECORD* (West Chester, Penna.) Sep. 12, 1857.
9. Ibid., March 21, 1865.
10. Ibid., Oct. 4, 1870.
11. *AMERICAN REPUBLICAN* (West Chester, Penna.) May 21, 1872.
12. Ibid., Oct. 1, 1872.

13. Ibid., Oct. 1, 1872.
14. *DAILY LOCAL NEWS* (West Chester, Penna.) Dec. 9, 1873.
15. *AMERICAN REPUBLICAN* (West Chester, Penna.) June 10, 1873.
16. *VILLAGE RECORD* (West Chester, Penna.) April 1, 1876.

QUARRY

The newspapers mention:

1818 "WHITE MARBLE...quarry"[1] George Norman (Tredyffrin Twp.)

1822 "Quarry...White marble"[2] Jacob Fisher Est. (East Caln Twp.)

1835 "quantity of limestone and marble"[3] Hunt Downing Est. (West Whiteland Twp.)

1839 "extensive beds of MARBLE"[4] George Boyer Est. (West Whiteland Twp.)

1840 "marble quarry of superior dark marble"[5] Joseph Smith (East Whiteland Twp.)

1840 "large strata of cloud marble, dark and light"[6] Wm. Fahnestock (East Whiteland Twp.)

1847 "Marble and Limestone Quarry...West Chester affords a good market for curb stones and crossings, which are obtained from the quarry of the best quality"[7] Josiah Harmar (East Whiteland Twp.)

1853 "Marble Quarry"[8] James Torbert (East Caln Twp.)

1854 "Marble"[9] Rebecca Garrison, Susan H. King (East Whiteland Twp.)

1855 "Marble"[10] Townsend Hoopes (East Caln Twp.)

1857 "marble quarry"[11] Stephen Blatchford (East Caln Twp.)

1866 "about to open marble quarry"[12] Mr. Lockwood (West Whiteland Twp.)

1867 "specimen of Black Marble from the surface of Dr. George Thomas's quarry. It has all the indication of the imported Irish Black Marble, and they consider it superior in working quality. Dr. Thomas has three veins of marble on his farm — white, blue and black and he purposes working them in the spring. Most of the marble is this County is brought from the state of Vermont"[13] William B. Torbert (West Whiteland Twp.)

1869 "[drinking fountain] dove color Chester County Marble from quarries of Messrs. Thomas Brothers, West Whiteland"[14]

1873 "marble steps and caps from quarries of J. Preston Thomas, West Whiteland"[15]

1. *VILLAGE RECORD* (West Chester, Penna.) Oct. 28, 1818.
2. *AMERICAN REPUBLICAN* (West Chester, Penna.) Dec. 4, 1822.
3. Ibid., Sept. 22, 1835.
4. *VILLAGE RECORD* (West Chester, Penna.) Dec. 17, 1839.
5. *AMERICAN REPUBLICAN* (West Chester, Penna.) June 2, 1840.
6. Ibid., Nov. 24, 1840.
7. *VILLAGE RECORD* (West Chester, Penna.) July 17, 1847.

8. Ibid., Aug. 9, 1853.
9. Ibid., Oct. 24, 1854.
10. Ibid., Oct. 23, 1855.
11. Ibid., Oct. 31, 1857.
12. Ibid., June 12, 1866.
13. Ibid., Dec. 31, 1867.
14. Ibid., July 27, 1869.
15. Ibid., April 15, 1873.

METAL

The newspaper advertisements mention:

1854 "Three story Brick dwelling...and store room, metal roof"[1] James Galliner (West Chester)

Before 1877 the newspaper advertisements mention five other buildings having metal roofs. In 1886 a newspaper mentions that the house of N.T. Hayes, in West Chester, "within a day or two the roof has been painted and beautiful metallic ornaments placed on the combs of the roof."[2]

1. *VILLAGE RECORD* (West Chester, Penna.) Dec. 26, 1854.
2. *DAILY LOCAL NEWS* (West Chester, Penna.) May 6, 1886.

MILK HOUSE

The 1798 Direct Tax lists one hundred and forty-five milk houses: seventy-two of stone; the mean size being 132 square feet; seventy of log; the mean size being 102 square feet; one of brick 28 x 11 feet; one of frame 10 x 8 feet and one that did not mention the material of construction 10 x 10 feet. One milk house is mentioned as having a smoke house over it and three stone milk and wash houses are mentioned as being in the same building. The 1796 tax assessment for East Fallowfield Township lists six stone milk houses, the mean size being 234 square feet.

In 1817 Christian Zook, of Tredyffrin Township had a "stone milk house, with a large room above occupied as a store house, and is considered as an excellent stand for business."[1]

1. *AMERICAN REPUBLICAN* (West Chester, Penna.) Nov. 11, 1817.

MILLS

The 1798 Direct Tax lists nine mills: four of stone and frame, the mean size being 1567 square feet; three of stone, the mean size being 1702 square feet; one of frame 60 x 25 feet and one of log 24 x 24 feet. The 1799 tax assessment for West Nottingham Township lists one stone mill 30 x 26 feet. The newspaper advertisements between 1809 and 1824 list three stone mills the mean size being 1316 square feet and two that did not mention the material of construction the mean size being 1222 square feet.

MORTAR

Mortar is defined by Bailey (ed. 1735) as "Lime and Sand mixed together for Building", by Sheridan (ed. 1789) as "a cement for building" and by Webster (ed. 1828) as "A mixture of lime and sand with water, used as a cement for uniting stones and bricks in walls. If the lime is slaked and the materials mixed with lime water, the cement will be much stronger."

The newspaper advertisements mention:

1838 the cellar of a house "with a mortar floor"[1] John Commons (West Marlboro Twp.)

1847 "barn yard is enclosed with a new stone and mortar wall"[2] James Patton (West Goshen Twp.)

1853 "Brick smoke house, two stories with two mortar floors, the lower story arranged for drying apples"[3] Hayes Jackson (East Marlboro Twp.)

1858 "stone House...2 garrets, mortar floors"[4] Jackson & Bradley (East Bradford Twp.)

1883 "addition built to his residence...of pressed brick with red mortar"[5] Addison May (West Chester)

1885 "The handsome residence of Mowrey Latshaw...with its pressed brick front, black mortar and brown stone window caps and sills presents an attractive appearance"[6] (Spring City)

The newspaper advertisements before 1876 mention two other cellars with mortar floors and one other garret having a mortar floor.

1. *AMERICAN REPUBLICAN* (West Chester, Penna.) Aug. 13, 1839.
2. Ibid., June 20, 1847.
3. *VILLAGE RECORD* (West Chester, Penna.) Nov. 22, 1853.
4. Ibid., Jan. 23, 1858.
5. *DAILY LOCAL NEWS* (West Chester, Penna.) June 8, 1883.
6. Ibid., July 13, 1885.

MOULDINGS

Mouldings are defined by Bailey (ed. 1735) "are Ornaments either of Wood or Stone; also that Part which bears up an Arch" and by Sheridan (ed. 1789) as "ornamental cavities in wood or stone."

The newspapers mention:

1860 "new two story stone House 30 by 40 feet containing two parlors and a hall, the ceilings of which are finished with ornamental mouldings"[1] Francis E. Wilcox (Willistown Twp.)

1877 "House...Around the ceiling is a small gilt moulding"[2] Samuel Holmes (Oxford)

1. *AMERICAN REPUBLICAN* (West Chester, Penna.) Sept. 4, 1860.
2. *OXFORD PRESS* (Oxford, Penna.) June 27, 1877.

MUD

The 1798 Direct Tax for Coventry Township lists the house of Elizabeth Hofacker as "Sones Wols of Moth Cracked"; George Fritz with "one Barn of Mode Walls 60 x 30"; Christopher Holderman with "Barn Mode Walls"; Martin Rinehart with "Mud Walls of stone" kitchen 30 x 28, 1½ stories high"; John High with house "Moth wols of stone 33 x 26" and Rudolph Harles with house "Moth wols of stone 32 x 23 1 story". The same tax for Vincent Township lists the heirs of Laurence Hipple as having "Stone wols of Mode with kitchen 30 x 19." The 1796 tax assessment for New London Township lists Isaac Ryan as having a mud house and barn and Samuel Ramsey, of Londonerry Township, with "old mud wall house." The 1799 tax assessment lists Thomas Simmons, of Londonderry Township, with "old Mud house", Isaac Tyan, of New London Township, with "Mud wol House old" and Ezekiel Hopkins, of Upper Oxford Township, with one mud house.

OBSERVATORY

Observatory is defined by Sheridan (ed. 1789) as "a place built for astronomical observation" and by Webster (ed. 1828) as "A place or building for making observations on the heavenly bodies; as the royal observatory at Greenwich."

The newspapers mention:

1859 "new cottage...observatory on top...a model house"[1] Daniel Mamall (West Vincent Twp.)

1874 "on roof is promenade observatory 60 feet long"[2] Ercildon Seminary (East Fallowfield Twp.)

Before 1877 there are three other mentions of observatories in the newspaper advertisements.

1. *VILLAGE RECORD* (West Chester, Penna.) May 17, 1859.
2. *AMERICAN REPUBLICAN* (West Chester, Penna.) Feb. 17, 1874.

OFFSET

The newspaper advertisements mention:

1845 "2½ storied Brick House, 45 by 33 feet (with an offset of 8 feet the width of one room to make the kitchen larger"[1] John C. Dorat (Penn Twp.)

1849 "2½ story Brick store and dwelling adjoining 50 by 40 feet, with an offset of 10 feet of the dwelling"[2] John M. Mercer (Upper Oxford Twp.)

1. *AMERICAN REPUBLICAN* (West Chester, Penna.) Aug. 5, 1845.
2. *VILLAGE RECORD* (West Chester, Penna.) Aug. 28, 1849.

OIL MILL

The 1798 Direct Tax lists three oil mills: one of wood 20 x 18 feet; one old log 18 x 18 feet and one of frame 29 x 27 feet.

OUT BUILDINGS

Sometimes the inventories mention buildings other than the houses: outshed, John Roades,[1] Darby Township, 1701; workhouse, Henry Gibbons,[2] Darby Township, 1702; shed over well, Robert Scothome,[3] Darby Township, 1708; bolting house and bake house, Ralph Fishbourn,[4] Chester, 1708; granary, Elizabeth Fishbourn,[5] Chester, 1709; out house, John Smith,[6] Darby, 1714/15; oven house, Jane Smith,[7] Darby Township, 1716; brew house, John Hoskins,[8] Chester, 1716; chamber over the wash house and cidar house, David Lloyd,[9] Chester, 1731; milk house, James Jefferies,[10] East Bradford Township, 1745; spring house, Thomas Gihon,[11] Concord Township, 1750; still house, James Bourgoin,[12] East Bradford Township, 1764; malt house, John Rudulph,[13] Darby Township, 1769; oil house, William Crabb,[14] Chichester Township, 1770; salt house, James Rowan,[15] Lower Chichester Township, 1772; chair house, John Knowles,[16] Ridley Township, 1778; well house, William Garrett,[17] Darby Township, 1780; cart house, John Smith,[18] Lower Chichester Township, 1785; saddle house, George Ashbridge,[19] Goshen Township, 1785; smoke house, Jobb Ruston,[20] Oxford Township, 1785; ash house, Enoch Jones,[21] Tredyffrin Township, 1820; carriage house, Samuel Downing,[22] East Nantmeal Township, 1821; woodhouse, Joshua Sharpless,[23] East Bradford Township, 1826; shop, John Stern,[24] East Goshen Township, 1838; pump house, Abraham Pennock,[25] West Marlboro Township, 1840; privy, John Kenedy,[26] East Caln Township, 1841 and tool house, Jesse Grubb,[27] East Coventry Township, 1849.

1. Abstracts o wills and inventories Bk. B, p. 151, (Historical Society of Pennsylvania, Phila., Pa.)
2. Ibid., p. 201.
3. Ibid., Bk. C, p. 273.
4. Ibid., p. 115.
5. Ibid., p. 141.
6. Chester County Inventories #21.
7. Ibid., #38.
8. Ibid., #27.
9. Ibid., #394.
10. Ibid., #958.
11. Ibid., #1361.
12. Ibid., 2139.
13. Ibid., 2465.
14. Ibid., #2555.
15. Ibid., #2691.
16. Ibid., #3138.
17. Ibid., #3265.
18. Ibid., #3578.
19. Ibid., 3739.
20. Ibid., 3674.
21. Ibid., 6801.
22. Ibid., 6902.
23. Ibid., 7960.
24. Ibid., 9739.
25. Ibid., 10041.
26. Ibid., 10054.
27. Ibid., 11498.

OUT HOUSE — NECESSARY, PRIVY

The 1798 Direct Tax lists nine out houses: three of stone; the mean size being 236 square feet; five of frame; the mean size being 239 square feet and one of brick 14 x 14 feet. The 1796 tax assessments for Charlestown and West Whiteland Townships mention six frame necessaries, three stone necessaries and four out houses. Richard Thomas, of West Whiteland Township, had "1 Double Necessary of Brick" and George Massey, of West Whiteland Township, had "1 Old Necessary large loop Holes." The 1799 tax assessment for Charlestown Township lists three stone out houses, the mean size being 246 square feet. In 1861 the Mansion House Hotel, in West Chester, had a "brick out house enclosed by board fence."[1] In 1834 John Van Amringe, of Upper Oxford Township, advertised "a stone privy."[2]

1. *VILLAGE RECORD* (West Chester, Penna.) Feb. 23, 1861.
2. *AMERICAN REPUBLICAN* (West Chester, Penna.) Sept. 9, 1834.

OVEN

The will of Richard Maris, of Springfield Township, in 1745, gives to his wife "the free use of my old Parlour & new Parlour in my new Dwelling House and the new vault under the sd House and also such Priviledge in my wash-house annexed to sd Dwelling House and use of my Draw well and bake oven in the sd wash-house"[1]

The newspaper advertisements mention:

1850 "bake oven"[2] Peter Carl (East Vincent Twp.)

1850 "frame shed with patent oven and cooking range in"[3] John Keech (West Chester)

1850 "patent oven in kitchen"[4] John Keech (West Chester)

1852 "brick oven"[5] Thomas Lamborn (East Marlboro Twp.)

1852 "wood house and Bake oven therein"[6] J.K. Missimer (Uwchlan Twp.)

1852 "nearly new oven attached"[7] J.B. Stretch (West Chester)

1854 "oven in cellar kitchen, and a patent oven in the upper one"[8] John S. Sanford (West Chester)

1855 "bake house"[9] Wm. S. Parker Est. (North Coventry Twp.)

1856 "oven shed"[10] John Deisem (Honey Brook borough)

1858 "bake oven under cover"[11] John Traynor, Jr., (Lower Oxford Twp.)

1861 "Rumford oven"[12] Wm. M. Taylor (Birmingham Twp.)

The newspaper advertisements, before 1876 mention one other brick oven, four bake ovens, three ovens, one bake house and one patent oven and oven under cover.

Prices for building ovens are found in account books. In the account book[13] of Jacob Lightfoot in 1795 "To Building a Bakeoven 0 15 0"; in the account book of Jacob Lightfoot in 1803 "To Laying Bottom and mouth in oven — 1 3" and in the account book of Joseph Hawley in 1823 "By Building the Oven at thy House 2 days found thy dirt the tender $2.00 Ditto next day loading bark 60 I diet."

1. Chester County Will Book 2, p. 184.
2. *AMERICAN REPUBLICAN* (West Chester, Penna.) Oct. 22, 1850.
3. *VILLAGE RECORD* (West Chester, Penna.) March 26, 1850.
4. *AMERICAN REPUBLICAN* (West Chester, Penna.) Feb. 19, 1850.
5. Ibid., Nov. 30, 1852.
6. *VILLAGE RECORD* (West Chester, Penna.) Oct. 12, 1852.
7. Ibid., Dec. 21, 1852.
8. Ibid., Nov. 28, 1854.
9. Ibid., Sep. 29, 1855.
10. *AMERICAN REPUBLICAN* (West Chester, Penna.) June 24, 1856.
11. *VILLAGE RECORD* (West Chester, Penna.) March 6, 1858.
12. Ibid., March 16, 1861.
13. Ms. #76488, Chester County Historical Society.
14. Account Books. Diaries, vault, Chester County Historical Society.

PAPER MILL

The 1798 Direct Tax lists five paper mills: three of stone, the mean size being 1282 square feet and one stone and frame 75 x 30 feet and one that did not mention the material of construction 45 x 28 feet. The 1796 tax assessment for East Fallowfield Township lists one stone and frame paper mill 60 x 35 feet. The newspapers mention between 1815 and 1824 one three story mill 50 x 40 feet; between 1825 and 1849 twelve mills: seven of stone the mean size being 2825 square feet, one stone and frame 62 x 37 feet and four that did not mention the material of construction the mean size being 2793 square feet and between 1850 and 1876 the newspapers mention seventeen paper mills eleven of stone, the mean size being 3797 square feet; one frame 60 x 32 feet; two stone and frame, the mean size being 2087 square feet and three that did not mention the material of construction, the mean size being 2612 square feet.

PARTITION

The wills, before 1814, mention the following partitions:

1762 "unto my Son John Flower the East End of my Mansion House Beginning at the front at the Brick Partition...unto my son Richard Flower ye westerly part of my Mansion house from ye aforesaid Brick Wall"[1] Richard Flower (Chichester Twp.)

1764 "allow her a Room in my now dwelling House with a Chimney in it to be partitioned off from the kitchen door to Room door"[2] Thomas Yarnall (Edgemont Twp.)

1806 "One room below stairs beside the kitchen or the Room over the kitchen should she chuse the latter the partition to be moved the wreght of two Joices to enlarge her room priviledge in the kitchen and cellar"[3] John Showalter (Tredyffrin Twp.)

The newspaper advertisements mention:

1845 "new Brick dwelling house...three rooms on the first floor with draw partition"[4] Hayes Jackson (East Marlboro Twp.)

1845 "new stone house...built for a store house, front room is 36 by 20 feet (by moving temporary partition"[5] John Vanderslice (Phoenixville)

1875 "DWELLING HOUSES NOW AND THEN...walls more than two feet in thickness...Other houses, of modern build have partition walls, four and a half inches thick"[6] (Chester County)

1. Chester County Will Book 4, p. 360.
2. Ibid., p. 474.
3. Ibid., Book 11, p. 130.
4. *VILLAGE RECORD* (West Chester, Penna.) Sept. 30, 1845.
5. Ibid., Sept. 22, 1845.
6. *DAILY LOCAL NEWS* (West Chester, Penna.) July 19, 1875.

PASSAGE

Passage is defined by Bailey (ed. 1735) as "the Place thro' which one goes."

The will of Samuel Taylor, of East Bradford Township, in 1759 mentions:

"two Rooms in my Dwelling house at the Northwest end one above and another below stairs and the use of halfe my Cellar and the Previledge of a garden that lyeth on the west side of a passage from the house to a Run or stream of water and Likewise a small stone building that stands at the End of the Garden."[1]

1. Chester County Will Book 4, p. 160.

PEBBLE DASH

SEE ROUGH CAST

The newspaper advertisements mention:

1822 "two story brick house pebble dashed."[1] John Kennedy (Downingtown)

1822 "stone dwelling-house, pebble dashed"[2] Benjamin Warner Est. (Tredyffrin Twp.)

1829 "two story frame house, pebble dashed"[3] Charles Jones (West Chester)

1830 "two story log House, plastered and pebble-dashed"[4] Jacob Stem (East Nantmeal Twp.)

1834 "shop, pebble dashed...buildings are all new"[5] James Humphrey (Uwchlan Twp.)

1839 "barn built of stone and dashed"[6] David Knauser (West Nantmeal Twp.)

1841 "stone HOUSE, with a log end lathed and pebble dashed"[7] Charles J. Davis (East Whiteland Twp.)

1857 "new stone House...with Pebbled Roof"[8] Wm. White (Tredyffrin Twp.)

1861 "three story stone House 40 by 37 feet pebble dashed and pebble roofed"[9] James Beale, Exton Hotel (West Whiteland Twp.)

1867 "Baptist Church, stone 45 by 70 feet...dashed walls"[10] (Coatesville)

Before 1877 the newspapers mention thirty-two other houses that were pebble dashed; seventeen of stone, seven of frame, three of brick, three of log and two that did not mention the material of construction. One other shop was pebble dashed.

1. *VILLAGE RECORD* (West Chester, Penna.) Jan. 30, 1822.
2. Ibid., May 29, 1822.
3. *AMERICAN REPUBLICAN* (West Chester, Penna.) May 26, 1829.
4. Ibid., Oct. 26, 1830.
5. Ibid., Sept. 9, 1834.
6. Ibid., Aug. 27, 1839.
7. *VILLAGE RECORD* (West Chester, Penna.) Oct. 5, 1841.
8. *AMERICAN REPUBLICAN* (West Chester, Penna.) March 24, 1857.
9. Ibid., June 25, 1861.
10. Ibid., July 20, 1867.

PIAZZA, PORCH, PORTICO, STOOP, VERANDA

Piazza is defined by Bailey (ed. 1735) as a "broad open Place, as a Market", by Sheridan (ed. 1789) as "a walk under a roof supported by pillars" and by Webster (ed. 1828) as "In building, a portico or covered walk supported by arches or columns."

Porch is defined by Bailey (ed. 1735) as "the entrance of an House", by Sheridan (ed. 1789) as "a roof supported by pillars before a door, an entrance, a portico, a covered walk" and by Webster (ed. 1828) as "In architecture, a kind of vestibule, supported by columns at the entrance of temples, halls, churches, or other buildings. 2. A portico; a covered walk."

Portico is defined by Bailey (ed. 1735) as "a long Place covered over with a vaulted or plain Roof, and supported with Pillars", by Sheridan (ed. 1789) as "a covered walk, a piazza" and by Webster (ed. 1828) as "In architecture, a kind of gallery on the ground, or a piazza encompassed with arches supported by columns; a covered walk. The roof is sometimes flat; sometimes vaulted."

Stoop was not defined by Bailey (ed. 1735) or by Sheridan (ed. 1789). Webster (ed. 1828) defines it as "In America, a kind of shed, generally open, but attached to a house; also, an open place for seats at a door.

Veranda was not defined by Bailey (ed. 1735) or by Sheridan (ed. 1789). Webster (ed. 1828) defines it as "An oriental word denoting a kind of open portico, formed by extending a sloping roof beyond the main building."

The newspapers mention:

1770 "stone dwelling house, 2 stories, 57 feet front, and 36 in depth, a fine piazza in the front the whole breadth of the house, 8 or 9 feet wide"[1] Yellow Springs (Pikeland Twp.)

1789 "house, part square logs and part stone, with a stone piazza and kitchen"[2] John Kerlin, Est. (Willistown Twp.)

1815 "2 story stone building, with four rooms on each floor, with a semi circular Piazza embracing the greater part of the house"[3] Benjamin Jefferis, Inn, (West Chester)

1817 "house is two stories high...with a piazza and balcony in front, and a porch in the rear"[4] Printer (Downingtown)

1818 "stone dwelling house...with piazza 45 feet by 10, ceiled and painted"[5] Moses Hoopes, David Wilson (East Goshen Twp.)

1820 "stone dwelling house...a porch round three fourths of said house"[6] Adam Zell (Honey Brook Twp.)

1822 "the eastern and northern sides of the kitchen are completely embraced by a piazza"[7] John Kennedy (Downingtown)

1827 "house is 42 by 32 feet...porch two ways"[8] John & Thomas Roberts (East Nantmeal Twp.)

1830 "dwelling house...porch in front and end"[9] Richard Barnard (Newlin Twp.)

1832 "house...A piazza back, the whole length of the house"[10] Joshua Hoopes (Downingtown)

1832 "two story stone building...a piazza front and back"[11] Daniel Vondersmith (Downingtown)

1832 "Stone Mansion House...There is a porch at the door"[12] Jacob Jones Est. (New Garden Twp.)

1833 "stone Dwelling house 35 by 34...with piazza on each side."[13] John Latshaw (Pikeland Twp.)

1835 "two story stone dwelling House...a portico in front and large piazza back"[14] Samuel Dull (Uwchlan Twp.)

1836 "Public House...a handsome and permanent piazza 9 feet wide extends the whole front"[15] Joel Pennock (London Grove Twp.)

1838 "Dwelling House...Attached to said building is a handsome porch to the north, extending the full length, and on the south side is a PIAZZA, 12 feet in length"[16] William G. Wallace (Sadsbury Twp.)

1838 "modern built frame house...porch to the basement"[17] John S. Bowen (Sadsbury Twp.)

1838 "stone dwelling house with kitchen piazza"[18] Thomas Maule (West Whiteland Twp.)

1839 "STONE HOUSE, 60 by 30 feet...with a piazza on each front"[19] James B. M'Farlan (Downingtown)

1839 "stone Tavern house, 36 by 50 ft...and a piazza passes around three sides of the building"[20] Randall Evans, "Franklin Tavern" (Tredyffrin Twp.)

1839 "three story Dwelling House, with two porches in front"[21] Samuel A. Knauser (West Vincent Twp.)

1841 "three story frame HOUSE, recently built, with double piazza extending the whole length of the building, affording a most delightful retreat in summer where it had a full view of the cars passing and repassing at all hours"[22] R.R. Walter (Parkesburg)

1842 "frame HOUSE, 28 by 30 ft., 2 stories high with two porticoes"[23] John E. Hartman (Uwchlan Twp.)

1847 "frame dwelling house...a Portico the whole length of the east end"[24] Elhanan Benner (Downingtown)

1848 "log House...a 20 feet portico in front"[25] M. Hirst (Charlestown Twp.)

1849 "stone dwelling house...porch in back 12 feet wide"[26] Harman Pennypacker (West Pikeland Twp.)

1850 "two story stone House...2 story piazza in front"[27] Jonathan Jones Est. (North Coventry Twp.)

1850 "three story stone House, nearly new...double porch on one front, and a single one on the other"[28] David D. Mancill (West Vincent Twp.)

1850 "stone mansion house...piazza extending the entire front of the building, and one at each of the back doors"[29] Wm. Huey (Willistown Twp.)

1851 "stone dwelling house, 80 feet front, with Gothic portico"[30] Abigail Kimber (East Pikeland Twp.)

1852 "stone dwelling house...enclosed piazza attached... kitchen piazza"[31] Joseph Pennypacker (Schuylkill Twp.)

1854 "stone house...handsome Verandah front"[32] C.P. Morton (West Bradford Twp.)

1855 "elegant iron verandah"[33] M. Thomas & Sons (West Chester)

1856 "2 story stone building, 36 feet front with stoops at the door of entrance"[34] "Our House" Chester Springs (West Pikeland Twp.)

1857 "2 story stone dwelling...stone out kitchen connected to the main building by a porch"[35] James Wynn Est. (East Nantmeal Twp.)

1857 "3 story house...porch in front and back and a stairway along side of the house leading to front porch"[36] John O'Reilly (Phoenixville)

1858 "Frame House 18 x 28 portico and balcony"[37] Isaac Groff (Atglen)

1858 "House, rough cast...portico over side door"[38] George D. Rembough (Downingtown)

1858 "stone House, portico and porches in front"[39] William Sharpless (London Grove Twp.)

1859 "stone House...piazza extending the entire length, with a large flight of stairs ascending thereto"[40] Samuel Roberts (West Pikeland Twp.)

1859 "frame kitchen attached with lattice portico"[41] Chester Valley Rail Road Co. (Downingtown)

1861 "stone Hotel...porch and platform in front"[42] "Steam Boat Tavern" (East Whiteland Twp.)

1863 "stone House, double portico around three sides"[43] J. Wilson Wright (Atglen)

1866 "porch 50 feet long"[44] Jonas G. Bassart (East Pikeland Twp.)

1867 "verandah on second floor"[45] David Meconkey (West Chester)

1867 "House...Lattice arched verandahs covered with evergreens and grapes surround the entire premises"[46] William Torbert (West Whiteland Twp.)

1867 "Brick House...has two large porticoes with balconies attached"[47] A. Hodgson (West Fallowfield Twp.)

1868 "stone Hotel...iron porches on 3 sides"[48] Chandler Phillips (London Grove Twp.)

1868 "covered iron Verandah extending the entire length of the building"[49] "Mansion House" (West Chester)

1868 "House...double Verandah in front 25 by 93 feet"[50] "Eagle Hotel" (West Chester)

1869 "stone House 20 by 50 feet, 2 story verandah 12 by 50 feet front"[51] T.S.C. Lowe (Schuylkill Twp.)

1869 "Closed Porch"[52] Isaac McClure (East Brandywine Twp.)

1869 "stone House...porch 10 by 30 feet at front door"[53] George Y. Passmore (West Brandywine Twp.)

1870 "House...Portico south and west 92 feet front south"[54] John Crisman Est. (North Coventry Twp.)

1870 "Three porticoes, one upstairs and 2 down"[55] Eusebius Barnard (Kennett Twp.)

1870 "New Hotel...ornamented with towers and a highly ornamented verandah from the second story running the entire length"[56] (Downingtown)

1870 "two verandahs 10 feet wide with heavy iron columns, pilasters and railing mostly wrought"[57] L. Lee Englebert (West Chester)

1870 "Porch on the north side 36 by 11 feet"[58] Eusebius Barnard Est. (Kennett Twp.)

1871 "House...There is a piazza supported by columns over the main entrance"[59] Penrose W.B. Brinton Est. (West Whiteland Twp.)

1873 "stone House, a porch ten feet wide, running around three sides"[60] Bernard Kendig Est. (Sadsbury Twp.)

1873 "House...side entrance with lattice porch"[61] Sharpless & Hall (West Chester)

1873 "original hotel ca. 1794...large kitchen with a wide projecting porch...the outside of which was enclosed with a lattice work, over which in summer ran climbing vines"[62] "White Hall Hotel" (West Chester)

1874 "Frame house, iron porch on two sides, making two fronts"[63] Lewis Michener (London Grove Twp.)

1875 "House...porch 12 feet wide"[64] Jonathan Rees (Phoenixville)

1875 "porch in front 7 x 40"[65] "Yearsley's" (West Caln Twp.)

1876 "House...Porch in front 8 by 31 feet"[66] George H. Cope (Lower Oxford Twp.)

1876 "House...and double verandas ten feet wide at the side with iron railings and posts"[67] J.S. Futhey (West Chester)

In the newspaper advertisements between 1850 and 1877 three hundred and fifty-nine porches were mentioned, ninety-two piazzas, thirty-four buildings with one portico, seven buildings with two porticos, three stoops, ten verandas and three iron verandas in addition to those already quoted.

1. *PENNSYLVANIA GAZETTE* (Philadelphia, Penna.) March 1, 1770.
2. *PENNSYLVANIA PACKET* (Philadelphia, Penna.) March 26, 1789.
3. *CHESTER & DELAWARE FEDERALIST* (West Chester, Penna.) Jan. 4, 1815.
4. *AMERICAN REPUBLICAN* (West Chester, Penna.) Jan. 14, 1817.
5. *VILLAGE RECORD* (West Chester, Penna.) Sep. 16, 1818.
6. *AMERICAN REPUBLICAN* (West Chester, Penna.) March 7, 1820.
7. *VILLAGE RECORD* (West Chester, Penna.) Jan. 30, 1822.
8. Ibid., Dec. 26, 1827.
9. Ibid., Jan. 6, 1830.
10. Ibid., April 4, 1832.
11. Ibid., Nov. 7, 1832.
12. *AMERICAN REPUBLICAN* (West Chester, Penna.) Nov. 6, 1832.
13. *VILLAGE RECORD* (West Chester, Penna.) Oct. 30, 1833.
14. Ibid., Sep. 2, 1835.
15. *AMERICAN REPUBLICAN* (West Chester, Penna.) Nov. 29, 1836.
16. Ibid., July 24, 1838.
17. Ibid., Nov. 20, 1838.
18. Ibid., Sep. 11, 1838.
19. Ibid., Oct. 1, 1839.
20. Ibid., Nov. 5, 1839.
21. Ibid., Oct. 8, 1839.
22. Ibid., Nov. 9, 1841.
23. Ibid., Dec. 20, 1842.
24. *VILLAGE RECORD* (West Chester, Penna.) Nov. 23, 1847.
25. Ibid., Sept. 5, 1848.
26. Ibid., Sep. 11, 1849.
27. Ibid., Sep. 24, 1850.
28. *AMERICAN REPUBLICAN* (West Chester, Penna.) Nov. 12, 1850.
29. *VILLAGE RECORD* (West Chester, Penna.) Nov. 5, 1850.
30. *AMERICAN REPUBLICAN* (West Chester, Penna.) Sept. 16, 1851.
31. Ibid., Oct. 19, 1852.
32. *VILLAGE RECORD* (West Chester, Penna.) Oct. 31, 1854.
33. *AMERICAN REPUBLICAN* (West Chester, Penna.) April 24, 1855.
34. Ibid., Jan. 1, 1856.
35. Ibid., Sept. 29, 1857.
36. Ibid., Feb. 24, 1857.
37. Ibid., Sept. 16, 1851.
38. *VILLAGE RECORD* (West Chester, Penna.) Feb. 20, 1858.
39. Ibid., Sept. 25, 1858.
40. Ibid., Oct. 29, 1859.
41. *AMERICAN REPUBLICAN* (West Chester, Penna.) July 5, 1859.
42. *VILLAGE RECORD* (West Chester, Penna.) Nov. 12, 1861.
43. Ibid., Nov. 14, 1863.
44. Ibid., Nov. 13, 1866.
45. Ibid., Oct. 15, 1867.
46. Ibid., Dec. 31, 1867.
47. Ibid., Aug. 10, 1867.
48. Ibid., Nov. 10, 1868.
49. Ibid., Oct. 27, 1868.
50. Ibid., Dec. 29, 1868.
51. Ibid., Oct. 9, 1869.
52. Ibid., July 13, 1869.
53. Ibid., Dec. 25, 1869.
54. Ibid., Aug. 20, 1870.
55. Ibid., Nov. 26, 1870.
56. Ibid., March 15, 1870.
57. Ibid., Oct. 22, 1870.
58. Ibid., Nov. 26, 1870.
59. *AMERICAN REPUBLICAN* (West Chester, Penna.) Nov. 7, 1871.
60. *VILLAGE RECORD* (West Chester, Penna.) Sept. 16, 1873.
61. *DAILY LOCAL NEWS* (West Chester, Penna.) March 28, 1873.
62. *AMERICAN REPUBLICAN* (West Chester, Penna.) Oct. 21, 1873.
63. *VILLAGE RECORD* (West Chester, Penna.) Feb. 7, 1874.
64. *PHOENIXVILLE MESSENGER* (Phoenixville, Penna.) Feb. 27, 1875.
65. Ibid., Oct. 16, 1875.
66. *AMERICAN REPUBLICAN* (West Chester, Penna.) June 27, 1876.
67. *VILLAGE RECORD* (West Chester, Penna.) April 1, 1876.

PIGEON HOUSE

The 1799 tax assessment for New London Township lists one pigeon house.

PILASTER

Pilaster is defined by Bailey (ed. 1735) as "a kind of square Pillar made to jut out of a Wall" and by Webster (ed. 1828) as "A square column, sometimes insulated; but usually pilasters are set within a wall, projecting only one quarter of their diameter. Their bases, capitals and entablatures have the same parts as those of columns."

The newspaper advertisements mention:

1869 "New School, brick 48 by 50 feet...The walls are finished on the outside with pilasters which relieve the plainness of an otherwise smooth surface."[1] (Kennett Square)

1870 "two Verandahs 10 feet wide with heavy iron columns, pilasters and railing mostly wrought"[2] J. Lee Englebert (West Chester)

1. *AMERICAN REPUBLICAN* (West Chester, Penna.) Sept. 14, 1869.
2. *VILLAGE RECORD* (West Chester, Penna.) Oct. 22, 1870.

PILLARS & POSTS

The 1796 tax assessment for West Whiteland Township lists both George Gray and George Hoofman each with "a Cart House on Posts, Straw Roof" George Hoofman also had a "Cart House on Posts." William Fahnestock, "Warren Tavern", East Whiteland Township, advertised in 1840 a "large Shelter on stone pillars, near the spring house, under which the cows are chained to be milked through the summer."[1]

1. *AMERICAN REPUBLICAN* (West Chester, Penna.) Nov. 24, 1840.

PLATFORM

The newspapers mention:
1880 "He has erected a platform 40 x 50 feet, of planed boards, for dancing purposes"[1] Thomas Grove (West Goshen Twp.)

1. *DAILY LOCAL NEWS* (West Chester, Penna.) June 8, 1880.

PLAZA

The newspapers mention:
1883 "The homestead in itself with its peaked gables, its beetle-browed porches and extensive court serves to recall all the architectural intricacies of the reign of Queen Anne, while from its square plaza upon the roof-top one commands an impressive view of far-reaching valleys, moorlands of irregular shape and wood freighted slopes"[1] John Patterson "Glen Cairn" (Wallace Twp.)

1. *DAILY LOCAL NEWS* (West Chester, Penna.) Jan. 26, 1883.

POT HOUSE

The 1798 Direct Tax lists three pot houses: two of frame, the mean size being 1256 square feet and one of log 40 x 22 feet. The newspaper advertisements between 1830 and 1834 mention two stone and log pot houses: one, 2½ story, 30 x 20 feet and the other 22 x 22 feet. One Kiln house is mentioned, 2½ story, 25 x 25 feet.

POWDER MILL

The 1798 Direct Tax lists one powder mill but did not mention the material of construction 18 x 15 feet.

PRESS HOUSE

The newspaper advertisements, between 1820 and 1824, mention one press house that did not mention the material of construction, 38 x 18 feet.

PROMENADE

The newspapers mention:
1870 "On top of the hotel is a handsome premenade of seventy feet in length" "Mansion House"[1] (West Chester)
1873 "promenade"[2] McClellan's Institute (West Chester)

1. *AMERICAN REPUBLICAN* (West Chester, Penna.) Dec. 6, 1870.
2. Ibid., March 18, 1873.

PUMP HOUSE

The 1798 Direct Tax for East Caln and West Whiteland Townships lists one frame pump house.

ROOFING

Roof is defined by Bailey (ed. 1735) as "the Top of a House", by Sheridan (ed. 1789) as "the cover of a house; the vault, the inside of the arch that covers a building" and by Webster (ed. 1828) as "The cover or upper part of a house or other building, consisting of rafters covered with boards, shingles or tiles, with a side or sides sloping from the ridge, for the purpose of carrying off the water that falls in rain or snow..."

Henry Graham Ashmead, in 1883, describes the Boar's Head Inn, in Chester, built in 1682 as "One story and a half high, with peaked roof...The roof was of split shingles";[1] the Old Hoskins (Graham) house, in Chester, built in 1688 as "Two stories in height with attics...Steep roof,"[2] and the Logan house, in Chester, built in 1700, as "Built of brick, two stories in height, with a tent-like roof forming an attic within, with steep sides."[3] The Brinton diary mentions that the "Brinton 1704 house, Joseph Brinton 1712, William Brinton 1713, Ann Brinton Cox, Joseph Eavenson, Mercer house. They were the first stone houses. Very steep roofs, a story high, with garrett rooms..."[4]

The newspaper advertisements mention the materials used in roofing:
1762 "Stone House, Cedar roofed"[5] George Mitchell (East Nottingham Twp.)
1775 "Smith Shop well covered with Tiles"[6] Dennis Whelen (Uwchlan Twp.)

1813 "Stone Dwelling-House, well finished, covered with cypress shingles"[7] Michael March (Coventry Twp.)

1820 "Stone Mill House covered with pine shingles"[8] Evan Lewis (Honeybrook Twp.)

1831 "The buildings have nearly all been lately covered with pine and oak shingles"[9] John Babb (Sadsbury Twp.)

1831 "new...brick house...and a good and substantial slate roof"[10] James Grier (West Nottingham Twp.)

1833 "BRICK HOUSE...22 feet front by 30 back, roofed with tin"[11] Lewis W. Williams (West Chester)

1849 "all under metal roof"[12] Joseph Lukens (West Chester)

1861 "stone Hotel, covered with slate and pebble roof"[13] "Steam Boat Tavern (East Whiteland Twp.)

1863 "Barn...a large gravel roof"[14] G. Grover Lewis (West Marlboro Twp.)

1864 "Brick Grape House...with glazed roof"[15] Alexander Marshall (West Chester)

1866 "House...with a tin roof painted on both sides"[16] H. G. Malin (Tredyffrin Twp.)

1866 "School House...roof is of sheet iron"[17] (West Marlboro Twp.)

1868 "Brick House...covered with a Metalic roof"[18] Thomas W. Parker (Pocopson Twp.)

1869 "grist mill...covered with fire proof roof"[19] M'Quillin & Hoopes (New Garden Twp.)

1869 "Green House...20 by 60 feet, requiring 60,000 sq. feet of glass roof to cover same"[20] Kift (West Chester)

1874 "Frame car shop, 2 story, shingle roof 229 by 70 feet"[21] Oxford Cooperative Car Co. (Oxford)

1874 "tin roof 3000 square feet"[22] Factory (Downingtown)

1875 "ware house, roofed with iron"[23] David Mercer (Newlin Twp.)

1886 "house...and within a day or two the roof has been painted and beautiful metallic ornaments placed on the combs of the roof"[24] N. Hayes (West Chester)

1889 "James C. Smith, of Oakbourne, Westtown...handsome addition...It will be a stone structure with copper ornamental roof and cornices"[25]

In the newspaper advertisements, before 1876, thirty-two other buildings were roofed with cedar, thirteen with tin, one with cypress, three with pine, two with tile, thirty-four with slate, four with metal and one with pebble.

The will of Hugh Kerns, of Ridley Township, proven in 1780 mentions "Covering the house with Cedar"[26] and the will of Henry Shengle, of Coventry Township, proven in 1785 mentions "I do order a Small Stable to built for her twelve feet square to be covered Straw and to be Raised So high as will be Sufficient to hold Hay enough at one time to Winter her Cow."[27]

The 1799 tax assessment for Honeybrook Township lists Abraham Cartz with "A Dwelling house and barn of Logs Covered with Straw and Shingles under One Roof."

1. Henry Graham Ashmead, *HISTORICAL SKETCH OF CHESTER, ON DELAWARE* (The Republican Steam Printing House, 1883), p. 63.
2. Ibid., p. 67.
3. Ibid., p. 73.
4. John H. Brinton diary Vol #3, p. 24 under date Feb. 6, 1885. Chester County Historical Society (West Chester, Penna.)
5. *PENNSYLVANIA GAZETTE* (Philadelphia, Penna.) Jan. 28, 1762.
6. Ibid., April 12, 1775.
7. *AMERICAN REPUBLICAN* (West Chester, Penna.) Nov. 9, 1813.
8. *VILLAGE RECORD* (West Chester, Penna.) Feb. 16, 1820.
9. Ibid., Nov. 16, 1831.
10. *AMERICAN REPUBLICAN* (West Chester, Penna.) Dec. 20, 1831.
11. Ibid., June 11, 1833.
12. *VILLAGE RECORD* (West Chester, Penna.) Sept. 9, 1849.
13. Ibid., Nov. 12, 1861.
14. Ibid., Nov. 21, 1863.
15. Ibid., Oct. 11, 1864.
16. Ibid., Nov. 24, 1866.
17. Ibid., April 10, 1866.
18. Ibid., Dec. 1, 1868.
19. Ibid., Sept. 24, 1869.
20. *AMERICAN REPUBLICAN* (West Chester, Penna.) July 13, 1869.
21. *VILLAGE RECORD* (West Chester, Penna.) April 7, 1874.
22. *DAILY LOCAL NEWS* (West Chester, Penna.) Oct. 25, 1874.
23. *VILLAGE RECORD* (West Chester, Penna.) Jan. 12, 1875.
24. *DAILY LOCAL NEWS* (West Chester, Penna.) May 6, 1886.
25. Ibid., Nov. 26, 1889.
26. Chester County Will Book 6, p. 434.
27. Chester County Will Book 7, p. 339.

COTTAGE ROOF

The newspaper advertisements mention:

1872 "House...alterations...cottage roof"[1] William Butler (West Chester)

1873 "stable of brick, 36 by 56 feet, two stories high, with cottage beveled roof"[2] J. J. Parker (West Goshen Twp.)

1. *AMERICAN REPUBLICAN* (West Chester, Penna.) July 9, 1872.
2. Ibid., May 20, 1873.

HIPPED ROOF

Henry Graham Ashmead in 1883 mentions that the Black Bear Inn, built before 1733/4, in Chester had a hipped roof[1] and that the Friends Meeting House, built in 1738, in Springfield Township was "stone with a hipped roof and a pent-roof over the doors and windows at the ends."[2] The 1796 tax for Uwchlan Township lists Thomas David with "One stone house, 1 story hip roof" and John Gordon with "One stone house 1 story high with hip roof."

1. Henry Graham Ashmead, *HISTORICAL SKETCH OF CHESTER, ON DELAWARE* (The Republican Steam Printing House, 1883), p. 99.
2. Ibid., p. 716.

MANSARD & FRENCH ROOF

The newspaper advertisements mention:

1867 "planning to add story & put on French roof"[1] "Mansion House Hotel" (West Chester)

1869 "Hotel...with Mansard roof"[2] Col. Speakman (Coatesville)

1870 "Mansard...French...The roofs are all to be boarded over closely, the curved parts for slate, and the flat parts for tin"[3] Normal School (West Chester)

1874 "addition to parsonage, 2 story flat roof building... and will change the L. house into a square one with mansard roof"[4] St. James Church (Downingtown)

Before 1876 the newspaper advertisements mention seventeen other buildings with mansard roofs, three with French roofs and two buildings changing to mansard roofs and two buildings changing to French roofs. Between 1876 and 1899 the newspapers mention twenty-seven mansard roofs and seven French roofs on buildings.

1. *AMERICAN REPUBLICAN* (West Chester, Penna.) Sept. 3, 1867.
2. Ibid., July 20, 1869.
3. Ibid., July 12, 1870.
4. *DAILY LOCAL NEWS* (West Chester, Penna.) April 17, 1874.

PENT HOUSE, ROOF, EAVES

Pent house is defined by Bailey (ed. 1735) as "a Shelter over a Door or Window" and by Sheridan (ed. 1789) as "a shed hanging out aslope from the main wall."

Henry Graham Ashmead, in 1883, mentions that the Barber house, built between 1699 and 1708, in Chester had a "Pent roof over second story window,"[1] and that the Logan house built in 1700, in Chester, had "over first story windows was a pent roof."[2] The James Barber house, built in 1732, in Chester was "a Brick house, with pent roof extending over the window of the first story."[3]

The newspapers mention:

1862 "2 story stone House (Dashed) 25 by 30 feet...wide porch front and Pent eaves over kitchen door"[4] John dePettit (Highland Twp.)

1873 "station house...new...covered with an ornamental pent house roof"[5] (Malvern)

1. Henry Graham Ashmead, *HISTORICAL SKETCH OF CHESTER, ON DELAWARE* (The Republican Steam Printing House, 1883), p. 121.
2. Ibid., p. 73.
3. Ibid., p. 150.
4. *VILLAGE RECORD* (West Chester, Penna.) Dec. 2, 1862.
5. *AMERICAN REPUBLICAN* (West Chester, Penna.) Sept. 16, 1873.

PITCHED ROOF

The newspaper advertisements mention:

1875 "Church...with a pitched roof"[1] Berean Church (West Chester)

1. *AMERICAN REPUBLICAN* (West Chester, Penna.) April 13, 1875.

PYRAMIDAL ROOF

The newspapers mention:

1868 "office building formerly standing on court house lot with a pyramidal roof and chimney at the apex. First built 1820, now gone"[1] Court House (West Chester)

1891 "log school house...square one story structure, with a pyramidal roof having eaves on every side and the apex of the roof exactly in the center"[2] (West Whiteland Twp.)

1. *VILLAGE RECORD* (West Chester, Penna.) April 7, 1868.
2. *DAILY LOCAL NEWS* (West Chester, Penna.) March 11, 1891.

SHED ROOF

The newspaper advertisements mention:

1864 "Brick House, back buildings of brick, 1½ stories high with shed roof"[1] Bowman Taylor (Kennett Twp.)

1874 "1½ story frame House, shed roof, 16 by 16 feet"[2] Cornelius Green (West Chester)

1. *VILLAGE RECORD* (West Chester, Penna.) Sept. 13, 1864.
2. Ibid., July 21, 1874.

THATCHED ROOF

The 1798 Direct Tax for East Caln and West Whiteland Townships lists the following thatched buildings: "Round logs thatch'd Family stable 14 x 12" belonging to Richard Thomas; "Frame Barn thatched 30 x 16 wants repair" belonging to Francis Gardner; "small log stable thatched 16 x 12" belonging to Francis Gardner; "Small round logs thatched 35 x 18" belonging to Richard Thomas; "2 story stone & log Barn thatched 30 x 16" belonging to Richard Thomas; "Old Frame barn thatched 30 x 20 Bad repair" belonging to Nicholas Byers; "2 story Round log & stone Barn thatched 30 x 20" belonging to Jacob Souder; "1 story Round log stable thatched 25 x 18" belonging to Jacob Souder; "old round log Barn thatched 40 x 60" belonging to Jno Newlin; "Round logs Barn thatched 40 x 20 Bad repair" belonging to Jno Hoofman; "small barn part old thatched 30 x 18" belonging to Jno

Houder; "Barn thatched 30 x 18" Bad repair" belonging to D. Thompson; "thatched logs 22 x 18" belonging to Jacob Zook and "Hay house thatched" belonging to Griffith Lewis. The 1796 tax assessment for West Whiteland Township lists George Gray and George Hoofman as each having "1 Cart House on Posts, Straw Roof." The 1799 tax assessment for New London Township lists James Hutcheson with "log house & thatched" and John Kimble with "Brick house & thatching." In 1905 a newspaper mentions that "Councilman David T. Sharpless is having a rather unusual covering placed on a rustic summer house...The thatched roof needed repairing, and Mr. Sharpless and his gardener covered it with rye straw, thatched after the manner of cottages in the old countries."[1]

The account book[2] of Job M. Seeds mentions:
10th 26th 1829
To 1 day a thatching   .40

1. *DAILY LOCAL NEWS* (West Chester, Penna.) April 8, 1905.
2. Ms. #3037, Chester County Historical Society (West Chester, Penna.)

VAULTED ROOF

A newspaper mentions:
1872 "vaulted roof, covered with tin"[1] Church Street Market House (West Chester)

1. *VILLAGE RECORD* (West Chester, Penna.) Oct. 8, 1872.

ROOMS

The first mention of rooms found in inventories are as follows: parlor, parlor chamber, kitchen and garret, William Wood, Darby Township, 1685; chamber, cork loft and shed, John Harding, Chichester Township, 1688; upper chamber and cellar, Richard Flow, Chester County, 1689; large parlor and little parlor, Joshua Fearn, Darby Township, 1693; hall, hall chamber and lower chamber, Maurice Trent, Chester County, 1697; common room below, dining room, great room above stairs and buttery, John Hodgessins, Chester County 1699; chamber on the ground floor and servant's room, Robert Wade, Chester County, 1698; shed chamber and kitchen chamber, Henry Gibbons, Darby Township, 1702; lodging room, Nathaniel Parcks, Concord Township, 1702; house and house chamber, Edmond Pritchard, Ridley Township, 1703/4; passage and passage chamber, Thomas Smith, Darby Township, 1705/6; common house and back kitchen, Richard Woodward, Middletown Township, 1706/7; porch, closet, corn mill chamber, garret chamber, cellar under the hall and cellar under the old house, John Bethell, Darby Township, 1707/8; great chamber, Thomas Hope, Kennett Township,

1708; dwelling house, Isaac Bartram, Darby Township, 1708; chamber where he died, Francis Chadds, Birmingham Township, 1713; room over ye porch, Thomas Powell, Chester, 1714; best room, loft and leanto, Edward Beeson, Nottingham Township, 1714; bed chamber, Thomas Powell, Upper Providence Township, 1714; blue room, John Hoskins, Chester County, 1716; passage between the house and shop, Thomas Hood, Darby Township, 1717; end shed and back shed, Walter Martin, Chichester Township, 1719; study and chamber closet, John Cartlidge, Conestoga, 1723; children's room, Joseph Coeburn, Aston Township, 1723; porch chamber, John Blunston, Darby Township, 1723; junior room and lower kitchen, Israel Taylor, Mattineconck, 1726; pantry, John Hannum, Concord Township, 1730; outward room in the kitchen and inward room in the kitchen, Nathaniel Newlin, Concord Township, 1731; chamber over the vault, Josiah Ffearn, Darby Township, 1731; stove room, William Lewis, Newtown Township, 1731; shed room, Joseph Rhoades, Marple Township, 1732; room at the stairs head, Robert Johnson, New Garden Township, 1732; out room, John Willis, junior, Thornbury Township, 1732; kitchen loft, Robert Johnson, New Garden Township, 1732; common lodging room and clock room, William Treherne, Chester County, 1739; closet in the parlor, shop in the house and out cellar, John Wilson, Chichester Township, 1741; big room, Elizabeth Swayne, East Marlboro Township, 1742; common room above stairs and entry, Richard Whitting, London Britain Township, 1743; passage between the two houses, public room, bed room below stairs and bar; James Trego, Whiteland Township, 1745; bed room up stairs, Anthony Arnold, East Bradford Township and mansion house, William Beaumont, East Bradford Township, 1747.

After 1750, fire room upstairs, David Jones, Tredyffrin Township, 1759; linen chamber, Peter Dicks, Lower Providence Township, 1760; passage room, Henry Howard, Edgmont Township, 1760; front parlor and back parlor, Thomas Pearson, Darby Township, 1763; room upstairs in the kitchen, Aaron Mendenhall, Sr., Caln Township, 1765; office, Philip Ford, Chester County, 1766; kitchen upstairs and down, William Miller, New Garden Township, 1768; stair closet, Peter Elliott, Darby Township, 1769; girl's room, John Hurford, New Garden Township, 1774; brick room, John Cox, Chester, 1771; kitchen cellar, Joseph James, Westtown Township, 1772; blue parlor, south room over the yard and milk room, Joseph Hoskins, Chester, 1773; common apartment, John Buffington, West Bradford Township, 1774; boy's room, Ellis Davis, Goshen Township 1774; bell room, Valentine Weaver, Chester, 1774; common house, Daniel Sharpless, Nether Providence Township, 1775; long room, John Richards, Darby Township, 1778; hall or front house, garret stairs, green parlor, common sitting room, yellow room up stairs, press closet and saddle and stove room, John Knowles, Ridley Township, 1778; woman's room, Edward Brinton, Birmingham Township,

1779; middle story and third story, William Miller, New Garden Township, 1781; room with a fireplace, Samuel Worth, East Bradford Township, 1782; balcony room upstairs, Archibald Dick, Lower Chichester Township, 1782; fire room lower floor, John McKissack, Oxford Township, 1783; room on the left of the front door and the room on the right hand of the front door, William Moore, Charlestown Township, 1783; glass room and blue chamber, John Smith, Lower Chichester Township, 1784; library room, and common hall, John Carmichael, East Caln Township, 1785; common parlour, Charles Humphrey, Haverford Township, 1786; maid's room and men's room, John Kerlin, East Whiteland Township, 1787; cider cellar, little cellar and wine cellar, William Garrett, Darby Township, 1788; old kitchen and back cellar, William Jones, Birmingham Township, 1789; store room down stairs, William Hunt, Westtown Township, 1790; in the room where he laid, Joseph Gatchel, East Nottingham Township, 1793; common room or kitchen, Joseph Hobson, New Garden Township, 1797 and entry up stairs, Benjamin Hutton, New Garden Township, 1799.

After 1800: observatory, Humphrey Marshall, West Bradford Township, 1801; garret back room west, garret front room west, garret front room east and garret east back room, James Jackson, West Chester, 1808; shed loft, Thomas Taylor, Westtown Township, 1811; out kitchen, George Pearson, West Chester, 1814; end closet, John Norris, East Whiteland Township, 1814; entry closet, kitchen closet and cellar closet, Thomas Wistar, Pennsbury Township, 1814; bar in the garret, John Gemmill, West Chester, 1815; up stairs kitchen, Elisha Baily, West Marlboro Township, 1816; back entry, Jehu Roberts, West Whiteland Township, 1818; inner cellar, front cellar and outer cellar, Joseph Walker, Tredyffrin Township, 1818; shed adjoining the house, Passmore Williamson, Thornbury Township, 1819; locked room, Richard Downing, East Caln Township, 1820; kitchen porch, Frederick Halman, Pikeland Township, 1821; second apartment, Hananiah Walker, Tredyffrin Township, 1821; workmen's room, Jno. Boyer, West Whiteland Township, 1822; cellar under stairs, Isaac Sharpless, East Bradford Township, 1822; workmen's lodging room, Jacob Valentine, Chester, 1823; meal room and lumber room, Israel Jackson, London Grove Township, 1823; cave, Thomas Mason, Charlestown Township, 1823; kitchen shed, Joshua Sharpless, East Bradford Township, 1826; garret up kitchen stairs, Aaron Davis, East Bradford Township, 1826; boy's garret, Joseph Malin, East Whiteland Township, 1826; white room, Jacob Bennett, Birmingham Township, 1826; school room, Joseph Strode, East Bradford Township, 1827; white chamber, William Clinglan, West Fallowfield Township, 1827; small room next the roof, Mary Paxson, Sadsbury Township, 1829; meal room or larder, George Peirce, Brandywine Township, 1831; cheese room, Lowdnes Taylor, West Goshen Township,

1833; doctor's room and shed rooms on second floor, John B. Cochran, West Fallowfield Township, 1834; chimney room, Jesse Dehaven, London Britain Township, 1835; sleeping chamber, Dania Stephens, Jr., New London Township, 1836; portico, Isaiah Matlack, Tredyffrin Township, 1838; common house apartment, Allen Chandler, London Grove Township, 1838; square room, Abner Pyle, East Marlboro Township, 1839; kitchen and wash house, Nicholas Boyers, East Caln Township, 1839; stair case, Caleb North, Coventry Township, 1840; mineral room, Joel Swayne, East Marlboro Township, 1840; wash kitchen, William Evans, Willistown Township, 1843; vault, James Baily, East Bradford Township, 1844; office garret, Mathew Stanley, West Brandywine Township, 1844; out house kitchen, John Kugler, Tredyffrin Township, 1844; water closet, Benjamin Funk, Schuylkill Township, 1845; driver's room, attic story room number one, breakfast or old bar room and bee room, Joshua Evans, Tredyffrin Township, 1846; back porch, Peter Stroud, West Fallowfield Township, 1847; frame kitchen, Bershaba Dickison, East Goshen Township, 1847, recess in room and kitchen recess, David Marys, East Vincent Township, 1847 and three story back building, Sarah Lukens, West Chester, 1849.

BALL ROOM

The newspaper advertisements mention:
1829 "two story stone house, 58 feet long, by 26 wide with four rooms and a bar room on the first floor, seven on the second, one of which is a large ball room"[1] Jacob Pyle Est. "Drovers Tavern" (East Marlboro Twp.)

1839 "two story stone house, 26 by 40 feet...six [rooms] on the second floor, two of which by raising the partition, can be converted into a ball, society or lecture room"[2] Samuel D. Moore "Moore Tavern" (Schuylkill Twp.)

1843 "Stone Tavern House, 60 by 30 feet, with bar room, ball room, dining room"[3] Jonathan Willett Est. "Drovers Tavern" (East Marlboro Twp.)

1856 "ball room"[4] Chester Springs Hotel (West Pikeland Twp.)

1. *AMERICAN REPUBLICAN* (West Chester, Penna.) Dec. 31, 1839.
2. Ibid., Dec. 17, 1839.
3. *VILLAGE RECORD* (West Chester, Penna.) Dec. 19, 1843.
4. *AMERICAN REPUBLICAN* (West Chester, Penna.) Jan. 1, 1856.

BATH ROOM

The newspaper advertisements mention:
1856 "Bath room"[1] John Clark (West Chester)

1869 "Frame Wash House and Bath Room 12 by 14 feet"[2]
Wm. R. Hoopes (West Chester)

Before 1865 the newspapers mention eighteen other bathrooms.

1. *AMERICAN REPUBLICAN* (West Chester, Penna.) Oct. 28, 1856.
2. *VILLAGE RECORD* (West Chester, Penna.) April 6, 1869.

BILLIARD ROOM

The newspaper advertisements mention:
1821 "billiard"[1] Dennis Whelen Est. (Pikeland Twp.)
1856 "Frame Billiard Saloon and Ten Pin Alley"[2] Chester Springs Hotel (West Pikeland Twp.)
1872 "billiard room 20 by 32 feet"[3] Reeves Mansion (Phoenixville)
1873 "livery stable...removing billiard room to front of building"[4] W. H. Huddleson (West Chester)

Before 1877 the newspaper advertisements mention three other billiard rooms but they are not described. Between 1877 and 1899 one billiard room was mentioned as being 40 x 20 feet.

1. *AMERICAN REPUBLICAN* (West Chester, Penna.) March 13, 1821.
2. Ibid., Jan. 1, 1856.
3. *PHOENIXVILLE MESSENGER* (Phoenixville, Penna.) April 27, 1872.
4. *DAILY LOCAL NEWS* (West Chester, Penna.) March 13, 1873.

BOUDOIR

The newspaper advertisements mention:
1875 "boudoir"[1] James Griffin (Phoenixville)

1. *PHOENIXVILLE MESSENGER* (Phoenixville, Penna.) Aug. 28, 1875.

BUTTERY

Buttery is defined by Bailey (ed. 1735) as "a Place where Victuals is set up", by Sheridan (ed. 1789) as "the room where provisions are laid up" and by Webster (ed. 1828) as "An apartment in a house, where butter, milk, provisions and utensils are kept."

John Brinton, of Kennett Township, in 1748 in his will mentions giving the "use of the new building at the East end of my said house with the buttery thereto adjoining and suitable privilege in the cellar and spring house"[1] to his wife.

1. Chester County Will Book 3, p. 21.

CELLAR

Cellar is defined by Bailey (ed. 1735) as "the lowest Part of a Building under Ground", by Sheridan (ed. 1789) as "a place under ground, where stores are reposited; where liquors are kept" and by Webster (ed. 1828) as "A room under a house or other building, used as a repository of liquors, provisions, and other stores for a family."

The Boar's Head Inn, in Chester, where William Penn resided in 1682-1683 had a "cellar, which was under the front part of the building...It was of dressed stone, the joints were true, every stone set square."[1]

The wills before 1813 had the following descriptions of cellars:
1739 "Vault in the Cellar under the New house"[2] Richard Eveson (Thornbury Twp.)
1752 "of the inner apartment of my seller which hath a lock to it"[3] Thomas James, (Willistown Twp.)
1769 "Cellar Room"[4] William Woodward (West Bradford Twp.)
1803 "the Celler Called the Milk Celler and a Small one with Stone Steps leading out of the kitchen part of this house"[5] Joel Baily (East Marlboro Twp.)
1806 "also a closet in the Celler with a lock on it which is under the old Barrall which she is to have"[6] T. Samuel Cunningham (East Caln Twp.)
1808 "and allow her the South West appartment in the Celler"[7] Isaac Baily (East Marlboro Twp.)
1811 "the priviledge of the Kitchen Oven Cellar and Closet and the Arch"[8] Thomas Cheyney (Thornbury Twp.)

In the wills before 1813 there were four other vaults and one other apartment in the cellar mentioned.

The newspaper advertisements mention:
1767 "all cellared under, and paved with brick"[9] Rees Peters (Concord Twp.)
1770 "A cellar under the whole with a partition in it"[10] Jonathan Richards (Aston Twp.)
1777 "cellared all under, and divided into 4 apartments"[11] Wm Gibbons (West Nantmeal Twp.)
1783 "cyder works for convenience as to convey the cyder from the press house into the cellar with a short spout"[12] Robert M'Elhenny (West Fallowfield Twp.)
1815 "with a good cellar divided into two parts by a stone wall"[13] Thomas Vickers (East Caln Twp.)
1815 "the cellar is divided into two apartments, one half of which is completely covered with mortar and is impregnable to rats"[14] Dennis Whelen (West Chester)
1829 "a kitchen...with a milk house underneath communicating with the cellar"[15] Ephraim Taylor (East Whiteland Twp.)
1832 "there are four good cellars, three of which have mortar floors, and also a deep vault to keep milk in"[16] Joshua Hoopes (Downingtown)
1838 "cellar is divided into 9 apartments, with smoke,

apple and potato houses, and floor all laid with lime and sand"[17] Brinton Jacobs (West Whiteland Twp.)

1839 "a dry cellar under the whole, in one corner of which is an ice house"[18] Samuel D. Moore, "Moore Tavern" (Schuylkill Twp.)

1840 "The cellars are about 7 feet high under the whole house"[19] Wm. Fahnestock "Warren Tavern" (East Whiteland Twp.)

1846 "A part of the celler is conveniently finished so as to answer for a mechanic's shop"[20] Andrew Terrill (West Bradford Twp.)

1852 "basement divided into three apartments, one is used as a spring house, one a kitchen the other a cellar"[21] William King (East Brandywine Twp.)

1853 "cellar, vault...floor of which, together with one under dwelling is plastered"[22] Catharine Evans Est. (West Chester)

1855 "wine cellar"[23] M. Thomas & Sons (West Chester)

1855 "cellar under the whole house, ceiled and plastered, with a mortar floor"[24] Isabella Furnace (West Nantmeal Twp.)

1856 "House is two story with a raised basement 45 x 25"[25]

1858 "cellar divided by stone wall, one part of which is paved with brick and contains a stone vault"[26] Enoch Passmore (Kennett Square)

1873 "cellar mortar floor and outside entrances"[27] J. B. Roecker (West Chester)

The newspaper advertisements before 1877 mention two cellars with brick floors, four with mortar floors, one rat proof, one with plastered floor, three that were divided into apartments, two with vaults and one wine cellar in addition to those already quoted.

1. Henry Graham Ashmead, *HISTORICAL SKETCH OF CHESTER, ON DELAWARE* (The Republican Steam Printing House, 1883) p. 63.
2. Chester County Will Book 2, p. 49.
3. Chester County Will Book 3, p. 344.
4. Chester County Will Book 5, p. 150.
5. Chester County Will Book 10, p. 441.
6. Chester County Will Book 11, p. 147.
7. Ibid., p. 220.
8. Ibid., p. 357.
9. *PENNSYLVANIA GAZETTE* (Philadelphia, Penna.) Jan. 22, 1767.
10. Ibid., June 7, 1770.
11. Ibid., April 9, 1777.
12. Ibid., March 5, 1783.
13. *VILLAGE RECORD* (West Chester, Penna.) Sept. 30, 1815.
14. *CHESTER & DELAWARE FEDERALIST* (West Chester, Penna.) May 24, 1815.
15. *AMERICAN REPUBLICAN* (West Chester, Penna.) Dec. 8, 1829.
16. *VILLAGE RECORD* (West Chester, Penna.) April 4, 1832.
17. *AMERICAN REPUBLICAN* (West Chester, Penna.) Dec. 18, 1838.
18. Ibid., Dec. 19, 1839.
19. Ibid., Nov. 29, 1840.
20. Ibid., Dec. 1, 1846.
21. Ibid., Feb. 10, 1852.
22. *VILLAGE RECORD* (West Chester, Penna.) Feb. 13, 1853.
23. *AMERICAN REPUBLICAN* (West Chester, Penna.) April 24, 1855.
24. Ibid., April 3, 1855.
25. Ibid., Jan. 22, 1856.
26. *VILLAGE RECORD* (West Chester, Penna.) Feb. 6, 1858.
27. *AMERICAN REPUBLICAN* (West Chester, Penna.) Dec. 23, 1873.

CONSERVATORY

The newspaper advertisements mention:

1858 "Frame conservatory"[1] S. Snyder & Asher S. Leidy (Westtown Twp.)

1867 "two conservatories and verandah on second floor"[2] David McConkey (West Chester)

1872 "House...Conservatory...house and conservatory are warmed by good furnaces"[3] James H. Bradford (West Chester)

In the newspaper advertisements before 1876 there are four other mentions of conservatories.

1. *VILLAGE RECORD* (West Chester, Penna.) June 12, 1858.
2. Ibid., Oct. 15, 1867.
3. Ibid., Sept. 17, 1872.

DINING ROOM

Dining room is defined by Sheridan (ed. 1789) as "the principle apartment of the house" and by Webster (ed. 1828) as "A room for a family or for company to dine in; a room for entertainments."

The newspaper advertisements mention:

1792 "stone house, four rooms and an entry on a floor...kitchen adjoining, with a large dining room over the same"[1] Adam Siter "Spread Eagle" (Tredyffrin Twp.)

1803 "the second story has four rooms calculated for dining or lodging rooms"[2] David Llewellyn "Spring House Tavern" (Easttown Twp.)

1835 "dining room about 50 feet long"[3] "Green Tree Hotel" (West Chester)

1843 "a brick dining room 16 by 24, two stories high, nearly new"[4] John Twaddle (West Chester)

1844 "sitting and dining room, which can be thrown together"[5] B. H. Wiley (Kennett Square)

1847 "Dining room over the kitchen, and a sitting room over that...Hydrant in the kitchen and dining room"[6] David McConkey (West Chester)

1847 "with a dining room 40 by 20 feet"[7] "Green Tree Hotel" (West Chester)

1848 "dining room in the basement story"[8] W. Pennock (Lower Oxford Twp.)

1852 "two story kitchen and dining room adjoining 25 by 15 feet running back"[9] Susan Lungren (West Chester)

1854 "dining room 14 x 17 feet"[10] Enos Smedley (West Chester)

1870 "dining room 25 by 15 feet"[11] Evan P. Trego

(Sadsbury Twp.)

1870 "Dining Room in Walnut 13 by 17"[12] J. Lee Englebert (West Chester)

1871 "dining room 42 x 60"[13] Normal School, (West Chester)

1871 "lecture room and dining hall being frescoed"[14] Normal School, (West Chester)

1875 "dining room 13 feet by 21 feet"[15] B.I.V. Miller Est. (Caln Twp.)

1875 "front room walnut and dining room oak grained, wide wash boards"[16] Hiram Sturgis (Phoenixville)

1876 "the dining room can be enlarged for extra occassions by pushing back the sliding doors"[17] J. R. Gilpin (Birmingham Twp.)

The newspaper advertisements before 1876 mention twenty-nine other dining rooms, one dining room with hydrant water and one other dining room in the basement. Between 1878 and 1899 the newspapers mention one dining room being 15 x 12 feet and another 30 x 21 feet.

1. *PENNSYLVANIA GAZETTE* (Philadelphia, Penna.) Jan. 25, 1792.
2. Ibid., Feb. 2, 1803.
3. *AMERICAN REPUBLICAN* (West Chester, Penna.) Oct. 20, 1835.
4. Ibid., Dec. 5, 1843.
5. Ibid., Dec. 3, 1844.
6. Ibid., Nov. 16, 1847.
7. Ibid., Nov. 23, 1847.
8. *VILLAGE RECORD* (West Chester, Penna.) Jan. 4, 1848.
9. *AMERICAN REPUBLICAN* (West Chester, Penna.) Feb. 10, 1852.
10. *VILLAGE RECORD* (West Chester, Penna.) Dec. 19, 1854.
11. Ibid., Sept. 27, 1870.
12. Ibid., Oct. 22, 1870.
13. *KENNETT ADVANCE* (Kennett Square, Penna.) March 4, 1871.
14. *AMERICAN REPUBLICAN* (West Chester, Penna.) July 18, 1871.
15. *VILLAGE RECORD* (West Chester, Penna.) Oct. 9, 1875.
16. *PHOENIXVILLE MESSENGER* (Phoenixville, Penna.) Feb. 27, 1875.
17. *VILLAGE RECORD* (West Chester, Penna.) April 15, 1876.

DORMITORY

The newspaper advertisements mention:

1836 "and a large dormitory on the third floor"[1] Joel Pennock "Chatham" (London Grove Twp.)

1837 "house...divided into 60 parlors and dormatories"[2] Margaret Holman "Mansion House" (West Chester)

1858 "double floored Barn 36 x 51 with dormitory... having a second story lathed and plastered suitable for a school room"[3] Thomas Lamborn (New Garden Twp.)

1. *AMERICAN REPUBLICAN* (West Chester, Penna.) Nov. 29, 1836.
2. Ibid., July 31, 1837.
3. *VILLAGE RECORD* (West Chester, Penna.) Dec. 11, 1858.

ENTRY & HALL

Entry is defined by Bailey (ed. 1735) as "a Passage" and by Sheridan (ed. 1789) as "the passage by which any one enters a house." Hall is defined by Bailey (ed. 1735) as "a large Room at the Entrance of an House", by Sheridan (ed. 1789) as "the first large room at the entrance of a house" and by Webster (ed. 1828) as "In architecture, a large room at the entrance of a house or palace."

The newspaper advertisements mention:

1831 "with an entry 7 ft in width...brick dwelling house"[1] George B. Norris (West Chester)

1831 "brick dwelling house...entry six feet wide"[2] Wm. Work Est. (West Chester)

1831 "half entry on the first floor"[3] James Grier (West Nottingham Twp.)

1834 "two story stone dwelling house...45 feet by 35 in depth, with a nine feet entry on the ground floor"[4] Thomas J. Maxwell (Tredyffrin Twp.)

1843 "Mansion...of brick...The hall or entry passing through the whole length of the building is 10 ft wide, with stairing leading to the upper entry of the same width"[5] John S. Bowen (West Goshen Twp.)

1848 "brick tavern...including a large hall nine feet wide"[6] Benjamin Seal "Franklin House" (New London Twp.)

1866 "hall 8 feet wide"[7] Joshua Menough (New London Twp.)

1868 "Brick Hotel 70 by 60 feet, hall 20 by 40 feet"[8] Chalkley Phillips (Franklin Twp.)

1875 "hall 9 feet wide with walnut staircase"[9] B.I.V. Miller Est. (Caln Twp.)

In the newspaper advertisements before 1877 there were three other entries 7 feet wide, two others 9 feet wide, one other through the center of the house 10 feet wide, one other ten feet wide and two other half entries.

1. *AMERICAN REPUBLICAN* (West Chester, Penna.) April 19, 1831.
2. *VILLAGE RECORD* (West Chester, Penna.) Nov. 30, 1831.
3. *AMERICAN REPUBLICAN* (West Chester, Penna.) Dec. 20, 1831.
4. Ibid., Aug. 26, 1834.
5. Ibid., Oct. 17, 1843.
6. Ibid., Nov. 21, 1848.
7. *VILLAGE RECORD* (West Chester, Penna.) Jan. 20, 1866.
8. Ibid., Dec. 26, 1868.
9. Ibid., Oct. 9, 1875.

GARRET

Garret is defined by Bailey (ed. 1735) as "the uppermost Floor in an House" and by Sheridan (ed. 1789) as "a room on the highest floor of the house."

The newspaper advertisements describe two garrets:

1831 "the garret floor is laid with mortar for security"[1] Jesse Meredith (Downingtown)

1851 "stone dwelling house, 2 stories high, with a raised garret"[2] George W. Freshcorn (West Nantmeal Twp.)

1. *VILLAGE RECORD* (West Chester, Penna.) Dec. 7, 1831.
2. Ibid., Nov. 4, 1851.

IRONING ROOM

The newspaper advertisements mention:
1855 "ironing room"[1] M. Thomas & Sons (West Chester)
The newspaper advertisements before 1876 mention one other ironing room.

1. *AMERICAN REPUBLICAN* (West Chester, Penna.) April 24, 1855.

KITCHEN

Kitchen is defined by Bailey (ed. 1735) as "a Room where Meat is dressed, &c., also Kitchen Stuff, i.e. Grease", by Sheridan (ed. 1789) as "the room in a house where the provisions are cooked" and by Webster (ed. 1828) as "A cook-room; the room of a house appropriated to cookery."

The newspapers mention kitchens quite regularly. To quote a few:
1763 "Brick Dwelling-house...There is a back Shed new built to the House, wherein is a good back kitchen and one Lodging Room"[1] Robert M'Mallin (Upper Darby Twp.)
1785 "leanto kitchen"[2] Benjamin Bartholomew (East Whiteland Twp.)
1828 "stone House, with stone kitchen adjoining, under which there is a milk house."[3] David West (East Goshen Twp.)
1829 "a Kitchen in the rear...with a milk house underneath communicating with the cellar"[4] Ephraim Taylor (East Whiteland Twp.)

1. *PENNSYLVANIA GAZETTE* (Philadelphia, Penna.) Feb. 10, 1763.
2. Ibid., Jan. 19, 1785.
3. *AMERICAN REPUBLICAN* (West Chester, Penna.) Nov. 4, 1828.
4. Ibid., Dec. 8, 1829.

KITCHEN   SUMMER

The newspapers mention, in 1839, a summer kitchen belonging to John Townsend, in Kennett Township.[1] Between 1839 and 1860 thirty-two other summer kitchens were mentioned as well as three out kitchens.

1. *VILLAGE RECORD* (West Chester, Penna.) Jan. 15, 1839.

LAUNDRY

The newspaper advertisements mention:
1878 "House...Laundry on second floor"[1] Hannah Markley Est. (East Nantmeal Twp.)
Between 1879 and 1899 one other laundry is mentioned as being 24 x 12 feet in the newspaper advertisements.

1. *DAILY LOCAL NEWS* (West Chester, Penna.) Dec. 17, 1878.

LECTURE ROOM

The newspaper advertisements mention:
1866 "second floor lecture room 40 by 60 feet height of ceiling 18 ft."[1] Major Kames (Downingtown)
1871 "lecture room and dining hall being frescoed"[2] Normal School (West Chester)

1. *AMERICAN REPUBLICAN* (West Chester, Penna.) Aug. 14, 1866.
2. Ibid., July 18, 1871.

LIBRARY

Library is defined by Bailey (ed. 1735) as "a Study or Place where Books are kept", by Sheridan as "the place where a collection of books is kept" and by Webster (ed. 1828) as "A collection of books belonging to a private person, or to a public institution or a company. An edifice or an apartment for holding a collection of books."

The newspaper advertisements mention:
1846 "that he has fitted up, in connection with it, an extensive Reading Room, which will be supplied daily, with the leading papers of both political parties, from the different cities of the United States"[1] L. K. Brown "Mansion House" (West Chester)
1855 "library"[2] M. Thomas & Sons (West Chester)
1863 "Two story Brick House, recently occupied by West Chester Library Co."[3] Col. McIntire (West Chester)
1866 "library and reading room...third floor to be used as the reading room and library, to be constructed in the Italian style, slate elevators with dormer windows"[4] Major Kimes (Downingtown)
1870 "Library in walnut"[5] J. Lee Englebert (West Chester)
1872 "House...library with permanent book cases"[6] J. W. Barnard (West Chester)
1872 "House...library with open Fire Place"[7] James H. Bradford (West Chester)
1875 "library 17 feet by 16 feet"[8] B. I. V. Miller Est. (Caln)
1876 "library with permanent book cases...is heated with

low down grate"[9] J. S. Futhey (West Chester)

1890 "stone Mansion House...with a one-story Library Annex 12 by 12 feet"[10] Warwick Furnace Farm (Warwick Twp.)

1894 "The library is wainscotted, ceiled and panelled in white oak"[11] Richard T. Elliott Est. (West Chester)

The newspaper advertisements before 1877 mentioned nine other libraries.

1. *AMERICAN REPUBLICAN* (West Chester, Penna.) Sept. 29, 1846.
2. Ibid., April 24, 1855.
3. *VILLAGE RECORD* (West Chester, Penna.) March 10, 1863.
4. *AMERICAN REPUBLICAN* (West Chester, Penna.) Aug. 14, 1866.
5. *VILLAGE RECORD* (West Chester, Penna.) Oct. 22, 1870.
6. Ibid., Oct. 8, 1872.
7. Ibid., Sept. 17, 1872.
8. Ibid., Oct. 9, 1875.
9. Ibid., April 1, 1876.
10. *DAILY LOCAL NEWS* (West Chester, Penna.) Sept. 30, 1890.
11. *CHESTER COUNTY DEMOCRAT* (West Chester, Penna.) Sept. 30, 1894.

LOBBY

Lobby is defined by Bailey (ed. 1735) as "(the Porch of an House) a kind of Passage, a Room, or Gallery", by Sheridan (ed. 1789) as "an opening before a room" and by Webster (ed. 1828) as "An opening before a room, or an entrance into a principal apartment, where there is a considerable space between that and the portico or vestibule. 2. A small hall or waiting room. 3. A small apartment taken from a hall or entry."

The newspaper advertisements mention:

1847 "two story Brick house...with an entry running from the front into a lobby"[1] C. Nields (West Chester)

Before 1877 there are seven other mentions of lobbies in the newspaper advertisements.

1. *AMERICAN REPUBLICAN* (West Chester, Penna.) Dec. 7, 1847.

MEAL ROOM

The newspaper advertisements mention:

1845 "brick kitchen adjoining, with a lodging room and meal room over it"[1] Thomas W. Boyd (West Fallowfield Twp.)

1846 "also meal rooms and kitchen adjoining"[2] Isaac Chambers (New Garden Twp.)

1852 "meal room and kitchen"[3] Isaac Chambers (New Garden Twp.)

1856 "meal room at one end of the back porch"[4] Thomas Phillips (West Nottingham Twp.)

1. *AMERICAN REPUBLICAN* (West Chester, Penna.) March 11, 1845.
2. *VILLAGE RECORD* (West Chester, Penna.) Dec. 15, 1846.
3. *AMERICAN REPUBLICAN* (West Chester, Penna.) Sept. 28, 1852.
4. Ibid., Sept. 9, 1856.

OFFICE

Office is defined by Bailey (ed. 1735) as "a Place where any Business is managed."

The 1798 Direct Tax lists five offices: two of brick, the mean size being 332 square feet; two of stone, the mean size being 188 square feet and one that did not mention the material of construction 11 x 9 feet. In the newspaper advertisements between 1835 and 1839 four offices are mentioned: one of stone 18 x 16 feet; two of brick, the mean size being 403 square feet and one that did not mention the material of construction 18 x 16 feet. Between 1865 and 1874 seven offices are mentioned: two of brick, two story, the mean size being 630 square feet and five that did not mention the material of construction the mean size being 351 square feet.

PANTRY

Pantry is defined by Bailey as "a Room or Closet where Bread and cold Meat are Kept", by Sheridan (ed. 1789) as "the room in which provisions are reposited" and by Webster (ed. 1828) as "An apartment or closet in which provisions are kept."

The newspaper advertisements mention:

1843 "stone dwelling HOUSE...4 rooms and pantry on the first floor"[1] George Pierce Est. (Brandywine Twp.)

1852 "pump in pantry"[2] George B. Ewart (Kennett Twp.)

1873 "[cellar] it is divided and subdivided into vault and pantry"[3] Henry Buckwalter (West Chester)

Before 1877 there were four other mentions of pantries in the newspaper advertisements.

1. *VILLAGE RECORD* (West Chester, Penna.) Sept. 19, 1843.
2. Ibid., Dec. 7, 1852.
3. *DAILY LOCAL NEWS* (West Chester, Penna.) Dec. 5, 1873.

SERVANT'S ROOM

The newspaper advertisements mention:

1855 "servants rooms"[1] M. Thomas & Sons (West Chester)

Before 1877 one other servant's room is mentioned in the newspaper advertisements.

1. *AMERICAN REPUBLICAN* (West Chester, Penna.) April 24, 1855.

STOVE

The 1798 Direct Tax lists 1 stove room adjoining 21 x 10. 1 stove room adjoining 20 x 16, 1 stove room 15 x 12, 1 stone shed stove 20 x 17, 1 stove room adjoining 20 x 14 and 1 kitchen and stove room 27 x 18. The 1799 tax assessment for Charlestown Township lists one stove room and kitchen 54 x 37.

The newspaper advertisements mention:

1763 "Saw'd Log Loom Shop and Kitchen, with a good Stone Chimney and Stove"[1] Robert McCallin (Upper Darby Twp.)

1786 "dweling houses...with stove and lodging rooms"[2] John Francis (Pikeland Twp.)

1810 "a kitchen and stove room adjoining"[3] Matthew Stanley (Brandywine Twp.)

In the newspaper advertisements there were two other mentions of stove rooms.

1. *PENNSYLVANIA GAZETTE* (Philadelphia, Penna.) Feb. 10, 1763.
2. Ibid., Nov. 16, 1786.
3. *AMERICAN REPUBLICAN* (West Chester, Penna.) June 17, 1810.

VESTIBULE

Vestibule is defined by Bailey (ed. 1735) as "a Porch or Entry into a House", by Sheridan (ed. 1789) as "the porch or first entrance of a house" and by Webster (ed. 1828) as "The porch or entrance into a house, or a large open space before the door, but covered. Vestibules for magnificence are usually between the court and garden."

The newspaper advertisements mention:

1851 "Brick dwelling House...vestibule"[1] C. B. Hatch (West Chester)

1864 "Brick Cottage House...front vestibule entrance"[2] Alexander Marshall (West Chester)

1870 "vestibules to the front doors"[3] J. W. Barnard (West Chester)

1874 "vestibule with self closing doors"[4] Presbyterian Church (West Chester)

In the newspaper advertisements before 1877 there were five other mentions of vestibules.

1. *AMERICAN REPUBLICAN* (West Chester, Penna.) March 11, 1851.
2. *VILLAGE RECORD* (West Chester, Penna.) Oct. 11, 1864.
3. Ibid., Sept. 20, 1870.
4. *DAILY LOCAL NEWS* (West Chester, Penna.) Sept. 16, 1874.

	1684	1700	1710	1720	1730	1740	1750	1760	1770	1780	1790	1800	1810	1820	1830	1840/49
Chamber	5	9	4	6	12	15	18	8		7				1		
Cork Loft	1															
Kitchen	5	13	11	11	12	10	15	20	16	34	15	15	53	122	119	160
Shed	2	1	1			2		1		1			1			1
Upper Chamber	2		1	1	3									5		
Lower Chamber	1								11	18						
Back room	2		4	1	5			14	11	18	5	19	29	32	34	68
Cellar	2	11	10	5	11	13	10	17	8	26	12	6	29	68	77	119
Parlour	2	11	5	7	9	8	8		6	17	5	7	26	58	57	105
Back chamber	1						1	3		2	5	8	22			
Little parlour	1			2	1					2	1					
Ground floor chamber	2															
Servant's room	1															
Lodging room	1	1	2		7	4	3	7	1	10	4		2	8	3	4
Parlour chamber	1	4	1	2	3	1	3	5		3			1	2		
Hall	1	7	5	5	3	2	3	2	1				1	2		
Hall chamber	1	1														
Buttery	1	1	1	1												
Dining room	1						1	1	2	3			2	7	15	21

	1684	1700	1710	1720	1730	1740	1750	1760	1770	1780	1790	1800	1810	1820	1830	1840/49
Closet	3	1	3	3	1		2	2	2							
Room over kitchen	1	1											12	23	27	
Garret	8	4	3	7	6	7	12	16	29	9	14	31	80	85	118	
Old chamber	1															
New chamber	2															
Common room	1			4	4	3	2		2							
Middle room	1	1	1	1	1	6	4	2	6	4	3	6	3			
Out shed	2												1	5	6	
House chamber	2															
Second chamber	1	2	2				1	1	3		2	1				4
Hall chamber	4	1	4	2	1	1	1									
Passage	1		1	1												
Passage chamber	1		1													
Old room	1															

	1700	1710	1720	1730	1740	1750	1760	1770	1780	1790	1800	1810	1820	1830	1840/49
Common house	1														
Back kitchen	1						1					1	2		
Shed chamber	2														
Kitchen chamber	2	3	4		1	1	6	2	6	1	2	5		1	3
Little chamber	1														
Lower room	1		1		2	2		1	2						
Garrett chamber	1														
Shed over well	1														
Porch	1														
Outer room	2										1				
Best room		1			1			3	1	4	2	2	6	9	5
Upper room	1	1		3					1	2					
Room over porch	1														
Room over hall	1														
2nd room	1			1									4	4	
3rd room	1			1									4	3	
Blue room	1									1		1	2	1	
1st chamber	2	1	1					1	1	3		2	1		4
3rd chamber	2									2		2	1		4
4th chamber	2									2		2	1		4
Room below stairs	1									2		2	1		3

	1700	1710	1720	1730	1740	1750	1760	1770	1780	1790	1800	1810	1820	1830	1840/49
Back shed	1		1												
End shed	1														
Study		1		2											
Front chamber		1				5	12	8	7	13	13	29			
Chamber closet		1													
Children's room		1													
New room above stairs		1													
Porch chamber		1													
Cellar chamber		1													
Old house		1													
Lower kitchen		1													
Junior room		1													
Front room		1					9	9	11	5	9	25	16	29	40
Best chamber			1						1						
Pantry			1				1						6	4	9
Room over cellar			1												
Shop chamber			1												
Chamber over vault			1												
Stove room			1			1	2	2	4	2	2	8	12	10	8
Outward room in kitchen			1												
Inward room in kitchen			1									1	3	3	10
Out kitchen			1										1	1	
Shed room			1	1			1			1			1	1	
Kitchen loft			1		3			7	10	5	1	8	26	21	17
Middle chamber			1				1								
Clock room			1		1				1		1				
Out cellar				1									1		
Big room				1			1	1	1					2	

	1740	1750	1760	1770	1780	1790	1800	1810	1820	1830
Entry	1		2	2	2		3	11	32	43
Little room	1	2	2	6	18	4	7	9	15	16
Loft	1	4	4	1	2	1	1	3	1	
New room	1	2	1							
Bar	1	3	1	3	1	3		9	11	12
Public room	1									
Great room above stairs	1									
Fire room upstairs		1								
South east room		1								
North east room		1								
Lower front chamber		1								
Middle upper chamber		1								
Fire room			1		3	1	1	1		
Kitchen upstairs and down			1							
Stair closet			1							
Back chamber			1	12	10	5	8	27		
Linen chamber			1							
Little room in kitchen			1		1		1			
Passage room			1							
Office			1			1		1	7	3
Front parlour			1	2	2	1	3	4	11	9
Back parlour			1				1	3	5	8
Big room upstairs			2			2				
North chamber			1	1		1	1	4		
South chamber			1	1			1	3		
East chamber			2	2	5	4	1	9		
West chamber			1	1	4	8	1	7		
Brick room			1							
Blue parlour			1						7	13
North room			1							
East room			2	3	1			6	16	21
West room			2		2			4	9	19
South room			1						6	6
South room over yard			1							
Boy's room			2	3		1			4	1
Girl's room			2							
Outer room upstairs			1							
Green parlour			1							
Yellow room upstairs			1	1						
Press closet			1							
Garrett stairs			1							
New room			1	4						
Long room			2	1			1	1	2	1
Room head of stairs			2					2	1	1
Wine cellar				1				1		
Cider cellar				1						
Little cellar				1						
Bell room				1						
S.E. room				2			1		7	10

	1780	1790	1800	1810	1820	1830	1840 1849
S. W. room	4				10	12	16
N. W. room	2				9	8	20
N. E. room	2			1	10	9	13
Room with fire place	1						
Balcony room upstairs	1						
Woman's room	1				1		
Kitchen upstairs	1				2		
East room 3rd story	1						1
West room 3rd story	2						1
Entry upstairs	1	2	1	2	7	12	22
John's room	4					3	4
Common sitting room	1			2			
Sitting room	2			2	13	29	70
3rd story	1			1	1	2	6
Library	1						3
Dark room	1						
5th chamber	1		1				2
6th chamber	1		1				2
7th chamber	1						2
Men's room	1						
Maid's room	1						
Blue chamber	1						
Glass room	1						
Stone room down stairs			1				
Milk cellar			1				
Common room or kitchen			1				
Observatory				1			
Shed loft				1			
Bar in garrett				1			
Entry closet				1			
End closet				1			
Kitchen stairs				1			
Bed room				1		3	3
Back entry				1			
West parlour					2	1	3
East parlour					1	2	7
Parlour #1					1		
Parlour #2					2	1	
Small parlour					1		
North parlour					1		
Kitchen porch					1		
Back cellar					5		
Out room					2		
Lower bed chamber					1	2	4
Men's work room					1		
Middle cellar					1		
Kitchen shed					2		
Workmen's lodging room					1		
Inner cellar					1		1
Old gentleman's room					1		
School room					1		
Stair room					1		

	1820	1830	1840 1849		1820	1830	1840 1849
Second apartment	1			3 rooms on 3rd story		1	3
White room	1			Entry on 3rd story			2
Large room	1			Mineral room			1
Small room up stairs	10	4	12	Stair case			1
Bed room #7	1			Stair way			1
Bed room #8	1			Back stair way			1
Lumber room	1			Cellar stairs			1
Meal room	1	1		Kitchen stairs			1
Cave	1			S.E. parlour			1
Portico		1		Wash kitchen			1
Square room		1		Cook Kitchen			1
Store room		3	2	North room upstairs			1
Common house apartment		1		Entry at head of stairs			1
Doctor's room		1	1	Out room over kitchen			1
Closet under stairs		4		Bed room in garrett			1
Cheese room		1		Chamber #8			2
Chimney room		1		Large room upstairs	1	2	1
Drawer under window		1		Back room upstairs	31	30	50
Cupboard under kitchen stairs		1		South room upstairs	7	12	11
Shed room upstairs		1		East room upstairs	17	25	18
Over sitting room		4	2	Room over parlour	3	5	4
Lodging room in garrett		1		West room upstairs	13	27	15
Over dining room		1	2	Middle room upstairs	10	9	13
Sleeping chamber		1	1	Front room upstairs	26	25	55
Parlour upstairs		1		2nd story	9	13	18
Front room 3rd story		1	1	North room upstairs	13	11	

	1820	1830	1840 1849		1820	1830	1840 1849
N.E. room upstairs	12	19	14	Bed room #9			1
N.W. room upstairs	8	14	12	Chamber #10			1
S.E. room upstairs	6	17	15	Chamber #11			1
S.W. room upstairs	8	12	14	Hall upstairs			1
Room over bar	1	1		Vault			2
Room over stove room	1			Office garrett			1
1st room upstairs	7	2		Water closet			1
2nd room upstairs	7	2		Over pantry			1
3rd room upstairs	7	2		Breakfast or old bar room			1
4th room upstairs		1		Bee room			1
New room upstairs	1			Driver's room			1
Boy's room upstairs	1	1	3	Dark room on 2nd floor			1
Father's room	1			Back porch			1
Best room upstairs	1			Recess in room			1
Front chamber	1			Kitchen recess			1
Back chamber	1			Frame kitchen			1
Parlour garrett	1			Arch in cellar			1
Boy's garrett	1			Attic story			2
White chamber	1			1st room in attic			1
Long room upstairs	2		1	2nd room in attic			1
Blue room upstairs				3rd room in attic			1
Lodging room upstairs	1	1		4th room in attic			1
Over front door	1			Hall in attic			1
Bed room #1	1		1	Attic over kitchen			1
Bed room #3	1		1	Window cupboard			2
Bed room #4	1		1	Cupboard in wall			7
Bed room #5	1		1	Cupboard over fire place			1
Bed room #6	1			Cupboard & arch in cellar			1

ROUGH CAST

(Also see PEBBLE DASH)

Rough cast is defined by Bailey (ed. 1735) as "Rough, uneven, rugged", by Sheridan (ed. 1789) as "a kind of rough plaster" and by Webster (ed. 1828) as "A plaster with a mixture of shells or pebbles, used for covering buildings."

The 1798 Direct Tax lists John Ross, of Haverford Township, with a two story house "Roughcast 72 x 21" and William Williams, of Radnor Township, with a house "Logs & Roughcast 24 x 17."

The newspaper advertisements mention:

1809 "a new frame House, two stories high, rough cast and well finished"[1] Caleb Shaw (West Whiteland Twp.)

1818 "new stone House, rough cast"[2] John Smith, Alexander Hampton, Richard Peters, Jr. (Charlestown Twp.)

1822 "log, ruff cast, 34 feet square"[3] Jacob Weiler (Honey Brook Twp.)

1854 "Two story stone dwelling, Barn, stone Stable, Carriage house, all rough cast"[4] John E. Fox (East Caln Twp.)

1858 "Brick House, rough cast"[5] Abner & Susan Harlan (East Fallowfield Twp.)

1859 "Frame and log House, plastered in and rough cast out"[6] Isaac & Mary Miller (Honey Brook Twp.)

1870 "House...rough coated walls, lined and perfectly dry on first floor"[7] Ben. Phillips (New Garden Twp.)

1871 "rough cast east side"[8] M. E. Church (Coatesville)

Before 1877 the newspaper advertisements mention twenty-four other houses being rough cast; thirteen of stone, four of log, three of frame and four houses that did not mention the material of construction. Two other buildings, that did not mention the material of construction, were rough cast.

In 1856 J.B. wrote in referecne to rough casting:

HOW TO KEEP DRY HOUSES. — Mr. Evans — As this is the best time of the year to rough cast or plaster the outside of houses, I purpose to give your readers the plan I took last year, which has proved to be effectual in keeping the wall inside perfectly dry. The house is a stone one, some fifty years old. The east end had been rough cast a long time ago, but had nearly all scaled off. In the first place all the old mortar and painting was picked off, and the wall swept and washed clean, and left stand a month to get a dashing rain or two. Good fresh lime and sharp clean creek sand free from loam was used to make the mortar; after the plaster dried thoroughly two coats of paint were put on. The first was Ohio paint, the second was White lead and brown zinc, mixed equally, which gives a color resembling Ct. Brown Stone, and is very much admired; however, any color can be made to suit the fancy. There is no more dampness on the wall inside now, in a wet spell, than there is on an inside partition. J.B.[9]

1. *AMERICAN REPUBLICAN* (West Chester, Penna.) Oct. 3, 1809.
2. *VILLAGE RECORD* (West Chester, Penna.) March 4, 1818.
3. *AMERICAN REPUBLICAN* (West Chester, Penna.) Sept. 18, 1822.
4. *VILLAGE RECORD* (West Chester, Penna.) Sept. 5, 1854.
5. Ibid., Sept. 25, 1858.
6. Ibid., Dec. 13, 1859.
7. Ibid., Oct. 4, 1870.
8. *AMERICAN REPUBLICAN* (West Chester, Penna.) Aug. 22, 1871.
9. *VILLAGE RECORD* (West Chester, Penna.) May 24, 1856.

SADDLE HOUSE

The 1798 Direct Tax for Newtown and part of Marple Townships lists one wood saddle house 9 x 9 feet.

SAW MILL

The 1798 Direct Tax lists twenty-nine saw mills: the mean size being 536 square feet. The newspaper advertisements between 1840 and 1849 list two saw mills, the mean size being 595 square feet and between 1850 and 1875 eight saw mills had a mean size of 779 square feet. One frame saw mill was 66 x 14 feet and one frame one and a half story saw mill was 45 x 12 feet.

SCHOOL

Henry Graham Ashmead, in 1884, mentions

1745 Church of England adherents purchased 1702 a rude frame building from John and Tobias Hendrickson, which had been used as a blacksmith shop, for which they paid about 5 lbs. moved it, whitewashed it inside and out and constructed rude benches...[1745] Old frame structure then used as school house.[1] (Chichester Twp.)

1750 log school house having rude desks fastened to the sides of the building in use in 1750 in old Newtown Square. 1749 a stone school house erected near St. David's Church. It was warmed by a wood fire built on the hearth, and a high chimney-stack being constructed to afford a large wide-mouthed fireplace.[2] (Newtown Twp.)

1760 One of the first schools built about 1760 of stone, the mortar being a composition of clay and straw[3] (Edgemont Twp.)

1770 "Built of brick laid in headers and stretchers, the ends of the headers being burnt black. It was two stories in height. It is said the bricks were imported from England — in the south gable the large numerals 1770 were inserted in the wall, being formed by the black ends of the headers."[4] (Chester)

John H. Brinton, in his diary, mentions that the school house was an old log building in Thornbury Township in 1795.[5]

The 1796 tax assessment for West Whiteland Township lists Richard Thomas with "Log School House for Publick Use", John Jacobs with "1 stone school house for public use" and for Uwchlan Township Enos Miles with "stone school house."

The newspapers mention:

1813 "dwelling house with two rooms on a floor, adjoining which there is a frame building 25 by 30 feet, occupied as a school house"[6] John Wolley (West Chester)

1822 "a frame house lately made use of as a school house but may easily be converted into a dwelling"[7] Thomazine Kennedy (Sadsbury Twp.)

1836 "log dwelling with a log building adjoining, occupied for a school room"[8] John Worth (West Bradford Twp.)

1838 "frame shop lathed and plastered...now occupied as a school house"[9] John R. Shortlidge Est. (New Garden Twp.)

1852 "New Building joined to the dwelling, 35 by 24 feet, and two stories high, which has been occupied as a Boarding School"[10] William Butler (West Fallowfield Twp.)

1854 "House was lately erected for the purpose of a school, 32 by 26, kitchen and bath room attached"[11] Ezra Michener (East Marlboro Twp.)

1855 "2 story Brick Academy Building, with 2 school rooms on each floor, cellar under and portico attached in front...2 story Brick dwelling and Boarding House with portico in front and one and a half story Brick Dining hall and kitchen attached back to which is attached a frame or Shed Wash house...a frame Ball-alley and Play-House, weatherboarded on the outside"[12] Unionville Academy (East Marlboro Twp.)

1856 "House 85 by 25 feet, stone and frame, 2 stories, basement. The school room is 25 feet square...every apartment warmed by heaters, kitchen has cooking range...The play grounds are laid out in walks and well supplied with shade trees, flowers &c."[13] Sunnyside Seminary (East Fallowfield Twp.)

1856 "Notice to Builders and Contractors — School House at Chestnut Grove — house to be built of brick, about 26 by 30 feet, story not less than ten feet high, with benches, desks, and everything necessary for a convenient and substantial school house"[14] C. Coates

(Highland Twp.)

1858 "double floored Barn 36 x 51 with dormitory... having a second story lathed and plaster suitable for a school room"[15] Thomas Lamborn (New Garden Twp.)

1858 "School House 22 x 26"[16] Frederick Deimer (Spring City)

1859 "school house to be erected is to be 60 feet square, two stories high, with four rooms and a class room attached to each room. Mr. John Yeager is to build."[17] (Phoenixville)

1859 "school house to be erected 45 by 48 feet, 2 stories, classroom attached to one room...Spara & Maxwell to build"[18] (Phoenixville)

1860 "stone House 25 feet square known as Grim's School House"[19] (Upper Uwchlan Twp.)

1861 "frame COTTAGE SCHOOL HOUSE"[20] Edith B. Chalfant (East Marlboro Twp.)

1864 "STONE BUILDING, some twenty five feet square and one story high, built and now used for a School House"[21] C. H. Bradley (Vincent Twp.)

1864 "Schoolroom is 25 feet square. The Play grounds are laid out in walks, well supplied with shade trees, flowers &c."[22] Samuel H. Harry (East Fallowfield)

1865 "Cottage School frame 24 x 36 feet"[23] (East Whiteland Twp.)

1865 "one a half story frame Building, stone foundation, 22½ by 38 feet, formerly used as a school House"[24] Benjamin Swayne (London Grove Twp.)

1866 "new school to be built near Exton station 30 by 40 feet stone"[25]

1869 "School House 60.4 by 33.4"[26] (Honey Brook)

1869 "New School, brick 48 by 50 feet, 2 story, each 13 feet high in the clear: the walls are finished on the outside with pilasters, which relieve the plainness of an otherwise smooth surface"[27] (Kennett Square)

1869 "Principal building brick 165 by 55 feet...new structure 64 x 58 feet"[28] Westtown School (Westtown Twp.)

1869 "New School 30 x 38, stories 13 ft high, will cost $2449.50"[29] (Willistown Twp.)

1870 "House 39 by 33 feet, ceilings corniced...17 rooms"[30] Toughkenamin Boarding School (New Garden Twp.)

1870 "School House to be 33 by 47 feet, 2 story"[31] (West Nantmeal Twp.)

1871 "Graded School 32 x 40, 2 story almost finished"[32] (Charlestown Twp.)

1871 "The School was built many years ago, and was of the Octagon style — quite fashionable at the time it was built, but rather out of date now"[33] (West Marlboro Twp.)

1872 "school house to replace old octagonal house"[34] (Schuylkill Twp.)

1872 "Building school house 30 by 40 feet with basement"[35] (West Whiteland Twp.)

1872 "new two story school house, stone, upper room 30 by 40 feet, 11 feet high"[36] (Westtown Twp.)

1875 "New school 32 by 45 feet, 2 story"[37] (East Vincent Twp.)

1875 "new school 26 by 36 feet"[38] (Penn Twp.)

1875 "This building which is to used exclusively for primary purposes, is sixty by fifty feet, two stories high, the height of each of which is fourteen feet in the clear, while the basement partially above ground is nine feet high, and will be used in wet and cold weather for playing purposes for which it is admirably adapted, being divided into two parts one of which will be used by the boys and the other by the girls. The first story contains two class rooms, divided by a regular partition, in which will be taught the third and fourth primaries. The fourth primary room contains fifty-five seats, which will accommodate one hundred and ten children without the least crowding. In the other room the third primary class will be taught and that will accommodate ninety scholars. The second story is divided by a glass partition and can be thrown into one. There will be taught the first and second primaries, and there are seats for one hundred and eighty children.

The exterior of the building is plain, without any pretensions to architectural display, while the inside is fitted up neatly and with an eye single to the comfort of children and teachers. Each floor is amply provided with water and gas, and is heated by heaters placed in the basement, and has all the modern arrangements for light and ventilation, while the school furniture is constructed upon the most approved and scientific principles. The cost of the building proper was $9,700, but by the time the lot is fully graded, fenced and paved the cost of all will reach $12,000. The contractor was Mr. John Yeager, under whose supervision the carpenter work was well done. Mr. T. L. Snyder did the brick work, Mr. John Prince the plastering, which by the way is a most excellent piece of work, Mr. Jos. Lukens the painting, and Caswell & Moore put in the heaters and water fixtures, and did the tin work and gas fitting."[39]

1875 "designs furnished by Mr. N. B. Dobb of New York...two new school rooms 28 by 21 feet"[40] Mason Street School (Phoenixville)

1875 "Brick, 1 story, 29 x 36"[41] (Goshen Twp.)

An old log school house, on the farm owned in 1891, by Richard Ashbridge, in West Whiteland Township was described as "A PRIMITIVE STRUCTURE. As we have stated it was a log building and a very primitive looking structure. It was a square one-story structure, with a pyramidal roof having eaves on every side and the open of

the roof exactly in the centre. There were five windows. A small one was on either side of the door in front. These had sash which moved up and down in the ordinary manner. In each of the other sides of the building there was one large window the sash of which slid longitudianally past each other. The desks were arranged around the walls and the benches were made of slabs turned upside down with holes bored in them to admit the feet. An old ten-plate stove stood in the center of the room and supplied the heat."[42]

1. Henry Graham Ashmead, *HISTORY OF DELAWARE COUNTY, PENNSYLVANIA* (Phila., Penna. 1884), p. 461.
2. Ibid., p. 641.
3. Ibid., p. 556.
4. Ibid., p. 349.
5. John H. Brinton Diary #1, p. 92 under date November 12, 1859. Chester County Historical Society (West Chester, Penna.)
6. *CHESTER & DELAWARE FEDERALIST* (West Chester, Penna.) Jan. 18, 1813.
7. *VILLAGE RECORD* (West Chester, Penna.) Nov. 13, 1822.
8. Ibid., Feb. 10, 1836.
9. Ibid., Feb. 13, 1838.
10. Ibid., Sept. 28, 1852.
11. Ibid., Dec. 16, 1854.
12. *AMERICAN REPUBLICAN* (West Chester, Penna.) Dec. 25, 1855.
13. Ibid., Nov. 25, 1856.
14. *VILLAGE RECORD* (West Chester, Penna.) May 24, 1856.
15. Ibid., Dec. 11, 1858.
16. Ibid., June 26, 1858.
17. Ibid., Sept. 6, 1859.
18. Ibid., Sept. 6, 1859.
19. Ibid., Oct. 13, 1860.
20. Ibid., Dec. 10, 1861.
21. Ibid., Nov. 8, 1864.
22. Ibid., Aug. 16, 1864.
23. Ibid., Oct. 21, 1865.
24. Ibid., Sept. 30, 1865.
25. *AMERICAN REPUBLICAN* (West Chester, Penna.) Dec. 26, 1866.
26. *VILLAGE RECORD* (West Chester, Penna.) Oct. 5, 1869.
27. *AMERICAN REPUBLICAN* (West Chester, Penna.) Sept. 14, 1869.
28. *VILLAGE RECORD* (West Chester, Penna.) Dec. 18, 1869.
29. *AMERICAN REPUBLICAN* (West Chester, Penna.) Aug. 3, 1869.
30. *VILLAGE RECORD* (West Chester, Penna.) Sept. 10, 1870.
31. Ibid., March 22, 1870.
32. Ibid., May 30, 1871.
33. Ibid., Dec. 16, 1871.
34. *PHOENIXVILLE MESSENGER* (Phoenixville, Penna.) May 25, 1872.
35. *AMERICAN REPUBLICAN* (West Chester, Penna.) Aug. 6, 1872.
36. *VILLAGE RECORD* (West Chester, Penna.) Feb. 13, 1872.
37. *DAILY LOCAL NEWS* (West Chester, Penna.) Aug. 2, 1875.
38. *VILLAGE RECORD* (West Chester, Penna.) April 24, 1875.
39. *PHOENIXVILLE MESSENGER* (Phoenixville, Penna.) Jan. 2, 1875.
40. Ibid., Aug. 7, 1875.
41. *VILLAGE RECORD* (West Chester, Penna.) July 17, 1875.
42. *DAILY LOCAL NEWS* (West Chester, Penna.) March 11, 1891.

SHED

Shed is defined by Bailey (ed. 1735) as "a Penthouse or Shelter made of Boards", by Sheridan (ed. 1789) as "a slight temporary covering" and by Webster (ed. 1828) as "A slight building; a covering of timber and boards, &c. for shelter against rain and the inclemencies of weather; a poor house or hovel; as a horse-shed."

The 1798 Direct Tax lists sixty-six sheds: twenty-five of stone, the mean size being 862 square feet; eighteen of frame, the mean size being 432 square feet; six of log, the mean size being 241 square feet; three of wood, the mean size being 327 square feet; one of stone and frame 20 x 12 feet and three that did not mention the material of construction, the mean size being 296 square feet. The 1799 tax assessment for Charlestown Township lists one log shed 18 x 15 feet and one shed that did not mention the material of construction 60 x 12 feet; for London Britain Township the tax assessment lists one stone shed 33 x 12 feet and for West Marlboro Township one stone and frame shed 30 x 8 feet and for Pikeland Township one frame shed 30 x 8 feet, one log shed 23 x 9 feet and one stone shed 25 x 9 feet.

The newspaper advertisements mention:

1763 "Brick Dwelling-house...There is a back Shed new built to the House, wherein is a good back kitchen and one Lodging Room"[1] Robert M'Mallin (Upper Darby Twp.)

1777 "stone shed (part of which is converted into stabling) 147 feet long divided and contains 12 teams"[2] William Gibbons (West Nantmeal Twp.)

1785 "stone shed 52 feet long and 14 feet wide, and 20 feet high...two stories high"[3] Samuel Vanleer (Easttown Twp.)

1810 "STORE-HOUSE, with two shed rooms adjoining the same"[4] William Dilworth (Birmingham Twp.)

1811 "new stone house, 40 feet front, 20 feet back, with a kitchen and shed room back"[5] Abraham Wells (Uwchlan Twp.)

1840 "shed kitchen"[6] David Brown (New Garden Twp.)

1841 "Store House...pump therein with a shed over the same, 11 feet long, running back the whole length of the house"[7] J. Meredith Est. (Kennett Twp.)

1868 "shed 16 by 60 feet enclosed by sliding doors"[8] Joseph Baugh (Downingtown)

The newspaper advertisements between 1809 and 1849 mention two sheds that do not give the material of construction, the mean size being 2120 square feet, one manure shed 60 x 20 feet and one stone shed 70 x 20 feet and between 1850 and 1870 one frame hitching shed 36 x 18 feet and one frame shed 80 x 14 feet.

1. *PENNSYLVANIA GAZETTE* (Philadelphia, Penna.) Feb. 10, 1763.
2. Ibid., April 9, 1777.
3. Ibid., Aug. 31, 1785.
4. *CHESTER AND DELAWARE FEDERALIST* (West Chester, Penna.) Feb. 21, 1810.
5. *AMERICAN REPUBLICAN* (West Chester, Penna.) Jan. 20. 1811.
6. Ibid., Nov. 10, 1840.
7. *VILLAGE RECORD* (West Chester, Penna.) Sept. 28, 1841.
8. Ibid., Nov. 24, 1868.

SHOP

Shop is defined by Bailey (ed. 1735) as "an office for selling Wares", by Sheridan (ed. 1789) as "place where any thing is sold; a room in which manufactures are carried on" and by Webster (ed. 1828) as "A building in which goods, wares, drugs, &c. are sold by retail."

The 1798 Direct Tax lists two hundred and eighteen shops: ninety-eight of log, the mean size being 228 square feet; forty of stone, the mean size being 393 square feet; twenty-four of wood, the mean size being 315 square feet; twenty-one that did not mention the material of construction, the mean size being 239 square feet; seventeen of frame, the mean size being 263 square feet; six of brick, the mean size being 227 square feet; five of timber, the mean size being 245 square feet; two of stone and frame, the mean size being 315 square feet; two of log and stone, the mean size being 282 square feet; one of slab 35 x 15 feet; one of plank 18 x 18 feet and one of stone and wood 30 x 25 feet. The 1796 tax assessment for East Fallowfield Township lists seven shops: three of log, the mean size being 266 square feet and four that did not mention the material of construction, the mean size being 141 square feet. The 1799 tax assessments for Charlestown, London Britain, Pikeland and West Marlboro Townships lists thirty-nine shops: thirty-two of log, the mean size being 231 square feet and two of stone, the mean size being 294 square feet.

The newspaper advertisements between 1809 and 1824 mention thirteen shops: five of stone, the mean size being 410 square feet; four of frame, the mean size being 404 square feet; one log 22 x 20 feet; one hewed log 20 x 11 feet; one plank 18 x 14 feet and one that did not mention the material of construction 18 x 15 feet. Between 1825 and 1849 the newspapers mention nine shops: four of frame, the mean size being 361 square feet; three of stone, the mean size being 773 square feet; one of stone and frame 30 x 24 feet and one that did not mention the material of construction 16 x 16 feet. Between 1850 and 1869 the newspapers mention fifteen shops: eight that did not mention the material of construction, the mean size being 421 square feet; three of frame, the mean size being 326 square feet; two of stone, the mean size being 352 square feet and two of brick, the mean size being 572 square feet.

COOPER

Cooper is defined by Bailey (ed. 1735) as "one who makes Tubs, Calks, Barrels, &c.", by Sheridan (ed. 1789) as "one who makes coops or barrels" and by Webster (ed. 1828) as "One whose occupation is to make barrels, hogsheads, butts, tubs and casks of various kinds."

The newspaper advertisements mention between 1870 and 1875 one three story cooper shop 40 x 24 feet.

CURRYING

Currier is defined by Bailey (ed. 1735) as "one who dresses, liquors and colours tanned Leather, to make it gentle, &c.", by Sheridan (ed. 1789) as "one who dresses and pares leather for those who make shoes, or other things" and by Webster (ed. 1828) as "A man who dresses and colors leather, after it is tanned."

The newspaper advertisements between 1836 and 1839 mention one currying shop 25 x 18 feet.

HATTER

The newspaper advertisements between 1845 and 1849 mention one hatter's shop 32 x 16 feet.

MACHINE

The newspaper advertisements between 1809 and 1814 mention one machine shop 45 x 25 feet; between 1840 and 1849 two machine shops, the mean size being 320 square feet. Between 1855 and 1864 four machine shops are mentioned: one of stone 90 x 20 feet, one of brick, three story, 50 x 40 feet, one of stone and frame 80 x 18 feet and one that did not mention the material of construction 30 x 20 feet.

PLUMBER

John Romans, of West Bradford Township, advertised in 1858 "frame Plumber Shop 12 by 13 feet with Tailor shop above."[1]

1. *VILLAGE RECORD* (West Chester, Penna.) Jan. 12, 1858.

SADDLER

The newspaper advertisements between 1850 and 1859 mention two saddler shops, the mean size being 256 square feet.

SHOEMAKER

The newspaper advertisements mention between 1845 and 1849 one one and a half story shoemaker shop 15½ x 14 feet.

SMITH

The newspaper advertisements mention between 1750 and 1774 one stone smith shop 40 x 30 feet; between 1775 and 1799 one of stone, one story 18 x 17 feet and between 1835 and 1839 three smith shops are mentioned: one of stone 28 x 19 feet and two that did not mention the material of construction, the mean size being 620 square feet.

TAILOR

John Romans, of West Bradford Township, advertised in 1858 a "frame Plumber Shop 12 x 13 feet with Tailor shop above."[1]

1. *VILLAGE RECORD,* West Chester, Penna.) Jan. 12, 1858.

WAGON MAKER

The newspaper advertisements mention:
1832 "Wagon-maker's Shop 16 by 24 feet, two stories high, with a large platform for drying"[1] Samuel Ross (Lower Oxford Twp.)

1. *AMERICAN REPUBLICAN* (West Chester, Penna.) Jan. 10, 1832.

WHEELWRIGHT

The newspaper advertisements mention between 1835 and 1849 seven wheelwright shops: two of frame the mean size being 495 square feet and five that did not mention the material of construction, the mean size being 565 square feet. Between 1850 and 1876 eleven wheelwright shops are mentioned: four of frame the mean size being 548 square feet; two of stone, the mean size being 643 square feet and five that did not mention the material of construction, the mean size being 774 square feet. In 1853 Samuel S. Walley, of Charlestown Townshi, advertised "wheelwright shop, 2 stories, 25 x 30, lower shop has 3 benches, upper story has trimming room and varnishing and painting room"[1] and in 1858 Samuel Hughes, of East Nottingham Township, advertised "frame wheelwright shop, 2 stories high, painting scaffold attached 25 by 30 feet."[2]

1. *VILLAGE RECORD* (West Chester, Penna.) Nov. 1, 1853.
2. Ibid., Nov. 6, 1858.

WORK

The newspaper advertisements mention between 1830 and 1834 one stone, two story, work shop 40 x 25 feet.

SILO

The first silo in a newspaper advertisement to be mentioned is in West Whiteland Township in 1883. It was 33 x 35 feet and 14 feet deep.[1]

1. *DAILY LOCAL NEWS* (West Chester, Penna.) Jan. 12, 1883.

SKYLIGHT

The newspaper advertisements mention:
1861 "one of the rooms on the first floor is 11 by 12 feet with a good sky light"[1] A. M. Cochran (Oxford Twp.)
Before 1877 four other sky lights are mentioned in the newspaper advertisements.

1. *VILLAGE RECORD* (West Chester, Penna.) Feb. 19, 1861.

SLAB

The 1798 Direct Tax lists Eliz. Price, of Chester, as having "1 Slab Chair house 15 x 10"; William Johnson, of Haverford Township, with "Slabs spring 10 x 10"; Seth Thomas, of Middletown Township and part of Lower Providence Township with "Slabs spring 10 x 10"; Jno Patterson of Middletown Township and part of Lower Prividence Township with "Slab stable 16 x 14"; Mary Vernon, of Springfield and part of Lower Providence Townships with "Slab House very indifferent 24 x 20"; John Worall, of Springfield and part of Lower Providence Townships, with "Slab House very ordinary 20 x 12"; Saml Armor Jr., of Upper and Lower Chichester Townships, with "Cedar slabs stable 12 x 10." The 1799 tax assessment for Charlestown Township lists James Bodley as having a "Slab spring 9 x 9."

Two slab stables were advertised in the newspapers: one in 1856 of Charles T. Glashow's, of East Nottingham Township[1] and one of Neal Patton's, of Kennett Township.[2]

1. *VILLAGE RECORD* (West Chester, Penna.) June 12, 1858.
2. Ibid., March 5, 1861.

SLATE

Slate is defined by Bailey (ed. 1735) as "a scaly Sort of stoney Substance for Roofing Houses, and other uses", by Sheridan as "a grey soffle stone, easily broke into thin plates, which are used to cover houses, or to write upon" and by Webster (ed. 1828) as "A piece of smooth argillaceous stone, used for covering buildings."

The newspapers mention:
1831 "forge is fifty feet square of stone covered with slate"[1] Ellis Passmore (New London Twp.)
1831 "new...brick house...with a good and substantial slate roof"[2] James Grier (West Nottingham Twp.)
1837 "blacksmith shop covered with slate"[3] David & Joe Lamborn (London Grove Twp.)
1846 "two houses, 1 log and the other stone, covered with slate"[4] Anthony Steel, Sr., (West Nottingham Twp.)
1850 "stone Barn covered with slate"[5] William Noble (Sadsbury Twp.)
1858 "2 story stone saw, plaster & cider mill 21 by 53 feet roofed with slate"[6] Wm. & John J. McCrery (Lower Oxford Twp.)
1861 "stone Hotel...covered with slate and pebble roof"[7] "Steam Boat" (East Whiteland Twp.)
1862 "SCHOOL ROOM, roofed with slate"[8] Samuel Harper (London Britain Twp.)
1864 "Brick Machine shops...Brick Foundry...covered with slate & tin roofs"[9] S.M. Pennock & Co. (Kennett Square)
1865 "House...(fire proof) being covered with slate"[10] W. E. Haines (Franklin Twp.)
1866 "new building...to be constructed in the Italian style, slate elevators with dormer windows"[11] Major Kames, (Downingtown)
1870 "slate & tin mansard"[12] Normal School (West Chester)
1871 "30 cottages...roofs plain and slated"[13] Joshua Kames (Downingtown)
1871 "stone grist mill...roofed with slate"[14] Halliday Hoopes (New Garden Twp.)
1873 "frame warehouse...slate roof"[15] William H. Curtis (Oxford)
1873 "Parlor...with marbleized slate mantle"[16] J. B. Hoecker (West Chester)
1873 "Paper mill...slate roof"[17] D. & J. C. Dickey (Upper Oxford Twp.)
1873 "House...slate mantle"[18] Sharpless & Hall (West Chester)
1874 "woollen mill...slate roof"[19] Joseph Fisher Est. (London Britain Twp.)
1874 "A Six-acre Rolling Mill. — The Phoenix Iron Company, whose great works are at Phoenixville, have nearly completed a new rolling-mill building, which is noteworthy in several respects. It is believed to be the largest single mill building, under one roof, in this country. The ground plan covering about six and a quarter acres of ground. Its longest dimension is nine hundred and thirty-eight feet and its breadth is two hundred and ninety feet, or nearly three-fourths of the length of State House row, from Fifth to Sixth sts., Philadela. The principal material of the building is rolled or wrought iron, the roof being slate.

Considering the heavy character of the principal material, it is difficult to conceive the light and airy appearance of the immense structure. The whole of the upper part of the building rests upon about two hundred and fifty wrought-iron flange columns of three-eights thickness of iron of the well-known Phoenixville pattern. These rise about thirty feet to the eaves of the roof, and are but eight and a half inches in diameter from the tip of one flange to the tip of the flange on the opposite side of the column. At a short distance they look very slender, considering the great expanse and weight of the superstructure they have to support, but they have been proved to be capable of sustaining many times the greatest weight or force they are ever likely to have to resist. The roof rises to the height of sixty feet at the ridge, the framework being exclusively of wrought iron, firmly braced and tied with rods and links. The building is erected simply for shelter for the engines, furnaces, rolls and other machinery found to be necessary for the enlarged business of the company, a great deal of which is iron for bridge building, to fill orders of Clark, Reeves & Co. The furnaces, engines and machinery will cost nearly a million of dollars. The cost of the six and a quarter acre building, when completed will be about $280,000. It is light, airy, strong and economical. It seems to combine the maximum of strength with the minimum expenditure of materials, and may be considered a fine specimen of American progress in structures for iron mill purposes."

1. *AMERICAN REPUBLICAN* (West Chester, Penna.) Oct. 11, 1831.
2. Ibid., Dec. 20, 1831.
3. *VILLAGE RECORD* (West Chester, Penna.) Feb. 8, 1837.
4. Ibid., Nov. 3, 1846.
5. Ibid., Oct. 8, 1850.
6. Ibid., Oct. 2, 1858.
7. Ibid., Nov. 12, 1861.
8. Ibid., Sept. 20, 1862.
9. Ibid., July 26, 1864.
10. Ibid., Jan. 7, 1865.
11. *AMERICAN REPUBLICAN* (West Chester, Penna.) Aug. 14, 1866.
12. Ibid., July 12, 1870.
13. *PHOENIXVILLE MESSENGER* (Phoenixville, Penna.) Jan. 27, 1871.
14. *VILLAGE RECORD* (West Chester, Penna.) Nov. 7, 1871.
15. Ibid., Jan. 7, 1873.
16. *AMERICAN REPUBLICAN* (West Chester, Penna.) Dec. 23, 1873.
17. Ibid., June 24, 1873.
18. *DAILY LOCAL NEWS* (West Chester, Penna.) March 20, 1873.
19. *VILLAGE RECORD* (West Chester, Penna.) May 9, 1874.
20. Ibid., April 28, 1874.

SLAUGHTER HOUSE

The 1798 Direct Tax lists four slaughter houses: three

of frame, the mean size being 193 square feet and one of wood 13 x 10 feet. The newspaper advertisements, between 1850 and 1876 list one wood slaughter house 16 x 14 feet and three that did not mention the material of construction, the mean size being 394 square feet. Between 1877 and 1899 the newspapers mention one frame slaughter house 60 x 20 feet and one that did not mention the material of construction 33 x 22 feet. In 1856 Chalkley J. Walton, of London Grove Township, advertised a "slaughter house 20 feet square with boiler shed attached."[1]

1. *VILLAGE RECORD* (West Chester, Penna.) Dec. 30, 1856.

SLITTING MILL

Slitting mill is defined by Webster (ed. 1828) as "A mill where iron bars are slit into nail rods, &c."

The 1799 tax assessment for West Marlboro Township lists two slitting mills, but did not mention the material of construction, the mean size being 885 square feet.

SMOKE HOUSE

The 1798 Direct Tax lists fifty-three smoke houses: thirty-nine of stone, the mean size being 187 square feet; eight of log, the mean size being 112 square feet; two of brick, the mean size being 122 square feet; two of plank, the mean size being 144 square feet; one of brick 12 x 11 feet and one of log and plank 10 x 10 feet. The 1799 tax assessment for Charlestown and West Marlboro Townships lists fourteen smoke houses: ten of stone, the mean size being 147 square feet; three of log, the mean size being 147 square feet and one that did not mention the material of construction 12 x 12 feet.

The newspaper advertisements mention:

1818 "stone smoke house with oven enclosed"[1] Philip Filman (East Nantmeal Twp.)

1828 "garret with plastered floor and smoke house in the same"[2] Ezekial White (East Goshen Twp.)

1842 "two story STONE HOUSE, 40 by 31 feet...cellar under the whole, and piazza in front...attached a new kitchen, 22 by 20 feet, with lodging room and smoke house on the end floor..."[3] Amos Garrett (Warwick Twp.)

1853 "Brick smoke house, 2 stories, with two mortar floors, the lower story arranged for drying apples"[4] Hayes Jackson (East Marlboro Twp.)

1860 "smoke house in garret, perfectly safe"[5] Emmor G. Griffith (Tredyffrin Twp.)

The newspaper advertisements between 1860 and 1864 mention one stone smoke house 12 x 12 feet.

1. *AMERICAN REPUBLICAN* (West Chester, Penna.) June 30, 1818.
2. *VILLAGE RECORD* (West Chester, Penna.) Jan. 9, 1828.
3. Ibid., Sept. 27, 1842.
4. Ibid., Nov. 22, 1853.
5. Ibid., Sept. 15, 1860.

SNUFF MILL

The 1798 Direct Tax lists four snuff mills: three of stone, the mean size being 1140 square feet and one that did not mention the material of construction 40 x 30 feet.

SPRING HOUSE

The 1798 Direct Tax lists seven hundred and twelve spring houses: five hundred and eighty of stone the mean size being 170 square feet; eighty-nine of log the mean size being 113 square feet; eleven of stone and log the mean size being 196 square feet; nine that did not mention the material of construction the mean size being 131 square feet; seven of wood the mean size being 180 square feet; three stone and frame the mean size being 213 square feet; two of frame the mean size being 82 square feet; two of brick the mean size being 156 square feet; two of slabs the mean size being 100 square feet; one of stone and wood 20 x 12 feet; one of plank 10 x 10 feet; one brick and stone 18 x 16 feet and one stone and timber 15 x 12 feet. The 1796 tax assessment for Uwchlan Township lists John Bound with "1 log dwelling house with spring house under", Esther Byers with "1 stone spring house with a dwelling over" and Enos Miles with "1 stone spring house with Joiner shop over". The 1799 tax assessment for Charlestown, Pikeland and West Marlboro Townships lists fifty-eight spring houses: forty-two of stone the mean size being 184 square feet; eight that did not mention the material of construction the mean size being 229 square feet; seven of log the mean size being 202 square feet and one of slabs 9 x 9 feet.

The newspapers mention:

1781 "stone spring house 18 by 20 feet with four granaries"[1] John Kerlin (East Whiteland Twp.)

1789 "stone spring house with one story above for grain"[2] Samuel Vanleer (Easttown Twp.)

1790 "stone spring house with an excellent cheese room over"[3] Benjamin Powell (East Bradford Twp.)

1809 "a stone Milk house, arched above for a smokehouse"[4] Julius Anderson (Charlestown Twp.)

1810 "a stone milk house, 18 by 16 feet, with a room and a fire place above"[5] Mathew Stanley (Brandywine Twp.)

1814 "springhouse, with a never failing spring of water under the same, 60 feet long and divided into 9 separate apartments and nearly in the center of the buildings"[6] Ellis Passmore "Pleasant Garden Forge" (New London Twp.)

1814 "a stone Spring House, sufficient to hold the milk of twenty cows paved with marble set in terrass"[7] John Miller Est. (Tredyffrin Twp.)

1815 "stone spring house fitted up so as to be occupied by a small family"[8] Jno. Duer (Sadsbury Twp.)

1818 "stone spring house, two stories high, the upper part suitable for a tenant"[9] George Norman (Tredyffrin Twp.)

1824 "a two story stone spring house the upper part a convenient tenant house"[10] James Jones (Brandywine Twp.)

1847 "spring house was repaired and painted last spring"[11] Alfred Weeks (East Marlboro Twp.)

1851 "spring house 27 by 14 feet with a shed adjoining 14 feet wide, in which Cope's Horse Power Churn is placed"[12] J. Kersey Marsh (East Brandywine Twp.)

1. *PENNSYLVANIA GAZETTE* (Philadelphia, Penna.) Aug. 8, 1781.
2. Ibid., Aug. 12, 1789.
3. Ibid., Oct. 6, 1790.
4. *AMERICAN REPUBLICAN* (West Chester, Penna.) Nov. 14, 1809.
5. Ibid., July 17, 1810.
6. Ibid., Oct. 11, 1814.
7. *CHESTER & DELAWARE FEDERALIST* (West Chester, Penna.) Dec. 14, 1814.
8. *AMERICAN REPUBLICAN* (West Chester, Penna.) April 4, 1815.
9. *VILLAGE RECORD* (West Chester, Penna.) Oct. 28, 1818.
10. Ibid., July 24, 1824.
11. *AMERICAN REPUBLICAN* (West Chester, Penna.) Oct. 19, 1847.
12. Ibid., Nov. 11, 1851.

STABLE

Stable is defined by Bailey as "a Place to keep Horses in", by Sheridan (ed. 1789) as "a house for beasts" and by Webster (ed. 1828) as "A house or shed for beasts to lodge and feed in. In large towns, a stable is usually a building for horses only, or horses and cows, and often connected with a coach house. In the northern towns in the northern states of America, a stable is usually an apartment in a barn in which hay and grain are deposited."

At a Court of Quarter Sessions held at Chester for the said County on August 28 and 29, 1705 the testimony mentions that James Gibbons "...with force and arms &c. a certain stable being part of the dwelling and mansion house of John Hoskins at Chester in the County aforesaid about the hour of two in the night of the same day feloniously and burglariously did break and enter and one gelding of a sorril color of the price of eight pounds of the goods & chattels of the said John Hoskins then and there being found then & there feloniously and burglarly did steal take & lead away against the peace of our said lady the Queen her crown and dignity."[1] Another mention of a dwelling house and barn being connected was in the 1798 Direct Tax for East Caln and West Whiteland Townships were Joseph Downing is listed as having "1 dwelling house and Barn Connect[d]." The 1798 Direct Tax lists four hundred and sixty stables: two hundred and fifty of log, the mean size being 276 square feet; seventy eight of frame, the mean size being 369 square feet; forty-eight of stone, the mean size being 664 square feet; forty of wood, the mean size being 176 square feet; eighteen that did not mention the material of construction, the mean size being 359 square feet; nine of stone and frame, the mean size being 677 square feet; eight of stone and log, the mean size being 348 square feet; three of timber the mean size being 424 square feet; two of brick, the mean size being 195 square feet; two of slab, the mean size being 172 square feet; one of wood and stone, the mean size being 357 square feet and one of log and frame of 216 square feet. The 1796 tax assessment for East Fallowfield Township lists seven log stables, the mean size being 366 square feet. The 1799 tax assessments for Charlestown, London Britain and West Marlboro Townships lists forty-three stables; thirty-four of log, the mean size being 286 square feet; five of frame, the mean size being 258 square feet; three of stone, the mean size being 203 square feet and one of stone and log of 225 square feet. The will of Henry Shengle, of Coventry Township, proven in 1785 instructs that "my Estate Shall Build...I do order a Small Stable be built for her [his wife] twelve feet Square to be covered Straw and to be Raised So high as will be Sufficient to hold Hay enough at one time to Winter her Cow."[2]

1. Colonial Society of Pennsylvania, *RECORD OF THE COURTS OF CHESTER COUNTY PENNSYLVANIA 1681-1697* (Patterson & White Co., Philadelphia, Penna., 1910), p. 132.
2. Chester County Will Book 7, p. 339.

STAIR CASE

Henry Graham Ashmead mentions in 1883 that the Old Hoskins (Graham) house, in Chester, built in 1688 had "Hallway runs through the center of the building...wide easily ascended staircase rises from the rear of the entry...Balustrade is fashioned of hard wood and is very massive...steps of ash."[1]

The newspaper advertisements mention:

1833 "Stone House...and two stair cases on the first floor"[2] "Washington Hotel" (West Pikeland Twp.)

1838 "Brick Building recently erected...with an open stair case"[3] Cheyney & Amos Nields (West Chester)

1843 "Frame Dwelling House, 2 stories high, calculated for one or two families, having two pair of stairs from cellar to garret"[4] Thos. Wood (West Fallowfield Twp.)

1843 "Mansion...of brick...The hall or entry passing the whole length of the building is 10 ft. wide, with stairing leading to the upper entry of the same width"[5] John S. Bowen (West Goshen Twp.)

1857 "porch in front and back, and a stairway along side of the house leading to front porch"[6] John O'Reilly (Phoenixville)

1859 "3 story stone Factory 30 by 60 feet, with stone stairway about 16 feet square containing overshoot wheel"[7] John & Aaron P. Osmond (London Britain Twp.)

1860 "House...piazza extending the entire length, with a large flight of stairs ascending thereto"[8] Samuel Roberts (West Pikeland Twp.)

1863 "two and a half story stone Mansion...with baluster stairs leading to second story"[9] George W. Richards (Phoenixville)

1863 "hall and stairways neatly papered"[10] Washington Yates (West Sadsbury Twp.)

1866 "front and back stairway"[11] M. Thomas & Sons (East Bradford Twp.)

1872 "3 story stone House, Open Stair Case and Railings to third story"[12] Jacob Rawle (Easttown Twp.)

1872 "open stairway from hall to 3d story"[13] Sarah M. Hickman (West Chester)

1872 "open stairs, Walnut Baluster"[14] Charles L. Warner (West Chester)

1873 "House...open stairway on first floor, Private stairs from dining room to third floor"[15] C. Marshall Ingram (Newlin Twp.)

1873 "The second story is reached by back and front stair-ways, with massive railings and ash steps"[16] Henry Buckwalter (West Chester)

1876 "The main stairway stands in a tower which rises above the surrounding roof and the rear building is carried up in the same style to correspond in appearance with the stair tower"[17] J. R. Gilpin (Birmingtown Twp.)

1880 "The stairs leading to the rooms in the upper stories are of solid walnut"[18] Dr. Ingram (West Chester)

Before 1877 the newspaper advertisements mention twenty-three houses with open stairs, eight houses with two staircases, three houses with front and back staircases and two houses with stairs having balusters in addition to those already listed.

The only advertisement found thus far of a man making stairs in the county is the following advertisement in 1875:

BUILDERS TAKE NOTICE
STAIR BUILDING IN ALL ITS BRANCHES
West Chester
D. W. C. Lewis.[19]

1. Henry Graham Ashmead, *HISTORICAL SKETCH OF CHESTER, ON DELAWARE* (The Republican Steam Printing House, 1883) p. 67.
2. *AMERICAN REPUBLICAN* (West Chester, Penna.) Dec. 17, 1833.
3. Ibid., Jan. 9, 1838.
4. Ibid., Sept. 26, 1843.
5. Ibid., Oct. 17, 1843.
6. Ibid., Feb. 24, 1857.
7. *VILLAGE RECORD* (West Chester, Penna.) Dec. 3, 1859.
8. Ibid., Oct. 2, 1860.
9. Ibid., June 9, 1863.
10. Ibid., Oct. 17, 1863.
11. Ibid., April 21, 1866.
12. Ibid., Nov. 2, 1872.
13. Ibid., March 19, 1872.
14. Ibid., Jan. 13, 1872.
15. Ibid., Sept. 9, 1873.
16. *DAILY LOCAL NEWS* (West Chester, Penna.) Dec. 5, 1873.
17. *VILLAGE RECORD* (West Chester, Penna.) April 15, 1876.
18. *DAILY LOCAL NEWS* (West Chester, Penna.) Oct. 1, 1880.
19. Ibid., Jan. 14, 1875.

STILL

The 1798 Direct Tax lists nineteen stills: seven of stone, the mean size being 562 square feet; seven of log, the mean size being 391 square feet; two of log and stone, the mean size being 278 square feet; one of wood 20 x 15 feet and one that did not mention the material of construction 26 x 20 feet. The newspaper advertisements between 1775 and 1799 mention one stone still 24 x 18 feet.

STONE

AVONDALE

The newspapers mention:

1900 "residence for Charles Walker...It is being built of Avondale stone, and is the first private residence to be erected in West Chester in that stone"[1]

1. *DAILY LOCAL NEWS* (West Chester, Penna.) Aug. 15, 1900.

BROWN

The newspapers mention:

1868 "Bank, three stories high, pressed brick front trimmed with Connecticut brown stone and 22 feet front by 58 feet back"[1] (Oxford)

1870 "House, brick with brownstone sills and lintels to the doors and windows"[2] J. W. Barnard (West Chester)

1872 "stone quarry of Brown and Grey sand quality"[3] Mary Evans (East Pikeland Twp.)

1873 "Two 3 story brick Houses...brown stone window and door caps and sills"[4] (West Chester)

1885 "The handsome residence of Mowrey Latshaw...with its pressed brick front, black mortar and brown stone window caps and sills presents an attractive appearance"[5] (Spring City)

1. *VILLAGE RECORD* (West Chester, Penna.) Dec. 5, 1868.
2. *AMERICAN REPUBLICAN* (West Chester, Penna.) Sept. 20, 1870.
3. *VILLAGE RECORD* (West Chester, Penna.) Sept. 28, 1872.
4. *AMERICAN REPUBLICAN* (West Chester, Penna.) Aug. 12, 1873.
5. *DAILY LOCAL NEWS* (West Chester, Penna.) July 13, 1885.

FLAG

Henry Graham Ashmead, in 1883, describes the Boar's Head Inn, in Chester, where Penn resided in 1682-1683 as "the kitchen floor was laid in flagging some of which were as large as 6 by 8 feet, under these was a body of eighteen inches of sand on which they rested."[1]

The newspaper advertisements mention:

1822 "in the cellar of which is a milk house handsomely flagged"[2] Hannah B. Stalker (East Caln Twp.)

1840 "quarry of superior flag and building stone"[3] Jonathan Smith Est. (Sadsbury Twp.)

1859 "frame Hog House, with pen flaged and enclosed by a stone wall"[4] David Wells (East Vincent Twp.)

1. Henry Graham Ashmead, *HISTORICAL SKETCH OF CHESTER, ON DELAWARE* (The Republican Steam Printing House, 1883), p. 63.
2. *VILLAGE RECORD* (West Chester, Penna.) July 17, 1822.
3. *AMERICAN REPUBLICAN* (West Chester, Penna.) Dec. 22, 1840.
4. *VILLAGE RECORD* (West Chester, Penna.) Dec. 11, 1858.

GRANITE

The newspapers mention:

1833 "three story Brick Building, fifty three by 32, plastered in front in imitation of granite"[1] Odd Fellows (West Chester)

1834 "two story Brick House...nearly new, granitized in front"[2] Outten D. Jester (West Chester)

1875 "granite steps"[3] Normal School (West Chester)

1885 "a handsome residence to be built of granite from the Fox Hill quarries, that township. The main building will be square, 32 by 22 feet, with mansard roof...but it could have been improved by having the trimmings of some other stone"[4] Dr. J. H. Latshaw (Warwick Twp.)

1886 "new portion of the house of John Wyeth, Thornbury...built of French Creek granite"[5]

1. *AMERICAN REPUBLICAN* (West Chester, Penna.) Dec. 3, 1833.
2. Ibid., April 1, 1834.
3. *DAILY LOCAL NEWS* (West Chester, Penna.) Aug. 18, 1875.
4. Ibid., Sept. 10, 1885.
5. Ibid., June 18, 1886.

SAND

The 1798 Direct Tax lists one sand stone house.

The newspapers mention:

1836 "sand stone barn"[1] Frederick March (Coventry Twp.)

1858 "new brown sand stone building belonging to our townsman, David Meconkey"[2] (West Chester)

1871 "sand stone steps"[3] Episcopal Church (Phoenixville)

1872 "stone quarry of Brown or Grey sand quality"[4] Mary Evans (East Pikeland Twp.)

1882 "house...which will be of Easttown gray sand stone"[5] (Tredyffrin Twp.)

1893 "A very handsome building will be erected...The front of the building will be of Pompeian brick, which is that long, narrow brick, used for some of the interior decorative work in the Court House. The base and trimmings will be of light red sandstone"[6]

1. *REGISTER & EXAMINER* (West Chester, Penna.) Oct. 11, 1836.
2. *VILLAGE RECORD* (West Chester, Penna.) Sept. 28, 1858.
3. *PHOENIXVILLE MESSENGER* (Phoenixville, Penna.) March 25, 1871.
4. *VILLAGE RECORD* (West Chester, Penna.) Sept. 28, 1872.
5. *DAILY LOCAL NEWS* (West Chester, Penna.) Jan. 4, 1882.
6. Ibid., March 23, 1893.

SOAP

A newspaper mentions:

1855 "Soapstone"[1] Benjamin Kugler Est. (Charlestown Twp.)

1. *AMERICAN REPUBLICAN* (West Chester, Penna.) Sept. 25, 1855.

SERPENTINE

The newspapers mention:

1837 "STONE HOUSE, built of the serpentine rock"[1] David Hoopes (West Goshen Twp.)

1856 "Rectory or Parsonage...built of green serpentine stone of this locality"[2] Church of Holy Trinity (West Chester)

1869 "Granite — The working of the Brinton Serpentine Quarry in Birmingham has developed a very fine bed of granite. The specimens are said to be equal to the finest granite in the market. Mr. Brinton we believe intends to make all arrangements to furnish the stone in large blocks."[3]

1870 "SERPENTINE STONE. — From certain articles which we have recently noticed in the Philadelphia Press, it would seem that some little feeling exists among the parties who furnish this beautiful stone. The following is a description of the Birmingham deposit, now being worked by the Messrs. BRINTON & CO:

This stone is found in Chester county, a mile and a half from the Street road station on the West Chester and Philadelphia Railroad, and near the Friends' meeting-house of Birmingham, from which it derives its name. It is claimed for this serpentine that in addition to being a non-conductor of heat it combines many other desirable qualities for building purposes. The other serpentine in this portion of the State occur in ridges parallel, or nearly so, to the general course of the Alleghanies, from north-east to south-west. The Birmingham deposit, on the contrary, is an isolated knob, elliptical in form, the long axis being east and west, at a distance of more than four miles from any distinct ridge. The knob rises about a hundred feet above the stream at its base, and covers an area of about six acres, thus furnishing a large supply of this building material. Several peculiar minerals are found in the Birmingham serpentine. Among them are clincochlore, asbestos, a limited amount of hydrated sillicate of magnesia (the true meerschaum, used for tobacco pipes), and many others. As would naturally be expected from this, the serpentine itself presents unusual and characteristic traits, and they are such as adapt it admirably for building purposes. Its prevailing color is a light, cheerful, permanent green; its texture is very uniform and firm; it occurs in large masses, some having been taken from the quarry eight or ten feet in length and three or four feet in thickness; and it is free from any mixture of iron or flint. When first quarried, it is so soft that it can readily be turned in a lathe, or cut into any desired form. Soon, however, it hardens, and then no exposure to water will soften it, as when the sillicates held in solution by the "quarry water" once crystalize, they become entirely insoluble. It will then bear a fine polish. These properties suggest its fitness for interior decorations, and for rich exterior designs. This serpentine has already been used in the construction of many handsome dwellings and church edifices. The new church at Broad and Spruce streets, Philadelphia, is built of this stone, and is one of the finest structures of its kind in the city."[4]

1870 "All exterior walls faced with serpentine stone"[5] Normal School (West Chester)

1871 "Brinton quarry supplying stone for Pennsylvania University building"[6]

1872 "quarry serpentine stone"[7] Lewis Garret (East Goshen Twp.)

1872 "serpentine stone chapel"[8] Lincoln University (Lower Oxford Twp.)
"building House...Fronts serpentine stone from Brinton's"[9] Market Street (West Chester)
"building is 3 story, and the front is built of serpentine stone from Birmingham quarries. The stones are dressed smooth and the painting is pure white, making a very clean appearance"[10] Hammond & Kervey Drugs (West Chester)

1873 Serpentine stone from Brinton quarry for Singer Sewing Machine Company in New York City[11]

"brick cottage, with serpentine stone front...The brick work to be painted in imitation of stone"[12] Dr. Joseph E. Jones (West Chester)

"brick cottage...serpentine stone window and door caps and sills and corner mountings"[12] J. J. Parker (West Goshen Twp.)

"Martin & Dunlap serpentine stone quarry"[14] (West Nottingham Twp.)

1874 Joseb Kidd discovered serpentine stone[15] (Elk Twp.)

1874 "CHESTER COUNTY SERPENTINE. —...But now, nearly a century later a different light presents itself, and the bloody battle ground is a scene of peaceful industry, the eye is greeted with a huge piles of earth and debris, tall derricks, the smoke of the steam engine, and all the appurtenance belonging to an enterprising quarry. The ridge has been laid bare in two places about 300 yards apart, and seems to be a solid mass of rock nearly to the surface, covering an area of 8 acres.

When first quarried the stone is soft, but rapidly hardens on exposure, so that in less than a year it is as difficult to cut as many of the sandstones.

This characteristic eminently adapts it to being worked by machinery at the quarry, and for this purpose a large steam mill has been erected on the ground. The Proprietor, Mr. Joseph H. Brinton is a gentleman of scientific education, being a graduate of the Sheffield school of Arts of Yale College, and one of those practical workers eminently fitted to develope the resources of the country. What he has accomplished here within the five years in advancing the art of stone cutting by machinery, seems to be worth more than the efforts of other inventions in this line for the past quarter of a century. We venture to say that no other stone works in the county contains as many curious and original mechanical devices. Here we can see a block of stone perhaps two feet thick and weighing over a ton sawed through under a gang of circular saws at the astonishing rate of over one foot per minute. Another powerful machine, one casting of which weighs over two tons, is used for facing the rough stone and saves the labor of at least twenty stone cutters. The mill is connected with the quarry by a railroad track and fitted with every convenience for handling the stone with facility. A 30 horse vertical engine and 50 horse cylinder boiler gives ample power to run all the machinery. Among the prominent buildings lately erected in Philadelphia with this stone we might mention the University of Pennsylvania, the Academy of National Science as well as several Churches on Broad street."[16]

1. *AMERICAN REPUBLICAN* (West Chester, Penna.) Sept. 5, 1837.
2. Ibid., Sept. 16, 1856.
3. *VILLAGE RECORD* (West Chester, Penna.) Aug. 17, 1869.
4. *AMERICAN REPUBLICAN* (West Chester, Penna.) Jan. 4, 1870.
5. Ibid., July 12, 1870.
6. Ibid., April 11, 1871.
7. *VILLAGE RECORD* (West Chester, Penna.) Nov. 16, 1872.
8. *AMERICAN REPUBLICAN* (West Chester, Penna.) May 7, 1872.
9. Ibid., April 16, 1872.
10. Ibid., Oct. 1, 1872.
11. *PHOENIXVILLE MESSENGER* (Phoenixville, Penna.) July 5, 1873.
12. *AMERICAN REPUBLICAN* (West Chester, Penna.) Aug. 12, 1873.
13. Ibid., May 20, 1873.
14. *DAILY LOCAL NEWS* (West Chester, Penna.) Sept. 15, 1873.
15. Ibid., April 8, 1874.
16. *AMERICAN REPUBLICAN* (West Chester, Penna.) March 24, 1874.

STORE

The 1798 Direct Tax lists seventeen store houses: eight of stone the mean size being 430 square feet; two frame the mean size being 414 square feet; one brick 2000 square feet; one log 288 square feet and five that did not mention the material of construction the mean size being 409 square feet.

The newspapers mention:

1831 "STORE ROOM...The rooms are separated by a partition which can be removed if required"[1] (West Chester)

1834 "frame store house lined inside with boards"[2] Thomas H. B. Jacobs (Charlestown Twp.)

1850 "STORE HOUSE which is well bolted and barred; stone cellar, has a lodging room in second story"[3] Isaac Evans (Uwchlan Twp.)

1850 "store room 20 by 40 feet with double counters and shelves"[4] John Keech (West Chester)

1855 "Bulk Window Awning with Frame, Shelves, Counter, Show case"[5] David Fields (West Chester)

1858 "The only Iron Front Store, No. 7 Church street... containing nine large and convenient rooms. The store room is 48 feet deep with two large Show Windows, and Glass Door in center"[6] L. W. H. Kervey (West Chester)

1858 "The only Iron Front Store, No. 7 Church street... containing nine large and convenient rooms. The store room is 48 feet deep with two large Show Windows, and Glass Door in center"[6] L. W. H. Kervey (West Chester)

1. *AMERICAN REPUBLICAN* (West Chester, Penna.) May 17, 1831.
2. Ibid., Dec. 16, 1834.
3. Ibid., Sept. 10, 1850.
4. Ibid., Feb. 19, 1850.
5. *VILLAGE RECORD* (West Chester, Penna.) July 24, 1855.
6. *AMERICAN REPUBLICAN* (West Chester, Penna.) Aug. 3, 1858.

STUDIO

The newspaper advertisements mention:
1859 "two story Frame Office and Studio, wood"[1] Mifflin Lewis Est. (Tredyffrin Twp.)

1.   *VILLAGE RECORD* (West Chester, Penna.) Oct. 1, 1859.

STYLE

A newspaper mentions:
1887 "Two More Handsome Houses...The architecture is somewhat different from any house in town and they will be built after the style of those along the W.C. & P.R.R. at 49th street..."[1] (West Chester)

1.   *DAILY LOCAL NEWS* (West Chester, Penna.) April 8, 1887.

COLONIAL

A newspaper mentions:
1889 "Since Daniel Newhall erected a fine residence at Strafford in the Colonial style of architecture the design has become quite popular. The houses are long, low but very substantial looking"[1] (Easttown Twp.)

1.   *DAILY LOCAL NEWS* (West Chester, Penna.) Aug. 6, 1889.

COMPOSITE

The newspapers mention:
1873 "three story brick cottage in the composite style"[1] J. J. Parker (West Goshen Twp.)

1.   *AMERICAN REPUBLICAN* (West Chester, Penna.) May 20, 1873.

CYCLOPEAN

The newspapers mention:
1893 "residence of Joseph Murtagh, on North Church street. It is the only building in West Chester constructed of unhewn boulders and is peculiar and unique in appearance. For the information of those unfamiliar with these things it may be worth while to state that it is of the style known as Cyclopean."[1]

1.   *DAILY LOCAL NEWS* (West Chester, Penna.) July 8, 1893.

ENGLISH

The newspapers mention:
1879 "Model Chester County Farm...The entrance to the buildings is through an iron gate, hung on granite posts...mansion of the manor, built of brick, in English style of architecture...A wide iron veranda the whole length of the house"[1] Samuel Morris (London Grove Twp.)
1881 "Henry Faucett has just completed a new mansion... The building is of the old English style"[2] (Birmingham Twp.)
1884 "Rev. Thomas Aitken, Berwin is erecting...houses... stone and brick and in the old English style"[3] (Easttown Twp.)

1.   *DAILY LOCAL NEWS* (West Chester, Penna.) Jan. 16, 1879.
2.   Ibid., Dec. 6, 1881.
3.   Ibid., May 20, 1884.

FRENCH

The newspapers mention:
1880 "[house] that of Mary Thomas...The building is much broken up, and resembles somewhat a French chateau"[1] (West Chester)
1889 "I. D. King, of Pennsbury Township, has just completed a house that will compare favorably with any dwelling in Chester County. It is of French construction both within and without."[2]

1.   *DAILY LOCAL NEWS* (West Chester, Penna.) June 10, 1880.
2.   Ibid., Aug. 27, 1889.

GOTHIC

The newspapers mention:
1851 "stone dwelling house, 80 feet front, with Gothic portico"[1] Abigail Kimber, (East Pikeland Twp.)
1861 "The building will be put up with stone, and finished in part Grecian and Gothic"[2] Zion's Church (East Vincent Twp.)
1870 "House...long deep windows Gothic style, plate and stained Glass"[3] J. Lee Englebert (West Chester)
1871 "Episcopalians about to erect new Church, frame and Gothic"[4] (Kennett Square)
1871 "The elegant Gothic Cottage erection on Church street, in our borough last summer is machine worked stone" [serpentine stone from Brinton's quarry] [5] (Phoenixville)
1872 "new Catholic Church to be Gothic style 45 by 90 feet"[6] (Coatesville)

1872 "stone Barn 48 by 45 feet, gothic windows back. It is built in English style"[7] Henry Webster (Highland Twp.)

1872 "style will be Gothic"[8] Reformed Mennonites Church (Phoenixville)

1873 "stone, built in Gothic style, 42 by 94 feet, tower and spire 100 feet high"[9] Methodist Episcopal Church (Wallace Twp.)

1875 "windows are Gothic with stained glass"[10] Berean Church (West Chester)

1882 "Gothic Cottage"[11] J. Atwood Pyle (London Grove Twp.)

1884 "The house will be two and a half stories high and will be of the Gothic style of architecture, gable front and back, with slate roof, and a porch on three sides"[12] James D. Peck (West Whiteland Twp.)

1889 "Next week C. W. Ash will give to the lowest Coatesville bidder the contract for the erection of his new house on Chestnut Street. The house, which will be of cottage Gothic style, 30 x 56 feet, and three stories high, will be an ornament and credit to our town. The first story will be of pointed stone, with marble caps for windows and doors. From the first story to the gables will be used pressed brick, and the gables and Gothic points will be finished in California cedar shingles. The rooms of the building will be large and well lighted. The hall, which will extend through the entire length of the building will be ten feet wide..."[13] (Coatesville)

1892 "one of the finest mansions in Chester County, Pa., built of brick, slate roof (Gothic style)"[14] "Cedarcroft" (East Marlboro Twp.)

1. *AMERICAN REPUBLICAN* (West Chester, Penna.) Sept. 16, 1851.
2. *VILLAGE RECORD* (West Chester, Penna.) March 12, 1861.
3. Ibid., Oct. 22, 1870.
4. Ibid., Feb. 14, 1871.
5. *PHOENIXVILLE MESSENGER* (Phoenixville, Penna.) Feb. 18, 1871.
6. *AMERICAN REPUBLICAN* (West Chester, Penna.) May 7, 1872.
7. *VILLAGE RECORD* (West Chester, Penna.) Nov. 19, 1872.
8. *PHOENIXVILLE MESSENGER* (Phoenixville, Penna.) July 20, 1872.
9. *DAILY LOCAL NEWS* (West Chester, Penna.) July 30, 1873.
10. *AMERICAN REPUBLICAN* (West Chester, Penna.) April 13, 1875.
11. *DAILY LOCAL NEWS* (West Chester, Penna.) Jan. 19, 1882.
12. Ibid., Sept. 30, 1884.
13. Ibid., March 23, 1892.
14. *COATESVILLE WEEKLY TIMES* (Coatesville, Penna.) March 30, 1889.

GRECIAN

The newspapers mention that the parishioners planned in 1861 that the new Zion Church, in East Vincent Township, be "put up with stone, and finished in part Grecian and Gothic."[1]

1. *VILLAGE RECORD* (West Chester, Penna.) March 12, 1861.

IONIC

The newspapers mention:

1859 "Two-storied frame Dwelling House with Ionic Front"[1] Chester Valley Railroad Company (Downingtown)

1. *AMERICAN REPUBLICAN* (West Chester, Penna.) July 5, 1859.

ITALIAN

The newspapers mention in 1866 that Major Kames, of Downingtown, was planning a "new building for holding lectures, musical, library and reading room 40 by 60 feet...to be constructed in the Italian style, slate elevators with dormer windows."[1]

1. *AMERICAN REPUBLICAN* (West Chester, Penna.) Aug. 14, 1866.

L SHAPED

The newspaper advertisements mention:

1847 "STONE MANSION (in the form of an L) 43 feet each front by 23 feet deep, 2 stories high"[1] Henry Buckwalter (Uwchlan Twp.)

1848 "stone house (in the form of an L) 37 feet front by 36 deep (two fronts) two stories"[2] Joseph Lukens (Willistown Twp.)

1856 "stone House in the shape of an L. The L is 29 feet by 34 feet other part 40 3/4 by 28 feet"[3] William Crosley Est. (Tredyffrin Twp.)

1856 "Frame House, built 6 years ago 36 by 15 feet, with an L 18 by 15 feet, all two stories, cellar 26 by 18 feet"[4] Thomas Phillips (West Nottingham Twp.)

1861 "2 story stone House in the form of an L, pebble dashed"[5] James Welsh (East Brandywine Twp.)

1866 "two story stone dwelling house L shaped 64 by 50 feet, ends 22 feet"[6] Marshall W. Aitken Est., (Upper Oxford Twp.)

1867 "3 story Brick House 48 by 30 feet, the ell is 20 by 18 feet"[7] Thomas S. Young (Coatesville)

1869 "stone House 42 by 21 feet...with an L extending back 40 feet"[8] Silas D. Yerkes (Downingtown)

1871 "New building in the shape of an L 197 by 60 feet, 2 story with wing 40 by 43"[9] Phoenix Iron Works (Phoenixville)

1872 "new stone House 20 by 30 feet with an L 18 by 11 feet, 2 story"[10] Levi Walleight (East Nantmeal Twp.)

1. *VILLAGE RECORD* (West Chester, Penna.) Nov. 2, 1847.
2. Ibid., Jan. 4, 1848.
3. Ibid., Oct. 25, 1856.
4. *AMERICAN REPUBLICAN* (West Chester, Penna.) Sept. 9, 1856.
5. Ibid., Sept. 24, 1861.
6. *VILLAGE RECORD* (West Chester, Penna.) Sept. 4, 1866.
7. Ibid., Feb. 2, 1867.
8. Ibid., Jan. 30, 1869.
9. *PHOENIXVILLE MESSENGER* (Phoenixville, Penna.) Jan. 14, 1871.
10. *AMERICAN REPUBLICAN* (West Chester, Penna.) May 14, 1872.

LAKESIDE

The newspapers mention:

1883 "The plans and specifications for the new frame residence of Samuel Butler, Uwchlan Township, has been completed and the work of building will commence this week. The house is to be 36 feet front, 2½ stories high and the interior is to be of hard wood or something on the Lakeside style of finishing. The roof will be of slate and a porch will surround the dwelling."[1]

1. *DAILY LOCAL NEWS* (West Chester, Penna.) Dec. 17, 1883.

OCTAGONAL

The newspapers mention:

1839   "Showplace of Chester County

This three-story house, with the huge basement, is constructed in the form of an octagon.

Lukens Pierce ordered the construction of this house at Towerville in 1839.

How can you manage to build square rooms in a house like that?

Each of the eight large rooms in the building has the same dimensions and the same appearance. A small wing built on the back of the house increases the number of rooms, including those on the third floor, to fifteen...

Rooms in the building open off a central shaft extending from the first to the third floors. A circular stairway leads from one floor to another.

Surmounting the house is a good-sized tower containing windows for lighting and ventilation purposes.

When the house was built a porch was constructed around the building. Windows in all the rooms were so designed that it was possible to raise the sash, open two small doors at the base of the window and walk onto the porch. In recent years those small doors have been permanently closed.

Not the least interesting fact concerning the construction of the house lay in the fact that only small stones were used...At that time cement was not used. Benjamin Vandever, of Coatesville, who built the house used a wooden frame as a mold, placed the stones within this frame in a mixture of lime, sand and water.

Approximately one foot was added to the height of the building each day."[1] (East Fallowfield Twp.)

1871 "The School House was built many years ago and was of the Octagon style — quite fashionable at the time it was built, but rather out of date now"[2] (West Marlboro Twp.)

1871 "Octagonal School House burned...nearly new"[3] (West Marlboro Twp.)

1872 "RESIDENCE, octagonal in shape"[4] Lukens Peirce Est. (East Fallowfield Twp.)

1872 "school house to replace old octagonal house"[5] (Schuylkill Twp.)

1893 "To-day masons began work on the foundation for a spacious addition to the old farm house which belonged to the Mayfield property, in the West Ward, which is now in the possession of Timothy Black. The addition will be of brick, 33 x 17 feet, and will be a handsome style of architecture, with an octagon front."[6] (West Chester)

1. *COATESVILLE RECORD* (Coatesville, Penna.) Aug. 18, 1939.
2. *VILLAGE RECORD* (Coatesville, Penna.) Dec. 16, 1871.
3. *AMERICAN REPUBLICAN* (West Chester, Penna.) Dec. 19, 1871.
4. *VILLAGE RECORD* (West Chester. Penna.) Nov. 12, 1872.
5. *PHOENIXVILLE MESSENGER* (Phoenixville, Penna.) May 25, 1872.
6. *DAILY LOCAL NEWS* (West Chester, Penna.) March 20, 1893.

QUEEN ANNE

The newspapers mention:

1883 "The homestead in itself with its peaked gables, its beetle-browed porches and extensive court serves to recall all the architectural intricacies of the reign of Queen Anne, while from the square plaza upon the roof-top one commands an impressive view of far-reaching valleys, moorlands of irregular shape and wood freighted slopes"[1] John Patterson (Wallace Twp.)

1884 "The new residence of Dr. C. P. Jackson, of East Nottingham...The building is of Queen Anne style of architecture, contains 12 rooms. It is two and a half stories high, with a two-story bay window on one side and a veranda is to be built on three sides of it...In the attic is a tank that contains 100 gallons of water...The interior of the house is finished in oiled pine and is very pretty. The entire structure is different from any building in that section and is greatly admired"[2]

1885 "Building in Downingtown. A gentleman from Downingtown says that there is an unusually large amount of building going on in that borough...The style of architecture which seems to please the eye of the citizens is either the French mansard roof or Queen Anne style"[3]

1885 "David Barrick...Devon...It will be of the Queen Anne style of architecture, and its size will be 36 by 40 feet"[4] (Easttown Twp.)

1885 "Charles McClees is erecting a handsome house...in the Queen Anne style"[5] (Wallace Twp.)

1886 "Edlwood Thorn, Pocopson...elegant mansion. It will be built in the Queen Anne style and will be finished throughout with hard wood"[6]

1886 "John Underwood...When completed the building will be of the Queen Anne style"[7] (Pocopson Twp.)

1887 "3 houses...all Queen Anne style"[8] David Berrick (Easttown Twp.)

1889 "The residence of George D. Peters...Queen Anne style of architecture"[9] (Spring City)

1893 "The two houses which S. J. Sharpless...The roofs of these houses or cottages are Hipped or pitched a little after the plan of the Queen Anne style...They are finished in cypress throughout the lower story and have cypress doors in the upper stories and cypress shingles are used in roofing"[10] (West Chester)

1. *DAILY LOCAL NEWS* (West Chester, Penna.) Jan. 26, 1883.
2. Ibid., Aug. 20, 1884.
3. Ibid., May 15, 1885.
4. Ibid., Jan. 13, 1885.
5. Ibid., Nov. 23, 1885.
6. Ibid., May 20, 1886.
7. Ibid., June 8, 1886.
8. Ibid., May 28, 1887.
9. Ibid., Jan. 26, 1889.
10. Ibid., Feb. 28, 1893.

T SHAPE HOUSE

The newspapers mention:

1885 "Modern House, T Shape, 2½ stories high, main building of brick 34 by 22 feet...back building frame 18 feet square...frame kitchen 18 by 14"[1] Enoch Moore, (London Grove Twp.)

1894 "To Build a Fine Barn...The one destroyed was one of the largest and finest double-decker barns in the country, being built in the form of the letter T: was 125 feet long by 100 wide; the main building was of stone, nearly 50 feet to square, being covered with slate roof, and would hold 200 tons of hay besides the other crops of the farm. It was the only barn in the county with stables three stories high that you could enter from the ground to all of them.[2] N.P.

Boyer "Ercildoun Stock Farm" (East Fallowfield Twp.)

1. *DAILY LOCAL NEWS* (West Chester, Penna.) Nov. 2, 1885.
2. Ibid., Aug. 24, 1894.

VILLA

The newspapers mention:
1875 "Brick Villa"[1] Joshua Kames (West Bradford Twp.)

1. *VILLAGE RECORD* (West Chester, Penna.) June 1, 1875.

SUMMER HOUSE

James Dilworth, of Birmingham Township, in his will written in 1769 left to his wife "that House and Kitchen where my Son Charles now lives with a yard inclosed before the Door also Ground for a Garden to be laid of by A line to Run from the oven along a pale fence round to a corner to be made near the Summer House thence parreled with the road across to the pale fence runing by the Sadlers Shop thence down the said Fence to the said Road with the use of the well belonging to my Dwelling House."[1] The 1798 Direct Tax listed George Massey, of West Whiteland Township, with "1 frame Summer House Grape Vine roof" and John Jacobs, of West Whiteland Township, with "1 Summer House.' £ In 1905 a newspaper mentions that "Councilman David T. Sharpless [of West Chester] is having a rather unusual covering placed on a rustic summer house...The thatched roof needed repairing, and Mr. Sharpless and his gardener covered it with rye straw, thatched after the manner of cottages in the old countries."[2]

1. Chester County Will Book 5, p. 146.
2. *DAILY LOCAL NEWS* (West Chester, Penna.) April 8, 1905.

TAN HOUSE – TANNARY

The 1798 Direct Tax lists five tan houses: four of log, the mean size being 476 square feet and one that did not mention the material of construction 45 x 25 feet. In the newspaper advertisements, between 1830 and 1849 four tan houses were mentioned: two of frame, two story, the mean size being 1295 square feet; one of stone 100 x 44 feet and one that did not mention the material of construction 40 x 25 feet. Between 1850 and 1876 the newspaper advertisements mention one frame tan house 30 x 20 feet.

TEN PIN ALLEY

The newspapers mention:

1850 "Frame Building now used as a ten pin alley"[1] John Sharpless (Phoenixville)

1851 "frame and weather boarded ten pin alley"[2] John Clift "Western Hotel" (Phoenixville)

1856 "Frame Billiard Saloon and Ten-Pin Alley"[3] Chester Springs (West Pikeland Twp.)

Before 1876 the newspapers mention one other frame ten pin alley and four others that did not mention the material of construction.

1. *VILLAGE RECORD* (West Chester, Penna.) March 12, 1850.
2. Ibid., Sept. 30, 1851.
3. *AMERICAN REPUBLICAN* (West Chester, Penna.) Jan. 1, 1856.

TILE

Tile is defined by Bailey (ed. 1735) as "a square earthen Plate for covering Houses", by Sheridan (ed. 1789) as "thin plates of baked clay used to cover houses" and by Webster (ed. 1828) as "A plate or piece of baked clay, used for covering the roofs of buildings...A piece of baked clay used in drains."

EXTERIOR

The newspaper advertisements mention:

1775 "Smith Shop well covered with Tiles"[1] Dennis Whelen (Uwchlan Twp.)

1829 "a large blacksmith shop built of stone and roofed with tile, including a tilt mill"[2] Joseph Buffington (East Bradford Twp.)

1861 "stone oven covered with tile"[3] Jeremiah Reifsneider (North Coventry Twp.)

Before 1877 the newspaper advertisements mention two other buildings having tile roofs.

1. *PENNSYLVANIA GAZETTE* (Philadelphia, Penna.) April 12, 1775.
2. *AMERICAN REPUBLICAN* (West Chester, Penna.) Sept. 22, 1829.
3. *VILLAGE RECORD* (West Chester, Penna.) Nov. 19, 1861.

INTERIOR

Henry Graham Ashmead, in 1883, mentions that the Barber House, in Chester, built between 1699 and 1708 had "fireplaces and hearths in the hall-room and the parlor were laid in blue tiles, presenting scenes from Scriptural history,"[1] and that the Logan house, in Chester, built in 1700 had "Under the high wooden mantel pieces in the parlour and the room opposite, across the hall, the fireplaces were lined with illuminated tiles, delineating incidents of Scriptural history."[2]

The newspaper advertisements mention:

1871 "directors contemplate...tile floor"[3] Phoenixville Bank (Phoenixville)

1872 "The ground floor is beautifully laid with marble tile"[4] Hammond & Kervey drug store (West Chester)

1873 "just remodelled store...The floor is handsomely laid with tri-colored tile"[5] Jesse Thatcher (West Chester)

1873 "The first story has a hall 7 feet wide, with a vestibule about 7 feet square, handsomely inlaid with tile of rare finish and exquisite design."[7] Henry Buckwalter (West Chester)

1879 "Fine Improvement — J. Curtis Smith Esq...A very pretty floor has been laid in the vestibule of Minton tile, by Mr. A. M. Garrett, proprietor, of the Marble Works, corner of Market and Matlack streets"[6] (West Chester)

1. Henry Graham Ashmead *HISTORICAL SKETCH OF CHESTER, ON DELAWARE,* (The Republican Steam Printing House, 1883) p. 121.
2. Ibid., p. 73.
3. *PHOENIXVILLE MESSENGER* (Phoenixville, Penna.) Aug. 5, 1871.
4. *AMERICAN REPUBLICAN* (West Chester, Penna.) Oct. 8, 1872.
5. *DAILY LOCAL NEWS* (West Chester, Penna.) Dec. 9, 1873.
6. Ibid., Dec. 5, 1873.
7. Ibid., March 26, 1879.

TILT MILL

The 1798 Direct Tax lists six tilt mills: five of stone, the mean size being 657 square feet and one of log 20 x 20 feet. The 1799 tax assessment for West Nottingham Township lists one log tilt mill 18 x 15 feet. The newspaper advertisements between 1835 and 1839 mention one tilt mill 32 x 25 feet.

TIN

The newspaper advertisements mention:

1860 "Barn...recently roofed with tin"[1] Cadwallader Evans (Willistown Twp.)

1863 "entire buildings covered with tin roofs"[2] J. Wilson Wright (Atglen)

1864 "Brick Machine Shops...Brick Foundry...covered with slate and tin roofs"[3] S. & M. Pennock & Co. (Kennett Square)

1866 "House...with a tin roof painted on both sides"[4] H. G. Malin (Tredyffrin Twp.)

1868 "stone house, tin roof"[5] George B. Temple (Birmingham Twp.)

1869 "Brick house, tin roof"[6] James Humphrey (Downingtown)

1870 "slate and tin mansard roof"[7] Normal School (West Chester)

1872 "vaulted roof covered with tin"[8] Market House (West Chester)

1873 "new brick stable...tin roof with heavy cornice and ornamental brackets"[9] Mansion House (West Chester)

1874 "tin roof 3000 square feet"[10] Factory (Downingtown)

1876 "planing mill...roofed with tin"[11] Fox & Egolf (Phoenixville)

Before 1877 the newspaper advertisements mention seven other houses roofed with tin; three of brick, one of frame and three houses that did not mention the material of construction. One brick barn was roooofed with tin.

1. *VILLAGE RECORD* (West Chester, Penna.) Nov. 6, 1860.
2. Ibid., Nov. 14, 1863.
3. Ibid., July 26, 1864.
4. Ibid., Nov. 24, 1866.
5. Ibid., June 23, 1868.
6. Ibid., March 9, 1869.
7. *AMERICAN REPUBLICAN* (West Chester, Penna.) July 12, 1870.
8. *VILLAGE RECORD* (West Chester, Penna.) Oct. 8, 1872.
9. *AMERICAN REPUBLICAN* (West Chester, Penna.) May 20, 1873.
10. *DAILY LOCAL NEWS* (West Chester, Penna.) Oct. 25, 1874.
11. *VILLAGE RECORD* (West Chester, Penna.) Sep. 30, 1876.

TOBACCO SHED

The first description of a tobacco house found was in 1880; "Mr. L. W. Kitzleman, of Dilworthtown...erecting a large shed for the covering of tobacco leaf...37 x 90.'[1]

1. *DAILY LOCAL NEWS* (West Chester, Penna.) March 3, 1880.

TOMB STONES

The wills, before 1815, give the following instructions pertaining to tomb stones:

1794 "A Good Suitable Tomb Stone with my name Age and time of dealth Engraved thereon"[1] James Black (Willistown Twp.)

1795 "that a Head Stone & foot Stone such as is over my son Phillips grave be set over my grave"[2] Philip Thomas (East Nottingham Twp.)

1799 "that twenty Pounds remain in my Executors hands to enable them to place over my Grave A decent tomb Stone that may be so fitted as to cover my wife also"[3] Daniel Cornog (Willistown Twp.)

1802 "I do order my Executors to bury me at the Log Meeting House and for to wall in a piece of ground at least eight by ten feet in the clear with Stone and lime"[4] Robert Lindsays (Pennsbury Twp.)

1806 "Executors shall provide a handsome Tombstone and

have it set over the grave of my late husband deceased and myself"[5] Sarah Cunningham (East Caln Twp.)

1812 "Executors Shall after my decease place a large marble Tomb Stone over my Grave together with my Beloved wifes"[6] Alexander Mitchell (West Fallorfield Twp.)

1. Chester County Will Book 9, p.
2. Ibid., p. 327.
3. Ibid., Book 10, p. 313.
4. Ibid., p. 339.
5. Ibid., Book 11, p. 165.
6. Ibid., p. 499

TOWER

The newspapers mention:

1880 "erection of a large building for Jermoe B. Gray and wife. It is being built of a grey stone, and will have at one corner a large tower...plans drawn by R. Williamson, a former resident of West Chester"[1] (West Chester)

1890 "Philip M. Sharples is improving his residence on North Franklin street by the addition of a brick back building and a handsome shingled two story bay window at the south, surmounted by a turret"[2] (West Chester)

1893 "A handsome tower is being erected upon the new residence of Mrs. Mary Grugg, South High street. It will be quite conspicuous, and is in keeping with the numerous styles of architecture in that neighborhood"[3] (West Chester)

1893 "house...at the west end of which a tower 18 x 20 feet and 45 feet high is being constructed"[4] Col Brinton, "Bellevue", (West Goshen Twp.)

1. *DAILY LOCAL NEWS* (West Chester, Penna.) June 10, 1880.
2. Ibid., April 20, 1890.
3. Ibid., July 25, 1893.
4. Ibid., Dec. 14, 1893.

TRADES

Trades, professions and manufactories pertaining to the art of building are not regularly indicated in the tax assessment transcripts until 1796. Before that they are sometimes mentioned in deeds, wills and inventories. The following list is the first appearance, as yet found, of occupations pertaining to building taken from the wills, deeds, tax assessment lists, mortgages and the 1842 and 1850 census: architect (1817), blacksmith (1682), brass founder (1764), brick layer (1696), brick maker (1705), cabinet maker (1772), carpenter (1687), engineer (1842), fence maker (1838), gardener (1810), glazier (1719), house carpenter (1695), house joiner (1800), house painter

(1837), house plasterer (1827), joiner (1692), lime burner (1767), lime kiln (1803), lime stone quarry (1804), lock smith (1812), lumber man (1842), lumber merchant (1820), lumber yard (1842), marble mason (1842), mason (1697), nail cutter (1809), nailer (1756), nail factory (1803), nail header (1811), nail maker (1796), nail manufacturer (1829), nail mill (1806), nail shop (1811), nurseryman (1799), painter (1759), plaster mill (1803), plasterer (1769), plaster works (1813), plumber (1847), post and railer (1808), post fence maker (1806), pump maker (1799), quarry (1806), quarryman (1764), saw mill (1764), sawyer (1708), shingle manufacturer (1803), shop joiner (1761), sign painter (1846), smith (1693), stone cutter (1801), stone mason (1806), stone quarrier (1842), stove finisher (1842), stove maker (1768), stove manu-factory (1842), stove merchant (1849), thatcher (1766), tin manufacturer (1768), tin plate worker (1764), turner (1698), turning mill (1771) and well mason (1820).

In 1796, when the assessors first were directed to list the trade of each man, there were 107 carpenters, 94 masons, one brickmaker and one bricklayer in the county.

TURNING MILL

The 1798 Direct Tax lists five turning mills: one of stone 30 x 20 feet; one of frame 20 x 20 feet; two of log, the mean size being 172 square feet and one that did not mention the material of construction 28 x 18 feet.

VAT HOUSE

The 1798 Direct Tax lists two vat houses but did not mention the material of construction, the mean size being 144 square feet. The 1796 tax assessment for East Fallowfield Township lists two stone vat houses, the mean size being 320 square feet. That of James Gibbons was described as "...and two Vatt House of Stone adjoining Each 16 by 20 feet two Stories high With One Vatt only."

VAULT

Vault is defined by Bailey as "an arched Building, a round Roof built like an Arch; a vaulted Cellar for Wines", by Sheridan (ed. 1789) as "a continued arch; a cellar; a cavern" and by Webster (ed. 1828) as "A continued arch, or an arched roof. Vaults are of various kinds, circular, elliptical, single, double, cross, diagonal, Gothic, &c. 2. A cellar. 3. A cave or cavern."

The newspapers mention a number of houses with vaults, few are described:

1762 "house...cellar under it, with two large Vaults"[1] William Lindsey (Lower Providence Twp.)

1782 "Cellar, which in its course out is vaulted over and makes a fine milk house"[2] Dugaud Cameron (Uwchlan Twp.)

1814 "two story frame Dwelling House, with a vault adjoining the back door"[3] John Lindsey (West Chester)

1824 "Stone house...a new vault of 15 Cubic feet, and cellar"[4] James Jones (Brandywine Twp.)

1824 "in the cellar are two deep milk vaults adopting the house to the accommodation of two families"[5] David Brown Est. (New Garden Twp.)

1839 "milk vault communicating with the well"[6] John Townsend (Kennett Twp.)

1841 "vault or milk house one story below, and extending to the well 15 ft. below the surface"[7] Benedict Darlington (Westtown Twp.)

1853 "cellars, vault...floor of which, together with one under the dwelling, is plastered"[8] Catharine Evans Est. (West Chester)

1855 "vault or cave"[9] Arthur Queen (Phoenixville)

1860 "new vault 14 by 16 feet"[10] John Stephens (West Nottingham Twp.)

1. *PENNSYLVANIA GAZETTE* (Philadelphia, Penna.) Sept. 23, 1762.
2. Ibid., Aug. 21, 1782.
3. *CHESTER & DELAWARE FEDERALIST* (West Chester, Penna.) Jan. 26, 1814.
4. *VILLAGE RECORD* (West Chester, Penna.) July 28, 1824.
5. Ibid., Nov. 24, 1824.
6. Ibid., Sept. 17, 1839.
7. *AMERICAN REPUBLICAN* (West Chester, Penna.) Sept. 21, 1841.
8. *VILLAGE RECORD* (West Chester, Penna.) Feb. 13, 1853.
9. *AMERICAN REPUBLICAN* (West Chester, Penna.) Feb. 20, 1855.
10. *VILLAGE RECORD* (West Chester, Penna.) Oct. 30, 1860.

WAGON HOUSE

Wagon is defined by Bailey (ed. 1735) as "a long Cart with four Wheels", by Sheridan (ed. 1789) as "a heavy carriage for burthens" and by Webster (ed. 1828) as "A vehicle moved on four wheels, and usually drawn by horses; used for the transportation of heavy commodities. In America, light wagons are used for the conveyance of families, and for carrying light commodities to market, particularly a very light kind drawn by one horse."

The 1798 Direct Tax lists one hundred and three wagon houses: fifty-two of stone, the mean size being 512 square feet; twenty-one of frame, the mean size being 396 square feet; seven of log, the mean size being 240 square feet; four of stone and frame, the mean size being 830 square feet; three of wood, the mean size being 180 square feet and sixteen that did not mention the material of construction the mean size being 374 square feet. The 1796 tax assessment for East Fallowfield Township lists one frame wagon house of 300 square feet and the 1799 tax assessment for West Marlboro Township lists four wagon houses that did not mention the material of construction, the mean size being 385 square feet.

The newspaper advertisements mention between 1775 and 1800 one wagon house, that did not mention the material of construction, 30 x 15 feet; between 1809 and 1824 three are mentioned: two of stone, the mean size being 843 square feet and one that did not mention the material of construction 24 x 18 feet. Between 1830 and 1849 twenty-four wagon houses are mentioned with dimensions: twelve of frame, the mean size being 753 square feet; ten of stone, the mean size being 912 square feet and two of stone and frame, the mean size being 670 square feet.

WAINSCOT

Wainscot is defined by Bailey (ed. 1735) as "a lining of Walls made of Boards within side of a Room", by Sheridan as "the inner wooden covering of a wall" and by Webster (ed. 1828) as "In building, timber-work serving to line the walls of a room, being made in panels."

Henry Graham Ashmead, in 1883, mentions that the Logan house, in Chester, built in 1700 had a "wainscoted hallway...All the rooms were wainscoted also, and the panels were painted or stained in imitation of mahogany."[1]

The account book[2] of Joseph Hawley mentions:

> 1810 3d 6th To 81 feet of Wenyscantling .75

The newspapers mention:

1874 "The wainscotting of yellow pine, is surrounded with walnut moulding...The whole of the woodwork being oiled"[3] Goshen Baptist Church (West Goshen Twp.)

1882 "The new residence of Mr. Stephen Darlington...the elaborate decoration in the way of panels, wainscoting"[4] (West Chester)

1885 "Four Rooms...alterations in the rooms where the post office was recently located (in Smedley Darlington's building)...Around each room is oak wainscotting, and the walls and ceilings are to be covered with the latest handsome wall paper that the market affords"[5] (West Chester)

1894 "The library is wainscotted, ceiled and panelled in white oak"[6] Richard T. Elliott (West Chester)

1. Henry Graham Ashmead, *HISTORICAL SKETCH OF CHESTER, ON DELAWARE* (The Republican Steam Printing House, 1883), p. 73.
2. Account Book and Diaries, Vault, Chester County Historical Society (West Chester, Penna.)
3. *AMERICAN REPUBLICAN* (West Chester, Penna.) Dec. 1, 1874.
4. *DAILY LOCAL NEWS* (West Chester, Penna.) April 28, 1882.
5. Ibid., April 1, 1885.
6. *CHESTER COUNTY DEMOCRAT* (West Chester, Penna.) Sept. 30, 1894.

WALL

Wall is defined by Bailey (ed. 1735) as "an Inclosure of Brick, Stone or Earth", by Sheridan (ed. 1789) as "a series of brick or stone carried upwards and cemented with mortar. The sides of a building" and by Webster (ed. 1828) as "...Walls of stone, with or without cement, are much used in America for fences on farms; walls are laid as the foundations of houses and the security of cellars. Walls of stone or brick form the exterior of buildings..."

The newspaper advertisements mention:

1845 "2½ storied Brick House...said house is a 14 inch wall, from the cellar to garret"[1] John C. Dorat (Penn Twp.)

1854 "new Brick House...House is divided in the center by a brick wall"[2] John McCool (Phoenixville)

1865 "Brick House...walls 23 inches in thickness to the second story"[3] Wm. Wheeler Est. (New London Twp.)

1868 "stone House, rough cast, interlined all through"[4] M. Pennypacker (Tredyffrin Twp.)

1870 "House...rough coated walls, lined and perfectly dry on first floor"[5] Benjamin Phillips (New Garden Twp.)

1870 "House...The walls are extra thick, the joists extra heavy, the floors are "deafened"[6] J. W. Barnard (West Chester)

1870 "House...all the outside walls being one third thicker than is usually built, and stripped within, and is entirely clear of dampness"[7] E. V. Garrett (West Chester)

1871 "frame cottage...The inside is lathed and plastered in the usual manner, but the outside is first covered with boards, which are overlaid with a sheet of felting, and then covered with slate from Vermont after the fashion of the mansard roof"[8] Thomas H. Hall (West Chester)

1872 "BRICK COTTAGE...lined north and south"[9] Wm. B. Haslett (Parkesburg)

1872 "Spikesworks — The building was a frame and the space between the weatherboarding and the lining was filled with sawdust to make it as near air tight as possible. It was an old structure"[10] Hoopes Bros. & Darlington (West Chester)

1873 "new stable...and the walls are strengthened by four inch ballusters between the windows"[11] Mansion House (West Chester)

1873 "The walls of the building are all hollow and hence they are dry and pleasant, the vacuum carrying off all dampness, which otherwise would find its way into the inner apartments"[12] Henry Buckwalter (West Chester)

1. *AMERICAN REPUBLICAN* (West Chester, Penna.) Aug. 5, 1845.
2. *VILLAGE RECORD* (West Chester, Penna.) Aug. 29, 1854.

3. Ibid., Nov. 18, 1865.
4. Ibid., March 28, 1868.
5. Ibid., Oct. 4, 1870.
6. *AMERICAN REPUBLICAN* (West Chester, Penna.) Sept. 20, 1870.
7. *VILLAGE RECORD* (West Chester, Penna.) Aug. 30, 1870.
8. *AMERICAN REPUBLICAN* (West Chester, Penna.) Dec. 12, 1871.
9. *VILLAGE RECORD* (West Chester, Penna.) Nov. 30, 1872.
10. *AMERICAN REPUBLICAN* (West Chester, Penna.) Oct. 8, 1872.
11. Ibid., May 20, 1873.
12. *DAILY LOCAL NEWS* (West Chester, Penna.) Dec. 5, 1873.

WALL PAPER

The newspaper advertisements mention:

1833 "BRICK DWELLING HOUSE...contains two rooms and a kitchen below, both rooms papered, and each having a marble mantle"[1] I. D. Barnard (West Chester)

Before 1875 the advertisements mention thirty-eight other houses having wall paper. The newspaper advertisements, of the stores, mention the different kinds of wall paper available:

1843 "JUST received and at reduced prices, a beautiful assortment of PAPER HANGINGS — new and splendid patterns, curtain paper &c...S. M. PAINTER"[2] (West Chester)

1844 "Premium Paper Hangings. We are now prepared and well pleased to exhibit to the Citizens of Chester county, our large assortment of the latest Spring Patterns of WALLPAPER, Fresco's Panels, Columns, Foulard and Plain papers for Parlor's, Chambers, Halls, &c. all offered at very reduced prices...Belrose, Son & Blanchard"[3] (Philadelphia)

1846 "JUST received and opening, a new and splendid lot of Wall Paper, both French and American Manufacture...T. R. HATCH"[4] (West Chester)

1846 "THE subscriber has just received a large assortment of WALL PAPER, among which are some new and splendid patterns. Also, an entire new article of paper windows; Fire Board patterns, &c., at Phila. prices. S. M. PAINTER"[5] (West Chester)

1847 "FAYE & BELROSE...Manufacturers and Importers of every American and French Paper Hangings. The subscribers have just received from their own extensive Factory, as well as from the most celebrated manufacturers of France and Germany, a large collection of new and beautiful designs of the most costly and magnificent Paper Hangings, with Borders and other appendages to match — comprising DECORATIONS of every style. FRESCOES of a variety of patterns. PANELS of all orders. EMBOSSED Gold and Silver Parlor Sets. RICH DOUBLE Satin Paper, plain and in colors. GOTHIC PATTERNS adopted for Dining Rooms and Halls. Plain and Color Ceilings. Marble Pillars, Cornices, &c. and every other style both antique and modern. F. & B. keep constantly on hand the largest assortment of cheap Glazed and unglazed Parlor, Dining Room, Chamber and Entry PAPERS..."[6] (Philadelphia)

1847 "Wide window curtain paper, fire board prints, borders, &c. FAYE & BELROSE...F. & B. Manufacture Statues and Ornamental papers for Halls and Vestibules, as well as Gold, Silver and Velvet papers and Borders..."[7] (Philadelphia)

1850 "WALL PAPER ONLY 2½ CENTS PER PIECE — A large assortment of Wall Paper has been received at Worrall's Bookstore. Glazed Paper at 25 cents per piece. Chamber do at 12½ cents per piece. Green slat Window Blinds..."[8] (West Chester)

1851 "THE subscribers are now prepared to furnish glazed and unglazed Wall Paper at Philadelphia prices; also Curtain Paper, Fire Board patterns, painted oil shades, green Window Blinds, &c. G. F. & E. P. WORRALL"[9] (West Chester)

1852 "WALL PAPER! WALL PAPER! A COMPLETE assortment of Wall and Entry Paper, comprising over 100 new patterns, glazed and unglazed, just received and for sale at city prices. House keepers about papering their rooms, would do well to call and select from the best assortment ever offered in the borough. W. H. PRICE"[10] (West Chester)

1853 "Paper Hangings. W. WILDON, No 1 South Fourth street...Fine satin papers Cheap papers Borders and moulding Fire board prints Fine gold papers Fine decorative papers Marble paper Oak paper..."[11] (Philadelphia)

1859 "Wall Paper. J. E. VANMETER, Successor to Samuel Baker, INTENDS making this store a branch of his Philadelphia store...latest styles, simultaneous with their appearance in Philadelphia or New York, at the lowest rates. PAPER HANGING...A New preparation to prevent dampness in walls &c. — Also, a large variety of Oil, Gilt, and Paper Shades, Green Gum Cloth, Curtain Fixtures &c..."[12] (West Chester)

1860 "Wall Paper. OF entirely new design...GLAZED PAPER for 17 cents and upwards; Unglazed 6 cents and upwards, with borders to match. Gold and Velvet Papers and Borders, Fire Board Prints, Decorations, &c...J. E. VANMETER Practical Paper Hanger"[13] (West Chester)

1873 "A new style of wall paper for dining-rooms has large medallions of game birds, real skin and real feathers being used. The figures are raised on light background which is very effective. Flowers are also introduced of wax and linen tied together with bright colored ribbon."[14]

1. *AMERICAN REPUBLICAN* (West Chester, Penna.) Jan. 29, 1833.

2. *VILLAGE RECORD* (West Chester, Penna.) April 4, 1843.
3. Ibid., April 9, 1844.
4. Ibid., Aug. 4, 1846.
5. Ibid., March 24, 1846.
6. Ibid., April 6, 1847.
7. Ibid., March 9, 1847.
8. Ibid., June 11, 1850.
9. *AMERICAN REPUBLICAN* (West Chester, Penna.) April 1, 1851.
10. *VILLAGE RECORD* (West Chester, Penna.) May 11, 1852.
11. Ibid., Jan. 25, 1853.
12. Ibid., March 29, 1859.
13. Ibid., Dec. 18, 1860.
14. *DAILY LOCAL NEWS* (West Chester, Penna.) Oct. 30, 1873.

WAREHOUSE

The newspaper advertisements between 1830 and 1849 mention four ware houses: two of stone, the mean size being 115 square feet; one of frame 70 x 50 feet and one, that did not mention the material of construction, 70 x 30 feet. Between 1850 and 1875, the newspaper advertisements mention ten ware houses: one of brick 24 x 18½ feet; one of stone 60 x 40 feet; four of frame, the mean size being 2222 square feet and four that did not mention the material of construction, the mean size being 1207 square feet.

WASH HOUSE

Richard Maris, of Springfield Township, in his will in 1745 gave to his wife "the free use of my old Parlour in my new Dwelling House and the new vault under the sd House and also such Priviledge in my wash-house annexed to sd Dwelling House and use of my Draw well and bake oven in the sd wash-house."[1]

The 1798 Direct Tax lists forty-two wash houses: twenty-nine of stone, the mean size being 340 square feet; three of log, the mean size being 292 square feet; five of frame, the mean size being 312 square feet; three of brick, the mean size being 220 square feet; one of brick and stone 19 x 19 feet and one of stone and frame 18 x 12 feet. The 1799 tax assessment for Charlestown Township lists one stone wash house.

The newspaper advertisements between 1830 and 1849 list one brick was house 16 x 16 feet and between 1850 and 1876 five wash houses that did not mention the material of construction had a mean size of 175 square feet.

1. Chester County Will Book 2, p. 184.

WASTE HOUSE

The 1798 Direct Tax lists one waste house that did not mention the material of construction 22 x 16 feet.

WATER CLOSET

The newspaper advertisements mention:

1857 "water closet, clapboarded"[1] William White (Tredyffrin Twp.)

Before 1862 seven other water closets were mentioned in the newspaper advertisements.

1. *AMERICAN REPUBLICAN* (West Chester, Penna.) March 24, 1857.

WEATHERBOARD

Weather board is defined by Webster (ed. 1828) as "The act of nailing up boards against a wall; or the boards themselves."

The newspaper advertisements mention:

1771 "new log house, weatherboarded and painted, well finished with sash windows, about 35 feet front, and 18 deep, two stories high"[1] Yellow Springs (Pikeland Twp.)

1815 "a barn 45 feet in length and 25 in depth, the stabling of stone, the upper part frame lately weatherboarded"[2] James Given (East Caln Twp.)

1815 "two dwelling houses, one of log, lately weatherboarded"[3] Wm. Dunwoody (West Whiteland Twp.)

1839 "frame house, 2 stories high...plastered inside and weatherboarded out"[4] Wm. Preston (East Marlboro Twp.)

1843 "a swisser barn...built of pleted logs and weather boarded, stone stabling"[5] Wm S. Michener (Upper Oxford Twp.)

1850 "house and shop all frame and weatherboarded"[6] John & Wm. Patrick (Sadsbury Twp.)

1851 "frame and weather boarded ten pin alley"[7] John Clift, "Western Hotel" (Phoenixville)

1854 "frame shed weather boarded on the outside"[8] John Conway (West Chester)

1855 "Play house, weather boarded on the outside"[9] Unionville Academy (East Marlboro Twp.)

1856 "Frame washing House weatherboarded. Frame Chinging House weatherboarded"[10] Keystone Mining Co. (Schuylkill Twp.)

1856 "1 frame refining house weatherboarded"[11] Chester County Mining Co.

1857 "Frame Rolling Mill with stone foundation 60 by 40 feet, weatherboarded on the outside...1½ story frame office weatherboarded"[12] Pleasant Garden Iron Works (New London Twp.)

1858 "Carriage House, weatherboarded"[13] George D. Rembaugh (Downingtown)

1858 "Frame stable, weather boarded"[14] Thomas Peck (East Brandywine Twp.)

1859 "carriage & wagon house weather boarded with stone foundation"[15] William Mullin (London Grove Twp.)

1859 "Frame corn crib and shelling house weather boarded"[16] Wm. Tuton (East Fallowfield Twp.)

1859 "stone ice house, frame cover, weather boarded"[17] John P. & Aaron P. Osmond (London Britain Twp.)

1859 "frame smelting House, weatherboarded...frame ore crushing House weatherboarded"[18] Penna. Smelting Co. (Schuylkill Twp.)

1862 "Frame House 16 by 24 feet, weatherboarded and filled in with brick"[19] Oliver Stoops (East Nottingham Twp.)

1863 "new two storied Frame House weatherboarded and painted. Also a two Storied Frame End adjoining the above described building, weatherboarded and painted in front."[20] Jacob Smith (West Brandywine Twp.)

1866 "two storied FRAME HOUSE weather-boarded and stripped"[21] Abner Keech (West Chester)

The newspaper advertisements mention forty-eight weather boarded houses: twenty-seven of frame, seventeen of log, three of stone and frame, one log and frame; twenty-seven barns, fourteen stables, one carriage house, two shops and one shed as being weatherboarded before 1860 as well as those already quoted. Between 1860 and 1875 the newspapers mention as being weatherboarded thirty-three houses; nineteen of log, twelve of frame, one frame house painted and one house that did not mention the material of construction; three summer kitchens, twenty-two barns, ten stables and carriage houses; four frame stables, two carriage houses, one hay house, one wagon and carriage house, one work shop, one tool house, two pump houses, one lumber house, three shed and two shops.

1. *PENNSYLVANIA GAZETTE* (Philadelphia, Penna.) March 1, 1771.
2. *AMERICAN REPUBLICAN* (West Chester, Penna.) Aug. 29, 1815.
3. *CHESTER & DELAWARE FEDERALIST* (West Chester, Penna.) Oct. 18, 1815.
4. *VILLAGE RECORD* (West Chester, Penna.) June 4, 1839.
5. *AMERICAN REPUBLICAN* (West Chester, Penna.) Dec. 19, 1843.
6. Ibid., July 2, 1850.
7. *VILLAGE RECORD* (West Chester, Penna.) Sept. 30, 1851.
8. Ibid., Nov. 28, 1854.
9. *AMERICAN REPUBLICAN* (West Chester, Penna.) Dec. 25, 1855.
10. Ibid., March 18, 1856.
11. Ibid., Aug. 19, 1856.
12. Ibid., March 10, 1857.
13. *VILLAGE RECORD* (West Chester, Penna.) Feb. 20, 1858.
14. Ibid., July 10, 1858.
15. Ibid., March 26, 1859.
16. Ibid., Dec. 17, 1859.
17. Ibid., Dec. 3, 1859.
18. Ibid., Oct. 18, 1859.
19. *AMERICAN REPUBLICAN* (West Chester, Penna.) June 24, 1862.
20. *VILLAGE RECORD* (West Chester, Penna.) May 30, 1863.
21. Ibid., March 3, 1866.

WELL – WELL HOUSE

The 1798 Direct Tax lists four well houses: two of stone, the mean size being 297 square feet and two of log, the mean size being 142 square feet.

The newspaper advertisements mention:

1828 "well dug and walled"[1] John Hoopes, Jr., Est. (Downingtown)

1829 "one well in the bar-room"[2] Joseph Vandersmith Est. (Downingtown)

1832 "a mineral spring 4½ feet deep, newly enclosed by both house and dressing room"[3] Stephen S. Speakman (Pikeland Twp.)

1855 "well of water at kitchen door, 26 feet deep"[4] Timothy Downing (Penn Twp.)

1. *AMERICAN REPUBLICAN* (West Chester, Penna.) Feb. 12, 1828.
2. Ibid., March 31, 1829.
3. Ibid., Oct. 16, 1832.
4. Ibid., Dec. 4, 1855.

WHARF

The 1798 Direct Tax lists the following wharfs:

"1 Wharf 45 by 30 on Chester Creek" Jos. Ashbridge (Chester)

"1 Stone Store and Wharf almost gone to Decay" David Bevan (Chester)

"1 Wharf & lot in Chester Creek" John Wall (Chester)

"Wharf" J. Pearson (Chester)

"1 Wharf 20 by 30 ft in Chester Creek" Wm. Siddons (Chester)

"1 Wharf 32 by 40 ft on Chester Creek" Thos. Sharpless (Chester)

"1 Wharf 20 by 50 ft on Chester Creek" P. West (Chester)

WIND MILL

Wind mill is defined by Sheridan (ed. 1789) as "a mill turned by the wind."

The newspapers mention:

1847 "wind mill and forcing pump at the barn"[1] William Romans (West Bradford Twp.)

1851 "pump worked by wind power"[2] Milton Conard (New London Twp.)

1883 "windmill forty feet in height...three sleeping apartments, the largest of which is 15 feet square"[3] George Brinton, Sr., (Pennsbury Twp.)

1884 "They [windmill] are getting to be very numerous through the county"[4]

1. *AMERICAN REPUBLICAN* (West Chester, Penna.) March 9, 1847.
2. Ibid., Sept. 16, 1851.
3. *DAILY LOCAL NEWS* (West Chester, Penna.) Aug. 24, 1883.
4. Ibid., Dec. 9, 1884.

WINDOW

Window is defined by Bailey (ed. 1735) as "an open Place in the Side of a House to let in Air and Light", by Sheridan (ed. 1789) as "an aperture in a building by which air and light are admitted; the frame or glass or any other materials that covers the aperture" and by Webster (ed. 1828) as "an opening in the wall of a building for the admission of light, and of air when necessary. This opening has a frame on the sides, in which are set movable sashes, containing panes of glass. In the U. States the sashes are made to rise and fall, for the admission or exclusion of air...Lattice or casement; or the network of wire used before the invention of glass."

Henry Graham Ashmead, in 1883, in describing houses in Chester, mentions that the Boar's Head Inn, where Penn resided in 1682-1683, that "The windows, with the exception of the one in the kitchen were small; the glasses 4 by 3 in 'size, were set in lead. The sashes were not hung with weights, a comparatively modern improvement, and when it was desired that the lower sashes should be raised, they were supported by pieces of wood which fitted into the groves in the frames, or a turn buckle placed half way up sustained the weight. The large window in the kitchen was made to slide one sash past the other."[1] The Old Hoskins (Graham) house, built in 1688, had "Windows in lower room deeply recessed and old-time seats constructed therein."[2] The Logan house, built in 1700, had "many small diamond-shaped panes of glass set in lead, in the large window sashes...and casements at the head of the stair landing."[3] In 1884 Henry Graham Ashmead in describing Haverford Friends Meeting mentions that the "old end built 1700 at a cost of £158 as an addition. First section replaced 1800. The pitch of the roof was changed and they substituted wooden sash for those of lead in the window frames of the section built in 1700."[4]

The Brinton diary mentions that the "Brinton 1704 house, Joseph Brinton 1712, William Brinton 1713, Ann Brinton Cox, Joseph Eavenson, Mercer house. They were the first stone houses. Very steep roofs, a story high, with garrett rooms, fire places for wood cord length, with seat in the corner, lead sash, very thick walls, small one pane windows in places."[5] The "Old house on Caleb Brinton's. It had a large fireplace on the east side, & sleeping room on the west side downstairs, and rooms overhead. Windows had lead sash; roof very steep. Probably built 1713."[6] "Edward Brinton (1726) built a house, steep roof, small windows, lead sash."[7] The Bettle house "The sash of its windows were lead."[8] The diary mentions that in the masonry house of John Hoopes built in 1734 "sash was of lead, 4 in by 6 in., for the windows."[9]

The newspaper advertisements mention:

1770 "new log house, weather-boarded and painted, well finished with sash windows...the buildings are neat and make an elegant appearance having glass windows, front and back" Yellow Springs[10] (Pikeland Twp.)

1831 "new...brick house...with 15 light windows, 10 by 12 glass together with side glass at the front door and large handsome top...slate roof and dormer windows"[11] James Grier (West Nottingham Twp.)

1838 "garret large and comfortable, with three dormer windows in front"[12] Wm. G. Wallace (Sadsbury Twp.)

1844 "two story dwelling...has been occupied for many years as a fancy store; it has two front doors and a bulk window"[13] Joseph Jones (West Chester)

1850 "brick Coachmaker's Shop and dwelling, shop 23 by 28 feet, 2 stories, cellar, eight windows in each story"[14] Isaac Clark (West Marlboro Twp.)

1870 "Inside shutters to all the windows"[15] J. W. Barnard (West Chester)

1872 "stone Barn...gothic windows...built in English style"[16] Henry Webster (Highland Twp.)

1872 "Brick COTTAGE...Shutters and blinds all around latest style windows"[17] Wm. B. Haslett (Parkesburg)

1872 "Walnut Doors and Inside Blinds in first story front, Segment head window heads in front with Marble Heads and Sills"[18] Charles L. Warner (West Chester)

1873 "two 2½ story stone houses 30 by 40 feet with bay windows"[19] L. Harry Richards (Phoenixville)

1873 "wire screens to cellar windows"[20] Sharpless & Hall (West Chester)

1873 "original hotel ca. 1794...with a steep roof, ornamented in the then prevalent style, with dormer windows to light the attic"[21] "White Hall" (West Chester)

1875 "House...dormer windows...double hung sash"[22] Hiram Sturgis (Phoenixville)

1875 "Varnished doors, sash &c."[23] John Griffin (Phoenixville)

1875 "windows are Gothic with stained glass"[24] Berean Church (West Chester)

1876 "Cottage style, with broad projecting eaves and headed dormer windows"[25] J. R. Gilpin (Birmingham Twp.)

Before 1877 the newspaper advertisements mention fifteen other houses with dormer windows and one other window with frames and sash.

1. Henry Graham Ashmead, *HISTORICAL SKETCH OF CHESTER, ON DELAWARE* (The Republican Steam Printing House, 1883), p. 63.
2. Ibid., p. 67.
3. Ibid., p. 73.
4. Henry Graham Ashmead, *HISTORY OF DELAWARE COUNTY, PENNSYLVANIA* (Phila., Penna. 1884) p. 574.
5. John H. Brinton diary Vol 3, p. 24 under date Feb. 6, 1885. Chester County Historical Society (West Chester, Penna.)
6. Ibid.
7. John H. Brinton, Account of William Brinton, p. 5. Chester County Historical Society (West Chester, Penna.)

8. John H. Brinton diary Vol 1, p. 38 & 40 under date Feb. 1843. Chester County Historical Society (West Chester, Penna.)
9. John H. Brinton diary Vol 3, p. 2 under date March 31, 1871. Chester County Historical Society (West Chester, Penna.)
10. *PENNSYLVANIA GAZETTE* (Philadelphia, Penna.) March 1, 1770.
11. *AMERICAN REPUBLICAN* (West Chester, Penna.) Dec. 20, 1831.
12. Ibid., July 24, 1838.
13. Ibid., Feb. 6, 1844.
14. Ibid., Dec. 10, 1850.
15. Ibid., Sept. 20, 1870.
16. *VILLAGE RECORD* (West Chester, Penna.) Nov. 19, 1872.
17. Ibid., Nov. 30, 1872.
18. Ibid., Jan. 13, 1872.
19. Ibid., Jan. 7, 1873.
20. *DAILY LOCAL NEWS* (West Chester, Penna.) March 28, 1873.
21. *AMERICAN REPUBLICAN* (West Chester, Penna.) Oct. 21, 1873.
22. *PHOENIXVILLE MESSENGER* (Phoenixville, Penna.) Feb. 27, 1875.
23. Ibid., Aug. 28, 1875.
24. *AMERICAN REPUBLICAN* (West Chester, Penna.) April 13, 1875.
25. *VILLAGE RECORD* (West Chester, Penna.) April 15, 1876.

WINDOW BLINDS — SHUTTERS

The newspaper advertisements mention:

1841 "shutter blinds to the upper windows"[1] R. R. Walter (Parkesburg)

1848 "brick dwelling house...with shutters or blinds to all the windows"[2] Elizabeth Kent Est. (Upper Oxford Twp.)

1870 "Inside shutters to all the windows"[3] J. W. Barnard
There were three other mentions of houses with inside blinds and shutters in the newspaper advertisements before 1876.

1. *AMERICAN REPUBLICAN* (West Chester, Penna.) Nov. 9, 1841.
2. Ibid., Oct. 10, 1848.
3. Ibid., Sept. 20, 1870.

WINGS

The newspapers mention:

1832 "stone dwelling house with extensive wings"[1] Israel Davis Est. (Tredyffrin Twp.)

1834 "Stone barn 53 by 39 with a large wing adjoining thereto of frame"[2] Jacob Wersler (Schuylkill Twp.)

1842 "factory...built of stone, the main building is 71 by 29 feet with a wing attached 64 by 31 feet, three stories high"[3] Wm. Umpley (Charlestown Twp.)

1845 "Factory has been lately rebuilt...being 172 feet in the main by 35 feet wide, with a wing 60 by 30, three stories high"[4] John Umpleby (Charlestown Twp.)

1855 "2 story Dwelling House, lathed and plastered out and inside...attached to main building a two story brick end or wing with a portico in front"[5] Dr. David Myerle (Kennett Twp.)

1855 "Front 140 by 53 feet with two wings running back 57 by 30 feet"[6] Poor House (Newlin Twp.)

1857 "New 2½ story stone mansion house 40 by 50 feet, with a stone wing, 30 by 25 feet, extending back to which is attached a brick milk house with portico in front and porch back"[7] Pleasant Garden Iron Works (New London Twp.)

1858 "4 story Cotton Factory 40 by 30 feet, 2 story stone wing"[8] Francis Bonner (Phoenixville)

1859 "stone stable with wing attached"[9] Joseph Gaines (East Whiteland Twp.)

1859 "Frame Ware House and passage Depot 150 feet in length with a frame wing about 30 by 30 attached, containing ware rooms, offices, restaurants & weight scales"[10] Chester Valley Rail Road Company (Downingtown)

1860 "new stone Barn 105 feet and frame straw house in front forming a wing with the Barn"[11] Edwin A. Yarnall (West Nantmeal Twp.)

1870 "four story stone House 33 by 33 feet. Brick 4 story wing adjoining 17 by 40 feet"[12] Washington House (Phoenixville)

In the newspaper advertisements, before 1876, there were three other mentions of houses with wings.

1. *AMERICAN REPUBLICAN* (West Chester, Penna.) Oct. 2, 1832.
2. Ibid., Nov. 18, 1834.
3. Ibid., Nov. 8, 1842.
4. Ibid., Sept. 16, 1845.
5. Ibid., Dec. 4, 1855.
6. *VILLAGE RECORD* (West Chester, Penna.) Sept. 18, 1855.
7. *AMERICAN REPUBLICAN* (West Chester, Penna.) March 10, 1857.
8. *VILLAGE RECORD* (West Chester, Penna.) Sept. 18, 1858.
9. Ibid., Sept. 24, 1859.
10. *AMERICAN REPUBLICAN* (West Chester, Penna.) July 5, 1859.
11. *VILLAGE RECORD* (West Chester, Penna.) May 19, 1860.
12. Ibid., June 4, 1870.

WOOD HOUSE — WOOD SHED

The 1798 Direct Tax lists six wood houses: five of frame, the mean size being 248 square feet and one that did not mention the material of construction 20 x 15 feet. The newspaper advertisements between 1865 and 1874 mention one wood shed 26 x 16 feet and one wood house 16 x 14 feet.

WOODS

ASH

Henry Graham Ashmead, in 1883, mentions that the Old Hoskins (Graham) house, in Chester, built in 1688 had "steps of ash."[1]

The newspapers mention:

1872 "The ceilings of each room have massive cornices run with plaster paris while the wood work of the new building is trimmed with walnut and ash, having a beautiful grain and evidently selected with great care"[2] Reeves Mansion (Phoenixville)

1873 "The second story is reached by back and front stair-ways, with massive railings and ash steps"[3] Henry Buckwalter (West Chester)

1874 "Dr. Jones laying floor, alternate strips of ash and cherry"[4] (West Chester)

1. Henry Graham Ashmead, *HISTORICAL SKETCH OF CHESTER, ON DELAWARE* (The Republican Steam Printing House, 1883) p. 67.
2. *PHOENIXVILLE MESSENGER* (Phoenixville, Penna.) April 27, 1872.
3. *DAILY LOCAL NEWS* (West Chester, Penna.) Dec. 5, 1873.
4. Ibid., March 17, 1874.

CALIFORNIA RED WOOD

The newspaper advertisements mention:

1886 "A Handsome House, C. H. Hannum...and will be finished with California red wood"[1] (West Chester)

1. *DAILY LOCAL NEWS* (West Chester, Penna.) July 27, 1886.

CEDAR

Henry Graham Ashmead in 1884 mentions that the Morris Ferry House, in Ridley Township built in 1729/30 "The figures 1698 are carved on the inner side of the mantelpiece of the northwest end of the building, and no doubt indicate the date of its erection. It is built of white-cedar log, flattened. Between this end and the other wooden end there is a space built up with stone. Through this space, and between the two wooden ends of the present building, the road formerly passed to the ferry."[1] In Birmingham Township the Friends Meeting house "First house, cedar logs, erected in 1722, on land given by Elizabeth Webb."[2]

The newspapers mention:

1765 "Shop built of Cedar"[3] John Smith (Chester)

1772 "[farm buildings] being covered with cedar shingles"[4] William Dogfrey (Great Valley)

1784 "barn, part of which is newly covered and boarded with cedar"[5] Samuel Briggs (Haverford Twp.)

1824 "a large Garden walled in under cedar roof"[6] James Jones (Brandywine Twp.)

In the newspapers, before 1877, twenty-nine other buildings are mentioned as either roofed or shingled with cedar and two other gardens fenced with cedar.

1. Henry Graham Ashmead, *HISTORY OF DELAWARE COUNTY, PENNSYLVANIA* (Philadelphia, Penna. 1884), p. 743.
2. Ibid., p. 317.
3. *PENNSYLVANIA GAZETTE* (Philadelphia, Penna.) July 18, 1765.
4. Ibid., Jan. 2, 1772.
5. Ibid., March 31, 1784.
6. *VILLAGE RECORD* (West Chester, Penna.) July 28, 1824.

CHERRY

The newspapers mention:

1874 "Dr. Jones laying new floor, alternate strips of ash and cherry"[1]

1. *DAILY LOCAL NEWS* (West Chester, Penna.) March 17, 1874.

CHESTNUT

The newspaper advertisements mention:

1770 "a barn, 70 feet in length, 23 in breadth, of good peeled chestnut logs"[1] Wm. Graham (Londonderry Twp.)

1814 "chestnut log Barn"[2] Samuel Cochran (Upper Oxford Twp.)

1814 "chestnut log Dwelling House"[3] Samuel Cochran (West Fallowfield Twp.)

1. *PENNSYLVANIA GAZETTE* (Philadelphia, Penna.) May 31, 1770.
2. *CHESTER AND DELAWARE FEDERALIST* (West Chester, Penna.) Dec. 14, 1814.
3. Ibid., Dec. 14, 1814.

CYPRESS

The newspaper advertisements mention:

1813 "Stone Dwelling House...covered with cypress shingles"[1] Michael March (Coventry Twp.)

1855 "Handsome library — Workmen are about finishing up...It is finished in cypress"[2] Charles W. Roberts (East Goshen Twp.)

1893 "The two houses which S. J. Sharpless...The roofs of these houses or cottages are hipped or pitched a little after the plan of the Queen Anne style...They are finished in cypress throughout the lower story and have cypress doors in the upper stories and cypress shingles are used in roofing"[3] (West Chester)

The newspaper, before 1877, mention one other building having cypress shingles.

1. *AMERICAN REPUBLICAN* (West Chester, Penna.) Nov. 9 1813.
2. *AMERICAN LOCAL* (West Chester, Penna.) April 1, 1855
3. *DAILY LOCAL NEWS*, Feb. 28, 1893.

MAHOGANY

The newspaper advertisements mention:

1841 "2 parlors on the first floor one of which is finished with mahogany folding doors"[1] John Aitken Est. (Upper Oxford Twp.)

1. *AMERICAN REPUBLICAN* (West Chester, Penna.) Sept. 21, 1841.

OAK

The newspapers mention:

1831 "The buildings have nearly all been lately covered with pine and oak shingles"[1] John Babb (Sadsbury Twp.)

1865 "The wood work of the room is beautifully oaked, and the ceiling handsomely corniced."[2] First National Bank (West Chester)

1885 "Four Handsome Houses...They are three stories high, with mansard roofs; contain good sized rooms and elegantly laid out with Olympic arches between the parlor and sitting room. The dining rooms are finished in grained oak and are 16 x 18, with 8 feet ceilings, and a door opening out on a side porch. All the rooms have cupboards and closets with hooks and other arrangements"[3] (West Chester)

1887 "Samuel J. Sharpless, Thornbury, is having one of the rooms in the new portion of his residence fitted up with oak finish"[4] (Thornbury Twp.)

1894 "The library is wainscotted, ceiled and panelled in white oak"[5] Richard T. Elliott (West Chester)

1. *VILLAGE RECORD* (West Chester, Penna.) Nov. 16, 1831.
2. Ibid., March 21, 1865.
3. *DAILY LOCAL NEWS* (West Chester, Penna.) Oct. 2, 1885.
4. Ibid., May 5, 1887.
5. *CHESTER COUNTY DEMOCRAT* (West Chester, Penna.) Sept. 30, 1894.

PINE

The newspaper advertisements mention:

1762 "Frame Barn of a well grown Pine"[1] Edward Bennett (Thornbury Twp.)

1820 "Stone Mill House covered with pine shingles"[2] Evan Lewis (Honey Brook Twp.)

1825 "the barn is new...well built and boarded with pine"[3] (West Fallowfield Twp.)

1831 "The buildings have all nearly all been lately covered with pine and oak shingles"[4] John Babb (Sadsbury Twp.)

1840 "barn 45 by 48 ft. boarded and roofed with pine"[5] John Swayne (West Marlboro Twp.)

1859 "Barn...the whole of the threshing story is laid tight with white pine"[6] Mary R. Cox (West Whiteland Twp.)

1874 "The wainscotting of yellow pine, is surrounded with walnut moulding...The whole of the woodwork being oiled"[7] Goshen Baptist Church (West Goshen Twp.)

In the newspaper advertisements, before 1877 there were four other mentions of pine roofing or shingles.

1. *PENNSYLVANIA GAZETTE* (Philadelphia, Penna.) Aug. 19, 1762.
2. *VILLAGE RECORD* (West Chester, Penna.) Feb. 16, 1820.
3. *AMERICAN REPUBLICAN* (West Chester, Penna.) Aug. 31, 1825.
4. *VILLAGE RECORD* (West Chester, Penna.) Nov. 16, 1831.
5. *AMERICAN REPUBLICAN* (West Chester, Penna.) Aug. 25, 1840.
6. *VILLAGE RECORD* (West Chester, Penna.) Oct. 11, 1859.
7. *AMERICAN REPUBLICAN* (West Chester, Penna.) Dec. 1, 1874.

POPLAR

The Brinton diary mentions that the early cabins of the settlers were made of poplar plank. The Brinton cabin was "Poplar plank 4½ inches thick, by some 15 inches wide – sawed G.B. thinks with a whip saw – yellow poplar – which the Emigrants selected always"[1] and the Thatcher cabin "was built of 3 inch yellow poplar plank, sawed by a whip saw & remained sound to the last."[2]

1. John H. Brinton Diary #1, p. 86, under date Nov. 4, 1857, Chester County Historical Society (West Chester, Penna.)
2. Ibid., #3, p. 23, under date May 13, 1884, Chester County Historical Society (West Chester, Penna.)

WALNUT

1870 "Dining Room in Walnut 13 by 17...Library in walnut"[1] J. Lee Englebert (West Chester)

1872 "Walnut Doors and Inside Blinds in first story front...open stairs, Walnut Baluster"[2] Charles L. Warner (West Chester)

1873 "The windows all have elegant stone caps, lintels and castings, while the inside finish is walnut...The large massive walnut doors leading from High street entrance, are the work of Mr. Baldwin of sash factory renown, and are a credit to his skill as a finished workman"[3] Henry Buckwalter (West Chester)

1874 "The wainscotting of yellow pine, is surrounded with walnut moulding. The pulpit also of the same material is finished with walnut...The pews are of pine with walnut moulding, and capped with walnut"[7] Goshen Baptist Church.

1875 "walnut staircase"[4] B. I. V. Miller Est. (Caln Twp.)

1880 "The vestibule is entirely of walnut...The floor of the hallways, both up and down stairs, is composed of a combination of walnut and ash, as is also the two bath room floors...The stairs leading to the rooms in the upper stories are of solid walnut"[5] Dr. Ingram (West Chester)

1882 "The new residence...is to be finished in red walnut"[6] William Penn Darlington (West Chester)

1. *VILLAGE RECORD* (West Chester, Penna.) Oct. 22, 1870.
2. Ibid., Jan. 13, 1872.
3. *DAILY LOCAL NEWS* (West Chester, Penna.) Dec. 5, 1873.
4. *VILLAGE RECORD* (West Chester, Penna.) Oct. 9, 1875.
5. Ibid., Oct. 1, 1880.
6. *DAILY LOCAL NEWS* (West Chester, Penna.) July 26, 1882.
7. *AMERICAN REPUBLICAN* (West Chester, Penna.) Dec. 1, 1874.

WOOLEN FACTORY

The newspaper advertisements between 1820 and 1824 mention one stone, three story woolen factory 50 x 45 feet: between 1825 and 1849 measurements were given of six woolen factories; one stone 80 x 37 feet, one three story stone and frame 43 x 21 feet and four that did not mention the material of construction the mean size being 1220 square feet. The newspapers between 1850 and 1874 mention ten woolen factories: seven of stone the mean size being 2726 square feet and three that did not mention the material of construction, the mean size being 1801 square feet. In 1865 one was described as "stone woolen mill 30 x 40 feet, with stone stairway about 16 feet square."[1]

1. *VILLAGE RECORD* (West Chester, Penna.) Sept. 19, 1865.

BRINTON 1704 HOUSE, Birmingham Township

John Hill Brinton, a West Chester attorney, collected the following data pertaining to the Brinton 1704 House, between 1830 and 1892, with the hope that members of the family would restore the house to its original condition.

1845 Ziba Darlington says —

I recollect the old Cabin built by William Brinton the Emigrant. It was removed to my lane end, on the Wilmington road, and was existing in the year 1800. I was a lad then.

The site of the Cabin was kept known by the old pear tree, planted by the Emigrant in his garden (unfortunately cut down by mistake of a laborer in 1852.) It was built of yellow poplar. The trees were sawed into plank with a whip saw. The Emigrant and his family lived in it for a number of years, and he died in it before his son, William Brinton the younger, built his house in 1704.

Some of the children of William the younger were born in the Cabin. He married in 1690 Jean Thatcher, the daughter of a neighboring colonist and William, the father and wife, Ann, and the son and his wife occupied the Cabin together for awhile.

The house of William the Younger had in the West Gable end, the letters

$$W \quad \overset{\displaystyle B}{\text{and}} \quad J$$
$$1704$$

They were not cut in the plastering but merely painted on it. Some years ago, before Thomas Brinton sold it, he whitewashed over them. They are however yet visible by getting a ladder and ascending to them.

1857 Ziba Darlington —

I have found remains of the Barn which belonged to the house of William Brinton the son built 1704. The plough turned them up, between the house and the road (Wilmington)——pieces of mortar.

1850 Catharine G. Brinton —

Your Father was 3 years old at Battle of Brandywine. Grandfather, George Brinton, sent Grandmother and the children over to their relatives, Peirces.

The house was turned upside down and plundered — beds cut open — the clock case split, and its works taken — found six months afterwards in Parry woods, wrapped in a blanket. These works were probably brought from England, when first settlement made. Father got a new case and face. The clock is now Henry's.

January 26, 1865 —

Spoke to Ziba Darlington of my examining the title to the Edward Brinton Mill Premises which led to a conversation about olden times matters. Ziba was born 1788, and is now in his 78th year.

He said the old 1704 house of William Brinton, the younger, was built of stone got out of a quarry near Thornbury School House, west of it four hundred yards in a woods of old George Brinton's farm. The old house of George Brinton and of Eavenson were built of stone got from the same quarry.

Ziba found the remains of the foundation of the Barn, which belonged to the old 1704 house. It was west of the house and between it and the present Wilmington road.

He says the land about the house is unusually rich, raised grain and corn such as he hardly ever saw equalled. In laying down a mortar floor in the old 1704 house, he found the soil was sand. This old house at one time had three dormer windows in the south roof and two in the north roof. It was quite an undertaking to build such a house at that time (1704).

January 16, 1867 —

An interesting talk this evening with Ziba Darlington, which I now note down, though not so much given to doing so of late. He was born in 1788 — and forty years ago owned and lived in the old Brinton House of 1704 — built by William the son.

Ziba says "I recollect distinctly the remains of the Brinton Cabin (of 1684). It is as far back as 1802 or 1804. The plank of the cabin was removed from its original site, and put up into a new building at my lane end or near the end on the north side of the lane.

I learned from William Brinton, (born 1754 or 6) that it was the remains of the Cabin, and most likely William's father, George, the son of old Edward Brinton (Edward born in 1704) moved this plank and reconstructed them. It was used for stock in its new form.

The plank was probably three inches thick, and

pinned together when they formed the Cabin, with modern pins for they would not spike such plank. The roof of the cabin most likely was made of oak riven like shingles and not shaven (called   ) and held on by poles.

This cabin may have been there in its new form as late as the War of 1812 — but not later. The old Wilmington road took off to the east by my lane end originally and curved round to near — and west of the site of the Cabin — then came out near by the present Tavern at Dilworthtown, south of the Tavern.

The Barn belonging to the 1704 house, I discovered — or its site, rather. It stood twenty yards from the Wilmington road and some ten or fifteen north of my lane. The foundation I discovered — remains of masonry. This was when I owned the premises.

The old pear tree by the Cabin was probably natural fruit. I placed some of its pears on exhibition at an Agricultural Fair at West Chester once, as those of a Tree as old as the Battle of the Boyne.

The pears were not of such a quality as would lead one to believe that the tree was brought over from England.

The present Barn of the 1704 house was built about 1775, William Brinton cut his initials on a stone of it in 1775 — they were to be seen when I was the owner — and may be yet. The upper part was frame.

July 27, 1867 —

Ziba Darlington further said, I took down the front eaves and cornice of the 1704 Brinton house, in 1828 when I bought there. It was decayed entirely — and came down by a slight effort. The upper floor, the rafters of the roof, and the floor downstairs, west room, are the original. I put in new door south of the house — but left the north door which is the old original. Sash of the windows I put in. Old partitions (board) I took out and put in new.

The porch, at first, was a Stoop, a small porch over the south door with side seats. This William Brinton (Wm 1754) told me he recollects, when a boy it was there.

August 23, 1860 —

The old 1704 house has just been roofed anew by its present occupant, Mr. Faucett, and he has put an ornamental chimney and added a small north and south gable in the middle of the roof over the doors.

The date has thus been removed, but in the west chimney he has the date copied on a marble piece and inserted. (W. & J.B.)
1704

I measured some corn stalks in his field north-

west of the house, 12 feet high, ears 7 feet to the commencement of them, lower end. But in my brother Henry's far field I found stalks (four times the length of my cane) and ears 7 feet 6 inches to the butt from the ground. I could not reach them. Ears 14 inches long, that is the cob.

Ziba Darlington says that in 1828, he took possession of the 1704 as its owner by purchase from Thomas Brinton. It was in bad repair. He renewed the floor of the sitting room, the south doors (sitting room and the door to the cellar kitchen) the stairs, window frames, renewed the roof, walled up the two small windows first floor west end, and put a shed over the pump, and dug a cistern by the southeast end of the house, and added a small frame addition to the east of the house.

He saw these woodworks were gone entirely, so decayed that he pushed the pent eaves down with his cane.

What remains of the old house is the floor of the west room first story. The floor of the second story, the north door. This pretty much all of the woodwork. The sleepers of the first story, of the second story and of the roof are of the original building; have not been renewed. These rafters are hewn, not sawed, that is the roof rafters.

The north door of the first floor is an old hardy fellow, is of double thickness, has its old iron hinges and painted red. This red coat was renewed in 1828 by Ziba Darlington. The latch is wood, but that is a successor of the earlier latch and was made by Thomas Cox in 1828.

Mr. Darlington says that the appearance of the house in 1828 was extremely venerable. The outside of the walls was covered with green mould; the chimneys (brick) were long necked, five feet above the comb of the roof with a white moulding below the top, and then below was the date W. & J.B.
1704
plainly visible.

Mr. D. reduced the chimneys 18 inches; he also took down all the pent eaves, renewed the roof and woodwork, as stated; mortared the kitchen (cellar) floor and adjoining cellar. Originally the kitchen floor was flags and the cellar floor earth. The whitewash took off the green mould and then he whitewashed anew, which has been renewed.

Mr. D. states that William Brinton (born there in 1755 and died after 1830) told him the old house had pent eaves round the north, south and west sides, and a porch over the south door with seats at right angles with the front of the house. It was a "stoop" and its similar may yet be seen in old houses in this county and in England.

Brother Henry says that Father told him in

1831 (the year of the decease) that the old burial place of the Colonist and his wife was a little north of his fence (Henry's fence) which strikes the Township line from the east, that is, rather on the north slope of the high ground by the line. Father blamed much the ploughing of the field where their remains lay, and was willing to contribute and have it enclosed in perpetual memory of their resting place. I reason now that there is the exact spot. I also always hears so, though I placed the place a little further up the hill by the line. I reason that brother Henry is right from these considerations.

There was no pump by the cabin as anybody ever heard of. The Colonist drew his water (must have done so) from the nearest spring head of the site of the cabin, near Faucett's north line but on the Parry or Ruth Brinton Johnson farm. To that spring there would be a road from the cabin, road or path, and that road extended east, would reach the burial spot, and most likely they would not go further up the slope of the hill than Father indicated. Then it was woods I suppose; now 1868, August 23, a tilled well grassed extremely fertile field.

I thus relate these facts minutely in order that some future Brinton, descended from the Colonist (if he so minds) may restore the old house to its primitive aspect and plant memorial stones where these settlers rest. Brother Henry added that some years ago a hand of his, renewing the fence along there, in setting up the posts, found a bone like a rib bone, a piece of it was so horrified that he avoided the place henceafter.

Could this be a human bone, the remains of the dead interned there? The ground must have been much abraded from its natural surface in 1699 & 1700, the dates of the burial, or the interment must have been shallow. But in 150 years would not all traces of the skeletons be gone?

These are speculations, — But there is their cabin's site; there is the spot where grew their pear tree; there is their burial spot; and there is the 1704 house (which they never saw) built by their son William) which remains pretty much as he put it up. In the southeast corner, some 10 feet up, is a crack in the wall, south face. It will stand, however, if not torn down, a comfortable dwelling for another 164 years, and be a valuable relic of the first settlement in these distant and secluded wilds.

Ziba Darlington says that stream which flows through your brother Henry's farm and also through Caleb Brinton's was called many years ago "The Sand Run."

July 3, 1869 —

Ziba Darlington says that Faucett is making sad alterations in the old 1704 Brinton house; has taken out the large chimney jambs, and made two doors on the west front of the house and extended the porch around on that side. Very sorry to hear of it.

In reference to the persons by whom this 1704 house has been occupied, the following notice prepared by Ziba Darlington appears in the Village Record of July 1869. Mr. Darlington completed his 81st year on the 1st day of June 1869.

The Old Brinton House: — "Just five miles from West Chester, on the Wilmington Road, many of our readers have doubtless noticed a farm house standing surrounded by trees, and looking the picture of neatness. It is now in Birmingham Township, Delaware County, yet it at one time was in our County, and its history is part of ours. It is, we think, the oldest house now standing in either Chester or Delaware Counties, and is besides the old homestead of one of our largest and most influential Chester County families. The house was erected in 1704 by William Brinton, son of William and Ann Brinton, who, with his parents, came from Birmingham, England, in the year 1684, the parents being very old at the time of their arrival. The mother died in 1699 and the father in 1700, and they were buried on these premises. It is believed that all the name in Pennsylvania descended from this pair. They all occupied a log cabin during the life of the parents and till the erection of the mansion in 1704. William Jr. married Jane Thatcher in the year 1690. The house remains very much the same as in their day, and since its erection, has been occupied by the following persons, for the length of time affixed to their names: William Brinton, 47 years; George Brinton, 42 years; Joseph Brinton, 12 years; Joseph Brinton, Esq., 24 years; Ziba Darlington, 32 years; Henry Faucett, 8 years."

West Chester, Sunday, Dec. 4, 1870. At about noon I started with Ziba Darlington for a drive to Chadds Ford and back... We then came to the old Brinton house of 1704, got out, went in and examined it. Mr. Faucett was very kind and permitted us to gratify our curiosity. The mantelpiece in the east room is ancient; the great sleeper supporting the second story (165 years old) floor remains solid and strong. Mr. D. says he had it planed to remove the cuts of the axe so visible then but some yet remain. There were two similar sleepers in the west room, but they were hewed off to a level with the ceiling, and still support the upper floor. Mr. D. said there were partitions with sides of an entry running from the south to the north door.

The walls are 22 inches thick. Mr. Faucett says similar stone are found in brother Henry W. Brinton's woods, adjoining him, a very fine, smooth, large building stone. They can be seen in the stream in the woods.

West Chester, Jan. 12, 1872 —

Mrs. Faucett, whose husband resides in the old 1704 Brinton house, brought me a picture frame.

The sill of the north door of the house had been removed, new sills or rather frame and door had been made this last summer.

By the sill or frame, I mean the upright piece of wood to which the door is swung by hinges.

Out of this frame, the present picture frame is made and presented to me. It is of walnut, sound and hard, and looks ancient. It was hard to work up. In the lower strip, inside, is the mark of a nail.

This wood was made up for the door 168 years ago. The nails used were wrought nails. The door was walnut also and three boards thick, nailed securely together. It is preserved by Mr. Faucett.

Ziba Darlington, born 1788, says the door and frame were the original. He knows the house for 70 years back and lived in it a number of years.[1]

1.   Diaries, Chester County Historical Society (West Chester, Pa.)

ABIAH TAYLOR HOUSE, East Bradford Township

A Relic. — Reuben John, of this borough, has shown us a piece of leaden window sash and glass taken from the little and old brick dwelling-house which stands near to the Strasburg Road and a short distance this side of Cope's Bridge, on the Brandywine. Relating to thos relic, Mr. John furnishes us with the following:

"This house was built in 1724. The bricks were made from clay procured a little way south of where the house stands. The house is located on a mound which is said to have been once a regular slope all around, but the road running on the west side disfigured it to some extent. The walls are yet sound and give promise of continuing to stand as long as the Egyptian pyramids if vandal hands will but permit them to do so. At the time of this building being ready for occupancy the family residing therein had their nearest neighbors at Dilworthtown, and of course they were on good terms. Why should they not be at such a long distance apart? This house was built by Abiah Taylor, and the tract which he "took up" remained in the name for a long time, but all are now gone, and it descended in title to the Baily Brothers. The mortar is almost as hard as the brick, and it is indeed a flinty sort of a structure. The windows on the west side were four in number. The north side had two, which were very small, and all had leaden sash. The eyesight of these people was good, hence no French-plate glass was used. The mound upon which the house stands I have heard was made by some people of a more ancient race, but this I am unable to say to a certainty. I have portions of the sash referred to and it was brought from England. I am unable to ascertain the date of the Taylor's coming to this country, but I think it was about the year 1700. I have also a large oaken chest, which they brought with them and which contained all their wardrobe. It would not be large enough to supply the pants of a family in these times."

We may add that Mr. John is a descendant of the man who erected the house, of which he furnishes us the above scrap of local history.'

1.   *VILLAGE RECORD,* (West Chester, Penna.) Jan. 20, 1883.

WOODSTOCK, Radnor Township

Mr James Hunter I understnad Humphry
Wayne and you have agread about the building
of a house we have agreed to take great part
of it. peice work if he and you agrees and
we do expect we will further as fast as
as any hand of the number but we hope you
wont Stop us for the want of Stuf or money
March 16th 1776

                                                      James Davis
                                                      Enoch Davis

To Mr. James Hunter
in Second Street philadelphia

March 17th 1776

Mr.
Hunter I Do intend to Asist Mr Wayn all as I posable Can
At youer Bilding in Radnor this is from your friend
                                                      Benjamin Davis Car

Humphery Waynes Article of Aggreem for Carpenter Work
of Jas Hunters House

May 11th 1776

For the Consideration of Sixty five pounds of Cash to be
paid by James Hunter Merchant of Philadelphia, to me the

subscriber I am to Do all the Carpenter Work of a house as mentioned under for him the House to be 32 foot by 23 foot Two door in Selar one back door to Selar 3 out side doors in the walls 3 door frames 5 windows in the first story 18 Lights Each with Shuters 7 windows in Second Story 15 Lights Each with sashes 4 windows in the garett 8 Lights Each to Cornish and Roof the said House and a pent House at Each End Even with the Roof the 3 floors to be plaind on one Side and groved the Lower Story to be devided in two Roms and a Entry Stairs in the Entry Selar Stairs under other Stairs the Second Story to be devided in three Rooms and a Entry at the foot of the garret Stairs doors out of Entry into Each Room the garet to be devided in two Rooms all the Pertitions to be Rough boards for Plastering to be with Sirbases and wash boards where there is any need of them through the whole House windows to be hung with weights all windows and door Jambs to be Cased and breasts to Chimneys if Mr Hunter Chuses at Every fire place to paint and glaze all S^d House to Square plates and Girders and Rising pices Said Hunter to find all materials at the Place in Radnor where the House is to be built with all hawling so as I Shall not be Hindred and to pay Cash as the work goes on the garret pertition to be plaind and groved a drawer under the two End windows and Closits where there may be any place for them I am to find out to paint and Coulars Except white Lead S^d Hunter is to find a trap door to be in the Roof, all the above work I do agree to finish against the first day of august next without Sickness or Some unavoidable acksident hapens I do agree to finish all the work in a workman like maner and in testimony of the Same I Subscribe my name this 11th day of May 1776

Humphrey Wayne

6 Egg nob Locks V
2 Large thum Latches
5 Thumb Latches
12 HL pair of HL Hinges
6 pair of smaler dito
7 pair of hooks and Hinges for doors outside
5 Sett of Shutter Hinges Stay backs fasnings Rings and Staples
2 Large Locks for out side doors
16 pair of puleys and pins 48 yards of puley cords
2000 4d peny Sprigs
2000 3 peny dito
2000 2 peny dito
3000 3 peny trunk nails
2 pound of Glue

RADNOR BUILDING AGREEM^T &C W^H HUMP WAYNE

To
Mr James Hunter
Merchant in Second
Street Philadelphia

[inside leaf:]

Mr Hunter as I have Cons[. .]ed and sent you a plan I think acording to what you told me and as to what work it will be when finished Less than what you spoke or agreed with me in the former Plan I will make an abatement acording to what it will mesuere Less but I canot justly compute it now for if there is Less in somethings there is more in others To what I Canot make the ods but little but you and I will not differ for any Small mater but my opinion is that You ought to make it twenty one feet as it would make the Houe better the back Room perticularly would be one foot Longer if that was done I am yours to Serve April the 5 1776

Humphrey Wayne [1]

1.   Charles J. Bonman Collection.

DIAMOND ROCK SCHOOL, Tredyffrin Township

The costs for Building Diamond Rock School were

1818 Diamond Rock Schoolhouse	Dr.	D C
To Mason work		46.00
To Carpenters Bill		70.00
To Sawyers Bill		10.00
To Wm Scholfield for lime		12.00
To Smith's Bill		3.75
To Pine boards		9.25
To Store Bill		6.03
To hinges & screws		3.96
To Stove		18.00
To Nails		5.60
To Brick		4.00
To Shingles & boards		53.84
To white lead		2.00
To hawling boards		4.50
To hawling		1.50
To bruch, Buckets, tin & lock		1.37½
To Plaisterer's Bill		9.12½
		260.93 [1]

1.   Ms. Diamond Rock School, Chester County Historical Society (West Chester, Penna.)

CHESTER SPRINGS, West Pikeland Township

A newspaper mentions in 1722:

A Letter came to us last Post, dated from Hamstead Harbour in Long Island, requesting a particular Account of the New Bath or Mineral Water found in the Great Valley about (2)0 Miles Westward of this City, for the Satisfaction of the Public in general, and of several Gentlemen in particular who are inclined to come to it from these Parts for Relief; though we have by us Several Instances of remarkable Cures done by the said Water, we are obliged to defer answering the Gentleman's Letter till another Paper, when we hope to give a true and demonstrative Account of its Virtues and Cures.[1]

In 1750 Robert Prichard petitioned the Justices of the Court of Quarter Sessions for a license for a tavern:

To the Honourable Justices of the Court of Quarter Sessions to be held for the County of Chester yᵉ 28th of Aug 1750

The Petition of Robert Prichard Humbly Sheweth:

That Your Petitioner is in Possession of a Farm in the township of Pikeland in the said County on which is that Medicinal Water Called the Yellow Springs unto which there is Frequently a Great Concourse of people on account of Health and also many others Travviling about their Occasions on a Publick Road Laid Out and Opened Near the same & also another Road is Ordered to be Laid from Uwchlan which may Cross the above Said Road near Said Spring. All which Occurrences Render it Necessary to Procure Accomodations for such as have Occasion to Come to the Said Place. And as your Petitioner hath already been at a Considerable Charge in Building & Improving and is yet Willing further to Build and Improve in order to Serve the people Grant him a Recommendation In order to obtain License to Keep a House of Entertainment at yᵉ said Place and Your Petitioner as in Duty Bound Shall Ever Pray, &c.

Robert Prichard

Allowed.[2]

A newspaper mentions in 1774:

To be Lett: any may be entered on the first day of April next; That noted INN at the Yellow Springs, together with 150 acres of excellent land, about 25 acres of extraordinary good meadow well watered; a large dwelling house and a large new stone barn.

The Baths and outhouses are in good repair; also a saw-mill, rebuilt last summer. The advantage of these Baths is well known to the public, an incontestible proof of which is the great concourse of people — from four to six hundred persons have convened there in one day in the summer season.

DR. SAMUEL KENNEDY[3]

In 1814:

LOTS FOR SALE, in the Town of BATH.

The subscriber having laid out a Town, at that celebrated watering place and farm, long known by the name of the YELLOW SPRINGS, situate in the Township of Pikeland, in the County of Chester, and Commonwealth of Pennsylvania, offers to sell One Hundred Lots, (containing altogether 154 acres and 44 perches) at two hundred and fifty Dollars each, one-half of which is to be paid, when Deeds in fee simple are made or tendered to them; and the other half in one year from that date, without interest, for which the purchaser must give his bond and security if required. Deeds for the Lots will be delivered to the purchasers at one dollar each.

The town of BATH, is 28 miles from Philadelphia, 15 from Norristown, 7 from Downingtown and 11 from West Chester; a turnpike road is authorized from this town to the Little Conestogo turnpike road, and a new turnpike road is contemplated from Pawlingsford Bridge and Norristown, thro' this town to the Little Conestogo turnpike road. The celebrity of the *Yellow Springs,* the medicinal qualities of their waters, and the salubrity of the air, have been so long known, and so generally resorted to and approved, as to render it unnecessary to describe them particularly.

On Lot No. 38, is the Mansion House, a stone building, two stories high, 70 feet by 45, commodiously divided into rooms, &c. estimated at six thousand dollars value.

On Lot No. 43, is a large and commodious Frame building, three stories high, 106 feet by 26, commodiously divided into dining rooms, drawing rooms and chambers, estimated at five thousand dollars value.

On Lot No. 41, is a good Stone Barn, containing stabling for 48 horses, estimated at eighteen hundred dollars value.

On Lot No. 42, is a two story Frame House, and a Frame Stable of 70 feet long, capable of containing 20 horses, estimated at eighteen hundred dollars value.

On Lot No. 39, is an excellent Ice House estimated at one thousand dollars value.

On Lot No. 17, is a two story Frame Dwelling House, estimated at sixteen hundred dollars value.

On Lot No. 16, is a Stone Spring House, over an excellent spring.

On Lot No. 13, is another Stone Spring House and Smoke House.

On Lot No. 7, is an excellent Bath, the water of as good quality as the Old Yellow Springs.

On Lot No. 4, is an excellent Mill Seat;

the owner of this Lot will be entitled to the right of the old dam in Lot No. 21, and to convey this water from it along the ancient race through Lots 21, 22, 23, 23, 19, 18, 17, 16, 15, 14, 13, 12, through the Bath Lot No. 11, 6, 5, 4, 3, 2, into the said Lot No. one, and the privilege to keep the said race and dam in repair. This Lot is estimated at three thousand dollars value.

On Lot No. 78, is an excellent Spring of Water which may be conveyed without difficulty to all the principal parts of the town.

A number of the Lots are covered with excellent timber, they are of different sizes, containing from about four acres to fifty perches each, according to their situation on the streets, and it is believed the least valuable of the Lots, are worth the money demanded for them.

The Old Yellow Springs Bath Lot, is reserved for the use of all proprietors of the town in common, the holder of each lot will have this secured to him by deed.

The timber *on the streets* is reserved by the subscriber. As soon as the Certificates are sold, their situationwill be determined by Lo t, to be drawn under the superintendence of three disinterested gentlemen, viz:—Isaac Wayne, Esq. William Everhart Esq. and Isaac Darlington, Esq.

It is confidently expected the Drawing will take place, on or before the 20th March next, of which due notice will be given.

James Bones[4]

In 1826:

YELLOW SPRINGS HOTEL, and BOARDING HOUSE

Mrs. Holman, proprietor of the above establishment, wishes to inform her friends and the public, that it has just undergone a thorough repair, and is now fitted up in a style not inferior to any establishment of the kind in the United States, to entertain visitors and Boarders the present season. Her buildings are extensive: In addition to the late improvements, she has added one story to the main dwelling, containing twenty-four additional Lodging rooms, enlarged the Dining-Rooms, Ball Room, &c. and she pledges herself that no exertions shall be wanting to procure every necessary, and even luxury, for the table, and choice Liquors, so as to give general satisfaction. . .

THE MINERAL SPRINGS

of this place have always sustained a high reputation for their medicinal qualities and powerful effect in restoring health and vigour to debilitated persons. She has repaired the GROVE and BATHS, and added an additional dressing room, particularly fitted for ladies. . .[5]

In 1839:

THE YELLOW SPRINGS

On a visit to Chester county, a few days ago, finding myself within an hour's drive of the Yellow Springs, I determined to stop there a few hours, in order to see how things looked towards the approaching season. I was much gratified to find that Mrs. Holman was still there, and that she is now the owner of all the property at that place, and will have completed, by the first of June, one of the handsomest and most extensive bathing establishments probably in the United States. The building, the plan of which was furnished by Hugh Walters, of this city, is 85 feet in length by 25 feet deep, divided into separate apartments, comprising shower, warm, moderate and cold baths and a portico the whole length, with columns in front, which will make a beautiful appearance. . .[6]

In 1855:

SHERIFF'S SALE OF VALUABLE PERSONAL PROPERTY,, — By virtue of sundry writs of Fieri Facias to me directed, will be sold at Public Sale, commencing on WEDNESDAY, the 24th day of October, A.D., 1855, at 12 o'clock M., and continuing each day thereafter until all the hereinafter mentioned Personal Property shall have been sold, at the Hotel and premises of Mrs. Marie L. Neef, Chester or Yellow Springs, in the township of West Pikeland, and county of Chester, the following Personal Property, to wit: — One broad wheeled Wagon with wood bed, 1 two horse Carriage, 1 Dearborn, 2 four horse STAGES, 1 new and superior Vermont built four horse STAGE COACH, cost $600, 1 York Wagon, 4 sets of Stage Harness, 2 sets of double Carriage Harness, 3 Plows, 2 Harrows, 1 Wheelbarrow, lot of Saddle and side Saddles, lot of Bridles, 2 sets of plow gears, 1 set of cart gears, 5 made of oak post, lot of forks, rakes, spades, shovels, &c., about 250 hair, cane and moss mattresses, about 200 pillows, 118 bolsters, 56 double bedsteads, 65 single bedsteads, 106 basins and ewers, 155 wash stands, 25 cot bedsteads, 90 LOOKING GLASSES, 45 Bureaus, 325 Windsor Chairs, 80 chambers, 4 tables, 1 mahogany Wardrobe, 1 poplar Wardrobe, 1 cane seated Settee, 8 mahogany Card Tables, 1 Mantle Glass, 35 cane seated Chairs, 12 camp stools, 5 chamber buckets, 14 cases of drawers, 4 sofas, 14 Lounges, 5 rush-bottom Chairs, 8 cane-seated arm Chairs, 2 marble top Centre Tables, 12 bar-room Chairs, 1 cane-seated rocking chair, 2 rocking chairs, 2 chairs for invalids, 2 bathing tubs, about 515 yards of matting, 95 candlesticks, 15 Britannia chamber Lamps, about 25 yds. Carpeting, 5 tin buckets, 36 blankets, about 75 quilts, 25 Chandeliers, and side Lamps, 3 hall Lamps, 15 long pine dining tables, 3 fire fenders, 2 iron sofas, 1 ice box, 1 water cooler and drainer, 1 gallon measure, 1 settee, 14 milk pans, 2 mahogany work stands, 1 superior PIANO (Shumaker's make) piano stool and cover, music stand, about 20 dozen tumblers, 10 wash tubs, 3 clothes baskets, 2 large menglers, 1 cask gin, 1 key and sherry brandy, 9 demi-johns, 16 barrels and white sugar, 1 barrel and brown sugar, 36 doz. white plates, 8 doz. meat dishes, 1 doz. glass fruit stands, 1½ doz. pitchers, 23 sets of cups and saucers, 16 dozen wine glasses, 1 dozen white sugar bowls, 2 dinner bells, lot of oil cloth for stairs and hall, 4 benches, 2 doughtrays, 1 dresser, 1 Clock, 3 waiters, 1 large COOKING STOVE and Fixtures, cost $300, made by Potts & Yocum, 4 ice cream cans, 4 Coal Stoves, 1 Wood Stove, 25 dozen chamber towels, lot of calico window curtains, lot of plain white window curtains, lot of figured white window curtains, 135 linen sheets, 225 muslin sheets, 12 dozen linen pillow cases, 7 dozen muslin pillow cases, 20 dozen knives and forks, 90 white counterpanes, 7 figured table covers, 13 bed sacking, 42 white linen table covers, 14 dozen linen napkins, 10 dozen German silver teaspoons, 10 salt spoons, 9 dozen plated forks, 5 dozen plated table spoons, 6 mahogany chairs, 2 side tables, 8 hand scrubs, fish box, lot of spices, jars, &c., superior Billiard Tables, together with various other articles appertaining to a Hotel and bathing establishment, not herein enumerated. Sized and taken in execution as the property of Maria L. Neef, and to be sold by

L. HEFFELFINGER,
Sheriff

Sheriff's Office
West Chester, Oct. 23-lt[7]

In 1856:

SHERIFF'S SALE OF THE CELEBRATED WATERING PLACE, KNOWN AS CHESTER OR YELLOW SPRINGS. — By virtue of a writ Benditioni Exponas to me directed, will be sold at Public Sale, on THURSDAY, January 24, 1856, at 1 o'clock, P.M., on the premises, the following described Real Estate, to wit: — all those certain Messuages, Tenements, Public Inn Buildings, and Tract of Piece of Land, known as the *Chester* (or *Yellow Springs Property*), situate in the township of West Pikeland, in the county of Chester, and State of Pennsylvania, bounded by lands of Isaac Tustin, Margaret Holman, dec'd (now Wm. W. Holman.) Harmen Pennypacker, and others,

containing 37 ACRES and 64 perches, (37 A & 64 P.) be the same more or less, with the appurtenances, late the estate of Dr. George Lingen. The improvements are:

No. 1. — Hotel, a three story STONE BUILDING about 95 feet in front with a porch extending along its sides and front; on the first floor are a parlor, large ball room, large dining room, store room, bar room with the fixtures, and water introduced under the counter. There is also in this building a wine and storage cellar, and attached to it is another large dining room, a kitchen with all the necessary water fixtures therein, and a bake house, the second and third stories are divided into pleasant chambers for boarders.

No. 2. — "HALL", — a three story STONE HOUSE, about 40 feet in front, with a large private dining room on the first floor, and second and third floors are divided into chambers.

No. 3. — "Cottage" — a two story STONE BUILDING, about 85 ft. front with two ends or wings extending back; on the first floor are a large parlor, a large drawing room, 3 bath rooms, with fixtures for showers, plunge and rising and falling douche baths, used for hydropathic purposes, two water closets and other rooms; the second story is divided into chambers; there are two cellars under the building, and a porch extending along the sides and the front; it is also connected with the 'Hotel" and "Hall" by a covered promenade of about 120 feet in length.

No. 4. — "Washington House" — a two story Frame BUILDING, clapboarded on the outside, about 90 feet in front, with basement story, in which is a plunge bath and water closet; the residue of the house being divided into chambers; there is also a porch extending along the front and ends of the house.

No. 5. — "Our House" — a two story STONE BUILDING, about 36 feet front, with stoops at the door of entrance, a basement story in which is a pantry room, ironing room and storage cellar—the upper stories being divided into chambers. There is also attached to it a Barber Shop and Ice Cream Saloon.

No. 6. — A Stone Stable, with hay loft and stalls sufficient for the accommodation of from 80 to 100 horses, with a hydrant and water trough at the door, and a Carriage and Wagon House attached.

The water which supplies Hotel, Cottage, Washington House and Stable, is collected from the springs by iron pipes into a reservoir, situated at an elevation sufficient to carry a stream of water over said buildings, and to which it is conducted through iron and disseminated through leaden pipes.

The Baths are: No. 1 — BATH HOUSE, about 75 feet long, containing 1 plunge, 4 warm, 1 Russian steam, rising and falling douche, and several shower baths, dressing rooms, and boiler and furnaces for heating water. No. 2 — Bath House with plunge bath; water supplied to baths in houses No. 1 and No. 2 from the Iron and Yellow Spring. No. 3 — Bath House containing plunge, shower, rising and falling douche baths, and dressing rooms; water supplied by the celebrated Diamond Spring. ——Bath Houses No. 1 and 2, and the "Iron or Yellow" and "Sulphur Springs" are in a grove laid out with walks, containing summer houses and swings, and is situated in front of the main or Hotel building. There is also upon the premises a FRAME BILLIARD SALOON and TEN-PIN ALLEY, a two story Stone Wash House, a frame cow shed, sufficiently large to accommodate about 15 Cows, a Stone spring house with smoke house in the upper story, 3 ice houses sufficiently large to contain a supply of ice during the business season, large dam for making ice, a cave, a vault, a frame pit pen, a large APPLE ORCHARD, with a variety of other FRUIT TREES, 2 kitchen gardens with hot beds and a flower garden. The buildings are in good repair, and the land is divided into convenient fields by good fences, and is in a good state of cultivation.

The Chester (or Yellow) Springs, is one of the oldest and most successful watering places in the country, is remarkable for the salubrity of the air, and excellence and variety of its waters. General Washington, during the war of the Revolution, appreciating these advantages, established here a military hospital for his invalid soldiers. It is accessible by two railroads and stage routes, by the Reading Railroad to Phoenixville, and the Columbia Railroad to the Steamboat Station, thence by stages — time from Philadelphia about 3 hours, from Baltimore 8 hours.

Seized and taken in execution as the property of DR. GEORGE LINGEN, and to be sold by
L. HEFFELFINGER, Sheriff[8]

James L. Paul writes in 1876:
CHESTER SPRINGS SCHOOL

This school is situated in the northern part of Chester county, near the Pickering Valley branch of the Philadelphia and Reading Railroad.

The buildings, as represented in the plate, are on the slope of a hill, facing southeast. The one on the right is called the Washington building, because it was built by General Washington, and used by him as a hospital for his sick and wounded soldiers from Valley Forge and Brandywine. It is a frame building,

and rough weather-boarded on the outside. Dents in the steps of the old stairways are still visible, and can be pointed out to the visitor as the marks of the crutches of the wounded patriots.

A wing has been added for the accomodation of the school, thus making the main study-hall 48 x 53 feet, with small adjacent rooms for class-rooms. They have all been painted, which gives them a cheerful appearance.

The central building is known as the cottage, and is used for the girls' sleeping apartments, sitting-room, wash- and bathing-rooms, library for the use of boys and girls, and music-room. The lady Principal and female members of the faculty also occupy this building.

The girls' sitting-room is 20 x 60 feet. It is nicely carpeted and well furnished, and made attractive by pictures and mottoes on the walls. Adjacent to this are the library and music-rooms. The bath-room is furnished with an abundance of warm and cold water, and all that is necessary to promote the health and cleanliness of the children. The dormitories are well ventilated, clean and comfortable.

The large building on the left, known as the "Hotel" was originally a small, two-story house, and for some time the head-quarters of General Washington. An old Franklin stove, used by him, may still be seen in one of the central rooms, which is used now as the boys' clothes-room. The building is used by the male members of the faculty and the boys. In addition to the dormitories, it contains sitting-rooms and bath-room, also the kitchen and dining-room.

Between the hotel and the cottage, standing back a few feet, and not visible in the engraving, is the "Hall" in which are the sewing-room, boys' mending-room and infirmary. These buildings are connected by a covered promenade.

In front of the cottage is a lawn of about one and a half acres, used as the girls' play-ground, in which are a number of shade trees and a beautiful magnesia spring called "diamond spring". South of the "Hotel" is the boys' play-ground, embracing several acres, in which are the chalybeate spring and bath houses. These grounds are finely shaded by grand old sycamore and other trees. . .

The school was organized in 1868. . .[9]

In 1920 The Pennsylvania Academy of Fine Arts announces:
THE PENNSYLVANIA ACADEMY OF FINE ARTS owns a tract of 40 acres at Chester Springs, Chester County, Pennsylvania, where it conducts an open air school for fine art instrcution. . .[10]

Dr. James E. Graham mentions in 1937:
Yellow Springs (now Chester Springs), situated some

ten or twelve miles west of Valley Forge, was a health resort of reputation, with medicinal springs and baths. It had many advantages to recommend it for the army hospital headquarters, and possession was immediately taken. The springs and baths, with some usable houses, were located on a farm belonging to Dr. Samuel Kennedy, who was among the first physicians ordered to Chester Springs, where he established hospitals in three barns. Dr. Kennedy became an early victim of the malignant putrid fever. A year after his death, Congress directed that his widow be paid $5,000 for the use of the property.

By order of General Washington, the construction of a commodious building was immediately started, to serve both as the Yellow Springs Medical Department headquarters and the principal hospital unit for the camp. "Washington Hall," as it was later called, was the only specially designed hospital erected for the soldiers of the Continental Army, with the exception of those small log huts constructed in various camps for temproary use.

Washington Hall was 106 feet long, 36 feet wide, and three full stories and attic high. The third floor was divided into many small rooms, while the second contained two large wards. The kitchen, dining room, and all the utilitarian quarters were located on the first or ground floor. Nine-foot porches surrounded the first two stories on three sides. Here, Dr. Bodo Otto was ordered to take charge of the new hospital which was filled with the sick from Valley Forge, even before construction work was finished. There he remained after the army broke camp, as director of the district and, assisted by his three sons, he continued in this important post until the hospital was discontinued by order of the Board of War, in the late winter of 1781.[11]

In 1955 a newspaper mentions:

FAITH ON FILM MAKING MOVIES FOR THE CHURCH

On a 160-acre estate at Chester Springs, not far from Phoenixville, young men and women are putting their faith on film. They are members of Good News Productions, Inc., a movie company which makes films based on religious and charitable themes. They sell these to churches and television programss. . .[12]

1. *AMERICAN WEEKLY MERCURY* (Philadelphia, Penna.) May 31, 1722.
2. Tavern Petitions, Vol. 8, p. 124, 125, Chester County Historical Society (West Chester, Penna.)
3. *PENNSYLVANIA GAZETTE* (Philadelphia, Penna.) February 4, 1774.
4. *CHESTER & DELAWARE FEDERALIST* (West Chester, Penna.) March 30, 1814.
5. *AMERICAN REPUBLICAN* (West Chester, Penna.) July 4, 1826.
6. *REGISTER & EXAMINER* (West Chester, Penna.) April 23, 1839.
7. *AMERICAN REPUBLICAN* (West Chester, Penna.) October 23, 1855.
8. Ibid., January 1, 1856.
9. James L. Paul, *PENNSYLVANIA'S SOLDIERS' ORPHAN SCHOOLS. . .* (Philadelphia, Penna.) pp. 409-411.
10. *PENNSYLVANIA ACADEMY OF FINE ARTS SUMMER SCHOOL. . .* 1920.
11. James E. Graham, *DR. BODO OTTO AND THE MEDICAL BACKGROUND OF THE AMERICAN REVOLUTION,* (Baltimore, Md., 1937), p. 152-153.
12. *PHILADELPHIA INQUIRER MAGAZINE* (Philadelphia, Penna.) January 9, 1955.

ARTICLES OF AGREEMENT Made this thirty first of the fifth month in the year A.D. one thousand Eight hundred and twenty five Between William Garrett (Smith) on the one part and Isaac Garrett Junr. on the other part all of Willistown Chester County Pennsylvania Witnesseth that the said Isaac Garrett Junr. for the considerations hereinafter mentioned, doth for himself, his exectors and administrators, covenant, promise and agree, to and with the said William Garrett, his exectors administrators and assigns that he the said Isaac Garrett Junr. shall and will, against the first day of the fourth month next ensuing after the date hereof in Good, substantial and workman like manner, and according to modern plan & Architect, well and substantially, erect, build set up and finish one stone house or messuage on the tract of land surveyed to the said William Garrett by his father Isaac Garrett Senr. of the dimensions following—twenty six feet by thirty two feet, two stories high and cellared underneath the roof to be of white pine shingles, the kitchen floor to be of good white oak board and finished with wash boards dressers, (and a cupboard if there is a convenient place) the windows to be cased and jambs to have corner strips and mantle over the fire place harth to be laid with mortar; and ceiled,—the parlor to be finished in the following manner the floor to be of good Yellow pine wash boards and surbase, the windows half jamb cased and double Archetives, a mantle or chimeny piece like the one in Doctor Joseph Roberts house in the front room over the parlor in the new end of said house——the room down stairs the floor to be of good Yellow pine the windows to be cased and have corner strips on the jambs, one door into it from the parlor and from the Kitchen and a fire place in said room——the rooms up stairs are to be finished in all respects like the one down stairs with the exception of white pine floors and a chenney and fire place in the front room——the house is to be plastered culed and painted and the wall outside to be plastered or dashed & whitewashed——And also the said Isaac Garrett Junr. shall and will at his own proper expense find and provide all the stone, brick, lime, morter, timber scantling, boards glass, putty, paint, painting, nails, sprigs screws, and in fine, every other article that may be required for the erecting, building, and finishing the said house (not otherwise specified hereafter) that is the said William Garrett is to find all the hinges locks, bolts and revits for the doors and shutters——And In Consideration whereof the said William Garrett doth, for himself his exectors and administrators, covenant and promise to and with the said Isaac Garrett Junr. his exectors administrators and assigns, well and truly to pay or cause to be paid unto the said Isaac Garrett his exectors, administrators and assigns, the sum of Eight Hundred & fifty dollars, in manner following (to wit). four hundred and twenty five dollars, a part thereof when the said building shall be completely finished, Two hundred and twelve dollars and fifty cents more thereof in one year after the finishing of said building and Two hundred and twelve dollars and fifty cents in full for the said work in one year after the second payment or two years after the finishing of said house——And for the true performance of all and singular the covenants and agreements aforesaid, each of the said parties bindeth himself his heirs exectors and administrators, unto the other, his exectors, administrators and assigns in the penal sum of two thousand dollars firmly by these presents——In witness whereof we have interchangeably set our hands and seals the day and year above written

Witness) N.B. the Kitchen and the (Isaac Garret Junr
present) two rooms over the Ketchen   /Seal/
at   ) are to be finished against (
) the first of the tenth   (
George) month next ensuing — was (
W. Hall) written befor signing and (Wm. Garrett
) sealing   (/Seal/

March 28th 1826
Paid on the within article the
Sum of two hundred and fifty two dollars

William Garrett

June 24th 1826
Paid on the within article the
Sum of one hundred and seventy three
dollars with its interest

Wm Garrett

Aprial 3rd 1827
Paid on the within articles the sum of two hundred
and twelve dollars & fifty cents

William Garrett

Aprial 5th 1828
Paid on the within article the sum of two
hundred & twelve dollars & fifty cents in full
of the within article

W. Garrett[1]

1. Ms., Lands (Chester County Historical Society (West Chester, Penna.)

MARKET HOUSE, West Chester

June 6, 1831

The Committee on the subject of a Market house Report that after much enquiry and reflection it was judged best to procure a plan from an Architect in the City. Through the Agency of Samuel Haines who evinced much interest in the subject, Mr. Thomas U. Walter was employed for this purpose and the prior reports together with all the documents in relation to it, were placed in his hands. Owing to previous engagements Mr. Walters was unable to give his immediate attention to it. On Saturday evening a draft was received from him which is satisfactory to the Committee and which they recommend to your adoption. The draft is herewith submitted. It will be perceived that there is some variation from the plan originally approved. This your Committee are satisfied is an improvement and trust will be sanctioned.

Your Committee have been unable to procure a detailed statement of the expense, but submit an extract from the letter of Mr. Haines, a judicious man. "From the best information I can collect it would cost in this city from $800 to $1000 to execute the work according to the draft, including curbstone and pavement within the floor of the building." The same work it is believed can be done for a less sum in this Borough.

It is recommended that the ground should be prepared and the paving and curbing of the floor done under the direction of the Street Commissioner, independent of the proposals for a contract and that such proposal be immediately issued by the Chief Burgess, as follows:

PROPOSALS

for erecting a Market houss 100 feet long in the Borough of West Chester, on the site designated by the corporation, will be received by the Chief Burgess at his office, until the 17th inst. at 5 o'clock P.M.

The building to be according to the plan adopted and deposited in his office for inspection to be finished before the 17th day of September next of the materials and in the manner following:

FOUNDATION

of pillars to be built of good stone with lime mortar, two and a half feet deep from top of Curb.

PILLARS

to be built of brick, faced with front brick of the best quality, with mortar made of fresh lime and road, creek or valley sand.

CEILING

to be lathed and plaistered of the best materials and in the best manner.

ROOF

two plates on each side to be 6 by 8 inches, of good

oak or pine, resting upon the pillars and extending the whole length to support the roof. PURLOIN on each side 6 inches square, of same material. Sixty one pair of rafters 3 inches by 4 at top and 3 by 5 at bottom of same material. Ceiling joists three inches by six of same material. The collar beams to each rafter 3 inches by five of same material — the plate and purloin to be framed together with studs at every other rafter — the rafters to be lathed with good oak lath 1 1/8 by 2½ inches, and covered with pine shingles of 28 inches 8 inch courses and three thicknesses — heels of rafters and ceiling joists to be bolted together with half inch iron bolts — joists to be well pinned or spiked to the plates.

BENCHES

to be framed together of good white oak scantling 4 inches square, enclosed at sides so as to form a box with a door at one end. The tops to be of white oak plank one and a half inches thick.

MEAT-RAILS

three to every stall 4 inches by 1½, of white oak, with an upright post 4 inches square of same material, to be framed into the end of the bench and ceiling above, in such a manner as to be taken down every night, — the rails to be let into mortices in the pillars for that purpose. Eight iron hooks to each rail.

THE FRONTS

to be finished with white pine boards of good quality, conformably to the front elevation of draft.

PAINTING

fronts and cornices to be white lead, venetians, green — Stalls (except top) lead colour.

SPOUTING

of tin to conduct the water from centre to each end and down each corner pillar to the ground.

The work to be done under the Superintendance of a committee of the Corporation, and the dimensions, proportions and architecture to conform in all respects to the draft.

June 17th 1831

Thomas U. Walter's bill for draft and plan of a Market house amounting to $8 was allowed and ordered to be paid.

The proposals received by the Chief Burgess for building a Market house were presented and opened, whereby it appeared that the following named persons offered to erect a Market for the sums annexed to their respective names viz

John H Bradley)		
& John Marshall)	for	$1000
David Haines	for	963.05
Daniel Buckwalter	for	889.99 including paving
John T. Haines	for	940. including 2 inch benches & 12 pair scale beam eyes

George Hughes
Alanson Watson &
Noah Harris   for   750

June 18th 1831

The board proceeeded to consider the proposals offered at last meeting for erecting a Market house, and agreed to accept the proposal of George Hughes, Alanson Watson and Noah Harris to erect the said building for the sum of Seven hundred and fifty dollars.

On motion resolved that a Committee be appointed to superintend the building of the Market house; whereupon Thos. S. Bell, James Tillum and Dr. Worthington were appointed.[1]

1.   Council Minutes 1824-1838, pp. 117-119, Municipal Building, (West Chester, Penna.)

MANSION HOUSE

A newspaper mentions in 1832:

CHESTER COUNTY HOTEL FOR RENT THE Hotel of the subscriber situate in the Borough of West Chester, opposite the New Market House, and within 150 feet of the Public buildings, is now nearly finished. It contains upwards of 60 rooms, and is calculated for the accommodation of visitors, private Families, Travellers, &c.

The establishment is to be conducted on Temperance principles, or in other words to vend no ardent spirits and it will be rented only to a person qualified to keep a first rate House.

WILLIAM EVERHART[1]

In 1842:

CHESTER COUNTY HOTEL at PRIVATE SALE. — The subscribers offer at private sale, that large and commodious PUBLIC HOUSE, in the Borough of West Chester, Chester co, Penna., known as the "CHESTER COUNTY HOTEL." It is situate in a central and business part of the Borough, but a few rods from the court house and public offices, on a lot 135 feet front on Market street, and 300 feet in depth on Church st. planted with flourishing trees and shrubbery, and laid out in walks so as to form a beautiful garden.

The Hotel was built by Wm. Everhart, Esq., in 1832, under the direction of Wm. Strickland, Esq. Architect, in the most approved and finished style. It is 70 feet front by 90 feet in depth, and contains sixty eight rooms and parlors, including two spacious dining rooms and kitchen. Attached to it is a large brick stable, carriage house, sheds and every other convenience for the accomodation of travellers.

Being situated in one of the most healthy and thriving inland towns in the state of Pennyslvania, within 22 miles of Philadelphia, accessible by railroad in a few hours ride, the Chester County Hotel commands not only an excellent country custom, but during the summer session, is resorted to by a large number of persons from Philadelphia, and other more southern cities. It is on the whole a most desirable property for any individual desirous of devoting his attention to the business for which it is calculated or a company wishing to make a profitable investment.

If not sold before the 25th of December next, it will then be for rent. — For terms enquire of J.D. Pettit, Esq. West Chester, or of

F. & S. HALLMAN.[2]

In 1850:

FIRE. — The Bowling Saloon, in the rear of the Mansion House, in this Borough, was discovered about 7½ o'clock on Saturday evening, to be on fire, and was entirely destroyed. . .[3]

In 1851:

A Good Substitute. — The proprietors of the Mansion House, in this borough, are erecting a brick stable and carriage house upon the site of the Ball Alley, which was burnt down about a year ago. The stable will be about one hundred feet long.[4]

In 1856:

A FINE IMPROVEMENT. — The proprietor of the Mansion House Hotel, in this Borough, is erecting a fine verandah, extending along the entire Market Street front of the building. It is for the pleasure and accommodation of ladies sojourning at the house. The windows of the parlours at each end of the building are intended to open out on the floor of the verandah, thus affording an agreeable promenade. It is built on cast iron brackets securely fastened in the walls, and from the outer edge will run a railing or balustrade to protect people from falling down on the heads of the gentlemen enjoying the shade below. When the roof and all is arranged it will be very pretty and a new inducement for Philadelphians to come out and spend the Summer with us.[5]

In 1861:

. . .The improvements are the above three storied brick "MANSION HOUSE HOTEL," fronting on Market street about 70 feet, and extending back from the corner of Market and Church streets along said Church st., about 100 feet, and containing billiard, bar, reading and dining rooms, hall and kitchen, with cooking range and hot and cold water therein, on the 1st floor; parlor, 14 chambers, 2 bath rooms with tubs, hot and cold water and shower baths, hall and water closet on 2nd floor; 22 chambers and hall on 3rd floor; the attic being finished and also divided into 20 chambers, and the cellar contains oyster saloon, cellar, and vault, kitchen, 2 vegetable, wood, coat and wine cellars; there is a verandah extending the whole length of front, wash shed at kitchen door and water and waste pipe in the bar, brick stable, about 85 by 46 feet, with 32 single and double stalls, harness room and hydrant on 1st floor and hay loft and garners on 2d floor; frame log house and chicken house attached to stable, frame and stone ice house about 25 feet deep by 12 feet square brick out house enclosed by board fence, yard enclosed by pale and board fence and set with largeshade and ornamental trees. This is the best located and arranged Public House in the borough.[6]

1. *AMERICAN REPUBLICAN* (West Chester, Penna.) Sept. 4, 1832.
2. *VILLAGE RECORD* (West Chester, Penna.) Jan. 18, 1842.
3. *AMERICAN REPUBLICAN* (West Chester, Penna.) Sept. 17, 1850.
4. *VILLAGE RECORD* (West Chester, Penna.) Oct. 21, 1851.
5. *AMERICAN REPUBLICAN* (West Chester, Penna.) June 3, 1856.
6. *CHESTER COUNTY TIMES* (West Chester, Penna.) Feb. 23, 1861.

FIRST PRESBYTERIAN CHURCH, West Chester

A newspaper mentions in 1832:

WEST CHESTER, JULY 6, 1832.

The Corner Stone of a Presbytarian Church in this Borough, was laid on the 3d instant, in the presence of a large concourse of citizens of both sexes.

The ceremony consisted of a statement from WILLIAM H. DILLINGHAM, Chairman of the Building Committee, explaining their plan, resources, views and objects, with some remarks upon the importance of the work. The document to be deposited was then read by THOMAS S. BELL, Esq., a member of the Committee, who was followed by the Rev. Mr. STEVENS in a highly appropriate prayer, invoking the blessing of Heaven upon the enterprise.

The stone was then adjusted by the Master Builders and Architect, when a concluding prayer was offered up by Elder SIMEON SIEGFRIED.

Copy of the DOCUMENT deposited.

On Tuesday July 3d, one thousand eight hundred and thirty-two this Corner Stone of the

PRESBYTERIAN CHURCH,

was laid by the Rev. WILLIAM A. STEVENS, officiating Presbyterian Clergyman in this Borough.

Attended by

William H. Dillingham,

Henry Fleming,

Asher Miner,
Joseph A. Davidson, and
Thomas S. Bell.
Building Committee.
And assisted by the Rev. Levi Scott and
Thomas Sovereign of the Methodist Church, and
Elder Simeon Siegfried, of the Baptist Denomination
— in the presence of numerous other citizens
assembled on the occasion.
Architect — Thomas U. Walter
Carpenters — David Haines and James Powell
Stone Mason — Eli Pyle
President of the United States — Andrew Jackson
Governor of the Commonwealth of Pennsyl-
vania — George Wolf
Population of West Chester, 1500
Corresponding Committee —
Rev. Wm. A. Stevens,
Gen. John W. Cunningham
Collecting Committee —
William Everhart, Esq.
Gen. John W. Cunningham,
Robert Ralston,
John T. Denny.
Trustees —
Ziba Pyle, Esq.,
Robert Ralston
Henry Fleming,
THOMAS WILLIAMSON, Scripsit
Then followed the names of subscribers to the
fund.

Mr. John Cornog is the Marble Mason. The
contract with him not having been made until after
laying the Corner Stone, his name does not appear on
the document deposited.

The following is a copy of the address, which
by request of the Building Committee has been
furnished for publication.

WE have assembled to lay the corner stone of a
Presbyterian Church. The plan of the house we
propose to erect has been furnished by a competent
architect who will superintend its execution, and
whose efforts thus far, have inspired general confi-
dence. The building is to be of stone, rough cast, 75
feet long by 45 fee wide, and 23 feet in height. It is
calculated to seat 500 people on the ground floor;
and galleries can hereafter be erected, to accommodate 300 more, if occasion should require. The
foundation will be a few feet above the pavement;
and a sufficient excavation has been made to admit of
the construction of a basement story. The architecture is Grecian, in good taste, and there is to be a
cupola, if our funds will admit, 73 feet in height from
the ground.

The estimated cost as we propose now to finish
it, is $5000. Of this sum $3000 is already subscribed
— $2100 of it in this borough; $200 in other parts of
the county, and $700 in the city of Philadelphia. We
are encouraged to hope, that we shall be able to raise
the balance before our building is completed.

In the site we are happily all united, and our lot
84 feet front by 145 feet deep, has been procured
upon favourable terms. In connexion with it, and
within two squares distance, we have presented to us
from William Everhart, Esq. besides his handsome
subscription, half an acre of land for a burial ground.
Our contracts with the carpenters, mason, and for
stone, have been advantageously made. The work is
to be commenced immediately, and prosecuted
vigorously, will be covered in this fall, and finished in
less than a year.

In the stone now to be laid there will be
deposited a glass vase, hermetically sealed, containing
an account of the proceedings of this day, the names
of the clergymen attending, the different committees,
architect, carpenters, mason, and the subscribers to
our fund, all handsomely written on fine paper,
together with a copy of the constitution of the
Presbyterian Church in the United States, the
confession of faith, and a copy of the Holy Bible. As
historical mementos, we have also inscribed upon the
paper the names of the President of the United States
and the Governor of the Commonwealth, and
deposited therewith one of each denomination of
silver coin struck in the year 1832.[1]

In 1874:

The Presbyterian Church Improvements
The work of remodeling the inside apartments of the
Presbyterian Church of this Borough, is progressing
finely, and so extended and creditable is the change
which is fast taking shape at the hands of the skilled
mechanic, that we deem it worthy of more than a
passing notice.

At present the audience room is divested of its
former entire outfit, and presents a wide, clear scope
for the putting in of the handsome new walnut pews,
which are expeditiously being fashioned at the
planing mill of Mr. Henry Baldwin. These pews are
being constructed with a view to both comfort and
elegance, and in the way of arrangement will be
located in semi-circular tiers, so that all the audience
will face the speaker with ease. The aisles will not be
materially changed from the old plan; there being one
on either side with a wider or main one in the centre.
The pulpit will be located about the height of the
pew backs from the floor, and its position will be
nearer the congregation than the one of old. In front
of the pulpit a semi-circular aisle will be formed by

the front pews and the pulpit platform. Back of the pulpit and in the enlarged recess, the organ and choir will be handsomely provided for, both in the way of ample room and beauty of surroundings. At the front entrance of the room it is intended to have a small vestibule with self-closing doors, which will render the rear portion of the room as agreeable as the front. The ungainly projection now attached to the gallery, will be removed, as will also the pillars supporting the same from the floor below. All of the pews will be provided with cushions made of the same material and after the same design. The pews will have no doors, and the partitions will only be so far as the seat is concerned; the entrance passage in each one being clear and unobstructed from one end to the other, thus presenting and affording more social facilities and greater comforts than is proffered in the old stiff style of pews. The carpet over the whole room, inside of pews included, will be of one style, kind and pattern, the bottoms of the pews being so arranged as to allow of its being put down and taken up without difficulty or injury to the material. There is a desire also to extend the work of improvement to the windows, and by means of dividing them lengthwise, arching their tops and supplying finely stained glass in the place of the small plain panes now in use, will render harmony and finish in keeping with the other work above described. The walls and ceiling, too, will also put on a new dress at the hands of the fresco artist. The ceiling will be clad in sky blue for a body tint, with neat ornamentations of hues to contrast in pleasing and decorative relief in the developing of the scroll and panel designs, which the improvement committee have selected. The walls will be similarly decorated, only the body color will be of different shade — that of a light purple tint.

The gas fixtures, too, will receive a change from their present arrangement. In this feature no definite plan has been as yet agreed upon, but the one receiving the most consideration points to a long gas pipe connecting the two present ceiling burners at a distance of about six feet from the ceiling, and from which jets to protrude on either side at distance of about 15 or 18 inches. It is thought that this plan will serve to do away with the present side lights.

In the lower or basement story of the new addition erected to form a recess back of the pulpit for choir purposes, some providing mind has carefully studied what may be frequently needed, in the way of fitting up this apartment with flue, pipe hole and water sink, and which on the occasion of a fair, festival, sociable, or some such happy event, will amply serve the purpose of a coffee or cook room. From this room also a stairway leads up into the

choir apartment so that the performers may come or retire without annoyance either to the minister, the congregation or themselves. The outside of the entire structure will receive a full and liberal coat of paint in imitation of granite, which, with a general freshening up of the exterior wood work, will complete a very elaborate and creditable improvement, not only to the church, but to West Chester.

The cost of this thorough siege of renovation and repair is estimated at about $3,000, and the date for the applying of the final touches has been fixed at or about the first of next November.[2]

In 1893:

THE PRESBYTERIAN CHAPEL. CARPENTERS ARE FINISHING THEIR WORK ON THE BUILDING.

Beautiful Windows Dedicated to the Dead and Presented by the Living, Who Are the Donors:

The carpenters are putting the finishing touches on the new chapel of the Presbyterian Church, and soon their work will be complete. A few weeks will yet be required for the furnishing of the different rooms, this delay being the only serious obstacle in the way of occupying the building at once.

The large main room, with the infant room adjoining and separated from the general apartment by folding doors, which can be opened during the exercises in which all in the building may desire to take part, is cheerful, light and comfortable. The numerous light tints on the stained glass present that dim effect which is so common in places of worship.

Above the infant room a large apartment, like a broad gallery, opens into the main room, and there the pastor's Bible class will be located, affording the adult pupils an opportunity to look down upon the younger ones and at the same time to set them a good example by way of deportment and regular attendance. This class is by far the largest in the school, and its members claim for it that the lessons are made more interesting than in any other. The teacher, Rev. W. R. Laird, seldom misses a Sunday. This body of workers has in the infant room a handsome memorial window dedicated to Miss Caroline Williamson, who for a long time was connected with the Sunday School.

Another window in the infant room has been placed there in memory of the late Theodore P. Apple, whose family take much interest in the church. The emblems are a cross and crown.

The pupils of the Sunday School, by general collection, have raised the money for two handsome windows, one of which will be marked with the name of a former pastor, Rev. Dr. J. C. Caldwell.

Two windows, bearing pictures of winged

cherubs flying amidst a bank of clouds, are in memory of Thomas W. Marshall, Jr., whose life lasted from 1879 to 1884. Another, showing a descending dove, is in memory of Robert H. Thorp, a son of Dr. W. K. Thorp. Easter lilies mark a window which is in memory of Sallie F. Moore, who lived from 1864 to 1886, and there is another fine piece of ornamental work dedicated to Robert S. Mercer.

WELL KNOWN CITIZENS HONORED

In the large room two of the most prominent windows are dedicated to the remembrance of Dr. Wilmer Worthington, who lived from 1804 to 1873, and his wife, Elizabeth Worthington, who was born in 1810 and died in 1875. They were the parents of Casper S. Worthington, of West Chester.

The late Hon. J. Smith Futhey, President Judge of the Courts of Chester County, is kept in mind by two windows, the one bearing the Greek letter Omega and the date 1820, and the other having the letter Alpha and the date 1888.

The Mission Band of William Hands has a window bearing the text "A Little Child Shall Lead Them." The organization is composed of active little girls who raised the money by a fair.

Hon. William McCullough is remembered by the token of an open Bible illumined by a star which shines above. This window, which is on the western side of the building, was presented by Mrs. S. D. Ramsey's class and Mrs. McCullough and daughter.[3]

In 1955:
A contract for the construction of a large addition to the First Presbyterian Sunday School, Miner and Darlington sts., and a general overhauling and renovating of the present building has been awarded to Earl Thomas, building contractor, 24 S. High st., by a committee which has been at work on the project for several months. It is for the sum of $152,410. . .Complete New Front

Plans call for the removal of the apartment house at 128 W. Miner st., standing immediately to the east of the church and which the church has owned for many years. Two smaller houses to the rear of this property will also be razed to make room for new construction and extension of the present Sunday School property.

The brown stone front of the Sunday School which was completed more than a half-century ago will be replaced with a front which will harmonize with the church proper. In making this change a hope that has been expressed for many years will finally be fulfilled.[4]

1. *CHESTER COUNTY DEMOCRAT* (West Chester, Penna.) July 10, 1832.
2. *DAILY LOCAL NEWS* (West Chester, Penna.) Sept. 16, 1874.
3. Ibid., July 12, 1893.
4. Ibid., Oct. 5, 1955.

CHESTER COUNTY PRISON, WEST CHESTER

West Chester July 7, 1836

To the Commissioners of Chester County Pa.
Gentlemen
In compliance with your request I herewith submit a plan and elevation for the Chester County Prison.

I have estimated the expense of executing the work in accordance with said design and find that the whole will cost $32,000, understanding that all the exterior will be composed of rubble, masonry except the Entrance porch, which I propose to construct of hewn granite — All the cell doors and windows to be faced with iron, the galleries to be supported on iron brackets, and all the necessary arrangements to be made for heating, hydrants, water closets &c — I have also calculated for covering the roof with leaded tin or zink

All of which is respectfully submitted
With great regard
Your ob. serv.
Tho. U. Walter Arch

To
Jno Mellin
Walker Yarnall
& S. Taylor Esquire
Commissioners of Chester co.

Specifications for building Chester County Prison at West Chester Pa.

August 30, 1837
The whole work to be executed according to the plans furnished by the Architect, and every part of the building to be done under his directions and subject to his approval together with the approval of the Commissioners of Chester County.

The dimensions and form of the building and enclosing walls to be the same as are represented by the drawings.

All the outside wall to be 2 ft. 4 in. thick above the ground and 2.10 below — All the partition walls to be of Stone 1.4 in. thick except the Corridor walls which will be composed of bricks — The exterior walls will all be composed of good rubble Stone well laid in strong mortar and pointed on the outside — The chimneys will all be built of bricks and the fireplaces Rumfordized.

The Prison to be heated by means of warm air

generated by 4 furnaces: — a cellar will be made under the whole corridor, and the furnaces placed at each end — the smoke flues of one end will be carried horizontally through the Air Chamber to the other end to assist in equalizing the heat — these flues to be covered substantially with cast iron plates similar to those of the new County prison and vagrants apartment at Philadelphia. The furnaces to be of S. P. Morris' construction and so arranged as to be used separately or together.

Flues to be constructed in the corridor walls of nine inches square to convey the heat to each cell, and the apertures in the cells to be finished with revolving grates fixed in runs of cast iron 4 inches deep: — all the flues to be worked with *"followers."*

A flue for ventilation to be carried from the ceiling of each cell to the roof of the building and *"topped"* out like a chimney.

Each cell to have a hole through the outside wall near the floor for the admission of cold air, these flues to be secured with cast iron funnells similar to those of the vagrants apartment at Philadelphia.

Each cell to have a Hydrant with a brass ground *"bib-cock"* of the best quality and a water closet with horizontal pipes of 8 inches calibre similar to those of the Eastern Penitentiary and the new County prison aforesaid.

All the hydrants and water closets to be supplied with water from reservoirs to be placed near the roof of the building: these reservoirs to be lined with lead and furnished with brass ground valves, cocks, ball cocks, over flow pipes and all the necessary machinery for supplying the hydrants, cleaning the water closets &c. the rain water from the roof to be turned into these reservoirs.

Each of the water closet pipes to be emptied by a toggle jointed lever stop cock, similar to those of the aforesaid new County Prison.

The cell doors to be fixed in cast iron frames similar to those of the Eastern Penitentiary — the inside doors to consist of iron grates hung on pivots with a small wicket gate near the top to feed the prisoners through: — the outside doors to be oak or Carolina pine with a substantial lock and latch on each, of the best American manufacture.

Each cell to be 9 feet wide, 9 feet high and 12 feet long in the clear — the flooring to consist of seasoned oak joists 12 inches deep and 16 inches from centre to centre, the whole substantially counter ceiled with stone and mortar — the floors will be dirst quality Carolina pine boards free from sap and unsound knots.

All the cell doors to open in the corridor, those of the 2d and 3d stories to be approached by means

of galleries to be supported on strong cast iron brachers running through the walls.

The floors of the galleries to be 2½ inch white pine plank — the balusters to be of iron with a substantial hand rail.

The block of cells to be 3 stories high each ten feet from floor to floor and the descent of the roof 5 feet — the height of the front building will be according to the front elevation.

A cellar of 8 feet in the clear to be made under the whole of the front building, but no cellar under the cells.

The whole establishment to be roofed with metalized tin or zink.

A coal grate and marble mantel to be placed in the keeper's parlour.

The front door to be 4 inches thick lined with boiler iron and secured with a substantial lock and bolts — all the locks in the building to be of the best American manufacture.

The whole work to be well plastered and painted, and the glass to be best American manufacture.

The cell windows to be 3 feet high cased with iron, with a sash to open inside similar to those of the vagrants apartment at Philadelphia.

The corridor to be paved with bricks, and to be lighted by horizontal sky lights placed upon the roof, and so arranged as to be raised by small cords from the galleries — there will be 8 of these lights each of which will consist of a single plate of glass ½ inch thick 2 ft. 6 in. long & 14 in. wide.

The Portico at the front door to be composed of Chissel dressed Granite and the steps to be of the same material.

All the details of the building, the character of the work and the finish of the various parts not here specified will be similar to the finish of the aforesaid New County Prison at Philadelphia.

Tho. U. Walter, Archt.

Phila., Aug 30/37[1]

Specifications for a County Prison in West Chester, Pa. Tho. U. Walter architect Phil: March 27/28

Cellars to be made under every part of the building except 14 of the cells as indicated on the *"plans of the foundations"*, these cellars to be seven feet in the clear. — Foundations for all the cellar walls to be dug one foot below the bottom of the cellars, and for the Yard walls at least four feet below the surface of the ground.

All the walls to be constructed to the *depth, height* and thickness described on the several plans, elevations and sections, and to be composed of the best rubble stone well laid in mortar consisting of sharp sand or of gravel and wood burnt lime, except the corridor walls of the cells which will be composed of bricks for the purpose of affording facility for constructing the flues — All the flues for ventilation and heat to be built around followers.

All the walls of the building to be pointed on the outside and well dashed on the inside, and all the yard walls to be well pointed on both sides.

All the foundations to be composed of large building stone well bedded in mortar.

The frontispiece around the front door, the steps, cheek blocks, window heads and sills and the water table to the height of 2F.8 inches to be composed of best granite, finely wrought and well laid, jointed and penciled the shafts of the columns to be composed of a single piece.

Note. The estimate for the Granite frontis piece should be kept separate so as to afford a choice of either adopting it or dispensing with it.

All the doorways of the cells to be trimmed with cast iron frames and secured on the outside with substantial yellow pine or oak doors with strong locks and latches of American manufacture; and to have inside doors of wrought iron composed of bars 3/8 by 2 inches and three inches apart, with connecting kneed bolts so as to fasten up and down and sideways at the same time, these bolts to be so arranged as to be secured by the outside locks.

The cell windows to be four inches wide by 3.6 high and to have a facing of cast iron of 6 inches on the square and 6 inches on the splay thus these windows as well as the doors to be exactly similar in every particular to those of the New County Prison at Philadelphia.

The cells to be warmed by means of furnaces constructed according to plans No. 2; — the horizontal smoke pipes or flues c.c.c.c. are to be formed of bricks and covered with cast iron plates secured together with screws and arranged like those of the new vagrants apartment at Philadelphia.

A separate flue for ventilation to be constructed from the apex of the arch in each room and carried up to the top of the building and topped out as an ordinary chimney with a flat stone on the top of the weths to prevent the rain beating down.

Flues for conveying the warm air to the cells, will be constructed from the apex of arch in the air chamber to each cell and the outlet secured with a cast iron revolving valve fixed in a circular frame similar to those of the vagrants apartment in Philadelphia.

Flues of six inches in diameter for admitting cold air into the cells to be made through the outside wall and secured around with cast iron — these flues to be formed with a knee of 18 inches long thus, for the purpose of preventing the communication of sound from one cell to another.

Each cell to be furnished with a brass ground bib cock hydrant supplied from a half inch branch from an inch and a quarter leader main — these mains to extend along the corridor walls under the door sills in every story and to communicate with reservoirs in the third story.

The reservoirs to be four in number, and to be fixed in the front cells of the 3rd story, two will be arranged for the hydrants and two for the Water closets: — the reservoirs for the hydrants will be 4 feet deep, 8 feet long and 2 feet wide, and those for the water closets 12 ft. long, 6 feet deep and 4 feet wide; they must all be lined with thick sheet lead and furnished with all the valves, cocks, levers, pullies & necessary to perfect the arrangement Similar to that of the Philadelphia County Prison.

Each cell will be furnished with a water closet similar to those in all the Philadelphia Prisons — the pipes to be all of the best iron 8 inches calibre and 5/8 thick with good sound gubs and substantial lead joints — the stop cocks for letting off the water to be like those of the Philadelphia County Prison.

The cell doors will be approached by means of galleries of 3 feet in width composed of 2 inch cedar or white pine plank planned on both sides and supported on cast iron brackets 3 feet apart — these galleries to be finished with a handrail supported on square wrought iron ballusters secured in every bracket.

The corridor to be lighted by 10 horizontal sky lights placed upon the roof and arranged with toggle jointed levers so as to be raised by means of small cords from the galleries; each skylight to consist of a single light of thick glass secured in a wooden frame and fastened to the roof with hinges.

The roof will consist of spruce pine rafters sheathed with boards suitable for the purpose and securely covered with the best *"musselman"* zink — the conductors to be composed of tin not less than four inches in diameter.

All the cells to be vaulted with quick arches and the abutments filled up solid with bricks well laid in mortar: — the two end cells in every story to be groin arched and strapped all around the iron bars 3/4 of an inch by three, secured around stone posts so as to prevent lateral pressure on the end walls, — none of the apartments in the front building will be arched with bricks; the groin over the vestibule will be made of wood plastered.

All the floors in the whole establishment to be composed of Carolina pine or Oak, grooved and tongued.

The stairway in the front building to be composed of yellow pine with cherry rail square balusters and cherry newel — the stairs in the corridor to be composed of best heart pine with square wooden balusters and cherry rail.

The 6 windows at the end of the corridor the 4 in the back of the 1st story, the 3 in the 2nd story and 4 in the 3rd story to be each 12 lights 8 x 10 — The 6 windows in the front of the 1st story to be 12 lights 10 x 18 the 5 in the 2nd story to be 12 lights 10 x 17 the 5 in the front of the 3rd story to be 9 lights 10 x 16 and the 8 in the wings to be 3 lights 10 x 14.

All these windows to be secured with iron gratings; — the perpendicular bars to be one and half inches square and five inches apart, and the horizontal bars to be ½ inch thick and 3 inches wide.

The four windows under the portico and on each side of the door into the corridor to be 2 feet wide and 6 feet high and to be secured with bars similar to the other windows.

The door opening into the corridor to be composed of wrought iron bars ½ inch thick 3 inches wide and 3 inches apart; and to be secured with a massy lock and bolt; the front door to be composed of oak lined with boiler iron and well studded with iron rivets. — The rest of the doors to be 2 inches thick, 4 pannels without mouldings; all the openings in the front building to be trimmed inside with flat ovels, and all the board jambs to be plastered.

The two fireplaces in the front rooms lower story to have marble mantles to cost not less than $30 each, and all the rest of the fireplaces to have plastered jambs with a marble shelf; — all the fireplaces in the building to be rumfordized with good strechers and all the chimneys to be built of bricks.

All the cornices to be composed of wood, the joists of the first story to be oak well seasoned and those of the upper stories to be hemlock pine or oak — all the joists to be 3 x 12 and to be 16 inches from centre to centre.

The yard walls to be capped with wood and to project 2 feet inside of the walls — all these cappings to be secured to the walls by strong iron screws at least 2 feet long and eight feet apart — the roof of these walls to be covered with zink and the under side of the 2 feet projection to be plastered.

All the rooms and cells to be well plastered without stucco cornices and all the wood work to have 3 coats of paint of best pure lead.

A strip of 4 feet wide to be paved with bricks around the whole building in the yard and the entire front pavement as well as the floor of the corridor to be paved with the first quality paving bricks.

All the cellar windows to be secured with window Bars at least 1½ inches square and not more than 4 inches apart.

The whole of the work to be done under the direction and subject to the approval of the Architect and no extra charge to be made under any circumstances whatever.

Should the party of the second part at any time decide upon having any work done or materials furnished that are not included in the plans and these specifications, or should the party of the second part agree to dispense with any workmanship or materials included in the said plans and specifications; all such additions or deductions to be valued by the Architect and either taken from or added to the sum specified as the case may be, according to the aforementioned estimate of the Architect.

We hereby acknowledge the foregoing specifications as the paper alluded to in the contract we have signed this day

William Ingram
Chalkley Jefferis
J.W. Passmore
John Beitler

West Chester May 18, 1838[2]

This agreement made the eighteenth day of May Anno Domini one thousand eight hundred and thirty eight, between William Ingram and Chalkley Jefferis of the county of Chester of the one part; and "The County of Chester" of the other part; witnesseth that the parties of the first part, in consideration of the matters hereinafter referred to and set out, covenant and agree to and with the party of the second part, to furnish and deliver the materials, and erect, at their own proper cost, on the lot recently purchased for that purpose at the north east corner of Market and New streets in the borough of West Chester, a county jail and workhouse, according to the plan and specifications furnished by Thomas U. Walter, architect, now in the possession of the Commissioners of said county; to commence the work without delay and prosecute it with all convenient despatch; to have the walls and building erected and under roof on or before the first day of January-next; to have the building and all necessary accompanying improvements embraced in the said plan and specifications fully completed on or before the first–day of January one thousand eight hundred and forty-; to procure all the iron pipes, and six large stop cocks to be used in the building, under the direction of the said architect; and faithfully, diligently, and in a good and workman-like manner under the control and direction of the said Commissioners and their Architect, to do execute and perform the office work and labor above mentioned.

And the party of the second part, in consideration of the premises, covenents and agrees to pay to the parties of the first part, the sum of thirty five thousand, nine hundred and forty nine dollars, in such proportions and at such times as may be agreeable to the parties.

Provided however. That in case the party of the second part shall at any time be of opinion that this contract is not duly complied with by the said parties of the first part, or that it is not in due progress of execution, or that the said parties of the first part are iregular, or negligent, in such case the said party of the second part shall be authorized to declare this contract forfeited, and thereupon the same shall become null; and the parties of the first part shall have no appeal from the opinion and decision aforesaid and they hereby release all right to except to, or question the same in any place or under any circumstances whatever; but the parties of the first part shall remain liable to the party of the second part for the damages occasioned to them by said non-compliance, iregularity or negligence.

And provided also, that in order to secure the faithful and punctual performance of the covenants above made by the parties of the first part, and to idennify and protect the party of the second part from loss in case of default and forfeiture of this contract, the said party of the second part shall be authorized to retain—until the completion of the contract, fifteen per cent on the amount of moneys at any time due to the said parties of the first part.

In witness whereof the said parties of the first part have hereunto set their hands and seals, and the party of the second part hath hereunto affixed the corporate seal of the County Commissioners attested by the signatures of the said Commissioners and their Clerk, the day and year first above written.

William Ingram
Chalkley Jefferis
J. W. Passmore
John Beitler
B. Parker
Clerk

Sealed & delivered in presence of
Wm. Darlington
William Embree[3]

A newspaper mentions in 1838:

We observe the enterprising contractors are going on rapidly with rogue's mansion house. We have observed several blocks of granite drawn past our door within the last week, designed for steps, columns, etc. This granite, we are told, is brought from way down east, the Maine quarries more than 500 miles distant, from whence it is brought cheaper than it can be gotten in this state.[4]

West Chester January 7, 1840
To the Commissioners of Chester County Pa.
Gentlemen

I have made a careful examination of the bill submitted by Ingram & Jefferis for extra work done and materials furnished in the construction of the Chester County Prison and find it composed of three kinds of charges: — the *first* embraces those that are covered by the contract and should not be paid for; — the *second,* those that were not called for by the contract, nor ordered by the Commissioners nor Architect, but that really make the building better; and the *third,* those that are truly extra, and of course should be paid for. In order to bring the subject fully before you I have divided the bill into these three separate parts, each item of which I will now consider.

In the first division of the bill which included such items as are not extras we have

1. extra work on Blocking course and sills; neither of which contains the least extra work, as the drawings plainly show.

2. Head and sill corridor door. — No cheaper head and sill could be used than the one we have, and as the door could not be made without a head and sill of some kind, these items cannot be extra.

3. Arch in cellar. This is a part of the Plan, it belongs to the building, and the design could not have been executed without it, and it should by no means be charged as an extra.

4. An extra furnace; This charge is altogether out of the question; the prison could not be warmed at all without it, and it was originally intended to have two at each end, but instead of that we have two at one end, and one at the other. — The *two fireholes* do not certainly constitute *two furnacees:* they both stand in one chamber and together constitute one furnace. — But even supposing the *four* mentioned in the contract to be constructed into *two* as this extra charge implies, and the same clause in the contract settles the question by holding up the vagrants apartment at Phila. as the pattern, of which these are exact duplicates.

5. Making large gate in Yard wall. This upon the whole is not an extra: — but it having been originally intended to make it on the eastern side, and upon consultation we decided that the Western side would be more convenient for the Prison, the Contractors were directed to be more particular with its strength and finish being on a street. I think, therefore, that the

dressing should be paid for, the stone sill, which was a subsequent order and say $25 for extra work on Arch, doors, and iron work, which make $61.12 of this item to be paid and $160.75 not to be paid.

6. Inside shutters in Vestibule. These shutters it is true are not particularly mentioned in the contract, neither are the nails, the hinges, the putty, and a thousand other things; but the house was to be made, and that too in the best manner, and these shutters are as necessary to its completion as any thing else.

7. Extra weight of Cell doors. This item is claimed because the Contract happens vaguely to mention a different sized iron from that used, but the clause finishes in these words *"the doors to be exactly similar in every particular to those of the New County Prison at Philadelphia."* The doors *are* exactly similar to those referred to, and of course nothing extra can be claimed.

8. Iron bars for Corridor walls. — These irons are necessary to the strength of the building, and as it was to be built in the most permanent manner, I know not how these bars can be extra work. The *second* division of the bill contains those items that claim some consideration as to the propriety of making some allowance for them. The first charge is marked on the bill number.

9. and consists of a charge for extra work on front. — That the building is the better in point of taste at least of this additional work no one will deny; but as it was done without any directions either from the Commissioners or the Architect, the contractors can have no legal claim whatever for it — hence it becomes a question whether the county would be justifiable in receiving from the contractors that which beautifies it, and consequently renders it more valuable, without making some compansation. — This is however a question that must be settled wholly by yourselves, and I will only venture to suggest whether it would not be justice to all parties to allow the iron windows that were left out of the front to ballance the extra work the contractores put upon it — their charge for extra work is $1201.11, and I find the Iron windows to be worth $609.92 — this however as I said before is a matter entirely for your decision.

10. Granite window heads and sills. — These items are also of advantage to the building, although they were unordered either by the commis-

sioner or the Architect, it therefore remains with you to say whether they shall be paid for or not — the power is in your own hands.

11. Door and window heads and sills for back of building; these are also under the same circumstances; wooden ones would have answered, and these were neither ordered nor in the contract; the building is however better of having them, but the Commissioners are by no means bound to pay for them.

12. Extra work digging and removing dirt in yard — if this earth came out of the foundations, or has been made by the work, the contractors should remove it without charge but if it was originally on the lot, it belongs to the county to take it away.

We have now the Third division of the bill to consider which consists of such items as are really extras; it commences with number

13. Curb stones and setting — This was an after order by the commissioners — the price is reasonable.

14. Extra work on step and cheek blocks; in consequence of a resolution of the Board to make a greater elevation to the building after the contract was made.

15. Building out Kitchen — This relates altogether to the additional Kitchen — the charges are correct, and the over is not included, an appendage of that kind being in the contract.

16. Is the culvery; this also is a correct charge.

17. Includes all the paving beyond that named in the contract and is principally caused by the additional Kitchen.

18. Making cellar door all of which is extra.

19. Forcing pump and appurtenances, which is also extra and directed to be paid by the Commissioners.

20. Extra work on large gate, explained in the 5th item.

21. Rain water cistern, an after consideration and of course an extra.

22. Extra work on cupola — This work was ordered to be done by all the Commissioners with the Architect under the impression that it belonged to the Contract; — but upon reflection I find that the cupolas of the Phila. Prisons, which were the patterns as regards finish, for this, are both unplastered, and in as rough a state as we found that on our Prison when we ordered a better finish to be given to it.

23. Stairs in Debtors Apartment — This was an alteration of the Plan, and of course an extra.

24. Lightning rod, cleaning well, digging &c con-

nected with additional kitchen, and extra window in Kitchen all of these charges are really extras — the window in the kitchen which wants perhaps the most explanation, takes the place of the door, and the door is where the oven was to have been.

25. Extra work on 39 doors — These doors were to have had each 4 pannels, but when I came to examine the Lumber which by the way was the best in the market, I was fearful that it would shrink and warp, and to prevent such a result I gave directions to have these doors all made in 6 equal panels to give them greater strength; the charge is therefore correct and reasonable.

26. Pipes connected with the rain water cistern, all of which is additional to the contract.

27. Painting roof and chimneys — this was ordered to be done to render the roof more durable, and it constitutes a proper extra charge.

28. Hanging of swinging gates in basement windows — the contract calls for straight bars in these windows, but gates were afterwards ordered and of course are extra.

29. Irons to fasten the roof on the yard wall — upon reflection I find this item to be strictly correct; — the contract specifies 8 feet between the irons which is the distance we have them apart in the city but when these irons were being placed on the walls at this distance I became apprehensive that the greater exposure here would probably give the wind such an influence on them as to tear them off: and the roof being also heavier than those in Phila furnished additional reasons for greater precaution, I therefore ordered an iron for every intermediate space, which renders this charge a correct one.

There yet remains to be done before the Prison is entirely completed, the repaving of the corridor; the plastering of the inside of the air chambers, and some slight changes in the furnaces; also the painting of the front door the fixing of the cords to the skylights, the fastenings of the cell windows and the plugs to the ventilators.

I believe all the work to be done in the best possible manner, and the contracts to have been most faithfully executed. The building is as good a one as could be made for the purpose, the arrangements for suppling the Prisoners with water, and the water closets are perfect in their execution, and the performance of the furnaces is beyond what we could expect in the present state of the building: — the cells on the west side are now as well warmed as will ever be desirable, but the eastern ones require an increase

in the funnel which supplies cold air, and they too will be amply warmed.

It will be proper for me here to remark that upon careful calculation I find the main items charged by the contractors as extras are put down at cost.

All of which is respectfully submitted
by Your Ob. Serv
Tho. U. Walter Arch
To the Commissioners of Chester County Pa.[5]

At a meeting of the Commissioners of Chester County held Feby. 18. 1840 in conjunction with Messrs. Ingram & Jefferis contractors for the erection of a New County Prison in West Chester it was agreed unanimously by both parties after great deliberation that a compromise of the extra charges should be made so as to allow $1900- dollars over and above the contract which it is understood will be in full for all extra demands whatever; — it is further understood by both parties that if any part of the work should prove defective, the Contractory bind themselves to make it perfect at their own expense — The Commissioners also agree to receive the building from

the Contractors this day.
Tho. U. Walter Arch
Feby 18. 1840[6]

A newspaper mentions in 1871:

PROGRESSING. — The work of building an addition to our county Prison is going on finely, under the supervising of Mr. D. H. Taylor, and will in a few weeks be completed. The new addition comprises eighteen new cells and other improvements. The stonework has been done by Mr. John Coburn, the brick laying Messrs. Taylor & Hampton, and the carpenter work by Mr. Joseph Hunt, Col. H. R. Guss & Son furnishing the brick. Although the fact of our authorities being obliged to make this addition is not calculated to inspire us with a pride for dimishing evils, we nevertheless feel proud of the improvement, as we always do in anything pertaining to add to the comforts of those who may desire to make our Borough a transcient home.[7]

In 1874:   Our Prison Improvements
The improvements in the way of remodeling some of the departments of our prison, which have been in progress for some few weeks past, are fast nearing completion, and will, in a few days more, be

successfully concluded. The changes consist of making three stairways, — one leading from the dining room of the keeper's dwelling department to the second story — the second to the cellar, and the third to the attic or lookout on the top of the building. The oven has been removed to the kitchen apartment of the prison proper, which is located on the western wing of the structure, which change has left a very neat and commodious kitchen for the uses of the keeper's family, in the eastern wing, which heretofore has been devoted to the oven and boilers. This new order of things is a decided improvement and the workmanship is very creditable. The carpenter work deserves special mention, both for its fine finish and for the fact of its being accomplished by one of the prisoners — Jones by name. On the second floor immediately over the dining room a very complete bath room for private uses has been fitted up, in which some of T.P. Apple's first class plumbing is exhibited. On the other side of the building, in the oven room the Palmer Bros., have displayed their work in the same creditable manner.

This change when completed, will influence a dedication of two rooms — one on the first story and the other on the second, immediately above — for the storage of carpets. By this change customers having business in the carpet department will not be brought in contact with the prison cooks in the kitchen, as is the case at present. In each of the yards, on the east and west sides of the prison, a large reflector is placed against the opposite wall fronting the cell extension of the building. These reflectors are kept lighted during each and every night after 10 o'clock, and which floods the yards with light, thus affording assistance to the night watchman to detect any demonstration that, might be made during the nighttime, on the part of the prisoners.

The whole improvement is one to be commended, and will not only insure a greater degree of comfort to the Warden and his family but will also afford the assistant keepers a more perfect control over the entire building.[8]

In 1875:
Improvements at Our Prison
The work of remodelling the kitchen department of our County Prison is progressing very fast, and bids fair to be completed in a week or two. The change and improvement is a very marked and creditable one and when finished will allow of prisoners being taken to and from their cells to work in the kitchen without their being brought in contact with the outer world, as is the case at present, and by which one or more prisoners have made their escape.

The new kitchen will be formed out of what was the "back office room," and about two-thirds of the execution yard, and door-ways will lead therefrom into the prison corridor. The oven has already been removed to the new quarters, and the remaining portion of the yard yet devoted for executions is only about 12 x 15 feet in proportion, while over the whole a roof has been placed, so as to make the awful enclosure perfectly private. The old oven room will be fitted up as a sort of receptacle for such persons as may come under the head of "drunk", and the old kitchen department proper will be converted into an "Inspection Room." The fitting up of the new kitchen is being done in such a manner as accords with good judgement, and when ready for use will be a long want well supplied.[9]

1. Ms. Public Offices, Prison, Chester County Historical Society (West Chester, Penna.)
2. Ibid.,
3. Ibid.
4. *VILLAGE RECORD* (West Chester, Penna.) July 31, 1838.
5. Ms. Public Ofices, Prison, Chester County Historical Society (West Chester, Penna.)
6. Ibid.
7.. *JEFFERSONIAN* (West Chester, Penna.) Aug. 26, 1871.
8. *DAILY LOCAL NEWS* (West Chester, Penna.) July 13, 1874.
9. Ibid., Nov. 1, 1875.

NATIONAL BANK OF CHESTER COUNTY & TRUST CO., WEST CHESTER

West Chester Pa. April 18, 1836

To the Directors of the Chester County Bank,

Gentlemen,

I have the pleasure of presenting to you the accompanying sketch of your Banking house.

This drawing exhibits the appearance the building would present, if the brick houses on the north were removed.

I have selected this position for the purpose of enabling me to give you an idea of the architectural effect of the whole structure. — this could not have been effected without omitting some of the adjoining houses, as in reality, very little more than the front of the Bank will be seen Your Wisdom in originating, and your liberality in executing, so laudable a work of art, as that in which we are now engaged, has emboldered me to lay before you this humble effort of my pencil; the acceptance of which, will be considered as an honour conferred on
Your Ob. serv
Thomas U. Walter[1]

A newspaper mentions in 1854:

DECORATIVE OIL PAINTING. — Many of the business men of this community have already had the opportunity of admiring the beautiful manner in which the Banking room of the Bank of Chester County has been painted, by a family of Swedes who landed in this county in September last. The two principal artists, father and son, are nephew and grand-nephew to our venerable townsman, Olof Stromberg, who left Sweden about the year 1800 and has been a resident of this town for more than half a century. His grand-nephew, Nils Stromberg, a lad of some 20 years of age, came to this country more than a year since, and shortly after presented himself before his uncle as one of his relatives from Sweden, from whom the old gentleman had not heard for many years. His uncle gave him a warm and hearty welcome, and after several months residence in the United States, the son concluded to urge his father to come over and bring with him his mother, brothers, and sisters. As before stated, his father landed in September last, bringing a wife, five children and a yound lad an apprentice to his art, who was willing also to risk his fortunes in the new country with his employer. The father, Carl Stromberg, has been engaged all his life, and he is a man of more than fifty years of age, in the art of decorative painting in oil, and he certainly must have occupied a high position at home as an artist if we are to judge by his first work in this country.

Very soon after arriving here the officers of the Bank desiring to re-paint the walls and ceiling of their Banking Room, engaged their services, and after eight weeks of constant labor they have produced a work that is highly creditable to their skill, and which must at once secure to them permanent and profitable employement. In some of our larger cities this mode of painting has been in use for a few years, but for the most part the art is new to us, our people generally covering the walls of their houses with ornamented paper.

The ceiling of the room is painted in two shades of delicate blue, and the side walls with a subdued tint of rose color. On these two ground colors, are series of beautiful designs representing for the most part combinations of leaves, fruit and flowers. The stucco centre piece on the ceiling is gilt, and so also a carved wreath surrounding the clock. Around an indented square panel occupying the greater part of the ceiling of the Banking Room, is a continuous vine representing grape leaves and rich clusters of grapes, with a design springing from each corner of the panel towards the centre of the ceiling. The gilt centre piece is also surrounded by a wreath of leaves and graceful

figures, all of these designs being painted in colors to produce the effect of, and represent plaster or stucco work. Just under the heavy cornice, at the angle formed by the ceiling and the side walls, there extends around the entire room, a highly ornamented arabesque border about eighteen inches or two feet wide.

The side walls are then laid off in panels with decorated corners, and in the centre of the largest of them is an elaborate wreath of leaves forming a kind of medallion frame work for a very beautiful landscape, each panel illustrating a different scene or subject.

It so happens, and the co-incidence is a rare one, that the President of the Bank, Dr. William Darlington, and the ex-Cashier, David Townsend, Esq., are both very distinguished Botanists, — thorough and enthusiastic followers and admirers of the science of the great Linnoeous. These two gentlemen are so widely known amongst scientific Botanists, particularly Dr. Darlington, that they have each had plants named after them, and some one with very good tasts suggested the idea that these plants should be represented by the artists in a panel over the door of the rooms of the President and Cashier, and the idea has been as handsomely carried out, as the compliment to those gentlemen is delicate and well deserved. Accordingly we have in the panel over the door of the President's room, the "Darlingtonis Californica," and in that of the door of the Cashier's room, the "Townsendis Sericea."

Our description of the work performed by these artists is necessarily meagre and imperfect, but we are anxious to draw particular attention to their first effort, so that people may make a visit to the Bank, to see how really beautiful this style of decorative painting is. When they look at the fine effect, and learn that it is not so expensive as to be beyond the means of some of our wealthy citizane, we think these worthy people from Northern Europe will find that their skill and taste will meet with constant and liberal employment.[2]

1.   Ms. Bank of Chester County, Chester County Historical Society (West Chester, Penna.)
2.   *AMERICAN REPUBLICAN* (West Chester, Penna.) Dec. 19, 1954.

VILLA MARIA CONVENT, WEST CHESTER

A newspaper mentions in 1838:

The "West Chester Young Ladies SEMINARY," IN WEST CHESTER. (Pa.)

Under the supervision of Dr. J. W. COOK and

wife, with whom is associated as principal of the literary department, Mrs. A. H. Lincon Phelps, late of the Female Seminary at Troy.

THE boro' of West Chester, in which this Seminary is located, is situated near the Brandywine river, four miles above the battle ground, and is one of the most salubrious, thriving, and pleasant villages in the state. It is a distance of 24 miles west of Philadelphia, and easy of access at all times by means of two daily lines of cars, on the Columbia and West Chester rail roads.

The buildings have been erected at a large expenditure, on a plan furnished by Thomas U. Walter, Esq. The principal building is 130 feet in length, by 45 in depth, and 4 stories in height, with two galleries, each 100 feet long, and 2 stories high, being sufficient fully to accommodate 200 pupils.

The extensive grounds, surrounding the school, will be laid out in walks, and planted with trees and shrubbery, for the recreation of the pupils, thereby securing to them all the comforts of a rural dwelling.

The seminary will be opened on Thursday, the first of November next.

In 1839:

SAMUEL DAY vs. The West Chester Young Ladies Seminary

In the Court of Common Plese of Chester county of August term, 1839, No. 72, scire facias, sur Mechanics' Lien, issued July 20, 1839, for work and labor done as a house carpenter in erecting and constructing a certain brick building, the central part thereof fifty feet square and five stories high, with a wing attached to each end, each forty feet long and forty-five feet deep, being four stories high; also two galleries attached, one to each end of the said wings, on the north-westerly side built of brick, each one hundred feet in length, sixteen feet wide, two stories high, together with wash house and oven attached to the north gallery; and known by the name of "The West Chester Young Ladies' Seminary," situate in the borough of West Chester, and county aforesaid, on a tract or lot of land, containing about twenty one acres, adjoining lands of the Chester County Silk Company, Abner Hoopes, Joshua Hoopes, and others, together with work and labor done in erecting a fence round the yard and garden attached to the same. Also for work and labor done as a house carpenter, in erecting and constructing a certain spring house, a few perches from the said Seminary, on the same lot, and belonging to the same parties, being two stories high, sixteen by thirty-two feet in size. Also for work and labor done as a house carpenter in erecting and constructing a certain barn a few perches from the said Seminary, on the same lot and belonging to the

same parties; being thirty-six feet, one story stone and frame above.

NOTICE is hereby given to claiments and persons interested in the aforesaid property, that a writ of scire facise, sur mechanics' lien, has issued in the above stated action, to me directed, returnable to said court on the first Monday of August next, when and where they may attend if they think proper, and enter on record their suggestions according to law.

JOSEPH TAYLOR, Sherriff.[2]

1. *VILLAGE RECORD* (West Chester, Penna.) Sept. 11, 1838.
2. *REGISTER & EXAMINER* (West Chester, Penna.) July 23, 1839.

OCTAGONAL HOUSE, EAST FALLOWFIELD TOWNSHIP

A newspaper mentions in 1939:

Showplace of Chester County

This three-story house, with the huge basement, is constructed in the form of an octagon. Lukens Pierce ordered the construction of this house at Towerville in 1839.

How can you manage to build square rooms in a house like this?

Each of the eight large rooms in the building has the same dimensions and the same appearance. A small wing built on the back of the house increased the number of rooms, including those on the third floor, to fifteen. . .

Rooms in the building open off a central shaft extending from the first to the third floors. A circular stairway leads from one floor to another. Surmounting the house is a good-sized tower containing windows for lighting and ventillation purposes.

When the house was built a porch was constructed around the building. Windows in all the rooms were so designed that it was possible to raise the sash, open two small doors at the base of the window and walk onto the porch. In recent years those small doors have been permanently closed.

Not the least interesting fact concerning the construction of the house lay in the fact that only small stones were used. . .At that time cement was not used. Benjamin Vanever, of Coatesville, who built the house used a wooden frame, placed the stones within this frame in a mixture of lime, sand and water.

Approximately one foot was added to the height of the building each day.[1]

1. *COATESVILLE RECORD*, (Coatesville, Penna.) Aug. 18, 1939.

1724 COURT HOUSE, Chester

MEMORANDUM that the Commissioners & Assessors of Chester County have (ye first day of March 1737/8) Agreed with John Owen to repair the Court House after the Manner herein Mentioned (Viz[t]) The Lower floor and the Bar and to provide Convenient Seats for the Petty Jury to Sitt on, when in Court, and to repair the Windows and Shutters below Stairs and above and the Chimney case in the Grand Jury room and to repair the Three Tables belonging to the Several rooms above Stairs and the Benches, and to fix a Turn'd Column or Pillar to Suport the Ceiling where the Bellrops come thro, And to Cause the Ceiling to be Repair'd, And to Provide as many Boards as may lay a floor over the Sd Ceiling and to make & put up Shutters for the Belfry (or place where the Bell hangs) and Likewise to Make a Window in the Gable End in the Garret or upper Room and glaze the Same, and to Endeavour to procure (with the help of Joseph Parker) the Chairs that is wanting belonging to the Court House as Also the Tongs and fire Shovels, And that the Said John Owen accomplish or Cause to be accomplish'd the aboves[d] respective articles by the first day of Next May Court to be held at this County of Chester In Consideration of the Performance of the said Work the Said John Owen hath been Allowed an Order on the Treasurer for five Pounds towards the Same & providing Materials

Chester March ye 1 1737:8

John Owen[1]

1786 COURT HOUSE, WEST CHESTER

October 1786 By 2021 feet Board by Wm Hawley @ 10/	10. 2. 0
By smith work by Gideon Williamson	72.13.11½
By Duting Hands by Worthington	18.10. 0
By 33 days Casting By Pusy Woolfe	37. 2. 6
By Casting By Ryan	2. 8. 0
By do By George Entrikin	13. 2. 6
By Carpentor Worke Timber Drying) Boards by Wm Sharpless)	92. 7. 3
By 4 Months By Loyd Powel @ 40/	8. 0. 0
By 78 days By John Sanders @ 2/6	9.15. 0
By 112 do By I. Doloss @ 2/6	14. 0. 0
By do By I. Molony @ do	14. 0. 0
By Iron By Thomas May @ 30 Pound) p Tim and casting – 3.11 6)	94. 5. 6
By 190 Bushell lime By Thompson	7.14. 2
By 270 do By George Thomas @ 9 d	10. 7. 9
By 80 By Bond	3. 0. 0
By 80 By Downing at 1/1 – 200 @ 9 d	11.16. 8

By shingles Board, & Plank by McClelan	60. 5. 6
By 70 Days Worke By Cornelius McCawley	8.15. 0
By 52 days Worke by E. Daugherty &	6.10. 0
By 12 days Casting By Jn⁰ Hannum	15. 0. 0
By 200 Bushells Lime By Rogers 100 @ 1/3	10. 0. 0
By 25 Days Casting By Sewil @ 22/6 p	28. 2. 6
By 7 3/4 days By Darlington & Evenson	6.15. 0
By 1 do By Richd Strode	1. 0. 0
By 4000 feet Board By Abram Sharpless	20. 0. 0
By Carpenter Worke By I. Hains	102.10. 6
By Sundry of smith worke by A Darlington	72. 5. 9
By Sundry of nails glass & sundry) by Jameson)	199.15. 0
By Locks By David Henderson	31.10. 0
By	25.15. 0
By Timber for Lath By Thomas Hoops	8. 0. 0
By Sundrys of Worke By McArther	10.16. 6
By Dut and Casting By Nathan Schofield	8.18. 9
By 60 Bushells By Jesse Hoops @ 1/6 p	4.10. 0
By sundry of Worke By William Speakman	16. 3.10
By laying the Dungen Flore By Wm Sharpless	4. 2. 6
By Drawing shingles By Isaac Speakman	1.10. 0
By 120 Scaffold Poles @ 6d	3. 0. 0
By 300 with @ 15/p	2. 5. 0
By sundry Expences in Precuring Materials at Philad.	3. 4. 2
By do for Boards	0.11. 0
By d at Turk when agree with workmen	2. 6. 3
By do at Dillworths waiting on the Commissioner 3 days	1. 7. 6
By 50 Bushell Han of Mellin	3.15. 0
By 10 of Gibbon	0.15. 0
By 15 do of Isaac Jacobs	1. 2. 6
By 2 spades	1. 2. 6
By a Barr & Pick	1.15. 0
By Cash Paid Cooper Harrison & company for 600 feet board	4.15. 0
By Cash to Beaumont for smith worke	11. 0. 0
By Expence atending Commissions – 29 May	0.10. 9
By Rope	0. 7. 6
By Expenses at Willmington & Hawling Load Boards	1. 7. 6
By do Philadelphia Pucuring Locks	1.10. 0
By Expense atending Comms Jun 30	0.11. 0
By 20 Bushell Han Strode	1.10. 0
By 40 Harlan & Strode	3. 0. 0
By Expenses for guard at James Request	1.10. 0
By Cash to Viegil Eachus for Lining nail 30 lb	2. 5. 0
By 203 Load stone Wm Eachus @ 6 d p	5. 1. 3
By sundry Expences at schofield Hous &	9. 0. 0
By 860 feet Board & scantlin By George Davis	36.10.10
By glazing windows By Wm Townsend	2.12. 6

By 20 Bushell Lime By Caleb Baldwin	0.15. 0
By Load Cut Hay for Plastering By Lewis	1. 2. 0
By 120 Bushell Lime By Danl	4.10. 0
By 120 John Jacobs	4.10. 0
By 4 Days Casting By Isaac Taylor	5. 0. 0
By 7 Days Attendance By Do	3.10. 0
By Expences By Isaac Taylor	0. 9. 6
By 37 Days atendance By John Jacobs	18.10. 0
By Expences By John Jacobs	2.10. 0
By casting 12 days By Ryan	15. 0. 0
By superintending By Jno Hannum	100. 0. 0
By sundry of Plastering & mason work	213. 7.11
By sundry Boards & shingles James Mclelan	7.12. 3
By 20 20 feet Boards By Hawley & Harry	10. 2. 0
By 1000 feet Boards for Ruff By J Hannu	3.15. 0
	1604.17.02

The above is the Acct of Last years Worke about the Court House the omissions and other allowances you are Posessed of

Jno Hannum

John Hannum &
other's Commissioners
for Building the
Court House &c
Their Account of
Sundries[1]

1.　Ms., Court House. Chester County Historical Society (West Chester, Pa.)

1786 COURT HOUSE, WEST CHESTER

Articles of agreement made & agreed to by and Between Evan Evans, John Menough Junr & Titus Taylor Commissioners of the County of Chester of the one part and James Bones Sheriff of said County of the other part Witnesseth that the said James Bones agrees to take down thirty feet in length of the front and back Walls of the Goal Yard next adjoining the Court House, lower than the Surface of the Ground, and build a Wall across the Goal Yard at the end of the said thirty feet of as deep a foundation as the other walls uniting it with the parts left standing so as to compleat a Goal Yard, leaving a clear passage on the West side of the Court House of thirty feet, and shall compleat said Wall in a workmanlike manner & shall cover the same as the other parts of the Yard Wall is covered and shall Plaister the inside of the Wall so built with good Mortar of lime and Creek sand, he agrees also to build up and compleat the corners of the Court House and break out and put in two Windows in the said West side, of the same Size and Dimensions as the other Windows in the

Court House, and to correspond with the two opposite Windows and compleated in the same manner, with Glazing, Shutters Springs &c, & the walls compleated about the frames. And the said Commissioners agree to pay the said James Bones two Dollars and Sixty Seven Cents for each perch of Wall of Mason Measure contained in the said Goal yard wall so compleated, and further allow him all the Stone and covering of the Wall so taken down as shall be necessary to compleat the wall to be built as aforesaid reserving for the use of the County the extra Materials not used, and shall further pay him the Cost he is at in building & Compleating the corners of the Court House and, all the expence of Breaking and putting in and compleating the two Windows in the West side of the Court House, And the said James Bones shall compleat all the Work above mentioned on his part before the third Monday of August next, and the said Commissioners shall pay the said James Bones the amount of the Contract aforesaid when the same is compleated in manner aforesaid And for the True performance of all and Singular the agreements aforesaid each of the parties bindeth themselves unto the other in the Sum of two Hundred Dollars In Witness whereof the said parties have herunto set their hands and Seals this 18th day of June 1801 ——

Josa Weaver

Titus Taylor /seal/
Jno Menough Jnr /seal/
　　　　　　　/seal/
James Bones /seal/

Articles
Between
James Bones Shff
　　　&
the Commis rs
to take down a part &
build Yard Wall &c
Dated June 18th 1801[1]

1.　Ms., Court House. Chester County Historical Society (West Chester, Pa.)

1846 COURT HOUSE, WEST CHESTER

In 1846:

NEW COURT HOUSE

The Commissioners of Chester county advertise for proposals, it will be seen, for putting up the new county buildings. We understand the plan fixed is as follows: The building is oblong in form — 119 feet by 62 — main entrance on High Street, with a portico; and an entrance in the centre of the Southern front. The Southern front, is finished with pilasters which extend from the ground to the roof. The Court room is on the 2nd story, 60 ½ by 57 feet in the clear; the county offices below. The capacity of the Court room is about double that of the present. The plan was drawn by Walters.

The building will be constructed of brick, with six columns on High street somewhat in the style of the Bank of Chester county. The building will be commenced early in the spring.[1]

In 1848:

The workmen are busily engaged in erecting walls around the new Court House, in this Borough. The wall will be surmounted with a broad coping, and upon that will be erected a handsome iron railing. Everything is done with taste and substantiability.[2]

West Chester Sep. 12. 1848

Commissioners of Chester County
      To Thomas U. Walter Dr.

1847-Dec. 23.	To detail drawings of Court house and superintendence of the work contracted for by Ingram Jefferes & Co as per agreement	$1100.00
1848-Sep. 12	designs and superintendence of work done in fitting up the offices, yard walls, privies, Iron railing coping &c from Jan. 1 to Sep. 12. 1848	400.00
	travelling expenses incurred in visiting the court house from Feb. 2. 1846 to Sep. 12. 1848	311.70
		1811.70

Pr.

1846-Oct. 17.	By Cash	$500.00	
1848-Jan. 5.	” ”	500.00	
Aug. 3	” ”	100.00	
Sep. 13	” ”		1100.00
			$ 711.70
			400.00
			311.70

Recd payment in full
West Chester Nov. 16. 1848
      Tho. U. Walter[3]

Names of Persons furnishing Materials and Labour in the Construction of the Chester County Court House

Stone
Townsend Eachus
Charles M. Layman
Edward Shields
Henry Jackson

Sand
Enos Smedley

Marble
James McCann
Amos B. McFarland

Bricks
Nicholas Mendenhall
Philip P. Sharpless
William Everhart

Lime
Abner Baldwin Jr.
Timothy Denny
Mordecai Lee
Amos B. McFarland
Joseph Sheppard
John Todd

Excavating Cellar
George Jones

Masonry
William Brown
George Bugless, Jr.
Ezekiel Benner
Elhamman Benner
John Battin
Oliver Farra
Samuel Good
James Hannum
Perry Peck
Thomas Pharoah
Emmor Ramage
Washington Simcox
Townsend Entrikin
Moses Walker

Bricklayers
James Bayard Jefferis
Alban Ingram
William Hoopes
Jasper Darlington
Philip Price
Marshall Battin
John Burns

Carpenters
Benjamin Gregg
John Sellars Dresser
Samuel Davis
Abel Green
James Ingram
William Lamborne
Emmor Townsend

Houston Way
Joel Woodward
William Slack

Labourers
Charles Burnett
Richard Crosslow
Levi Cummins
John Hall
Samuel Sowder
James Moore
Owen McDonough
John Porsel
Henry Ruthven
Dominick Rogers
Charles Smith
John Sandford
Solomon Burton
William Gibbons
Jacob Harris
Israel Hill
Joseph Miller
Orange Milby
George Nixon

Iron Work
Edge J. Cope

Painter
J. H. Hardy

Marble Masons
James Parke
Matthew Parke
William Brannan
Patrick Hasson
Hugh Lafferty
Robert Graham
Gilpin Williams

Marble Sawyers
William Clay
James Fox
John Laughlin
Thomas Callahan[4]

A newspaper mentions in 1857:

A HANDSOME DONATION. — Mr. John Hall, one of the oldest and most respectable citizens, who has for many years been following the business of a Watchmaker, has erected in the Court House yard at his own expense a most beautiful Sun Dial. It is set in the most substantial manner, and will remain a fit and appropriate monument, we hope, for years of the generous donor. This Dial is made by mr. Young the mathematical instrument maker of Philadelphia, the plate being of plated silver, and the index or arm that casts the shadow, of heavy brass. The plate is marked with Roman numerals from 1 to X11 and on it is engraved, "ERECTED BY JOHN HALL, JUNE 1857." Mr. Hall had everything prepared and wished to have it erected last June when there was no equation, but he failed to get the work done until recently. This is a handsome improvement, and the whole county will feel indebted to Mr. Hall for that which may be used by all who visit West Chester.[5]

In 1858:

REPAIRING THE COURT HOUSE

Mr. EDITOR: — There is an old saying "that a stitch in time will save nine," if properly done. This might be aptly applied to the Court House in your borough.

The architect who planned it, I understand recommended to the County Commissioners to have the outside of it finished in mastic work, considering that a neat, and at the same time, durable finish. In this it would seem that he did not understand his business, or misled them for the work did not last more than about five years before it commenced peeling off; and it has been repaired within the last four years at an expense of about $2000, and now looks worse than ever. This mastic work now hangs about the building in shreds not unlike a snake shedding its skin in the spring of the year. I think it would have looked much better, been cheaper, and more durable had it been made of dressed stone of some kind, or even pressed bricks, in the first instance. This patching up is "like the Indian's gun, costing more than it comes to." All repairs done to such a building ought to be durable ones, and then little re-pairing would be needed. I was in the Commissioners' office a few days ago, and was much pleased with a plan they had there, which was submitted to them by a practical stone cutter, showing how a handsome, and at the same time durable, finish on the outside of this building, with dressed freestone 4½ inches thick, could be made, and fastened firmly in the wall with iron clamps, and at a cost less than most people could suppose. Every person who saw it seemed pleased with it, and thought that this was the most feasible plan, and would make the most durable job.

All agree that there will have to be something done before long, or the building will be a sad looking picture, and that no more patching up ought to be done, as it would be expense thrown away. The principle difficulty in the minds of the Commissioners, it would seem, is the scarcity of funds in the County Treasury, and they being careful men, are opposed to running the county in debt any more than they can well help.

On the score of Economy, if it should be thought advisable to adopt the above mentioned plan, I would suggest the propriety of the Commissioner's putting the Building under contract, to be completed in two or three years, as might be thought most advisable. This would enable them to pay for it by instalments; and by using prudent economy in other matters, the Treasury would not feel it sensibly. We would then have a neat, chaste, and durable Court House and public offices for the benefit of the people of the county to transact their business, and at the same time would be a credit to their intelligence and good taste.

ECONOMIST[6]

This indenture made the sixteenth day of March AD one thousand eight hundred and fifty nine between William Gray John Paul, trading under the firm of Gray & Paul of the City of Philadelphia, of the one part and Joseph Russell, Titus Gheen and Benj. Hartmen, Commissioners of Chester County of the other part; witnesseth that the said Gray & Paul, for and in consideration of the sum of twelve thousand dollars do for themselves, their executors and administrators covenant, promise and agree to and with the Commissioners of Chester County as aforesaid that they the said Gray & Paul, shall & will on or before the fifteenth day of October next, in a good and workmanlike manner, and to the entire satisfaction of said Commissioners, well and substantially set up and face, the south & west sides of the Court House of said County situate in the Borough of West Chester, with blocks of the best pictou stone not less than four inches thick. the East and North west corner to be returned with stone, in accordance with plans adopted & furnished by said Commissioners.

In consideration whereof the said Commissioners of Chester County for themselves, and their successors do covenant & promise to and with the said Gray & Paul their executors & administrators well & truly to pay or cause to be paid unto the said Gray & Paul, their executors & administrators, the sum of twelve thousand dollars in manner following, to wit; one thousand dollars, part thereof when the first course of stone is laid: one thousand dollars other part thereof, when the window sills of the first story are set: two thousand dollars other part thereof, when the window heads of the first story are set: two thousand dollars, other part thereof when the window sills of the second story are set: three thousand dollars other part thereof when the caps of the pilasters are set thereon: and the remaining three thousand dollars in full for said work when the same shall be completely and satisfactorily finished: it being understood, that each and any of the foregoing payments shall be withheld at the times specified if the work so far done is unsatisfactory to said Commissioners.

And it is further covenanted and agreed by and between the parties aforesaid that the said Gray & Paul are to cut out and remove four inches of the brick work from the external face of the wall of the said south and west sides of said Court House from the marble base to the cornice: to completely take down and remove the pediments and buttresses on the south side and rebuild the same solidly of brick in the best manner and with the best material, facing them with stone as aforesaid: to remove the whole or so much of the principle cornice as may be necessary for the improvements & replace the same in a workmanlike manner: to furnish the best yellow pine beams 10 x 14 inches to support said pediments, should they be required, but if not necessary, then the value thereof is to be deducted from the last payment: to furnish all the stone on the ground and set the same with the best refined hydraulic cement or oil putty, securing them to the wall properly with iron clamps made for the purpose: to protect said sides of said building from the weather while the work is in progress and until it is completed, and upon the completion thereof to remove all dirt & rubbish from the premises and replace the pavements & fence.

In testimony whereof the said Gray & Paul have hereunto set their hand & seal & the said Commissioners have also respectively set their hands & caused the seal of the said County to be attached. The day & year first above written.

>Gray & Paul
>Joseph Russell
>Titus W. Gheen
>Benj. Hartman

Witness present, The interlination on the first page made before signing

>Robert Marshe
>David Meconkey

It is hereby covenanted and agreed by and between the parties to the within Indentures that the provisions and specifications therein set forth by and they are hereby extended so as to embrace the North side and East front of said Court House: the work thereon to be done and completed by the first day of January AD 1860: the said Commissioners to pay the said Gray & Paul their executors and administrators therefore, the additional sum of nine thousand three

hundred dollars in manner following, to wit, eight hundred dollars part thereof when the first course of stone is laid: eight hundred dollars (?) part thereof when the window sills of the first story are laid: seventeen hundred dollars other part thereof when the window heads of the first story are set: seventeen hundred dollars other part thereof when the window sills of the second story are set: eighteen hundred dollars other part thereof when the caps of the pilasters are set thereon, and the remaining twenty five hundred dollars when the said work shall be fully and satisfactorily finished: the work on said side and front to be carried up uniformally.

In witness whereof the said Gray & Paul have hereunto set their hand & seal, and the Commissioners have also respectively set their hands & caused the seal of the said County to be attached this fourth day of May. AD 1859

>Gray & Paul
>Joseph Russell
>Titus W. Gheen
>Benj. Hartman

Witness present

>Henry M. McIntire
>Wm. Bell Waddell[7]

December 31st 1859

Charles Fairlamb County Treasurer pay to Gray and Paul Four thousand eight hundred dollars, balance in full for repairs at Court House agreeably to the annexed Contracts, dated March 16th 1859, and May 4th 1859 —

>Joseph Russell
>Titus W Gheen   Commissioners
>Benjn Hartman

Received December 31st 1859 of Charles Fairlamb County Treasurer the sum of Four thousand eight hundred dollars being the balance in full for repairs at Court House, agreeable to the annexed Contracts dated March 16th and May 4th AD 1859 — $4,800

>Gray & Paul[8]

In 1859:

Nobody has visited West Chester lately, that has not lamented the awful breaking out all over the Court House. It is going to be repaired. The Commissioners have contracted to have the exterior faced with Pictou stone, of a brownish gray color. If well done, it will give the building a handsome substantial appearance.[9]

A TAX PAYER

We beg leave to protest against the removal of the pilasters from the south front of the Court House. Of course, the stone-cutter would accept such a suggestion, for it would diminish his labor and increase his profits. But such an alteration would make the building resemble the Horticultural Hall. It would make it appear too low and too long. These pilasters conceal defective symmetry, and were intended for that purpose. They compensate for the want of proportion. Take them away and you only turn "the cocked hat" into a "tarpoliam."[10]

In 1868:

"GIVE US WE AIR."

In the South-east half of our Court room lays the negro quarter. At every Quarter Sessions, the Black Brigade takes possession of it, not allowing a single white man to invade its sacred precincts. At least one hundred of the colored friends of Stevens, Sumner and Hickman, are found sitting there regularly during court hours, eating pea nuts, squirting tobacco juice, sweating from the heat of the furnace, and filling the atmosphere with Africa's balmy odors. The door keeper gets mad; the constables walk about pointing their long poles among the greasy crows; and the care-taker of the room, after adjournment, goes with his broom gathering up the rubbish of pea nut shells, and washing off pools of spittle.

This week the black brigade were out in full force, and the other parts of the room were densely crowded. The weather being cold the furnace sent up its volumn of heated air beyond what is customary even. The Court was annoyed, and ordered the Constables — "Give us air — open that window in the South-east corner, and that one opposite in the North-east corner." This afforded some relief from the stifling atmosphere.

Now the Jeffersonian adopts this order as a good one for the next campaign: "Give us air." Yes, Messrs. Stevens & Co., the county wants air, and will have it. New Hampshire, in a few days, will open the window and give you fresh air from the North-east, abating the stench of this vile negro business.

"Give us air!" Yes, says Ohio, we will, from our prairies. "Air you want?" says Pennsylvania, and the current comes from the valleys and mountain tops, driving off noisome smells from her borders. The country wants wholesome air, and a sounding storm sweeps from West to East, relieving the political health of the people.

The cry is a capital one, "Air, air, give us air." The black brigade and its commanders must move to Raccoon Hollows.[11]

In 1884:

The Old Town Clock

There are but a very few of our citizens as they tread the Court House pavement on their way to the post office and look up at the old town clock, to note the passing time or to set their watches thereby, that know anything of the excitements that attended the selection of the mechanic who should be entrusted with its construction.

Nearly fifty years ago the following subscription book was circulated amongst the citizens of West Chester, viz: "We whose names are hereunto subscribed to promise to pay David Townsend, an order, the sums set opposite our respective names, to be appropriated towards the erection of a TOWN CLOCK, to be placed upon the Court House, in the borough of West Chester, as soon as a sufficient sum can be obtained for that purpose. September 29, 1835". . .[12]

1. *VILLAGE RECORD* (West Chester, Penna.) Feb. 24, 1846.
2. Ibid., May 16, 1848.
3. Ms. Public Offices, Court House, Chester County Historical Society (West Chester, Penna.)
4. Ibid.
5. *AMERICAN REPUBLICAN* (West Chester, Penna.) Aug. 4, 1857.
6. *VILLAGE RECORD* (West Chester, Penna.) Feb. 16, 1858.
7. Ms. Public Offices, Court House, Chester County Historical Society (West Chester, Penna.)
8. Ibid.
9. *JEFFERSONIAN* (West Chester, Penna.) April 2, 1859.
10. Ibid., May 16, 1859.
11. Ibid., Feb. 1, 1868.
12. *VILLAGE RECORD* (West Chester, Penna.) May 27, 1884.

DAVID TOWNSEND HOUSE, WEST CHESTER

May 4, 1849

David Townsend agrees to employ Thomas Bateman to build an addition to the house of the said David Townsend on Matlack Street in West Chester, of the following dimensions and description, an outline of which is hereto annexed. The said Thomas is to find all the materials and labor and finish the said building in a plain and substantial manner. The materials all to be of good quality. The building is to be attached to the eastern wall of the north wing of the present house. The south wall is to commence upon or in a line with the north wall of the main building. The dimensions to be thirty one feet by sixteen, extending six feet further northwardly than the north wall of the said north wing, the walls to be of the same height and same pitch of roof as the said wing. The cellar to be of the same depth as the cellar of the said wing and the earth therefrom removed to the south side of the main building. The cellar walls to be of stone, and the walls above ground to be of brick well burned all to be laid in good sand and lime mortar; the brick walls to be nine inches thick, and the stone walls fourteen inches thick, and plastered inside and outside to correspond with the said main building. The first floor and stairs leading to the second story to be of good white oak or yellow pine boards. Both stories to be ceiled. The first story to have a partition across it running from east to west at the distance of eleven feet from the north wall, which partition is to be studed and well braced to prevent sinking, and lathed and plastered, on the north side with one coat of mortar on the partition and walls, and the partition, and the walls south of it, to be well plastered and white coated, on the inside. The floor of the apartment north of said partition, in the first story to be laid with undressed white oak or yellow pine boards of good quality. The joists to be of pine, three inches by ten and not more than sixteen inches apart. The southern portion on the first floor to have one door with marble sill and one window in the south wall, two windows in the east wall and one door in the partition; and one door in the north wall and one window in the east wall north of said partition. The doors and windows correspond in style of finish with those of the said wing and to be of the same size. The southern apartment ot have a cupboard the height of the story, five feet wide with two doors with suitable fastenings, and stile up the middle, and with five shelves sixteen inches deep. A chimney, and fireplace of suitable construction to insert a kitchen range or boilers, is to be carried up to the height of one foot above the comb of the roof of the main building, and to be of such construction as to prevent the smoke from issueing into the apartments or rooms. The stairway to the second floor is to be a closed one, three feet inside in the clear, also a stairway of same width of passage, and stairs, to the cellar. The second story to be partitioned off by a partition dividing it in the same manner as the first story, to have two windows in the south wall, three in the east wall and one in the north wall, one door in the partition and two doors inserted in the west wall, being the east wall of said wing before mentioned. The windows in the north and south walls to be of the same size as those in the first story, and those in the east wall to be of half the same size. One window in the said west wall to be removed and the opening well built up and plastered on the west side thereof and white coated. At the head of the stairs on the second floor is to be a suitable railing for a guard. The said second story to be plastered ceiled and white coated. The roof to be of good pine shingles well put on, and to weather not more than nine inches with tin gutter & spout. All the window

shutters of the first story, and the north and south ones of the second story, are to be close ones, to be hung with good strap hinges and have good fastenings for each. Those for the windows in the east wall in the second story to be plain, hung inside with good butt hinges and fastened with suitable bolts. There are to be three cellar windows, one in the south wall and two in the east wall, large enough to give sufficient light to the cellar; the south to be hung with butt hinges so as to swing upward. A door to be opened in the eastern wall so as to communicate with the adjoining cellar. The walls of the cellar, the joists and floor above, to be whitewashed. The pump is to be taken out of the wall, the well wall to be taken down two feet below the bottom of the cellar and then built up level with the bottom, with stone or brick laid in good lime and sand mortar, and a cast iron grate framed over the opening so as to open and shut with convenience. All the woodwork of the building above ground including all the windows, to be painted with three coats of white lead and oil on the outside, and two inside. A prive to be built, with put under of at least eight feet in depth, walled with stone or hard burned brick laid in good mortar. The house to be of wood, close framed and jointed, plained inside and outside, seven feet high, five feet eight inches long, and four feet seven inches wide in the clear inside, and painted with white lead and oil inside and outside. To the building first mentioned are to be tin spouts to carry the water from the roof to the ground. The said reserves liberty to furnish such materials as he has about the buildings before mentioned to be accounted for at the usual price of such materials, by the said Thomas. In consideration of the foregoing premises the said David agrees to pay the said Thomas or his order the sum of five hundred and twenty-five dollars when the said building is wholly finished and receipt or discharges for materials furnished for said buildings are exhibited to him the said David. And the said Thomas doth obligate himself to complete the said buildings within ten weeks from the date hereof. In witness whereof the parties hereto have set their hands and seals this fourth day of May Anno Domini one thousand eight hundred and forty nine.

David Townsend
Thos. Bateman[1]

1.   West Chester, Streets, Matlack, Chester County Historical Society (West Chester, Pa.).

CHESTER COUNTY HISTORICAL SOCIETY BUILDING, WEST CHESTER

A newspaper mentions in 1848:
HORTICULTURE

A stated meeting of the Chester County Horticultural Society was held in the Cabinet on Saturday last, and we are happy to state that it is in flourishing anticipation of successful experiment. A considerable amount of money has been subscribed and committees appointed to enquire into the cost and report plans for erecting a spacious building for the accommodation of the monthly and annual exhibitions of the Society. They design, we understand, to erect a building for useful purposes, that will afford accommodation to the various lectures, audience, &c., that may require a larger and more convenient building than the Cabinet. We hope they may succeed.[1]

In 1870:

HORTICULTURAL HALL — The owners of the Horticultural Hall, West Chester, have determined upon remodelling and improvement of the building: the floor is to be raised and made more substantial, and a gallery extending from the front around the sides half the depth of the building is to be erected at once, while an extension to the rear is to be added for staging and dressing rooms. Improvement in the mode of heating the Hall has also been decided upon. Indeed, the effort is intended to make a hall for lectures and other amusements suitable to the wants of the place. The undertakers will have this advantage; they will find it a hard matter to spoil the building.[2]

In 1871:

BUILDING MOVING — Mr. C. Frame, of this borough, is the most successful building raiser we hear of. Some few weeks ago, he raised the roof of the Horticultural Hall. Everybody said it would be a failure — it would fall — it would be twisted, etc., but when Clint got his screws set up, it went gradually to the height of about six feet and not a twist or crack about it.[3]

DRAMATIC COMPANY — The Horticultural Hall, in this Borough, after being closed nearly all winter, has been again opened for public exhibitions. Two nights last week, the Presbyterian choir gave concerts and tableaux to appreciative audiences. Since then, the stage has been cleared and drop curtains put up, and very handsome scenery arranged in the most approved style. This is a new feature in the hall, indeed; a new thing in West Chester. Heretofore all plays requiring a change of scenery could be but imperfect-

ly represented on account of the absence of appropriate apparatus. Hereafter this will not be the case. In the rear of the hall, an additional building has been erected, which has been divided into two large and airy dressing or green rooms communicating immediately with the rear part of the state. Indeed all the paraphernalia of a theatre has been provided for the benefit of actors. Four large private boxes have been erected and properly fitted up, for the gratification of those who choose to be more exclusive in their attendance. A large number of new and improved seats have also been placed in the gallery, and new seats will be provided for the main body of the building. The gallery affords room for the accommodation of a large number of persons. The hall is heated from large furnaces in the cellar, and the ante-rooms each side of the entrance are dispensed with, thus largely increasing the capacity of the hall. Outside, the building is much improved in appearance. The six or eight feet added to its height, takes away its former "squatty" appearance, and it is now really a fine building. The great large windows still extend to the floor, affording ready and safe egress to the people inside in case of accident.[4]

HORTICULTURAL HALL
SEATS 1,200
WEST CHESTER, PENN.

Population about 7,000. Twenty-six miles, by rail, from Philadelphia. RECONSTRUCTED WITH GALLERY AND STAGE; ELEGANT SCENERY AND DROP CURTAIN BY PROF. SEAVEY: two large dressing rooms, with rear entrance. Just opened. Only large hall in the town to rent. First class shows are well-patronized.

Apply to: G. McCARTNEY,

Janitor.[5]

In 1872:

A CREDITABLE IMPROVEMENT — The managers of our Horticultural Hall have recently erected a lobby addition to the entrance, which effectually shuts out the "cold chilly blasts of December." Our good people who have heretofore shrinked from visiting this hall owing to the cold blasts which were permitted to enter without opposition, will be happy to learn of this important improvement.[6]

In 1873:

SHERIFF'S SALE OF REAL ESTATE.

By virtue of a writ of Lev. Pa. Sur. Mech. Lien, to me directed, will be sold at Public Sale on MONDAY, MARCH 17th, A.D. 1873, at the Court House, in the borough of WEST CHESTER, Chester County, Pennsylvania, between the hours of 10 o'clock a.m. and 12 m., the following described Real Estate, to wit: All that certain Lot or Piece of ground situate on the East side of High street, between Chestnut and Washington streets, in the Borough of West Chester, Chester County, Pa., being about 65 feet in front on High Street, and extending back of that width about 153 feet to an alley, containing about 9945 Feet of Land, more or less, with the appurtenances. The improvements are a one-story building, having a front of about 65 feet and a depth of about 145 feet, and a one-story rear building about 14 feet deep, known as the Chester County HORTICULTURAL HALL. This is a large Hall building with gallery and large stage, suitable for entertainments of any description.

Seized and taken in execution as the property of "The Chester County Horticultural Society," and to be sold by

DAVIS GILL, Sheriff.

Sheriff's Office, West Chester, February 19, 1873.
N.B. — $100 of the purchase money must be paid at the time and place of sale, and satisfactory security given for the payment of the balance thereof to the Sheriff on or before the last Monday in April 1873.
D. G., Sheriff[7]

In 1880:

A coat of blue calcimine is being put on the walls and ceiling of Horticultural Hall. The building is otherwise being improved.[8]

In 1882:

Fire Escapes — The managers of Horticultural Hall are now making an improvement to the building for which their patrons will be truly thankful. It consists of four pairs of stairs, two on each side, which will answer the double purpose of fire escapes, and for emptying the hall quickly when crowded. The two first ones lead to the gallery, and the two back ones to the first door.[9]

In 1883:

Horticultural Hall to be Improved — The proprietors of Horticultural Hall are making arrangements to add considerable improvement to that building, the work to be commenced in a few days. Among the alterations to be made is the doing away with the inside projection now at the door and running the benches back to the front wall. This will necessitate the removal of the ticket office from its present position, and it will be arranged on the outside of the building entirely. This alteration will increase the seating capacity of the hall very much.[10]

In 1885:

The Opening — The West Chester Cornet Band opened its new roller skating rink in Horticultural Hall Friday evening under very flattering auspices. The new floor was as smooth as glass and the newly-painted and papered walls were favorable commented upon by the two hundred persons

present. The members of the band in full uniform flitted about during the evening doing what they could to make their patrons feel at home and enjoy themselves. The Coatesville Cornet Band came down and gave their West Chester brethren a house-warming. There were seventeen of them, and at eleven o'clock, after they had performed several beautiful airs and tried the skates awhile, they started on the return trip homeward in a large sleigh. During the evening, a barrel race was won by Masters Hemphill and Harlan and the hurdle race by Masters Heck and Strickland. The new malleable skates were much admired.[11]

Horticultural Hall — Workmen are still engaged on the tower U. H. Painter is building at the northwest corner of Horticultural Hall from plans furnished by E. F. Bertolette, of Phoenixville, which were some time ago fully described in the columns of the LOCAL NEWS. On Wednesday, Mr. Painter received a modification of the plan, which he has adopted. This plan changes greatly the external appearance of the building, making one door eight feet wide instead of two doors four feet each, while the second story will be decorated with one triple window instead of single ones as in the former plans. The shape of the roof has been changed. The whole will look very neat and pretty. The present entrance door will be closed except at the end of an entertainment, when it will be opened to aid in emptying the hall quickly. The internal arrangement of the tower and vestibule will not be materially altered from our former description, with the exception that there will be two sets of swinging doors before entering the auditorium, which will completely prevent any sudden or severe drafts of wind blowing on those seated in the hall. Mr. Painter tells us that he will have the whole completed and in readiness for the Teachers' Institute. He has also ordered one hundred additional folding chairs to fill the space allowed by these changes in the building.[12]

The brick work of the tower now being erected at the northwest corner of Horticultural Hall, West Chester, was completed on Wednesday afternoon. Carpenters are now at work laying floors in the first and second stories of the building and also putting on the rafters for the roof. The tower is 17 feet square and 35 feet high to the square. The latter will be run up from the four corners to a peak and covered with shingles painted red. At the east side of the tower, there will be a flight of stairs that will lead into the northwest corner of the second story. About midway of the lower room there will be a partition with swinging doors, while another door of the same kind will be placed in the doorway leading from the tower into the main audience room of the building. This, it is thought, will effectually prevent the draughts of air which were so objectionable heretofore. The ticket office will be placed under the stairway in the tower. It is so arranged that one person will be able to take the tickets for both the main room and the gallery. Mr. Painter has had the hall wired for a large number of electric lights around the sides of the main audience room, also for floorlights, and during the holding of the Teacher Institute will have, in addition to the above, a large chandelier hanging a short distance from the state.[13]

In 1894:

Next week the work of tearing out and rebuilding the rear portion of the Opera House will commence in earnest, the bricklayers having been notified to work at that time. A large and commodious stage is to be erected, in the rear of which will be several dressing and waiting rooms.[14]

1. *JEFFERSONIAN* (West Chester, Penna.) March 21, 1848.
2. Ibid., Nov. 5, 1870.
3. Ibid., March 25, 1871.
4. Ibid., May 6, 1871.
5. *NEW YORK CLIPPER* (New York, N.Y.) May 13, 1871.
6. *DAILY LOCAL NEWS* (West Chester, Penna.) Jan. 4, 1872.
7. *AMERICAN REPUBLICAN* (West Chester, Penna.) Feb. 25, 1873.
8. *DAILY LOCAL NEWS* (West Chester, Penna.) Sept. 1, 1880.
9. Ibid., July 25, 1882.
10. Ibid., Oct. 24, 1883.
11. Ibid., Feb. 21, 1885.
12. Ibid., Sept. 10, 1885.
13. Ibid., Oct. 1, 1885.
14. Ibid., May 5, 1894.

PENNSYLVANIA RAILROAD STATION, WEST CHESTER

A newspaper mentions in 1885:

THE ALTERATIONS AT THE DEPOT — This (Friday) morning a corps of surveyors and mechanics began tearing out the present interior arrangements at the Market Street P.R.R. depot, West Chester, preparatory to making the alterations which Superintendent L.K. Lodge designed whilst in the borough on Thursday. The surveyors are under the superintendency of Chief Engineer Feldpauche, who is a son-in-law of David Gill, of Duffryn Mawr. A decided change is made in the rooms and offices of the building, which are as follows: The ladies' department will be moved to where the gentleman's waiting-room now is, in the central part of the building, and the gentleman's will be changed into the room now occupied by the ticket office. A partition will be run from the front of the building to the right of the entrance to the present ladies' waiting-room back of

the freight department. The rooms thus separated will be used for the ticket and freights offices, the former to be separated by a partition or railing about two feet high. The freight clerk's apartment will, therefore, be divided for the ticket clerks. An entry will be run alongside the gentleman's waiting-room, through which the ladies, after purchasing their tickets, can pass to their waiting-room across the present main hallway which will not be disturbed. There will be two windows in the ticket office, one for ladies and one for gentlemen. The latter will purchase their tickets at a window which will be separated from the former by a railing, and will return to their room for the train by the entrance way now serving as an exit for the ladies' apartment to the train. The gentleman's private room will be where the cupboards were in which the late fire first started; the ladies' where the gentleman's are at present. This is about the sum and substance of the alterations to be made; and the work is to be pushed rapidly toward completion. By this arrangement, there need be no waiting in a large open hallway with a draft blowing through while passengers are purchasing their tickets, and so far the change is very acceptable to those employed at the depot.[1]

In 1917:

SOME CHANGES AT OLD DEPOT
Warehouse and Sheds to be extended. Indicating that New Station is yet a Dream — Looking Backward.

Several cart loads of bricks have been delivered at the P.R.R. passenger station, on East Market Street, which, it is stated, are to be used in making an extension to the warehouse and office of the Adams Express Company. These occupy the south end of the railway car sheds. This movement would seem to indicate that the old sheds at least are not to be removed and replaced by new ones, as a part of "our new passenger station."

What changes have been made in the old "depot" as it was called away back fifty years or so ago, when it was looked upon as a thing of beauty, and a metropolitan railway station.

Passenger cars, the old time cars, with very low ceilings, or roofs, with pictures painted over the windows, a stove in one end, no ventilators to speak of, etc., were shunted into one side of a raised platoform, while the baggage car was switched into the car shed on another track.

As stated, the platforms were on a level with the car floors. The side of the station now used by the express company was the passenger shed. The freight was delivered in the shed on the other side. The ticket office was where the women's waiting room now is. Some years after incoming passenger trains were run on a track on the east side of the sheds, without the locomotive being detached; the passenger train shed was used only for out going trains. The passengers alighted under this new deal dodged posts holding up an overshoot, which on many days shed showers down passenger's necks.

Then the freight warehouse was placed on the west side, the passenger station on the east on the main sheds, and platforms lowered. When the P.R.R. acquired the P.B. & W. the trains of the Frasier branch, which used to run into the "new depot" on East Gay Street, were transferred to the Market Street Station, and a new shed erected outside the old sheds. These are as open as the traditional saw mill.

These and many more changes have been made in the half-centur of the railway station. When the fire of 1888, or thereabouts, occured some improvements were made, and later the freight depot on East Union street was erected and the whole old depot given up to passenger and express business.[2]

1. *DAILY LOCAL NEWS* (West Chester, Penna.) Jan. 9, 1885.
2. Ibid., Jan. 23, 1917.

BAPTIST CHURCH, WEST CHESTER

A newspaper mentions in 1854:

NOTICE TO CONTRACTORS — Sealed proposals will be received for the erection of a baptist house of worship, in the Borough of West Chester, until the 6th day of April next inclusive. Plans and specifications will be exhibited on and after the 22nd inst., at the house of E.P. Worrall, corner of High & Chestnut Streets, in said Borough.

E.P. WORRALL
Chairman of Committee.[1]

THE CORNER STONE of the New Baptist Church at West Chester will be laid on Tuesday, the 4th of July at 2½ o'clock. The Rev. Dr. Dowling and Rev. J.H. Kennard of Philadelphia, and A.S. Patton will officiate.[2]

In 1855:

BAPTIST CHURCH — The Lecture room of the new Baptist Church of West Chester will be opened for Divine Service on Sunday morning next. Sermons will be preached in the morning at 10½ o'clock, and in the evening at 7 by ministering brethren from abroad. Collections will be taken up during the day to help defray the Church debt. When completed, it will be decidedly the handsomest church edifice in the borough.[3]

In 1856:

FRESCO PAINTING — The principal room of the Baptist church has recently been beautifully frescoes by two German artists from Reading. We had the opportunity of examining it some time since, and were greatly astonished at the fine effect produced. The ceiling and side walls are both elaborately finished, probably too much so for a room of no larger dimensions. The recess back of the pulpit is painted so as to deceive the eye entirely. One can scarely realize that it is a flat surface. There are no pews or seats as yet in the room, the congregation still worshipping in the basement story. We were glad to see that the church is provided with a fine baptismal font suitable for immersion. This will do away with the necessity of going out to a mill dam to per form this solemn rite of the christian church.[4]

In 1857:

DEDICATION — The principal room of the Baptist Church, in West Chester, was consecrated to the worship of the Lord on Sunday last. The Rev. Mr. Patton, Rev. Mr. Parmely, and other Divines assisted in the exercises. The Church, which is now entirely completed, is a large and handsome brick edifice.[5]

In 1886:

Church to be Enlarged — At the Wednesday evening meeting of the First Baptist Church of West Chester plans were submitted for the proposed enlargement of the building. The following is a brief detail of the change. There will be an addition built on the south side, extending about half the depth of the building. In this addition, on the second floor, it is proposed to place the pulpit, the baptistry and rooms for candidates to prepare for baptism and change their apparel after the ordinance has been administered, while on the first floor there will be a large parlor, which will be used for society meetings, and a studio for the pastor. The main auditorium will be converted into an amphitheatre, plain but neat in finish, with individual seats. In the space now occupied by the pulpit and baptistry, a gallery will be erected in order to give balance to the one now in the front part of the church. There will be a pavement laid along the north side of the building to an entrance to be made on that side. The preent stairways will also be made wider. The contemplated improvements will cost about $4000, and when finished, will make the interior of the building very comfortable, with a seating capacity of 800. It is expected that the work will be begun in a very short time.[6]

Hurried Glances at the Great Change Effected by Hammer, Saw and Trowel

The announcement that services will be hald in the main room of the First Baptist Church, of this place, on Sunday next is evidence that the extensive improvements there recently inaugurated are about completed.

Thursday evening busy men and women were engaged therein pushing ahead the final work, and the scene was an energetic one, in which the pastor, Rev. Mr. Meedham, conspicuously figured. Carpenters were engaged in placing the handsome perforated chairs in amphitheatre position upon the main floor, which work as it progressed shaped the handsome room and made it grow in coziness and attractiveness as if some magic hand was employed in the undertaking.

The brick addition on the south side of the building is a grand feature of the structure proper and through it the main room has been changed from the old stiff plan to one of the most easy and graceful order. In this addition the pastor has his nicely-furnished study, it being on the lower floor, fronting High street. Adjoining it is a reception or waiting room quite invitingly arranged while above are two spacious preparing rooms set aside for the uses of candidates for baptism, one for ladies and the other for gentlemen, each with a spacious wardrobe and other features of comfort and accommodation. These rooms lead to the baptismal pool, which is in the alcove back of the pulpit. The arrangements of these apartments connected with the pool are perfect. The candidate for the pool is conducted from the waiting room down a short flight of steps into the rear of pool proper and enters the water before he or she is brought before the congregation to receive the ordinance. The retiring is of the same private character and in every way have the objectionable or unpleasant features of this ordinance of the church been put aside and the nervous person who shall ask to receive this ordinance will find the way easy and agreeable.

The pulpit, a neat and prettily designed one, is placed upon a slight semi-circular elevation and the pastor is thereby brought in the midst of his people while teaching them the spirit of the Divine Word. A handsome chair for his comfort adorns the stand and the whole effect is very pretty. We expect the heavy curtains are to be tastefully arranged back of the pulpit and across the lower part of the pool recess, which will greatly add to the beauty and home-like surroundings of the room. Unless this is done there will be a feature wanting which will be very apparent to the congregation. Over where the pulpit formerly stood a tastefully constructed gallery has been erected capable of comfortably seating 174 persons, while the one on the west side has been remodeled to conform to the general fine appearance of the room and will seat nearly 100 more.

The whole floor of the main room is handsomely covered with Brussels carpet of a very pretty and serviceable pattern, while upon it are placed the easy chairs in such a manner as to impart a decidedly cheerful effect to the whole interior. The galleries are also carpeted in fine style, and in the building on the north and south sides small windows for ventilating purposes have been made. The walls have been artistically painted, and nicely conform to the decorations of the ceiling, and the profuse display of electric light jets rendors the whole still more inviting. There are many additional means of ingress and egress, and in every feature the improvement is a credit not only to the people of that church but to the town.

This hastily prepared description falls far short of doing justice to the great change now about being completed to the structure, and what we have failed to notice we trust, our readers will go and see and enjoy for themselves.[7]

1. *AMERICAN REPUBLICAN* (West Chester, Penna.) March 21, 1854.
2. Ibid., June 27, 1854.
3. *REGISTER & EXAMINER* (West Chester, Penna.) Jan. 6, 1855.
4. *AMERICAN REPUBLICAN* (West Chester, Penna.) Dec. 9, 1856.
5. Ibid., Sept. 8, 1857.
6. *DAILY LOCAL NEWS* (West Chester, Penna.) March 4, 1886.
7. Ibid., Aug. 27, 1886.

CEDARCROFT, EAST MARLBORO TOWNSHIP

A newspaper mentions in 1860:

I have been to Oxford, and, if not a graduate, have at least obtained some honors. But I gorget, it is not that noted place whence theologians come forth with greater dignity, but a remote yet thriving borough in the southwest of this county. Nearly all the houses are of brick, of good size, some quite handsome, a bank, two or three churches, a seminary, and other schools, six or eight stores, one storeroom, the largest in the county of Chester. I learn much of the improvement is in anticipation of the Baltimore and Central Railroad soon being in operation this far. Passing after a long drive, through the intellectual town of Kennett Square your correspondent is fully warranted in certifying to the aforesaid appellation, in not being able to procure, in the whole array of stores, even a handful of crackers, wherewith to sustain his more material organization. Alas! my good friend from Old Chester has just removed. Bayard Taylor's house, (nearly finished) some distance north of town, is a rectangular building of plain brick, the corners faced with granite. In front is a square tower, five stories high, with a balcony around near the top, from which an extensive view is obtained in all directions. The building is without exterior ornament, and the style is much like a portion of Independence Hall, Philadelphia. The workmen are about finishing the interior. The cornices upon the ceilings, are very fine, that of the central hall being a rope-vine; that of the parlors, an oak vine or wreath with rich center pieces; whilst the hall separating these rooms, having a large window with a semicircular top, at the end of it, has a Grecian cornice around the ceiling, the perfection of beauty and chasteness of design. The walls look as if they would endure as long as brick and granite can keep company, and yet they will crumble and fall ere the name of Bayard Taylor shall cease to be.[1]

In 1879:

WHO WILL GET CEDARCROFT? A GREAT CHANCE OF SOMEONE

Mrs. Bayard Taylor does not find it desirable since the death of her husband to retain permanently so large a country place as Cedarcroft. It is accordingly offered for private sale, and an unusual opportunity is thus offered to any gentleman wishing an attractive country seat in the most beautiful part of Chester County, near Philadelphia. It would also be admirably adapted for a girls' boarding school or any similar institution.

The farm consists of about 150 acres, of which a large part is in a good state of cultivation. The woodlands are covered with a heavy growth of native forest trees, chiefly hickory, oak and chestnut. The house is a spacious brick structure, containing all modern improvements, with eleven fine rooms on the second and third floors, besides four rooms for servants and several store rooms. It is beautifully situated, so as to command a fine view of the woodland through which the driveway from the high road approaches it on the one side, and of over a quarter of a mile of lawn and meadows immediately in front. There are large piazzas, a green-house, an effective tower and a *porte-cochere*. The architectural effect of the house is exceedingly fine, and it was built in the most substantial manner by day's work under Mr. Taylor's personal supervision. Less than a year before he went to Germany, he had it carefully overhauled by a competent architect and put in a condition of thorough repair, so that as, he said himself, it was good for a century without much further expense. There, are, besides, a stable, carriage-house and workshop in the rear, with a farmhouse two stories high, a spring and dairy-house, two story gardner's house with small stable and small one story

house for a workman and his family. There is a fine orchard in good bearing condition, a large vineyard and cold grapery, a terraced garden and a small pond for ice supply.

The climate is considered extremely healthy, and the large number of people living to an advanced age is always noticed by strangers. The place is thirty-two miles southwest from Philadelphia by rail, and four or five miles less by the post roads. It is within one mile of the telegraph and railroad station of Kennett Square, on the Baltimore Central Railroad. . .[2]

In 1886, Benjamin Prince was quoted:

. . .I assisted in the erection of Bayard Taylor's residence from the commencement to the completion. It was named "Cedarcroft," I suppose, from the number of cedar trees upon the place. The bricks were burned on the property. Yes, I consider it a well planned and firmly constructed house. Bayard was not frequently on the spot while the building was in progress, but I think he showed considerable judgement in the expression of his views when he was present. His friend and traveling companion, Mr. Braisted, exercised most constant supervision over the work.[3]

---

1. *VILLAGE RECORD* (West Chester, Penna.) April 17, 1860.
2. *DAILY LOCAL NEWS* (West Chester, Penna.) Oct. 11, 1879.
3. Ibid., July 27, 1886.

LOCH AERIE, WEST WHITELAND TOWNSHIP

OUR GENTLEMAN FARMERS
No. XX

A visit to "Glen-Loch", the country seat of W. E. Lockwood, Esq., in Chester County — Description of one of the largest estates in Pennsylvania.

One of the beauty spots of Eastern Pennsylvania and the peer of any of the suburban homes and vast farms and resided on by prominent citizens of Philadelphia, along the line of the Pennsylvania Railroad, is "Glen-Loch," the country seat of Mr. William E. Lockwood, of the firm of W. E. & E. Dunbar Lockwood, manufacturers of patent folding boxes, envelopes, tage, etx., Nos. 251 & 253 South Third Street, Philadelphia, Pennsylvania.

"Glen-Lock" is a fraction over twenty-five miles from Philadelphia, five miles from West Chester, seven miles from Downingtown, and there is a large circle of railroad connections of main roads and branches for thirteen miles around. No homestead in Chester County is more charmingly situated than

"Glen-Loch", and the delightful natural location is enhanced by the artistic taste displayed by Mr. Lockwood in improving his large estate, and the practival scientific skill he has shown in providing his country house with every available comfort and convenience, and health giving arrangements. The estate is contiguous to the most beautiful portions of the lovely Chester Valley, and from the windows of the tall, massive, stone tower that surmounts the family mansion a scene of rural beauty spreads out in a broad panarama for over twenty miles around, such as the eye rarely gets an opportunity to feast itself upon. Through the courtesy of Mr. Lockwood the writer was not only enabled to enjoy the beautiful prospect from the tower, but was afforded an opportunity to learn something about the characteristics of the estate.

The mansion mentioned stands in the center of a splendid lawn of about six acres in extent, the surpassing beauty of which is due in part to the skill of Mr. Charles P. Miller, the Fairmount Park Landscape Artist. The mansion, which is one of the stateliest structures in Chester County, was built by Mr. Lockwood in 1865 from designs furnished by Addison Hutton, Architect. It is built of Pennyslvania blue marble and blue limestone quarried on the estate. It is of mixed architecture and combines the "German Schloss," the French Cottage orne, and English Swiss Villa styles. Only mention can be made in the limits of this article of the scientific knowledge displayed by Mr. Lockwood in the drainageand ventilating plans adopted by him in making the residence perfectly healthy, the exclusion of all foul air and gases and the presence of plenty of pure, fresh air in every room and an abundance of light. The cellar is perfectly dry, and the continued excellent health of Mr. Lockwood and all the members of the family is a proof of the true hygienic principles used in the construction of the building. The mansion has two stories and an alpine roof. The bay windows are provided with stained glass, and a feature is the spacious hall, from which runs upwards to the top floor a wide and massive stairway. There are several porches around the building commanding fine views, and so arranged as not to exclude the sunlight from the building. The rooms are all large and airy, and furnished in superior style. Burgular alarms in teh bedrooms connect with the residences of employees on the estate, and the heating is furnished by ordinary heaters and several low grates. There is hot and cold water in every room and plenty of bathing facilities. Under the tower is a large iron tank holding 900 gallons of water, and the water pipes are tapped thirty five feet below to supply fresh water to the lower part of the house. That the mansion stands on high ground may be known from the fact that water will run one way towards the Schuylkill and the other way towards Brandywine Creek, poured on the ground near the building. On the lawn and in front of the residence is a very pretty miniature lake, large enough for boating purposes. It has a stone embarkment around covered with creeping plants, and in the center stands a huge crane, a fine work of art, and a four inch pipe produces a spray that completely covers the crane with water. Near the lake is a handsome marble fountain imported by the late Vito Viti, and which cost $750.00. The springs that supply water for the lake and fountain and other purposes is at an elevation of one hundred feet and 2600 feet distant. The water is forced by gravity through two and three inch pipes, and runs 12,400 gallons in twenty four hours, and there is a constant supply.

The water supply of "Glen-Loch" is a peculiarity. It comes from a point south of the Lancaster Turnpike and Pennsylvania Railroad and from mica slate and flint rock, twenty five in number and at such elevation that 17,000 feet of pipe supplies the entire estate with water by the force of gravity. It can be carried twenty feet above the highest elevation where it is used, and the water is of the purest and softest kind. There are some twelve or fourteen other springs on the estate that yield hard water, but none of them are used to any extent. The thermometrical tests of these springs during hot weather vary from 52-65 degrees.

The "Glen-Loch" tract covers an extent of 684 acres of very superior land. There are four railroad stations on the estate, viz: Glen-Loch Station Pennsylvania R.R.; Woodland Station West Chester Branch Penna. R.R.; Swedesford Station on the Schuylkill Branch Penns Branch Penna. R.R., and the White-Horse Station on the Chester Valley branch of the Reading R.R. The 684 acres include the ground for railroad turnpike and public road purposes. The shape of the tract is irregular, but may be said to be bounded on the north by the Chester Valley Railroad; east and south by the Schuylkill and West Chester branches of the Penna. R.R., and the large tract of Mr. William Weightsman, of Powers and Weightman, and on the west by the large holdings of Mr. George Jacobs, Dr. Carey and others. The elevation extends in a straight line along the entire width of the Great Valley and from this elevation the entire view of the valley, which is thirty five miles long,, may be obtained, extending from Bridgeport and Norristown to its entrance into the Piqua or Small valley near Coatesville.

The estate was formerly a Welsh tract of 500

acres, and the title deeds say it was held on a lease from W. Penn to Peter Young and from Peter Young to Hugh Roberts, of whom President George B. Roberts of the Penna. R. R. is a lineal descendant. The tract has been subdivided and has been in the possession of General Persifor Frazer of the Revolution and also of the family of P. Frazer Smith. The purchase of the estate was made by Elon Dunbar, Mr. W. E. Lockwood's step-father, from estate of William Harmer, in 1849, and Mr. Lockwood from Mr. Dunbar in April 1863. When Mr. Dunbar purchased, there was 113 acres. Mr. Lockwood has been making purchases adjoining the original tract at different times and from 136 acres it has increased to 684 acres.

Mr. Lockwood states that the preservation of his health and that of his family was his main motive in becoming one of what are known as "Gentlemen Farmers", and now tips the beam at 185 pounds; he is satisfied that he has made an advantageous change from town to country.

The "Glen-Loch" acres have been analyzed by I. Slogett Brittain Esq. with the following results: Brown Rematite — pure metalic iron 50.67 sulphur none. Phosphorus 298. Protesquidoxide of Manganese 267. After iron ores come the blue marble and blue limestone quarries or Hornblende. There is a deposit of magnesia limestone for building purposes; also a deposit of sand for glass, and north of that is a deposit of "Kaolin" and an inferior quality of iron ore, and the summit of the north valley is sandstone.

Mr. Lockwood began to pay some attention to live stock in 1868, when he purchased twenty five head of Ayrshires, but about that time he was elected president of the Union Paper Collar Co. and had to reside in New York for ten years. He was thus forced to relinquish the raising of stock, but he secured the services of competent farmers who attended to what stock he required for domestic purposes. Mr. Lockwood intends to divide his tract into three small farms, consisting of the property south of the Penna. R R and will include twelve acres of woodland, which will be kept to preserve the water supply. Four hundred acres north of the Penna. R R will be retained as the homestead farms of two hundred acres each. On the western most tract is St. Paul's Episcopal Church erected in 1828 by the Rev. Dr. Levi Bull and which was improved in 1874 at the expense of $8000. A fine parsonage will be erected during the coming summer.

It is estimated that large portions of Mr. Lockwood's estate are worth $1000 an acre for mining purposes, and Mr. Lockwood argues that Farmers are the largest consumers of iron.

Mr. Lockwood has his own system of slushing and ventilation, and he claims that his plan of slushing will remove all solid matter whatever deposited that causes impurities. He studies his plan of ventilation for three years and his ventilation pipes are known as *"Lockwood's Gallons."*

A considerable portion of Glen-Loch is devoted to raising grain, and the regular orthodox system is pursued in grain planting and raising. A fine tennant house, a spacious stable, a gas house, two ice houses, and a number of other buildings are situated on the property.

The Pennsylvania Railroad cuts directly through Mr. Lockwood's estate, and the portion on the Lancaster avenue has a hemlock hedge and barbed wire fence. On the lawn are a number of rare trees, including ash, sycamores, European beech, blue spruce, American tulip poplar, weeping spruce, etc., etc., etc.

The estate is connected over the Pennsylvania Railroad by a number of bridges, one of which was built of iron cost $15,000. The railroad company has a water reservoir near Glen-Loch station that holds 250,000 gallons and water comes from Mr. Lockwood's estate.[1]

A newspaper mentions in 1877:

Wm. E. Lockwood, of Glenlock, has a telephone in his house; also one in the P.R.R. tower so that in case of invasion of his domicile by burglars or tramps, he can call the P.R.R. hands to his assistance. The Railroad Company also keep a police car on the siding there to lock up all loaders and tramps from in the vicinity. Mr. Lockwood also has a very complete "burglar alarm", which connects with every door and window in his house, and burrows his neighbor's "bull dogs" for outside alarm at night. Also he has a formidable array of repeating revolving and breech loading pistols and rifles and we understand he thinks of adding a gattling gun and jackass howitzer, and yet he retires to his little bed very uneasy as to his safety during the night. We should think the tramp would give his place a wide berth in their travels but through his influence they are gobbled up at the rate of a dozen per night in and about Glenloch.[2]

In 1935:

One of the most interesting houses in the Chester Valley is that of the late William E. Lockwood, at Glen Loch. It was built in the year 1865, with its towers and bull's-eye windows. William A. Stephenson, late of West Barnard Street, West Chester, was the boss stone mason, and the walls were well built. The architect was Addison Hutton, who, five years later, designed the first building for what is now State Teachers College. Mr. Hutton, as the story goes, was on his way to Glen Loch in response to a summons from Mr. Lockwood to consult with him in regard to the plans when he was told that Abraham Lincoln, President of the United States, had been shot. All the people were so shocked and horrified that there was no talk about house plans that day, and the dwelling was not erected until some months later. One of the art treasures in the home today is a painting of George Washington on horseback — a handsome piece of work which once was loaned to the late John Wanamaker, long ago, to be exhibited in his Market street window. [3]

1. *GERMANTOWN TELEGRAPH* (Philadelphia, Penna.) Oct. 12, 18??.
2. *DAILY LOCAL NEWS* (West Chester, Penna.) Oct. 19. 1877.
3. Ibid., May 1, 1936.

HOLY TRINITY PROTESTANT EPISCOPAL CHURCH, WEST CHESTER

A newspaper mentions in 1868:

New Church — Workmen have commenced digging the foundation for the new Episcopal church, at the corner of High and Union Sts., this Borough. It will be the largest building in the Borough.[1]

In 1869:

The new Episcopal church, West Chester, one of the largest buildings, perhaps, in the State, is rapidly approaching completion. The interior is highly ornamented, and everything about it is of the substantial order.[2]

In 1871:

A TOWER: — The Episcopal congragation of this borough have begun the erection of a large and beautiful tower to their church. It is destined to be 150 feet high and built cheifly of Serpentine stone. It bids fair to be a very handsome addition.[3]

In 1874:

NEW FURNACE — A new and additional furnace has lately been placed in the basement of the Church of the Holy Trinity in this place, by which means that congregation will be kept comfortable during the coming winter. This will be cheering news to those who have heretofore complained of the too cool atmosphere of this church.[4]

In 1886:

The New Rectory — We understand that it has been virtaully decided to purchase 40 or 60 feet of the Buckwalter lot at the corner of Union and High streets, fronting on High. Upon this, after all the necessary agreements have been signed, a rectory will be built, which will be in keeping with the

architectural beauty of the church buildings across the way. It will be built this fall, and the architect will be the rector, Rev. John Bolton.[5]

The Protestant Episcopal Parsonage — Rapid progress is being made in the work of excavating for the cellar of the Protestant Episcopal parsonage to be erected on the newly pruchased lot at the corner of Union and High streets, West Chester. It is probable that part of the work will be completed today. The dirt is being used for filling in around the rising walls of the public school building nearby. It appears that some very erroneous impressions have gone abroad as to the character of the building that is under contract as a parsonage. We are informed that is is to be a plain brick structure 35 x 42 feet, two stories and an attic. There will be no hard wood finish as one report has stated. The work will be pushed as rapidly as possible to completion.[6]

In 1887:

Stained Glass — On Saturday last, Rev. John Bolton had placed in the front doors of the parsonage where he lives on South High street two very handsome glass panels which he stained and burned when a young man working at the profession of an architect. They are as bright and beautiful as the day they were made, and in speaking of them to a friend Mr. Bolton said: "They will be just the same if they are kept a thousand years. I have myself seen specimens of glass prepared in the same way that were over 500 years old and not affected in the least by the lapse of time.[7]

In 1888:

Memorial Windows — On the east and west sides of the unfinished tower at the Church of the Holy Trinity this borough, are left spaces for windows to light up the entrance into the church, but as yet they ahve not been closed in. The lower portion of the tower is to be completed at once and used as another entrance to the body of the church. . . S,8

In 1889:

The tower of the Episcopal Church, now building, has a history of faith and charity not to be forgotten. The first donation was $500 by the late Mr. John Tweddle, one of the originators and first Vestrymen of the church. This, with other contributions, especially by the late Mr. Isaac Lea and family, was used in laying the foundations in 1872. Mrs. Ebbs, a munificent subscriber to the church at its erection, bequeathed $500 for the building of the tower, which was lost. Another lady who has been a great benefactor of the church, supplied the means by which it was carried to its present height. Two members of the Tweddle family and the lady alluded to and Mr. James C. Brooks finished it last year at the main entrance to the church; memorial windows being placed in it to the late Mrs. Farley, the late Mrs. W. W. Jefferis, the late Mr. B. F. Pyle and to the late Mr. Wm. McCormick. It is now being completed by the bequest of $5000 from the late James Neely, under the direction of the accomplished architect, Mr. T. Roney Williamson.

It is to be faced with serpentine stone and will be 113 feet from the ground to the top of the vane. At the height of 60 feet it is proposed to place a set of chimes, consisting of ten bells. A chime with a peal in a set of musical bells attuned to each other so as to play tunes to call to worship, to peal for marriages and to toll at funerals. There is nothing sweeter than the music of a good chime of bells floating out upon the stillness of the evening air, attuning the thoughts to higher things, to the praise of God; there is nothing gayer than a marriage peal, or more solemn than the deep reminder of the mortality of us all. A chime is a public benefaction, serving alike for the call to worship and carrying the charm of music into the sick chamber, the cabin of the poor and to the cell of the prisoner; like the birds of the air offering to heaven a song of gratitude and praise. Some one said: "Let me make the music of a people and I will form their character." Mr. Bolton is endeavoring to raise the necessary funds by asking public-spirited individuals to give for the bells. He has already secured half the necessary funds. $150 will pay for a bell.[9]

The stone-work of the Protestant Episcopal tower, on South High street, was finished yesterday.[10]

In 1890:

Arc Lights For the Holy Trinity — Heretofore there have been 1000 incandescent electric light power in the Church of the Holy Trinity. It is expected that by next Sunday the Electric Light Company will have taken the incandescent lights out and will have substituted for them four large arc lights, as per order of the Vestry at a recent meeting.[11]

1. *JEFFERSONIAN* (West Chester, Penna.) March 21, 1868.
2. Ibid., Oct. 2, 1869.
3. Ibid., Oct. 14, 1871.
4. *DAILY LOCAL NEWS*, (West Chester, Penna.) Nov. 14, 1874.
5. Ibid., July 3, 1886.
6. Ibid., July 14, 1886.
7. Ibid., July 18, 1887.
8. Ibid., Oct. 29, 1888.
9. Ibid., Sept. 10, 1889.
10. Ibid., Dec. 14, 1889.
11. Ibid., Aug. 7, 1890.

FOUNTAIN, WEST CHESTER

This fountain is described in a newspaper in 1869:

DRINKING FOUNTAIN IN WEST CHESTER — We have been shown the design for the Drinking Fountain, to be erected on High street, in front of the Court House, in this Borough. It will be erected close to the curb, about half-way between the corner of High and Market streets and the gate leading into the Court House yard. Already an opening has been made in the pavement to receive it, and Messrs. Garrett & Jones, Marble Manufacturers, West Chester, are now busily at work upon it, and expect to complete it in a manner creditable to their establishment in about two weeks. It is being made from Chester county marble—dove color—from the quarries of the Messrs. Thomas Brothers, West Whiteland. The design, gotten up by Rev. John Bolton, is to represent Rock-Work; it will have a basin facing the pavement for the use of individuals, and on the side fronting the street there will be a trough for watering horses, immediately beneath which and close to the ground will be another basin or trough, at which thirsty and panting 'Carlo" and other members of the canine family can stop and quench their thirst. The whole will be surmounted by a neat ornament, and when complete will be about eight feet in height, and will cost in the neighborhood of $350. The inscriptions have not yet been decided on. The idea of erecting a public fountain in West Chester originated with Mrs. John Hickman, who had been kindly assisted in the laudable work by other ladies of our Borough, all of whom are certainly entitled to much praise, and they will no doubt receive the heartfelt thanks of many a weary traveler as he refreshes himself with a cold drink of water. Aside from its usefulness it will be a pretty ornament to our town.

Since the above was put in type we understand the following inscription will be put on the fountain:

Thirsty traveler, see in Me
An emblem of true charity;
My life I give,
That you may live—
And I've a fresh supple from Heaven,
For every cup of water given.[1]

In 1879 a newspaper mentions:
ALTERING THE FOUNTAIN — The cross and circle that formerly adorned the top of the fountain in front of the Court House became broken last winter from some cause. Workmen are engaged in placing upon it a round urn.[2]

In 1881:
Broke the Fountain — A young lad who was playing in front of the Court House last evening about 7 o'clock got upon the fountain and accidentally pulled the top off and broke the marble ball, both the boy and ball falling to the ground together.[3]

In 1882:

> Major D. Jones, marble cutter, has been making some improvements to the marble fountain in front of the Court House, which have been completed, and the fountain is now being re-erected.[4]

In 1960:

> A landmark is missing from in front of the county Court House in West Chester. Last week the marble drinking fountain for horses, on the west side of the street, near High, was finally moved. It is now on the grounds of the Townsend House on N. Matlack st. There it will ultimately become an ornamental addition to the formal garden which lies behind the historic home. The fountain stood on High st. since 1860. It had been about 50 years, however, since it was used for its original purpose of watering horses. As a matter of fact, its supply of water had been cut off for more than a quarter of a century. About the only incident attendant upon its removal was the finding of an 1800 penny by the workmen filling in the hole from which the base of the fountain was removed. For what it is worth, Old Ed was told, the penny too, was turned over to the Chester County Historical Society.[5]

1. *VILLAGE RECORD* (West Chester, Penna.) July 27, 1869.
2. *DAILY LOCAL NEWS* (West Chester, Penna.) July 2, 1879.
3. Ibid., May 28, 1881.
4. Ibid., May 20, 1882.
5. Ibid., Oct. 10, 1960.

NORMAL SCHOOL, WEST CHESTER

A newspaper mentions in 1870:

> NORMAL SCHOOL — Every body about West Chester is interested in the erection of the Normal School. A good deal has been said about the selection of the site. Some like it, others do not. We like the idea of its location in West Chester; and just at this point our likes and dislikes are at a stand. The contract for its erection has been awarded to the lowest bidder; we hope he may be the best.
>
> Mr. Addison Hutton, of Philadelphia, is the architect. We shall know more about him when the building is up. The general idea or plan of the building is furnished of course by the committee; the minutia by the architect.
>
> The structure, as determined upon, will have a total front of one hundred and fifty feet, four stories high, with the French roof. The central building will be forty-six feet front and one hundred and twelve deep, with two wings, each fifty-two feet front by forty-four deep. The first story will be twelve feet high; the second story of the central building

fourteen feet, and of the wings eleven feet; and the fourth nine feet and a half — clear of the floors and ceilings. The cellar will be eight feet clear in height. All the exterior walls of the building from the first floor line to the roof, will be faced with serpentine stone. The base of the building, from the ground to the line of the first floor, will be faced with white marble. The steps, window and door sills, are all to be of white marble. The roofs are all to be boarded over closely, by the curved parts for slate, and the flat parts for tin. The Act of the Legislature requires that one of the rooms shall be large enough to seat one thousand persons. This room is sixty by forty-two feet, with gallery on three sides—the ceiling twenty-six feet in the clear.

> Here is the general outline, and the ground work of a handsome edifice; and plenty of room for a bungler to spoil.

> The ground has been staked off, and work of excavation for cellar commended. It is to be finished by the last of September, 1871, unless the building committee ask a delay of one year. The building stone comes from the Birmingham quarries, and B. J. Roberts will be the superintendent.

> It will be a good thing for the Borough when finished.[1]

> THE NORMAL SCHOOL — The workmen are very busy at work on the Normal School in this Borough, and they are making rapid headway with the foundations. The force employed consists of about 40 men, thirteen of them are Masons. Between 30 and 40 horses in hauling. The foundation, it is said, will be ready in about three weeks for the first tier of joists. The Governor and State Superintendent, and other prominent men are expected to be present at the laying of the corner stone.[2]

> NORMAL SCHOOL — The ceremony of laying the corner stone of the Normal School House, in this Borough, took place on Wednesday last. Governor Geary and Ex-Governor Pollock were not present, as expected, and the ceremonies devolved on Dr. Worthington, Professor Wickersham — (by the way, what a small amount it takes to make a professor), Revs. Mr. Moore and John Bolton. It didn't strike very deep. We hope the School may be a success to the Borough in a pecuniary point.[3]

> NORMAL SCHOOL — The new Normal School Building in our Borough, is now in course of roofing. It has quite an imposing appearance, and will be quite an ornament to the Borough.[4]

In 1871:

> NORMAL SCHOOL — A committee of nine appointed by the Governor, to examine the new Normal School building in West Chester, met on Wednesday

the 22nd for the purpose. Six of the committee were present, namely Mr. Wickersham, State Superintendent, Senator Turner, John W. Forney, Mr. Baker, Superintendent of Common Schools of Delaware, Mr. Eastburn, do., of Bucks, and Mr*Maris of Chester. A thorough examination of the building was made from cellar to roof, and both admiration and satisfaction expressed.

The capacity of the building is worthy of note. The entire building contains over one hundred rooms, all of which are well ventilated, and roomy; a large dining room chapel or lecture room capable of holding, we should judge, fifteen hundred people; it is built of Serpentine and presents a handsome substantial and ornamental appearance, and reflects credit upon the workmen and contractors. There may be room for criticism as to taste and symmetry, but we would not like to be called upon to improve it. [5]

1. *JEFFERSONIAN* (West Chester, Penna.) July 16, 1870.
2. Ibid., Aug. 6, 1870.
3. Ibid., Sept. 19, 1870.
4. Ibid., Dec. 3, 1870.
5. Ibid., Feb. 25, 1871.

MONAGHAN HOUSE PLANS, WEST CHESTER

The architect of this house, built in 1872,[1] was Addison Hutton.[2]

Specifications

Of the workmanship and materials required in the erection of a dwelling house on Miner St., West Chester, Penna. for R. E. Monaghan Esqr.

Description

To be a frame structure with foundations of Stone and roofed with slate. Two Storeys high with cellar and finished attic story.

Dimensions

Main Building 38'.0" x 32'.0" exterior measurement of frame.

Back Building 26'.0" x 16'.0" — same measurement.

Back Porch &c. 14'.6" x 7'.0".

Veranda to front and flanks of main building 9'.0" wide.

Heights

Cellar	7'.0" in the clear
1st Storey main building	11'.0" in the clear
2nd Storey main building	10'.0" in the clear
Attic Storey main building	8'.6" in the clear
1st Storey back building	8'.6" in the clear
2nd Storey back building	8'.6" in the clear

And the pitch of the roofs as shown by the drawings. Refer also to the drawings for further particulars of the arrangement of the Rooms, Stairs, Doors.

Excavations

Excavate beneath the entire area of the building to a depth of 4'.6" below the established grade first removing and piling the top soil for future use.

Sink for an ice vault 15'.0" x 15'.0" adjoining the kitchen cellar to a depth of 6'.0" below cellar bottom also for a cess-pool 6 feet diam. and at least 15 feet deep — Excavate cellar-way and for steps to ice-vault. Also for all peirs and foundations for porch and verandas and all wall trenches 6 in. below cellar bottom.

Clear up and cart away all the earth from the excavations, and all rubbish accumulating from waste material of construction.

Stone work

All the walls indicated on the plans by the blur tint will be constructed with the best quarry building Stone laid on their broadest beds and thoroughly bedded in mortar and of the thicknesses figured thereon.

All the mortar for the stone work will be composed of the best fresh lime and sharp sand or screened gravel.

Cut Stone

Provide and set a flag stone 2'.6" x 1'.6" x 4" on each pier of the veranda to receive the iron posts. Also flag steps for the cellar entrance — and to ice-vault from the cellar.

Brick work

Construct flues as indicated on the plans of sound square well burned brikcs — parged throughout their entire heights and topped out above the roof with pressed bricks, to receive the Terracotta chimney tops. The greatest attention will be paid to making secure from fire.

Also turn an arch of two 4-inch rings over the ice vault.

All the mortar for the brickwork will be composed of the best fresh lime and sharp sand.

Carpenter's work and Lumber

Provide for the frame work

Sills around the entire building	6" x 8"
Wall plates the entire building	6" x 4"
Corner post for every angle	6" x 6"
Girders beneath hall partitions	9" x 12"
Girders beneath Sliding doors	6" x 12"
Studding for Main Building	3" x 6"
Studding for Back Building	3" x 4"
Joist for 1st and 2nd floors and veranda	3" x 10"
Joist for Back Building, and 3rd floor front Build	3" x 9"
Collar beams and rafters	3" x 5"
All other Studding, ceiling joist and rafters for veranda for back porch	3" x 4"

All the above to be Hemlock wood.

The studding will be framed into the sills and plates — bottom and top — spaced 16 inches mid. to mid. corner posts and window studs pinned top and bottom. All 6" x 6" posts will have angle braces tenoned and pinned. Frame all cripples — and fill in studs under and over the window frames.

The joists of the first floor will rest on the sills, those of the main building will be framed into the middle girders. The 2nd and 3rd teirs of joists will be secured together by planks spiked on their sides over their bearing on the hall partitions, and notched and spiked on bearers at their outer ends.

All the joists throughout placed 16 inches from mid. to mid. and where the span exceeds 8 feet, they will have a course of lattice bridging through the middle. Make all requisite framings for stairways, flues and hearth in the parlor double the trimmer wherever more than two tail joist are required.

The rafters will be notched and spiked on the wall plate. Secured and supported at the top by the partition studding to prevent side thrust on the walls — spaced 2 feet from mid. to mid. closely sheathed over with 1-inch boards to receive the slate roofing. All the joists and rafters to be of Hemlock wood.

Weather-boarding

Sheathe the entire surface of the exterior walls with two thicknesses of cane-fibre-felt secured by a shingle lath nailed vertically on each studding to this lath will be nailed 3/4-inch rebated mill-worked, clear, well-seasoned, white prime weather-boards, one nail to each stud in each board.

Cornices

The cornices including that of veranda will be constructed in accordance with the design and detail drawings, of clear, well-seasoned white pine wood, all nearly and smoothly cleaned off for painting.

Floors

All the floor boards for the 1st and 2nd floors will be narrow, mill-worked, well-seasoned white-yellow pine boards, securely secret nailed to the joists, and afterwards, smoothed off. Those for the 1st floor and veranda to be 1¼ inches thick. The attic Storey will be floored with narrow, seasoned white pine boards secret nailed, and smoothed off. The veranda floor to be yellow pine.

Fill the joints of the veranda floor with white lead paint in laying it.

Floor the vestibule with encaustic tiles of neat patterns laid in the best manner. The counter floor to be sunk 3" and filled in with best mortar.

Windows

All the window frames for the principal storeys of the main building will be made to receive 1¾" sash, double hung with sham-axle pullies, patent cord and weights. All the other window frames to be made in the same manner. For sash, 1-3/8" thick.

Nine windows opening on the veranda will be finished to the floor, the lower sash to fly up in the treact. All the windows to have an exterior finish of 1½ x 6 inches. All the lumber for the frames, sash and exterior finish to be white pine thoroughly seasoned; for the sash and finish to be clear.

Construct the dormers and Bay window in accordance with the design and detail drawings.

Doors

All the exterior door frames will be made with 2-inch pine plank and (except back-kitchen door) to have headlight over exterior, finish the same as the windows. Case all the inside doorways with 1-inch white pine plank, securely fastened to the studding with hinge blocks and rebate strips nailed on.

The front doors will be in two leaves 2¼ inches thick — in two thicknesses — paneled and boldly boulded. The vestibule doors in two leaves 2 inches thick, paneled and moulded below the lock rail and glazed above; also to have head light over.

These doors to be hung with 5" x 5" butts and secured with 6-inch mortice rebate locks and French bolts bottom and top. All the furniture for them to be copper bronze.

The doors between the parlor and library will be arched and will be 2¼ inches thick, paneled and moulded on both sides, hung in the tract with 5-inch shieves to run on iron warps and secured with the best sliding door locks with countersunk handles. Provide all the requisite guides and stops to make them complete. Arch finish at bay window.

All the other doors of passage for the first floor of main building to be 1¾ inches thick, 6-panel moulded on both sides, hung with 4" x 4" butts, three to each door and secured with 4-inch mortise locks.

All the other doors to be 1½ inches thick, 6-panel moulded on both sides (except for closets, which will be moulded on one side only) hung with 3½" x 3½" butts and secure with 4-inch mortise locks.

All the furniture for these doors to be white porcelain and the wood for all the doors will be of the best clear white pine thoroughly seasoned, interior doors to be finished for staining and varnishing.

Shutters

All the windows of the first story, except bay, and the front and flanks of the second storey of the main building, will have outside shutters. Those of the 1st storey to be 1½" thick, paneled and moulded on both sides, hung with parliament butts and secured with galvanized shutter bolts, two to each of the fly-head windows. Those of the 2nd storey will be 1½" thick, venitian rolling slats hung and secured as those of the first story.

The Bay window will have inside venitian blinds 1-inch thick, in four folds, cut at the meeting rail of the sash to fold into boxes formed in the jambs, hung and secured with copper bronze hinges and fastenings.

All the wood for the shutters will be white pine, clear and well-seasoned. The shutters for the bay windows will be finished for staining and varnishing.

Stairways

The main stair from first to third floor will have 3" x 12" carriages, three to the going, firmly secured to the floors and landings. The steps will be 1-3/8" thick, moulded, grooved tongued and blocked to the risers and let into the wall string.

The first newel will be 7 inches, those at the landings 5 inches square, moulded and chambered, the rail 3½" x 5" moulded, close string boltly moulded 2½-inch turned balusters. The newel rail and mouldings of string, will be walnut wood; the steps, risers and balusters and string will be ash wood, all thoroughly seasoned and finished for oiling.

The back stairs to 2nd story and cellar will be constructed in the usual manner, with yellow pine treads and white pine risers.

Veranda

The posts will be cast iron, two post together as shown by the design, and to rest on a stone sill at the floor with a bar to carry the floor beams and shouldered to receive the plate.

The floor joists will rest on walls be framed into bearers at each of the posts. These bearers will be framed into the sills of the main building. The ceiling joists will be secured to the studding of main building and will form the outlookers for the cornice. Frame rafters and board over the roof closely for tinning.

The gutter will be formed by the sheathing.

Ceil with narrow well seasoned mill-worked white pine boards, with beaded pannels made with mouldings and to have a moulding in the angle of the plate.

Enclose beneath the veranda with paneling and perforated work as shown.

Exterior Steps

All exterior steps will be constructed with yellow pine wood with good strong carriages, supported on stone foundations. Steps 1½" thick, nosed and moulded and securely nailed to carriages and risers.

Roofs

The Roof of the main building and kitchen to be overlaid with the best Chapman's No. 1 Slates laid on felt and secured with 4 D. nails boiled in oil.

Variagated with best Vermont green Slates.

Tin work

The roof of the veranda, bay-window and back porch, all the valleys gutters, ridges and conductors and the flashings of chimneys Dormers, and connection of kitchen with main building will be of the best I.C. charcoal tin put on in the best manner, painted on both sides, the upper side will have two coats.

Provide tin flues 5" x 12" for parlor, library, halls and dining room.

Interior

Fit up all the closets as shown on the drawings with shelves and wardrobes hooks as directed. The pantry will have shelving on one side with doors to one set of shelving and drawers beneath.

Bath-rooms

The floor of the bath room in the main building will be laid alternate walnut & ash and wainscoted to a height of three feet with alternate ash and walnut narrow white pine mill-worked boards with beaded joints and moulded walnut capping. The water closet, wash basin and bath tubs will be cased with white pine wood — all finished for oiling and painting.

The other bath-room will be fitted up in like manner with yellow pine finished for oiling.

Dressings

The wash boards throughout the first floor of the main building and second storey of hall will be 10 inches high including 2½ inch sub. and 2½ inch top moulding. The dressings of the doors and windows of the same will be 1½" x 6" chamfered and reeded.

The wash boards of the chambers will be 8 inches high including 2 inch sub and 2 inch top moulding. The dressings for these rooms will be 1¼" x 4" moulded.

The kitchesn and rooms over will have 6-inch washboards including 1½-inch sub and moulding worked on with 4-inch moulded dressings to the doors and windows. Finish the Attic storye with 5-inch wash boards moulded and no sub. dress the openings with 3-inch mouldings.

Plastering

All the walls and ceilings throughout to have two coats of brown mortar and one of white; in the parlor, library and halls to be finished in sand-hard for painting. The laths to be of good quality free from bark and rot and securely nailed on.

Run cornices of 14 inches girt in parlor dining room, library and 12-inch girt in halls. Provide center pieces for parlor library and dining room to cost $2.00 each.

All the mortar for the plastering will be composed of the best fresh lime and sharp sand thoroughly mixed with best slaughter hair.

Painting and Glazing

All the interior wood work (except the doors, bay-window blinds and small bath room fitting, and hard wood work), and all the exterior including the iron posts of the veranda will receive three coats of pure white lead and linseed oil — boiled and of such tints as may be directed. All the interior doors, the blinds of the bay window and fitting up of water closet to have a coat of light stain and two coats of varnish. The hard wood will receive three coats of linseed oil.

The glass for the vestibule doors and the head light for these and the front doors will be French plate of best quality. All the glass for the windows and other head lights will be of the best American manufacture all bedded, bradded and back-puttied and cleaned off; that of the first story of main building will be double thick.

Mantles

Provide and set up two marble or enameled slate mantels, one in dining room and one in the parlor, of selected pattern, to cost $125.00 each.

The parlor to have a slate hearth.

Plumbing and Gas-fitting

The water will be introduced to the following:

To Two tinned-copper lined Philadelphia made bath tubs of New York pattern, supply of hot and cold water, 1¼ inch waste and in large room silver plated fixtures.

To two best pan pattern water closets with 4-inch cast iron soil pipes leading to main 6" terra-cotta drain beneath the cellar floow, and extended to cess-pool near stable.

To a soap-stone sink in the kitchen with skirting and drip board with supply of hot and cold water, large waste and brass fixtures. To a tinned-copper sink in the pantry, supply of hot and cold water, large waste and brass fixtures.

To a circulating coiler placed in the bathroom, with copper connections to water back of cook in stove in the kitchen.

Gas-pipe

Conceal in the walls and ceilings gas pipes of sufficient size to supply the following burners, all proved and prepared to connect with the meter and burners:

To one Harp light in the hall
To two 4-light chandeliers in parlor and Library
To one 2-light Bracket in each parlor and library
To one 3-light Chandelier in dining room
To one 1-light Bracket in each kitchen and the pantry

To one 2-light Toilet in each front chamber
To one 1-light Bracket in each of the other chambers
To one 1-light Bracket in the Dewing room and passage
To one 1-light Bracket in the 2nd story hall
To one 1-light Bracket in the kitchen cellar

Miscellaneous Items

Provide and set Terra-cotta chimney tops of approved pattern.

Provide and set our Baltimore parlor stove with all the requisite dampers flues and summer pieces.

Put up a half-inch copper cable lightning rod in the best manner.

Put screens of close wire work to all the cellar windows. Fit up fins &c. for coal in cellar.

Heating

Put a Reynolds heater in brick work in the cellar. Provide cold-air supply Smoke flue, hot-air connections, and registers complete.[3]

1. Ms. West Chester Streets, Minor, Chester County Historical Society (West Chester, Penna.)
2. *JEFFERSONIAN* (West Chester, Penna.) July 20, 1872.
3. Ms., Chester County Historical Society (West Chester, Penna.)

Architectural Drawings
of
Historic Buildings

in

Southeastern Pennsylvania

prepared by the office

of

John D. Milner, AIA, Architect
National Heritage Corporation
West Chester, Pennsylvania

Prepared in conjunction with the recording and restoration of certain buildings in southeastern Pennsylvania, these architectural drawings serve as a visual record of a stylistic, cultural and temporal cross section of the region's residential architecture of the late seventeenth, eighteenth and early nineteenth centuries. The photographs are by George Eisenman, James L. Dillon & Co., Inc.

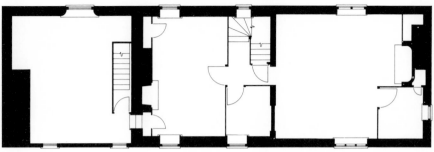

Second Floor Plan

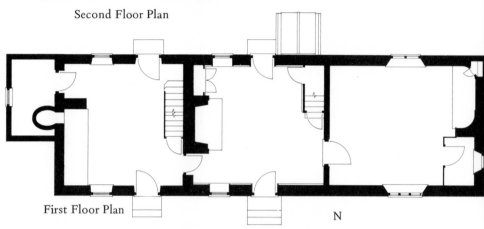

First Floor Plan   N

Thomas Massey House
Lawrence Road, Broomall, Delaware County, Pennsylvania
Owner: The Township of Marple
Delineator: Stuart MacDonald

The Massey House was constructed in four distinct sections
as follows: brick (c. 1696); center stone (c. 1730); end
stone, first floor (c. 1730) and end stone, second floor -
partially frame (c. 1860). The building represents a
rare combination of three centuries of modest residential
architecture and, as such, has unique interpretative value.

Plate 1

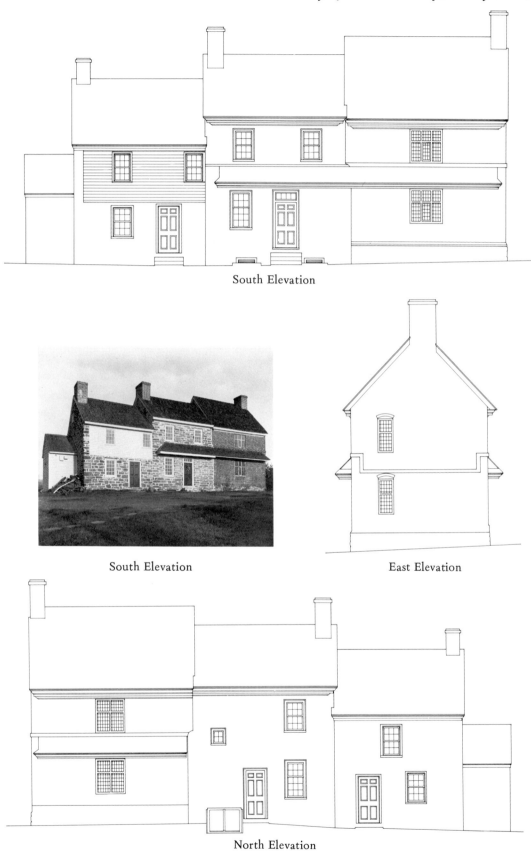

South Elevation

South Elevation

East Elevation

North Elevation

Plate No. 1 (continued)

375

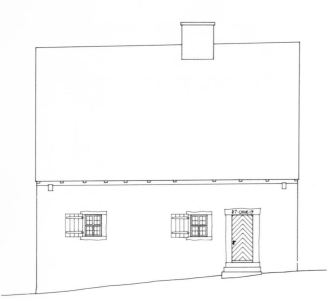

South Elevation

East Elevation

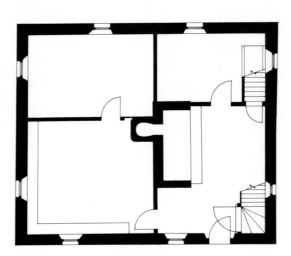

N

First Floor Plan

Hans Herr House
Willow Street, Lancaster County, Pennsylvania
Owner: Lancaster Mennonite Conference Historical Society
Delineator: Jeffrey C. Bourke

Built in 1719 as a residence and Mennonite Meeting House, this primitive stone building is one of the earliest surviving structures of Germanic origin in the country. Erected by emigrants from Switzerland and the Palatinate region of Germany, the house contains many details reflecting the European traditions of its builders.

Plate No. 2

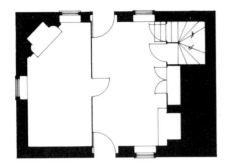

First Floor Plan

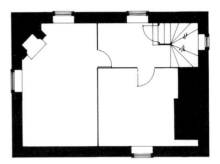

Second Floor Plan

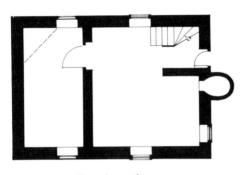

Cellar Floor Plan

View From Southwest

N

John Chad House
Route 100, Chadds Ford, Delaware County, Pennsylvania
Owner: The Chadds Ford Historical Society
Delineator: John T. Parks

Built about 1720, this small stone "bank house" was the home of John Chad, the originator of the ferry service crossing the Brandywine River in Chadds Ford. It is one of a group of significant buildings surviving in the area of the Revolutionary Battle of the Brandywine.

Plate No. 3

South Elevation

East Elevation

View from the Southeast

Plate No. 3 (continued)

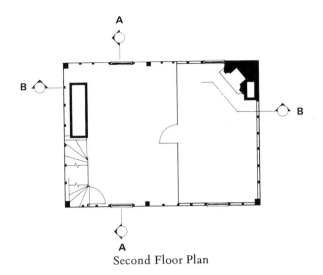

Second Floor Plan

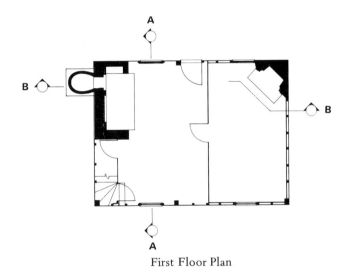

First Floor Plan

N

Mendenhall-Peeling House
Original Location: Route 1, Concordville, Delaware County,
      Pennsylvania
New Location: Route 401, Malvern, Chester County, Pennsylvania
Owner: Chester County Historical Society
Delineator: Michael F. Lynch

Probably constructed during the third decade of the eighteenth century, this building is a rare and extremely fine example of early frame construction in southeastern Pennsylvania. Although construction in wood was prevalent during the seventeenth and eighteenth centuries, few buildings of this type and style have survived.

Plate No. 4

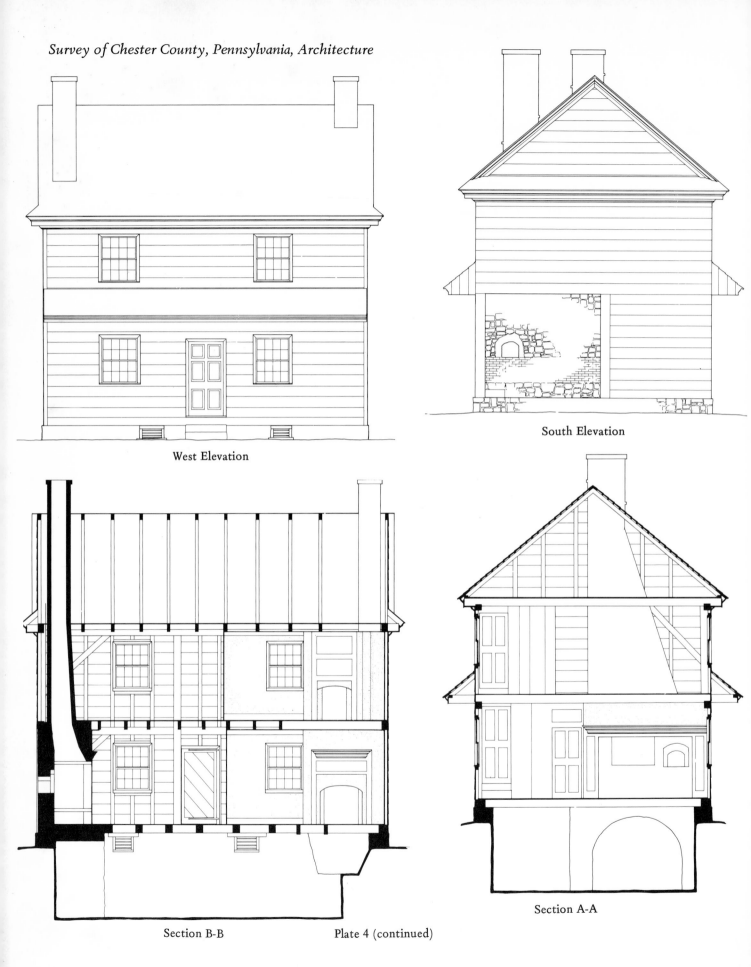

West Elevation

South Elevation

Section B-B   Plate 4 (continued)

Section A-A

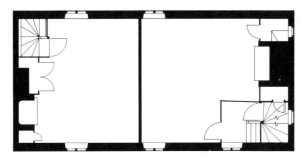

Second Floor Plan

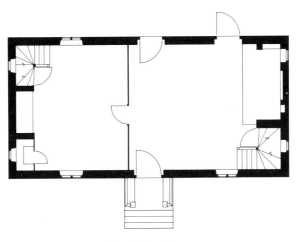

First Floor Plan

Barns Brinton House
Route 1, Pennsbury Township, Chester County, Pennsylvania
Owner: Chadds Ford Historical Society
Delineator: Stuart MacDonald

Built in the 1720's by William Barns, this fine early red brick building served as a combination tavern-residence on the Great Road to Nottingham. The floor plans are clearly divided by central partitions into a "public area" and a "private area". Most of the building's extraordinary architectural details have survived intact including Flemish bond brickwork (on the two principal elevations), elaborate woodwork and wrought iron hardware.

Plate No. 5

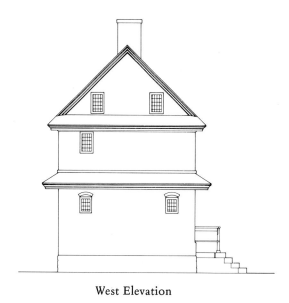

West Elevation

South Elevation

Plate No. 5 (continued)

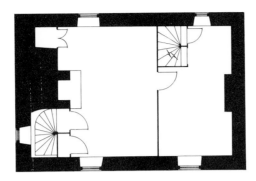

Second Floor Plan

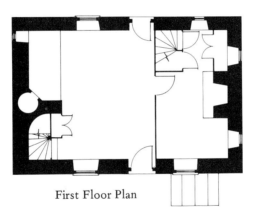

First Floor Plan

General Varnum's Quarters (Edwards-Stephens House)
Valley Forge State Park, Chester County, Pennsylvania
Owner: Commonwealth of Pennsylvania
Delineator: James L. Mullahy

Built before 1736 by one of the Welsh-Baptist settlers in
the Great Valley, this small stone building is representative
of the transitional "hall and parlor" house of the
southeastern Pennsylvania region. Probably the oldest
surviving structure in the Park, this house served as the
quarters for the famous general from Rhode Island during
Washington's encampment at Valley Forge during the
winter of 1777-78.

Plate No. 6

East Elevation

South Elevation

Plate No. 6 (continued)

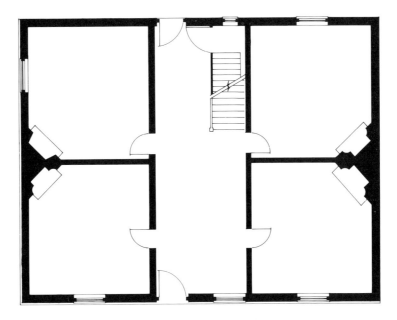

First Floor Plan

N

Primitive Hall
Chatham, Chester County, Pennsylvania
Owner: Primitive Hall Foundation
Delineator: John T. Parks

Built in 1738 by Joseph Pennock, member of the Assembly
and famous land holder of the eighteenth century, this
building stands without peers as an example of a house on
the grand scale built in the hinterland in the period prior to
1745. Its significant architectural features include fine
Flemish bond brickwork, a deep plaster cove exterior
cornice, wide central hallway on each of two floors
(flanked by two rooms on each side) and woodwork of
simple but bold design.

Plate No. 7

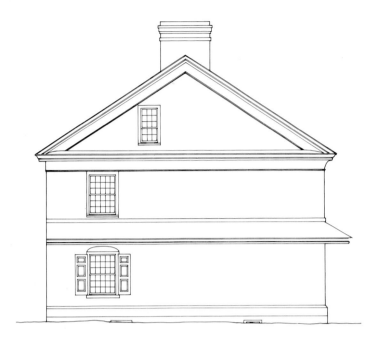

West Elevation

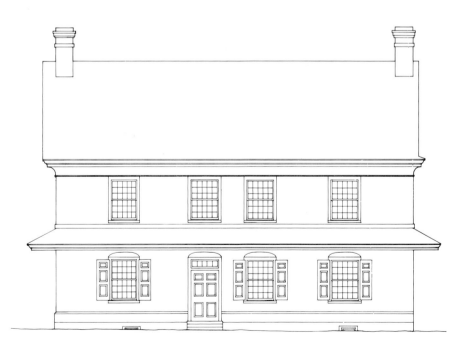

South Elevation

Plate No. 7 (continued)

Central Hall — Second Floor

View from the Southwest

Central Hall — First Floor

Southeast Room — Second Floor

Plate No. 7 (continued)

New Addition

Courtyard

Dilworthtown Inn
Dilworthtown, Chester County, Pennsylvania
Owner: Dilworthtown Inn, Inc., Timothy W. McCarthy,
    Innkeeper
Delineator: John T. Parks

Built during the 1750's as an inn on the important road connecting Wilmington, Delaware and West Chester, Pennsylvania, the Dilworthtown Inn served in that capacity for two centuries. The building was restored, with additions, in 1972 to serve as a restaurant.

Plate No. 8

South Elevation

View from the Southwest

View from the Northwest

Plate No. 8 (continued)

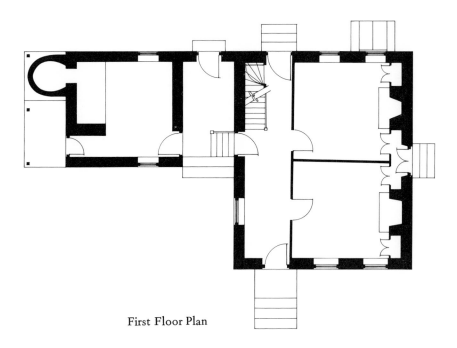

First Floor Plan

General Washington's Headquarters (The Isaac Potts House)
Valley Forge State Park, Chester County, Pennsylvania
Owner: Commonwealth of Pennsylvania
Delineator: James L. Mullahy

Constructed just prior to the Revolution as a country residence for Isaac Potts, one of the heirs of John Potts of Pottsgrove, this fine stone building bears stylistic similarities to contemporary residences in Germantown. Because it served as General Washington's headquarters during the winter encampment of 1777-78, the structure has been the object of extensive study and a series of restoration efforts over a period of 100 years.

Plate No. 9

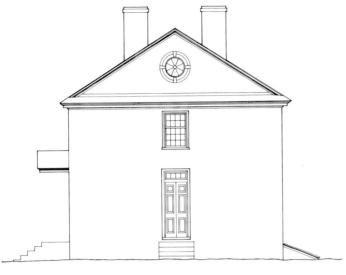

South Elevation

West Elevation

Plate No. 9 (continued)

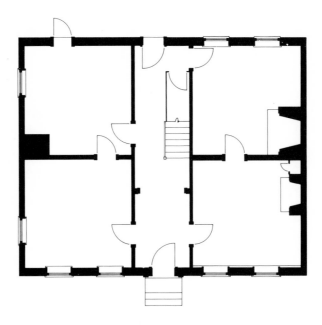

First Floor Plan

John Sebastian Goundie House
Main Street, Bethlehem, Northampton County, Pennsylvania
Owner: Historic Bethlehem, Inc.
Delineator: Stuart MacDonald

This fine brick townhouse was constructed in 1810 as the residence of John Sebastian Goundie, a prominent brewer in Bethlehem. One unique architectural feature is the stucco which covers the exterior stone foundation and is scored and painted red to simulate brickwork.

Plate No. 10

East Elevation

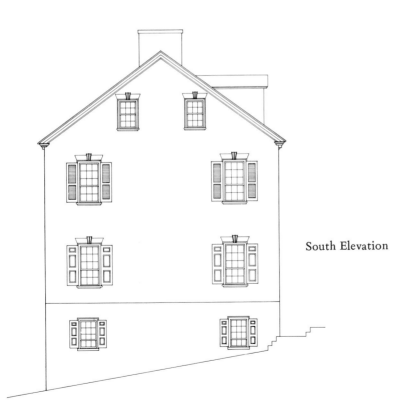

South Elevation

Plate No. 10 (continued)

INDEX TO ILLUSTRATIONS